Modern Information Retrieval

ACM PRESS BOOKS

This book is published as part of ACM Press Books – a collaboration between the Association for Computing (ACM) and Addison Wesley Longman Limited. ACM is the oldest and largest educational and scientific society in the information technology field. Through its high-quality publications and services, ACM is a major force in advancing the skills and knowledge of IT professionals throughout the world. For further information about ACM, contact:

ACM Member Services
1515 Broadway, 17th Floor
New York, NY 10036-5701
Phone: 1-212-626-0500
Fax: 1-212-944-1318
E-mail: acmhelp@acm.org
URL: http://www.acm.org/

ACM European Service Center
108 Cowley Road
Oxford OX4 1JF
United Kingdom
Phone: +44-1865-382388
Fax: +44-1865-381388
E-mail: acm_europe@acm.org
URL: http://www.acm.org/

Modern Information Retrieval

Ricardo Baeza-Yates
Berthier Ribeiro-Neto

ACM Press
New York

Harlow, England • London • New York • Boston • San Francisco • Toronto • Sydney • Singapore • Hong Kong
Tokyo • Seoul • Taipei • New Delhi • Cape Town • Madrid • Mexico City • Amsterdam • Munich • Paris • Milan

Pearson Education Limited

Edinburgh Gate
Harlow
Essex CM20 2JE
England

and Associated Companies throughout the world

Visit us on the World Wide Web at:
www.pearsoned.co.uk

Typeset in Computer Modern by 56
Printed and bound in the United States of America

First printed 1999

ISBN 0-201-39829-X

British Library Cataloguing-in-Publication Data
A catalogue record for this book is available from the British Library

Library of Congress Cataloging-in-Publication Data
Baeza-Yates, R. (Ricardo)
   Modern information retrieval / Ricardo Baeza-Yates, Berthier Ribeiro-Neto.
     p. cm.
   Includes bibliographical reference and index.
   ISBN 0-201-39829-X
   1. Information storage and retrieval systems. I. Ribeiro, Berthier de Araûjo
   Neto, 1960-. II. Title.
   Z667.B34 1999
   025.04–dc21

                              99-10033
                                CIP

10 9 8
07 06 05 04

Preface

Information retrieval (IR) has changed considerably in recent years with the expansion of the World Wide Web and the advent of modern and inexpensive graphical user interfaces and mass storage devices. As a result, traditional IR textbooks have become quite out of date and this has led to the introduction of new IR books. Nevertheless, we believe that there is still great need for a book that approaches the field in a rigorous and complete way from a computer-science perspective (as opposed to a user-centered perspective). This book is an effort to partially fulfill this gap and should be useful for a first course on information retrieval as well as for a graduate course on the topic.

The book comprises two portions which complement and balance each other. The core portion includes nine chapters authored or coauthored by the designers of the book. The second portion, which is fully integrated with the first, is formed by six state-of-the-art chapters written by leading researchers in their fields. The same notation and glossary are used in all the chapters. Thus, despite the fact that several people have contributed to the text, this book is really much more a textbook than an edited collection of chapters written by separate authors. Furthermore, unlike a collection of chapters, we have carefully designed the contents and organization of the book to present a cohesive view of all the important aspects of modern information retrieval.

From IR models to indexing text, from IR visual tools and interfaces to the Web, from IR multimedia to digital libraries, the book provides both breadth of coverage and richness of detail. It is our hope that, given the now clear relevance and significance of information retrieval to modern society, the book will contribute to further disseminate the study of the discipline at information science, computer science, and library science departments throughout the world.

Ricardo Baeza-Yates, Santiago, Chile
Berthier Ribeiro-Neto, Belo Horizonte, Brazil
January, 1999

To Helena, Rosa, and our children

território de homens livres
que será nosso país
e será pátria de todos.
Irmãos, cantai ese mundo
que não verei, mas virá
um dia, dentro de mil anos,
talvez mais. . . não tenho pressa.

de **Cidade Prevista** no livro
A Rosa do Povo, 1945

Carlos Drummond de Andrade

Amo los libros
exploradores,
libros con bosque o nieve,
profundidad o cielo

de **Oda al Libro (I)**,

Pablo Neruda

territory of free men
that will be our country
and will be the nation of all
Brothers, sing this world
which I'll not see, but which will come
one day, in a thousand years,
maybe more. . . no hurry.

from **Prevised City** in the book
The Rose of the People, 1945

Carlos Drummond de Andrade

I love books
that explore,
books with a forest or snow,
depth or sky

from **Ode to the Book (I)**,

Pablo Neruda

Acknowledgements

We would like to deeply thank the various people who, during the several months in which this endeavor lasted, provided us with useful and helpful assistance. Without their care and consideration, this book would likely not have matured.

First, we would like to thank all the chapter contributors, for their dedication and interest. To Elisa Bertino, Eric Brown, Barbara Catania, Christos Faloutsos, Elena Ferrari, Ed Fox, Marti Hearst, Gonzalo Navarro, Edie Rasmussen, Ohm Sornil, and Nivio Ziviani, who contributed with writings that reflect expertise we certainly do not fully profess ourselves. And for all their patience throughout an editing and cross-reviewing process which constitutes a rather difficult balancing act.

Second, we would like to thank all the people who demonstrated interest in publishing this book, particularly Scott Delman and Doug Sery.

Third, we would like to commend the interest, encouragement, and great job done by Addison Wesley Longman throughout the overall process, represented by Keith Mansfield, Karen Sutherland, Bridget Allen, David Harison, Sheila Chatten, Helen Hodge and Lisa Talbot. The reviewers they contacted read an early (and rather preliminary) proposal of this book and provided us with good feedback and invaluable insights. The chapter on Parallel and Distributed IR was moved from the part on Applications of IR (where it did not fit well) to the part on Text IR due to the objective argument of an unknown referee. A separate chapter on Retrieval Evaluation was only included after another zealous referee strongly made the case for the importance of this subject.

Fourth, we would like to thank all the people who discussed this project with us. Doug Oard provided us with an early critique of the proposal. Gary Marchionini was an earlier supporter and provided us with useful contacts during the process. Bruce Croft encouraged our efforts from the beginning. Alberto Mendelzon provided us with an initial proposal and a compilation of references for the chapter on searching the Web. Ed Fox found time in a rather busy schedule to provide us with an insightful review of the introduction (which resulted in a great improvement) and a thorough review of the chapter on Modeling. Marti Hearst demonstrated interest in our proposal early on, provided assistance throughout the editing process, and has been an enthusiastic supporter and partner.

Fifth, we thank the support of our institutions, the Departments of Computer Science of the University of Chile and of the Federal University of Minas Gerais, as well as the funding provided by national research agencies (CNPq in Brazil and CONICYT in Chile) and international collaboration projects, in particular CYTED project VII.13 AMYRI (Environment for Information Managing and Retrieval in the World Wide Web) and Finep project SIAM (Information Systems for Mobile Computers) under the Pronex program.

Most important, to Helena, Rosa, and our children, who put up with a string of trips abroad, lost weekends, and odd working hours.

List of Trademarks
Alta Vista is a trademark of Compaq Computer Corporation
FrameMaker is a trademark of Adobe Systems Incorporated
IBM SP2 is a trademark of International Business Machines Corporation
Netscape Communicator is a trademark of Netscape Communications Corporation
Solaris, Sun 3/50 and Sun UltraSparc-1 are trademarks of Sun Microsystems, Inc.
Thinking Machines CM-2 is a trademark of Thinking Machines Corporation
Unix is licensed through X/Open Company Ltd
Word is a trademark of Microsoft Corporation
WordPerfect is a trademark of of Corel Corporation

Contents

Biographies

Biographies of Main Authors

Ricardo Baeza-Yates received a bachelor degree in Computer Science in 1983 from the University of Chile. Later, he received an MSc in Computer Science (1985), a professional title in electrical engineering (1985), and an MEng in EE (1986) from the same university. He received his PhD in Computer Science from the University of Waterloo, Canada, in 1989. He has been the president of the Chilean Computer Science Society (SCCC) from 1992 to 1995 and from 1997 to 1998. During 1993, he received the Organization of the American States award for young researchers in exact sciences. Currently, he is a full professor at the Computer Science Department of the University of Chile, where he was the chairperson in the period 1993 to 1995. He is coauthor of the second edition of the *Handbook of Algorithms and Data Structures*, Addison-Wesley, 1991; and coeditor of *Information Retrieval: Algorithms and Data Structures*, Prentice Hall, 1992. He has also contributed several papers to journals published by professional organizations such as ACM, IEEE, and SIAM.

His research interests include algorithms and data structures, text retrieval, graphical interfaces, and visualization applied to databases. He currently coordinates an IberoAmerican project on models and techniques for searching the Web financed by the Spanish agency Cyted. He has been a visiting professor or an invited speaker at several conferences and universities around the world, as well as referee for several journals, conferences, NSF, etc. He is a member of the ACM, AMS, EATCS, IEEE, SCCC, and SIAM.

Berthier Ribeiro-Neto received a bachelor degree in Math, a BS degree in Electrical Engineering, and an MS degree in Computer Science, all from the Federal University of Minas Gerais, Brazil. In 1995, he was awarded a Ph.D. in Computer Science from the University of California at Los Angeles. Since then, he has been with the Computer Science Department of the Federal University of Minas Gerais where he is an Associate Professor.

His main interests are information retrieval systems, digital libraries, interfaces for the Web, and video on demand. He has been involved in a number of research projects financed through Brazilian national agencies such as the Ministry of Science and Technology (MCT) and the National Research Council (CNPq). From the projects currently underway, the two main ones deal with wireless information systems (project SIAM financed within program PRONEX) and video on demand (project ALMADEM financed within program PROTEM III). Dr Ribeiro-Neto is also involved with an IberoAmerican project on information systems for the Web coordinated by Professor Ricardo Baeza-Yates. He was the chair of SPIRE'98 (String Processing and Information Retrieval South American Symposium), is the chair of SBBD'99 (Brazilian Symposium on Databases), and has been on the committee of several conferences in Brazil, in South America and in the USA. He is a member of ACM, ASIS, and IEEE.

Biographies of Contributors

Elisa Bertino is Professor of Computer Science in the Department of Computer Science of the University of Milano where she heads the Database Systems Group. She has been a visiting researcher at the IBM Research Laboratory (now Almaden) in San Jose, at the Microelectronics and Computer Technology Corporation in Austin, Texas, and at Rutgers University in Newark, New Jersey. Her main research interests include object-oriented databases, distributed databases, deductive databases, multimedia databases, interoperability of heterogeneous systems, integration of artificial intelligence and database techniques, and database security. In those areas, Professor Bertino has published several papers in refereed journals, and in proceedings of international conferences and symposia. She is a coauthor of the books *Object-Oriented Database Systems — Concepts and Architectures*, Addison-Wesley 1993; *Indexing Techniques for Advanced Database Systems*, Kluwer 1997; and *Intelligent Database Systems*, Addison-Wesley forthcoming. She is or has been on the editorial boards of the following scientific journals: the *IEEE Transactions on Knowledge and Data Engineering*, the *International Journal of Theory and Practice of Object Systems*, the *Very Large Database Systems (VLDB) Journal*, the *Parallel and Distributed Database Journal*, the *Journal of Computer Security*, *Data & Knowledge Engineering*, and the *International Journal of Information Technology*.

Eric Brown has been a Research Staff Member at the IBM T.J. Watson Research Center in Yorktown Heights, NY, since 1995. Prior to that he was a Research Assistant at the Center for Intelligent Information Retrieval at the University of Massachusetts, Amherst. He holds a BSc from the University of Vermont and an MS and PhD from the University of Massachusetts, Amherst. Dr. Brown conducts research in large scale information retrieval systems, automatic text categorization, and hypermedia systems for digital libraries and knowledge management. He has published a number of papers in the field of information retrieval.

Barbara Catania is a researcher at the University of Milano, Italy. She received an MS degree in Information Sciences in 1993 from the University of

Genova and a PhD in Computer Science in 1998 from the University of Milano. She has also been a visiting researcher at the European Computer-Industry Research Center, Munich, Germany. Her main research interests include multimedia databases, constraint databases, deductive databases, and indexing techniques in object-oriented and constraint databases. In those areas, Dr Catania has published several papers in refereed journals, and in proceedings of international conferences and symposia. She is also a coauthor of the book *Indexing Techniques for Advanced Database Systems*, Kluwer 1997.

Christos Faloutsos received a BSc in Electrical Engineering (1981) from the National Technical University of Athens, Greece and an MSc and PhD in Computer Science from the University of Toronto, Canada. Professor Faloutsos is currently a faculty member at Carnegie Mellon University. Prior to joining CMU he was on the faculty of the Department of Computer Science at the University of Maryland, College Park. He has spent sabbaticals at IBM-Almaden and AT&T Bell Labs. He received the Presidential Young Investigator Award from the National Science Foundation in 1989, two 'best paper' awards (SIGMOD 94, VLDB 97), and three teaching awards. He has published over 70 refereed articles and one monograph, and has filed for three patents. His research interests include physical database design, searching methods for text, geographic information systems, indexing methods for multimedia databases, and data mining.

Elena Ferrari is an Assistant Professor at the Computer Science Department of the University of Milano, Italy. She received an MS in Information Sciences in 1992 and a PhD in Computer Science in 1998 from the University of Milano. Her main research interests include multimedia databases, temporal object-oriented data models, and database security. In those areas, Dr Ferrari has published several papers in refereed journals, and in proceedings of international conferences and symposia. She has been a visiting researcher at George Mason University in Fairfax, Virginia, and at Rutgers University in Newark, New Jersey.

Dr Edward A. Fox holds a PhD and MS in Computer Science from Cornell University, and a BS from MIT. Since 1983 he has been at Virginia Polytechnic Institute and State University (Virginia Tech), where he serves as Associate Director for Research at the Computing Center, Professor of Computer Science, Director of the Digital Library Research Laboratory, and Director of the Internet Technology Innovation Center. He served as vice chair and chair of ACM SIGIR from 1987 to 1995, helped found the ACM conferences on multimedia and digital libraries, and serves on a number of editorial boards. His research is focused on digital libraries, multimedia, information retrieval, WWW/Internet, educational technologies, and related areas.

Marti Hearst is an Assistant Professor at the University of California Berkeley in the School of Information Management and Systems. From 1994 to 1997 she was a Member of the Research Staff at Xerox PARC. She received her BA, MS, and PhD degrees in Computer Science from the University of California at Berkeley. Professor Hearst's research focuses on user interfaces and robust language analysis for information access systems, and on furthering the understanding of how people use and understand such systems.

Gonzalo Navarro received his first degrees in Computer Science from ESLAI (Latin American Superior School of Informatics) in 1992 and from the University of La Plata (Argentina) in 1993. In 1995 he received his MSc in Computer Science from the University of Chile, obtaining a PhD in 1998. Between 1990 and 1993 he worked at IBM Argentina, on the development of interactive applications and on research on multimedia and hypermedia. Since 1994 he has worked in the Department of Computer Science of the University of Chile, doing research on design and analysis of algorithms, textual databases, and approximate search. He has published a number of papers and also served as referee on different journals (*Algorithmica*, *TOCS*, *TOIS*, etc.) and at conferences (SIGIR, CPM, ESA, etc.).

Edie Rasmussen is an Associate Professor in the School of Information Sciences, University of Pittsburgh. She has also held faculty appointments at institutions in Malaysia, Canada, and Singapore. Dr Rasmussen holds a BSc from the University of British Columbia and an MSc degree from McMaster University, both in Chemistry, an MLS degree from the University of Western Ontario, and a PhD in Information Studies from the University of Sheffield. Her current research interests include indexing and information retrieval in text and multimedia databases.

Ohm Sornil is currently a PhD candidate in the Department of Computer Science at Virginia Polytechnic and State University and a scholar of the Royal Thai Government. He received a BEng in Electrical Engineering from Kasetsart University, Thailand, in 1993 and an MS in Computer Science from Syracuse University in 1997. His research interests include information retrieval, digital libraries, communication networks, and hypermedia.

Nivio Ziviani is a Professor of Computer Science at the Federal University of Minas Gerais in Brazil, where he heads the laboratory for Treating Information. He received a BS in Mechanical Engineering from the Federal University of Minas Gerais in 1971, an MSc in Informatics from the Catholic University of Rio in 1976, and a PhD in Computer Science from the University of Waterloo, Canada, in 1982. He has obtained several research funds from the Brazilian Research Council (CNPq), Brazilian Agencies CAPES and FINEP, Spanish Agency CYTED (project AMYRI), and private institutions. He currently coordinates a four year project on Web and wireless information systems (called SIAM) financed by the Brazilian Ministry of Science and Technology. He is cofounder of the Miner Technology Group, owner of the Miner Family of agents to search the Web. He is the author of several papers in journals and conference proceedings covering topics in the areas of algorithms and data structures, information retrieval, text indexing, text searching, text compression, and related areas. Since January of 1998, he is the editor of the 'News from Latin America' section in the Bulletin of the European Association for Theoretical Computer Science. He has been chair and member of the program committee of several conferences and is a member of ACM, EATICS and SBC.

Chapter 1
Introduction

1.1 Motivation

Information retrieval (IR) deals with the representation, storage, organization of, and access to information items. The representation and organization of the information items should provide the user with easy access to the information in which he is interested. Unfortunately, characterization of the *user information need* is not a simple problem. Consider, for instance, the following hypothetical user information need in the context of the World Wide Web (or just the Web):

> Find all the pages (documents) containing information on college tennis teams which: (1) are maintained by an university in the USA and (2) participate in the NCAA tennis tournament. To be relevant, the page must include information on the national ranking of the team in the last three years and the email or phone number of the team coach.

Clearly, this full description of the user information need cannot be used directly to request information using the current interfaces of Web search engines. Instead, the user must first translate this information need into a *query* which can be processed by the search engine (or IR system).

In its most common form, this translation yields a set of keywords (or index terms) which summarizes the description of the user information need. Given the user query, the key goal of an IR system is to retrieve information which might be useful or relevant to the user. The emphasis is on the retrieval of *information* as opposed to the retrieval of *data*.

1.1.1 Information versus Data Retrieval

Data retrieval, in the context of an IR system, consists mainly of determining which documents of a collection contain the keywords in the user query which, most frequently, is not enough to satisfy the user information need. In fact, the user of an IR system is concerned more with retrieving *information* about a

1

subject than with retrieving data which satisfies a given query. A data retrieval language aims at retrieving all objects which satisfy clearly defined conditions such as those in a regular expression or in a relational algebra expression. Thus, for a data retrieval system, a single erroneous object among a thousand retrieved objects means total failure. For an information retrieval system, however, the retrieved objects might be inaccurate and small errors are likely to go unnoticed. The main reason for this difference is that information retrieval usually deals with natural language text which is not always well structured and could be semantically ambiguous. On the other hand, a data retrieval system (such as a relational database) deals with data that has a well defined structure and semantics.

Data retrieval, while providing a solution to the user of a database system, does not solve the problem of retrieving information about a subject or topic. To be effective in its attempt to satisfy the user information need, the IR system must somehow 'interpret' the contents of the information items (documents) in a collection and rank them according to a degree of relevance to the user query. This 'interpretation' of a document content involves extracting syntactic and semantic information from the document text and using this information to match the user information need. The difficulty is not only knowing how to extract this information but also knowing how to use it to decide relevance. Thus, the notion of *relevance* is at the center of information retrieval. In fact, the primary goal of an IR system is to retrieve all the documents which are relevant to a user query while retrieving as few non-relevant documents as possible.

1.1.2 Information Retrieval at the Center of the Stage

In the past 20 years, the area of information retrieval has grown well beyond its primary goals of indexing text and searching for useful documents in a collection. Nowadays, research in IR includes modeling, document classification and categorization, systems architecture, user interfaces, data visualization, filtering, languages, etc. Despite its maturity, until recently, IR was seen as a narrow area of interest mainly to librarians and information experts. Such a tendentious vision prevailed for many years, despite the rapid dissemination, among users of modern personal computers, of IR tools for multimedia and hypertext applications. In the beginning of the 1990s, a single fact changed once and for all these perceptions — the introduction of the World Wide Web.

The Web is becoming a universal repository of human knowledge and culture which has allowed unprecedent sharing of ideas and information in a scale never seen before. Its success is based on the conception of a standard user interface which is always the same no matter what computational environment is used to run the interface. As a result, the user is shielded from details of communication protocols, machine location, and operating systems. Further, any user can create his own Web documents and make them point to any other Web documents without restrictions. This is a key aspect because it turns the Web into a new publishing medium accessible to everybody. As an immediate consequence, any Web user can push his personal agenda with little effort and almost at no cost. This universe without frontiers has attracted tremendous attention from millions of people everywhere since the very beginning. Furthermore, it is causing a revolution in the way people use computers and perform their daily tasks. For instance, home shopping and home banking are becoming very popular and have generated several hundred million dollars in revenues.

Despite so much success, the Web has introduced new problems of its own. Finding useful information on the Web is frequently a tedious and difficult task. For instance, to satisfy his information need, the user might navigate the space of Web links (i.e., the *hyperspace*) searching for information of interest. However, since the hyperspace is vast and almost unknown, such a navigation task is usually inefficient. For naive users, the problem becomes harder, which might entirely frustrate all their efforts. The main obstacle is the absence of a well defined underlying data model for the Web, which implies that information definition and structure is frequently of low quality. These difficulties have attracted renewed interest in IR and its techniques as promising solutions. As a result, almost overnight, IR has gained a place with other technologies at the center of the stage.

1.1.3   Focus of the Book

Despite the great increase in interest in information retrieval, modern textbooks on IR with a broad (and extensive) coverage of the various topics in the field are still difficult to find. In an attempt to partially fulfill this gap, this book presents an overall view of research in IR from a computer scientist's perspective. This means that the focus of the book is on computer algorithms and techniques used in information retrieval systems. A rather distinct viewpoint is taken by librarians and information science researchers, who adopt a human-centered interpretation of the IR problem. In this interpretation, the focus is on trying to understand how people interpret and use information as opposed to how to structure, store, and retrieve information automatically. While most of this book is dedicated to the computer scientist's viewpoint of the IR problem, the human-centered viewpoint is discussed to some extent in the last two chapters.

We put great emphasis on the integration of the different areas which are closed related to the information retrieval problem and thus, should be treated together. For that reason, besides covering text retrieval, library systems, user interfaces, and the Web, this book also discusses visualization, multimedia retrieval, and digital libraries.

1.2   Basic Concepts

The effective retrieval of relevant information is directly affected both by the *user task* and by the *logical view of the documents* adopted by the retrieval system, as we now discuss.

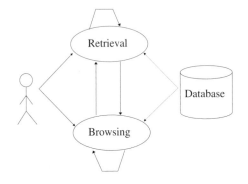

Figure 1.1 Interaction of the user with the retrieval system through distinct tasks.

1.2.1 The User Task

The user of a retrieval system has to translate his information need into a query in the language provided by the system. With an information retrieval system, this normally implies specifying a set of words which convey the semantics of the information need. With a data retrieval system, a query expression (such as, for instance, a regular expression) is used to convey the constraints that must be satisfied by objects in the answer set. In both cases, we say that the user searches for useful information executing a *retrieval* task.

Consider now a user who has an interest which is either poorly defined or which is inherently broad. For instance, the user might be interested in documents about car racing in general. In this situation, the user might use an interactive interface to simply look around in the collection for documents related to car racing. For instance, he might find interesting documents about Formula 1 racing, about car manufacturers, or about the '24 Hours of Le Mans.' Furthermore, while reading about the '24 Hours of Le Mans', he might turn his attention to a document which provides directions to Le Mans and, from there, to documents which cover tourism in France. In this situation, we say that the user is *browsing* the documents in the collection, not searching. It is still a process of retrieving information, but one whose main objectives are not clearly defined in the beginning and whose purpose might change during the interaction with the system.

In this book, we make a clear distinction between the different tasks the user of the retrieval system might be engaged in. His task might be of two distinct types: information or data *retrieval* and *browsing*. Classic information retrieval systems normally allow information or data retrieval. Hypertext systems are usually tuned for providing quick browsing. Modern digital library and Web interfaces might attempt to combine these tasks to provide improved retrieval capabilities. However, combination of retrieval and browsing is not yet a well established approach and is not the dominant paradigm.

Figure 1.1 illustrates the interaction of the user through the different tasks we identify. Information and data retrieval are usually provided by most modern information retrieval systems (such as Web interfaces). Further, such systems might also provide some (still limited) form of browsing. While combining information and data retrieval with browsing is not yet a common practice, it might become so in the future.

Both retrieval and browsing are, in the language of the World Wide Web, 'pulling' actions. That is, the user requests the information in an interactive manner. An alternative is to do retrieval in an automatic and permanent fashion using software agents which *push* the information towards the user. For instance, information useful to a user could be extracted periodically from a news service. In this case, we say that the IR system is executing a particular retrieval task which consists of *filtering* relevant information for later inspection by the user. We briefly discuss filtering in Chapter 2.

1.2.2 Logical View of the Documents

Due to historical reasons, documents in a collection are frequently represented through a set of index terms or keywords. Such keywords might be extracted directly from the text of the document or might be specified by a human subject (as frequently done in the information sciences arena). No matter whether these representative keywords are derived automatically or generated by a specialist, they provide a *logical view of the document*. For a precise definition of the concept of a document and its characteristics, see Chapter 6.

Modern computers are making it possible to represent a document by its full set of words. In this case, we say that the retrieval system adopts a *full text* logical view (or representation) of the documents. With very large collections, however, even modern computers might have to reduce the set of representative keywords. This can be accomplished through the elimination of *stopwords* (such as articles and connectives), the use of *stemming* (which reduces distinct words to their common grammatical root), and the identification of noun groups (which eliminates adjectives, adverbs, and verbs). Further, compression might be employed. These operations are called *text operations* (or transformations) and are covered in detail in Chapter 7. Text operations reduce the complexity of the document representation and allow moving the logical view from that of a full text to that of a set of *index terms*.

The full text is clearly the most complete logical view of a document but its usage usually implies higher computational costs. A small set of categories (generated by a human specialist) provides the most concise logical view of a document but its usage might lead to retrieval of poor quality. Several intermediate logical views (of a document) might be adopted by an information retrieval system as illustrated in Figure 1.2. Besides adopting any of the intermediate representations, the retrieval system might also recognize the internal structure normally present in a document (e.g., chapters, sections, subsections, etc.). This

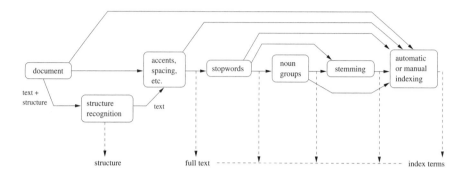

Figure 1.2   Logical view of a document: from full text to a set of index terms.

information on the structure of the document might be quite useful and is required by structured text retrieval models such as those discussed in Chapter 2.

As illustrated in Figure 1.2, we view the issue of logically representing a document as a continuum in which the logical view of a document might shift (smoothly) from a full text representation to a higher level representation specified by a human subject.

1.3   Past, Present, and Future

1.3.1   Early Developments

For approximately 4000 years, man has organized information for later retrieval and usage. A typical example is the table of contents of a book. Since the volume of information eventually grew beyond a few books, it became necessary to build specialized data structures to ensure faster access to the stored information. An old and popular data structure for faster information retrieval is a collection of selected words or concepts with which are associated pointers to the related information (or documents) — the *index*. In one form or another, indexes are at the core of every modern information retrieval system. They provide faster access to the data and allow the query processing task to be speeded up. A detailed coverage of indexes and their usage for searching can be found in Chapter 8.

For centuries, indexes were created manually as categorization hierarchies. In fact, most libraries still use some form of categorical hierarchy to classify their volumes (or documents), as discussed in Chapter 14. Such hierarchies have usually been conceived by human subjects from the library sciences field. More recently, the advent of modern computers has made possible the construction of large indexes automatically. Automatic indexes provide a view of the retrieval problem which is much more related to the system itself than to the user need.

In this respect, it is important to distinguish between two different views of the IR problem: a computer-centered one and a human-centered one.

In the computer-centered view, the IR problem consists mainly of building up efficient indexes, processing user queries with high performance, and developing ranking algorithms which improve the 'quality' of the answer set. In the human-centered view, the IR problem consists mainly of studying the behavior of the user, of understanding his main needs, and of determining how such understanding affects the organization and operation of the retrieval system. According to this view, keyword based query processing might be seen as a strategy which is unlikely to yield a good solution to the information retrieval problem in the long run.

In this book, we focus mainly on the computer-centered view of the IR problem because it continues to be dominant in the market place.

1.3.2   Information Retrieval in the Library

Libraries were among the first institutions to adopt IR systems for retrieving information. Usually, systems to be used in libraries were initially developed by academic institutions and later by commercial vendors. In the first generation, such systems consisted basically of an automation of previous technologies (such as card catalogs) and basically allowed searches based on author name and title. In the second generation, increased search functionality was added which allowed searching by subject headings, by keywords, and some more complex query facilities. In the third generation, which is currently being deployed, the focus is on improved graphical interfaces, electronic forms, hypertext features, and open system architectures.

Traditional library management system vendors include Endeavor Information Systems Inc., Innovative Interfaces Inc., and EOS International. Among systems developed with a research focus and used in academic libraries, we distinguish Okapi (at City University, London), MELVYL (at University of California), and Cheshire II (at UC Berkeley). Further details on these library systems can be found in Chapter 14.

1.3.3   The Web and Digital Libraries

If we consider the search engines on the Web today, we conclude that they continue to use indexes which are very similar to those used by librarians a century ago. What has changed then?

Three dramatic and fundamental changes have occurred due to the advances in modern computer technology and the boom of the Web. First, it became a lot cheaper to have access to various sources of information. This allows reaching a wider audience than ever possible before. Second, the advances in all kinds of digital communication provided greater access to networks. This implies that the information source is available even if distantly located and that the access can be done quickly (frequently, in a few seconds). Third, the freedom to post whatever information someone judges useful has greatly contributed to the popularity of the Web. For the first time in history, many people have free access to a large publishing medium.

Fundamentally, low cost, greater access, and publishing freedom have allowed people to use the Web (and modern digital libraries) as a highly *interactive* medium. Such interactivity allows people to exchange messages, photos, documents, software, videos, and to 'chat' in a convenient and low cost fashion. Further, people can do it at the time of their preference (for instance, you can buy a book late at night) which further improves the convenience of the service. Thus, high interactivity is the fundamental and current shift in the communication paradigm. Searching the Web is covered in Chapter 13, while digital libraries are covered in Chapter 15.

In the future, three main questions need to be addressed. First, despite the high interactivity, people still find it difficult (if not impossible) to retrieve information relevant to their information needs. Thus, in the dynamic world of the Web and of large digital libraries, which techniques will allow retrieval of higher quality? Second, with the ever increasing demand for access, quick response is becoming more and more a pressing factor. Thus, which techniques will yield faster indexes and smaller query response times? Third, the quality of the retrieval task is greatly affected by the user interaction with the system. Thus, how will a better understanding of the user behavior affect the design and deployment of new information retrieval strategies?

1.3.4 Practical Issues

Electronic commerce is a major trend on the Web nowadays and one which has benefited millions of people. In an electronic transaction, the buyer usually has to submit to the vendor some form of credit information which can be used for charging for the product or service. In its most common form, such information consists of a credit card number. However, since transmitting credit card numbers over the Internet is not a safe procedure, such data is usually transmitted over a fax line. This implies that, at least in the beginning, the transaction between a new user and a vendor requires executing an off-line procedure of several steps before the actual transaction can take place. This situation can be improved if the data is encrypted for security. In fact, some institutions and companies already provide some form of encryption or automatic authentication for security reasons.

However, security is not the only concern. Another issue of major interest is privacy. Frequently, people are willing to exchange information as long as it does not become public. The reasons are many but the most common one is to protect oneself against misuse of private information by third parties. Thus, privacy is another issue which affects the deployment of the Web and which has not been properly addressed yet.

Two other very important issues are copyright and patent rights. It is far from clear how the wide spread of data on the Web affects copyright and patent laws in the various countries. This is important because it affects the business of building up and deploying large digital libraries. For instance, is a site which supervises all the information it posts acting as a publisher? And if so, is it responsible for a misuse of the information it posts (even if it is not the source)?

Additionally, other practical issues of interest include scanning, optical character recognition (OCR), and cross-language retrieval (in which the query is in one language but the documents retrieved are in another language). In this book, however, we do not cover practical issues in detail because it is not our main focus. The reader interested in details of practical issues is referred to the interesting book by Lesk [501].

1.4   The Retrieval Process

At this point, we are ready to detail our view of the retrieval process. Such a process is interpreted in terms of component subprocesses whose study yields many of the chapters in this book.

To describe the retrieval process, we use a simple and generic software architecture as shown in Figure 1.3. First of all, before the retrieval process can even be initiated, it is necessary to define the text database. This is usually done by the manager of the database, which specifies the following: (a) the documents to be used, (b) the operations to be performed on the text, and (c) the text model (i.e., the text structure and what elements can be retrieved). The text operations transform the original documents and generate a logical view of them.

Once the logical view of the documents is defined, the database manager (using the DB Manager Module) builds an index of the text. An index is a critical data structure because it allows fast searching over large volumes of data. Different index structures might be used, but the most popular one is the *inverted file* as indicated in Figure 1.3. The resources (time and storage space) spent on defining the text database and building the index are amortized by querying the retrieval system many times.

Given that the document database is indexed, the retrieval process can be initiated. The user first specifies a *user need* which is then parsed and transformed by the same text operations applied to the text. Then, *query operations* might be applied before the actual *query*, which provides a system representation for the user need, is generated. The query is then processed to obtain the *retrieved documents*. Fast query processing is made possible by the index structure previously built.

Before been sent to the user, the retrieved documents are ranked according to a *likelihood* of relevance. The user then examines the set of ranked documents in the search for useful information. At this point, he might pinpoint a subset of the documents seen as definitely of interest and initiate a *user feedback* cycle. In such a cycle, the system uses the documents selected by the user to change the query formulation. Hopefully, this modified query is a better representation

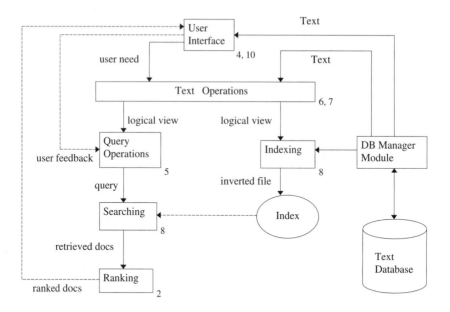

Figure 1.3 The process of retrieving information (the numbers beside each box indicate the chapters that cover the corresponding topic).

of the real user need.

The small numbers outside the lower right corner of various boxes in Figure 1.3 indicate the chapters in this book which discuss the respective subprocesses in detail. A brief introduction to each of these chapters can be found in section 1.5.

Consider now the user interfaces available with current information retrieval systems (including Web search engines and Web browsers). We first notice that the user almost never declares his information need. Instead, he is required to provide a direct representation for the query that the system will execute. Since most users have no knowledge of text and query operations, the query they provide is frequently inadequate. Therefore, it is not surprising to observe that poorly formulated queries lead to poor retrieval (as happens so often on the Web).

1.5   Organization of the Book

For ease of comprehension, this book has a straightforward structure in which four main parts are distinguished: text IR, human-computer interaction (HCI) for IR, multimedia IR, and applications of IR. *Text IR* discusses the classic problem of searching a collection of documents for useful information. *HCI for IR* discusses current trends in IR towards improved user interfaces and better data visualization tools. *Multimedia IR* discusses how to index document images and other binary data by extracting features from their content and how to search them efficiently. On the other hand, document images that are predominantly text (rather than pictures) are called *textual images* and are amenable to automatic extraction of keywords through metadescriptors, and can be retrieved using text IR techniques. *Applications of IR* covers modern applications of IR such as the Web, bibliographic systems, and digital libraries. Each part is divided into topics which we now discuss.

1.5.1 Book Topics

The four parts which compose this book are subdivided into eight topics as illustrated in Figure 1.4. These eight topics are as follows.

The topic *Retrieval Models & Evaluation* discusses the traditional models of searching text for useful information and the procedures for evaluating an information retrieval system. The topic *Improvements on Retrieval* discusses techniques for transforming the query and the text of the documents with the aim of improving retrieval. The topic *Efficient Processing* discusses indexing and searching approaches for speeding up the retrieval. These three topics compose the first part on Text IR.

The topic *Interfaces & Visualization* covers the interaction of the user with the information retrieval system. The focus is on interfaces which facilitate the process of specifying a query and provide a good visualization of the results.

The topic *Multimedia Modeling & Searching* discusses the utilization of multimedia data with information retrieval systems. The focus is on modeling, indexing, and searching multimedia data such as voice, images, and other binary data.

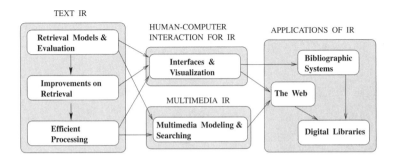

Figure 1.4 Topics which compose the book and their relationships.

The part on applications of IR is composed of three interrelated topics: *The Web, Bibliographic Systems*, and *Digital Libraries*. Techniques developed for the first two applications support the deployment of the latter.

The eight topics distinguished above generate the 14 chapters, besides this introduction, which compose this book and which we now briefly introduce.

1.5.2   Book Chapters

Figure 1.5 illustrates the overall structure of this book. The reasoning which yielded the chapters from 2 to 15 is as follows.

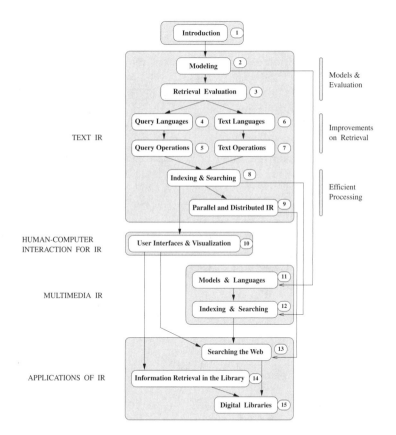

Figure 1.5   Structure of the book.

In the traditional keyword-based approach, the user specifies his information need by providing sets of keywords and the information system retrieves the documents which best approximate the user query. Also, the information system might attempt to rank the retrieved documents using some measure of relevance. This ranking task is critical in the process of attempting to satisfy the user information need and is the main goal of *modeling* in IR. Thus, information retrieval models are discussed early in Chapter 2. The discussion introduces many of the fundamental concepts in information retrieval and lays down much of the foundation for the subsequent chapters. Our coverage is detailed and broad. Classic models (Boolean, vector, and probabilistic), modern probabilistic variants (belief network models), alternative paradigms (extended Boolean, generalized vector, latent semantic indexing, neural networks, and fuzzy retrieval), structured text retrieval, and models for browsing (hypertext) are all carefully introduced and explained.

Once a new retrieval algorithm (maybe based on a new retrieval model) is conceived, it is necessary to evaluate its performance. Traditional evaluation strategies usually attempt to estimate the costs of the new algorithm in terms of time and space. With an information retrieval system, however, there is the additional issue of evaluating the relevance of the documents retrieved. For this purpose, text reference collections and evaluation procedures based on variables other than time and space are used. Chapter 3 is dedicated to the discussion of *retrieval evaluation*.

In traditional IR, queries are normally expressed as a set of keywords which is quite convenient because the approach is simple and easy to implement. However, the simplicity of the approach prevents the formulation of more elaborate querying tasks. For instance, queries which refer to both the structure and the content of the text cannot be formulated. To overcome this deficiency, more sophisticated query languages are required. Chapter 4 discusses various types of *query languages*. Since now the user might refer to the structure of a document in his query, this structure has to be defined. This is done by embedding the description of a document content and of its structure in a text language such as the Standard Generalized Markup Language (SGML). As illustrated in Figure 1.5, Chapter 6 is dedicated to the discussion of *text languages*.

Retrieval based on keywords might be of fairly low quality. Two possible reasons are as follows. First, the user query might be composed of too few terms which usually implies that the query context is poorly characterized. This is frequently the case, for instance, in the Web. This problem is dealt with through transformations in the query such as query expansion and user relevance feedback. Such *query operations* are covered in Chapter 5. Second, the set of keywords generated for a given document might fail to summarize its semantic content properly. This problem is dealt with through transformations in the text such as identification of noun groups to be used as keywords, stemming, and the use of a thesaurus. Additionally, for reasons of efficiency, text compression can be employed. Chapter 7 is dedicated to *text operations*.

Given the user query, the information system has to retrieve the documents which are related to that query. The potentially large size of the document collection (e.g., the Web is composed of millions of documents) implies that specialized indexing techniques must be used if efficient retrieval is to be achieved. Thus, to speed up the task of matching documents to queries, proper *indexing* and *search-*

ing techniques are used as discussed in Chapter 8. Additionally, query processing can be further accelerated through the adoption of *parallel and distributed IR* techniques as discussed in Chapter 9.

As illustrated in Figure 1.5, all the key issues regarding Text IR, from modeling to fast query processing, are covered in this book.

Modern user interfaces implement strategies which assist the user to form a query. The main objective is to allow him to define more precisely the context associated to his information need. The importance of query contextualization is a consequence of the difficulty normally faced by users during the querying process. Consider, for instance, the problem of quickly finding useful information in the Web. Navigation in hyperspace is not a good solution due to the absence of a logical and semantically well defined structure (the Web has no underlying logical model). A popular approach for specifying a user query in the Web consists of providing a set of keywords which are searched for. Unfortunately, the number of terms provided by a common user is small (typically, fewer than four) which usually implies that the query is vague. This means that new user interface paradigms which assist the user with the query formation process are required. Further, since a vague user query usually retrieves hundreds of documents, the conventional approach of displaying these documents as items of a scrolling list is clearly inadequate. To deal with this problem, new data visualization paradigms have been proposed in recent years. The main trend is towards visualization of a large subset of the retrieved documents at once and direct manipulation of the whole subset. *User interfaces* for assisting the user to form his query and current approaches for *visualization* of large data sets are covered in Chapter 10.

Following this, we discuss the application of IR techniques to multimedia data. The key issue is how to model, index, and search structured documents which contain multimedia objects such as digitized voice, images, and other binary data. *Models and query languages* for office and medical information retrieval systems are covered in Chapter 11. *Efficient indexing and searching* of multimedia objects is covered in Chapter 12. Some readers may argue that the models and techniques for multimedia retrieval are rather different from those for classic text retrieval. However, we take into account that images and text are usually together and that with the Web, other media types (such as video and audio) can also be mixed in. Therefore, we believe that in the future, all the above will be treated in a unified and consistent manner. Our book is a first step in that direction.

The final three chapters of the book are dedicated to applications of modern information retrieval: the Web, bibliographic systems, and digital libraries. As illustrated in Figure 1.5, Chapter 13 presents the Web and discusses the main problems related to the issue of searching the Web for useful information. Also, our discussion covers briefly the most popular search engines in the Web presenting particularities of their organization. Chapter 14 covers commercial document databases and online public access catalogs. Commercial document databases are still the largest information retrieval systems nowadays. LEXIS-NEXIS, for instance, has a database with 1.3 billion documents and attends to over 120 million query requests annually. Finally, Chapter 15 discusses modern digital libraries. Architectural issues, models, prototypes, and standards are all covered. The discussion also introduces the '5S' model (streams, structures, spaces, scenarios and societies) as a framework for providing theoretical and practical unification of digital libraries.

1.6   How to Use this Book

Although several people have contributed chapters for this book, it is really a textbook. The contents and the structure of the book have been carefully designed by the two main authors who also authored or coauthored nine of the 15 chapters in the book. Further, all the contributed chapters have been judiciously edited and integrated into a unifying framework that provides uniformity in structure and style, a common glossary, a common bibliography, and appropriate cross-references. At the end of each chapter, a discussion on research issues, trends, and selected bibliography is included. This discussion should be useful for graduate students as well as for researchers. Furthermore, the book is complemented by a Web page with additional information and resources.

1.6.1   Teaching Suggestions

This textbook can be used in many different areas including computer science (CS), information systems, and library science. The following list gives suggested contents for different courses at the undergraduate and graduate level, based on syllabuses of many universities around the world:

- **Information Retrieval** (Computer Science, undergraduate): this is the standard course for many CS programs. The minimum content should include Chapters 1 to 8 and Chapter 10, that is, most of the part on Text IR complemented with the chapter on user interfaces. Some specific topics of those chapters, such as more advanced models for IR and sophisticated algorithms for indexing and searching, can be omitted to fit a one term course. The chapters on Applications of IR can be mentioned briefly at the end.

- **Advanced Information Retrieval** (Computer Science, graduate): similar to the previous course but with more detailed coverage of the various chapters particularly modeling and searching (assuming the previous course as a requirement). In addition, Chapter 9 and Chapters 13 to 15 should be covered completely. Emphasis on research problems and new results is a must.

- **Information Retrieval** (Information Systems, undergraduate): this course is similar to the CS course, but with a different emphasis. It should include Chapters 1 to 7 and Chapter 10. Some notions from Chapter 8 are useful but not crucial. At the end, the system-oriented parts of the chapters on Applications of IR, in particular those on Bibliographic Systems and Digital Libraries, must be covered (this material can be complemented with topics from [501]).

- **Information Retrieval** (Library Science, undergraduate): similar to the previous course, but removing the more technical and advanced material of Chapters 2, 5, and 7. Also, greater emphasis should be put on the chapters on Bibliographic Systems and Digital Libraries. The course should be complemented with a thorough discussion of the user-centered view of the IR problem (for example, using the book by Allen [13]).

- **Multimedia Retrieval** (Computer Science, undergraduate or graduate): this course should include Chapters 1 to 3, 6, and 11 to 15. The emphasis could be on multimedia itself or on the integration of classical IR with multimedia. The course can be complemented with one of the many books on this topic, which are usually more broad and technical.

- **Topics in IR** (Computer Science, graduate): many chapters of the book can be used for this course. It can emphasize modeling and evaluation or user interfaces and visualization. It can also be focused on algorithms and data structures (in that case, [275] and [825] are good complements). A multimedia focus is also possible, starting with Chapters 11 and 12 and using more specific books later on.

- **Topics in IR** (Information Systems or Library Science, graduate) similar to the above but with emphasis on non-technical parts. For example, the course could cover modeling and evaluation, query languages, user interfaces, and visualization. The chapters on applications can also be considered.

- **Web Retrieval and Information Access** (generic, undergraduate or graduate): this course should emphasize hypertext, concepts coming from networks and distributed systems and multimedia. The kernel should be the basic models of Chapter 2 followed by Chapters 3, 4, and 6. Also, Chapters 11 and 13 to 15 should be discussed.

- **Digital Libraries** (generic, undergraduate or graduate): This course could start with part of Chapters 2 to 4 and 6, followed by Chapters 10, 14, and 15. The kernel of the course could be based on the book by Lesk [501].

More bibliography useful for many of the courses above is discussed in the last section of this chapter.

1.6.2   The Book's Web Page

As IR is a very dynamic area nowadays, a book by itself is not enough. For that reason (and many others), the book has a Web home page located and mirrored in the following places (mirrors in USA and Europe are also planned):

- Brazil: `http://www.dcc.ufmg.br/irbook`
- Chile: `http://sunsite.dcc.uchile.cl/irbook`

Comments, suggestions, contributions, or mistakes found are welcome through email to the contact authors given on the Web page.

The Web page contains the Table of Contents, Preface, Acknowledgements, Introduction, Glossary, and other appendices to the book. It also includes exercises and teaching materials that will be increasing in volume and changing with time. In addition, a reference collection (containing 1239 documents on Cystic Fibrosis and 100 information requests with extensive relevance evaluation [721]) is available for experimental purposes. Furthermore, the page includes useful pointers to IR syllabuses in different universities, IR research groups, IR publications, and other resources related to IR and this book. Finally, any new important results or additions to the book as well as an errata will be made publicly available there.

1.7   Bibliographic Discussion

Many other books have been written on information retrieval, and due to the current widespread interest in the subject, new books have appeared recently. In the following, we briefly compare our book with these previously published works.

Classic references in the field of information retrieval are the books by van Rijsbergen [785] and Salton and McGill [698]. Our distinction between data and information retrieval is borrowed from the former. Our definition of the information retrieval process is influenced by the latter. However, almost 20 years later, both books are now outdated and do not cover many of the new developments in information retrieval.

Three more recent and also well known references in information retrieval are the book edited by Frakes and Baeza-Yates [275], the book by Witten, Moffat, and Bell [825], and the book by Lesk [501]. All these three books are complementary to this book. The first is focused on data structures and algorithms for information retrieval and is useful whenever quick prototyping of a known algorithm is desired. The second is focused on indexing and compression, and covers images besides text. For instance, our definition of a textual image is borrowed from it. The third is focused on digital libraries and practical issues such as history, distribution, usability, economics, and property rights. On the issue of computer-centered and user-centered retrieval, a generic book on information systems that takes the latter view is due to Allen [13].

There are other complementary books for specific chapters. For example, there are many books on IR and hypertext. The same is true for generic or specific multimedia retrieval, as images, audio or video. Although not an information retrieval title, the book by Rosenfeld and Morville [682] on information architecture of the Web, is a good complement to our chapter on searching the

Web. The book by Menasce and Almeida [554] demonstrates how to use queueing theory for predicting Web server performance. In addition, there are many books that explain how to find information on the Web and how to use search engines.

The reference edited by Sparck Jones and Willet [414], which was long awaited, is really a collection of papers rather than an edited book. The coherence and breadth of coverage in our book makes it more appropriate as a textbook in a formal discipline. Nevertheless, this collection is a valuable research tool. A collection of papers on cross-language information retrieval was recently edited by Grefenstette [323]. This book is a good complement to ours for people interested in this particular topic. Additionally, a collection focused on intelligent IR was edited recently by Maybury [550], and another collection on natural language IR edited by Strzalkowski will appear soon [748].

The book by Korfhage [451] covers a lot less material and its coverage is not as detailed as ours. For instance, it includes no detailed discussion of digital libraries, the Web, multimedia, or parallel processing. Similarly, the books by Kowalski [459] and Shapiro *et al.* [719] do not cover these topics in detail, and have a different orientation. Finally, the recent book by Grossman and Frieder [326] does not discuss the Web, digital libraries, or visual interfaces.

For people interested in research results, the main journals on IR are: *Journal of the American Society of Information Sciences (JASIS)* published by Wiley and Sons, *ACM Transactions on Information Systems, Information Processing & Management* (IP&M, Elsevier), *Information Systems* (Elsevier), *Information Retrieval* (Kluwer), and *Knowledge and Information Systems* (Springer). The main conferences are: ACM SIGIR International Conference on Information Retrieval, ACM International Conference on Digital Libraries (ACM DL), ACM Conference on Information Knowledge and Management (CIKM), and Text REtrieval Conference (TREC). Regarding events of regional influence, we would like to acknowledge the SPIRE (South American Symposium on String Processing and Information Retrieval) symposium.

Chapter 2
Modeling

2.1 Introduction

Traditional information retrieval systems usually adopt index terms to index and retrieve documents. In a restricted sense, an index term is a keyword (or group of related words) which has some meaning of its own (i.e., which usually has the semantics of a noun). In its more general form, an index term is simply any word which appears in the text of a document in the collection. Retrieval based on index terms is simple but raises key questions regarding the information retrieval task. For instance, retrieval using index terms adopts as a fundamental foundation the idea that the semantics of the documents and of the user information need can be naturally expressed through sets of index terms. Clearly, this is a considerable oversimplification of the problem because a lot of the semantics in a document or user request is lost when we replace its text with a set of words. Furthermore, matching between each document and the user request is attempted in this very imprecise space of index terms. Thus, it is no surprise that the documents retrieved in response to a user request expressed as a set of keywords are frequently irrelevant. If one also considers that most users have no training in properly forming their queries, the problem is worsened with potentially disastrous results. The frequent dissatisfaction of Web users with the answers they normally obtain is just one good example of this fact.

Clearly, one central problem regarding information retrieval systems is the issue of predicting which documents are relevant and which are not. Such a decision is usually dependent on a ranking algorithm which attempts to establish a simple ordering of the documents retrieved. Documents appearing at the top of this ordering are considered to be more likely to be relevant. Thus, ranking algorithms are at the core of information retrieval systems.

A ranking algorithm operates according to basic premises regarding the notion of document relevance. Distinct sets of premises (regarding document relevance) yield distinct information retrieval models. The IR model adopted determines the predictions of what is relevant and what is not (i.e., the notion of relevance implemented by the system). The purpose of this chapter is to cover the most important information retrieval models proposed over the years. By doing so, the chapter also provides a conceptual basis for most of the remaining chapters in this book.

We first propose a taxonomy for categorizing the 15 IR models we cover. Second, we distinguish between two types of user retrieval tasks: ad hoc and filtering. Third, we present a formal characterization of IR models which is useful for distinguishing the various components of a particular model. Last, we discuss each of the IR models included in our taxonomy.

2.2   A Taxonomy of Information Retrieval Models

The three classic models in information retrieval are called Boolean, vector, and probabilistic. In the Boolean model, documents and queries are represented as sets of index terms. Thus, as suggested in [327], we say that the model is *set theoretic*. In the vector model, documents and queries are represented as vectors in a t-dimensional space. Thus, we say that the model is *algebraic*. In the probabilistic model, the framework for modeling document and query representations is based on probability theory. Thus, as the name indicates, we say that the model is *probabilistic*.

Over the years, alternative modeling paradigms for each type of classic model (i.e., set theoretic, algebraic, and probabilistic) have been proposed. Regarding alternative set theoretic models, we distinguish the fuzzy and the extended Boolean models. Regarding alternative algebraic models, we distinguish the generalized vector, the latent semantic indexing, and the neural network models. Regarding alternative probabilistic models, we distinguish the inference network and the belief network models. Figure 2.1 illustrates a taxonomy of these information retrieval models.

Besides references to the text content, the model might also allow references to the structure normally present in written text. In this case, we say that we have a structured model. We distinguish two models for structured text retrieval namely, the non-overlapping lists model and the proximal nodes model.

As discussed in Chapter 1, the user task might be one of *browsing* (instead of retrieval). In Figure 2.1, we distinguish three models for browsing namely, flat, structure guided, and hypertext.

The organization of this chapter follows the taxonomy of information retrieval models depicted in the figure.We first discuss the three classic models. Second, we discuss the alternative models for each type of classic model. Third, we cover structured text retrieval models. At the end, we discuss models for browsing.

We emphasize that the IR model (Boolean, vector, probabilistic, etc.), the logical view of the documents (full text, set of index terms, etc.), and the user task (retrieval, browsing) are orthogonal aspects of a retrieval system as detailed in Chapter 1. Thus, despite the fact that some models are more appropriate for a certain user task than for another, the same IR model can be used with distinct document logical views to perform different user tasks. Figure 2.2 illustrates the retrieval models most frequently associated with each one of six distinct combinations of a document logical view and a user task.

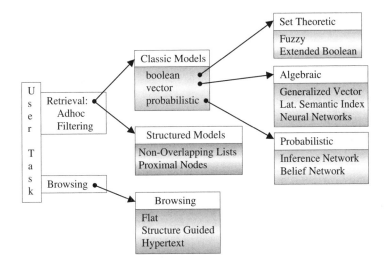

Figure 2.1 A taxonomy of information retrieval models.

LOGICAL VIEW OF DOCUMENTS

	Index Terms	Full Text	Full Text + Structure
Retrieval	Classic Set Theoretic Algebraic Probabilistic	Classic Set Theoretic Algebraic Probabilistic	Structured
Browsing	Flat	Flat Hypertext	Structure Guided Hypertext

(USER TASK)

Figure 2.2 Retrieval models most frequently associated with distinct combinations of a document logical view and a user task.

2.3   Retrieval: Ad hoc and Filtering

In a conventional information retrieval system, the documents in the collection remain relatively static while new queries are submitted to the system. This operational mode has been termed *ad hoc* retrieval in recent years and is the most common form of user task. A similar but distinct task is one in which the queries remain relatively static while new documents come into the system (and leave). For instance, this is the case with the stock market and with news wiring services. This operational mode has been termed *filtering*.

In a filtering task [74], a *user profile* describing the user's preferences is constructed. Such a profile is then compared to the incoming documents in an attempt to determine those which might be of interest to this particular user. For instance, this approach can be used to select a news article among thousands of articles which are broadcast each day. Other potential scenarios for the application of filtering include the selection of preferred judicial decisions, or the selection of articles from daily newspapers, etc.

Typically, the filtering task simply indicates to the user the documents which might be of interest to him. The task of determining which ones are really relevant is fully reserved to the user. Not even a ranking of the filtered documents is provided. A variation of this procedure is to rank the filtered documents and show this ranking to the user. The motivation is that the user can examine a smaller number of documents if he assumes that the ones at the top of this ranking are more likely to be relevant. This variation of filtering is called *routing* (see Chapter 3) but it is not popular.

Even if no ranking is presented to the user, the filtering task can compute an internal ranking to determine potentially relevant documents. For instance, documents with a ranking above a given threshold could be selected; the others would be discarded. Any IR model can be adopted to rank the documents, but the vector model is usually preferred due to its simplicity. At this point, we observe that filtering is really a type of user task (or operational mode) and not a model of information retrieval. Thus, the task of filtering and the IR model adopted are orthogonal aspects of an IR system.

In a filtering task, the crucial step is not the ranking itself but the construction of a user profile which truly reflects the user's preferences. Many approaches for constructing user profiles have been proposed and here we briefly discuss a couple of them.

A simplistic approach for constructing a user profile is to describe the profile through a set of keywords and to require the user to provide the necessary keywords. The approach is simplistic because it requires the user to do too much. In fact, if the user is not familiar with the service which generates the upcoming documents, he might find it fairly difficult to provide the keywords which appropriately describe his preferences in that context. Furthermore, an attempt by the user to familiarize himself with the vocabulary of the upcoming documents might turn into a tedious and time consuming exercise. Thus, despite its feasibility, requiring the user to precisely describe his profile might be impractical. A more elaborate alternative is to collect information from the user about his preferences and to use this information to build the user profile dynamically. This can be accomplished as follows.

In the very beginning, the user provides a set of keywords which describe an initial (and primitive) profile of his preferences. As new documents arrive, the system uses this profile to select documents which are potentially of interest and shows them to the user. The user then goes through a relevance feedback cycle (see Chapter 5) in which he indicates not only the documents which are really relevant but also the documents which are non-relevant. The system uses this information to adjust the user profile description such that it reflects the new preferences just declared. Of course, with this procedure the profile is continually changing. Hopefully, however, it stabilizes after a while and no longer changes drastically (unless, of course, the user's interests shift suddenly). Chapter 5 illustrates mechanisms which can be used to dynamically update a keyword-based profile.

From the above, it should be clear that the filtering task can be viewed as a conventional information retrieval task in which the documents are the ones which keep arriving at the system. Ranking can be computed as before. The difficulty with filtering resides in describing appropriately the user's preferences in a user profile. The most common approaches for deriving a user profile are based on collecting relevant information from the user, deriving preferences from this information, and modifying the user profile accordingly. Since the number of potential applications of filtering keeps increasing, we should see in the future a renewed interest in the study and usage of the technique.

2.4   A Formal Characterization of IR Models

We have argued that the fundamental premises which form the basis for a ranking algorithm determine the IR model. Throughout this chapter, we will discuss different sets of such premises. However, before doing so, we should state clearly what exactly an IR model is. Our characterization is as follows.

Definition   *An information retrieval model is a quadruple* $[\mathbf{D}, \mathbf{Q}, \mathcal{F}, R(q_i, d_j)]$ *where*

(1) $\mathbf{D}$ *is a set composed of logical views (or representations) for the documents in the collection.*

(2) $\mathbf{Q}$ *is a set composed of logical views (or representations) for the user in-formation needs. Such representations are called* queries.

(3) $\mathcal{F}$ *is a framework for modeling document representations, queries, and their relationships.*

(4) $R(q_i, d_j)$ *is a ranking function which associates a real number with a query* $q_i \in \mathbf{Q}$ *and a document representation* $d_j \in \mathbf{D}$. *Such ranking defines an ordering among the documents with regard to the query* q_i.

To build a model, we think first of representations for the documents and for the user information need. Given these representations, we then conceive the framework in which they can be modeled. This framework should also provide the intuition for constructing a ranking function. For instance, for the classic Boolean model, the framework is composed of sets of documents and the standard operations on sets. For the classic vector model, the framework is composed of a t-dimensional vectorial space and standard linear algebra operations on vectors. For the classic probabilistic model, the framework is composed of sets, standard probability operations, and the Bayes' theorem.

In the remainder of this chapter, we discuss the various IR models shown in Figure 2.1. Throughout the discussion, we do not explicitly instantiate the components $\mathbf{D}$, $\mathbf{Q}$, $\mathcal{F}$, and $R(q_i, d_j)$ of each model. Such components should be quite clear from the discussion and can be easily inferred.

2.5   Classic Information Retrieval

In this section we briefly present the three classic models in information retrieval namely, the Boolean, the vector, and the probabilistic models.

2.5.1   Basic Concepts

The classic models in information retrieval consider that each document is described by a set of representative keywords called index terms. An *index term* is simply a (document) word whose semantics helps in remembering the document's main themes. Thus, index terms are used to index and summarize the document contents. In general, index terms are mainly nouns because nouns have meaning by themselves and thus, their semantics is easier to identify and to grasp. Adjectives, adverbs, and connectives are less useful as index terms because they work mainly as complements. However, it might be interesting to consider all the distinct words in a document collection as index terms. For instance, this approach is adopted by some Web search engines as discussed in Chapter 13 (in which case, the document logical view is *full text*). We postpone a discussion on the problem of how to generate index terms until Chapter 7, where the issue is covered in detail.

Given a set of index terms for a document, we notice that not all terms are equally useful for describing the document contents. In fact, there are index terms which are simply vaguer than others. Deciding on the importance of a term for summarizing the contents of a document is not a trivial issue. Despite this difficulty, there are properties of an index term which are easily measured and which are useful for evaluating the potential of a term as such. For instance, consider a collection with a hundred thousand documents. A word which appears in each of the one hundred thousand documents is completely useless as an index term because it does not tell us anything about which documents the user might be interested in. On the other hand, a word which appears in just five documents is quite useful because it narrows down considerably the space of documents which might be of interest to the user. Thus, it should be clear that distinct index terms have varying relevance when used to describe document contents. This effect is captured through the assignment of numerical *weights* to each index term of a document.

Let k_i be an index term, d_j be a document, and $w_{i,j} \geq 0$ be a *weight* associated with the pair (k_i, d_j). This weight quantifies the importance of the index term for describing the document semantic contents.

Definition   *Let t be the number of index terms in the system and k_i be a generic index term. $K = \{k_1, \ldots, k_t\}$ is the set of all index terms. A weight $w_{i,j} > 0$ is associated with each index term k_i of a document d_j. For an index term which does not appear in the document text, $w_{i,j} = 0$. With the document d_j is associated an index term vector $\vec{d_j}$ represented by $\vec{d_j} = (w_{1,j}, w_{2,j}, \ldots, w_{t,j})$. Further, let g_i be a function that returns the weight associated with the index term k_i in any t-dimensional vector (i.e., $g_i(\vec{d_j}) = w_{i,j}$).*

As we later discuss, the index term weights are usually assumed to be mutually independent. This means that knowing the weight $w_{i,j}$ associated with the pair (k_i, d_j) tells us nothing about the weight $w_{i+1,j}$ associated with the pair (k_{i+1}, d_j). This is clearly a simplification because occurrences of index terms in a document are not uncorrelated. Consider, for instance, that the terms *computer* and *network* are used to index a given document which covers the area of computer networks. Frequently, in this document, the appearance of one of these two words attracts the appearance of the other. Thus, these two words are correlated and their weights could reflect this correlation. While mutual independence seems to be a strong simplification, it does simplify the task of computing index term weights and allows for fast ranking computation. Furthermore, taking advantage of index term correlations for improving the final document ranking is not a simple task. In fact, none of the many approaches proposed in the past has clearly demonstrated that index term correlations   are advantageous (for ranking purposes) with general collections. Therefore, unless clearly stated otherwise, we assume mutual independence among index terms. In Chapter 5 we discuss modern retrieval techniques which are based on term correlations and which have been tested successfully with particular collections. These successes seem to be slowly shifting the current understanding towards a more favorable view of the usefulness of term correlations for information retrieval systems.

The above definitions provide support for discussing the three classic information retrieval models, namely, the Boolean, the vector, and the probabilistic models, as we now do.

2.5.2 Boolean Model

The Boolean model is a simple retrieval model based on set theory and Boolean algebra. Since the concept of a set is quite intuitive, the Boolean model provides a framework which is easy to grasp by a common user of an IR system. Furthermore, the queries are specified as Boolean expressions which have precise semantics. Given its inherent simplicity and neat formalism, the Boolean model received great attention in past years and was adopted by many of the early commercial bibliographic systems.

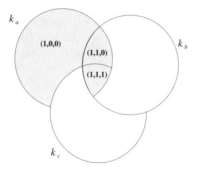

Figure 2.3 The three conjunctive components for the query $[q = k_a \land (k_b \lor \neg k_c)]$.

Unfortunately, the Boolean model suffers from major drawbacks. First, its retrieval strategy is based on a binary decision criterion (i.e., a document is predicted to be either relevant or non-relevant) without any notion of a grading scale, which prevents good retrieval performance. Thus, the Boolean model is in reality much more a data (instead of information) retrieval model. Second, while Boolean expressions have precise semantics, frequently it is not simple to translate an information need into a Boolean expression. In fact, most users find it difficult and awkward to express their query requests in terms of Boolean expressions. The Boolean expressions actually formulated by users often are quite simple (see Chapter 10 for a more thorough discussion on this issue). Despite these drawbacks, the Boolean model is still the dominant model with commercial document database systems and provides a good starting point for those new to the field.

The Boolean model considers that index terms are present or absent in a document. As a result, the index term weights are assumed to be all binary, i.e., $w_{i,j} \in \{0, 1\}$. A query q is composed of index terms linked by three connectives: *not, and, or*. Thus, a query is essentially a conventional Boolean expression which can be represented as a disjunction of conjunctive vectors (i.e., in *disjunctive normal form* — DNF). For instance, the query $[q = k_a \land (k_b \lor \neg k_c)]$ can be written in disjunctive normal form as $[\vec{q}_{dnf} = (1, 1, 1) \lor (1, 1, 0) \lor (1, 0, 0)]$, where each of the components is a binary weighted vector associated with the tuple (k_a, k_b, k_c). These binary weighted vectors are called the conjunctive components of $\vec{q}_{dnf}$. Figure 2.3 illustrates the three conjunctive components for the query q.

Definition   *For the Boolean model, the index term weight variables are all binary i.e.,* $w_{i,j} \in \{0, 1\}$. *A query q is a conventional Boolean expression. Let $\vec{q}_{dnf}$ be the disjunctive normal form for the query q. Further, let $\vec{q}_{cc}$ be any of the conjunctive components of $\vec{q}_{dnf}$. The similarity of a document d_j to the query q is defined as*

$$sim(d_j, q) = \begin{cases} 1 & if\ \exists \vec{q}_{cc}\ |\ (\vec{q}_{cc} \in \vec{q}_{dnf}) \land (\forall_{k_i},\ g_i(\vec{d_j}) = g_i(\vec{q}_{cc})) \\ 0 & otherwise \end{cases}$$

If $sim(d_j, q) = 1$ then the Boolean model predicts that the document d_j is relevant to the query q (it might not be). Otherwise, the prediction is that the document is not *relevant.*

The Boolean model predicts that each document is either *relevant* or *non-relevant*. There is no notion of a *partial match* to the query conditions. For instance, let d_j be a document for which $\vec{d_j} = (0, 1, 0)$. Document d_j includes the index term k_b but is considered non-relevant to the query $[q = k_a \wedge (k_b \vee \neg k_c)]$.

The main *advantages* of the Boolean model are the clean formalism behind the model and its simplicity. The main *disadvantages* are that exact matching may lead to retrieval of too few or too many documents (see Chapter 10). Today, it is well known that index term weighting can lead to a substantial improvement in retrieval performance. Index term weighting brings us to the vector model.

2.5.3   Vector Model

The vector model [697, 695] recognizes that the use of binary weights is too limiting and proposes a framework in which partial matching is possible. This is accomplished by assigning *non-binary* weights to index terms in queries and in documents. These term weights are ultimately used to compute the *degree of similarity* between each document stored in the system and the user query. By sorting the retrieved documents in decreasing order of this degree of similarity, the vector model takes into consideration documents which match the query terms only partially. The main resultant effect is that the ranked document answer set is a lot more precise (in the sense that it better matches the user information need) than the document answer set retrieved by the Boolean model.

Definition   *For the vector model, the weight $w_{i,j}$ associated with a pair (k_i, d_j) is positive and non-binary. Further, the index terms in the query are also weighted. Let $w_{i,q}$ be the weight associated with the pair $[k_i, q]$, where $w_{i,q} \geq 0$. Then, the query vector $\vec{q}$ is defined as $\vec{q} = (w_{1,q}, w_{2,q}, \ldots, w_{t,q})$ where t is the total number of index terms in the system. As before, the vector for a document d_j is represented by $\vec{d_j} = (w_{1,j}, w_{2,j}, \ldots, w_{t,j})$.*

Therefore, a document d_j and a user query q are represented as t-dimensional vectors as shown in Figure 2.4. The vector model proposes to evaluate the degree of similarity of the document d_j with regard to the query q as the correlation between the vectors $\vec{d_j}$ and $\vec{q}$. This correlation can be quantified, for instance, by the *cosine of the angle* between these two vectors. That is,

$$
\begin{aligned}
sim(d_j, q) &= \frac{\vec{d_j} \bullet \vec{q}}{|\vec{d_j}| \times |\vec{q}|} \\
&= \frac{\sum_{i=1}^{t} w_{i,j} \times w_{i,q}}{\sqrt{\sum_{i=1}^{t} w_{i,j}^2} \times \sqrt{\sum_{j=1}^{t} w_{i,q}^2}}
\end{aligned}
$$

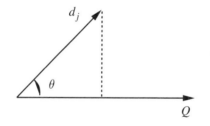

Figure 2.4   The cosine of θ is adopted as $sim(d_j, q)$.

where $|\vec{d_j}|$ and $|\vec{q}|$ are the norms of the document and query vectors. The factor $|\vec{q}|$ does not affect the ranking (i.e., the ordering of the documents) because it is the same for all documents. The factor $|\vec{d_j}|$ provides a normalization in the space of the documents.

Since $w_{i,j} \geq 0$ and $w_{i,q} \geq 0$, $sim(q, d_j)$ varies from 0 to +1. Thus, instead of attempting to predict whether a document is relevant or not, the vector model ranks the documents according to their *degree of similarity* to the query. A document might be retrieved even if it matches the query only *partially*. For instance, one can establish a threshold on $sim(d_j, q)$ and retrieve the documents with a degree of similarity above that threshold. But to compute rankings we need first to specify how index term weights are obtained.

Index term weights can be calculated in many different ways. The work by Salton and McGill [698] reviews various term-weighting techniques. Here, we do not discuss them in detail. Instead, we concentrate on elucidating the main idea behind the most effective term-weighting techniques. This idea is related to the basic principles which support clustering techniques, as follows.

Given a collection C of objects and a *vague* description of a set A, the goal of a simple clustering algorithm might be to separate the collection C of objects into two sets: a first one which is composed of objects related to the set A and a second one which is composed of objects not related to the set A. Vague description here means that we do not have complete information for deciding precisely which objects are and which are not in the set A. For instance, one might be looking for a set A of cars which have a price *comparable* to that of a Lexus 400. Since it is not clear what the term *comparable* means exactly, there is not a precise (and unique) description of the set A. More sophisticated clustering algorithms might attempt to separate the objects of a collection into various clusters (or classes) according to their properties. For instance, patients of a doctor specializing in cancer could be classified into five classes: terminal, advanced, metastasis, diagnosed, and healthy. Again, the possible class descriptions might be imprecise (and not unique) and the problem is one of deciding to which of these classes a new patient should be assigned. In what follows, however, we only discuss the simpler version of the clustering problem (i.e., the one which considers only two classes) because all that is required is a decision on which documents are predicted to be relevant and which ones are predicted to be not relevant (with regard to a given user query).

To view the IR problem as one of clustering, we refer to the early work of Salton. We think of the documents as a collection C of objects and think of the user query as a (vague) specification of a set A of objects. In this scenario, the IR problem can be reduced to the problem of determining which documents are in the set A and which ones are not (i.e., the IR problem can be viewed as a clustering problem). In a clustering problem, two main issues have to be resolved. First, one needs to determine what are the features which better describe the objects in the set A. Second, one needs to determine what are the features which better distinguish the objects in the set A from the remaining objects in the collection C. The first set of features provides for quantification of *intra-cluster* similarity, while the second set of features provides for quantification of *inter-cluster* dissimilarity. The most successful clustering algorithms try to balance these two effects.

In the vector model, intra-clustering similarity is quantified by measuring the raw frequency of a term k_i inside a document d_j. Such term frequency is usually referred to as the *tf factor* and provides one measure of how well that term describes the document contents (i.e., intra-document characterization). Furthermore, inter-cluster dissimilarity is quantified by measuring the inverse of the frequency of a term k_i among the documents in the collection. This factor is usually referred to as the *inverse document frequency* or the *idf factor*. The motivation for usage of an idf factor is that terms which appear in many documents are not very useful for distinguishing a relevant document from a non-relevant one. As with good clustering algorithms, the most effective term-weighting schemes for IR try to balance these two effects.

Definition   *Let N be the total number of documents in the system and n_i be the number of documents in which the index term k_i appears. Let $freq_{i,j}$ be the raw frequency of term k_i in the document d_j (i.e., the number of times the term k_i is mentioned in the text of the document d_j). Then, the normalized frequency $f_{i,j}$ of term k_i in document d_j is given by*

$$f_{i,j} = \frac{freq_{i,j}}{max_l \ freq_{l,j}} \tag{2.1}$$

where the maximum is computed over all terms which are mentioned in the text of the document d_j. If the term k_i does not appear in the document d_j then $f_{i,j} = 0$. Further, let idf_i, inverse document frequency for k_i, be given by

$$idf_i = \log \frac{N}{n_i} \tag{2.2}$$

The best known term-weighting schemes use weights which are given by

$$w_{i,j} = f_{i,j} \times \log \frac{N}{n_i} \tag{2.3}$$

or by a variation of this formula. Such term-weighting strategies are called tf-idf schemes.

Several variations of the above expression for the weight $w_{i,j}$ are described in an interesting paper by Salton and Buckley which appeared in 1988 [696]. However, in general, the above expression should provide a good weighting scheme for many collections.

For the query term weights, Salton and Buckley suggest

$$w_{i,q} = \left(0.5 + \frac{0.5 \; freq_{i,q}}{max_l \; freq_{l,q}} \right) \times \log \frac{N}{n_i} \tag{2.4}$$

where $freq_{i,q}$ is the raw frequency of the term k_i in the text of the information request q.

The main *advantages* of the vector model are: (1) its term-weighting scheme improves retrieval performance; (2) its partial matching strategy allows retrieval of documents that *approximate* the query conditions; and (3) its cosine ranking formula sorts the documents according to their degree of similarity to the query. Theoretically, the vector model has the *disadvantage* that index terms are assumed to be mutually independent (equation 2.3 does *not* account for index term dependencies). However, in practice, consideration of term dependencies might be a disadvantage. Due to the locality of many term dependencies, their indiscriminate application to all the documents in the collection might in fact *hurt* the overall performance.

Despite its simplicity, the vector model is a resilient ranking strategy with general collections. It yields ranked answer sets which are difficult to improve upon without query expansion or relevance feedback (see Chapter 5) within the framework of the vector model. A large variety of alternative ranking methods have been compared to the vector model but the consensus seems to be that, in general, the vector model is either superior or almost as good as the known alternatives. Furthermore, it is simple and fast. For these reasons, the vector model is a popular retrieval model nowadays.

2.5.4 Probabilistic Model

In this section, we describe the classic probabilistic model introduced in 1976 by Roberston and Sparck Jones [677] which later became known as the *binary independence retrieval* (BIR) model. Our discussion is intentionally brief and focuses mainly on highlighting the key features of the model. With this purpose in mind, we do not detain ourselves in subtleties regarding the binary independence assumption for the model. The section on bibliographic discussion points to references which cover these details.

The probabilistic model attempts to capture the IR problem within a probabilistic framework. The fundamental idea is as follows. Given a user query, there is a set of documents which contains exactly the relevant documents and no other. Let us refer to this set of documents as the *ideal* answer set. Given the description of this ideal answer set, we would have no problems in retrieving its documents. Thus, we can think of the querying process as a process of specifying the properties of an ideal answer set (which is analogous to interpreting the IR problem as a problem of clustering). The problem is that we do not know exactly what these properties are. All we know is that there are index terms whose semantics should be used to characterize these properties. Since these properties are not known at query time, an effort has to be made at initially guessing what they could be. This initial guess allows us to generate a preliminary probabilistic description of the ideal answer set which is used to retrieve a first set of documents. An interaction with the user is then initiated with the purpose of improving the probabilistic description of the ideal answer set. Such interaction could proceed as follows.

The user takes a look at the retrieved documents and decides which ones are relevant and which ones are not (in truth, only the first top documents need to be examined). The system then uses this information to refine the description of the ideal answer set. By repeating this process many times, it is expected that such a description will evolve and become closer to the real description of the ideal answer set. Thus, one should always have in mind the need to guess at the beginning the description of the ideal answer set. Furthermore, a conscious effort is made to model this description in probabilistic terms.

The probabilistic model is based on the following fundamental assumption.

Assumption (Probabilistic Principle)   Given a user query q and a document d_j in the collection, the probabilistic model tries to estimate the probability that the user will find the document d_j interesting (i.e., relevant). The model assumes that this probability of relevance depends on the query and the document representations only. Further, the model assumes that there is a subset of all documents which the user prefers as the answer set for the query q. Such an *ideal* answer set is labeled R and should maximize the overall probability of relevance to the user. Documents in the set R are predicted to be *relevant* to the query. Documents not in this set are predicted to be *non-relevant*.

This assumption is quite troublesome because it does not state explicitly how to compute the probabilities of relevance. In fact, not even the sample space which is to be used for defining such probabilities is given.

Given a query q, the probabilistic model assigns to each document d_j, as a measure of its similarity to the query, the ratio $P(d_j$ relevant-to $q)/P(d_j$ non-relevant-to $q)$ which computes the odds of the document d_j being relevant to the query q. Taking the odds of relevance as the rank minimizes the probability of an erroneous judgement [282, 785].

Definition   *For the probabilistic model, the index term weight variables are all binary i.e., $w_{i,j} \in \{0,1\}$, $w_{i,q} \in \{0,1\}$. A query q is a subset of index terms. Let R be the set of documents known (or initially guessed) to be relevant. Let $\overline{R}$ be the complement of R (i.e., the set of non-relevant documents). Let $P(R|\vec{d_j})$*

be the probability that the document d_j is relevant to the query q and $P(\overline{R}|\vec{d_j})$ be the probability that d_j is non-relevant to q. The similarity $sim(d_j, q)$ of the document d_j to the query q is defined as the ratio

$$sim(d_j, q) = \frac{P(R|\vec{d_j})}{P(\overline{R}|\vec{d_j})}$$

Using Bayes' rule,

$$sim(d_j, q) = \frac{P(\vec{d_j}|R) \times P(R)}{P(\vec{d_j}|\overline{R}) \times P(\overline{R})}$$

$P(\vec{d_j}|R)$ stands for the probability of randomly selecting the document d_j from the set R of relevant documents. Further, $P(R)$ stands for the probability that a document randomly selected from the entire collection is relevant. The meanings attached to $P(\vec{d_j}|\overline{R})$ and $P(\overline{R})$ are analogous and complementary.

Since $P(R)$ and $P(\overline{R})$ are the same for all the documents in the collection, we write,

$$sim(d_j, q) \quad \sim \quad \frac{P(\vec{d_j}|R)}{P(\vec{d_j}|\overline{R})}$$

Assuming independence of index terms,

$$sim(d_j, q) \quad \sim \quad \frac{(\prod_{g_i(\vec{d_j})=1} P(k_i|R)) \times (\prod_{g_i(\vec{d_j})=0} P(\overline{k_i}|R))}{(\prod_{g_i(\vec{d_j})=1} P(k_i|\overline{R})) \times (\prod_{g_i(\vec{d_j})=0} P(\overline{k_i}|\overline{R}))}$$

$P(k_i|R)$ stands for the probability that the index term k_i is present in a document randomly selected from the set R. $P(\overline{k_i}|R)$ stands for the probability that the index term k_i is not present in a document randomly selected from the set R. The probabilities associated with the set $\overline{R}$ have meanings which are analogous to the ones just described.

Taking logarithms, recalling that $P(k_i|R) + P(\overline{k_i}|R) = 1$, and ignoring factors which are constant for all documents in the context of the same query, we can finally write

$$sim(d_j, q) \quad \sim \quad \sum_{i=1}^{t} w_{i,q} \times w_{i,j} \times \left(\log \frac{P(k_i|R)}{1 - P(k_i|R)} + \log \frac{1 - P(k_i|\overline{R})}{P(k_i|\overline{R})} \right)$$

which is a key expression for ranking computation in the probabilistic model.

Since we do not know the set R at the beginning, it is necessary to devise a method for initially computing the probabilities $P(k_i|R)$ and $P(k_i|\overline{R})$. There are many alternatives for such computation. We discuss a couple of them below.

In the very beginning (i.e., immediately after the query specification), there are no retrieved documents. Thus, one has to make simplifying assumptions such as: (a) assume that $P(k_i|R)$ is constant for all index terms k_i (typically, equal to 0.5) and (b) assume that the distribution of index terms among the non-relevant documents can be approximated by the distribution of index terms among all the documents in the collection. These two assumptions yield

$$P(k_i|R) = 0.5$$
$$P(k_i|\overline{R}) = \frac{n_i}{N}$$

where, as already defined, n_i is the number of documents which contain the index term k_i and N is the total number of documents in the collection. Given this initial guess, we can then retrieve documents which contain query terms and provide an initial probabilistic ranking for them. After that, this initial ranking is improved as follows.

Let V be a subset of the documents initially retrieved and ranked by the probabilistic model. Such a subset can be defined, for instance, as the top r ranked documents where r is a previously defined threshold. Further, let V_i be the subset of V composed of the documents in V which contain the index term k_i. For simplicity, we also use V and V_i to refer to the number of elements in these sets (it should always be clear when the used variable refers to the set or to the number of elements in it). For improving the probabilistic ranking, we need to improve our guesses for $P(k_i|R)$ and $P(k_i|\overline{R})$. This can be accomplished with the following assumptions: (a) we can approximate $P(k_i|R)$ by the distribution of the index term k_i among the documents retrieved so far, and (b) we can approximate $P(k_i|\overline{R})$ by considering that all the non-retrieved documents are not relevant. With these assumptions, we can write,

$$P(k_i|R) = \frac{V_i}{V}$$
$$P(k_i|\overline{R}) = \frac{n_i - V_i}{N - V}$$

This process can then be repeated recursively. By doing so, we are able to improve on our guesses for the probabilities $P(k_i|R)$ and $P(k_i|\overline{R})$ without any assistance from a human subject (contrary to the original idea). However, we can also use assistance from the user for definition of the subset V as originally conceived.

The last formulas for $P(k_i|R)$ and $P(k_i|\overline{R})$ pose problems for small values of V and V_i which arise in practice (such as $V = 1$ and $V_i = 0$). To circumvent these problems, an adjustment factor is often added in which yields

$$P(k_i|R) = \frac{V_i + 0.5}{V + 1}$$
$$P(k_i|\overline{R}) = \frac{n_i - V_i + 0.5}{N - V + 1}$$

An adjustment factor which is constant and equal to 0.5 is not always satisfactory. An alternative is to take the fraction n_i/N as the adjustment factor which yields

$$P(k_i|R) \;\;=\;\; \frac{V_i + \frac{n_i}{N}}{V + 1}$$

$$P(k_i|\overline{R}) \;\;=\;\; \frac{n_i - V_i + \frac{n_i}{N}}{N - V + 1}$$

This completes our discussion of the probabilistic model.

The main *advantage* of the probabilistic model, in theory, is that documents are ranked in decreasing order of their *probability* of being relevant. The *disadvantages* include: (1) the need to guess the initial separation of documents into relevant and non-relevant sets; (2) the fact that the method does *not* take into account the frequency with which an index term occurs inside a document (i.e., all weights are binary); and (3) the adoption of the independence assumption for index terms. However, as discussed for the vector model, it is not clear that independence of index terms is a bad assumption in practical situations.

2.5.5   Brief Comparison of Classic Models

In general, the Boolean model is considered to be the weakest classic method. Its main problem is the inability to recognize partial matches which frequently leads to poor performance. There is some controversy as to whether the probabilistic model outperforms the vector model. Croft performed some experiments and suggested that the probabilistic model provides a better retrieval performance. However, experiments done afterwards by Salton and Buckley refute that claim. Through several different measures, Salton and Buckley showed that the vector model is *expected* to outperform the probabilistic model with general collections. This also seems to be the dominant thought among researchers, practitioners, and the Web community, where the popularity of the vector model runs high.

2.6   Alternative Set Theoretic Models

In this section, we discuss two alternative set theoretic models, namely the fuzzy set model and the extended Boolean model.

2.6.1   Fuzzy Set Model

Representing documents and queries through sets of keywords yields descriptions which are only partially related to the real semantic contents of the respective documents and queries. As a result, the matching of a document to the query terms is approximate (or vague). This can be modeled by considering that each query term defines a *fuzzy* set and that each document has a *degree of membership* (usually smaller than 1) in this set. This interpretation of the retrieval process (in terms of concepts from fuzzy theory) is the basic foundation of the various fuzzy set models for information retrieval which have been proposed over the years. Instead of reviewing several of these models here, we focus on a particular one whose description fits well with the models already covered in this chapter. Thus, our discussion is based on the fuzzy set model for information retrieval proposed by Ogawa, Morita, and Kobayashi [616]. Before proceeding, we briefly introduce some fundamental concepts.

Fuzzy Set Theory

Fuzzy set theory [846] deals with the representation of classes whose boundaries are not well defined. The key idea is to associate a membership function with the elements of the class. This function takes values in the interval [0,1] with 0 corresponding to no membership in the class and 1 corresponding to full membership. Membership values between 0 and 1 indicate *marginal* elements of the class. Thus, membership in a fuzzy set is a notion intrinsically *gradual* instead of abrupt (as in conventional Boolean logic).

Definition   *A fuzzy subset A of a universe of discourse U is characterized by a membership function $\mu_A : U \to [0,1]$ which associates with each element u of U a number $\mu_A(u)$ in the interval [0,1].*

The three most commonly used operations on fuzzy sets are: the *complement* of a fuzzy set, the *union* of two or more fuzzy sets, and the *intersection* of two or more fuzzy sets. They are defined as follows.

Definition   *Let U be the universe of discourse, A and B be two fuzzy subsets of U, and $\overline{A}$ be the complement of A relative to U. Also, let u be an element of U. Then,*

$$\mu_{\overline{A}}(u) = 1 - \mu_A(u)$$
$$\mu_{A \cup B}(u) = max(\mu_A(u), \mu_B(u))$$
$$\mu_{A \cap B}(u) = min(\mu_A(u), \mu_B(u))$$

Fuzzy sets are useful for representing vagueness and imprecision and have been applied to various domains. In what follows, we discuss their application to information retrieval.

Fuzzy Information Retrieval

As discussed in Chapters 5 and 7, one additional approach to modeling the information retrieval process is to adopt a thesaurus (which defines term relationships). The basic idea is to expand the set of index terms in the query with related terms (obtained from the thesaurus) such that additional relevant documents (i.e., besides the ones which would be normally retrieved) can be retrieved by the user query. A thesaurus can also be used to model the information retrieval problem in terms of fuzzy sets as follows.

A thesaurus can be constructed by defining a *term-term correlation matrix* $\vec{c}$ (called *keyword connection matrix* in [616]) whose rows and columns are associated to the index terms in the document collection. In this matrix $\vec{c}$, a normalized correlation factor $c_{i,l}$ between two terms k_i and k_l can be defined by

$$c_{i,l} = \frac{n_{i,l}}{n_i + n_l - n_{i,l}}$$

where n_i is the number of documents which contain the term k_i, n_l is the number of documents which contain the term k_l, and $n_{i,l}$ is the number of documents which contain both terms. Such a correlation metric is quite common and has been used extensively with clustering algorithms as detailed in Chapter 5.

We can use the term correlation matrix $\vec{c}$ to define a fuzzy set associated to each index term k_i. In this fuzzy set, a document d_j has a degree of membership $\mu_{i,j}$ computed as

$$\mu_{i,j} = 1 - \prod_{k_l \in d_j} (1 - c_{i,l})$$

which computes an algebraic sum (here implemented as the complement of a negated algebraic product) over all terms in the document d_j. A document d_j belongs to the fuzzy set associated to the term k_i if its own terms are related to k_i. Whenever there is at least one index term k_l of d_j which is strongly related to the index k_i (i.e., $c_{i,l} \sim 1$), then $\mu_{i,j} \sim 1$ and the index k_i is a good fuzzy index for the document d_j. In the case when all index terms of d_j are only loosely related to k_i, the index k_i is not a good fuzzy index for d_j (i.e., $\mu_{i,j} \sim 0$). The adoption of an algebraic sum over all terms in the document d_j (instead of the classic *max* function) allows a smooth transition for the values of the $\mu_{i,j}$ factor.

The user states his information need by providing a Boolean-like query expression. As also happens with the classic Boolean model (see the beginning of this chapter), this query is converted to its disjunctive normal form. For instance, the query $[q = k_a \wedge (k_b \vee \neg k_c)]$ can be written in disjunctive normal form as $[\vec{q}_{dnf} = (1, 1, 1) \vee (1, 1, 0) \vee (1, 0, 0)]$, where each of the components is a binary weighted vector associated to the tuple (k_a, k_b, k_c). These binary weighted vectors are the conjunctive components of $\vec{q}_{dnf}$. Let cc_i be a reference to the i-th conjunctive component. Then,

$$\vec{q}_{dnf} = cc_1 \vee cc_2 \vee \ldots \vee cc_p$$

where p is the number of conjunctive components of $\vec{q}_{dnf}$. The procedure to compute the documents relevant to a query is analogous to the procedure adopted

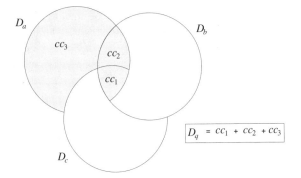

Figure 2.5 Fuzzy document sets for the query $[q = k_a \wedge (k_b \vee \neg k_c)]$. Each cc_i, $i \in \{1,2,3\}$, is a conjunctive component. D_q is the query fuzzy set.

by the classic Boolean model. The difference is that here we deal with fuzzy (instead of *crispy* or Boolean) sets. We proceed with an example.

Consider again the query $[q = k_a \wedge (k_b \vee \neg k_c)]$. Let D_a be the fuzzy set of documents associated to the index k_a. This set is composed, for instance, by the documents d_j which have a degree of membership $\mu_{a,j}$ greater than a predefined threshold K. Further, let $\overline{D}_a$ be the complement of the set D_a. The fuzzy set $\overline{D}_a$ is associated to $\overline{k}_a$, the negation of the index term k_a. Analogously, we can define fuzzy sets D_b and D_c associated to the index terms k_b and k_c, respectively. Figure 2.5 illustrates this example. Since the sets are all fuzzy, a document d_j might belong to the set D_a, for instance, even if the text of the document d_j does not mention the index k_a.

The query fuzzy set D_q is a union of the fuzzy sets associated with the three conjunctive components of $\vec{q}_{dnf}$ (which are referred to as cc_1, cc_2, and cc_3). The membership $\mu_{q,j}$ of a document d_j in the fuzzy answer set D_q is computed as follows.

$$
\begin{aligned}
\mu_{q,j} &= \mu_{cc_1+cc_2+cc_3,j} \\
&= 1 - \prod_{i=1}^{3}(1 - \mu_{cc_i,j}) \\
&= 1 - (1 - \mu_{a,j}\mu_{b,j}\mu_{c,j}) \times \\
&\quad\; (1 - \mu_{a,j}\mu_{b,j}(1 - \mu_{c,j})) \times (1 - \mu_{a,j}(1 - \mu_{b,j})(1 - \mu_{c,j}))
\end{aligned}
$$

where $\mu_{i,j}$, $i \in \{a,b,c\}$, is the membership of d_j in the fuzzy set associated with k_i.

As already observed, the degree of membership in a disjunctive fuzzy set is computed here using an *algebraic sum*, instead of the more common *max* function. Further, the degree of membership in a conjunctive fuzzy set is computed here using an *algebraic product*, instead of the more common *min* function. This adoption of algebraic sums and products yields degrees of membership which vary more smoothly than those computed using the *min* and *max* functions and thus seem more appropriate to an information retrieval system.

This example illustrates how this fuzzy model ranks documents relative to the user query. The model uses a term-term correlation matrix to compute correlations between a document d_j and its fuzzy index terms. Further, the model adopts algebraic sums and products (instead of *max* and *min*) to compute the overall degree of membership of a document d_j in the fuzzy set defined by the user query. Ogawa, Morita, and Kobayashi [616] also discuss how to incorporate user relevance feedback into the model but such discussion is beyond the scope of this chapter.

Fuzzy set models for information retrieval have been discussed mainly in the literature dedicated to fuzzy theory and are not popular among the information retrieval community. Further, the vast majority of the experiments with fuzzy set models has considered only small collections which make comparisons difficult to make at this time.

2.6.2   Extended Boolean Model

Boolean retrieval is simple and elegant. However, since there is no provision for term weighting, no ranking of the answer set is generated. As a result, the size of the output might be too large or too small (see Chapter 10 for details on this issue). Because of these problems, modern information retrieval systems are no longer based on the Boolean model. In fact, most of the new systems adopt at their core some form of vector retrieval. The reasons are that the vector space model is simple, fast, and yields better retrieval performance. One alternative approach though is to extend the Boolean model with the functionality of partial matching and term weighting. This strategy allows one to combine Boolean query formulations with characteristics of the vector model. In what follows, we discuss one of the various models which are based on the idea of extending the Boolean model with features of the vector model.

The *extended Boolean model*, introduced in 1983 by Salton, Fox, and Wu [703], is based on a critique of a basic assumption in Boolean logic as follows. Consider a conjunctive Boolean query given by $q = k_x \wedge k_y$. According to the Boolean model, a document which contains either the term k_x or the term k_y is as irrelevant as another document which contains neither of them. However, this binary decision criteria frequently is not in accordance with common sense. An analogous reasoning applies when one considers purely disjunctive queries.

When only two terms are considered, we can plot queries and documents in a two-dimensional map as shown in Figure 2.6. A document d_j is positioned in this space through the adoption of weights $w_{x,j}$ and $w_{y,j}$ associated with the pairs $[k_x, d_j]$ and $[k_y, d_j]$, respectively. We assume that these weights are normalized and thus lie between 0 and 1. For instance, these weights can be computed as normalized tf-idf factors as follows.

$$w_{x,j} = f_{x,j} \times \frac{idf_x}{max_i \ idf_i}$$

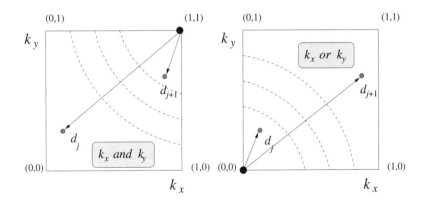

Figure 2.6 Extended Boolean logic considering the space composed of two terms k_x and k_y only.

where, as defined by equation 2.3, $f_{x,j}$ is the normalized frequency of term k_x in document d_j and idf_i is the inverse document frequency for a generic term k_i. For simplicity, in the remainder of this section, we refer to the weight $w_{x,j}$ as x, to the weight $w_{y,j}$ as y, and to the document vector $\vec{d_j} = (w_{x,j}, w_{y,j})$ as the point $d_j = (x, y)$. Observing Figure 2.6 we notice two particularities. First, for a disjunctive query $q_{or} = k_x \vee k_y$, the point $(0,0)$ is the spot to be avoided. This suggests taking the distance from $(0,0)$ as a measure of similarity with regard to the query q_{or}. Second, for a conjunctive query $q_{and} = k_x \wedge k_y$, the point $(1,1)$ is the most desirable spot. This suggests taking the complement of the distance from the point $(1,1)$ as a measure of similarity with regard to the query q_{and}. Furthermore, such distances can be normalized which yields,

$$
\begin{aligned}
sim(q_{or}, d) &= \sqrt{\frac{x^2 + y^2}{2}} \\
sim(q_{and}, d) &= 1 - \sqrt{\frac{(1-x)^2 + (1-y)^2}{2}}
\end{aligned}
$$

If the weights are all Boolean (i.e., $w_{x,j} \in \{0, 1\}$), a document is always positioned in one of the four corners (i.e., $(0,0)$, $(0,1)$, $(1,0)$, or $(1,1)$) and the values for $sim(q_{or}, d)$ are restricted to 0, $1/\sqrt{2}$, and 1. Analogously, the values for $sim(q_{and}, d)$ are restricted to 0, $1 - 1/\sqrt{2}$, and 1.

Given that the number of index terms in a document collection is t, the Boolean model discussed above can be naturally extended to consider Euclidean distances in a t-dimensional space. However, a more comprehensive generalization is to adopt the theory of vector norms as follows.

The *p-norm model* generalizes the notion of distance to include not only Euclidean distances but also p-distances, where $1 \leq p \leq \infty$ is a newly introduced parameter whose value must be specified at query time. A generalized disjunctive query is now represented by

$$q_{or} = k_1 \ \lor^p \ k_2 \ \lor^p \ \ldots \lor^p \ k_m$$

Analogously, a generalized conjunctive query is now represented by

$$q_{and} = k_1 \ \land^p \ k_2 \ \land^p \ \ldots \land^p \ k_m$$

The respective query-document similarities are now given by

$$sim(q_{or}, d_j) = \left(\frac{x_1^p + x_2^p + \ldots + x_m^p}{m} \right)^{\frac{1}{p}}$$

$$sim(q_{and}, d_j) = 1 - \left(\frac{(1 - x_1)^p + (1 - x_2)^p + \ldots + (1 - x_m)^p}{m} \right)^{\frac{1}{p}}$$

where each x_i stands for the weight $w_{i,d}$ associated to the pair $[k_i, d_j]$.

The p norm as defined above enjoys a couple of interesting properties as follows. First, when $p = 1$ it can be verified that

$$sim(q_{or}, d_j) = sim(q_{and}, d_j) = \frac{x_1 + \ldots + x_m}{m}$$

Second, when $p = \infty$ it can be verified that

$$sim(q_{or}, d_j) = max(x_i)$$
$$sim(q_{and}, d_j) = min(x_i)$$

Thus, for $p = 1$, conjunctive and disjunctive queries are evaluated by a sum of term-document weights as done by vector-based similarity formulas (which compute the inner product). Further, for $p = \infty$, queries are evaluated according to the formalism of fuzzy logic (which we view as a generalization of Boolean logic). By varying the parameter p between 1 and infinity, we can vary the p-norm ranking behavior from that of a vector-like ranking to that of a Boolean-like ranking. This is quite powerful and is a good argument in favor of the extended Boolean model.

The processing of more general queries is done by grouping the operators in a predefined order. For instance, consider the query $q = (k_1 \land^p k_2) \lor^p k_3$. The similarity $sim(q, d_j)$ between a document d_j and this query is then computed as

$$sim(q, d) = \left(\frac{\left(1 - \left(\frac{(1-x_1)^p + (1-x_2)^p}{2} \right)^{\frac{1}{p}} \right)^p + x_3^p}{2} \right)^{\frac{1}{p}}$$

This procedure can be applied recursively no matter the number of AND/OR operators.

One additional interesting aspect of this extended Boolean model is the possibility of using combinations of different values of the parameter p in a same query request. For instance, the query

$$(k_1 \vee^2 k_2) \wedge^\infty k_3$$

could be used to indicate that k_1 and k_2 should be used as in a vector system but that the presence of k_3 is required (i.e., the conjunction is interpreted as a Boolean operation). Despite the fact that it is not clear whether this additional functionality has any practical impact, the model does allow for it and does so in a natural way (without the need for clumsy extensions to handle special cases).

We should also observe that the extended Boolean model relaxes Boolean algebra interpreting Boolean operations in terms of algebraic distances. In this sense, it is really a hybrid model which includes properties of both the set theoretic models and the algebraic models. For simplicity, we opted for classifying the model as a set theoretic one.

The extended Boolean model was introduced in 1983 but has not been used extensively. However, the model does provide a neat framework and might reveal itself useful in the future.

2.7   Alternative Algebraic Models

In this section, we discuss three alternative algebraic models namely, the generalized vector space model, the latent semantic indexing model, and the neural network model.

2.7.1   Generalized Vector Space Model

As already discussed, the three classic models assume independence of index terms. For the vector model, this assumption is normally interpreted as follows.

Definition   *Let $\vec{k}_i$ be a vector associated with the index term k_i. Independence of index terms in the vector model implies that the set of vectors $\{\vec{k}_1, \vec{k}_2, \ldots, \vec{k}_t\}$ is linearly independent and forms a basis for the subspace of interest. The dimension of this space is the number t of index terms in the collection.*

Frequently, independence among index terms is interpreted in a more restrictive sense to mean pairwise orthogonality among the index term vectors i.e., to mean that for each pair of index term vectors $\vec{k}_i$ and $\vec{k}_j$ we have $\vec{k}_i \bullet \vec{k}_j = 0$. In 1985, however, Wong, Ziarko, and Wong [832] proposed an interpretation in which the index term vectors are assumed linearly independent but are not pairwise orthogonal. Such interpretation leads to the *generalized vector space model* which we now discuss.

In the generalized vector space model, two index term vectors might be non-orthogonal. This means that index term vectors are not seen as the orthogonal vectors which compose the basis of the space. Instead, they are themselves composed of *smaller* components which are derived from the particular collection at hand as follows.

Definition   *Given the set $\{k_1, k_2, \ldots, k_t\}$ of index terms in a collection, as before, let $w_{i,j}$ be the weight associated with the term-document pair $[k_i, d_j]$. If the $w_{i,j}$ weights are all binary then all possible patterns of term co-occurrence (inside documents) can be represented by a set of 2^t minterms given by $m_1 = (0, 0, \ldots, 0)$, $m_2 = (1, 0, \ldots, 0)$, $\ldots$, $m_{2^t} = (1, 1, \ldots, 1)$. Let $g_i(m_j)$ return the weight $\{0,1\}$ of the index term k_i in the minterm m_j.*

Thus, the minterm m_1 (for which $g_i(m_1) = 0$, for all i) points to the documents containing none of the index terms. The minterm m_2 (for which $g_1(m_2) = 1$, for $i = 1$, and $g_i(m_2) = 0$, for $i > 1$) points to the documents containing solely the index term k_1. Further, the minterm m_{2^t} points to the documents containing all the index terms. The central idea in the generalized vector space model is to introduce a set of pairwise orthogonal vectors $\vec{m}_i$ associated with the set of minterms and to adopt this set of vectors as the basis for the subspace of interest.

Definition   *Let us define the following set of $\vec{m}_i$ vectors*

$$
\begin{aligned}
\vec{m}_1 &= (1, 0, \ldots, 0, 0) \\
\vec{m}_2 &= (0, 1, \ldots, 0, 0) \\
&\vdots \\
\vec{m}_{2^t} &= (0, 0, \ldots, 0, 1)
\end{aligned}
$$

where each vector $\vec{m}_i$ is associated with the respective minterm m_i.

Notice that $\vec{m}_i \bullet \vec{m}_j = 0$ for all $i \neq j$ and thus the set of $\vec{m}_i$ vectors is, by definition, *pairwise* orthogonal. This set of $\vec{m}_i$ vectors is then taken as the orthonormal basis for the generalized vector space model.

Pairwise orthogonality among the $\vec{m}_i$ vectors does not imply independence among the index terms. On the contrary, index terms are now correlated by the $\vec{m}_i$ vectors. For instance, the vector $\vec{m}_4$ is associated with the minterm $m_4 = (1, 1, \ldots, 0)$ which points to the documents in the collection containing the index terms k_1, k_2, and no others. If such documents do exist in the collection under consideration then we say that the minterm m_4 is *active* and that a dependence between the index terms k_1 and k_2 is induced. If we consider this point more carefully, we notice that the generalized vector model adopts as a basic foundation the idea that co-occurrence of index terms inside documents in the collection induces dependencies among these index terms. Since this is an idea which was introduced many years before the generalized vector space model itself, novelty is not granted. Instead, the main contribution of the model is the establishment of a formal framework in which dependencies among index terms (induced by co-occurrence patterns inside documents) can be nicely represented.

The usage of index term dependencies to improve retrieval performance continues to be a controversial issue. In fact, despite the introduction in the 1980s of more effective algorithms for incorporating term dependencies (see Chapter 5), there is no consensus that incorporation of term dependencies in the model yields effective improvement with general collections. Thus, it is not clear that the framework of the generalized vector model provides a clear advantage in practical situations. Further, the generalized vector model is more complex and computationally more expensive than the classic vector model.

To determine the index term vector $\vec{k}_i$ associated with the index term k_i, we simply sum up the vectors for all minterms m_r in which the term k_i is in state 1 and normalize. Thus,

$$\vec{k}_i \;=\; \frac{\sum_{\forall r,\; g_i(m_r)=1} c_{i,r}\; \vec{m}_r}{\sqrt{\sum_{\forall r,\; g_i(m_r)=1} c_{i,r}^2}} \tag{2.5}$$

$$c_{i,r} \;=\; \sum_{d_j \;\mid\; g_l(\vec{d}_j)=g_l(m_r)\; for\; all\; l} w_{i,j}$$

These equations provide a general definition for the index term vector $\vec{k}_i$ in terms of the $\vec{m}_r$ vectors. The term vector $\vec{k}_i$ collects all the $\vec{m}_r$ vectors in which the index term k_i is in state 1. For each $\vec{m}_r$ vector, a correlation factor $c_{i,r}$ is defined. Such a correlation factor sums up the weights $w_{i,j}$ associated with the index term k_i and each document d_j whose term occurrence pattern coincides exactly with that of the minterm m_r. Thus, a minterm is of interest (in which case it is said to be *active*) only if there is at least one document in the collection which matches its term occurrence pattern. This implies that no more than N minterms can be active, where N is the number of documents in the collection. Therefore, the ranking computation does not depend on an exponential number of minterms as equation 2.5 seems to suggest.

Notice that the internal product $\vec{k}_i \bullet \vec{k}_j$ can now be used to quantify a degree of correlation between the index terms k_i and k_j. For instance,

$$\vec{k}_i \bullet \vec{k}_j = \sum_{\forall r \;\mid\; g_i(m_r)=1 \;\wedge\; g_j(m_r)=1} c_{i,r} \times c_{j,r}$$

which, as later discussed in Chapter 5, is a good technique for quantifying index term correlations.

In the classic vector model, a document d_j and a user query q are expressed by $\vec{d}_j = \sum_{\forall i} w_{i,j}\, \vec{k}_i$ and $\vec{q} = \sum_{\forall i} w_{i,q}\, \vec{k}_i$, respectively. In the generalized vector space model, these representations can be directly translated to the space of minterm vectors $\vec{m}_r$ by applying equation 2.5. The resultant $\vec{d}_j$ and $\vec{q}$ vectors are then used for computing the ranking through a standard cosine similarity function.

The ranking that results from the generalized vector space model combines the standard $w_{i,j}$ term-document weights with the correlation factors $c_{i,r}$. However, since the usage of term-term correlations does not necessarily yield improved retrieval performance, it is not clear in which situations the generalized model outperforms the classic vector model. Furthermore, the cost of computing the ranking in the generalized model can be fairly high with large collections because, in this case, the number of active minterms (i.e., those which have to be considered for computing the $\vec{k}_i$ vectors) might be proportional to the number of documents in the collection. Despite these drawbacks, the generalized vector model does introduce new ideas which are of importance from a theoretical point of view.

2.7.2   Latent Semantic Indexing Model

As discussed earlier, summarizing the contents of documents and queries through a set of index terms can lead to poor retrieval performance due to two effects. First, many unrelated documents might be included in the answer set. Second, relevant documents which are not indexed by any of the query keywords are not retrieved. The main reason for these two effects is the inherent vagueness associated with a retrieval process which is based on keyword sets.

The ideas in a text are more related to the concepts described in it than to the index terms used in its description. Thus, the process of matching documents to a given query could be based on concept matching instead of index term matching. This would allow the retrieval of documents even when they are not indexed by query index terms. For instance, a document could be retrieved because it shares concepts with another document which is relevant to the given query. Latent semantic indexing is an approach introduced in 1988 which addresses these issues (for clustering-based approaches which also address these issues, see Chapter 5).

The main idea in the *latent semantic indexing model* [287] is to map each document and query vector into a lower dimensional space which is associated with concepts. This is accomplished by mapping the index term vectors into this lower dimensional space. The claim is that retrieval in the reduced space may be superior to retrieval in the space of index terms. Before proceeding, let us define basic terminology.

Definition *As before, let t be the number of index terms in the collection and N be the total number of documents. Define $\vec{M}=(M_{ij})$ as a term-document association matrix with t rows and N columns. To each element M_{ij} of this matrix is assigned a weight $w_{i,j}$ associated with the term-document pair $[k_i, d_j]$. This $w_{i,j}$ weight could be generated using the tf-idf weighting technique common in the classic vector space model.*

Latent semantic indexing proposes to decompose the $\vec{M}$ association matrix in three components using singular value decomposition as follows.

$$\vec{M} = \vec{K}\vec{S}\vec{D}^t$$

The matrix $\vec{K}$ is the matrix of eigenvectors derived from the term-to-term correlation matrix given by $\vec{M}\vec{M}^t$ (see Chapter 5). The matrix $\vec{D}^t$ is the matrix of eigenvectors derived from the transpose of the document-to-document matrix given by $\vec{M}^t\vec{M}$. The matrix $\vec{S}$ is an $r \times r$ diagonal matrix of singular values where $r = min(t, N)$ is the *rank* of $\vec{M}$.

Consider now that only the s largest singular values of $\vec{S}$ are kept along with their corresponding columns in $\vec{K}$ and $\vec{D}^t$ (i.e., the remaining singular values of $\vec{S}$ are deleted). The resultant $\vec{M}_s$ matrix is the matrix of rank s which is closest to the original matrix $\vec{M}$ in the least square sense. This matrix is given by

$$\vec{M}_s = \vec{K}_s\vec{S}_s\vec{D}^t_s$$

where s, $s < r$, is the dimensionality of a reduced concept space. The selection of a value for s attempts to balance two opposing effects. First, s should be large enough to allow fitting all the structure in the real data. Second, s should be small enough to allow filtering out all the non-relevant representational details (which are present in the conventional index-term based representation).

The relationship between any two documents in the reduced space of dimensionality s can be obtained from the $\vec{M}_s^t\vec{M}_s$ matrix given by

$$
\begin{aligned}
\vec{M}_s^t\vec{M}_s &= (\vec{K}_s\vec{S}_s\vec{D}^t_s)^t\vec{K}_s\vec{S}_s\vec{D}^t_s \\
&= \vec{D}_s\vec{S}_s\vec{K}^t_s\vec{K}_s\vec{S}_s\vec{D}^t_s \\
&= \vec{D}_s\vec{S}_s\vec{S}_s\vec{D}^t_s \\
&= (\vec{D}_s\vec{S}_s)(\vec{D}_s\vec{S}_s)^t
\end{aligned}
$$

In the above matrix, the (i, j) element quantifies the relationship between documents d_i and d_j.

To rank documents with regard to a given user query, we simply model the query as a *pseudo-document* in the original $\vec{M}$ term-document matrix. Assume the query is modeled as the document with number 0. Then, the first row in the matrix $\vec{M}_s^t\vec{M}_s$ provides the ranks of all documents with respect to this query.

Since the matrices used in the latent semantic indexing model are of rank s, $s << t$, and $s << N$, they form an efficient indexing scheme for the documents in the collection. Further, they provide for elimination of noise (present in index term-based representations) and removal of redundancy.

The latent semantic indexing model introduces an interesting conceptualization of the information retrieval problem based on the theory of singular value decomposition. Thus, it has its value as a new theoretical framework. Whether it is superior in practical situations with general collections remains to be verified.

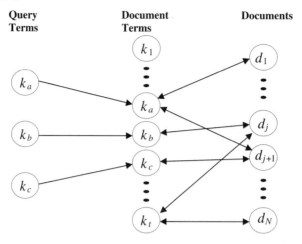

Figure 2.7   A neural network model for information retrieval.

2.7.3   Neural Network Model

In an information retrieval system, document vectors are compared with query vectors for the computation of a ranking. Thus, index terms in documents and queries have to be matched and weighted for computing this ranking. Since neural networks are known to be good pattern matchers, it is natural to consider their usage as an alternative model for information retrieval.

It is now well established that our brain is composed of billions of neurons. Each *neuron* can be viewed as a basic processing unit which, when stimulated by input signals, might emit output signals as a reactive action. The signals emitted by a neuron are fed into other neurons (through synaptic connections) which can themselves emit new output signals. This process might repeat itself through several layers of neurons and is usually referred to as a *spread activation* process. As a result, input information is processed (i.e., analyzed and interpreted) which might lead the brain to command physical reactions (e.g., motor actions) in response.

A *neural network* is an oversimplified graph representation of the mesh of interconnected neurons in a human brain. The nodes in this graph are the processing units while the edges play the role of the synaptic connections. To simulate the fact that the strength of a synaptic connection in the human brain changes over time, a *weight* is assigned to each edge of our neural network. At each instant, the state of a node is defined by its *activation level* (which is a function of its initial state and of the signals it receives as input). Depending on its activation level, a node A might send a signal to a neighbor node B. The strength of this signal at the node B depends on the weight associated with the edge between the nodes A and B.

A neural network for information retrieval can be defined as illustrated in Figure 2.7. The model depicted here is based on the work in [815]. We first observe that the neural network in Figure 2.7 is composed of three layers: one for the query terms, one for the document terms, and a third one for the documents themselves. Observe the similarity between the topology of this neural network and the topology of the inference and belief networks depicted in Figures 2.9 and 2.10. Here, however, the query term nodes are the ones which initiate the inference process by sending signals to the document term nodes. Following that, the document term nodes might themselves generate signals to the document nodes. This completes a first phase in which a signal travels from the query term nodes to the document nodes (i.e., from the left to the right in Figure 2.7).

The neural network, however, does not stop after the first phase of signal propagation. In fact, the document nodes in their turn might generate new signals which are directed back to the document term nodes (this is the reason for the bidirectional edges between document term nodes and document nodes). Upon receiving this stimulus, the document term nodes might again fire new signals directed to the document nodes, repeating the process. The signals become weaker at each iteration and the spread activation process eventually halts. This process might activate a document d_l even when such a document does not contain any query terms. Thus, the whole process can be interpreted as the activation of a built-in thesaurus.

To the query term nodes is assigned an initial (and fixed) activation level equal to 1 (the maximum). The query term nodes then send signals to the document term nodes which are attenuated by normalized query term weights $\overline{w}_{i,q}$. For a vector-based ranking, these normalized weights can be derived from the weights $w_{i,q}$ defined for the vector model by equation 2.4. For instance,

$$\overline{w}_{i,q} = \frac{w_{i,q}}{\sqrt{\sum_{i=1}^{t} w_{i,q}^2}}$$

where the normalization is done using the norm of the query vector.

Once the signals reach the document term nodes, these might send new signals out directed towards the document nodes. These signals are attenuated by normalized document term weights $\overline{w}_{i,j}$ derived from the weights $w_{i,j}$ defined for the vector model by equation 2.3. For instance,

$$\overline{w}_{i,j} = \frac{w_{i,j}}{\sqrt{\sum_{i=1}^{t} w_{i,j}^2}}$$

where the normalization is done using the norm of the document vector.

The signals which reach a document node are summed up. Thus, after the first round of signal propagation, the activation level of the document node associated to the document d_j is given by

$$\sum_{i=1}^{t} \overline{w}_{i,q}\, \overline{w}_{i,j} = \frac{\sum_{i=1}^{t} w_{i,q}\, w_{i,j}}{\sqrt{\sum_{i=1}^{t} w_{i,q}^2} \times \sqrt{\sum_{i=1}^{t} w_{i,j}^2}}$$

which is exactly the ranking provided by the classic vector model.

To improve the retrieval performance, the network continues with the spreading activation process after the first round of propagation. This modifies the initial vector ranking in a process analogous to a user relevance feedback cycle (see Chapter 5). To make the process more effective, a minimum activation threshold might be defined such that document nodes below this threshold send no signals out. Details can be found in [815].

There is no conclusive evidence that a neural network provides superior retrieval performance with general collections. In fact, the model has not been tested extensively with large document collections. However, a neural network does present an alternative modeling paradigm. Further, it naturally allows retrieving documents which are not initially related to the query terms — an appealing functionality.

2.8   Alternative Probabilistic Models

One alternative which has always been considered naturally appealing for quantifying document relevance is the usage of probability theory and its main streams. One such stream which is gaining increased attention concerns the *Bayesian belief networks* which we now discuss.

Bayesian (belief) networks are useful because they provide a clean formalism for combining distinct sources of evidence (past queries, past feedback cycles, and distinct query formulations) in support of the rank for a given document. This combination of distinct evidential sources can be used to improve retrieval performance (i.e., to improve the 'quality' of the ranked list of retrieved documents) as has been demonstrated in the work of Turtle and Croft [771].

In this chapter we discuss two models for information retrieval based on Bayesian networks. The first model is called *inference network* and provides the theoretical basis for the retrieval engine in the Inquery system [122]. Its success has attracted attention to the use of Bayesian networks with information retrieval systems. The second model is called *belief network* and generalizes the first model. At the end, we briefly compare the two models.

Our discussion below uses a style which is quite distinct from that employed by Turtle and Croft in their original writings. Particularly, we pay more attention to probabilistic argumentation during the development of the model. We make a conscious effort of consistently going back to the Bayesian formalism for motivating the major design decisions. It is our view that such an explanation strategy allows for a more precise argumentation which facilitates the task of grasping the subtleties involved.

Before proceeding, we briefly introduce Bayesian networks.

2.8.1   Bayesian Networks

Bayesian networks [630] are directed acyclic graphs (DAGs) in which the nodes represent random variables, the arcs portray causal relationships between these variables, and the strengths of these causal influences are expressed by conditional probabilities. The *parents* of a node (which is then considered as a *child* node) are those judged to be direct *causes* for it. This causal relationship is represented in the DAG by a link directed from each parent node to the child node. The *roots* of the network are the nodes without parents.

Let x_i be a node in a Bayesian network G and Γ_{x_i} be the set of parent nodes of x_i. The influence of Γ_{x_i} on x_i can be specified by any set of functions $F_i(x_i, \Gamma_{x_i})$ that satisfy

$$\sum_{\forall x_i} F_i(x_i, \Gamma_{x_i}) = 1$$

$$0 \leq F_i(x_i, \Gamma_{x_i}) \leq 1$$

where x_i also refers to the states of the random variable associated to the node x_i. This specification is complete and consistent because the product $\prod_{\forall i} F_i(x_i, \Gamma_{x_i})$ constitutes a joint probability distribution for the nodes in G.

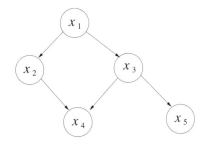

Figure 2.8   An example of a Bayesian network.

Figure 2.8 illustrates a Bayesian network for a joint probability distribution $P(x_1, x_2, x_3, x_4, x_5)$. In this case, the dependencies declared in the network allow the natural expression of the joint probability distribution in terms of local conditional probabilities (a key advantage of Bayesian networks) as follows.

$$P(x_1, x_2, x_3, x_4, x_5) = P(x_1)P(x_2|x_1)P(x_3|x_1)P(x_4|x_2, x_3)P(x_5|x_3)$$

The probability $P(x_1)$ is called the *prior* probability for the network and can be used to model previous knowledge about the semantics of the application.

2.8.2   Inference Network Model

The two most traditional schools of thought in probability are based on the *frequentist* view and the *epistemological* view. The frequentist view takes probability as a statistical notion related to the laws of chance. The epistemological

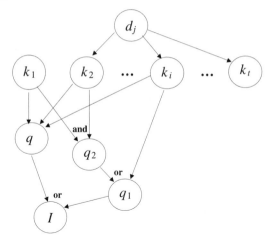

Figure 2.9   Basic inference network model.

view interprets probability as a degree of belief whose specification might be devoid of statistical experimentation. This second viewpoint is important because we frequently refer to probabilities in our daily lives without a clear definition of the statistical experiment which yielded those probabilities.

The inference network model [772, 771] takes an epistemological view of the information retrieval problem. It associates random variables with the index terms, the documents, and the user queries. A random variable associated with a document d_j represents the event of observing that document (i.e., the model assumes that documents are being observed in the search for relevant documents). The observation of the document d_j asserts a belief upon the random variables associated with its index terms. Thus, observation of a document is the *cause* for an increased belief in the variables associated with its index terms.

Index term and document variables are represented as nodes in the network. Edges are directed from a document node to its term nodes to indicate that observation of the document yields improved belief on its term nodes.

The random variable associated with the user query models the event that the information request specified by the query has been met. This random variable is also represented by a node in the network. The belief in this (query) node is a function of the beliefs in the nodes associated with the query terms. Thus, edges are directed from the index term nodes to the query node. Figure 2.9 illustrates an inference network for information retrieval.   The document d_j has k_2, k_i, and k_t as its index terms. This is modeled by directing the edges from the node d_j to the nodes k_2, k_i, and k_t. The query q is composed of the index terms k_1, k_2, and k_i. This is modeled by directing the edges from the nodes k_1, k_2, and k_i to the node q. Notice that Figure 2.9 also includes three extra nodes: q_2, q_1, and I. The nodes q_2 and q_1 are used to model an (alternative) Boolean formulation q_1 for the query q (in this case, $q_1 = (k_1 \wedge k_2) \vee k_i$). When such (additional) information is available, the user information need I is supported by both q and q_1.

In what follows, we concentrate our attention on the support provided to the query node q by the observation of a document d_j. Later on, we discuss the impact of considering multiple query representations for an information need I. This is important because, as Turtle and Croft have demonstrated, a keyword-based query formulation (such as q) can be combined with a Boolean-like query formulation (such as q_1) to yield improved retrieval performance for the same information need.

The complete inference network model also includes text nodes and query concept nodes but the model discussed above summarizes the essence of the approach.

A simplifying assumption is made which states that all random variables in the network are binary. This seems arbitrary but it does simplify the modeling task and is general enough to capture all the important relationships in the information retrieval problem.

Definition   *Let $\vec{k}$ be a t-dimensional vector defined by $\vec{k} = (k_1, k_2, \ldots, k_t)$ where k_1, k_2, ..., k_t are binary random variables i.e., $k_i \in \{0, 1\}$. These variables define the 2^t possible states for $\vec{k}$. Further, let d_j be a binary random variable associated with a document d_j and let q be a binary random variable associated with the user query.*

Notice that q is used to refer to the query, to the random variable associated with it, and to the respective node in the network. This is also the case for d_j and for each index term k_i. We allow this overloading in syntax because it should always be clear whether we are referring to either the query or to its associated random variable.

The ranking of a document d_j with respect to a query q is a measure of how much evidential support the observation of d_j provides to the query q. In an inference network, the ranking of a document d_j is computed as $P(q \wedge d_j)$ where q and d_j are short representations for $q = 1$ and $d_j = 1$, respectively. In general, such a ranking is given by

$$
\begin{aligned}
P(q \wedge d_j) &= \sum_{\forall \vec{k}} P(q \wedge d_j | \vec{k}) \times P(\vec{k}) \\
&= \sum_{\forall \vec{k}} P(q \wedge d_j \wedge \vec{k}) \\
&= \sum_{\forall \vec{k}} P(q | d_j \times \vec{k}) \times P(d_j \times \vec{k}) \\
&= \sum_{\forall \vec{k}} P(q | \vec{k}) \times P(\vec{k} | d_j) \times P(d_j) \qquad \textbf{(2.6)} \\
P(\overline{q \wedge d_j}) &= 1 - P(q \wedge d_j)
\end{aligned}
$$

which is obtained by basic conditioning and the application of Bayes' rule. Notice that $P(q|d_j \times \vec{k}) = P(q|\vec{k})$ because the k_i nodes separate the query node q from the document node d_j. Also, the notation $\overline{q \wedge d_j}$ is a short representation for $\neg(q \wedge d_j)$.

The instantiation of a document node d_j (i.e., the observation of the document) separates its children index term nodes making them mutually independent (see Bayesian theory for details). Thus, the degree of belief asserted to each index term node k_i by instantiating the document node d_j can be computed separately. This implies that $P(\vec{k}|d_j)$ can be computed in product form which yields (from equation 2.6),

$$P(q \wedge d_j) = \sum_{\forall \vec{k}} P(q|\vec{k}) \times$$

$$\left(\prod_{\forall i|g_i(\vec{k})=1} P(k_i|d_j) \times \prod_{\forall i|g_i(\vec{k})=0} P(\overline{k}_i|d_j) \right) \times P(d_j) \qquad \textbf{(2.7)}$$

$$P(\overline{q \wedge d_j}) = 1 - P(q \wedge d_j)$$

where $P(\overline{k}_i|d_j) = 1 - P(k_i|d_j)$. Through proper specification of the probabilities $P(q|\vec{k})$, $P(k_i|d_j)$, and $P(d_j)$, we can make the inference network cover a wide range of useful information retrieval ranking strategies. Later on, we discuss how to use an inference network to subsume the Boolean model and tf-idf ranking schemes. Let us first cover the specification of the $P(d_j)$ probabilities.

Prior Probabilities for Inference Networks

Since the document nodes are the root nodes in an inference network, they receive a *prior probability distribution* which is of our choosing. This prior probability reflects the probability associated to the event of observing a given document d_j (to simplify matters, a single document node is observed at a time). Since we have no prior preferences for any document in particular, we usually adopt a prior probability distribution which is uniform. For instance, in the original work on inference networks [772, 771], the probability of observing a document d_j is set to $1/N$ where N is the total number of documents in the system. Thus,

$$P(d_j) = \frac{1}{N}$$

$$P(\overline{d}_j) = 1 - \frac{1}{N}$$

The choice of the value $1/N$ for the prior probability $P(d_j)$ is a simple and natural specification given that our collection is composed of N documents. However, other specifications for $P(d_j)$ might also be interesting. For instance, in the cosine formula of the vector model, the contribution of an index term to the rank of the document d_j is inversely proportional to the norm of the vector $\vec{d_j}$. The larger the norm of the document vector, the smaller is the relative contribution of its index terms to the document final rank. This effect can be taken into account through proper specification of the prior probabilities $P(d_j)$ as follows.

$$P(d_j) = \frac{1}{|\vec{d_j}|}$$
$$P(\overline{d_j}) = 1 - P(d_j)$$

where $|\vec{d_j}|$ stands for the norm of the vector $\vec{d_j}$. Therefore, in this case, the larger the norm of a document vector, the smaller its associated prior probability. Such specification reflects a prior knowledge that we have about the behavior of vector-based ranking strategies (which normalize the ranking in the document space). As commanded by Bayesian postulates, previous knowledge of the application domain should be asserted in the specification of the priors in the network, as we have just done.

Inference Network for the Boolean Model

Here we demonstrate how an inference network can be tuned to subsume the Boolean model. First, for the Boolean model, the prior probabilities $P(d_j)$ are all set to $1/N$ because the Boolean model makes no prior distinction on documents. Thus,

$$P(d_j) = \frac{1}{N}$$
$$P(\overline{d_j}) = 1 - P(d_j)$$

Regarding the conditional probabilities $P(k_i|d_j)$ and $P(q|\vec{k})$, the specification is as follows.

$$P(k_i|d_j) = \begin{cases} 1 & \text{if } g_i(d_j) = 1 \\ 0 & \text{otherwise} \end{cases}$$
$$P(\overline{k_i}|d_j) = 1 - P(k_i|d_j)$$

which basically states that, when the document d_j is being observed, only the nodes associated with the index terms of the document d_j are *active* (i.e., have an induced probability greater than 0). For instance, observation of a document node d_j whose term vector is composed of exactly the index terms k_2, k_i, and k_t (see Figure 2.9) activates the index term nodes $\{k_2, k_i, k_t\}$ and no others.

Once the beliefs in the index term nodes have been computed, we can use them to compute the evidential support they provide to the user query q as follows.

$$P(q|\vec{k}) = \begin{cases} 1 & \text{if } \exists \vec{q}_{cc} \mid (\vec{q}_{cc} \in \vec{q}_{dnf}) \wedge (\forall_{k_i}, \ g_i(\vec{k}) = g_i(\vec{q}_{cc})) \\ 0 & \text{otherwise} \end{cases}$$

$$P(\bar{q}|\vec{k}) = 1 - P(q|\vec{k})$$

where $\vec{q}_{cc}$ and $\vec{q}_{dnf}$ are as defined for the classic Boolean model. The above equation basically states that one of the conjunctive components of the user query (expressed in disjunctive normal form) must be matched by the set of active terms in $\vec{k}$ (in this case, those activated by the document observed) exactly.

Substituting the above definitions for $P(q|\vec{k})$, $P(k_i|d_j)$, and $P(d_j)$ into equation 2.7, it can be easily shown that the set of documents retrieved is exactly the set of documents returned by the Boolean model as defined in section 2.5.2. Thus, an inference network can be used to subsume the Boolean model without difficulties.

Inference Network for tf-idf Ranking Strategies

For tf-idf ranking strategies (i.e., those related to the vector model), we adopt prior probabilities which reflect our prior knowledge of the importance of document normalization. Thus, we set the prior $P(d_j)$ to $1/|\vec{d_j}|$ as follows.

$$P(d_j) = \frac{1}{|\vec{d_j}|} \tag{2.8}$$

$$P(\bar{d_j}) = 1 - P(d_j)$$

Further, we have to decide where to introduce the tf (term-frequency) and the idf (inverse-document-frequency) factors in the network. For that purpose, we consider that the tf and idf factors are normalized (as in equation 2.1) and that these normalized factors are strictly smaller than 1.

We first focus on capturing the impact of the tf factors in the network. Normalized tf factors are taken into account through the beliefs asserted upon the index term nodes as follows.

$$P(k_i|d_j) = f_{i,j} \tag{2.9}$$

$$P(\bar{k_i}|d_j) = 1 - P(k_i|d_j)$$

These equations simply state that, according to the observed document d_j, the relevance of a term k_i is determined by its normalized term-frequency factor.

We are now in a position to consider the influence of idf factors. They are taken into account through the specification of the impact of index term nodes on the query node. Define a vector $\vec{k}_i$ given by,

$$\vec{k}_i = \vec{k} \mid (g_i(\vec{k}) = 1 \ \wedge \ \forall_{j \neq i} \ g_j(\vec{k}) = 0)$$

The vector $\vec{k}_i$ is a reference to the state of the vector $\vec{k}$ in which the node k_i is active and all others are inactive. The motivation is that tf-idf ranking strategies sum up the *individual* contributions of index terms and $\vec{k}_i$ allows us to consider the influence of the term k_i in isolation. We are now ready to define the influence of the index term nodes in the query node q as

$$
P(q|\vec{k}) = \begin{cases} idf_i & \text{if } \vec{k} = \vec{k}_i \wedge g_i(\vec{q}) = 1 \\ 0 & \text{if } \vec{k} \neq \vec{k}_i \vee g_i(\vec{q}) = 0 \end{cases} \tag{2.10}
$$

$$P(\overline{q}|\vec{k}) = 1 - P(q|\vec{k})$$

where idf_i here is a normalized version of the idf factor defined in equation 2.2. By applying equations 2.8, 2.9, and 2.10 to equation 2.7, we can then write

$$
\begin{aligned}
P(q \wedge d_j) &= \sum_{\forall \vec{k}_i} P(q|\vec{k}_i) \times P(k_i|d_j) \times \left(\prod_{\forall \ l \neq i} P(\overline{k}_l|d_j) \right) \times P(d_j) \\
&= \left(\prod_{\forall \ i} P(\overline{k}_i|d_j) \right) \times P(d_j) \times \sum_{\forall \vec{k}_i} P(k_i|d_j) \times P(q|\vec{k}_i) \times \frac{1}{P(\overline{k}_i|d_j)} \\
&= C_j \times \frac{1}{|\vec{d_j}|} \times \sum_{\forall i | g_i(\vec{d_j})=1 \wedge g_i(\vec{q})=1} f_{i,j} \times idf_i \times \frac{1}{1 - f_{i,j}}
\end{aligned}
$$

$$P(\overline{q \wedge d_j}) = 1 - P(q \wedge d_j)$$

which provides a tf-idf-like ranking. Unfortunately, C_j depends on a product of the various probabilities $P(\overline{k}_i|d_j)$ which vary from document to document and thus the ranking is distinct from the one provided by the vector model. Despite this peculiarity in the tf-idf ranking generated, it has been shown that an inference network is able to provide good retrieval performance with general collections. The reason is that the network allows us to consistently combine evidence from distinct evidential sources to improve the final ranking, as we now discuss.

Combining Evidential Sources

In Figure 2.9, the first query node q is the standard keyword-based query formulation for the user information need I. The second query q_1 is a Boolean-like query formulation for the same information need (i.e., an additional evidential source collected from a specialist). The joint support these two query formulations provide to the information need node I can be modeled through, for instance, an OR operator (i.e., $I = q \vee q_1$). In this case, the ranking provided by the inference network is computed as,

$$
\begin{aligned}
P(I \wedge d_j) &= \sum_{\vec{k}} P(I|\vec{k}) \times P(\vec{k}|d_j) \times P(d_j) \\
&= \sum_{\vec{k}} (1 - P(\bar{q}|\vec{k})\, P(\bar{q}_1|\vec{k})) \times P(\vec{k}|d_j) \times P(d_j)
\end{aligned}
$$

which might yield a retrieval performance which surpasses the retrieval performance obtained with each of the query nodes in isolation as demonstrated in [771].

2.8.3   Belief Network Model

The belief network model, introduced in 1996 by Ribeiro-Neto and Muntz [674], is also based on an epistemological interpretation of probabilities. However, it departs from the inference network model by adopting a clearly defined sample space. As a result, it yields a slightly different network topology which provides a separation between the document and the query portions of the network. This is the main difference between the two models and one which has theoretical implications.

The Probability Space

The probability space adopted was first introduced by Wong and Yao [830] and works as follows. All documents in the collection are indexed by *index terms* and the universe of discourse U is the set K of all index terms.

Definition   *The set $K = \{k_1, \ldots, k_t\}$ is the universe of discourse and defines the sample space for the belief network model. Let $u \subset K$ be a subset of K. To each subset u is associated a vector $\vec{k}$ such that $g_i(\vec{k}) = 1 \iff k_i \in u$.*

The introduction of the vector $\vec{k}$ is useful to keep the notation compatible with the one which has been used throughout this chapter.

Each index term is viewed as an *elementary concept* and K as a concept space. A concept u is a subset of K and might represent a document in the collection or a user query. In a belief network, set relationships are specified using random variables as follows.

Definition   *To each index term k_i is associated a binary random variable which is also referred to as k_i. The random variable k_i is set to 1 to indicate that the index k_i is a member of a concept/set represented by $\vec{k}$.*

This association of concepts with subsets is useful because it allows us to express the logical notions of conjunction, disjunction, negation, and implication as the more familiar set-theoretic notions of intersection, union, complementation, and inclusion. Documents and user queries can be defined as concepts in the sample space K as follows.

Definition   *A document d_j in the collection is represented as a concept (i.e., a set) composed of the terms which are used to index d_j. Analogously, a user query q is represented as a concept composed of the terms which are used to index q.*

A probability distribution P is defined over K as follows. Let c be a generic concept in the space K representing a document or user query. Then,

$$P(c) \;=\; \sum_u P(c|u) \times P(u) \tag{2.11}$$

$$P(u) \;=\; \left(\frac{1}{2}\right)^t \tag{2.12}$$

Equation 2.11 defines $P(c)$ as the *degree of coverage* of the space K by c. Such a coverage is computed by contrasting each of the concepts in K with c (through $P(c|u)$) and by summing up the individual contributions. This sum is weighted by the probability $P(u)$ with which u occurs in K. Since at the beginning the system has no knowledge of the probability with which a concept u occurs in the space K, we can assume that each u is equally likely which results in equation 2.12.

Belief Network Model

In the belief network model, the user query q is modeled as a network node to which is associated a binary random variable (as in the inference network model) which is also referred to as q. This variable is set to 1 whenever q completely covers the concept space K. Thus, when we assess $P(q)$ we compute the degree of coverage of the space K by q. This is equivalent to assessing the degree of belief associated with the following proposition: Is it true that q completely covers all possible concepts in K?

A document d_j is modeled as a network node with which is associated a binary random variable which is also referred to as d_j. This variable is 1 to indicate that d_j completely covers the concept space K. When we assess $P(d_j)$, we compute the degree of coverage of the space K by d_j. This is equivalent to assessing the degree of belief associated with the following proposition: Is it true that d_j completely covers all possible concepts in K?

According to the above formalism, the user query and the documents in the collection are modeled as subsets of index terms. Each of these subsets is interpreted as a *concept* embedded in the concept space K which works as a common *sample space*. Furthermore, user queries and documents are modeled

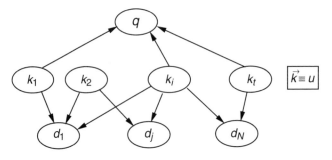

Figure 2.10   Basic belief network model.

identically. This is an important observation because it defines the topology of the belief network.

Figure 2.10 illustrates our belief network model. As in the inference network model, a query q is modeled as a binary random variable which is pointed to by the index term nodes which compose the query concept.   Documents are treated analogously to user queries (i.e., both are concepts in the space K). Thus, contrary to the inference network model, a document node is pointed to by the index term nodes which compose the document. This is the topological difference between the two models and one which has more implications than it seems at first glance.

The ranking of a document d_j relative to a given query q is interpreted as a concept matching relationship and reflects the degree of coverage provided to the concept d_j by the concept q.

Assumption   In the belief network model, $P(d_j|q)$ is adopted as the rank of the document d_j with respect to the query q.

By the application of Bayes' theorem, we can write $P(d_j|q) = P(d_j \wedge q)/P(q)$. Since $P(q)$ is a constant for all documents in the collection, we can write $P(d_j|q)$ $\sim P(d_j \wedge q)$ i.e., the rank assigned to a document d_j is directly proportional to $P(d_j \wedge q)$. This last probability is computed through the application of equation 2.11 which yields

$$P(d_j|q) \quad \sim \quad \sum_{\forall u} P(d_j \wedge q|u) \times P(u)$$

In the belief network of Figure 2.10, instantiation of the index term variables logically separates the nodes q and d making them mutually independent (i.e., the document and query portions of the network are logically separated by instantiation of the index term nodes). Therefore,

$$P(d_j|q) \sim \sum_{\forall u} P(d_j|u) \times P(q|u) \times P(u)$$

which can be rewritten as

$$P(d_j|q) \sim \sum_{\forall \vec{k}} P(d_j|\vec{k}) \times P(q|\vec{k}) \times P(\vec{k}) \tag{2.13}$$

To complete the belief network we need to specify the conditional probabilities $P(q|\vec{k})$ and $P(d_j|\vec{k})$. Distinct specifications of these probabilities allow the modeling of different ranking strategies (corresponding to different IR models). We now discuss how to specify these probabilities to subsume the vector model. For the vector model, the probabilities $P(q|\vec{k})$ and $P(d_j|\vec{k})$ are specified as follows. Let,

$$\vec{k}_i = \vec{k} \mid (g_i(\vec{k}) = 1 \land \forall_{j \neq i}\ g_j(\vec{k}) = 0)$$

as before. Also,

$$P(q|\vec{k}) = \begin{cases} \dfrac{w_{i,q}}{\sqrt{\sum_{i=1}^{t} w_{i,q}^2}} & \text{if } \vec{k} = \vec{k}_i \land g_i(q) = 1 \\ 0 & \text{otherwise} \end{cases}$$

$$P(\bar{q}|\vec{k}) = 1 - P(q|\vec{k})$$

Further, define

$$P(d_j|\vec{k}) = \begin{cases} \dfrac{w_{i,j}}{\sqrt{\sum_{i=1}^{t} w_{i,j}^2}} & \text{if } \vec{k} = \vec{k}_i \land g_i(\vec{d}_j) = 1 \\ 0 & \text{otherwise} \end{cases}$$

$$P(\overline{d_j}|\vec{k}) = 1 - P(d_j|\vec{k})$$

Then, the ordering of the retrieved documents (i.e., the ranking) defined by $P(d_j|q)$ coincides with the ordering generated by the vector model as specified in section 2.5.3. Thus, the belief network model can be tuned to subsume the vector model which cannot be accomplished with the inference network model.

2.8.4 Comparison of Bayesian Network Models

There is a close resemblance between the belief network model and the inference network model. However, this resemblance hides important differences between the two models. First, the belief network model is based on a set-theoretic view of the IR ranking problem and adopts a clearly defined sample space. The inference network model takes a purely epistemological view of the IR problem which is more difficult to grasp (because, for instance, the sample space is not clearly defined). Second, the belief network model provides a separation between the document and the query portions of the network which facilitates the modeling of additional evidential sources such as past queries and past relevance information. Third, as a result of this document-query space separation, the belief network model is able to reproduce any ranking strategy generated by the inference network model while the converse is not true.

To see that the belief network ranking subsumes any ranking generated by an inference network, compare equations 2.6 and 2.13. The key distinction is between the terms $P(d_j|\vec{k})$ and $P(\vec{k}|d_j)$. For the latter, instantiation of the document node d_j separates the index term nodes making them mutually independent. Thus, the joint probability $P(\vec{k}|d_j)$ can always be computed as the product of the individual probabilities $P(k_i|d_j)$. However, the computation of $P(d_j|\vec{k})$ might be non-decomposable in a product of term-based probabilities. As a result, $P(d_j|\vec{k})$ can express any probability function defined with $P(\vec{k}|d_j)$ while the converse is not true.

One should not infer from the above comparison that the inference network model is not a good model. On the contrary, it has been shown in the literature that the inference network model allows top retrieval performance to be accomplished with general collections. Further, it is the retrieval model used by the Inquery system. The point of the comparison is that, from a theoretical point of view, the belief network model is more general. Also, it provides a separation between the document space and the query space which simplifies the modeling task.

2.8.5   Computational Costs of Bayesian Networks

In the inference network model, according to equation 2.6, only the states which have a single document active node are considered. Thus, the cost of computing the ranking is linear on the number of documents in the collection. As with conventional collections, index structures such as inverted files (see Chapter 8) are used to restrict the ranking computation to those documents which have terms in common with the query. Thus, the cost of computing an inference network ranking has the same complexity as the cost of computing a vectorial ranking.

In the belief network model, according to equation 2.13, the only states (of the roots nodes) considered (for computing the rank of a document d_j) are the ones in which the active nodes are exactly those associated with the query terms. Thus, again, the cost of computing the ranking is linear on the number of documents in the collection. If index structures are used, the cost of computing a belief network ranking has the same complexity as the cost of computing a vectorial ranking.

Therefore, the Bayesian network models discussed here do not impose significant additional costs for ranking computation. This is so because the networks presented do not include cycles, which implies that belief propagation can be done in a time proportional to the number of nodes in the network.

2.8.6   The Impact of Bayesian Network Models

The classic Boolean model is based on a neat formalism but is not very effective for information retrieval. The classic vector model provides improved answer sets but lacks a more formal framework. Many attempts have been made in the past to combine the best features of each model. The extended Boolean model and the generalized vector space model are two well known examples. These past attempts are grounded in the belief that the combination of selected properties from distinct models is a promising approach towards improved retrieval.

Bayesian network models constitute modern variants of probabilistic reasoning whose major strength (for information retrieval) is a framework which allows the neat combination of distinct evidential sources to support a relevance judgement (i.e., a numerical rank) on a given document. In this regard, belief networks seem more appropriate than previous approaches and more promising. Further, besides allowing the combination of Boolean and vector features, a belief network can be naturally extended to incorporate evidential information derived from past user sessions [674] and feedback cycles [332].

The inference network model has been successfully implemented in the Inquery retrieval system [122] and compares favorably with other retrieval systems. However, despite these promises, whether Bayesian networks will become popular and widely used for information retrieval remains to be seen.

2.9   Structured Text Retrieval Models

Consider a user with a superior visual memory. Such a user might then recall that the specific document he is interested in contains a page in which the string '*atomic holocaust*' appears in italic in the text surrounding a Figure whose label contains the word 'earth.' With a classic information retrieval model, this query could be expressed as ['atomic holocaust' **and** 'earth'] which retrieves all the documents containing both strings. Clearly, however, this answer contains many more documents than desired by this user. In this particular case, the user would like to express his query through a richer expression such as

same-page (near ('*atomic holocaust*,' Figure (label ('earth'))))

which conveys the details in his visual recollection. Further, the user might be interested in an advanced interface which simplifies the task of specifying this (now complex) query. This example illustrates the appeal of a query language which allows us to combine the specification of strings (or patterns) with the specification of structural components of the document. Retrieval models which combine information on text content with information on the document structure are called *structured text retrieval* models.

For a query such as the one illustrated above, a structured text retrieval system searches for all the documents which *satisfy* the query. Thus, there is no notion of relevance attached to the retrieval task. In this sense, the current structured text retrieval models are data (instead of information) retrieval models. However, the retrieval system could search for documents which match the query conditions only partially. In this situation, the matching would be approximate and some ranking would have to be used for ordering the approximate answers. Thus, a structured text retrieval algorithm can be seen as an information retrieval algorithm for which the issue of appropriate ranking is not well established. In fact, this is an actual, interesting, and open research problem.

At the end of the 1980s and throughout the 1990s, various structured text retrieval models have appeared in the literature. Usually, the more expressive the model, the less efficient is its query evaluation strategy. Thus, selection of a structured model for a given application must be exercised with care. A good policy is to select the most efficient model which supports the functionality required by the application in view.

Here, we do not survey all the structured text retrieval models. Instead, we briefly discuss the main features of two of them, namely, a model based on *non-overlapping lists* and a model based on *proximal nodes*. These two models should provide a good overview of the main issues and tradeoffs in structured text retrieval.

We use the term *match point* to refer to the position in the text of a sequence of words which matches (or satisfies) the user query. Thus, if the user specifies the simple query ['atomic holocaust in Hiroshima'] and this string appears in three positions in the text of a document d_j, we say that the document d_j contains three match points. Further, we use the term *region* to refer to a contiguous portion of the text and the term *node* to refer to a structural component of the document such as a chapter, a section, a subsection, etc. Thus, a node is a region with predefined topological properties which are known both to the author of the document and to the user who searches the document system.

2.9.1   Model Based on Non-Overlapping Lists

Burkowski [132, 133] proposes to divide the whole text of each document in non-overlapping text regions which are collected in a *list*. Since there are multiple ways to divide a text in non-overlapping regions, multiple lists are generated. For instance, we might have a list of all chapters in the document, a second list of all sections in the document, and a third list of all subsections in the document. These lists are kept as separate and distinct data structures. While the text regions in the same (flat) list have no overlapping, text regions from distinct lists might overlap. Figure 2.11 illustrates four separate lists for the same document.

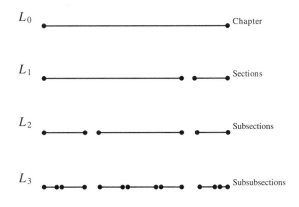

Figure 2.11   Representation of the structure in the text of a document through four separate (flat) indexing lists.

To allow searching for index terms and for text regions, a single inverted file (see Chapter 8 for a definition of inverted files) is built in which each structural component stands as an entry in the index. Associated with each entry, there is a list of text regions as a list of occurrences. Moreover, such a list could be easily merged with the traditional inverted file for the words in the text. Since the text regions are non-overlapping, the types of queries which can be asked are simple: (a) select a region which contains a given word (and does not contain other regions); (b) select a region A which does not contain any other region B (where B belongs to a list distinct from the list for A); (c) select a region not contained within any other region, etc.

2.9.2   Model Based on Proximal Nodes

Navarro and Baeza-Yates [41, 589, 590] propose a model which allows the definition of independent hierarchical (non-flat) indexing structures over the same document text. Each of these indexing structures is a strict hierarchy composed of chapters, sections, paragraphs, pages, and lines which are called *nodes* (see Figure 2.12). To each of these nodes is associated a text region. Further, two distinct hierarchies might refer to overlapping text regions.

Given a user query which refers to distinct hierarchies, the compiled answer is formed by nodes which all come from only one of them. Thus, an answer cannot be composed of nodes which come from two distinct hierarchies (which allows for faster query processing at the expense of less expressiveness). Notice, however, that due to the hierarchical structure, nested text regions (coming from the same hierarchy) are allowed in the answer set.

Figure 2.12 illustrates a hierarchical indexing structure composed of four

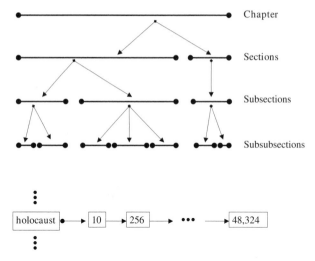

Figure 2.12 Hierarchical index for structural components and flat index for words.

levels (corresponding to a chapter, sections, subsections, and subsubsections of the same document) and an inverted list for the word 'holocaust.' The entries in this inverted list indicate all the positions in the text of the document in which the word 'holocaust' occurs. In the hierarchy, each node indicates the position in the text of its associated structural component (chapter, section, subsection, or subsubsection).

The query language allows the specification of regular expressions (to search for strings), the reference to structural components by name (to search for chapters, for instance), and a combination of these. In this sense, the model can be viewed as a compromise between expressiveness and efficiency. The somewhat limited expressiveness of the query language allows efficient query processing by first searching for the components which match the strings specified in the query and, subsequently, evaluating which of these components satisfy the structural part of the query.

Consider, for instance, the query [(*section) with ('holocaust')] which searches for sections, subsections, or subsubsections which contain the word 'holocaust.' A simple query processing strategy is to traverse the inverted list for the term 'holocaust' and, for each entry in the list (which indicates an occurrence of the term 'holocaust' in the text), search the hierarchical index looking for sections, subsections, and subsubsections containing that occurrence of the term. A more sophisticated query processing strategy is as follows. For the first entry in the list for 'holocaust,' search the hierarchical index as before. This implies traversing down the hierarchy until no more successful matches occur (or the bottom of the hierarchy is reached). Let the last matching structural component be referred to as the innermost matching component. Once this first search is concluded, do not start all over again for the following entry in the inverted list. Instead, verify whether the innermost matching component also matches the second entry in the list. If it does, we immediately conclude that the larger structural components above it (in the hierarchy) also do. Proceed then to the third entry in the list, and so on. Notice that the query processing is accelerated because only the nearby (or proximal) nodes in the list need to be searched at each time. This is the reason for the label *proximal nodes.*

The model based on proximal nodes allows us to formulate queries which are more complex than those which can be formulated in the model based on non-overlapping lists. To speed up query processing, however, only nearby (proximal) nodes are looked at which imposes restrictions on the answer set retrieved (all nodes must come from the same hierarchy). More complex models for structured retrieval have been proposed in the literature as discussed in [41, 590].

2.10   Models for Browsing

As already observed, the user might not be interested in posing a specific query to the system. Instead, he might be willing to invest some time in exploring the document space looking for interesting references. In this situation, we say that the user is *browsing* the space instead of searching. Both with browsing and searching, the user has goals which he is pursuing. However, in general, the goal of a searching task is clearer in the mind of the user than the goal of a browsing task. As is obvious, this is not a distinction which is valid in all scenarios. But, since it is simple and provides a clear separation between the tasks of searching and browsing, it is adopted here. We distinguish three types of browsing namely, flat, structure guided, and hypertext.

2.10.1   Flat Browsing

The idea here is that the user explores a document space which has a flat organization. For instance, the documents might be represented as dots in a (two-dimensional) plan or as elements in a (single dimension) list. The user then glances here and there looking for information within the documents visited. For instance, he might look for correlations among neighbor documents or for keywords which are of interest to him. Such keywords could then be added to the original query in an attempt to provide better contextualization. This is a process called *relevance feedback* which is discussed in detail in Chapter 5. Also, the user could explore a single document in a flat manner. For example, he could use a browser to look into a Web page, using the arrows and the scroll bar. One disadvantage is that in a given page or screen there may not be any indication about the context where the user is. For example, if he opens a novel at a random page, he might not know in which chapter that page is.

Web search engines such as 'Yahoo!' provide, besides the standard search interface, a hierarchical directory which can be used for browsing (and frequently, for searching). However, the organization is not flat as discussed below.

2.10.2 Structure Guided Browsing

To facilitate the task of browsing, the documents might be organized in a structure such as a directory. Directories are hierarchies of classes which group documents covering related topics. Such hierarchies of classes have been used to classify document collections for many centuries now. Thus, it seems natural to adapt them for use with modern browsing interfaces. In this case, we say that the user performs a structure guided type of browsing. The same idea can be applied to a single document. For example, if we are browsing an electronic book, a first level of content could be the chapters, the second level, all sections, and so on. The last level would be the text itself (flat). A good user interface could go down or up those levels in a focused manner, assisting the user with the task of keeping track of the context.

Besides the structure which directs the browsing task, the interface can also include facilities such as a history map which identifies classes recently visited. This might be quite useful for dealing with very large structures – an issue discussed in Chapters 10 and 13. When searching, the occurrences can also be displayed showing just the structure (for example, using the table of contents). This allows us to see the occurrences in a global context instead of in a page of text that may have no indication of where we are.

2.10.3 The Hypertext Model

One fundamental concept related to the task of writing down text is the notion of *sequencing*. Written text is usually conceived to be read sequentially. The reader should not expect to fully understand the message conveyed by the writer by randomly reading pieces of text here and there. One might rely on the text structure to skip portions of the text but this might result in miscommunication between reader and writer. Thus, a sequenced organizational structure lies underneath most written text. When the reader fails to perceive such a structure and abide by it, he frequently is unable to capture the essence of the writer's message.

Sometimes, however, we are looking for information which is subsumed by the whole text but which cannot be easily captured through sequential reading. For instance, while glancing at a book about the history of the wars fought by man, we might be momentarily interested solely in the regional wars in Europe. We know that this information is in the book, but we might have a hard time finding it because the writer did not organize his writings with this purpose (he might have organized the wars chronologically). In such a situation, a different organization of the text is desired. However, there is no point in rewriting the whole text. Thus, the solution is to define a new organizational structure besides the one already in existence. One way to accomplish such a goal is through the design of a hypertext.

Hypertext Definition and the Navigational Task

A *hypertext* is a high level interactive navigational structure which allows us to browse text non-sequentially on a computer screen. It consists basically of nodes which are correlated by directed links in a graph structure.

To each node is associated a text region which might be a chapter in a book, a section in an article, or a Web page. Two nodes A and B might be connected by a *directed link* l_{AB} which correlates the texts associated with these two nodes. In this case, the reader might move to the node B while reading the text associated with the node A.

In its most conventional form, a hypertext link l_{AB} is attached to a specific string inside the text for node A. Such a string is marked specially (for instance, its characters might appear in a different color or underlined) to indicate the presence of the underlying link. While reading the text, the user might come across a marked string. If the user clicks on that string, the underlying directed link is followed, and a new text region (associated with the node at the destination) is displayed on the screen.

The process of navigating the hypertext can be understood as a traversal of a directed graph. The linked nodes of the graph represent text nodes which are semantically related. While traversing this graph the reader visualizes a flow of information which was conceived by the designer of the hypertext. Consider our previous example regarding a book on the wars fought by man. One might design a hypertext composed of two distinct *webs* (here, a web is simply a connected component formed by a subset of all links in the hypertext). While the first web might be designed to provide access to the local wars fought in Europe in chronological order, the second web might be designed to provide access to the local wars fought by each European country. In this way, the user of this hypertext can access the information according to his particular need.

When the hypertext is large, the user might lose track of the organizational structure of the hypertext. The effect is that the user might start to take bad navigational decisions which might sidetrack him from his main goal (which usually consists of finding a piece of information in the hypertext). When this happens, the user is said to be *lost in hyperspace* [604]. To avoid this problem, it is desirable that the hypertext include a hypertext map which shows where the user is at all times. In its simplest form, this map is a directed graph which displays the current node being visited. Additionally, such a map could include information on the paths the user has traveled so far. This can be used to remind the user of the uselessness of following paths which have been explored already.

While navigating a hypertext, the user is restricted to the intended flow of information previously conceived by the hypertext designer. Thus, the task of designing a hypertext should take into account the needs of its potential users. This implies the execution of a requirement analysis phase before starting the actual implementation of the hypertext. Such a requirement analysis is critically important but is frequently overlooked.

Furthermore, during the hypertext navigation, the user might find it difficult to orient himself. This difficulty arises even in the presence of a guiding tool such as the hypertext map discussed above. One possible reason is an excessively complex hypertext organization with too many links which allow the user to travel back and forth. To avoid this problem, the hypertext can have a simpler structure which can be quickly remembered by the user at all times. For instance, the hypertext can be organized hierarchically to facilitate the navigational task.

Definition of the structure of the hypertext should be accomplished in a domain modeling phase (done after a requirement analysis phase). Further, after the modeling of the domain, a user interface design should be concluded prior to implementation. Only then, can we say that we have a proper hypertext structure for the application at hand. In the Web, however, pages are usually implemented with no attention paid to requirement analysis, domain modeling, and user interface design. As a result, Web pages are frequently poorly conceived and often fail to provide the user with a proper hypertext structure for assistance with the information seeking task.

With large hypertexts, it might be difficult for the user to position himself in the part of the whole graph which is of most interest to him. To facilitate this initial positioning step, a search based on index terms might be used. In [540], Manber discusses the advantages of this approach.

Hypertexts provided the basis for the conception and design of the hypertext markup language (HTML) and the hypertext transfer protocol (HTTP) which originated the *World Wide Web* (which we simply refer to as the Web). In Chapter 13, we discuss the Web in detail. We briefly discuss some of its features below.

About the Web

When one talks about the Web, the first concept which comes to mind is that of a hypertext. In fact, we frequently think of the Web as a huge distributed hypertext domain. However, the Web is not exactly a proper hypertext because it lacks an underlying data model, it lacks a navigational plan, and it lacks a consistently designed user interface. Each one of the millions of Web page designers devises his own interface with its own peculiar characteristics. Many times we visit a Web site simply looking for a phone number and cannot find it because it is buried in the least expected place of the local hypertext structure. Thus, the Web user has no underlying metaphor to assist him in the search for information of interest.

Instead of saying that the Web is a hypertext, we prefer to say that it is a pool of (partially) interconnected webs. Some of these webs might be characterized as a local hypertext (in the sense that they have an underlying structure which enjoys some consistency) but others might be simply a collection of pages designed separately (for instance, the web of a university department whose professors design their own pages). Despite not being exactly a hypertext, the Web has provided us with a new dimension in communication functionality because it is easily accessible world wide at very low cost. And maybe most important, the Web has no control body setting up regulations and censorship rules. As a result, for the first time in the history of mankind, any one person can publish his writings through a large medium without being subjected to the filtering of an editorial board.

For a more thorough discussion of these and many other issues related to the Web, the user is referred to Chapter 13.

2.11   Trends and Research Issues

There are three main types of products and systems which can benefit directly from research in models for information retrieval: library systems, specialized retrieval systems, and the Web.

Regarding library systems, there is currently much interest in cognitive and behavioral issues oriented particularly at a better understanding of which criteria the users adopt to judge relevance. From the point of view of the computer scientist, a main question is how this knowledge about the user affects the ranking strategies and the user interface implemented by the system. A related issue is the investigation of how models other than the Boolean model (which is still largely adopted by most large commercial library systems) affect the user of a library.

A specialized retrieval system is one which is developed with a particular application in mind. For instance, the LEXIS-NEXIS retrieval system (see Chapter 14), which provides access to a very large collection of legal and business documents, is a good example of a specialized retrieval system. In such a system, a key problem is how to retrieve (almost) all documents which might be relevant to the user information need without also retrieving a large number of unrelated documents. In this context, sophisticated ranking algorithms are highly desirable. Since ranking based on single evidential sources is unlikely to provide the appropriate answers, research on approaches for combining several evidential sources seems highly relevant (as demonstrated at the various TREC conferences, see Chapter 3 for details).

In the Web, the scenario is quite distinct and unique. In fact, the user of the Web frequently does not know what he wants or has great difficulty in properly formulating his request. Thus, research in advanced user interfaces is highly desirable. From the point of view of the ranking engine, an interesting problem is to study how the paradigm adopted for the user interface affects the ranking. Furthermore, it is now well established that the indexes maintained by the various Web search engines are almost disjoint (e.g., the ten most popular search engines have indexes whose intersection corresponds to less than 2% of the total number of pages indexed). In this scenario, research on meta-search engines (i.e., engines which work by fusing the rankings generated by other search engines) seems highly promising.

2.12   Bibliographic Discussion

Early in 1960, Maron and Kuhns [547] had already discussed the issues of relevance and probabilistic indexing in information retrieval. Twenty-three years later, Salton and McGill wrote a book [698] which became a classic in the field. The book provides a thorough coverage of the three classic models in information retrieval namely, the Boolean, the vector, and the probabilistic models. Another landmark reference is the book by van Rijsbergen [785] which, besides also covering the three classic models, presents a thorough and enjoyable discussion on the probabilistic model. The book edited by Frakes and Baeza-Yates [275] presents several data structures and algorithms for IR and is more recent. Further, it includes a discussion of ranking algorithms by Harman [340] which provides interesting insights into the history of information retrieval from 1960 to 1990.

Boolean operations and their implementation are covered in [803]. The inadequacy of Boolean queries for information retrieval was characterized early on by Verhoeff, Goffman, and Belzer [786]. The issue of adapting the Boolean formalism to operate with other frameworks received great attention. Bookstein discusses the problems related with merging Boolean and weighted retrieval systems [101] and the implications of Boolean structure for probabilistic retrieval [103]. Losee and Bookstein [522] cover the usage of Boolean queries with probabilistic retrieval. Anick *et al.* [21] propose an interface based on natural language for Boolean retrieval. A thesaurus-based Boolean retrieval system is proposed in [493].

The vector model is maybe the most popular model among the research community in information retrieval. Much of this popularity is due to the long-term research of Salton and his associates [697, 704]. Most of this research revolved around the SMART retrieval system developed at Cornell University [695, 842, 696]. Term weighting for the vector model has also been investigated thoroughly. Simple term weighting was used early on by Salton and Lesk [697]. Sparck Jones introduced the idf factor [409, 410] and Salton and Yang verified its effectiveness for improving retrieval [704]. Yu and Salton [842] further studied the effects of term weighting in the final ranking. Salton and Buckley [696] summarize 20 years of experiments in term weighting with the SMART system. Raghavan and Wong [665] provide a critical analysis of the vector model.

The probabilistic model was introduced by Robertson and Sparck Jones [677] and is thoroughly discussed in [785]. Experimental studies with the model were conducted by Sparck Jones [411, 412] which used feedback from the user to estimate the initial probabilities. Croft and Harper [199] proposed a method to estimate these probabilities without feedback from the user. Croft [198] later on added within-document frequency weights into the model. Fuhr discusses probabilistic indexing through polynomial retrieval functions [281, 284]. Cooper, Gey, and Dabney [186] and later on Gey [295] propose the use of logistic regression with probabilistic retrieval. Lee and Kantor [494] study the effect of inconsistent expert judgements on probabilistic retrieval. Fuhr [282] reviews various variants of the classic probabilistic model. Cooper [187], in a seminal paper, raises troubling questions on the utilization of the probabilistic ranking principle in information retrieval.

The inference network model was introduced by Turtle and Croft [772, 771] in 1990. Haines and Croft [332] discuss the utilization of inference networks for user relevance feedback (see Chapter 5). Callan, Lu, and Croft [139] use an inference network to search distributed document collections. Callan [138], in his turn, discusses the application of inference networks to information filtering. The belief network model, due to Ribeiro-Neto and Muntz [674], generalizes the inference network model.

The extended Boolean model was introduced by Salton, Fox, and Wu [703]. Lee, Kim, Kim, and Lee [496] discuss the evaluation of Boolean operators with the extended Boolean model, while properties of the model are discussed in [495]. The generalized vector space model was introduced in 1985 by Wong, Ziarko, and Wong [832, 831]. Latent semantic indexing was introduced in 1988 by Furnas, Deerwester, Dumais, Landauer, Harshman, Streeter, and Lochbaum [287]. In a subsequent paper, Bartell, Cottrell, and Belew [62] show that latent semantic indexing can be interpreted as a special case of multidimensional scaling.

Regarding neural network models for information retrieval, our discussion in this book is based mainly on the work by Wilkinson and Hingston [815]. But we also benefited from the writings of Kwok on the subject and related topics [466, 467, 469, 468].

The fuzzy set model (for information retrieval) covered in this book is due to Ogawa, Morita, and Kobayashi [616]. The utilization of fuzzy theory in information retrieval goes back to the 1970s with the work of Radecki [658, 659, 660, 661], of Sachs [691], and of Tahani [755]. Bookstein [102] proposes the utilization of fuzzy operators to deal with weighted Boolean searches. Kraft and Buel [461] utilize fuzzy sets to generalize a Boolean system. Miyamoto, Miyake, and Nakayama [567] discuss the generation of a pseudothesaurus using co-occurrences and fuzzy operators. Subsequently, Miyamoto and Nakayama [568] discuss the utilization of this thesaurus with information retrieval systems.

Our discussion on structured text is based on the survey by [41]. Another survey of interest (an older one though) is the work by MacLeod [533]. Burkowski [132, 133] proposed a model based on non-overlapping regions. Clarke, Cormack, and Burkowski [173] extended this model with overlapping capabilities. The model based on proximal nodes was proposed by Navarro and Baeza-Yates [589, 590]. In [534], MacLeod introduced a model based on a single hierarchy which also associates attributes with nodes in the hierarchy (for database-like querying) and hypertext links with pairs of nodes. Kilpelainen and Mannila [439] discuss the retrieval from hierarchical texts through the specification of partial patterns. In [183], Consens and Milo discuss algebras for querying text regions.

A classic reference on hypertexts is the book by Nielsen [604]. Another popular reference is the book by Shneiderman and Kearsley [727]. Conklin [181] presents an introductory survey of the area. The *Communications of the ACM* dedicated an special edition [177] to hypermedia which discusses in detail the Dexter model — a reference standard on the terminology and semantics of basic hypermedia concepts. A subsequent edition [178] was dedicated to the presentation of various models for supporting the design of hypermedia applications.

Chapter 3
Retrieval Evaluation

3.1 Introduction

Before the final implementation of an information retrieval system, an evaluation of the system is usually carried out. The type of evaluation to be considered depends on the objectives of the retrieval system. Clearly, any software system has to provide the functionality it was conceived for. Thus, the first type of evaluation which should be considered is a functional analysis in which the specified system functionalities are tested one by one. Such an analysis should also include an error analysis phase in which, instead of looking for functionalities, one behaves erratically trying to make the system fail. It is a simple procedure which can be quite useful for catching programming errors. Given that the system has passed the functional analysis phase, one should proceed to evaluate the performance of the system.

The most common measures of system performance are time and space. The shorter the response time, the smaller the space used, the better the system is considered to be. There is an inherent tradeoff between space complexity and time complexity which frequently allows trading one for the other. In Chapter 8 we discuss this issue in detail.

In a system designed for providing data retrieval, the response time and the space required are usually the metrics of most interest and the ones normally adopted for evaluating the system. In this case, we look for the performance of the indexing structures (which are in place to accelerate the search), the interaction with the operating system, the delays in communication channels, and the overheads introduced by the many software layers which are usually present. We refer to such a form of evaluation simply as *performance evaluation*.

In a system designed for providing information retrieval, other metrics, besides time and space, are also of interest. In fact, since the user query request is inherently vague, the retrieved documents are not exact answers and have to be ranked according to their relevance to the query. Such relevance ranking introduces a component which is not present in data retrieval systems and which plays a central role in information retrieval. Thus, information retrieval systems require the evaluation of how precise is the answer set. This type of evaluation is referred to as *retrieval performance evaluation*.

In this chapter, we discuss retrieval performance evaluation for information retrieval systems. Such an evaluation is usually based on a test reference collection and on an evaluation measure. The test reference collection consists of a collection of documents, a set of example information requests, and a set of relevant documents (provided by specialists) for each example information request. Given a retrieval strategy S, the evaluation measure quantifies (for each example information request) the *similarity* between the set of documents retrieved by S and the set of relevant documents provided by the specialists. This provides an estimation of the *goodness* of the retrieval strategy S.

In our discussion, we first cover the two most used retrieval evaluation measures: recall and precision. We also cover alternative evaluation measures such as the E measure, the harmonic mean, satisfaction, frustration, etc. Following that, we cover four test reference collections namely, TIPSTER/TREC, CACM, CISI, and Cystic Fibrosis.

3.2   Retrieval Performance Evaluation

When considering retrieval performance evaluation, we should first consider the retrieval task that is to be evaluated. For instance, the retrieval task could consist simply of a query processed in batch mode (i.e., the user submits a query and receives an answer back) or of a whole interactive session (i.e., the user specifies his information need through a series of interactive steps with the system). Further, the retrieval task could also comprise a combination of these two strategies. Batch and interactive query tasks are quite distinct processes and thus their evaluations are also distinct. In fact, in an interactive session, user effort, characteristics of the interface design, guidance provided by the system, and duration of the session are critical aspects which should be observed and measured. In a batch session, none of these aspects is nearly as important as the quality of the answer set generated.

Besides the nature of the query request, one has also to consider the setting where the evaluation will take place and the type of interface used. Regarding the setting, evaluation of experiments performed in a laboratory might be quite distinct from evaluation of experiments carried out in a real life situation. Regarding the type of interface, while early bibliographic systems (which still dominate the commercial market as discussed in Chapter 14) present the user with interfaces which normally operate in batch mode, newer systems (which are been popularized by the high quality graphic displays available nowadays) usually present the user with complex interfaces which often operate interactively.

Retrieval performance evaluation in the early days of computer-based information retrieval systems focused primarily on laboratory experiments designed for batch interfaces. In the 1990s, a lot more attention has been paid to the evaluation of real life experiments. Despite this tendency, laboratory experimentation is still dominant. Two main reasons are the repeatability and the scalability provided by the closed setting of a laboratory.

In this book, we focus mainly on experiments performed in laboratories. In this chapter in particular we discuss solely the evaluation of systems which operate in batch mode. Evaluation of systems which operate interactively is briefly discussed in Chapter 10.

3.2.1   Recall and Precision

Consider an example information request I (of a test reference collection) and its set R of relevant documents. Let $|R|$ be the number of documents in this set. Assume that a given retrieval strategy (which is being evaluated) processes the information request I and generates a document answer set A. Let $|A|$ be the number of documents in this set. Further, let $|Ra|$ be the number of documents in the intersection of the sets R and A. Figure 3.1 illustrates these sets.

The recall and precision measures are defined as follows.

- **Recall** is the fraction of the relevant documents (the set R) which has been retrieved i.e.,

$$Recall = \frac{|Ra|}{|R|}$$

- **Precision** is the fraction of the retrieved documents (the set A) which is relevant i.e.,

$$Precision = \frac{|Ra|}{|A|}$$

Recall and precision, as defined above, assume that all the documents in the answer set A have been examined (or seen). However, the user is not usually presented with all the documents in the answer set A at once. Instead, the

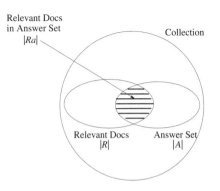

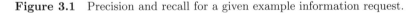

Figure 3.1   Precision and recall for a given example information request.

documents in A are first sorted according to a degree of relevance (i.e., a ranking is generated). The user then examines this ranked list starting from the top document. In this situation, the recall and precision measures vary as the user proceeds with his examination of the answer set A. Thus, proper evaluation requires plotting a precision versus recall curve as follows.

As before, consider a reference collection and its set of example information requests. Let us focus on a given example information request for which a query q is formulated. Assume that a set R_q containing the relevant documents for q has been defined. Without loss of generality, assume further that the set R_q is composed of the following documents

$$R_q = \{d_3, d_5, d_9, d_{25}, d_{39}, d_{44}, d_{56}, d_{71}, d_{89}, d_{123}\} \tag{3.1}$$

Thus, according to a group of specialists, there are ten documents which are relevant to the query q.

Consider now a new retrieval algorithm which has just been designed. Assume that this algorithm returns, for the query q, a ranking of the documents in the answer set as follows.

Ranking for query q:

1. d_{123} ●	6. d_9 ●	11. d_{38}
2. d_{84}	7. d_{511}	12. d_{48}
3. d_{56} ●	8. d_{129}	13. d_{250}
4. d_6	9. d_{187}	14. d_{113}
5. d_8	10. d_{25} ●	15. d_3 ●

The documents that are relevant to the query q are marked with a bullet after the document number. If we examine this ranking, starting from the top document, we observe the following points. First, the document d_{123} which is ranked as number 1 is relevant. Further, this document corresponds to 10% of all the relevant documents in the set R_q. Thus, we say that we have a precision of 100% at 10% recall. Second, the document d_{56} which is ranked as number 3 is the next relevant document. At this point, we say that we have a precision of roughly 66% (two documents out of three are relevant) at 20% recall (two of the ten relevant documents have been seen). Third, if we proceed with our examination of the ranking generated we can plot a curve of precision versus recall as illustrated in Figure 3.2. The precision at levels of recall higher than 50% drops to 0 because not all relevant documents have been retrieved. This precision versus recall curve is usually based on 11 (instead of ten) *standard* recall levels which are 0%, 10%, 20%, ..., 100%. For the recall level 0%, the precision is obtained through an interpolation procedure as detailed below.

In the above example, the precision and recall figures are for a single query. Usually, however, retrieval algorithms are evaluated by running them for several distinct queries. In this case, for each query a distinct precision versus recall curve is generated. To evaluate the retrieval performance of an algorithm over

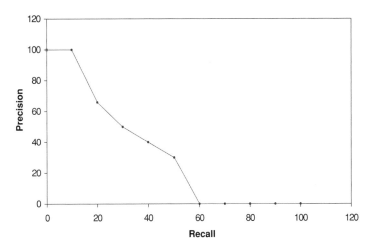

Figure 3.2   Precision at 11 standard recall levels.

all test queries, we average the precision figures at each recall level as follows.

$$\overline{P}(r) = \sum_{i=1}^{N_q} \frac{P_i(r)}{N_q} \tag{3.2}$$

where $\overline{P}(r)$ is the average precision at the recall level r, N_q is the number of queries used, and $P_i(r)$ is the precision at recall level r for the i-th query.

Since the recall levels for each query might be distinct from the 11 standard recall levels, utilization of an interpolation procedure is often necessary. For instance, consider again the set of 15 ranked documents presented above. Assume that the set of relevant documents for the query q has changed and is now given by

$$R_q = \{d_3, d_{56}, d_{129}\} \tag{3.3}$$

In this case, the first relevant document in the ranking for query q is d_{56} which provides a recall level of 33.3% (with precision also equal to 33.3%) because, at this point, one-third of all relevant documents have already been seen. The second relevant document is d_{129} which provides a recall level of 66.6% (with precision equal to 25%). The third relevant document is d_3 which provides a recall level of 100% (with precision equal to 20%). The precision figures at the 11 standard recall levels are interpolated as follows.

Let r_j, $j \in \{0, 1, 2, \ldots, 10\}$, be a reference to the j-th standard recall level (i.e., r_5 is a reference to the recall level 50%). Then,

$$P(r_j) = max_{\ r_j \leq r \leq r_{j+1}} \ P(r) \tag{3.4}$$

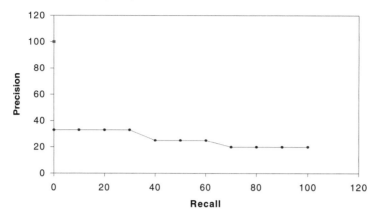

Figure 3.3 Interpolated precision at 11 standard recall levels relative to $R_q = \{d_3, d_{56}, d_{129}\}$.

which states that the interpolated precision at the j-th standard recall level is the maximum known precision at any recall level between the j-th recall level and the $(j + 1)$-th recall level.

In our last example, this interpolation rule yields the precision and recall figures illustrated in Figure 3.3. At recall levels 0%, 10%, 20%, and 30%, the interpolated precision is equal to 33.3% (which is the known precision at the recall level 33.3%). At recall levels 40%, 50%, and 60%, the interpolated precision is 25% (which is the precision at the recall level 66.6%). At recall levels 70%, 80%, 90%, and 100%, the interpolated precision is 20% (which is the precision at recall level 100%).

The curve of precision versus recall which results from averaging the results for various queries is usually referred to as precision versus recall figures. Such average figures are normally used to compare the retrieval performance of distinct retrieval algorithms. For instance, one could compare the retrieval performance of a newly proposed retrieval algorithm with the retrieval performance of the classic vector space model. Figure 3.4 illustrates average precision versus recall figures for two distinct retrieval algorithms. In this case, one algorithm has higher precision at lower recall levels while the second algorithm is superior at higher recall levels.

One additional approach is to compute average precision at given *document cutoff values*. For instance, we can compute the average precision when 5, 10, 15, 20, 30, 50, or 100 relevant documents have been seen. The procedure is analogous to the computation of average precision at 11 standard recall levels but provides additional information on the retrieval performance of the ranking algorithm.

Average precision versus recall figures are now a standard evaluation strategy for information retrieval systems and are used extensively in the information retrieval literature. They are useful because they allow us to evaluate

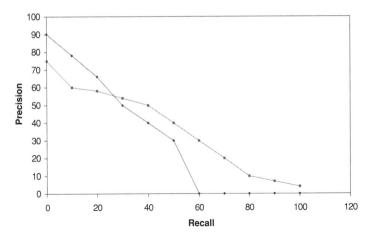

Figure 3.4 Average recall versus precision figures for two distinct retrieval algorithms.

quantitatively both the quality of the overall answer set and the breadth of the retrieval algorithm. Further, they are simple, intuitive, and can be combined in a single curve. However, precision versus recall figures also have their disadvantages and their widespread usage has been criticized in the literature. We return to this point later on. Before that, let us discuss techniques for summarizing precision versus recall figures by a single numerical value.

Single Value Summaries

Average precision versus recall figures are useful for comparing the retrieval performance of distinct retrieval algorithms over a set of example queries. However, there are situations in which we would like to compare the retrieval performance of our retrieval algorithms for the individual queries. The reasons are twofold. First, averaging precision over many queries might disguise important anomalies in the retrieval algorithms under study. Second, when comparing two algorithms, we might be interested in investigating whether one of them outperforms the other for each query in a given set of example queries (notice that this fact can be easily hidden by an average precision computation). In these situations, a single precision value (for each query) can be used. This single value should be interpreted as a summary of the corresponding precision versus recall curve. Usually, this single value summary is taken as the precision at a specified recall level. For instance, we could evaluate the precision when we observe the first relevant document and take this precision as the single value summary. Of course, as seems obvious, this is not a good approach. More interesting strategies can be adopted as we now discuss.

Average Precision at Seen Relevant Documents
The idea here is to generate a single value summary of the ranking by averaging the precision figures obtained after each new relevant document is observed (in the ranking). For instance, consider the example in Figure 3.2. The precision figures after each new relevant document is observed are 1, 0.66, 0.5, 0.4, and 0.3. Thus, the *average precision at seen relevant documents* is given by $(1+0.66+0.5+0.4+0.3)/5$ or 0.57. This measure favors systems which retrieve relevant documents quickly (i.e., early in the ranking). Of course, an algorithm might present a good average precision at seen relevant documents but have a poor performance in terms of overall recall.

R-Precision
The idea here is to generate a single value summary of the ranking by computing the precision at the R-th position in the ranking, where R is the total number of relevant documents for the current query (i.e., number of documents in the set R_q). For instance, consider the examples in Figures 3.2 and 3.3. The value of R-precision is 0.4 for the first example (because $R = 10$ and there are four relevant documents among the first ten documents in the ranking) and 0.33 for the second example (because $R = 3$ and there is one relevant document among the first three documents in the ranking). The R-precision measure is a useful parameter for observing the behavior of an algorithm for each individual query in an experiment. Additionally, one can also compute an average R-precision figure over all queries. However, using a single number to summarize the full behavior of a retrieval algorithm over several queries might be quite imprecise.

Precision Histograms
The R-precision measures for several queries can be used to compare the retrieval history of two algorithms as follows. Let $RP_A(i)$ and $RP_B(i)$ be the R-precision values of the retrieval algorithms A and B for the i-th query. Define, for instance, the difference

$$RP_{A/B}(i) = RP_A(i) - RP_B(i) \qquad (3.5)$$

A value of $RP_{A/B}(i)$ equal to 0 indicates that both algorithms have equivalent performance (in terms of R-precision) for the i-th query. A positive value of $RP_{A/B}(i)$ indicates a better retrieval performance by algorithm A (for the i-th query) while a negative value indicates a better retrieval performance by algorithm B. Figure 3.5 illustrates the $RP_{A/B}(i)$ values (labeled *R-Precision A/B*) for two hypothetical retrieval algorithms over ten example queries. The algorithm A is superior for eight queries while the algorithm B performs better for the two other queries (numbered 4 and 5). This type of bar graph is called a *precision histogram* and allows us to quickly compare the retrieval performance history of two algorithms through visual inspection.

Summary Table Statistics
Single value measures can also be stored in a table to provide a statistical summary regarding the set of all the queries in a retrieval task. For instance, these

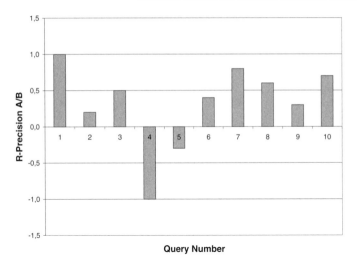

Figure 3.5   A precision histogram for ten hypothetical queries.

summary table statistics could include: the number of queries used in the task, the total number of documents retrieved by all queries, the total number of relevant documents which were effectively retrieved when all queries are considered, the total number of relevant documents which could have been retrieved by all queries, etc.

Precision and Recall Appropriateness

Precision and recall have been used extensively to evaluate the retrieval performance of retrieval algorithms. However, a more careful reflection reveals problems with these two measures [451, 664, 754]. First, the proper estimation of maximum recall for a query requires detailed knowledge of all the documents in the collection. With large collections, such knowledge is unavailable which implies that recall cannot be estimated precisely. Second, recall and precision are related measures which capture different aspects of the set of retrieved documents. In many situations, the use of a single measure which combines recall and precision could be more appropriate. Third, recall and precision measure the effectiveness over a set of queries processed in batch mode. However, with modern systems, interactivity (and not batch processing) is the key aspect of the retrieval process. Thus, measures which quantify the *informativeness* of the retrieval process might now be more appropriate. Fourth, recall and precision are easy to define when a linear ordering of the retrieved documents is enforced. For systems which require a weak ordering though, recall and precision might be inadequate.

3.2.2 Alternative Measures

Since recall and precision, despite their popularity, are not always the most appropriate measures for evaluating retrieval performance, alternative measures have been proposed over the years. A brief review of some of them is as follows.

The Harmonic Mean

As discussed above, a single measure which combines recall and precision might be of interest. One such measure is the harmonic mean F of recall and precision [422] which is computed as

$$F(j) = \frac{2}{\frac{1}{r(j)} + \frac{1}{P(j)}} \tag{3.6}$$

where $r(j)$ is the recall for the j-th document in the ranking, $P(j)$ is the precision for the j-th document in the ranking, and $F(j)$ is the harmonic mean of $r(j)$ and $P(j)$ (thus, relative to the j-th document in the ranking). The function F assumes values in the interval $[0, 1]$. It is 0 when no relevant documents have been retrieved and is 1 when all ranked documents are relevant. Further, the harmonic mean F assumes a high value only when both recall and precision are high. Therefore, determination of the maximum value for F can be interpreted as an attempt to find the best possible compromise between recall and precision.

The E Measure

Another measure which combines recall and precision was proposed by van Rijsbergen [785] and is called the E evaluation measure. The idea is to allow the user to specify whether he is more interested in recall or in precision. The E measure is defined as follows.

$$E(j) = 1 - \frac{1 + b^2}{\frac{b^2}{r(j)} + \frac{1}{P(j)}}$$

where $r(j)$ is the recall for the j-th document in the ranking, $P(j)$ is the precision for the j-th document in the ranking, $E(j)$ is the E evaluation measure relative to $r(j)$ and $P(j)$, and b is a user specified parameter which reflects the relative importance of recall and precision. For $b = 1$, the $E(j)$ measure works as the complement of the harmonic mean $F(j)$. Values of b greater than 1 indicate that the user is more interested in precision than in recall while values of b smaller than 1 indicate that the user is more interested in recall than in precision.

User-Oriented Measures

Recall and precision are based on the assumption that the set of relevant documents for a query is the same, independent of the user. However, different users might have a different interpretation of which document is relevant and which one is not. To cope with this problem, *user-oriented* measures have been proposed such as coverage ratio, novelty ratio, relative recall, and recall effort [451].

As before, consider a reference collection, an example information request I, and a retrieval strategy to be evaluated. Let R be the set of relevant documents for I and A be the answer set retrieved. Also, let U be the subset of R which is known to the user. The number of documents in U is $|U|$. The intersection of the sets A and U yields the documents known to the user to be relevant which were retrieved. Let $|Rk|$ be the number of documents in this set. Further, let $|Ru|$ be the number of relevant documents previously unknown to the user which were retrieved. Figure 3.6 illustrates the situation. The *coverage ratio* is defined as the fraction of the documents known (to the user) to be relevant which has actually been retrieved i.e.,

$$coverage = \frac{|Rk|}{|U|}$$

The *novelty ratio* is defined as the fraction of the relevant documents retrieved which was unknown to the user i.e.,

$$novelty = \frac{|Ru|}{|Ru| + |Rk|}$$

A high coverage ratio indicates that the system is finding most of the relevant documents the user expected to see. A high novelty ratio indicates that the system is revealing (to the user) many new relevant documents which were previously unknown.

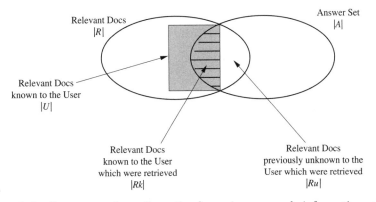

Figure 3.6   Coverage and novelty ratios for a given example information request.

Additionally, two other measures can be defined as follows. The *relative recall* is given by the ratio between the number of relevant documents found (by the system) and the number of relevant documents the user expected to find. In the case when the user finds as many relevant documents as he expected, he stops searching and the relative recall is equal to 1. The *recall effort* is given by the ratio between the number of relevant documents the user expected to find and the number of documents examined in an attempt to find the expected relevant documents.

Other Measures

Other measures which might be of interest include the *expected search length*, which is good for dealing with sets of documents weakly ordered, the *satisfaction*, which takes into account only the relevant documents, and the *frustration*, which takes into account only the non-relevant documents [451].

3.3   Reference Collections

In this section we discuss various reference collections which have been used throughout the years for the evaluation of information retrieval systems. We first discuss the TIPSTER/TREC collection which, due to its large size and thorough experimentation, is usually considered to be the *reference* test collection in information retrieval nowadays. Following that, we cover the CACM and ISI collections due to their historical importance in the area of information retrieval. We conclude this section with a brief discussion of the Cystic Fibrosis collection. It is a small collection whose example information requests were extensively studied by four groups of specialists before generation of the relevant document sets.

3.3.1   The TREC Collection

Research in information retrieval has frequently been criticized on two fronts. First, that it lacks a solid formal framework as a basic foundation. Second, that it lacks robust and consistent testbeds and benchmarks. The first of these criticisms is difficult to dismiss entirely due to the inherent degree of psychological *subjectiveness* associated with the task of deciding on the relevance of a given document (which characterizes information, as opposed to data, retrieval). Thus, at least for now, research in information retrieval will have to proceed without a solid formal underpinning. The second of these criticisms, however, can be acted upon. For three decades, experimentation in information retrieval was based on relatively small test collections which did not reflect the main issues present in a large bibliographical environment. Further, comparisons between various retrieval systems were difficult to make because distinct groups conducted experiments focused on distinct aspects of retrieval (even when the same test collection was used) and there were no widely accepted benchmarks.

In the early 1990s, a reaction to this state of disarray was initiated under the leadership of Donna Harman at the National Institute of Standards and Technology (NIST), in Maryland. Such an effort consisted of promoting a yearly conference, named TREC for Text REtrieval Conference, dedicated to experimentation with a large test collection comprising over a million documents. For each TREC conference, a set of reference experiments is designed. The research groups which participate in the conference use these reference experiments for comparing their retrieval systems.

A clear statement of the purpose of the TREC conferences can be found in the NIST TREC Web site [768] and reads as follows.

> The TREC conference series is co-sponsored by the National Institute of Standards and Technology (NIST) and the Information Technology Office of the Defense Advanced Research Projects Agency (DARPA) as part of the TIPSTER Text Program. The goal of the conference series is to encourage research in information retrieval from large text applications by providing a large test collection, uniform scoring procedures, and a forum for organizations interested in comparing their results. Attendance at TREC conferences is restricted to those researchers and developers who have performed the TREC retrieval tasks and to selected government personnel from sponsoring agencies.
>
> Participants in a TREC conference employ a wide variety of retrieval techniques, including methods using automatic thesauri, sophisticated term weighting, natural language techniques, relevance feedback, and advanced pattern matching. Each system works with the same test collection that consists of about 2 gigabytes of text (over 1 million documents) and a given set of information needs called 'topics.' Results are run through a common evaluation package so that groups can compare the effectiveness of different techniques and can determine how differences between systems affect performance.

Since the collection was built under the TIPSTER program, it is frequently referred to as the TIPSTER or the TIPSTER/TREC test collection. Here, however, for simplicity we refer to it as the TREC collection.

The first TREC conference was held at NIST in November 1992, while the second TREC conference occurred in August 1993. In November 1997, the sixth TREC conference was held (also at NIST) and counted the following participating organizations (extracted from [794]):

Apple Computer	City Univ., London
AT&T Labs Research	CLARITECH Corporation
Australian National Univ.	Cornell Univ./SaBIR Research, Inc.
Carnegie Mellon Univ.	CSIRO (Australia)
CEA (France)	Daimler Benz Res. Center, Ulm
Center for Inf. Res., Russia	Dublin Univ. Center

Duke Univ./Univ. of Colorado/Bellcore	Oregon Health Sciences Univ.
ETH (Switzerland)	Queens College, CUNY
FS Consulting, Inc.	Rutgers Univ. (2 groups)
GE Corp./Rutgers Univ.	Siemens AG
George Mason Univ./NCR Corp.	SRI International
Harris Corp.	TwentyOne
IBM T.J. Watson Res. (2 groups)	Univ. California, Berkeley
ISS (Singapore)	Univ. California, San Diego
ITI (Singapore)	Univ. Glasgow
APL, Johns Hopkins Univ.	Univ. Maryland, College Park
LEXIS-NEXIS	Univ. Massachusetts, Amherst
MDS at RMIT, Australia	Univ. Montreal
MIT/IBM Almaden Res. Center	Univ. North Carolina (2 groups)
MSI/IRIT/Univ. Toulouse	Univ. Sheffield/Univ. Cambridge
NEC Corporation	Univ. Waterloo
New Mexico State Univ. (2 groups)	Verity, Inc.
NSA (Speech Research Group)	Xerox Res. Centre Europe
Open Text Corporation	

The seventh TREC conference was held again at NIST in November of 1998.

In the following, we briefly discuss the TREC document collection and the (benchmark) tasks at the TREC conferences. As with most test collections, the TREC collection is composed of three parts: the documents, the example information requests (called *topics* in the TREC nomenclature), and a set of relevant documents for each example information request. Further, the TREC conferences also include a set of tasks to be used as a benchmark.

The Document Collection

The TREC collection has been growing steadily over the years. At TREC-3, the collection size was roughly 2 gigabytes while at TREC-6 it had gone up to roughly 5.8 gigabytes. In the beginning, copyright restrictions prevented free distribution of the collection and, as a result, the distribution CD-ROM disks had to be bought. In 1998, however, an arrangement was made which allows free access to the documents used in the most recent TREC conferences. As a result, TREC disk 4 and TREC disk 5 are now available from NIST at a small fee (US$200 in 1998) to cover distribution costs. Information on how to obtain the collection (which comes with the disks) and the topics with their relevant document sets (which have to be retrieved through the network) can be obtained directly from the NIST TREC Web site [768].

The TREC collection is distributed in six CD-ROM disks of roughly 1 gigabyte of compressed text each. The documents come from the following sources:

WSJ	→ *Wall Street Journal*
AP	→ Associated Press (news wire)
ZIFF	→ Computer Selects (articles), Ziff-Davis
FR	→ Federal Register

DOE   → US DOE Publications (abstracts)
SJMN   → *San Jose Mercury News*
PAT   → US Patents
FT   → *Financial Times*
CR   → Congressional Record
FBIS   → Foreign Broadcast Information Service
LAT   → *LA Times*

Table 3.1 illustrates the contents of each disk and some simple statistics regarding the collection (extracted from [794]). Documents from all subcollections are

Disk	Contents	Size Mb	Number Docs	Words/Doc. (median)	Words/Doc. (mean)
1	WSJ, 1987-1989	267	98,732	245	434.0
	AP, 1989	254	84,678	446	473.9
	ZIFF	242	75,180	200	473.0
	FR, 1989	260	25,960	391	1315.9
	DOE	184	226,087	111	120.4
2	WSJ, 1990-1992	242	74,520	301	508.4
	AP, 1988	237	79,919	438	468.7
	ZIFF	175	56,920	182	451.9
	FR, 1988	209	19,860	396	1378.1
3	SJMN, 1991	287	90,257	379	453.0
	AP, 1990	237	78,321	451	478.4
	ZIFF	345	161,021	122	295.4
	PAT, 1993	243	6,711	4,445	5391.0
4	FT, 1991-1994	564	210,158	316	412.7
	FR, 1994	395	55,630	588	644.7
	CR, 1993	235	27,922	288	1373.5
5	FBIS	470	130,471	322	543.6
	LAT	475	131,896	351	526.5
6	FBIS	490	120,653	348	581.3

Table 3.1 Document collection used at TREC-6. Stopwords are not removed and no stemming is performed (see Chapter 7 for details on stemming).

tagged with SGML (see Chapter 6) to allow easy parsing (which implies simple coding for the groups participating at TREC conferences). Major structures such as a field for the document number (identified by <DOCNO>) and a field for the document text (identified by <TEXT>) are common to all documents. Minor structures might be different across subcollections to preserve parts of the structure in the original document. This has been the philosophy for formatting decisions at NIST: preserve as much of the original structure as possible while providing a common framework which allows simple decoding of the data.

An example of a TREC document is the document numbered 880406-0090

```
<doc>

<docno> WSJ880406-0090 </docno>
<hl> AT&T Unveils Services to Upgrade Phone Networks Under
Global Plan </hl>
<author> Janet Guyon (WSJ Staff) </author>
<dateline> New York </dateline>

<text>
American Telephone & Telegraph Co. introduced the first of a new
generation of phone services with broad ...
</text>

</doc>
```

Figure 3.7   TREC document numbered WSJ880406-0090.

in the *Wall Street Journal* subcollection which is shown in Figure 3.7 (extracted
from [342]). Further details on the TREC document collection can be obtained
from [794, 768].

The Example Information Requests (Topics)

The TREC collection includes a set of example *information requests* which can
be used for testing a new ranking algorithm. Each request is a description of
an information need in natural language. In the TREC nomenclature, each test
information request is referred to as a *topic*. An example of an information request in TREC is the topic numbered 168 (prepared for the TREC-3 conference)
which is illustrated in Figure 3.8 (extracted from [342]).

The task of converting an information request (topic) into a system query
(i.e., a set of index terms, a Boolean expression, a fuzzy expression, etc.) must
be done by the system itself and is considered to be an integral part of the
evaluation procedure.

The number of topics prepared for the first six TREC conferences goes up to
350. The topics numbered 1 to 150 were prepared for use with the TREC-1 and
TREC-2 conferences. They were written by people who were experienced users
of real systems and represented long-standing information needs. The topics
numbered 151 to 200 were prepared for use with the TREC-3 conference, are
shorter, and have a simpler structure which includes only three subfields (named
Title, Description, and Narrative as illustrated in the topic 168 above). The
topics numbered 201 to 250 were prepared for use with the TREC-4 conference
and are even shorter. At the TREC-5 (which included topics 251-300) and
TREC-6 (which included topics 301-350) conferences, the topics were prepared
with a composition similar to the topics in TREC-3 (i.e., they were expanded
with respect to the topics in TREC-4 which were considered to be too short).

```
<top>

<num> Number: 168
<title> Topic: Financing AMTRAK

<desc> Description:
A document will address the role of the Federal Government in
financing the operation of the National Railroad Transportation Cor-
poration (AMTRAK).

<narr> Narrative: A relevant document must provide information on
the government's responsibility to make AMTRAK an economically
viable entity. It could also discuss the privatization of AMTRAK as
an alternative to continuing government subsidies. Documents com-
paring government subsidies given to air and bus transportation with
those provided to AMTRAK would also be relevant.

</top>
```

Figure 3.8 Topic numbered 168 in the TREC collection.

The Relevant Documents for Each Example Information Request

At the TREC conferences, the set of relevant documents for each example information request (topic) is obtained from a pool of possible relevant documents.
This pool is created by taking the top K documents (usually, $K = 100$) in the
rankings generated by the various participating retrieval systems. The documents in the pool are then shown to human assessors who ultimately decide on
the relevance of each document.

   This technique for assessing relevance is called the *pooling method* [794]
and is based on two assumptions. First, that the vast majority of the relevant
documents is collected in the assembled pool. Second, that the documents which
are not in the pool can be considered to be not relevant. Both assumptions have
been verified to be accurate in tests done at the TREC conferences. A detailed
description of these relevance assessments can be found in [342, 794].

The (Benchmark) Tasks at the TREC Conferences

The TREC conferences include two main information retrieval tasks [342]. In
the first, called *ad hoc* task, a set of new (conventional) requests are run against
a fixed document database. This is the situation which normally occurs in a
library where a user is asking new queries against a set of static documents. In
the second, called *routing* task, a set of fixed requests are run against a database
whose documents are continually changing. This is like a filtering task in which
the same questions are always being asked against a set of dynamic documents
(for instance, news clipping services). Unlike a pure filtering task, however, the
retrieved documents must be ranked.

For the ad hoc task, the participant systems receive the test information requests and execute them on a pre-specified document collection. For the routing task, the participant systems receive the test information requests and two distinct document collections. The first collection is used for training and allows the tuning of the retrieval algorithm. The second collection is used for testing the tuned retrieval algorithm.

Starting at the TREC-4 conference, new secondary tasks, besides the ad hoc and routing tasks, were introduced with the purpose of allowing more specific comparisons among the various systems. At TREC-6, eight (specific) secondary tasks were added in as follows.

- **Chinese** Ad hoc task in which both the documents and the topics are in Chinese.

- **Filtering** Routing task in which the retrieval algorithm has only to decide whether a new incoming document is relevant (in which case it is taken) or not (in which case it is discarded). No ranking of the documents taken needs to be provided. The test data (incoming documents) is processed in time-stamp order.

- **Interactive** Task in which a human searcher interacts with the retrieval system to determine the relevant documents. Documents are ruled relevant or not relevant (i.e., no ranking is provided).

- **NLP** Task aimed at verifying whether retrieval algorithms based on natural language processing offer advantages when compared to the more traditional retrieval algorithms based on index terms.

- **Cross languages** Ad hoc task in which the documents are in one language but the topics are in a different language.

- **High precision** Task in which the user of a retrieval system is asked to retrieve ten documents that answer a given (and previously unknown) information request within five minutes (wall clock time).

- **Spoken document retrieval** Task in which the documents are written transcripts of radio broadcast news shows. Intended to stimulate research on retrieval techniques for spoken documents.

- **Very large corpus** Ad hoc task in which the retrieval systems have to deal with collections of size 20 gigabytes (7.5 million documents).

For TREC-7, the NLP and the Chinese secondary tasks were discontinued. Additionally, the routing task was retired as a main task because there is a consensus that the filtering task is a more realistic type of routing task. TREC-7 also included a new task called *Query Task* in which several distinct query versions were created for each example information request [794]. The main goal of this task is to allow investigation of query-dependent retrieval strategies, a well known problem with the TREC collection due to the sparsity of the given information requests (which present very little overlap) used in past TREC conferences.

Besides providing detailed descriptions of the tasks to be executed, the TREC conferences also make a clear distinction between two basic techniques for transforming the information requests (which are in natural language) into query statements (which might be in vector form, in Boolean form, etc.). In the TREC-6 conference, the allowable query construction methods were divided into *automatic* methods, in which the queries were derived completely automatically from the test information requests, and *manual* methods, in which the queries were derived using any means other than the fully automatic method [794].

Evaluation Measures at the TREC Conferences

At the TREC conferences, four basic types of evaluation measures are used: summary table statistics, recall-precision averages, document level averages, and average precision histograms. Briefly, these measures can be described as follows (see further details on these measures in Section 3.2).

- **Summary table statistics** Consists of a table which summarizes statistics relative to a given task. The statistics included are: the number of topics (information requests) used in the task, the number of documents retrieved over all topics, the number of relevant documents which were effectively retrieved for all topics, and the number of relevant documents which could have been retrieved for all topics.

- **Recall-precision averages** Consists of a table or graph with average precision (over all topics) at 11 standard recall levels. Since the recall levels of the individual queries are seldom equal to the standard recall levels, interpolation is used to define the precision at the standard recall levels. Further, a non-interpolated average precision over seen relevant documents (and over all topics) might be included.

- **Document level averages** In this case, average precision (over all topics) is computed at specified document cutoff values (instead of standard recall levels). For instance, the average precision might be computed when 5, 10, 20, 100 relevant documents have been seen. Further, the average R-precision value (over all queries) might also be provided.

- **Average precision histogram** Consists of a graph which includes a single measure for each separate topic. This measure (for a topic t_i) is given, for instance, by the difference between the R-precision (for topic t_i) for a target retrieval algorithm and the average R-precision (for topic t_i) computed from the results of all participating retrieval systems.

3.3.2   The CACM and ISI Collections

The TREC collection is a large collection which requires time consuming preparation before experiments can be carried out effectively at a local site. Further, the testing itself is also time consuming and requires much more effort than that required to execute the testing in a small collection. For groups who are not interested in making this investment, an alternative approach is to use a smaller test collection which can be installed and experimented with in a much shorter time. Further, a small collection might include features which are not present in the larger TREC collection. For instance, it is well known that the example information requests at TREC present very little overlap among themselves and thus are not very useful for investigating the impact of techniques which take advantage of information derived from dependencies between the current and past user queries (an issue which received attention at the TREC-7 conference). Further, the TREC collection does not provide good support for experimenting with algorithms which combine distinct evidential sources (such as co-citations, bibliographic coupling, etc.) to generate a ranking. In these situations, alternative (and smaller) test collections might be more appropriate.

For the experimental studies in [271], five different (small) test collections were developed: ADI (documents on information science), CACM, INSPEC (abstracts on electronics, computer, and physics), ISI, and Medlars (medical articles). In this section we cover two of them in detail: the CACM and the ISI test collections. Our discussion is based on the work by Fox [272].

The CACM Collection

The documents in the CACM test collection consist of all the 3204 articles published in the *Communications of the ACM* from the first issue in 1958 to the last number of 1979. Those documents cover a considerable range of computer science literature due to the fact that the CACM served for many years as the premier periodical in the field.

Besides the text of the documents, the collection also includes information on structured *subfields* (called *concepts* by Fox) as follows:

- author names
- date information
- word stems from the title and abstract sections
- categories derived from a hierarchical classification scheme
- direct references between articles
- bibliographic coupling connections
- number of co-citations for each pair of articles.

The subfields 'author names' and 'date information' provide information on authors and date of publication. The subfield 'word stems' provides, for each document, a list of indexing terms (from the title and abstract sections) which have been stemmed (i.e., reduced to their grammatical roots as explained in Chapter 7). The subfield 'categories' assigns a list of classification categories (from the Computing Reviews category scheme) to each document. Since the categories are fairly broad, the number of categories for any given document is usually smaller than five. The subfield 'direct references' provides a list of pairs of documents $[d_a, d_b]$ in which each pair identifies a document d_a which includes a direct reference to a document d_b. The subfield 'bibliographic coupling' provides a list of triples $[d_1, d_2, n_{cited}]$ in which the documents d_1 and d_2 both include a direct reference to a same third document d_j and the factor n_{cited} counts the number of documents d_j cited by both d_1 and d_2. The subfield 'co-citations' provides a list of triples $[d_1, d_2, n_{citing}]$ in which the documents d_1 and d_2 are both cited by a same third document d_j and the factor n_{citing} counts the number of documents d_j citing both d_1 and d_2. Thus, the CACM collection provides a unique environment for testing retrieval algorithms which are based on information derived from cross-citing patterns — a topic which has attracted much attention in the past.

The CACM collection also includes a set of 52 test information requests. For instance, the information request numbered 1 reads as follows.

> What articles exist which deal with TSS (Time Sharing System), an operating system for IBM computers?

For each information request, the collection also includes two Boolean query formulations and a set of relevant documents. Since the information requests are fairly specific, the average number of relevant documents for each information request is small and around 15. As a result, precision and recall figures tend to be low.

The ISI Collection

The 1460 documents in the ISI (often referred to as CISI) test collection were selected from a previous collection assembled by Small [731] at the Institute of Scientific Information (ISI). The documents selected (which are about information sciences) were those most cited in a cross-citation study done by Small. The main purpose of the ISI collection is to support investigation of similarities based on terms and on cross-citation patterns.

The documents in the ISI collection include three types of subfields as follows.

- author names
- word stems from the title and abstract sections
- number of co-citations for each pair of articles.

The meaning of each of these subfields is as in the CACM collection.

The ISI collection includes a total of 35 test information requests (in natural language) for which there are Boolean query formulations. It also includes 41 additional test information requests for which there is no Boolean query formulation (only the version in natural language). The information requests are fairly general which resulted in a larger number of relevant documents to each request (around 50). However, many of these relevant documents have no terms in common with the information requests which implies that precision and recall figures tend to be low.

Statistics for the CACM and ISI Collections

Tables 3.2 and 3.3 provide comparative summary statistics for the CACM and the ISI test collections.

Collection	Num. Docs	Num. Terms	Terms/Docs.
CACM	3204	10,446	40.1
ISI	1460	7392	104.9

Table 3.2 Document statistics for the CACM and ISI collections.

Collection	Number Queries	Terms per Query	Relevants per Query	Relevants in Top 10
CACM	52	11.4	15.3	1.9
ISI	35 & 76	8.1	49.8	1.7

Table 3.3 Query statistics for the CACM and ISI collections.

We notice that, compared to the size of the collection, the ISI collection has a much higher percentage of relevant documents per query (3.4%) than the CACM collection (0.5%). However, as already discussed, many of the relevant documents in the ISI collection have no terms in common with the respective information requests which usually yields low precision.

Related Test Collections

At the Virginia Polytechnic Institute and State University, Fox has assembled together nine small test collections in a CD-ROM. These test collections have sizes comparable to those of the CACM and ISI collections, but include their own particularities. Since they have been used throughout the years for evaluation of information retrieval systems, they provide a good setting for the preliminary testing of information retrieval algorithms. A list of these nine test collections is provided in Table 3.4.

3.3.3   The Cystic Fibrosis Collection

The cystic fibrosis (CF) collection [721] is composed of 1239 documents indexed with the term 'cystic fibrosis' in the National Library of Medicine's MEDLINE database. Each document contains the following fields:

Collection	Subject	Num. Docs	Num. Queries
ADI	Information Science	82	35
CACM	Computer Science	3200	64
ISI	Library Science	1460	76
CRAN	Aeronautics	1400	225
LISA	Library Science	6004	35
MED	Medicine	1033	30
NLM	Medicine	3078	155
NPL	Elec. Engineering	11,429	100
TIME	General Articles	423	83

Table 3.4   Test collections related to the CACM and ISI collections.

- MEDLINE accession number
- author
- title
- source
- major subjects
- minor subjects
- abstract (or extract)
- references
- citations.

The collection also includes 100 information requests (generated by an expert with two decades of clinical and research experience with cystic fibrosis) and the documents relevant to each query. Further, 4 separate relevance scores are provided for each relevant document. These relevance scores can be 0 (which indicates non-relevance), 1 (which indicates marginal relevance), and 2 (which indicates high relevance). Thus, the overall relevance score for a document (relative to a given query) varies from 0 to 8. Three of the relevance scores were provided by subject experts while the fourth relevance score was provided by a medical bibliographer.

Table 3.5 provides some statistics regarding the information requests in the CF collection. We notice that the number of queries with at least one relevant document is close to the total number of queries in the collection. Further, for various relevance thresholds (the minimum value of relevance score used to characterize relevance), the average number of relevant documents per query is between 10 and 30.

The CF collection, despite its small size, has two important characteristics. First, its set of relevance scores was generated directly by human experts through a careful evaluation strategy. Second, it includes a good number of information requests (relative to the collection size) and, as a result, the respective query vectors present overlap among themselves. This allows experimentation

Relevance Threshold	Queries At Least 1 Rel. Doc	Min. Num. Rel. Docs	Max. Num. Rel. Docs	Avg. Num. Rel. Docs
1	100	2	189	31.9
2	100	1	130	18.1
3	99	1	119	14.9
4	99	1	114	14.1
5	99	1	93	10.7
6	94	1	53	6.4

Table 3.5 Summary statistics for the information requests in the CF collection.

with retrieval strategies which take advantage of past query sessions to improve retrieval performance.

3.4   Trends and Research Issues

A major trend today is research in interactive user interfaces. The motivation is a general belief that effective retrieval is highly dependent on obtaining proper feedback from the user. Thus, evaluation studies of interactive interfaces will tend to become more common in the near future. The main issues revolve around deciding which evaluation measures are most appropriate in this scenario. A typical example is the informativeness measure [754] introduced in 1992.

Furthermore, the proposal, the study, and the characterization of alternative measures to recall and precision, such as the harmonic mean and the E measures, continue to be of interest.

3.5   Bibliographic Discussion

A nice chapter on retrieval performance evaluation appeared in the book by Salton and McGill [698]. Even if outdated, it is still interesting reading. The book by Khorfage [451] also includes a full chapter on retrieval evaluation. A recent paper by Mizzaro [569] presents a very complete survey of relevance studies throughout the years. About 160 papers are discussed in this paper.

Two recent papers by Shaw, Burgin, and Howel [422, 423] discuss standards and evaluations in test collections for cluster-based and vector-based retrieval models. These papers also discuss the advantages of the harmonic mean (of recall and precision) as a single alternative measure for recall and precision. Problems with recall and precision related to systems which require a weak document ordering are discussed by Raghavan, Bollmann, and Jung [664, 663]. Tague-Sutcliffe proposes a measure of informativeness for evaluating interactive user sessions [754].

Our discussion of the TREC collection is based on the papers by Harman [342] and by Vorhees and Harman [794]. The TREC collection is the most important reference collection nowadays for evaluation of complex information requests which execute on a large collection. Our coverage of the CACM and ISI collections is based on the work by Fox [272]. These collections are small, require short setup time, and provide a good environment for testing retrieval algorithms which are based on information derived from cross-citing patterns — a topic which has attracted much attention in the past [94, 435, 694, 730, 732, 809] and which might flourish again in the context of the Web. The discussion on the Cystic Fibrosis (CF) collection is based on the work by Shaw, Wood, Wood, and Tibbo [721]. The CF collection is also small but includes a set of relevance scores carefully generated by human experts. Furthermore, its example information requests present overlap among themselves which allows the testing of retrieval algorithms that take advantage of past user sessions to improve retrieval performance.

Chapter 4
Query Languages

---

with Gonzalo Navarro

4.1 Introduction

We cover in this chapter the different kinds of queries normally posed to text retrieval systems. This is in part dependent on the retrieval model the system adopts, i.e., a full-text system will not answer the same kinds of queries as those answered by a system based on keyword ranking (as Web search engines) or on a hypertext model. In Chapter 8 we explain *how* the user queries are solved, while in this chapter we show *which* queries can be formulated. The type of query the user might formulate is largely dependent on the underlying information retrieval model. The different models for text retrieval systems are covered in Chapter 2.

As in previous chapters, we want to distinguish between information retrieval and data retrieval, as we use this dichotomy to classify different query languages. We have chosen to distinguish first languages that allow the answer to be ranked, that is, languages for information retrieval. As covered in Chapter 2, for the basic information retrieval models, keyword-based retrieval is the main type of querying task. For query languages not aimed at information retrieval, the concept of ranking cannot be easily defined, so we consider them as languages for data retrieval. Furthermore, some query languages are not intended for final users and can be viewed as languages that a higher level software package should use to query an on-line database or a CD-ROM archive. In that case, we talk about *protocols* rather than query languages. Depending on the user experience, a different query language will be used. For example, if the user knows exactly what he wants, the retrieval task is easier and ranking may not even be needed.

An important issue is that most query languages try to use the content (i.e., the semantics) and the structure of the text (i.e., the text syntax) to find relevant documents. In that sense, the system may fail to find the relevant answers (see Chapter 3). For this reason, a number of techniques meant to enhance the usefulness of the queries exist. Examples include the expansion of a word to the set of its synonyms or the use of a thesaurus and stemming to put together all the derivatives of the same word. Moreover, some words which are very frequent and do not carry meaning (such as 'the'), called *stopwords*, may be removed. This subject is covered in Chapter 7. Here we assume that all the query preprocessing has already been done. Although these operations are usually done for information retrieval, many of them can also be useful in a data retrieval context. When we want to emphasize the difference between words that can be retrieved by a query and those which cannot, we call the former 'keywords.'

Orthogonal to the kind of queries that can be asked is the subject of the *retrieval unit* the information system adopts. The retrieval unit is the basic element which can be retrieved as an answer to a query (normally a set of such basic elements is retrieved, sometimes ranked by relevance or other criterion). The retrieval unit can be a file, a document, a Web page, a paragraph, or some other structural unit which contains an answer to the search query. From this point on, we will simply call those retrieval units 'documents,' although as explained this can have different meanings (see also Chapter 2).

This chapter is organized as follows. We first show the queries that can be formulated with keyword-based query languages. They are aimed at information retrieval, including simple words and phrases as well as Boolean operators which manipulate sets of documents. In the second section we cover pattern matching, which includes more complex queries and is generally aimed at complementing keyword searching with more powerful data retrieval capabilities. Third, we cover querying on the structure of the text, which is more dependent on the particular text model. Finally, we finish with some standard protocols used on the Internet and by CD-ROM publishers.

4.2   Keyword-Based Querying

A query is the formulation of a user information need. In its simplest form, a query is composed of keywords and the documents containing such keywords are searched for. Keyword-based queries are popular because they are intuitive, easy to express, and allow for fast ranking. Thus, a query can be (and in many cases is) simply a word, although it can in general be a more complex combination of operations involving several words.

In the rest of this chapter we will refer to single-word and multiple-word queries as *basic queries*. Patterns, which are covered in section 4.3, are also considered as basic queries.

4.2.1   Single-Word Queries

The most elementary query that can be formulated in a text retrieval system is a word. Text documents are assumed to be essentially long sequences of words. Although some models present a more general view, virtually all models allow us to see the text in this perspective and to search words. Some models are also able to see the internal division of words into letters. These latter models permit the searching of other types of patterns, which are covered in section 4.3. The set of words retrieved by these extended queries can then be fed into the word-treating machinery, say to perform thesaurus expansion or for ranking purposes.

A word is normally defined in a rather simple way. The alphabet is split into 'letters' and 'separators,' and a word is a sequence of letters surrounded by separators. More complex models allow us to specify that some characters are not letters but do not split a word, e.g. the hyphen in `on-line.` It is good practice to leave the choice of what is a letter and what is a separator to the manager of the text database.

The division of the text into words is not arbitrary, since words carry a lot of meaning in natural language. Because of that, many models (such as the vector model) are completely structured on the concept of words, and words are the only type of queries allowed (moreover, some systems only allow a small set of words to be extracted from the documents). The result of word queries is the set of documents containing at least one of the words of the query. Further, the resulting documents are ranked according to a degree of similarity to the query. To support ranking, two common statistics on word occurrences inside texts are commonly used: 'term frequency' which counts the number of times a word appears inside a document and 'inverse document frequency' which counts the number of documents in which a word appears. See Chapter 2 for more details.

Additionally, the exact positions where a word appears in the text may be required for instance, by an interface which highlights each occurrence of that word.

4.2.2   Context Queries

Many systems complement single-word queries with the ability to search words in a given *context*, that is, near other words. Words which appear near each other may signal a higher likelihood of relevance than if they appear apart. For instance, we may want to form phrases of words or find words which are proximal in the text. Therefore, we distinguish two types of queries:

- **Phrase** is a sequence of single-word queries. An occurrence of the phrase is a sequence of words. For instance, it is possible to search for the word `enhance,` and then for the word `retrieval.` In phrase queries it is normally understood that the separators in the text need not be the same as those in the query (e.g., two spaces versus one space), and uninteresting words are not considered at all. For instance, the previous example could match a text such as '...enhance the retrieval...'. Although the notion of a phrase is a very useful feature in most cases, not all systems implement it.

- **Proximity** A more relaxed version of the phrase query is the proximity query. In this case, a sequence of single words or phrases is given, together

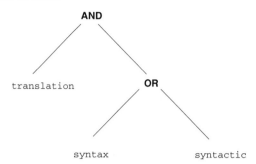

Figure 4.1   An example of a query syntax tree. It will retrieve all the documents which contain the word 'translation' as well as either the word 'syntax' or the word 'syntactic'.

with a maximum allowed distance between them. For instance, the above example could state that the two words should occur within four words, and therefore a match could be '...enhance the power of retrieval....' This distance can be measured in characters or words depending on the system. The words and phrases may or may not be required to appear in the same order as in the query.

Phrases can be ranked in a fashion somewhat analogous to single words (see Chapters 2 and 5 for details). Proximity queries can be ranked in the same way if the parameters used by the ranking technique do not depend on physical proximity. Although it is not clear how to do better ranking, physical proximity has semantic value. This is because in most cases the proximity means that the words are in the same paragraph, and hence related in some way.

4.2.3   Boolean Queries

The oldest (and still heavily used) form of combining keyword queries is to use Boolean operators. A *Boolean query* has a syntax composed of *atoms* (i.e., basic queries) that retrieve documents, and of *Boolean operators* which work on their operands (which are sets of documents) and deliver sets of documents. Since this scheme is in general *compositional* (i.e., operators can be composed over the results of other operators), a *query syntax tree* is naturally defined, where the leaves correspond to the basic queries and the internal nodes to the operators. The query syntax tree operates on an algebra over sets of documents (and the final answer of the query is also a set of documents). This is much as, for instance, the syntax trees of arithmetic expressions where the numbers and variables are the leaves and the operations form the internal nodes. Figure 4.1 shows an example.

The operators most commonly used, given two basic queries or Boolean subexpressions e_1 and e_2, are:

- **OR** The query (e_1 OR e_2) selects all documents which satisfy e_1 or e_2. Duplicates are eliminated.

- **AND** The query (e_1 AND e_2) selects all documents which satisfy both e_1 and e_2.

- **BUT** The query (e_1 BUT e_2) selects all documents which satisfy e_1 but not e_2. Notice that classical Boolean logic uses a NOT operation, where (NOT e_2) is valid whenever e_2 is not. In this case all documents not satisfying e_2 should be delivered, which may retrieve a huge amount of text and is probably not what the user wants. The BUT operator, instead, restricts the universe of retrievable elements to the result of e_1.†

Besides selecting the appropriate documents, the IR system may also sort the documents by some criterion, highlight the occurrences within the documents of the words mentioned in the query, and allow feedback by taking the answer set as a basis to reformulate the query.

With classic Boolean systems, no ranking of the retrieved documents is normally provided. A document either satisfies the Boolean query (in which case it is retrieved) or it does not (in which case it is not retrieved). This is quite a limitation because it does not allow for partial matching between a document and a user query. To overcome this limitation, the condition for retrieval must be relaxed. For instance, a document which partially satisfies an AND condition might be retrieved.

In fact, it is widely accepted that users not trained in mathematics find the meaning of Boolean operators difficult to grasp. With this problem in mind, a 'fuzzy Boolean' set of operators has been proposed. The idea is that the meaning of AND and OR can be relaxed, such that instead of forcing an element to appear in *all* the operands (AND) or at least in *one* of the operands (OR), they retrieve elements appearing in *some* operands (the AND may require it to appear in more operands than the OR). Moreover, the documents are ranked higher when they have a larger number of elements in common with the query (see Chapter 2).

4.2.4 Natural Language

Pushing the fuzzy Boolean model even further, the distinction between AND and OR can be completely blurred, so that a query becomes simply an enumeration of words and context queries. All the documents matching a portion of the user query are retrieved. Higher ranking is assigned to those documents matching more parts of the query. The negation can be handled by letting the user express

---

† Notice that the same problem arises in the relational calculus, which is shown similar to the relational algebra only when 'unsafe' expressions are avoided. Unsafe expressions are those that make direct or indirect reference to a universe of elements, as NOT does.

that some words are not desired, so that the documents containing them are penalized in the ranking computation. A threshold may be selected so that the documents with very low weights are not retrieved. Under this scheme we have completely eliminated any reference to Boolean operations and entered into the field of natural language queries. In fact, one can consider that Boolean queries are a simplified abstraction of natural language queries.

A number of new issues arise once this model is used, especially those related to the proper way to rank an element with respect to a query. The search criterion can be re-expressed using a different model, where documents and queries are considered just as a vector of 'term weights' (with one coordinate per interesting keyword or even per existing text word) and queries are considered in exactly the same way (context queries are not considered in this case). Therefore, the query is now internally converted into a vector of term weights and the aim is to retrieve all the vectors (documents) which are *close* to the query (where closeness has to be defined in the model). This allows many interesting possibilities, for instance a complete document can be used as a query (since it is also a vector), which naturally leads to the use of relevance feedback techniques (i.e., the user can select a document from the result and submit it as a new query to retrieve documents similar to the selected one). The algorithms for this model are totally different from those based on searching patterns (it is even possible that not every text word needs to be searched but only a small set of hopefully representative keywords extracted from each document). Natural language querying is also covered in Chapter 14.

4.3   Pattern Matching

In this section we discuss more specific query formulations (based on the concept of a *pattern*) which allow the retrieval of pieces of text that have some property. These data retrieval queries are useful for linguistics, text statistics, and data extraction. Their result can be fed into the composition mechanism described above to form phrases and proximity queries, comprising what we have called *basic queries*. Basic queries can be combined using Boolean expressions. In this sense we can view these data retrieval capabilities as enhanced tools for information retrieval. However, it is more difficult to rank the result of a pattern matching expression.

A *pattern* is a set of syntactic features that must occur in a text segment. Those segments satisfying the pattern specifications are said to 'match' the pattern. We are interested in documents containing segments which match a given search pattern. Each system allows the specification of some types of patterns, which range from very simple (for example, words) to rather complex (such as regular expressions). In general, as more powerful is the set of patterns allowed, more involved are the queries that the user can formulate and more complex is the implementation of the search. The most used types of patterns are:

- **Words** A string (sequence of characters) which must be a word in the text (see section 4.2). This is the most basic pattern.

- **Prefixes** A string which must form the beginning of a text word. For instance, given the prefix '`comput`' all the documents containing words such as '`computer`,' '`computation`,' '`computing`,' etc. are retrieved.

- **Suffixes** A string which must form the termination of a text word. For instance, given the suffix '`ters`' all the documents containing words such as '`computers`,' '`testers`,' '`painters`,' etc. are retrieved.

- **Substrings** A string which can appear within a text word. For instance, given the substring '`tal`' all the documents containing words such as '`coastal`,' '`talk`,' '`metallic`,' etc. are retrieved. This query can be restricted to find the substrings inside words, or it can go further and search the substring anywhere in the text (in this case the query is not restricted to be a sequence of letters but can contain word separators). For instance, a search for '`any flow`' will match in the phrase '`...many flowers....`'

- **Ranges** A pair of strings which matches any word lying between them in lexicographical order. Alphabets are normally sorted, and this induces an order into the strings which is called *lexicographical order* (this is indeed the order in which words in a dictionary are listed). For instance, the range between words '`held`' and '`hold`' will retrieve strings such as '`hoax`' and '`hissing`.'

- **Allowing errors** A word together with an error threshold. This search pattern retrieves all text words which are 'similar' to the given word. The concept of similarity can be defined in many ways. The general concept is that the pattern or the text may have errors (coming from typing, spelling, or from optical character recognition software, among others), and the query should try to retrieve the given word and what are likely to be its erroneous variants. Although there are many models for similarity among words, the most generally accepted in text retrieval is the *Levenshtein distance*, or simply *edit distance*. The edit distance between two strings is the minimum number of character insertions, deletions, and replacements needed to make them equal (see Chapter 6). Therefore, the query specifies the maximum number of allowed errors for a word to match the pattern (i.e., the maximum allowed edit distance). This model can also be extended to search substrings (not only words), retrieving any text segment which is at the allowed edit distance from the search pattern. Under this extended model, if a typing error splits '`flower`' into '`flo wer`' it could still be found with one error, while in the restricted case of words it could not (since neither '`flo`' nor '`wer`' are at edit distance 1 from '`flower`'). Variations on this distance model are of use in computational biology for searching on DNA or protein sequences as well as in signal processing.

- **Regular expressions** Some text retrieval systems allow searching for *regular expressions*. A regular expression is a rather general pattern built up by simple strings (which are meant to be matched as substrings) and the following operators:

- union: if e_1 and e_2 are regular expressions, then $(e_1|e_2)$ matches what e_1 or e_2 matches.
- concatenation: if e_1 and e_2 are regular expressions, the occurrences of $(e_1\ e_2)$ are formed by the occurrences of e_1 immediately followed by those of e_2 (therefore simple strings can be thought of as a concatenation of their individual letters).
- repetition: if e is a regular expression, then (e^*) matches a sequence of zero or more contiguous occurrences of e.

For instance, consider a query like 'pro (blem | tein) (s | ε) (0 | 1 | 2)*' (where ε denotes the empty string). It will match words such as 'problem02' and 'proteins.' As in previous cases, the matches can be restricted to comprise a whole word, to occur inside a word, or to match an arbitrary text segment. This can also be combined with the previous type of patterns to search a regular expression allowing errors.

- **Extended patterns** It is normal to use a more user-friendly query language to represent some common cases of regular expressions. Extended patterns are subsets of the regular expressions which are expressed with a simpler syntax. The retrieval system can internally convert extended patterns into regular expressions, or search them with specific algorithms. Each system supports its own set of extended patterns, and therefore no formal definition exists. Some examples found in many new systems are:

  - classes of characters, i.e. one or more positions within the pattern are matched by any character from a pre-defined set. This involves features such as case-insensitive matching, use of ranges of characters (e.g., specifying that some character must be a digit), complements (e.g., some character must not be a letter), enumeration (e.g., a character must be a vowel), wild cards (i.e., a position within the pattern matches with anything), among others.
  - conditional expressions, i.e., a part of the pattern may or may not appear.
  - wild characters which match any sequence in the text, e.g. any word which starts as 'flo' and ends with 'ers,' which matches 'flowers' as well as 'flounders.'
  - combinations that allow some parts of the pattern to match exactly and other parts with errors.

4.4   Structural Queries

Up to now we have considered the text collection as a set of documents which can be queried with regard to their text content. This model is unable to take advantage of novel text features which are becoming commonplace, such as the

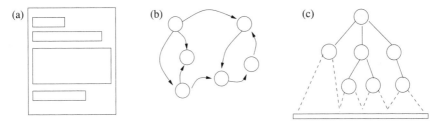

Figure 4.2 The three main structures: (*a*) form-like fixed structure, (*b*) hypertext structure, and (*c*) hierarchical structure.

text structure. The text collections tend to have some structure built into them, and allowing the user to query those texts based on their structure (and not only their content) is becoming attractive. The standardization of languages to represent structured texts such as HTML has pushed forward in this direction (see Chapter 6).

As discussed in Chapter 2, mixing contents and structure in queries allows us to pose very powerful queries, which are much more expressive than each query mechanism by itself. By using a query language that integrates both types of queries, the retrieval quality of textual databases can be improved.

This mechanism is built on top of the basic queries, so that they select a set of documents that satisfy certain constraints on their content (expressed using words, phrases, or patterns that the documents must contain). On top of this, some structural constraints can be expressed using containment, proximity, or other restrictions on the structural elements (e.g., chapters, sections, etc.) present in the documents. The Boolean queries can be built on top of the structural queries, so that they combine the sets of documents delivered by those queries. In the Boolean syntax tree (recall the example of Figure 4.1) the structural queries form the leaves of the tree. On the other hand, structural queries can themselves have a complex syntax.

We divide this section according to the type of structures found in text databases. Figure 4.2 illustrates them. Although structured query languages should be amenable for ranking, this is still an open problem.

In what follows it is important to distinguish the difference between the structure that a text may *have* and what can be *queried* about that structure. In general, natural language texts may have any desired structure. However, different models allow the querying of only some aspects of the real structure. When we say that the structure allowed is restricted in some way, we mean that only the aspects which follow this restriction can be queried, albeit the text may have more structural information. For instance, it is possible that an article has a nested structure of sections and subsections, but the query model does not accept recursive structures. In this case we will not be able to query for sections included in others, although this may be the case in the texts documents under consideration.

4.4.1   Fixed Structure

The structure allowed in texts was traditionally quite restrictive. The documents had a fixed set of *fields,* much like a filled form. Each field had some text inside. Some fields were not present in all documents. Only rarely could the fields appear in any order or repeat across a document. A document could not have text not classified under any field. Fields were not allowed to nest or overlap. The retrieval activity allowed on them was restricted to specifying that a given basic pattern was to be found only in a given field. Most current commercial systems use this model.

This model is reasonable when the text collection has a fixed structure. For instance, a mail archive could be regarded as a set of mails, where each mail has a sender, a receiver, a date, a subject, and a body field. The user can thus search for the mails sent to a given person with 'football' in the subject field. However, the model is inadequate to represent the hierarchical structure present in an HTML document, for instance.

If the division of the text into fields is rigid enough, the content of some fields can even be interpreted not as text but as numbers, dates, etc. thereby allowing different queries to be posed on them (e.g., month ranges in dates). It is not hard to see that this idea leads naturally to the relational model, each field corresponding to a column in the database table. Looking at the database as a text allows us to query the textual fields with much more power than is common in relational database systems. On the other hand, relational databases may make better use of their knowledge on the data types involved to build specialized and more efficient indices. A number of approaches towards combining these trends have been proposed in recent years, their main problem being that they do not achieve optimal performance because the text is usually stored together with other types of data. Nevertheless, there are several proposals that extend SQL (Structured Query Language) to allow full-text retrieval. Among them we can mention proposals by leading relational database vendors such as Oracle and Sybase, as well as SFQL, which is covered in section 4.5.

4.4.2   Hypertext

Hypertexts probably represent the maximum freedom with respect to structuring power. A hypertext is a directed graph where the nodes hold some text and the links represent connections between nodes or between positions inside the nodes (see Chapter 2). Hypertexts have received a lot of attention since the explosion of the Web, which is indeed a gigantic hypertext-like database spread across the world.

However, retrieval from a hypertext began as a merely navigational activity. That is, the user had to manually traverse the hypertext nodes following links to search what he wanted. It was not possible to query the hypertext based on its structure. Even in the Web one can search by the text contents of the nodes, but not by their structural connectivity.

An interesting proposal to combine browsing and searching on the Web is WebGlimpse. It allows classical navigation plus the ability to search by content in the neighborhood of the current node. Currently, some query tools have appeared that achieve the goal of querying hypertexts based on their content and their structure. This problem is covered in detail in Chapter 13.

4.4.3   Hierarchical Structure

An intermediate structuring model which lies between fixed structure and hypertext is the hierarchical structure. This model represents a recursive decomposition of the text and is a natural model for many text collections (e.g., books, articles, legal documents, structured programs, etc.). Figure 4.3 shows an example of such a hierarchical structure.

The simplification from hypertext to a hierarchy allows the adoption of faster algorithms to solve queries. As a general rule, the more powerful the model, the less efficiently it can be implemented.

Our aim in this section is to analyze and discuss the different approaches presented by the hierarchical models. We first present a selection of the most representative models and then discuss the main subjects of this area.

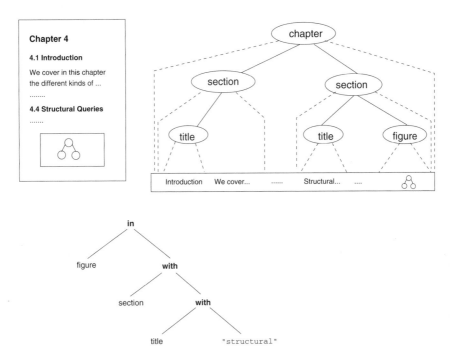

Figure 4.3   An example of a hierarchical structure: the page of a book, its schematic view, and a parsed query to retrieve the figure.

A Sample of Hierarchical Models

PAT Expressions

These are built on the same index as the text index, i.e. there is no special separate index on the structure. The structure is assumed to be marked in the text by *tags* (as in HTML), and therefore is defined in terms of initial and final tags. This allows a dynamic scheme where the structure of interest is not fixed but can be determined at query time. For instance, since tags need not to be especially designed as normal tags, one can define that the end-of-lines are the marks in order to define a structure on lines. This also allows for a very efficient implementation and no additional space overhead for the structure.

Each pair of initial and final tags defines a *region*, which is a set of contiguous text areas. Externally computed regions are also supported. However, the areas of a region cannot nest or overlap, which is quite restrictive. There is no restriction on areas of different regions.

Apart from text searching operations, it is possible to select areas containing (or not) other areas, contained (or not) in other areas, or followed (or not) by other areas.

A disadvantage is that the algebra mixes regions and sets of text positions which are incompatible and force complex conversion semantics. For instance, if the result of a query is going to generate overlapping areas (a fact that cannot be determined beforehand) then the result is converted to positions. Also, the dynamic definition of regions is flexible but requires the structure to be expressable using tags (also called 'markup', see Chapter 6), which for instance does not occur in some structured programming languages.

Overlapped Lists

These can be seen as an evolution of PAT Expressions. The model allows for the areas of a region to overlap, but not to nest. This elegantly solves the problems of mixing regions and sets of positions. The model considers the use of an inverted list (see Chapter 8) where not only the words but also the regions are indexed.

Apart from the operations of PAT Expressions, the model allows us to perform set union, and to combine regions. Combination means selecting the minimal text areas which include any two areas taken from two regions. A 'followed by' operator imposes the additional restriction that the first area must be before the second one. An '*n* words' operator generates the region of all (overlapping) sequences of *n* words of the text (this is further used to retrieve elements close to each other). If an operation produces a region with nested areas, only the minimal areas are selected. An example is shown in Figure 2.11.

The implementation of this model can also be very efficient. It is not clear, however, whether overlapping is good or not for capturing the structural properties that information has in practice. A new proposal allows the structure to be nested *and* overlapped, showing that more interesting operators can still be implemented.

Lists of References

These are an attempt to make the definition and querying of structured text uniform, using a common language. The language goes beyond querying structured text, so we restrict our attention to the subset in which we are interested.

The structure of documents is fixed and hierarchical, which makes it impossible to have overlapping results. All possible regions are defined at indexing time. The answers delivered are more restrictive, since nesting is not allowed (only the top-level elements qualify) and all elements must be of the same type, e.g. only sections, or only paragraphs. In fact, there are also hypertext links but these cannot be queried (the model also has navigational features).

A static hierarchical structure makes it possible to speak in terms of direct ancestry of nodes, a concept difficult to express when the structure is dynamic. The language allows for querying on 'path expressions,' which describe paths in the structure tree.

Answers to queries are seen as lists of 'references.' A reference is a pointer to a region of the database. This integrates in an elegant way answers to queries and hypertext links, since all are lists of references.

Proximal Nodes

This model tries to find a good compromise between expressiveness and efficiency. It does not define a specific language, but a model in which it is shown that a number of useful operators can be included achieving good efficiency.

The structure is fixed and hierarchical. However, many independent structures can be defined on the same text, each one being a strict hierarchy but allowing overlaps between areas of different hierarchies. An example is shown in Figure 2.12.

A query can relate different hierarchies, but returns a subset of the nodes of one hierarchy only (i.e., nested elements are allowed in the answers, but no overlaps). Text matching queries are modeled as returning nodes from a special 'text hierarchy.'

The model specifies a fully compositional language where the leaves of the query syntax tree are formed by basic queries on contents or names of structural elements (e.g., all chapters). The internal nodes combine results. For efficiency, the operations defined at the internal nodes must be implementable looking at the identity and text areas of the operands, and must relate nodes which are close in the text.

It has been shown that many useful operators satisfy this restriction: selecting elements that (directly or transitively) include or are included in others; that are included at a given position (e.g., the third paragraph of each chapter); that are shortly before or after others; set manipulation; and many powerful variations. Operations on content elements deliver a set of regions with no nesting, and those results can be fully integrated into any query. This ability to integrate the text into the model is very useful. On the other hand, some queries requiring non-proximal operations are not allowed, for instance *semijoins*. An example of a semijoin is 'give me the titles of all the chapters referenced in this chapter.'

Tree Matching
This model relies on a single primitive: tree inclusion, whose main idea is as follows. Interpreting the structure both of the text database and of the query (which is defined as a pattern on the structure) as trees, determine an embedding of the query into the database which respects the hierarchical relationships between nodes of the query.

Two variants are studied. *Ordered inclusion* forces the embedding to respect the left-to-right relations among siblings in the query, while *unordered inclusion* does not. The leaves of the query can be not only structural elements but also text patterns, meaning that the ancestor of the leaf must contain that pattern.

Simple queries return the roots of the matches. The language is enriched by Prolog-like variables, which can be used to express requirements on equality between parts of the matched substructure and to retrieve another part of the match, not only the root. Logical variables are also used for union and intersection of queries, as well as to emulate tuples and join capabilities.

Although the language is set oriented, the algorithms work by sequentially obtaining each match. The use of logical variables and unordered inclusion makes the search problem intractable (NP-hard in many cases). Even the good cases have an inefficient solution in practice.

Discussion

A survey of the main hierarchical models raises a number of interesting issues, most of them largely unresolved up to now. Some of them are listed below.

Static or dynamic structure
As seen, in a static structure there are one or more explicit hierarchies (which can be queried, e.g., by ancestry), while in a dynamic structure there is not really a hierarchy, but the required elements are built on the fly. A dynamic structure is implemented over a normal text index, while a static one may or may not be. A static structure is independent of the text markup, while a dynamic one is more flexible for building arbitrary structures.

Restrictions on the structure
The text or the answers may have restrictions about nesting and/or overlapping. In some cases these restrictions exist for efficiency reasons. In other cases, the query language is restricted to avoid restricting the structure. This choice is largely dependent on the needs of each application.

Integration with text
In many structured models, the text content is merely seen as a secondary source of information which is used only to restrict the matches of structural elements. In classic IR models, on the other side, information on the structure is the secondary element which is used only to restrict text matches. For an effective

integration of queries on text content with queries on text structure, the query language must provide for full expressiveness of both types of queries and for effective means of combining them.

Query language

Typical queries on structure allow the selection of areas that contain (or not) other areas, that are contained (or not) in other areas, that follow (or are followed by) other areas, that are close to other areas, and set manipulation. Many of them are implemented in most models, although each model has unique features. Some kind of standardization, expressiveness taxonomy, or formal categorization would be highly desirable but does not exist yet.

4.5   Query Protocols

In this section we briefly cover some query languages that are used automatically by software applications to query text databases. Some of them are proposed as standards for querying CD-ROMs or as intermediate languages to query library systems. Because they are not intended for human use, we refer to them as protocols rather than languages. More information on protocols can be found in Chapters 14 and 15. The most important query protocols are:

- **Z39.50** is a protocol approved as a standard in 1995 by ANSI and NISO. This protocol is intended to query bibliographical information using a standard interface between the client and the host database manager which is independent of the client user interface and of the query database language at the host. The database is assumed to be a text collection with some fixed fields (although it is more flexible than usual). The Z39.50 protocol is used broadly and is part, for instance, of WAIS (see below). The protocol does not only specify the query language and its semantics, but also the way in which client and server establish a session, communicate and exchange information, etc. Although originally conceived only to operate on bibliographical information (using the Machine Readable Cataloging Record (MARC) format), it has been extended to query other types of information as well.

- **WAIS** (Wide Area Information Service) is a suite of protocols that was popular at the beginning of the 1990s before the boom of the Web. The goal of WAIS was to be a network publishing protocol and to be able to query databases through the Internet.

In the CD-ROM publishing arena, there are several proposals for query protocols. The main goal of these protocols is to provide 'disk interchangeability.' This means more flexibility in data communication between primary information providers and end users. It also enables significant cost savings since it allows access to diverse information without the need to buy, install, and train users for different data retrieval applications. We briefly cover three of these proposals:

- **CCL** (Common Command Language) is a NISO proposal (Z39.58 or ISO 8777) based on Z39.50. It defines 19 commands that can be used interactively. It is more popular in Europe, although very few products use it. It is based on the classical Boolean model.

- **CD-RDx** (Compact Disk Read only Data exchange) uses a client-server architecture and has been implemented in most platforms. The client is generic while the server is designed and provided by the CD-ROM publisher who includes it with the database in the CD-ROM. It allows fixed-length fields, images, and audio, and is supported by such US national agencies as the CIA, NASA, and GSA.

- **SFQL** (Structured Full-text Query Language) is based on SQL and also has a client-server architecture. SFQL has been adopted as a standard by the aerospace community (the Air Transport Association/Aircraft Industry Association). Documents are rows in a relational table and can be tagged using SGML. The language defines the format of the answer, which has a header and a variable length message area. The language does not define any specific formatting or markup. For example, a query in SFQL is:

```
Select abstract from journal.papers where title
contains "text search"
```

The language supports Boolean and logical operators, thesaurus, proximity operations, and some special characters such as wild cards and repetition. For example:

```
...  where paper contains "retrieval" or like "info
%" and date > 1/1/98
```

Compared with CCL or CD-RDx, SFQL is more general and flexible, although it is based on a relational model, which is not always the best choice for a document database.

4.6   Trends and Research Issues

We reviewed in this chapter the main aspects of the query languages that retrieve information from textual databases. Our discussion covered from the most classic tools to the most novel capabilities that are emerging, from searching words to extended patterns, from the Boolean model to querying structures. Table 4.1 shows the different basic queries allowed in the different models. Although the probabilistic and the Bayesian belief network (BBN) models are based on word queries, they can incorporate set operations.

We present in Figure 4.4 the types of operations we covered and how they can be structured (not all of them exist in all models and not all of them have to be used to form a query). The figure shows, for instance, that we can form a query using Boolean operations over phrases (skipping structural queries), which

Model	Queries allowed
Boolean	word, set operations
Vector	words
Probabilistic	words
BBN	words

Table 4.1   Relationship between types of queries and models.

can be formed by words and by regular expressions (skipping the ability to allow errors).

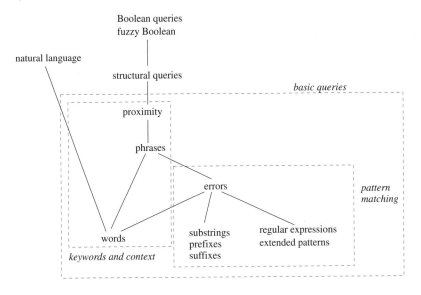

Figure 4.4   The types of queries covered and how they are structured.

The area of query languages for text databases is definitely moving towards higher flexibility. While text models are moving towards the goal of achieving a better understanding of the user needs (by providing relevance feedback, for instance), the query languages are allowing more and more power in the specification of the query. While extended patterns and searching allowing errors permit us to find patterns without complete knowledge of what is wanted, querying on the structure of the text (and not only on its content) provides greater expressiveness and increased functionality.

Another important research topic is visual query languages. Visual metaphors can help non-experienced users to pose complex Boolean queries. Also, a visual query language can include the structure of the document. This topic is related to user interfaces and visualization and is covered in Chapter 10.

4.7   Bibliographic Discussion

The material on classical query languages (most simple patterns, Boolean model, and fixed structure) is based on current commercial systems, such as Fulcrum, Verity, and others, as well as on non-commercial systems such as Glimpse [540] and Igrep [26].

The fuzzy Boolean model is described in [703]. The Levenshtein distance is described in [504] and [25]. Soundex is explained in [445]. A comparison of the effectiveness of different similarity models is given in [595]. A good source on regular expressions is [375]. A rich language on extended patterns is described in [837].

A classical reference on hypertext is [181]. The WebGlimpse system is presented in [539]. The discussion of hierarchical text is partially based on [41]. The original proposals are: PAT Expressions [693], Overlapped Lists [173] and the new improved proposal [206], Lists of References [534], Proximal Nodes [590], and Tree Matching [439]. PAT Expressions are the basic model of the PAT Text Searching System [309]. A simple structured text model is presented in [36] and a visual query language that includes structure is discussed in [44].

More information on Z39.50 can be obtained from [23]. More information on WAIS is given in [425]. For details on SFQL see [392].

Chapter 5
Query Operations

5.1 Introduction

Without detailed knowledge of the collection make-up and of the retrieval environment, most users find it difficult to formulate queries which are well designed for retrieval purposes. In fact, as observed with Web search engines, the users might need to spend large amounts of time reformulating their queries to accomplish effective retrieval. This difficulty suggests that the first query formulation should be treated as an initial (naive) attempt to retrieve relevant information. Following that, the documents initially retrieved could be examined for relevance and new improved query formulations could then be constructed in the hope of retrieving additional useful documents. Such query reformulation involves two basic steps: expanding the original query with new terms and reweighting the terms in the expanded query.

In this chapter, we examine a variety of approaches for improving the initial query formulation through query expansion and term reweighting. These approaches are grouped in three categories: (a) approaches based on feedback information from the user; (b) approaches based on information derived from the set of documents initially retrieved (called the *local* set of documents); and (c) approaches based on global information derived from the document collection. In the first category, user relevance feedback methods for the vector and probabilistic models are discussed. In the second category, two approaches for local analysis (i.e., analysis based on the set of documents initially retrieved) are presented. In the third category, two approaches for global analysis are covered.

Our discussion is not aimed at completely covering the area, neither does it intend to present an exhaustive survey of query operations. Instead, our discussion is based on a selected bibliography which, we believe, is broad enough to allow an overview of the main issues and tradeoffs involved in query operations. Local and global analysis are highly dependent on clustering algorithms. Thus, clustering is covered throughout our discussion. However, there is no intention of providing a complete survey of clustering algorithms for information retrieval.

5.2   User Relevance Feedback

Relevance feedback is the most popular query reformulation strategy. In a relevance feedback cycle, the user is presented with a list of the retrieved documents and, after examining them, marks those which are relevant. In practice, only the top 10 (or 20) ranked documents need to be examined. The main idea consists of selecting important terms, or expressions, attached to the documents that have been identified as relevant by the user, and of enhancing the importance of these terms in a new query formulation. The expected effect is that the new query will be moved towards the relevant documents and away from the non-relevant ones.

Early experiments using the Smart system [695] and later experiments using the probabilistic weighting model [677] have shown good improvements in precision for small test collections when relevance feedback is used. Such improvements come from the use of two basic techniques: query expansion (addition of new terms from relevant documents) and term reweighting (modification of term weights based on the user relevance judgement).

Relevance feedback presents the following main advantages over other query reformulation strategies: (a) it shields the user from the details of the query reformulation process because all the user has to provide is a relevance judgement on documents; (b) it breaks down the whole searching task into a sequence of small steps which are easier to grasp; and (c) it provides a controlled process designed to emphasize some terms (relevant ones) and de-emphasize others (non-relevant ones).

In the following three subsections, we discuss the usage of user relevance feedback to (a) expand queries with the vector model, (b) reweight query terms with the probabilistic model, and (c) reweight query terms with a variant of the probabilistic model.

5.2.1   Query Expansion and Term Reweighting for the Vector Model

The application of *relevance feedback* to the vector model considers that the term-weight vectors of the documents identified as relevant (to a given query) have similarities among themselves (i.e., relevant documents resemble each other). Further, it is assumed that non-relevant documents have term-weight vectors which are dissimilar from the ones for the relevant documents. The basic idea is to reformulate the query such that it gets closer to the term-weight vector space of the relevant documents.

Let us define some additional terminology regarding the processing of a given query q as follows,

> D_r: set of relevant documents, as identified by the user, among the *retrieved* documents;
> D_n: set of non-relevant documents among the *retrieved* documents;
> C_r: set of relevant documents among all documents in the collection;

$|D_r|, |D_n|, |C_r|$: number of documents in the sets D_r, D_n, and C_r, respectively;

α, β, γ: tuning constants.

Consider first the unrealistic situation in which the complete set C_r of relevant documents to a given query q is known in advance. In such a situation, it can be demonstrated that the best query vector for distinguishing the relevant documents from the non-relevant documents is given by,

$$\vec{q}_{opt} = \frac{1}{|C_r|} \sum_{\forall \vec{d}_j \in C_r} \vec{d}_j - \frac{1}{N - |C_r|} \sum_{\forall \vec{d}_j \notin C_r} \vec{d}_j \tag{5.1}$$

The problem with this formulation is that the *relevant* documents which compose the set C_r are not known a priori. In fact, we are looking for them. The natural way to avoid this problem is to formulate an initial query and to incrementally change the initial query vector. This incremental change is accomplished by restricting the computation to the documents *known* to be relevant (according to the user judgement) at that point. There are three classic and similar ways to calculate the modified query $\vec{q}_m$ as follows,

$$Standard\_Rochio: \quad \vec{q}_m = \alpha \, \vec{q} + \frac{\beta}{|D_r|} \sum_{\forall \vec{d}_j \in D_r} \vec{d}_j - \frac{\gamma}{|D_n|} \sum_{\forall \vec{d}_j \in D_n} \vec{d}_j$$

$$Ide\_Regular: \quad \vec{q}_m = \alpha \, \vec{q} + \beta \sum_{\forall \vec{d}_j \in D_r} \vec{d}_j - \gamma \sum_{\forall \vec{d}_j \in D_n} \vec{d}_j$$

$$Ide\_Dec\_Hi: \quad \vec{q}_m = \alpha \, \vec{q} + \beta \sum_{\forall \vec{d}_j \in D_r} \vec{d}_j - \gamma \, max_{non\text{-}relevant}(\vec{d}_j)$$

where $max_{non-relevant}(\vec{d}_j)$ is a reference to the highest ranked non-relevant document. Notice that now D_r and D_n stand for the sets of relevant and non-relevant documents (among the retrieved ones) according to the user judgement, respectively. In the original formulations, Rochio [678] fixed $\alpha = 1$ and Ide [391] fixed $\alpha = \beta = \gamma = 1$. The expressions above are modern variants. The current understanding is that the three techniques yield similar results (in the past, Ide Dec-Hi was considered slightly better).

The Rochio formulation is basically a direct adaptation of equation 5.1 in which the terms of the original query are added in. The motivation is that in practice the original query q may contain important information. Usually, the information contained in the relevant documents is more important than the information provided by the non-relevant documents [698]. This suggests making the constant γ smaller than the constant β. An alternative approach is to set γ to 0 which yields a *positive* feedback strategy.

The main advantages of the above relevance feedback techniques are simplicity and good results. The simplicity is due to the fact that the modified term weights are computed directly from the set of retrieved documents. The good results are observed experimentally and are due to the fact that the modified query vector does reflect a portion of the intended query semantics. The main disadvantage is that *no* optimality criterion is adopted.

5.2.2 Term Reweighting for the Probabilistic Model

The probabilistic model dynamically ranks documents similar to a query q according to the probabilistic ranking principle. From Chapter 2, we already know that the similarity of a document d_j to a query q can be expressed as

$$sim(d_j, q) \; \alpha \; \sum_{i=1}^{t} w_{i,q} \; w_{i,j} \; \left(\log \frac{P(k_i|R)}{1 - P(k_i|R)} + \log \frac{1 - P(k_i|\overline{R})}{P(k_i|\overline{R})} \right) \qquad (\mathbf{5.2})$$

where $P(k_i|R)$ stands for the probability of observing the term k_i in the set R of relevant documents and $P(k_i|\overline{R})$ stands for the probability of observing the term k_i in the set $\overline{R}$ of non-relevant documents.

Initially, equation 5.2 cannot be used because the probabilities $P(k_i|R)$ and $P(k_i|\overline{R})$ are unknown. A number of different methods for estimating these probabilities automatically (i.e., without feedback from the user) were discussed in Chapter 2. With user feedback information, these probabilities are estimated in a slightly different way as follows.

For the initial search (when there are no retrieved documents yet), assumptions often made include: (a) $P(k_i|R)$ is constant for all terms k_i (typically 0.5) and (b) the term probability distribution $P(k_i|\overline{R})$ can be approximated by the distribution in the whole collection. These two assumptions yield:

$$
\begin{aligned}
P(k_i|R) &= 0.5 \\
P(k_i|\overline{R}) &= \frac{n_i}{N}
\end{aligned}
$$

where, as before, n_i stands for the number of documents in the collection which contain the term k_i. Substituting into equation 5.2, we obtain

$$sim_{initial}(d_j, q) = \sum_{i}^{t} w_{i,q} \; w_{i,j} \; \log \frac{N - n_i}{n_i}$$

For the feedback searches, the accumulated statistics related to the relevance or non-relevance of previously retrieved documents are used to evaluate the probabilities $P(k_i|R)$ and $P(k_i|\overline{R})$. As before, let D_r be the set of relevant retrieved documents (according to the user judgement) and $D_{r,i}$ be the subset of D_r composed of the documents which contain the term k_i. Then, the probabilities $P(k_i|R)$ and $P(k_i|\overline{R})$ can be approximated by

$$P(k_i|R) = \frac{|D_{r,i}|}{|D_r|}; \quad P(k_i|\overline{R}) = \frac{n_i - |D_{r,i}|}{N - |D_r|} \qquad (\mathbf{5.3})$$

Using these approximations, equation 5.2 can rewritten as

$$sim(d_j, q) = \sum_{i=1}^{t} w_{i,q} \, w_{i,j} \, \log \left[\frac{|D_{r,i}|}{|D_r| - |D_{r,i}|} \div \frac{n_i - |D_{r,i}|}{N - |D_r| - (n_i - |D_{r,i}|)} \right]$$

Notice that here, contrary to the procedure in the vector space model, no query expansion occurs. The same query terms are being reweighted using feedback information provided by the user.

Formula 5.3 poses problems for certain small values of $|D_r|$ and $|D_{r,i}|$ that frequently arise in practice ($|D_r| = 1, |D_{r,i}| = 0$). For this reason, a 0.5 adjustment factor is often added to the estimation of $P(k_i|R)$ and $P(k_i|\overline{R})$ yielding

$$P(k_i|R) = \frac{|D_{r,i}| + 0.5}{|D_r| + 1}; \quad P(k_i|\overline{R}) = \frac{n_i - |D_{r,i}| + 0.5}{N - |D_r| + 1} \qquad (5.4)$$

This 0.5 adjustment factor may provide unsatisfactory estimates in some cases, and alternative adjustments have been proposed such as n_i/N or $(n_i - |D_{r,i}|)$ $/(N - |D_r|)$ [843]. Taking n_i/N as the adjustment factor (instead of 0.5), equation 5.4 becomes

$$P(k_i|R) = \frac{|D_{r,i}| + \frac{n_i}{N}}{|D_r| + 1}; \quad P(k_i|\overline{R}) = \frac{n_i - |D_{r,i}| + \frac{n_i}{N}}{N - |D_r| + 1}$$

The main advantages of this relevance feedback procedure are that the feedback process is directly related to the derivation of new weights for *query* terms and that the term reweighting is optimal under the assumptions of term independence and binary document indexing ($w_{i,q} \in \{0,1\}$ and $w_{i,j} \in \{0,1\}$). The disadvantages include: (1) document term weights are *not* taken into account during the feedback loop; (2) weights of terms in the previous query formulations are also disregarded; and (3) no query expansion is used (the same set of index terms in the original query is reweighted over and over again). As a result of these disadvantages, the probabilistic relevance feedback methods do *not* in general operate as effectively as the conventional vector modification methods.

To extend the probabilistic model with query expansion capabilities, different approaches have been proposed in the literature ranging from term weighting for query expansion to term clustering techniques based on spanning trees. All of these approaches treat probabilistic query expansion separately from probabilistic term reweighting. While we do not discuss them here, a brief history of research on this issue and bibliographical references can be found in section 5.6.

5.2.3   A Variant of Probabilistic Term Reweighting

The discussion above on term reweighting is based on the classic probabilistic model introduced by Robertson and Sparck Jones in 1976. In 1983, Croft extended this weighting scheme by suggesting distinct initial search methods and by adapting the probabilistic formula to include within-document frequency weights. This variant of probabilistic term reweighting is more flexible (and also more powerful) and is briefly reviewed in this section.

The formula 5.2 for probabilistic ranking can be rewritten as

$$sim(d_j, q) \; \alpha \; \sum_{i=1}^{t} w_{i,q} \; w_{i,j} \; F_{i,j,q}$$

where $F_{i,j,q}$ is interpreted as a factor which depends on the triple $[k_i, d_j, q]$. In the classic formulation, $F_{i,j,q}$ is computed as a function of $P(k_i|R)$ and $P(k_i|\overline{R})$ (see equation 5.2). In his variant, Croft proposed that the initial search and the feedback searches use distinct formulations.

For the initial search, he suggested

$$\begin{aligned} F_{i,j,q} &= (C + idf_i) \; \overline{f}_{i,j} \\ \overline{f}_{i,j} &= K + (1+K) \frac{f_{i,j}}{max(f_{i,j})} \end{aligned}$$

where $\overline{f}_{i,j}$ is a normalized within-document frequency. The parameters C and K should be adjusted according to the collection. For automatically indexed collections, C should be initially set to 0.

For the feedback searches, Croft suggested the following formulation for $F_{i,j,q}$

$$F_{i,j,q} = \left(C + \log \frac{P(k_i|R)}{1 - P(k_i|R)} + \log \frac{1 - P(k_i|\overline{R})}{P(k_i|\overline{R})} \right) \; \overline{f}_{i,j}$$

where $P(k_i|R)$ and $P(k_i|\overline{R})$ are computed as in equation 5.4.

This variant of probabilistic term reweighting has the following advantages: (1) it takes into account the within-document frequencies; (2) it adopts a normalized version of these frequencies; and (3) it introduces the constants C and K which provide for greater flexibility. However, it constitutes a more complex formulation and, as before, it operates solely on the terms originally in the query (without query expansion).

5.2.4   Evaluation of Relevance Feedback Strategies

Consider the modified query vector $\vec{q}_m$ generated by the Rochio formula and assume that we want to evaluate its retrieval performance. A simplistic approach is to retrieve a set of documents using $\vec{q}_m$, to rank them using the vector formula, and to measure recall-precision figures relative to the set of relevant documents (provided by the experts) for the original query vector $\vec{q}$. In general, the results show spectacular improvements. Unfortunately, a significant part of this improvement results from the higher ranks assigned to the set R of documents already identified as relevant during the feedback process [275]. Since the user has seen these documents already (and pointed them as relevants), such evaluation is unrealistic. Further, it masks any real gains in retrieval performance due to documents not seen by the user yet.

A more realistic approach is to evaluate the retrieval performance of the modified query vector $\vec{q}_m$ considering only the *residual collection* i.e., the set of all documents minus the set of feedback documents provided by the user. Because highly ranked documents are removed from the collection, the recall-precision figures for $\vec{q}_m$ tend to be lower than the figures for the original query vector $\vec{q}$. This is not a limitation because our main purpose is to compare the performance of distinct relevance feedback strategies (and not to compare the performance before and after feedback). Thus, as a basic rule of thumb, any experimentation involving relevance feedback strategies should always evaluate recall-precision figures relative to the residual collection.

5.3 Automatic Local Analysis

In a user relevance feedback cycle, the user examines the top ranked documents and separates them into two classes: the relevant ones and the non-relevant ones. This information is then used to select new terms for query expansion. The reasoning is that the expanded query will retrieve more relevant documents. Thus, there is an underlying notion of *clustering* supporting the feedback strategy. According to this notion, known relevant documents contain terms which can be used to describe a larger cluster of relevant documents. In this case, the description of this larger cluster of relevant documents is built interactively with assistance from the user.

A distinct approach is to attempt to obtain a description for a larger cluster of relevant documents automatically. This usually involves identifying terms which are related to the query terms. Such terms might be synonyms, stemming variations, or terms which are close to the query terms in the text (i.e., terms with a distance of at most k words from a query term). Two basic types of strategies can be attempted: global ones and local ones.

In a global strategy, all documents in the collection are used to determine a global thesaurus-like structure which defines term relationships. This structure is then shown to the user who selects terms for query expansion. Global strategies are discussed in section 5.4.

In a local strategy, the documents retrieved for a given query q are examined at query time to determine terms for query expansion. This is similar to a relevance feedback cycle but might be done without assistance from the user (i.e., the approach might be fully automatic). Two local strategies are discussed below: local clustering and local context analysis. The first is based on the work done by Attar and Fraenkel in 1977 and is used here to establish many of the fundamental ideas and concepts regarding the usage of clustering for query expansion. The second is a recent work done by Xu and Croft in 1996 and illustrates the advantages of combining techniques from both local and global analysis.

5.3.1 Query Expansion Through Local Clustering

Adoption of clustering techniques for query expansion is a basic approach which has been attempted since the early years of information retrieval. The standard approach is to build global structures such as association matrices which quantify term correlations (for instance, number of documents in which two given terms co-occur) and to use correlated terms for query expansion. The main problem with this strategy is that there is not consistent evidence that global structures can be used effectively to improve retrieval performance with general collections. One main reason seems to be that global structures do not adapt well to the local context defined by the current query. One approach to deal with this effect is to devise strategies which aim at optimizing the current search. Such strategies are based on *local clustering* and are now discussed. Our discussion is based on the original work by Attar and Fraenkel which appeared in 1977.

We first define basic terminology as follows.

Definition   *Let $V(s)$ be a non-empty subset of words which are grammatical variants of each other. A canonical form s of $V(s)$ is called a* stem. *For instance, if $V(s)$={polish,polishing,polished} then s=polish.*

For a detailed discussion on stemming algorithms see Chapter 7. While stems are adopted in our discussion, the ideas below are also valid for non-stemmed keywords. We proceed with a characterization of the local nature of the strategies covered here.

Definition   *For a given query q, the set D_l of documents retrieved is called the local document set. Further, the set V_l of all distinct words in the local document set is called the local vocabulary. The set of all distinct stems derived from the set V_l is referred to as S_l.*

We operate solely on the documents retrieved for the current query. Since it is frequently necessary to access the text of such documents, the application of local strategies to the Web is unlikely at this time. In fact, at a client machine, retrieving the text of 100 Web documents for local analysis would take too long, reducing drastically the interactive nature of Web interfaces and the satisfaction of the users. Further, at the search engine site, analyzing the text of 100 Web documents would represent an extra spending of CPU time which is not cost effective at this time (because search engines depend on processing a high number of queries per unit of time for economic survival). However, local strategies might be quite useful in the environment of intranets such as, for instance, the collection of documents issued by a large business company. Further, local strategies might also be of great assistance for searching information in specialized document collections (for instance, medical document collections).

Local feedback strategies are based on expanding the query with terms correlated to the query terms. Such correlated terms are those present in local clusters built from the local document set. Thus, before we discuss local query expansion, we discuss strategies for building local clusters. Three types of clusters are covered: association clusters, metric clusters, and scalar clusters.

Association Clusters

An association cluster is based on the co-occurrence of stems (or terms) inside documents. The idea is that stems which co-occur frequently inside documents have a synonymity association. Association clusters are generated as follows.

Definition   *The frequency of a stem s_i in a document d_j, $d_j \in D_l$, is referred to as $f_{s_i,j}$. Let $\vec{m}=(m_{ij})$ be an association matrix with $|S_l|$ rows and $|D_l|$ columns, where $m_{ij}=f_{s_i,j}$. Let $\vec{m}^t$ be the transpose of $\vec{m}$. The matrix $\vec{s}=\vec{m}\vec{m}^t$ is a local stem-stem association matrix. Each element $s_{u,v}$ in $\vec{s}$ expresses a correlation $c_{u,v}$ between the stems s_u and s_v namely,*

$$c_{u,v} = \sum_{d_j \in D_l} f_{s_u,j} \times f_{s_v,j} \tag{5.5}$$

The correlation factor $c_{u,v}$ quantifies the absolute frequencies of co-occurrence and is said to be unnormalized. Thus, if we adopt

$$s_{u,v} = c_{u,v} \tag{5.6}$$

then the association matrix $\vec{s}$ is said to be unnormalized. An alternative is to normalize the correlation factor. For instance, if we adopt

$$s_{u,v} = \frac{c_{u,v}}{c_{u,u} + c_{v,v} - c_{u,v}} \tag{5.7}$$

then the association matrix $\vec{s}$ is said to be normalized. The adoption of normalization yields quite distinct associations as discussed below.

Given a local association matrix $\vec{s}$, we can use it to build local association clusters as follows.

Definition   *Consider the u-th row in the association matrix $\vec{s}$ (i.e., the row with all the associations for the stem s_u). Let $S_u(n)$ be a function which takes the u-th row and returns the set of n largest values $s_{u,v}$, where v varies over the set of local stems and $v \neq u$. Then $S_u(n)$ defines a local association cluster around the stem s_u. If $s_{u,v}$ is given by equation 5.6, the association cluster is said to be unnormalized. If $s_{u,v}$ is given by equation 5.7, the association cluster is said to be normalized.*

Given a query q, we are normally interested in finding clusters only for the $|q|$ query terms. Further, it is desirable to keep the size of such clusters small. This means that such clusters can be computed efficiently at query time.

Despite the fact that the above clustering procedure adopts stems, it can equally be applied to non-stemmed keywords. The procedure remains unchanged except for the usage of keywords instead of stems. Keyword-based local clustering is equally worthwhile trying because there is controversy over the advantages of using a stemmed vocabulary, as discussed in Chapter 7.

Metric Clusters

Association clusters are based on the frequency of co-occurrence of pairs of terms in documents and do not take into account *where* the terms occur in a document. Since two terms which occur in the same sentence seem more correlated than two terms which occur far apart in a document, it might be worthwhile to factor in the distance between two terms in the computation of their correlation factor. Metric clusters are based on this idea.

Definition   *Let the distance $r(k_i, k_j)$ between two keywords k_i and k_j be given by the number of words between them in a same document. If k_i and k_j are in distinct documents we take $r(k_i, k_j) = \infty$. A local stem-stem metric correlation matrix $\vec{s}$ is defined as follows. Each element $s_{u,v}$ of $\vec{s}$ expresses a metric correlation $c_{u,v}$ between the stems s_u and s_v namely,*

$$c_{u,v} = \sum_{k_i \in V(s_u)} \sum_{k_j \in V(s_v)} \frac{1}{r(k_i, k_j)}$$

In this expression, as already defined, $V(s_u)$ and $V(s_v)$ indicate the sets of keywords which have s_u and s_v as their respective stems. Variations of the above expression for $c_{u,v}$ have been reported in the literature (such as $1/r^2(k_i, k_j)$) but the differences in experimental results are not remarkable.

The correlation factor $c_{u,v}$ quantifies absolute inverse distances and is said to be unnormalized. Thus, if we adopt

$$s_{u,v} = c_{u,v} \tag{5.8}$$

then the association matrix $\vec{s}$ is said to be unnormalized. An alternative is to normalize the correlation factor. For instance, if we adopt

$$s_{u,v} = \frac{c_{u,v}}{|V(s_u)| \times |V(s_v)|} \tag{5.9}$$

then the association matrix $\vec{s}$ is said to be normalized.

Given a local metric matrix $\vec{s}$, we can use it to build local metric clusters as follows.

Definition   *Consider the u-th row in the metric correlation matrix $\vec{s}$ (i.e., the row with all the associations for the stem s_u). Let $S_u(n)$ be a function which* *takes the u-th row and returns the set of n largest values $s_{u,v}$, where v varies over the set of local stems and $v \neq u$. Then $S_u(n)$ defines a local metric cluster around the stem s_u. If $s_{u,v}$ is given by equation 5.8, the metric cluster is said to be unnormalized. If $s_{u,v}$ is given by equation 5.9, the metric cluster is said to be normalized.*

Scalar Clusters

One additional form of deriving a synonymity relationship between two local stems (or terms) s_u and s_v is by comparing the sets $S_u(n)$ and $S_v(n)$. The idea is that two stems with similar *neighborhoods* have some synonymity relationship. In this case we say that the relationship is indirect or induced by the neighborhood. One way of quantifying such neighborhood relationships is to arrange all correlation values $s_{u,i}$ in a vector $\vec{s}_u$, to arrange all correlation values $s_{v,i}$ in another vector $\vec{s}_v$, and to compare these vectors through a scalar measure. For instance, the cosine of the angle between the two vectors is a popular scalar similarity measure.

Definition   *Let $\vec{s}_u = (s_{u,1}, s_{u,2}, \ldots, s_{u,n})$ and $\vec{s}_v = (s_{v,1}, s_{v,2}, \ldots, s_{v,n})$ be two vectors of correlation values for the stems s_u and s_v. Further, let $\vec{s} = (s_{u,v})$ be a scalar association matrix. Then, each $s_{u,v}$ can be defined as*

$$s_{u,v} = \frac{\vec{s}_u \cdot \vec{s}_v}{|\vec{s}_u| \times |\vec{s}_v|} \qquad (5.10)$$

The correlation matrix $\vec{s}$ is said to be induced by the neighborhood. Using it, a scalar cluster is then defined as follows.

Definition   *Let $S_u(n)$ be a function which returns the set of n largest values $s_{u,v}$, $v \neq u$, defined according to equation 5.10. Then, $S_u(n)$ defines a scalar cluster around the stem s_u.*

Interactive Search Formulation

Stems (or terms) that belong to clusters associated to the query stems (or terms) can be used to expand the original query. Such stems are called neighbors (of the query stems) and are characterized as follows.

A stem s_u which belongs to a cluster (of size n) associated to another stem s_v (i.e., $s_u \in S_v(n)$) is said to be a *neighbor* of s_v. Sometimes, s_u is also called a *searchonym* of s_v but here we opt for using the terminology *neighbor*. While neighbor stems are said to have a synonymity relationship, they are not necessarily synonyms in the grammatical sense. Often, neighbor stems represent distinct keywords which are though correlated by the current query context. The local aspect of this correlation is reflected in the fact that the documents and stems considered in the correlation matrix are all local (i.e., $d_j \in D_l$, $s_u \in V_l$).

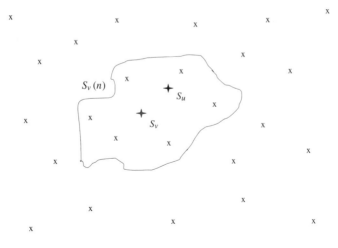

Figure 5.1   Stem s_u as a neighbor of the stem s_v.

Figure 5.1 illustrates a stem (or term) s_u which is located within a neighborhood $S_v(n)$ associated with the stem (or term) s_v. In its broad meaning, neighbor stems are an important product of the local clustering process since they can be used for extending a search formulation in a promising unexpected direction, rather than merely complementing it with missing synonyms.

Consider the problem of expanding a given user query q with neighbor stems (or terms). One possibility is to expand the query as follows. For each stem $s_v \in q$, select m neighbor stems from the cluster $S_v(n)$ (which might be of type association, metric, or scalar) and add them to the query. Hopefully, the additional neighbor stems will retrieve new relevant documents. To cover a broader neighborhood, the set $S_v(n)$ might be composed of stems obtained using correlation factors (i.e., $c_{u,v}$) normalized and unnormalized. The qualitative interpretation is that an unnormalized cluster tends to group stems whose ties are due to their large frequencies, while a normalized cluster tends to group stems which are more rare. Thus, the union of the two clusters provides a better representation of the possible correlations.

Besides the merging of normalized and unnormalized clusters, one can also use information about correlated stems to improve the search. For instance, as before, let two stems s_u and s_v be correlated with a correlation factor $c_{u,v}$. If $c_{u,v}$ is larger than a predefined threshold then a neighbor stem of s_u can also be interpreted as a neighbor stem of s_v and vice versa. This provides greater flexibility, particularly with Boolean queries. To illustrate, consider the expression $(s_u + s_v)$ where the $+$ symbol stands for disjunction. Let $s_{u'}$ be a neighbor stem of s_u. Then, one can try both $(s_{u'} + s_v)$ and $(s_u + s_{u'})$ as synonym search expressions, because of the correlation given by $c_{u,v}$.

Experimental results reported in the literature usually support the hypothesis of the usefulness of local clustering methods. Furthermore, metric clusters seem to perform better than purely association clusters. This strengthens the hypothesis that there is a correlation between the association of two terms and the distance between them.

We emphasize that all the qualitative arguments in this section are explicitly based on the fact that all the clusters are local (i.e., derived solely from the documents retrieved for the current query). In a global context, clusters are derived from all the documents in the collection which implies that our qualitative argumentation might not stand. The main reason is that correlations valid in the whole corpora might not be valid for the current query.

5.3.2   Query Expansion Through Local Context Analysis

The local clustering techniques discussed above are based on the set of documents retrieved for the original query and use the top ranked documents for clustering neighbor terms (or stems). Such a clustering is based on term (stems were considered above) co-occurrence inside documents. Terms which are the best neighbors of each query term are then used to expand the original query q. A distinct approach is to search for term correlations in the whole collection — an approach called global analysis. Global techniques usually involve the building of a thesaurus which identifies term relationships in the whole collection. The terms are treated as concepts and the thesaurus is viewed as a concept relationship structure. Thesauri are expensive to build but, besides providing support for query expansion, are useful as a browsing tool as demonstrated by some search engines in the Web. The building of a thesaurus usually considers the use of small contexts and phrase structures instead of simply adopting the context provided by a whole document. Furthermore, with modern variants of global analysis, terms which are closest to the whole query (and not to individual query terms) are selected for query expansion. The application of ideas from global analysis (such as small contexts and phrase structures) to the local set of documents retrieved is a recent idea which we now discuss.

Local context analysis [838] combines global and local analysis and works as follows. First, the approach is based on the use of noun groups (i.e., a single noun, two adjacent nouns, or three adjacent nouns in the text), instead of simple keywords, as document concepts. For query expansion, concepts are selected from the top ranked documents (as in local analysis) based on their co-occurrence with query terms (no stemming). However, instead of documents, passages (i.e., a text window of fixed size) are used for determining co-occurrence (as in global analysis).

More specifically, the local context analysis procedure operates in three steps.

- First, retrieve the top n ranked passages using the original query. This is accomplished by breaking up the documents initially retrieved by the

query in fixed length passages (for instance, of size 300 words) and ranking
these passages as if they were documents.

- Second, for each concept c in the top ranked passages, the similarity
  $sim(q,c)$ between the whole query q (not individual query terms) and the
  concept c is computed using a variant of tf-idf ranking.

- Third, the top m ranked concepts (according to $sim(q,c)$) are added to
  the original query q. To each added concept is assigned a weight given by
  $1 - 0.9 \times i/m$ where i is the position of the concept in the final concept
  ranking. The terms in the original query q might be stressed by assigning
  a weight equal to 2 to each of them.

Of these three steps, the second one is the most complex and the one which we
now discuss.

The similarity $sim(q,c)$ between each related concept c and the original
query q is computed as follows.

$$sim(q,c) = \prod_{k_i \in q} \left(\delta + \frac{\log(f(c,k_i) \times idf_c)}{\log n} \right)^{idf_i}$$

where n is the number of top ranked passages considered. The function $f(c,k_i)$
quantifies the correlation between the concept c and the query term k_i and is
given by

$$f(c,k_i) = \sum_{j=1}^{n} pf_{i,j} \times pf_{c,j}$$

where $pf_{i,j}$ is the frequency of term k_i in the j-th passage and $pf_{c,j}$ is the
frequency of the concept c in the j-th passage. Notice that this is the standard correlation measure defined for association clusters (by Equation 5.5) but
adapted for passages. The inverse document frequency factors are computed as

$$idf_i = max(1, \frac{\log_{10} N/np_i}{5})$$
$$idf_c = max(1, \frac{\log_{10} N/np_c}{5})$$

where N is the number of passages in the collection, np_i is the number of passages
containing the term k_i, and np_c is the number of passages containing the concept
c. The factor δ is a constant parameter which avoids a value equal to zero
for $sim(q,c)$ (which is useful, for instance, if the approach is to be used with
probabilistic frameworks such as that provided by belief networks). Usually, δ is
a small factor with values close to 0.1 (10% of the maximum of 1). Finally, the
idf_i factor in the exponent is introduced to emphasize infrequent query terms.

The procedure above for computing $sim(q,c)$ is a non-trivial variant of tf-
idf ranking. Furthermore, it has been adjusted for operation with TREC data

and did not work so well with a different collection. Thus, it is important to have in mind that tuning might be required for operation with a different collection.

We also notice that the correlation measure adopted with local context analysis is of type association. However, we already know that a correlation of type metric is expected to be more effective. Thus, it remains to be tested whether the adoption of a metric correlation factor (for the function $f(c, k_i)$) makes any difference with local context analysis.

5.4   Automatic Global Analysis

The methods of local analysis discussed above extract information from the local set of documents retrieved to expand the query. It is well accepted that such a procedure yields improved retrieval performance with various collections. An alternative approach is to expand the query using information from the whole set of documents in the collection. Strategies based on this idea are called global analysis procedures. Until the beginning of the 1990s, global analysis was considered to be a technique which failed to yield consistent improvements in retrieval performance with general collections. This perception has changed with the appearance of modern procedures for global analysis. In the following, we discuss two of these modern variants. Both of them are based on a thesaurus-like structure built using all the documents in the collection. However, the approach taken for building the thesaurus and the procedure for selecting terms for query expansion are quite distinct in the two cases.

5.4.1   Query Expansion based on a Similarity Thesaurus

In this section we discuss a query expansion model based on a global similarity thesaurus which is constructed automatically [655]. The similarity thesaurus is based on term to term relationships rather than on a matrix of co-occurrence (as discussed in section 5.3). The distinction is made clear in the discussion below. Furthermore, special attention is paid to the selection of terms for expansion and to the reweighting of these terms. In contrast to previous global analysis approaches, terms for expansion are selected based on their similarity to the whole query rather than on their similarities to individual query terms.

A *similarity thesaurus* is built considering term to term relationships. However, such relationships are not derived directly from co-occurrence of terms inside documents. Rather, they are obtained by considering that the terms are concepts in a concept space. In this concept space, each term is indexed by the documents in which it appears. Thus, terms assume the original role of documents while documents are interpreted as indexing elements. The following definitions establish the proper framework.

Definition *As before (see Chapter 2), let t be the number of terms in the collection, N be the number of documents in the collection, and $f_{i,j}$ be the frequency* *of occurrence of the term k_i in the document d_j. Further, let t_j be the number of distinct index terms in the document d_j and itf_j be the inverse term frequency for document d_j. Then,*

$$itf_j = \log \frac{t}{t_j}$$

analogously to the definition of inverse document frequency.

Within this framework, to each term k_i is associated a vector $\vec{k}_i$ given by

$$\vec{k}_i = (w_{i,1}, w_{i,2}, \ldots, w_{i,N})$$

where, as in Chapter 2, $w_{i,j}$ is a weight associated to the index-document pair $[k_i, d_j]$. Here, however, these weights are computed in a rather distinct form as follows.

$$w_{i,j} = \frac{(0.5 + 0.5 \frac{f_{i,j}}{max_j(f_{i,j})}) \; itf_j}{\sqrt{\sum_{l=1}^{N}(0.5 + 0.5 \frac{f_{i,l}}{max_l(f_{i,l})})^2 \; itf_j^2}} \tag{5.11}$$

where $max_j(f_{i,j})$ computes the maximum of all factors $f_{i,j}$ for the i-th term (i.e., over all documents in the collection). We notice that the expression above is a variant of tf-idf weights but one which considers inverse term frequencies instead.

The relationship between two terms k_u and k_v is computed as a correlation factor $c_{u,v}$ given by

$$c_{u,v} = \vec{k}_u \cdot \vec{k}_v = \sum_{\forall \; d_j} w_{u,j} \times w_{v,j} \tag{5.12}$$

We notice that this is a variation of the correlation measure used for computing scalar association matrices (defined by Equation 5.5). The main difference is that the weights are based on interpreting documents as indexing elements instead of repositories for term co-occurrence. The global similarity thesaurus is built through the computation of the correlation factor $c_{u,v}$ for each pair of indexing terms $[k_u, k_v]$ in the collection (analogously to the procedure in section 5.3). Of course, this is computationally expensive. However, this global similarity thesaurus has to be computed only once and can be updated incrementally.

Given the global similarity thesaurus, query expansion is done in three steps as follows.

- First, represent the query in the concept space used for representation of the index terms.

- Second, based on the global similarity thesaurus, compute a similarity $sim(q, k_v)$ between each term k_v correlated to the query terms and the whole query q.
- Third, expand the query with the top r ranked terms according to $sim(q, k_v)$.

For the first step, the query is represented in the concept space of index term vectors as follows.

Definition   *To the query q is associated a vector $\vec{q}$ in the term-concept space given by*

$$\vec{q} = \sum_{k_i \in q} w_{i,q} \vec{k_i}$$

where $w_{i,q}$ is a weight associated to the index-query pair $[k_i, q]$. This weight is computed analogously to the index-document weight formula in equation 5.11.

For the second step, a similarity $sim(q, k_v)$ between each term k_v (correlated to the query terms) and the user query q is computed as

$$sim(q, k_v) = \vec{q} \cdot \vec{k_v} = \sum_{k_u \in Q} w_{u,q} \times c_{u,v}$$

where $c_{u,v}$ is the correlation factor given in equation 5.12. As illustrated in Figure 5.2, a term might be quite close to the whole query while its distances to individual query terms are larger. This implies that the terms selected here for query expansion might be distinct from those selected by previous global analysis methods (which adopted a similarity to individual query terms for deciding terms for query expansion).

For the third step, the top r ranked terms according to $sim(q, k_v)$ are added to the original query q to form the expanded query q'. To each expansion term k_v in the query q' is assigned a weight $w_{v,q'}$ given by

$$w_{v,q'} = \frac{sim(q, k_v)}{\sum_{k_u \in q} w_{u,q}}$$

The expanded query q' is then used to retrieve new documents to the user. This completes the technique for query expansion based on a similarity thesaurus. Contrary to previous global analysis approaches, this technique has yielded improved retrieval performance (in the range of 20%) with three different collections.

It is worthwhile making one final observation. Consider a document d_j which is represented in the term-concept space by $\vec{d_j} = \sum_{k_i \in d_j} w_{i,j} \vec{k_i}$. Further, assume that the original query q is expanded to include all the t index terms

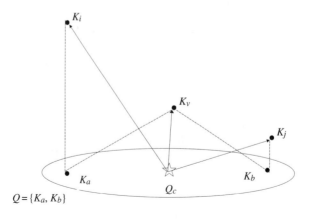

Figure 5.2   The distance of a given term k_v to the query centroid Q_c might be quite distinct from the distances of k_v to the individual query terms.

(properly weighted) in the collection. Then, the similarity $sim(q, d_j)$ between the document d_j and the query q can be computed in the term-concept space by

$$sim(q, d_j) \ \alpha \ \sum_{k_v \in d_j} \sum_{k_u \in q} w_{v,j} \times w_{u,q} \times c_{u,v}$$

Such an expression is analogous to the formula for query-document similarity in the generalized vector space model (see Chapter 2). Thus, the generalized vector space model can be interpreted as a query expansion technique. The main differences with the term-concept idea are the weight computation and the fact that only the top r ranked terms are used for query expansion with the term-concept technique.

5.4.2   Query Expansion based on a Statistical Thesaurus

In this section, we discuss a query expansion technique based on a global statistical thesaurus [200]. Despite also being a global analysis technique, the approach is quite distinct from the one described above which is based on a similarity thesaurus.

The global thesaurus is composed of classes which group correlated terms in the context of the whole collection. Such correlated terms can then be used to expand the original user query. To be effective, the terms selected for expansion must have high term discrimination values [699] which implies that they must be low frequency terms. However, it is difficult to cluster low frequency terms effectively due to the small amount of information about them (they occur in few documents). To circumvent this problem, we cluster documents into classes instead and use the low frequency terms in these documents to define our thesaurus classes. In this situation, the document clustering algorithm must produce small and tight clusters.

A document clustering algorithm which produces small and tight clusters is the *complete link algorithm* which works as follows (naive formulation).

(1) Initially, place each document in a distinct cluster.

(2) Compute the similarity between all pairs of clusters.

(3) Determine the pair of clusters $[C_u, C_v]$ with the highest inter-cluster similarity.

(4) Merge the clusters C_u and C_v.

(5) Verify a stop criterion. If this criterion is not met then go back to step 2.

(6) Return a hierarchy of clusters.

The similarity between two clusters is defined as the minimum of the similarities between all pairs of inter-cluster documents (i.e., two documents not in the same cluster). To compute the similarity between documents in a pair, the cosine formula of the vector model is used. As a result of this minimality criterion, the resultant clusters tend to be small and tight.

Consider that the whole document collection has been clustered using the complete link algorithm. Figure 5.3 illustrates a small portion of the whole cluster hierarchy in which $sim(C_u, C_v) = 0.15$ and $sim(C_{u+v}, C_z) = 0.11$ where C_{u+v} is a reference to the cluster which results from merging C_u and C_v. Notice that the similarities decrease as we move up in the hierarchy because high level clusters include more documents and thus represent a looser grouping. Thus, the tightest clusters lie at the bottom of the clustering hierarchy.

Given the document cluster hierarchy for the whole collection, the terms that compose each class of the global thesaurus are selected as follows.

- Obtain from the user three parameters: threshold class (TC), number of

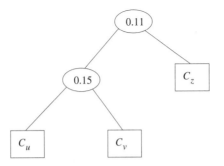

Figure 5.3 Hierarchy of three clusters (inter-cluster similarities indicated in the ovals) generated by the complete link algorithm.

documents in a class (NDC), and minimum inverse document frequency (MIDF).

- Use the parameter TC as a threshold value for determining the document clusters that will be used to generate thesaurus classes. This threshold has to be surpassed by $sim(C_u, C_v)$ if the documents in the clusters C_u and C_v are to be selected as sources of terms for a thesaurus class. For instance, in Figure 5.3, a value of 0.14 for TC returns the thesaurus class C_{u+v} while a value of 0.10 for TC returns the classes C_{u+v} and C_{u+v+z}.

- Use the parameter NDC as a limit on the size of clusters (number of documents) to be considered. For instance, if both C_{u+v} and C_{u+v+z} are preselected (through the parameter TC) then the parameter NDC might be used to decide between the two. A low value of NDC might restrict the selection to the smaller cluster C_{u+v}.

- Consider the set of documents in each document cluster preselected above (through the parameters TC and NDC). Only the lower frequency documents are used as sources of terms for the thesaurus classes. The parameter MIDF defines the minimum value of inverse document frequency for any term which is selected to participate in a thesaurus class. By doing so, it is possible to ensure that only *low frequency* terms participate in the thesaurus classes generated (terms too generic are not good synonyms).

Given that the thesaurus classes have been built, they can be used for query expansion. For this, an average term weight wt_C for each thesaurus class C is computed as follows.

$$wt_C = \frac{\sum_{i=1}^{|C|} w_{i,C}}{|C|}$$

where $|C|$ is the number of terms in the thesaurus class C and $w_{i,C}$ is a precomputed weight associated with the term-class pair $[k_i, C]$. This average term weight can then be used to compute a thesaurus class weight w_C as

$$w_C = \frac{wt_C}{|C|} \times 0.5$$

The above weight formulations have been verified through experimentation and have yielded good results.

Experiments with four test collections (ADI, Medlars, CACM, and ISI; see Chapter 3 for details on these collections) indicate that global analysis using a thesaurus built by the complete link algorithm might yield consistent improvements in retrieval performance.

The main problem with this approach is the initialization of the parameters TC, NDC, and MIDF. The threshold value TC depends on the collection and can be difficult to set properly. Inspection of the cluster hierarchy is almost always necessary for assisting with the setting of TC. Care must be exercised because a high value of TC might yield classes with too few terms while a low value of TC might yield too few classes. The selection of the parameter NDC can be decided more easily once TC has been set. However, the setting of the parameter MIDF might be difficult and also requires careful consideration.

5.5   Trends and Research Issues

The relevance feedback strategies discussed here can be directly applied to the graphical interfaces of modern information systems. However, since interactivity is now of greater importance, new techniques for capturing feedback information from the user are desirable. For instance, there is great interest in graphical interfaces which display the documents in the answer set as points in a 2D or 3D space. The motivation is to allow the user to quickly identify (by visual inspection) relationships among the documents in the answer. In this scenario, a rather distinct strategy for quantifying feedback information might be required. Thus, relevance strategies for dealing with visual displays are an important research problem.

In the past, global analysis was viewed as an approach which did not yield good improvements in retrieval performance. However, new results obtained at the beginning of the 1990s changed this perception. Further, the Web has provided evidence that techniques based on global analysis might be of interest to the users. For instance, this is the case with the highly popular 'Yahoo!' software which uses a manually built hierarchy of concepts to assist the user with forming the query. This suggests that investigating the utilization of global analysis techniques in the Web is a promising research problem.

Local analysis techniques are interesting because they take advantage of the local context provided with the query. In this regard, they seem more appropriate than global analysis techniques. Furthermore, many positive results have been reported in the literature. The application of local analysis techniques to the Web, however, has not been explored and is a promising research direction. The main challenge is the computational burden imposed on the search engine site due to the need to process document texts at query time. Thus, a related research problem of relevance is the development of techniques for speeding up query processing at the search engine site. In truth, this problem is of interest even if one considers only the normal processing of the queries because the search engines depend on processing as many queries as possible for economic survival.

The combination of local analysis, global analysis, visual displays, and interactive interfaces is also a current and important research problem. Allowing the user to visually explore the document space and providing him with clues which assist with the query formulation process are highly relevant issues. Positive results in this area might become a turning point regarding the design of user interfaces and are likely to attract wide attention.

5.6 Bibliographic Discussion

Query expansion methods have been studied for a long time. While the success of expansion methods throughout the years has been debatable, more recently researchers have reached the consensus that query expansion is a useful and little explored (commercially) technique. Useful because its modern variants can be used to consistently improve the retrieval performance with general collections. Little explored because few commercial systems (and Web search engines) take advantage of it.

Early work suggesting the expansion of a user query with closely related terms was done by Maron and Kuhns in 1960 [547]. The classic technique for combining query expansion with term reweighting in the vector model was studied by Rocchio in 1965 (using the Smart system [695] as a testbed) and published later on [678]. Ide continued the studies of Rocchio and proposed variations to the term reweighting formula [391].

The probabilistic model was introduced by Robertson and Sparck Jones [677] in 1976. A thorough and entertaining discussion of this model can be found in the book by van Rijsbergen [785]. Croft and Harper [199] suggested that the initial search should use a distinct computation. In 1983, Croft [198] proposed to extend the probabilistic formula to include within-document frequencies and introduced the C and K parameters.

Since the probabilistic model does not provide means of expanding the query, query expansion has to be done separately. In 1978, Harper and van Rijsbergen [345] used a term-term clustering technique based on a maximum spanning tree to select terms for probabilistic query expansion. Two years later, they also introduced a new relevance weighting scheme, called EMIM [344], to be used with their query expansion technique. In 1981, Wu and Salton [835] used relevance feedback to reweight terms (using a probabilistic formula) extracted from relevant documents and used these terms to expand the query. Empirical results showed improvements in retrieval performance.

Our discussion on user relevance feedback for the vector and probabilistic models in section 5.2 is based on four sources: a nice paper by Salton and Buckley [696], the book by van Rijsbergen [785], the book by Salton and McGill [698], and two book chapters by Harman [340, 339].

Regarding automatic query expansion, Lesk [500] tried variations of term-term clustering in the Smart system without positive results. Following that, Sparck Jones and Barber [413] and Minker, Wilson and Zimmerman [562] also observed no improvements with query expansion based on term-term global clustering. These early research results left the impression that query expansion based on global analysis is not an effective technique. However, more recent results show that this is not the case. In fact, the research results obtained by Vorhees [793], by Crouch and Yang [200], and by Qiu and Frei [655] indicate that query expansion based on global analysis can consistently yield improved retrieval performance.

Our discussion on query expansion through local clustering is based on early work by Attar and Fraenkel [35] from 1977. The idea of local context analysis is much more recent and was introduced by Xu and Croft [838] in 1996. The discussion on query expansion using a global similarity thesaurus is based on the work by Qiu and Frei [655]. Finally, the discussion on query expansion using a global statistical thesaurus is based on the work of Crouch and Yang [200] which is influenced by the term discrimination value theory introduced by Salton, Yang, and Yu [699] early in 1975.

Since query expansion frequently is based on some form of clustering, our discussion covered a few clustering algorithms. However, our aim was not to provide a thorough review of clustering algorithms for information retrieval. Such a review can be found in the work of Rasmussen [668].

Chapter 6
Text and Multimedia Languages and Properties

6.1 Introduction

Text is the main form of communicating knowledge. Starting with hieroglyphs, the first written surfaces (stone, wood, animal skin, papyrus, and rice paper), and paper, text has been created everywhere, in many forms and languages. We use the term *document* to denote a single unit of information, typically text in a digital form, but it can also include other media. In practice, a document is loosely defined. It can be a complete logical unit, like a research article, a book or a manual. It can also be part of a larger text, such as a paragraph or a sequence of paragraphs (also called a *passage* of text), an entry in a dictionary, a judge's opinion on a case, the description of an automobile part, etc. Furthermore, with respect to its physical representation, a document can be any physical unit, for example a file, an email, or a World Wide Web (or just Web) page.

A document has a given syntax and structure which is usually dictated by the application or by the person who created it. It also has a semantics, specified by the author of the document (who is not necessarily the same as the creator). Additionally, a document may have a presentation style associated with it, which specifies how it should be displayed or printed. Such a style is usually given by the document syntax and structure and is related to a specific application (for example, a Web browser). Figure 6.1 depicts all these relations. A document can also have information about itself, called *metadata*. The next section explains different types of metadata and their relevance.

The *syntax* of a document can express structure, presentation style, semantics, or even external actions. In many cases one or more of these elements are implicit or are given together. For example, a structural element (e.g., a section) can have a fixed formatting style. The semantics of a document is also associated with its use. For example, Postscript directives are designed for drawing.

The syntax of a document can be implicit in its content, or expressed in a simple declarative language or even in a programming language. For example, many editor formats are declarative while a TeX document uses a powerful typesetting language. Although a powerful language could be easier to parse than the data itself, it might be difficult to convert documents in that language to other formats. Many syntax languages are proprietary and specific, but open

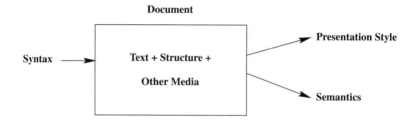

Figure 6.1   Characteristics of a document.

and generic languages are better because documents can be interchanged between applications and are more flexible. Text can also be written in natural
language. However, at present the semantics of natural language is still not easy
for a computer to understand. The current trend is to use languages which provide information on the document structure, format, and semantics while being
readable by humans as well as computers. The Standard Generalized Markup
Language (SGML), which is covered later on in this chapter, tries to balance all
the issues above. Metadata, markup, and semantic encoding represent different
levels of formalization of the document contents.

Most documents have a particular formatting style. However, new applications are pushing for external formatting such that information can be represented independently of style, and vice versa. The presentation style can be
embedded in the document, as in TeX or Rich Text Format (RTF). Style can
be complemented by macros (for example, LaTeX in the case of TeX). In most
cases, style is defined by the document author. However, the reader may decide
part of the style (for example, by setting options in a Web browser). The style
of a document defines how the document is visualized in a computer window or
a printed page, but can also include treatment of other media such as audio or
video.

In this chapter we first cover metadata. Following that we discuss text
characteristics such as formats and natural language statistics. Next we cover
languages to describe text structure, presentation style, or semantics. The last
part is devoted to multimedia formats and languages.

6.2   Metadata

Most documents and text collections have associated with them what is known as
metadata. Metadata is information on the organization of the data, the various
data domains, and the relationship between them. In short, metadata is 'data
about the data.' For instance, in a database management system, the schema

specifies some of the metadata, namely, the name of the relations, the fields or attributes of each relation, the domain of each attribute, etc.

Common forms of metadata associated with text include the author, the date of publication, the source of the publication, the document length (in pages, words, bytes, etc.), and the document genre (book, article, memo, etc.). For example, the Dublin Core Metadata Element Set [807] proposes 15 fields to describe a document. Following Marchionini [542], we refer to this kind of information as Descriptive Metadata, metadata that is external to the meaning of the document, and pertains more to how it was created. Another type of metadata characterizes the subject matter that can be found within the document's contents. We will refer to this as Semantic Metadata. Semantic Metadata is associated with a wide number of documents and its availability is increasing. All books published within the USA are assigned Library of Congress subject codes, and many journals require author-assigned key terms that are selected from a closed vocabulary of relevant terms. For example, biomedical articles that appear within the MEDLINE (see Chapter 3) system are assigned topical metadata pertaining to disease, anatomy, pharmaceuticals, and so on. To standardize semantic terms, many areas use specific *ontologies*, which are hierarchical taxonomies of terms describing certain knowledge topics.

An important metadata format is the Machine Readable Cataloging Record (MARC) which is the most used format for library records. MARC has several fields for the different attributes of a bibliographic entry such as title, author, etc. Specific uses of MARC are given in Chapter 14. In the USA, a particular version of MARC is used: USMARC, which is an implementation of ANSI/NISO Z39.2, the American National Standard for Bibliographic Information Interchange. The USMARC format documents contain the definitions and content for the fields that have to be used in records structured according to Z39.2. This standard is maintained by the Library of Congress of the USA.

With the increase of data in the Web, there are many initiatives to add metadata information to Web documents. In the Web, metadata can be used for many purposes. Some of them are cataloging (BibTeX is a popular format for this case), content rating (for example, to protect children from reading some type of documents), intellectual property rights, digital signatures (for authentication), privacy levels (who should and who should not have access to a document), applications to electronic commerce, etc. The new standard for Web metadata is the Resource Description Framework (RDF), which provides interoperability between applications. This framework allows the description of Web resources to facilitate automated processing of the information. It does not assume any particular application or semantic domain. It consists of a description of nodes and attached attribute/value pairs. Nodes can be any Web resource, that is, any Uniform Resource Identifier (URI), which includes the Uniform Resource Locator (URL). Attributes are properties of nodes, and their values are text strings or other nodes (Web resources or metadata instances). To describe the semantics, values from, for example, the Dublin Core library metadata URL can be used. Other predefined vocabularies for authoring metadata are expected, in particular for content rating and for digital signatures. In addition, currently, there are many Web projects on ontologies for different application domains (see also Chapters 13 and 15). Metadata is also useful for metadescriptions of non-textual objects. For example, a set of keywords that describe an image. These keywords can later be used to search for the image using classic text information retrieval techniques (on the metadescriptions).

6.3   Text

With the advent of the computer, it was necessary to code text in binary digits. The first coding schemes were EBCDIC and ASCII, which used seven bits to code each possible symbol. Later, ASCII was standardized to eight bits (ISO-Latin), to accommodate several languages, including accents and other diacritical marks. Nevertheless, ASCII is not suitable for oriental languages such as Chinese or Japanese Kanji, where each symbol might represent a concept and therefore thousands of them exist. For this case, a 16-bit code exists called Unicode (ISO 10616) [783].

In this section we cover different characteristics of text. First, the possible formats of text, ASCII being the simplest format. Second, how the information content of text can be measured, followed by different models for it. Finally, we mention briefly how we can measure similarity between strings or pieces of text.

6.3.1   Formats

There is no single format for a text document, and an IR system should be able to retrieve information from many of them. In the past, IR systems would convert a document to an internal format. However, that has many disadvantages, because the original application related to the document is not useful any more. On top of that, we cannot change the contents of a document. Current IR systems have filters that can handle most popular documents, in particular those of word processors with some binary syntax such as Word, WordPerfect or FrameMaker. Even then, good filters might not be possible if the format is proprietary and its details are not public. This is not the case for full ASCII syntax, as in TeX documents. Although documents can be in a binary format (for example, parts of a Word document), documents that are represented in human-readable ASCII form imply more portability and are easier to modify (for example, they can be edited with different applications).

Other text formats were developed for document interchange. Among these we should mention the Rich Text Format (RTF), which is used by word processors and has ASCII syntax. Other important formats were developed for displaying or printing documents. The most popular ones are the Portable Document Format (PDF) and Postscript (which is a powerful programming language for drawing). Other interchange formats are used to encode electronic mail, for example MIME (Multipurpose Internet Mail Exchange). MIME supports multiple character sets, multiple languages, and multiple media.

On top of these formats, nowadays many files are compressed. Text compression is treated in detail in Chapter 7, but here we comment on the most popular compression software and associated formats. These include Compress (Unix), ARJ (PCs), and ZIP (for example `gzip` in Unix and `Winzip` in Windows). Other tools allow us to convert binary files, in particular compressed text, to ASCII text such that it can be transmitted through a communication line using only seven bits. Examples of these tools are `uuencode/uudecode` and `binhex`.

6.3.2   Information Theory

Written text has a certain semantics and is a way to communicate information. Although it is difficult to formally capture how much information is there in a given text, the distribution of symbols is related to it. For example, a text where one symbol appears almost all the time does not convey much information. Information theory defines a special concept, *entropy*, to capture information content (or equivalently, information uncertainty). If the alphabet has σ symbols, each one appearing with probability p_i (probability here is defined as the symbol frequency over the total number of symbols) in a text, the entropy of this text is defined as

$$E = -\sum_{i=1}^{\sigma} p_i \log_2 p_i$$

In this formula the σ symbols of the alphabet are coded in binary, so the entropy is measured in bits. As an example, for $\sigma = 2$, the entropy is 1 if both symbols appear the same number of times or 0 if only one symbol appears. We say that the amount of information in a text can be quantified by its entropy. The definition of entropy depends on the probabilities (frequencies) of each symbol. To obtain those probabilities we need a *text model*. So we say that the amount of information in a text is measured with regard to the text model. This concept is also important, for example, in text compression, where the entropy is a limit on how much the text can be compressed, depending on the text model.

In our case we are interested in natural language, as we now discuss.

6.3.3   Modeling Natural Language

Text is composed of symbols from a finite alphabet. We can divide the symbols in two disjoint subsets: symbols that separate words and symbols that belong to words. It is well known that symbols are not uniformly distributed. If we consider just letters (a to z), we observe that vowels are usually more frequent than most consonants. For example, in English, the letter 'e' has the highest frequency. A simple model to generate text is the binomial model. In it, each symbol is generated with a certain probability. However, natural language has a dependency on previous symbols. For example, in English, a letter 'f' cannot appear after a letter 'c' and vowels or certain consonants have a higher probability of occurring. Therefore, the probability of a symbol depends on previous symbols. We can use a finite-context or Markovian model to reflect this dependency. The model can consider one, two, or more letters to generate the next symbol. If we use k letters, we say that it is a k-order model (so the binomial model is considered a 0-order model). We can use these models taking words as symbols. For example, text generated by a 5-order model using the distribution of words in the Bible might make sense (that is, it can be grammatically correct), but will be different from the original. More complex models include finite-state models (which define regular languages), and grammar models (which define context free and other languages). However, finding the right grammar for natural language is still a difficult open problem.

The next issue is how the different words are distributed inside each document. An approximate model is *Zipf's Law* [847, 310], which attempts to capture the distribution of the frequencies (that is, number of occurrences) of the words in the text. The rule states that the frequency of the i-th most frequent word is $1/i^\theta$ times that of the most frequent word. This implies that in a text of n words with a vocabulary of V words, the i-th most frequent word appears $n/(i^\theta H_V(\theta))$ times, where $H_V(\theta)$ is the harmonic number of order θ of V, defined as

$$
H_V(\theta) = \sum_{j=1}^{V} \frac{1}{j^\theta}
$$

so that the sum of all frequencies is n. The left side of Figure 6.2 illustrates the distribution of frequencies considering that the words are arranged in decreasing order of their frequencies. The value of θ depends on the text. In the most simple formulation, $\theta = 1$, and therefore $H_V(\theta) = O(\log n)$. However, this simplified version is very inexact, and the case $\theta > 1$ (more precisely, between 1.5 and 2.0) fits better the real data [26]. This case is very different, since the distribution is much more skewed, and $H_V(\theta) = O(1)$. Experimental data suggests that a better model is $k/(c + i)^\theta$ where c is an additional parameter and k is such that all frequencies add to n. This is called a Mandelbrot distribution [561].

Since the distribution of words is very skewed (that is, there are a few hundred words which take up 50% of the text), words that are too frequent, such as *stopwords*, can be disregarded. A stopword is a word which does not carry meaning in natural language and therefore can be ignored (that is, made not searchable), such as 'a,' 'the,' 'by,' etc. Fortunately the most frequent words are stopwords and therefore, half of the words appearing in a text do not need to be considered. This allows us, for instance, to significantly reduce the space overhead of indices for natural language texts. For example, the most frequent words in the TREC-2 collection (see Chapter 3 for details on this reference collection and others) are 'the,' 'of,' 'and,' 'a,' 'to' and 'in' (see also Chapter 7).

Another issue is the distribution of words in the documents of a collection. A simple model is to consider that each word appears the same number of times in every document. However, this is not true in practice. A better model is

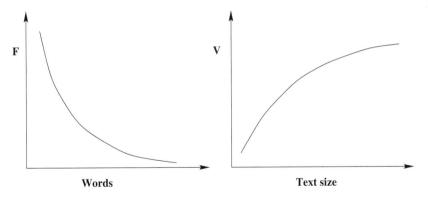

Figure 6.2 Distribution of sorted word frequencies (left) and size of the vocabulary (right).

to consider a negative binomial distribution, which says that the fraction of documents containing a word k times is

$$F(k) = \binom{\alpha + k - 1}{k} p^k (1 + p)^{-\alpha - k}$$

where p and α are parameters that depend on the word and the document collection. For example, for the Brown Corpus [276] and the word 'said', we have $p = 9.24$ and $\alpha = 0.42$ [171]. The latter reference gives other models derived from a Poisson distribution.

The next issue is the number of distinct words in a document. This set of words is referred to as the document *vocabulary*. To predict the growth of the vocabulary size in natural language text, we use the so-called *Heaps' Law* [352]. This is a very precise law which states that the vocabulary of a text of size n words is of size $V = Kn^\beta = O(n^\beta)$, where K and β depend on the particular text. The right side of Figure 6.2 illustrates how the vocabulary size varies with the text size. K is normally between 10 and 100, and β is a positive value less than one. Some experiments [26, 42] on the TREC-2 collection show that the most common values for β are between 0.4 and 0.6. Hence, the vocabulary of a text grows sublinearly with the text size, in a proportion close to its square root.

Notice that the set of different words of a language is fixed by a constant (for example, the number of different English words is finite). However, the limit is so high that it is much more accurate to assume that the size of the vocabulary is $O(n^\beta)$ instead of $O(1)$, although the number should stabilize for huge enough texts. On the other hand, many authors argue that the number keeps growing anyway because of typing or spelling errors.

Heaps' law also applies to collections of documents because, as the total text size grows, the predictions of the model become more accurate. Furthermore, this model is also valid for the World Wide Web (see Chapter 13).

The last issue is the average length of words. This relates the text size in words with the text size in bytes (without accounting for punctuation and other extra symbols). For example, in the different subcollections of the TREC-2 collection, the average word length is very close to 5 letters, and the range of variation of this average in each subcollection is small (from 4.8 to 5.3 letters). If we remove the stopwords, the average length of a word increases to a number between 6 and 7 (letters). If we take only the words of the vocabulary, the average length is higher (about 8 or 9). This defines the total space needed for the vocabulary.

Heaps' law implies that the length of the words in the vocabulary increases logarithmically with the text size and thus, that longer and longer words should appear as the text grows. However, in practice, the average length of the words in the overall text is constant because shorter words are common enough (e.g. stopwords). This balance between short and long words, such that the average word length remains constant, has been noticed many times in different contexts, and can also be explained by a finite-state model in which: (a) the space character has probability close to 0.2; (b) the space character cannot appear twice subsequently; and (c) there are 26 letters [561]. This simple model is consistent with Zipf's and Heaps' laws.

The models presented in this section are used in Chapters 8 and 13, in particular Zipf's and Heaps' laws.

6.3.4 Similarity Models

In this section we define notions of syntactic similarity between strings or documents. Similarity is measured by a *distance function*. For example, if we have strings of the same length, we can define the distance between them as the number of positions that have different characters. Then, the distance is 0 if they are equal. This is called the Hamming distance. A distance function should also be symmetric (that is, the order of the arguments does not matter) and should satisfy the triangle inequality (that is, $distance(a, c) \leq distance(a, b) + distance(b, c)$).

An important distance over strings is the edit or Levenshtein distance mentioned earlier. The edit distance is defined as the minimum number of characters, insertions, deletions, and substitutions that we need to perform in any of the strings to make them equal. For instance, the edit distance between 'color' and 'colour' is one, while the edit distance between 'survey' and 'surgery' is two. The edit distance is considered to be superior for modeling syntactic errors than other more complex methods such as the Soundex system, which is based on phonetics [595]. Extensions to the concept of edit distance include different weights for each operation, adding transpositions, etc.

There are other measures. For example, assume that we are comparing two given strings and the only operation allowed is deletion of characters. Then, after all non-common characters have been deleted, the remaining sequence of characters (not necessarily contiguous in the original string, but in the same order) is the longest common subsequence (LCS) of both strings. For example, the LCS of 'survey' and 'surgery' is 'surey.'

Similarity can be extended to documents. For example, we can consider lines as single symbols and compute the longest common sequence of lines between two files. This is the measure used by the `diff` command in Unix-like operating systems. The main problem with this approach is that it is very time consuming and does not consider lines that are similar. The latter drawback can be fixed by taking a weighted edit distance between lines or by computing the LCS over all the characters. Other solutions include extracting fingerprints (any piece of text that in some sense characterizes it) for the documents and comparing them, or finding large repeated pieces. There are also visual tools to see document similarity. For example, `Dotplot` draws a rectangular map where both coordinates are file lines and the entry for each coordinate is a gray pixel that depends on the edit distance between the associated lines.

6.4   Markup Languages

Markup is defined as extra textual syntax that can be used to describe formatting actions, structure information, text semantics, attributes, etc. For example, the formatting commands of TeX (a popular text formatting software) could be considered markup. However, formal markup languages are much more structured. The marks are called tags, and usually, to avoid ambiguity, there is an initial and ending tag surrounding the marked text. The standard metalanguage for markup is SGML, as already mentioned. An important subset of SGML is XML (eXtensible Markup Language), the new metalanguage for the Web. The most popular markup language used for the Web, HTML (HyperText Markup Language), is an instance of SGML. All these languages and examples of them are described below.

6.4.1   SGML

SGML stands for Standard Generalized Markup Language (ISO 8879) and is a metalanguage for tagging text developed by a group led by Goldfarb [303] based on earlier work done at IBM. That is, SGML provides the rules for defining a markup language based on tags. Each instance of SGML includes a description of the document structure called a document type definition. Hence, an SGML document is defined by: (1) a description of the structure of the document and (2) the text itself marked with tags which describe the structure. We will explain later the syntax associated with the tags.

The document type definition is used to describe and name the pieces that a document is composed of and define how those pieces relate to each other. Part of the definition can be specified by an SGML document type declaration (DTD).

Other parts, such as the semantics of elements and attributes, or application conventions, cannot be expressed formally in SGML. Comments can be used, however, to express them informally. This means that all of the rules for applying SGML markup to documents are part of the definition, and those that can be expressed in SGML syntax are represented in the DTD. The DTD does not define the semantics (that is, the meaning, presentation, and behavior), or intended use, of the tags. However, some semantic information can be included in comments embedded in the DTD, while more complete information is usually present in separate documentation. This additional documentation typically describes the elements, or logical pieces of data, the attributes, and information about those pieces of data. For example, two tags can have the same name but different semantics in two different applications.

Tags are denoted by angle brackets (`<tagname>`). Tags are used to identify the beginning and ending of pieces of the document, for example a quote in a literary text. Ending tags are specified by adding a slash before the tag name (e.g., `</tagname>`). For example, the tag `</author>` could be used to identify the element 'name of author,' which appears in italics and generates a link to a biographic sketch. Tag attributes are specified at the beginning of the element, inside the angle brackets and after the nametag using the syntax `attname=value`.

Figure 6.3 gives an example of a simple DTD and a document using it. While we do not intend to discuss SGML syntax here, we give a brief description of the example such that the reader can grasp the main ideas. Each ELEMENT represents a tag denoted by its name. The two following characters indicate if the starting and ending tags are compulsory (-) or optional (O). For example, the ending tag for `prolog` is necessary while for `sender` it is not. Following that, the inside portion of the content tag is specified using a regular expression style syntax where ',' stands for concatenation, '|' stands for logical or, '?' stands for zero or one occurrence, '*' stands for zero or more occurrences, and '+' stands for one or more occurrences of the preceding element. The content tag can be composed of the combination of other tag contents, ASCII characters (PCDATA), and binary data (NDATA), or EMPTY. The possible attributes of a tag are given in an attribute list (ATTLIST) identified by the tag name, followed by the name of each attribute, its type, and if it is required or not (otherwise, the default value is given). An SGML document instance is associated with the DTD so that the various tools working with the data know which are the correct tags and how they are organized.

The document description generally does not specify how a document should look, for example when it is printed on paper or displayed on a screen. Because SGML separates content from format, we can create very good models of data that have no mechanism for describing the format, hence, no standard way to output the data in a formatted fashion. Therefore, output specifications, which are directions on how to format a document, are often added to SGML documents. For this purpose, output specification standards such as DSSSL (Document Style Semantic Specification Language) and FOSI (Formatted Output Specification Instance) were devised. Both of these standards define mechanisms for associating style information with SGML document instances.

```
<!--SGML DTD for electronic messages -->

<!ELEMENT e-mail          - - (prolog, contents) >
<!ELEMENT prolog          - - (sender, address+, subject?, Cc*) >
<!ELEMENT (sender | address | subject | Cc) - O (#PCDATA) >
<!ELEMENT contents        - - (par | image | audio)+ >
<!ELEMENT par             - O (ref | #PCDATA)+ >
<!ELEMENT ref             - O EMPTY >
<!ELEMENT (image | audio) - - (#NDATA) >

<!ATTLIST e-mail
         id          ID              #REQUIRED
         date_sent   DATE            #REQUIRED
         status      (secret | public )  public >
<!ATTLIST ref
         id          IDREF           #REQUIRED >
<!ATTLIST (image | audio )
         id          ID              #REQUIRED >

<!--Example of use of previous DTD-->
<!DOCTYPE e-mail SYSTEM "e-mail.dtd">
<e-mail id=94108rby date_sent=02101998>
  <prolog>
  <sender> Pablo Neruda </sender>
  <address> Federico García Lorca </address>
  <address> Ernest Hemingway </address>
  <subject> Pictures of my house in Isla Negra
  <Cc> Gabriel García Márquez </Cc>
  </prolog>
  <contents>
      <par>
      As promised in my previous letter, I am sending two digital
      pictures to show you my house and the splendid view of the
      Pacific Ocean from my bedroom (photo <ref idref=F2>).
      </par>
      <image id=F1> "photo1.gif" </image>
      <image id=F2> "photo2.jpg" </image>
      <par>
      Regards from the South, Pablo.
  </contents>
</e-mail>
```

Figure 6.3 DTD for structuring electronic mails and an example of its use.

They are the components of an SGML system used for defining, for instance, that the data identified by a tag should be typeset in italics.

One important use of SGML is in the Text Encoding Initiative (TEI). The TEI is a cooperative project that started in 1987 and includes several US associations related to the humanities and linguistics. The main goal is to generate guidelines for the preparation and interchange of electronic texts for scholarly research, as well as for industry. In addition to the guidelines, TEI provides several document formats through SGML DTDs. One of the most used formats is TEI Lite. The TEI Lite DTD can be used stand-alone or together with the full set of TEI DTD files.

6.4.2 HTML

HTML stands for HyperText Markup Language and is an instance of SGML. HTML was created in 1992 and has evolved during the past years, 4.0 being the latest version, released as a recommendation at the end of 1997. Currently it is being extended in many ways to solve its many limitations, for example, to be able to write mathematical formulas. Most documents on the Web are stored and transmitted in HTML. HTML is a simple language well suited for hypertext, multimedia, and the display of small and simple documents.

HTML is based on SGML, and although there is an HTML DTD (Document Type Definition), most HTML instances do not explicitly make reference to the DTD. The HTML tags follow all the SGML conventions and also include formatting directives.

HTML documents can have other media embedded within them, such as images or audio in different formats. HTML also has fields for metadata, which can be used for different applications and purposes. If we also add programs (for example, using Javascript) inside a page, some people call it dynamic HTML (or DHTML). This should not be confused with a Microsoft proposal (also called dynamic HTML) of an Application Programming Interface (API) for accessing and manipulating HTML documents. Figure 6.4 gives an example of an HTML document together with its output in a Web browser.

Because HTML does not fix the presentation style of a document, in 1997, Cascade Style Sheets (CSS) were introduced. CSS offer a powerful and manageable way for authors, artists, and typographers to create visual effects that improve the aesthetics of HTML pages in the Web. Style sheets can be used one after another (called cascading) to define the presentation style for different elements of an HTML page. Style sheets separate information about presentation from document content, which in turn simplifies Web site maintenance, promotes Web page accessibility, and makes the Web faster. However, CSS support in current browsers is still modest. Another disadvantage is that two style sheets do not have to be consistent nor complete, so the stylistic result might not be good, in particular regarding color. CSS are supposed to balance the expectations of the author and of the reader regarding presentation issues. Nevertheless, it is not clear who or in which cases the author or the reader should define the presentation.

The evolution of HTML implies support for backward compatibility and also for forward compatibility, because people should also be able to see new documents with old browsers. HTML 4.0 has been specified in three flavors: strict, transitional, and frameset. Strict HTML only worries about non-presentational

```
<html>
<head>
<title>HTML Example</title>
<meta name=rby content="Just an example">
</head>
<body>
<h1>HTML Example</h1>
<p>
<hr>
<p>
HTML has many <i>tags</i>, among them:
<ul>
<li> links to other <a href=http://www.w3c.org/>pages</a>
     (a from anchor),
<li> paragraphs (p), headings (h1, h2, etc), font types (b, i),
<li> horizontal rules (hr), indented lists and items (ul, li),
<li> images (img), tables, forms, etc.
</ul>
<p>
<hr>
<p>
<img align=left src="at_work.gif">
This page is <b>always</b> under construction.
</body>
</html>
```

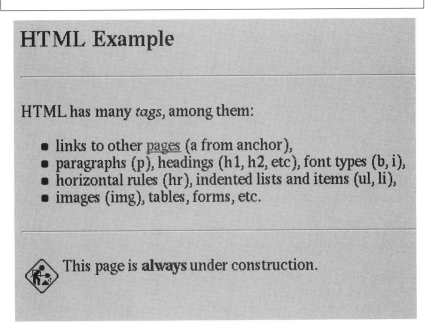

Figure 6.4   Example of an HTML document and how it is seen in a browser.

markup, leaving all the displaying information to CSS. Transitional HTML uses all the presentational features for pages that should be read for old browsers that do not understand CSS. Frameset HTML is used when you want to partition the browser window in two or more frames. HTML 4.0 includes support for style sheets, internationalization, frames, richer tables and forms, and accessibility options for people with disabilities.

Typical HTML applications use a fixed small set of tags in conformance with a single SGML specification. Fixing a small set of tags allows users to leave the language specification out of the document and makes it much easier to build applications, but this advantage comes at the cost of severely limiting HTML in several important aspects. In particular, HTML does not:

- allow users to specify their own tags or attributes in order to parameterize or otherwise semantically qualify their data;

- support the specification of nested structures needed to represent database schemas or object-oriented hierarchies;

- support the kind of language specification that allows consuming applications to check data for structural validity on importation.

In contrast to HTML stands generic SGML. A generic SGML application is one that supports SGML language specifications of arbitrary complexity and makes possible the qualities of extensibility, structure, and validation missing in HTML. SGML makes it possible to define your own formats for your own documents, to handle large and complex documents, and to manage large information repositories. However, full SGML contains many optional features that are not needed for Web applications and have proven to have a cost/benefit ratio unattractive to current vendors of Web browsers. All these reasons led to the development of XML, a simpler metalanguage that is described in the next section.

6.4.3   XML

XML stands for eXtensible Markup Language and is a simplified subset of SGML. That is, XML is not a markup language, as HTML is, but a metalanguage that is capable of containing markup languages in the same way as SGML. XML allows a human-readable semantic markup, which is also machine-readable. As a result, XML makes it easier to develop and deploy new specific markup, enabling automatic authoring, parsing, and processing of networked data. In some ways, XML allows one to do many things that today are done by Java scripts or other program interfaces.

XML does not have many of the restrictions imposed by HTML but on the other hand imposes a more rigid syntax on the markup, which becomes important at processing time. In XML, ending tags cannot be omitted. Also, tags for elements that do not have any content, like BR and IMG, are specially marked by a slash before the closing angle bracket. XML also distinguishes upper

```
<?XML VERSION="1.0" RMD="NONE" ?>
<e-mail id="94108rby" date_sent="02101998">
  <prolog>
  <sender> Pablo Neruda </sender>
  <address> Federico García Lorca </address>
  <address> Ernest Hemingway </address>
  <subject> Pictures of my house in Isla Negra
  <Cc> Gabriel García Márquez </Cc>
  </prolog>
  <contents>
      <par>
      As promised in my previous letter, I am sending two digital
      pictures to show you my house and the splendid view of the
      Pacific Ocean from my bedroom (photo <ref idref="F2"/>).
      </par>
      <image id="F1" ref="photo1.gif" />
      <image id="F2"> ref="photo2.jpg" />
      <par>
      Regards from the South, Pablo.
      </par>
  </contents>
</e-mail>
```

Figure 6.5 An XML document without a DTD analogous to the previous SGML example.

and lower case, so `img` and `IMG` are different tags (this is not true in HTML). In addition, all attribute values must be between quotes. This implies that parsing XML without knowledge of the tags is easier. In particular, using a DTD is optional. If there is no DTD, the tags are obtained while the parsing is done. With respect to SGML, there are a few syntactic differences, and many more restrictions. Listing all these differences is beyond the scope of this book, but Figure 6.5 shows an example of a DTDless XML document based on the previous electronic mail DTD given for SGML (see Figure 6.3). The `RMD` attribute stands for Required Markup Declaration, which indicates whether a DTD must be used or not (no DTD in this case). Other possible values are `INTERNAL` which means that the DTD is inside the document or `ALL` (default value) which allows the use of external sources for part or the whole DTD as in SGML.

XML allows any user to define new tags, define more complex structures (for example, unbounded nesting with the same rules of SGML) and has data validation capabilities. As XML is very new, there is still some discussion of how it will change or impact Internet applications. XML is a profile of SGML that eliminates many of the difficulties of implementing things, so for the most part it behaves just like SGML, as shown before. As mentioned, XML removes the requirement for the existence of a DTD, which can be parsed directly from the data. Removing the DTD places even more importance on the application documentation. This can also have a large impact on the functions that the software provides. For example, it means that if an XML editor does not use a DTD, how will it help the user to tag the documents consistently? These problems should be resolved in the near future. In the case of semantic ambiguity between tag names, one goal is to have a *namespace* such that there is a convention for its use.

The Extensible Style sheet Language (XSL) is the XML counterpart of Cascading Style Sheets. XSL is designed to transform and style highly-structured, data-rich documents written in XML. For example, with XSL it would be possible to automatically extract a table of contents from a document. The syntax of XSL has been defined using XML. In addition to adding style to a document, XSL can be used to transform XML documents to HTML and CSS. This is analogous to macros in a word processor.

Another extension to XML, defined using XML, is the Extensible Linking Language (XLL). XLL defines different types of links, including external and internal links. In particular, any element type can be the origin of a link and outgoing links can be defined on documents that cannot be modified. The behavior of the links is also more generic. The object linked can be embedded in, or replace the document. It is also possible to generate a new context without changing the current application (for example, the object is displayed in a new window).

Recent uses of XML include:

- **Mathematical Markup Language** (MathML): two sets of tags, one for presentation of formulas and another for the meaning of mathematical expressions.

- **Synchronized Multimedia Integration Language** (SMIL): a declarative language for scheduling multimedia presentations in the Web, where the position and activation time of different objects can be specified.

- **Resource Description Format** (already covered in section 6.2): metadata information for XML should be given using RDF.

The XML movement is one indication that a parseable, hierarchical object model will play an increasingly major role in the evolution of HTML. The next generation of HTML should be based on a suite of XML tag sets to be used together with mathematics, synchronized multimedia, and vector graphics (possibly using the XML-based languages already mentioned). That is, the emphasis will be on structuring and modeling data rather than on presentation and layout issues.

6.5   Multimedia

Multimedia usually stands for applications that handle different types of digital data originating from distinct types of media. The most common types of media in multimedia applications are text, sound, images, and video (which is an animated sequence of images). The digital data originating from each of these four types of media is quite distinct in volume, format, and processing requirements (for instance, video and audio impose real time constraints on their processing). As an immediate consequence, different types of formats are necessary for storing each type of media.

In this section we cover formats and standard languages for multimedia applications. In contrast with text formats, most formats for multimedia are partially binary and hence can only be processed by a computer. Also, the presentation style is almost completely defined, perhaps with the exception of some spatial or temporal attributes.

6.5.1   Formats

Multimedia includes images, audio and video, as well as other binary data. We now briefly survey the main formats used for all these data types. They are used mainly in the Web and in digital libraries (see Chapters 13 and 15).

There are several formats for images. The simplest formats are direct representations of a bit-mapped (or pixel-based) display such as XBM, BMP, or PCX. However, those formats consume too much space. For example, a typical computer screen which uses 256 colors for each pixel might require more than 1 Mb (one megabyte) in storage just for describing the content of a single screen frame. In practice, images have a lot of redundancy and can be compressed efficiently. So, most popular image formats incorporate compression such as Compuserve's Graphic Interchange Format (GIF). GIF is good for black and white pictures, as well as pictures that have a small number of colors or gray levels (say 256). To improve compression ratios for higher resolutions, lossy compression was developed. That is, uncompressing a compressed image does not give the original. This is done by the Joint Photographic Experts Group (JPEG) format, which tries to eliminate parts of the image that have less impact on the human eye. This format is parametric, in the sense that the loss can be tuned.

Another common image format is the Tagged Image File Format (TIFF). This format is used to exchange documents between different applications and different computer platforms. TIFF has fields for metadata and also supports compression as well as different numbers of colors. Yet another format is True-vision Targa image file (TGA), which is associated with video game boards. There are many more image formats, many of them associated to particular applications ranging from fax (bi-level image formats such as JBIG) to fingerprints (highly accurate and compressed formats such as WSQ) and satellite images (large resolution and full-color images). In 1996 a new bit-mapped image format was proposed for the Internet: Portable Network Graphics (PNG). This format could be important in the future.

Audio must be digitalized first in order to be stored properly. The most common formats for small pieces of digital audio are AU, MIDI, and WAVE. MIDI is an standard format to interchange music between electronic instruments and computers. For audio libraries other formats are used such as RealAudio or CD formats.

There are several formats for animations or moving images (similar to video or TV), but here we mention only the most popular ones. The main one is MPEG (Moving Pictures Expert Group) which is related to JPEG. MPEG works by coding the changes with respect to a base image which is given at fixed intervals. In this way, MPEG profits from the temporal image redundancy that any video has. Higher quality is achieved by using more frames and higher resolution. MPEG specifies different compression levels, but usually not all the applications support all of them. This format also includes the audio signal associated with the video. Other video formats are AVI, FLI, and QuickTime. AVI may include compression (CinePac), as well as QuickTime, which was developed by Apple. As for MPEG, audio is also included.

6.5.2   Textual Images

A particular class of images that is very important in office systems, multimedia retrieval, and digital libraries are images of documents that contain mainly typed or typeset text. These are called *textual images* and are obtained by scanning the documents, usually for archiving purposes — a procedure that also makes the images (and their associated text) available to anyone through a computer network. The fact that a large portion of a textual image is text can be used for retrieval purposes and efficient compression.

Although we do not cover image compression in this chapter, we have seen that the most popular image formats include some form of compression embedded in them. In the case of textual images, further compression can be achieved by extracting the different text symbols or marks from the image, building a library of symbols for them, and representing each one (within the image) by a position in the library. As many symbols are repeated, the compression ratio is quite good. Although this technique is lossy (because the reconstructed image is not equal to the original), the reconstructed image can be read without problems. Additional information can be stored to reproduce the original image, but for most applications this is not needed. If the image contains non-textual information such as logos or signatures, which might be necessary to reproduce, they may be extracted through a segmentation process, stored, and compressed separately. When needed, the textual and non-textual parts of the image can be combined and displayed together.

Regarding the retrieval of textual images, several alternatives are possible as follows:

- At creation time or when added to the database, a set of keywords that describe the image is associated with it (for example, metadata can be used). Later, conventional text retrieval techniques can be applied to those keywords. This alternative is valid for any multimedia object.

- Use OCR to extract the text of the image. The resultant ASCII text can be used to extract keywords, as before, or as a full-text description of the image. Depending on the document type, the OCR output could be reasonably good or actually quite bad (consider the first page of a newspaper, with several columns, different font types and sizes). In any case, many typos are introduced and a usual keyword-based query might miss many documents (in this case, an approximate search is better, but also slower).

- Use the symbols extracted from the images as basic units to combine image retrieval techniques (see Chapter 12) with sequence retrieval techniques (see Chapter 8). In this case, the query is transformed into a symbol sequence that has to match approximately another symbol sequence in the compressed image. This idea seems promising but has not been pursued yet.

6.5.3   Graphics and Virtual Reality

There are many formats proposed for three-dimensional graphics. Although this topic is not fully relevant to information retrieval, we include some information here for the sake of completeness. Our emphasis here is on the Web.

The Computer Graphics Metafile (CGM) standard (ISO 8632) is defined for the open interchange of structured graphical objects and their associated attributes. CGM specifies a two-dimensional data interchange standard which allows graphical data to be stored and exchanged between graphics devices, applications, and computer systems in a device-independent manner. It is a structured format that can represent vector graphics (for example, polylines or ellipses), raster graphics, and text. Although initially CGM was a vector graphics format, it has been extended to include raster capabilities and provides a very useful format for combined raster and vector images. A metafile is a collection of elements. These elements may be the geometric components of the picture, such as polyline or polygon; the appearance of these components; or how to interpret a particular metafile or a particular picture. The CGM standard specifies which elements are allowed to occur in which positions in a metafile.

The Virtual Reality Modeling Language (VRML, ISO/IEC 14772-1) is a file format for describing interactive 3D objects and worlds and is a subset of the Silicon Graphics OpenInventor file format. VRML is also intended to be a universal interchange format for integrated 3D graphics and multimedia. VRML may be used in a variety of application areas such as engineering and scientific visualization, multimedia presentations, entertainment and educational titles, Web pages, and shared virtual worlds. VRML has become the *de facto* standard modeling language for the Web.

6.5.4   HyTime

The Hypermedia/Time-based Structuring Language (HyTime) is a standard (ISO/IEC 10744) defined for multimedia documents markup. HyTime is an SGML architecture that specifies the generic hypermedia structure of documents.

Following the guiding principle of SGML, HyTime-defined structure is independent of any presentation of the encoded document. As an architecture, HyTime allows DTDs to be written for individual document models that use HyTime constructs, specifying how these document sets tailor the composition of these constructs for their particular representational needs. The standard also provides several metaDTDs, facilitating the design of new multimedia markup languages.

The hypermedia concepts directly represented by HyTime include

- complex locating of document objects,
- relationships (hyperlinks) between document objects, and
- numeric, measured associations between document objects.

The HyTime architecture has three parts: the base linking and addressing architecture, the scheduling architecture (derived from the base architecture), and the rendition architecture (which is an application of the scheduling architecture). The base architecture addresses the syntax and semantics of hyperlinks. For most simple hypermedia presentations, this should be enough. The scheduling module of HyTime defines the abstract representation of arbitrarily complex hypermedia structures, including music and interactive presentations. Its basic mechanism is a simple one: the sequencing of object containers along axes measured in temporal or spatial units. The rendition module is essentially an application of the scheduling architecture that defines a general mechanism for defining the creation of new schedules from existing schedules by applying special 'rendition rules' of different types.

HyTime does not directly specify graphical interfaces, user navigation, user interaction, or the placement of media on time lines and screen displays. These aspects of document processing are rendered from the HyTime constructs in a manner specified by mechanisms such as style sheets, as is done with SGML documents.

One application of HyTime, is the Standard Music Description Language (SMDL). SDML is an architecture for the representation of music information, either alone, or in conjunction with other media, also supporting multimedia time sequencing information. Another application is the Metafile for Interactive Documents (MID). MID is a common interchange structure, based on SGML and HyTime, that takes data from various authoring systems and structures it for display on dissimilar presentation systems, with minimal human intervention.

6.6 Trends and Research Issues

Many changes and proposals are happening, and very rapidly, in particular due to the advent of the Web. At this point, the reader must be lost in a salad of acronyms (we were too!), in spite of the fact that we have only mentioned the most important languages and formats. The most important of these are included in the Glossary at the end of this book. Some people believe that new

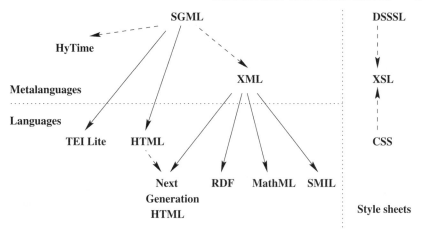

Figure 6.6 Taxonomy of Web languages.

format specifications such as CSS or XML take away the simplicity of HTML, which is the basis of its success. Only the future will tell. Figure 6.6 illustrates a taxonomy of the main languages considered. Solid lines indicate instances of a metalanguage (for example, HTML is an instance of SGML), while dashed lines indicate derived languages. The main trend is the convergence and integration of the different efforts, the Web being the main application.

A European alternative to SGML is the Open Document Architecture (ODA) which is also a standard (ISO 8613 [398]). ODA was designed to share documents electronically without losing control over the content, structure, and layout of those documents. ODA defines a logical structure (like SGML), a layout and the content (including vector and raster graphics). An ODA file can also be formatted, processable, or formatted processable. Formatted files cannot be edited and have information about content and layout. The other two types can be edited. Processable files also have logical information in addition to content, while formatted processable files have everything. ODA is not used very much nowadays (see also Chapter 11).

Recent developments include:

- An object model is being defined: the document object model (DOM). DOM will provide an interoperable set of classes and methods to manipulate HTML and XML objects from programming languages such as Java.

- Integration between VRML and Dynamic HTML, providing a set of evolving features and architecture extensions to HTML and Web browsers that includes cascading style sheets and document object models.

- Integration between the Standard Exchange for Product Data format (STEP, ISO 10303) and SGML. STEP covers product data from a broad range of industries, and provides extensive support for modeling, automated storage schema generation, life-cycle maintenance, and other management facilities.

- Efforts to convert MARC to SGML by defining a DTD, as well as converting MARC to XML. This has potential possibilities for enhanced access and navigation and presentation of MARC record data and the associated information.

- CGM has become of interest to Web researchers and commercial vendors for its use on the Internet, by developing a new encoding which can be parsed by XML.

- Several new proposals have appeared. Among them we can mention SDML (Signed Document Markup Language), VML (Vector Markup Language), and PGML (Precision Graphics Markup Language). The latter is based on the 2D imaging model of Postscript and PDF.

6.7   Bibliographic Discussion

The document model used in the introduction is based on [437]. Specific information on Web metadata is given in [487, 753]. Most of the information about markup languages and related issues is from the World Wide Web Consortium (see www.w3.org), in particular information on new developments such as DOM or SMIL. More information on SGML and XML is given by Goldfarb [303, 304]. Additional references in SGML are [369, 756] (in particular, the SGML example has been adapted from [24]). There are hundreds of books on HTML. Two sources for HTML 4.0 are [207, 796]. A book on CSS is [517]. For information on XML, XSL, and XLL see [795, 799, 798]. For a discussion about the advantages and disadvantages of XML and related languages see [182, 106, 455, 436]. More information on multimedia formats can be found in [501]. Formats for images and compression of textual images are covered in detail in [825].

Chapter 7
Text Operations

with Nivio Ziviani

7.1 Introduction

As discussed in Chapter 2, not all words are equally significant for representing the semantics of a document. In written language, some words carry more *meaning* than others. Usually, *noun* words (or groups of noun words) are the ones which are most representative of a document content. Therefore, it is usually considered worthwhile to preprocess the text of the documents in the collection to determine the terms to be used as *index terms*. During this preprocessing phase other useful text operations can be performed such as elimination of stop-words, stemming (reduction of a word to its grammatical root), the building of a thesaurus, and compression. Such text operations are discussed in this chapter.

We already know that representing documents by sets of index terms leads to a rather imprecise representation of the semantics of the documents in the collection. For instance, a term like '*the*' has no meaning whatsoever by itself and might lead to the retrieval of various documents which are unrelated to the present user query. We say that using the set of all words in a collection to index its documents generates too much *noise* for the retrieval task. One way to reduce this noise is to reduce the set of words which can be used to refer to (i.e., to index) documents. Thus, the preprocessing of the documents in the collection might be viewed simply as a process of controlling the size of the vocabulary (i.e., the number of distinct words used as an index terms). It is expected that the use of a controlled vocabulary leads to an improvement in retrieval performance.

While controlling the size of the vocabulary is a common technique with commercial systems, it does introduce an additional step in the indexing process which is frequently not easily perceived by the users. As a result, a common user might be surprised with some of the documents retrieved and with the absence of other documents which he expected to see. For instance, he might remember that a certain document contains the string '*the house of the lord*' and notice that such a document is not present among the top 20 documents retrieved in response to his query request (because the controlled vocabulary contains neither 'the' nor 'of'). Thus, it should be clear that, despite a potential improvement in retrieval performance, text transformations done at preprocessing time might make it more difficult for the user to interpret the retrieval task. In recognition of this problem, some search engines in the Web are giving up text operations entirely and simply indexing all the words in the text. The idea is that, despite a more noisy index, the retrieval task is simpler (it can be interpreted as a full text search) and more intuitive to a common user.

Besides document preprocessing, other types of operations on documents can also be attempted with the aim of improving retrieval performance. Among these we distinguish the construction of a thesaurus representing conceptual term relationships and the clustering of related documents. Thesauri are also covered in this chapter. The discussion on document clustering is covered in Chapter 5 because it is an operation which might depend on the current user query.

Text normalization and the building of a thesaurus are strategies aimed at improving the precision of the documents retrieved. However, in the current world of very large digital libraries, improving the efficiency (in terms of time) of the retrieval process has also become quite critical. In fact, Web search engines are currently more concerned with reducing query response time than with improving precision and recall figures. The reason is that they depend on processing a high number of queries per unit of time for economic survival. To reduce query response time, one might consider the utilization of text compression as a promising alternative.

A good compression algorithm is able to reduce the text to 30–35% of its original size. Thus, compressed text requires less storage space and takes less time to be transmitted over a communication link. The main disadvantage is the time spent compressing and decompressing the text. Until recently, it was generally understood that compression does not provide substantial gains in processing time because the extra time spent compressing/decompressing text would offset any gains in operating with compressed data. Further, the use of compression makes the overall design and implementation of the information system more complex. However, modern compression techniques are slowly changing this understanding towards a more favorable view of the adoption of compression techniques. By modern compression techniques we mean good compression and decompression speeds, fast random access without the need to decode the compressed text from the beginning, and direct searching on the compressed text without decompressing it, among others.

Besides compression, another operation on text which is becoming more and more important is *encryption*. In fact, due to the fast popularization of services in the Web (including all types of electronic commerce), key (and old) questions regarding security and privacy have surfaced again. More than ever before, impersonation and unauthorized access might result in great prejudice and financial damage to people and organizations. The solution to these problems is not simple but can benefit from the operation of encrypting text. Discussing encrypted text is beyond the scope of this book but an objective and brief introduction to the topic can be found in [501].

In this chapter, we first discuss five preprocessing text operations including thesauri. Following that, we very briefly summarize the problem of document clustering (which is discussed in detail in Chapter 5). Finally, a thorough discussion on the issue of text compression, its modern variations, and its main implications is provided.

7.2   Document Preprocessing

Document preprocessing is a procedure which can be divided mainly into five text operations (or transformations):

(1) Lexical analysis of the text with the objective of treating digits, hyphens, punctuation marks, and the case of letters.

(2) Elimination of stopwords with the objective of filtering out words with very low discrimination values for retrieval purposes.

(3) Stemming of the remaining words with the objective of removing affixes (i.e., prefixes and suffixes) and allowing the retrieval of documents containing syntactic variations of query terms (e.g., connect, connecting, connected, etc).

(4) Selection of index terms to determine which words/stems (or groups of words) will be used as an indexing elements. Usually, the decision on whether a particular word will be used as an index term is related to the syntactic nature of the word. In fact, noun words frequently carry more semantics than adjectives, adverbs, and verbs.

(5) Construction of term categorization structures such as a thesaurus, or extraction of structure directly represented in the text, for allowing the expansion of the original query with related terms (a usually useful procedure).

In the following, each of these phases is discussed in detail. But, before proceeding, let us take a look at the logical view of the documents which results after each of the above phases is completed. Figure 1.2 is repeated here for convenience as Figure 7.1. As already discussed, by aggregating the preprocessing phases, we are able to move the logical view of the documents (adopted by the system) from that of a full text to that of a set of high level indexing terms.

7.2.1   Lexical Analysis of the Text

Lexical analysis is the process of converting a stream of characters (the text of the documents) into a stream of words (the candidate words to be adopted as index terms). Thus, one of the major objectives of the lexical analysis phase is the identification of the words in the text. At first glance, all that seems to be involved is the recognition of spaces as word separators (in which case, multiple

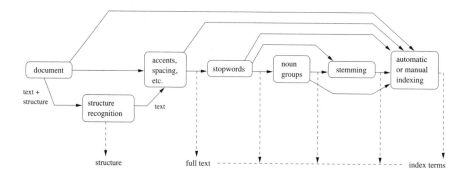

Figure 7.1 Logical view of a document throughout the various phases of text preprocessing.

spaces are reduced to one space). However, there is more to it than this. For instance, the following four particular cases have to be considered with care [263]: digits, hyphens, punctuation marks, and the case of the letters (lower and upper case).

Numbers are usually not good index terms because, without a surrounding context, they are inherently vague. For instance, consider that a user is interested in documents about the number of deaths due to car accidents between the years 1910 and 1989. Such a request could be specified as the set of index terms {deaths, car, accidents, years, 1910, 1989}. However, the presence of the numbers 1910 and 1989 in the query could lead to the retrieval, for instance, of a variety of documents which refer to either of these two years. The problem is that numbers by themselves are just too vague. Thus, in general it is wise to disregard numbers as index terms. However, we have also to consider that digits might appear mixed within a word. For instance, '510B.C.' is a clearly important index term. In this case, it is not clear what rule should be applied. Furthermore, a sequence of 16 digits identifying a credit card number might be highly relevant in a given context and, in this case, should be considered as an index term. A preliminary approach for treating digits in the text might be to remove all words containing sequences of digits unless specified otherwise (through regular expressions). Further, an advanced lexical analysis procedure might perform some date and number normalization to unify formats.

Hyphens pose another difficult decision to the lexical analyzer. Breaking up hyphenated words might be useful due to inconsistency of usage. For instance, this allows treating 'state-of-the-art' and 'state of the art' identically. However, there are words which include hyphens as an integral part. For instance, gilt-edge, B-49, etc. Again, the most suitable procedure seems to adopt a general rule and specify the exceptions on a case by case basis.

Normally, punctuation marks are removed entirely in the process of lexical analysis. While some punctuation marks are an integral part of the word (for instance, '510B.C.'), removing them does not seem to have an impact in retrieval performance because the risk of misinterpretation in this case is minimal. In fact, if the user specifies '510B.C' in his query, removal of the dot both in the query term and in the documents will not affect retrieval. However, very particular scenarios might again require the preparation of a list of exceptions. For instance, if a portion of a program code appears in the text, it might be wise to distinguish between the variables 'x.id' and 'xid.' In this case, the dot mark should not be removed.

The case of letters is usually not important for the identification of index terms. As a result, the lexical analyzer normally converts all the text to either lower or upper case. However, once more, very particular scenarios might require the distinction to be made. For instance, when looking for documents which describe details about the command language of a Unix-like operating system, the user might explicitly desire the non-conversion of upper cases because this is the convention in the operating system. Further, part of the semantics might be lost due to case conversion. For instance, the words *Bank* and *bank* have different meanings — a fact common to many other pairs of words.

As pointed out by Fox [263], all these text operations can be implemented without difficulty. However, careful thought should be given to each one of them because they might have a profound impact at document retrieval time. This is particularly worrisome in those situations in which the user finds it difficult to understand what the indexing strategy is doing. Unfortunately, there is no clear solution to this problem. As already mentioned, some Web search engines are opting for avoiding text operations altogether because this simplifies the interpretation the user has of the retrieval task. Whether this strategy will be the one of choice in the long term remains to be seen.

7.2.2 Elimination of Stopwords

As discussed in Chapter 2, words which are too frequent among the documents in the collection are not good discriminators. In fact, a word which occurs in 80% of the documents in the collection is useless for purposes of retrieval. Such words are frequently referred to as *stopwords* and are normally filtered out as potential index terms. Articles, prepositions, and conjunctions are natural candidates for a list of stopwords.

Elimination of stopwords has an additional important benefit. It reduces the size of the indexing structure considerably. In fact, it is typical to obtain a compression in the size of the indexing structure (for instance, in the size of an inverted list, see Chapter 8) of 40% or more solely with the elimination of stopwords.

Since stopword elimination also provides for compression of the indexing structure, the list of stopwords might be extended to include words other than articles, prepositions, and conjunctions. For instance, some verbs, adverbs, and adjectives could be treated as stopwords. In [275], a list of 425 stopwords is illustrated. Programs in C for lexical analysis are also provided.

Despite these benefits, elimination of stopwords might reduce recall. For instance, consider a user who is looking for documents containing the phrase '*to be or not to be.*' Elimination of stopwords might leave only the term *be* making it almost impossible to properly recognize the documents which contain the phrase specified. This is one additional reason for the adoption of a full text index (i.e., insert all words in the collection into the inverted file) by some Web search engines.

7.2.3   Stemming

Frequently, the user specifies a word in a query but only a variant of this word is present in a relevant document. Plurals, gerund forms, and past tense suffixes are examples of syntactical variations which prevent a perfect match between a query word and a respective document word. This problem can be partially overcome with the substitution of the words by their respective stems.

A *stem* is the portion of a word which is left after the removal of its affixes (i.e., prefixes and suffixes). A typical example of a stem is the word *connect* which is the stem for the variants *connected, connecting, connection,* and *connections.* Stems are thought to be useful for improving retrieval performance because they reduce variants of the same root word to a common concept. Furthermore, stemming has the secondary effect of reducing the size of the indexing structure because the number of distinct index terms is reduced.

While the argument supporting stemming seems sensible, there is controversy in the literature about the benefits of stemming for retrieval performance. In fact, different studies lead to rather conflicting conclusions. Frakes [275] compares eight distinct studies on the potential benefits of stemming. While he favors the usage of stemming, the results of the eight experimental studies he investigated do not allow us to reach a satisfactory conclusion. As a result of these doubts, many Web search engines do not adopt any stemming algorithm whatsoever.

Frakes distinguishes four types of stemming strategies: affix removal, table lookup, successor variety, and n-grams. Table lookup consists simply of looking for the stem of a word in a table. It is a simple procedure but one which is dependent on data on stems for the whole language. Since such data is not readily available and might require considerable storage space, this type of stemming algorithm might not be practical. Successor variety stemming is based on the determination of morpheme boundaries, uses knowledge from structural linguistics, and is more complex than affix removal stemming algorithms. N-grams stemming is based on the identification of digrams and trigrams and is more a term clustering procedure than a stemming one. Affix removal stemming is intuitive, simple, and can be implemented efficiently. Thus, in the remainder of this section we concentrate our discussion on algorithms for affix removal stemming only.

In affix removal, the most important part is suffix removal because most variants of a word are generated by the introduction of suffixes (instead of prefixes). While there are three or four well known suffix removal algorithms, the most popular one is that by Porter because of its simplicity and elegance. Despite being simpler, the Porter algorithm yields results comparable to those of the more sophisticated algorithms.

The Porter algorithm uses a suffix list for suffix stripping. The idea is to apply a series of rules to the suffixes of the words in the text. For instance, the rule

$$s \longrightarrow \phi \qquad\qquad (7.1)$$

is used to convert plural forms into their respective singular forms by substituting the letter s by nil. Notice that to identify the suffix we must examine the last letters in the word. Furthermore, we look for the longest sequence of letters which matches the left hand side in a set of rules. Thus, application of the two following rules

$$sses \longrightarrow ss \qquad\qquad (7.2)$$
$$s \longrightarrow \phi$$

to the word *stresses* yields the stem *stress* instead of the stem *stresse*. By separating such rules into five distinct phases, the Porter algorithm is able to provide effective stemming while running fast. A detailed description of the Porter algorithm can be found in the appendix.

7.2.4 Index Terms Selection

If a full text representation of the text is adopted then all words in the text are used as index terms. The alternative is to adopt a more abstract view in which not all words are used as index terms. This implies that the set of terms used as indices must be selected. In the area of bibliographic sciences, such a selection of index terms is usually done by a specialist. An alternative approach is to select candidates for index terms automatically.

Distinct automatic approaches for selecting index terms can be used. A good approach is the identification of noun groups (as done in the Inquery system [122]) which we now discuss.

A sentence in natural language text is usually composed of nouns, pronouns, articles, verbs, adjectives, adverbs, and connectives. While the words in each grammatical class are used with a particular purpose, it can be argued that most of the semantics is carried by the noun words. Thus, an intuitively promising strategy for selecting index terms automatically is to use the nouns in the text. This can be done through the systematic elimination of verbs, adjectives, adverbs, connectives, articles, and pronouns.

Since it is common to combine two or three nouns in a single component (e.g., *computer science*), it makes sense to cluster nouns which appear nearby in the text into a single indexing component (or concept). Thus, instead of simply using nouns as index terms, we adopt noun groups. A *noun group* is a set of nouns whose syntactic distance in the text (measured in terms of number of words between two nouns) does not exceed a predefined threshold (for instance, 3).

When noun groups are adopted as indexing terms, we obtain a conceptual logical view of the documents in terms of sets of non-elementary index terms.

7.2.5   Thesauri

The word *thesaurus* has Greek and Latin origins and is used as a reference to a treasury of words [261]. In its simplest form, this treasury consists of (1) a precompiled list of important words in a given domain of knowledge and (2) for each word in this list, a set of related words. Related words are, in its most common variation, derived from a synonymity relationship.

In general, however, a thesaurus also involves some normalization of the vocabulary and includes a structure much more complex than a simple list of words and their synonyms. For instance, the popular thesaurus published by Peter Roget [679] also includes *phrases* which means that concepts more complex than single words are taken into account. Roget's thesaurus is of a general nature (i.e., not specific to a certain domain of knowledge) and organizes words and phrases in categories and subcategories.

An example of an entry in Roget's thesaurus is as follows:

> **cowardly** *adjective*
> Ignobly lacking in courage: *cowardly turncoats.*
> **Syns:** chicken (slang), chicken-hearted, craven, dastardly, faint-hearted, gutless, lily-livered, pusillanimous, unmanly, yellow (slang), yellow-bellied (slang).

To the adjective *cowardly*, Roget's thesaurus associates several synonyms which compose a thesaurus class. While Roget's thesaurus is of a generic nature, a thesaurus can be specific to a certain domain of knowledge. For instance, the Thesaurus of Engineering and Scientific Terms covers concepts related to engineering and technical terminology.

According to Foskett [261], the main purposes of a thesaurus are basically: (a) to provide a standard vocabulary (or system of references) for indexing and searching; (b) to assist users with locating terms for proper query formulation; and (c) to provide classified hierarchies that allow the broadening and narrowing of the current query request according to the needs of the user. In this section, however, we do not discuss how to use a thesaurus for modifying the user query. This issue is covered on Chapter 5 which also discusses algorithms for automatic construction of thesauri.

Notice that the motivation for building a thesaurus is based on the fundamental idea of using a *controlled vocabulary* for the indexing and searching. A controlled vocabulary presents important advantages such as normalization of indexing concepts, reduction of noise, identification of indexing terms with a clear semantic meaning, and retrieval based on concepts rather than on words. Such advantages are particularly important in specific domains, such as the medical domain for which there is already a large amount of knowledge compiled. For general domains, however, a well known body of knowledge which can be associated with the documents in the collection might not exist. The reasons might be that the document base is new, that it is too large, or that it changes very dynamically. This is exactly the case with the Web. Thus, it is not clear how useful a thesaurus is in the context of the Web. Despite that, the success of the search engine named 'Yahoo!' (see Chapter 13), which presents the user with a term classification hierarchy that can be used to reduce the space to be searched, suggests that thesaurus-based techniques might be quite useful even in the dynamic world of the Web.

It is still too early to reach a consensus on the advantages of a thesaurus for the Web. As a result, many search engines simply use *all* the words in all the documents as index terms (i.e., there is no notion of using the concepts of a controlled vocabulary for indexing and searching purposes). Whether thesaurus-based techniques will flourish in the context of the Web remains to be seen.

The main components of a thesaurus are its index terms, the relationships among the terms, and a layout design for these term relationships. Index terms and term relationships are covered below. The layout design for term relationships can be in the form of a list or in the form of a bi-dimensional display. Here, we consider only the more conventional layout structure based on a list and thus, do not further discuss the issue of layout of the terms in a thesaurus. A brief coverage of topics related to this problem can be found in Chapter 10. A more detailed discussion can be found in [261].

Theasurus Index Terms

The terms are the *indexing* components of the thesaurus. Usually, a term in a thesaurus is used to denote a *concept* which is the basic semantic unit for conveying ideas. Terms can be individual words, groups of words, or phrases, but most of them are single words. Further, terms are basically nouns because nouns are the most concrete part of speech. Terms can also be verbs in gerund form whenever they are used as nouns (for instance, *acting, teaching,* etc.).

Whenever a concept cannot be expressed by a single word, a group of words is used instead. For instance, many concepts are better expressed by a combination of an adjective with a noun. A typical example is *ballistic missiles*. In this case, indexing the compound term directly will yield an entry under *balistic* and no entry under *missiles* which is clearly inadequate. To avoid this problem, the compound term is usually modified to have the noun as the first word. For instance, we can change the compound term to *missiles, ballistic*.

We notice the use of the plural form *missiles* instead of the singular form *missile*. The reasoning is that a thesaurus represents classes of things and thus it is natural to prefer the plural form. However, the singular form is used for compound terms which appear normally in the singular such as *body temperature*. Deciding between singular and plural is not always a simple matter.

Besides the term itself, frequently it is necessary to complement a thesaurus entry with a *definition* or an *explanation*. The reason is the need to specify the precise meanings of a term in the context of a particular thesaurus. For instance, the term *seal* has a meaning in the context of *marine animals* and a rather distinct meaning in the context of *documents*. In these cases, the definition might be preceded by a context explanation such as *seal (marine animals)* and *seal (documents)* [735].

Thesaurus Term Relationships

The set of terms related to a given thesaurus term is mostly composed of synonyms and near-synonyms. In addition to these, relationships can be induced by patterns of co-occurrence within documents. Such relationships are usually of a hierarchical nature and most often indicate broader (represented by BT) or narrower (represented by NT) related terms. However, the relationship might also be of a lateral or non-hierarchical nature. In this case, we simply say that the terms are related (represented by RT).

As discussed in Chapter 5, BT and NT relationships define a classification hierarchy where the broader term is associated with a class and its related narrower terms are associated with the instances of this class. Further, it might be that a narrower term is associated with two or more broader terms (which is not the most common case though). While BT and NT relationships can be identified in a fully automatic manner (i.e., without assistance from a human subject), dealing with RT relationships is much harder. One reason seems to be that RT relationships are dependent on the specific context and particular needs of the group of users and thus are difficult to identify without knowledge provided by specialists.

On the Use of Thesauri in IR

As described by Peter Roget [679, 261], a thesaurus is a classification scheme composed of words and phrases whose organization aims at facilitating the expression of ideas in written text. Thus, whenever a writer has a difficulty in finding the proper term to express an idea (a common occurrence in serious writing), he can use the thesaurus to obtain a better grasp on the fundamental semantics of terms related to his idea.

In the area of information retrieval, researchers have for many years conjectured and studied the usefulness of a thesaurus for helping with the query formation process. Whenever a user wants to retrieve a set of documents, he first builds up a conceptualization of what he is looking for. Such conceptualization is what we call his *information need*. Given the information need, the user still has to translate it into a query in the language of the IR system. This usually means that a set of index terms has to be selected. However, since the collection might be vast and the user inexperienced, the selection of such *initial* terms might be erroneous and improper (a very common situation with the largely unknown and highly dynamic collection of documents and pages which compose the Web). In this case, reformulating the original query seems to be a promising course of action. Such a reformulation process usually implies expanding the original query with related terms. Thus, it seems natural to use a thesaurus for assisting the user with the search for related terms.

Unfortunately, this approach does not work well in general because the relationships captured in a thesaurus frequently are not valid in the local context of a given user query. One alternative is to determine thesaurus-like relationships at query time. Unfortunately, such an alternative is not attractive for Web search engines which cannot afford to spend a lot of time with the processing of individual queries. This and many other interesting issues related to the use of thesaurus-based techniques in IR are covered in Chapter 5.

7.3   Document Clustering

Document clustering is the operation of grouping together similar (or related) documents in classes. In this regard, document clustering is not really an operation on the text but an operation on the collection of documents.

The operation of clustering documents is usually of two types: global and local. In a global clustering strategy, the documents are grouped accordingly to their occurrence in the whole collection. In a local clustering strategy, the grouping of documents is affected by the context defined by the current query and its *local* set of retrieved documents.

Clustering methods are usually used in IR to transform the original query in an attempt to better represent the user information need. From this perspective, clustering is an operation which is more related to the transformation of the user query than to the transformation of the text of the documents. In this book, document clustering techniques are treated as query operations and thus, are covered in Chapter 5 (instead of here).

7.4   Text Compression

7.4.1   Motivation

Text compression is about finding ways to represent the text in fewer bits or bytes. The amount of space required to store text on computers can be reduced significantly using compression techniques. Compression methods create a reduced representation by identifying and using structures that exist in the text. From the compressed version, the original text can be reconstructed exactly.

Text compression is becoming an important issue in an information retrieval environment. The widespread use of digital libraries, office automation systems, document databases, and the Web has led to an explosion of textual information available online. In this scenario, text compression appears as an attractive option for reducing costs associated with space requirements, input/output (I/O) overhead, and communication delays. The gain obtained from compressing text is that it requires less storage space, it takes less time to be transmitted over a communication link, and it takes less time to search directly the compressed text. The price paid is the time necessary to code and decode the text.

A major obstacle for storing text in compressed form is the need for IR systems to access text randomly. To access a given word in a compressed text, it is usually necessary to decode the entire text from the beginning until the desired word is reached. It could be argued that a large text could be divided into blocks that are compressed independently, thus allowing fast random access to each block. However, efficient compression methods need to process some text before making compression effective (usually more than 10 kilobytes). The smaller the blocks, the less effective compression is expected to be.

Our discussion here focuses on text compression methods which are suitable for use in an IR environment. For instance, a successful idea aimed at merging the requirements of compression algorithms and the needs of IR systems is to consider that the symbols to be compressed are words and not characters (character-based compression is the more conventional approach). Words are the atoms on which most IR systems are built. Moreover, it is now known that much better compression is achieved by taking words as symbols (instead of characters). Further, new word-based compression methods allow random access to words within the compressed text which is a critical issue for an IR system.

Besides the economy of space obtained by a compression method, there are other important characteristics to be considered such as compression and decompression speed. In some situations, decompression speed is more important than compression speed. For instance, this is the case with textual databases in which it is common to compress the text once and to read it many times from disk.

Another important characteristic of a compression method is the possibility of performing compressed pattern matching, defined as the task of performing pattern matching in a compressed text without decompressing it. In this case, sequential searching can be speeded up by compressing the search key rather than decoding the compressed text being searched. As a consequence, it is possible to search faster on compressed text because much less text has to be scanned. Chapter 8 presents efficient methods to deal with searching the compressed text directly.

When the text collection is large, efficient text retrieval requires specialized index techniques. A simple and popular indexing structure for text collections are the inverted files. Inverted files (see Chapter 8 for details) are especially adequate when the pattern to be searched for is formed by simple words. Since this is a common type of query (for instance, when searching the Web), inverted files are widely used for indexing large text collections.

An inverted file is typically composed of (a) a vector containing all the distinct words in the text collection (which is called the *vocabulary*) and (b) for each word in the vocabulary, a list of all documents (identified by document numbers) in which that word occurs. Because each list of document numbers (within the inverted file) is organized in ascending order, specific compression methods have been proposed for them, leading to very efficient index compression schemes. This is important because query processing time is highly related to index access time. Thus, in this section, we also discuss some of the most important index compression techniques.

We first introduce basic concepts related to text compression. We then present some of the most important statistical compression methods, followed by a brief review of compression methods based on a dictionary. At the end, we discuss the application of compression to inverted files.

7.4.2   Basic Concepts

There are two general approaches to text compression: *statistical* and *dictionary* based. *Statistical methods* rely on generating good probability estimates (of appearance in the text) for each symbol. The more accurate the estimates are, the better the compression obtained. A *symbol* here is usually a character, a text word, or a fixed number of characters. The set of all possible symbols in the text is called the *alphabet*. The task of estimating the probability on each next symbol is called *modeling*. A *model* is essentially a collection of probability distributions, one for each context in which a symbol can be coded. Once these probabilities are available the symbols are converted into binary digits, a process called *coding*. In practice, both the encoder and decoder use the same model. The decoder interprets the output of the encoder (with reference to the same model) to find out the original symbol.

There are two well known statistical coding strategies: Huffman coding and arithmetic coding. The idea of Huffman coding is to assign a fixed-length bit encoding to each different symbol of the text. Compression is achieved by assigning a smaller number of bits to symbols with higher probabilities of appearance. Huffman coding was first proposed in the early 1950s and was the most important compression method until the late 1970s, when arithmetic coding made higher compression rates possible.

Arithmetic coding computes the code incrementally, one symbol at a time, as opposed to the Huffman coding scheme in which each different symbol is pre-encoded using a fixed-length number of bits. The incremental nature does not allow decoding a string which starts in the middle of a compressed file. To decode a symbol in the middle of a file compressed with arithmetic coding, it is necessary to decode the whole text from the very beginning until the desired word is reached. This characteristic makes arithmetic coding inadequate for use in an IR environment.

Dictionary methods substitute a sequence of symbols by a pointer to a previous occurrence of that sequence. The pointer representations are references to entries in a dictionary composed of a list of symbols (often called phrases) that are expected to occur frequently. Pointers to the dictionary entries are chosen so that they need less space than the phrase they replace, thus obtaining compression. The distinction between modeling and coding does not exist in dictionary methods and there are no explicit probabilities associated to phrases. The most well known dictionary methods are represented by a family of methods, known as the Ziv-Lempel family.

Character-based Huffman methods are typically able to compress English texts to approximately five bits per character (usually, each uncompressed character takes 7-8 bits to be represented). More recently, a word-based Huffman method has been proposed as a better alternative for natural language texts. This method is able to reduce English texts to just over two bits per character. As we will see later on, word-based Huffman coding achieves compression rates close to the entropy and allows random access to intermediate points in the compressed text. Ziv-Lempel methods are able to reduce English texts to fewer than four bits per character. Methods based on arithmetic coding can also compress English texts to just over two bits per character. However, the price paid is slower compression and decompression, and the impossibility of randomly accessing intermediate points in the compressed text.

Before proceeding, let us present an important definition which will be useful from now on.

Definition Compression ratio *is the size of the compressed file as a fraction of the uncompressed file.*

7.4.3   Statistical Methods

In a statistical method, a probability is estimated for each symbol (the modeling task) and, based on this probability, a code is assigned to each symbol at a time (the coding task). Shorter codes are assigned to the most likely symbols.

The relationship between probabilities and codes was established by Claude Shannon in his source code theorem [718]. He showed that, in an optimal encoding scheme, a symbol that is expected to occur with probability p should be assigned a code of length $\log_2 \frac{1}{p}$ bits. The number of bits in which a symbol is best coded represents the *information content* of the symbol. The average amount of information per symbol over the whole alphabet is called the *entropy* of the probability distribution, and is given by:

$$E = \sum p_i \log_2 \frac{1}{p_i}$$

E is a *lower bound* on compression , measured in bits per symbol, which applies to any coding method based on the probability distribution p_i. It is important to note that E is calculated from the probabilities and so is a property of the model. See Chapter 6 for more details on this topic.

Modeling

The basic *function of a model* is to provide a probability assignment for the next symbol to be coded. High compression can be obtained by forming good models of the text that is to be coded. The probability assignment is explained in the following section.

Compression models can be *adaptive, static,* or *semi-static. Adaptive models* start with no information about the text and progressively learn about its statistical distribution as the compression process goes on. Thus, adaptive models need only one pass over the text and store no additional information apart from the compressed text. For long enough texts, such models converge to the true statistical distribution of the text. One major disadvantage, however, is that decompression of a file has to start from its beginning, since information on the distribution of the data is stored incrementally inside the file. Adaptive modeling is a good option for general purpose compression programs, but an inadequate alternative for full-text retrieval where random access to compressed patterns is a must. *Static models* assume an average distribution for all input texts. The modeling phase is done only once for all texts to be coded in the future (i.e., somehow a probability distribution is estimated and then used for all texts to be compressed in the future). These models tend to achieve poor compression ratios when the data deviates from initial statistical assumptions. For example, a model adequate for English literary texts will probably perform poorly for financial texts containing a lot of different numbers, as each number is relatively rare and so receives long codes.

Semi-static models do not assume any distribution on the data, but learn it in a first pass . In a second pass, they compress the data by using a fixed code derived from the distribution learned from the first pass. At decoding time, information on the data distribution is sent to the decoder before transmitting the encoded symbols. The disadvantages of semi-static models are that they must make two passes over the text and that information on the data distribution must be stored to be used by the decoder to decompress. In situations where interactive data communications are involved it may be impractical to make two passes over the text. However, semi-static models have a crucial advantage in IR contexts: since the same codes are used at every point in the compressed file, direct access is possible.

Word-based models take words instead of characters as symbols. Usually, a word is a contiguous string of characters in the set {A..Z, a..z} separated by other characters not in the set {A..Z, a..z}. There are many good reasons to use word-based models in an IR context. First, much better compression rates are achieved by taking words as symbols because words carry a lot of meaning in natural languages and, as a result, their distribution is much more related to the semantic structure of the text than the individual letters. Second, words are the atoms on which most information retrieval systems are built. Words are already stored for indexing purposes and so might be used as part of the model for compression. Third, the word frequencies are also useful in answering queries involving combinations of words because the best strategy is to start with the least frequent words first.

Since the text is not only composed of words but also of separators, a model must also be chosen for them. There are many different ways to deal with separators. As words and separators always follow one another, two different alphabets are usually used: one for words and one for separators. Consider the following example: each rose, a rose is a rose. In the word-based model, the set of symbols of the alphabet is {a, each, is, rose}, whose frequencies are 2, 1, 1, and 3, respectively, and the set of separators is {',⊔', ⊔}, whose frequencies are 1 and 5, respectively (where ⊔ represents a space). Once it is known that the text starts with a word or a separator, there is confusion about which alphabet to use.

In natural language texts, a word is followed by a single space in most cases. In the texts of the TREC-3 collection [342] (see Chapter 3), 70–80% of the separators are single spaces. Another good alternative is to consider the single space that follows a word as part of the same word. That is, if a word is followed by a space, we can encode just the word. If not, we can encode the word and then the following separator. At decoding time, we decode a word and assume that a space follows unless the next symbol corresponds to a separator. Notice that now a single alphabet for words and separators (single space excluded) is used. For instance, in the example above, the single alphabet is {',⊔', a, each, is, rose} and there is no longer an alphabet for separators. As the alphabet excludes the single space then the words are called *spaceless words*.

In some situations word-based models for full-text databases have a potential to generate a great quantity of different codes and care must be exercised to deal with this fact. For instance, as discussed in the section on lexical analysis (at the beginning of this chapter), one has to consider whether a sequence of digits is to be considered as a word. If it is, then a collection which contains one million documents and includes document numbers as identifiers will generate one million words composed solely of digits, each one occurring once in the collection. This can be very inefficient for any kind of compression method available. One possible good solution is to divide long numbers into shorter ones by using a null (or implicit) punctuation marker in between. This diminishes the alphabet size resulting in considerable improvements in the compression ratio and in the decoding time.

Another important consideration is the size of the alphabet in word-based schemes. How large is the number of different words in a full-text database? It is empirically known that the vocabulary V of natural language texts with n words grows sublinearly. Heaps [352] shows that $V = O(n^\beta)$, where β is a constant dependent on the particular text. For the 2 gigabyte TREC-3 collection [342], β is between 0.4 and 0.6 which means that the alphabet size grows roughly proportional to the square root of n. Even for this growth of the alphabet, the generalized Zipf law shows that the probability distribution is skewed so that the entropy remains constant. This implies that the compression ratio does not degrade as the text (and hence the number of different symbols) grows. Heaps' and Zipfs' laws are explained in Chapter 6.

Finally, it is important to mention that word-based Huffman methods need large texts to be effective (i.e., they are not adequate to compress and transmit a single Web page over a network). The need to store the vocabulary represents an important space overhead when the text is small (say, less than 10 megabytes). However, this is not a concern in IR in general as the texts are large and the vocabulary is needed anyway for other purposes such as indexing and querying.

Coding

Coding corresponds to the task of obtaining the representation (code) of a symbol based on a probability distribution given by a model. The main goal of a coder is to assign short codes to likely symbols and long codes to unlikely ones. As we have seen in the previous section, the entropy of a probability distribution is a lower bound on how short the average length of a code can be, and the quality of a coder is measured in terms of how close to the entropy it is able to get. Another important consideration is the speed of both the coder and the decoder. Sometimes it is necessary to sacrifice the compression ratio to reduce the time to encode and decode the text.

A semi-static Huffman compression method works in two passes over the text. In a first pass, the modeler determines the probability distribution of the symbols and builds a coding tree according to this distribution. In a second pass, each next symbol is encoded according to the coding tree. Adaptive Huffman compression methods, instead, work in one single pass over the text updating the coding tree incrementally. The encoding of the symbols in the input text is also done during this single pass over the text. The main problem of adaptive Huffman methods is the cost of updating the coding tree as new symbols are read.

As with Huffman-based methods, arithmetic coding methods can also be based on static, semi-static or adaptive algorithms. The main strength of arithmetic coding methods is that they can generate codes which are arbitrarily close to the entropy for any kind of probability distribution. Another strength of arithmetic coding methods is that they do not need to store a coding tree explicitly. For adaptive algorithms, this implies that arithmetic coding uses less memory than Huffman-based coding. For static or semi-static algorithms, the use of canonical Huffman codes overcomes this memory problem (canonical Huffman trees are explained later on).

In arithmetic coding, the input text is represented by an interval of real numbers between 0 and 1. As the size of the input becomes larger, the interval becomes smaller and the number of bits needed to specify this interval increases. Compression is achieved because input symbols with higher probabilities reduce the interval less than symbols with smaller probabilities and hence add fewer bits to the output code.

Arithmetic coding presents many disadvantages over Huffman coding in an IR environment. First, arithmetic coding is much slower than Huffman coding, especially with static and semi-static algorithms. Second, with arithmetic coding, decompression cannot start in the middle of a compressed file. This contrasts with Huffman coding, in which it is possible to index and to decode from any position in the compressed text if static or semi-static algorithms are used. Third, word-based Huffman coding methods yield compression ratios as good as arithmetic coding ones.

Consequently, Huffman coding is the method of choice in full-text retrieval, where both speed and random access are important. Thus, we will focus the remaining of our discussion on semi-static word-based Huffman coding.

Huffman Coding

Huffman coding is one of the best known compression methods [386]. The idea is to assign a variable-length encoding in bits to each symbol and encode each symbol in turn. Compression is achieved by assigning shorter codes to more frequent symbols. Decompression uniqueness is guaranteed because no code is a prefix of another. A word-based semi-static model and Huffman coding form a good compression method for text.

Figure 7.2 presents an example of compression using Huffman coding on words. In this example the set of symbols of the alphabet is {',⊔', a, each, for, is, rose}, whose frequencies are 1, 2, 1, 1, 1, and 3, respectively. In this case the alphabet is unique for words and separators. Notice that the separator '⊔' is not part of the alphabet because the single space that follows a word is considered as part of the word. These words are called *spaceless words* (see more about spaceless words in Section 7.4.3). The Huffman tree shown in Figure 7.2 is an example of a binary trie built on binary codes. Tries are explained in Chapter 8.

Decompression is accomplished as follows. The stream of bits in the compressed file is traversed from left to right. The sequence of bits read is used to also traverse the Huffman compression tree, starting at the root. Whenever a leaf node is reached, the corresponding word (which constitutes the decompressed symbol) is printed out and the tree traversal is restarted. Thus, according to the tree in Figure 7.2, the presence of the code 0110 in the compressed file leads to the decompressed symbol for.

To build a Huffman tree, it is first necessary to obtain the symbols that constitute the alphabet and their probability distribution in the text to be compressed. The algorithm for building the tree then operates bottom up and starts

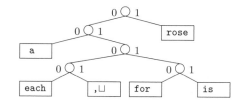

Original text: for each rose, a rose is a rose

Compressed text: 0110 0100 1 0101 00 1 0111 00 1

Figure 7.2 Huffman coding tree for spaceless words.

by creating for each symbol of the alphabet a node containing the symbol and its probability (or frequency). At this point there is a forest of one-node trees whose probabilities sum up to 1. Next, the two nodes with the smallest probabilities become children of a newly created parent node. With this parent node is associated a probability equal to the sum of the probabilities of the two chosen children. The operation is repeated ignoring nodes that are already children, until there is only one node, which becomes the root of the decoding tree. By delaying the pairing of nodes with high probabilities, the algorithm necessarily places them closer to the root node, making their code smaller. The two branches from every internal node are consistently labeled 0 and 1 (or 1 and 0). Given s symbols and their frequencies in the text, the algorithm builds the Huffman tree in $O(s \log s)$ time.

The number of Huffman trees which can be built for a given probability distribution is quite large. This happens because interchanging left and right subtrees of any internal node results in a different tree whenever the two subtrees are different in structure, but the weighted average code length is not affected. Instead of using any kind of tree, the preferred choice for most applications is to adopt a *canonical tree* which imposes a particular order to the coding bits.

A Huffman tree is canonical when the height of the left subtree of any node is never smaller than that of the right subtree, and all leaves are in increasing order of probabilities from left to right. Figure 7.3 shows the canonical tree for the example of Figure 7.2. The deepest leaf at the leftmost position of the Huffman canonical tree, corresponding to one element with smallest probability, will contain only zeros, and the following codes will be in increasing order inside each level. At each change of level we shift left one bit in the counting. The table in Figure 7.3 shows the canonical codes for the example of Figure 7.2.

A canonical code can be represented by an ordered sequence S of pairs (x_i, y_i), $1 \leq i \leq \ell$, where x_i represents the number of symbols at level i, y_i represents the numerical value of the first code at level i, and ℓ is the height of the tree. For our example in Figure 7.3, the ordered sequence is $S = \langle (1,1), (1,1), (0,\infty), (4,0) \rangle$. For instance, the fourth pair $(4,0)$ in S corresponds to the fourth level and indicates that there are four nodes at this level and that to the node most to the left is assigned a code, at this level, with value 0. Since this is the fourth level, a value 0 corresponds to the codeword 0000.

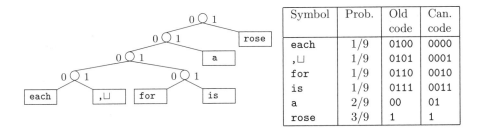

Symbol	Prob.	Old code	Can. code
each	1/9	0100	0000
,␣	1/9	0101	0001
for	1/9	0110	0010
is	1/9	0111	0011
a	2/9	00	01
rose	3/9	1	1

Figure 7.3 Canonical code.

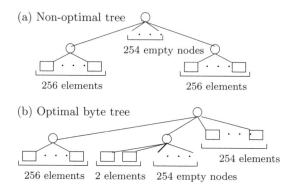

Figure 7.4   Example of byte Huffman tree.

One of the properties of canonical codes is that the set of codes having the same length are the binary representations of consecutive integers. Interpreted as integers, the 4-bit codes of the table in Figure 7.3 are 0, 1, 2, and 3, the 2-bit code is 1 and the 1-bit code is also 1. In our example, if the first character read from the input stream is 1, a codeword has been identified and the corresponding symbol can be output. If this value is 0, a second bit is appended and the two bits are again interpreted as an integer and used to index the table and identify the corresponding symbol. Once we read '00' we know that the code has four bits and therefore we can read two more bits and use them as an index into the table. This fact can be exploited to enable efficient encoding and decoding with small overhead. Moreover, much less memory is required, which is especially important for large vocabularies.

Byte-Oriented Huffman Code
The original method proposed by Huffman [386] leads naturally to binary coding trees. In [577], however, it is proposed to build the code assigned to each symbol as a sequence of whole bytes. As a result, the Huffman tree has degree 256 instead of 2. Typically, the code assigned to each symbol contains between 1 and 5 bytes. For example, a possible code for the word **rose** could be the 3-byte code '47 131 8.'

The construction of byte Huffman trees involves some details which must be dealt with. Care must be exercised to ensure that the first levels of the tree have no empty nodes when the code is not binary. Figure 7.4(a) illustrates a case where a naive extension of the binary Huffman tree construction algorithm might generate a non-optimal byte tree. In this example the alphabet has 512 symbols, all with the same probability. The root node has 254 empty spaces that could be occupied by symbols from the second level of the tree, changing their code lengths from 2 bytes to 1 byte.

A way to ensure that the empty nodes always go to the lowest level of the tree follows. We calculate beforehand the number of empty nodes that will arise.

We then compose these empty nodes with symbols of smallest probabilities (for moving the empty nodes to the deepest level of the final tree). To accomplish this, we need only to select a number of symbols equal to $1 + ((v - 256) \bmod 255)$, where v is the total number of symbols (i.e., the size of the vocabulary), for composing with the empty nodes. For instance, in the example in Figure 7.4(a), we have that 2 elements must be coupled with 254 empty nodes in the first step (because, $1 + ((512 - 256) \bmod 255) = 2$). The remaining steps are similar to the binary Huffman tree construction algorithm.

All techniques for efficient encoding and decoding mentioned previously can easily be extended to handle word-based byte Huffman coding. Moreover, no significant decrease of the compression ratio is experienced by using bytes instead of bits when the symbols are words. Further, decompression of byte Huffman code is faster than decompression of binary Huffman code. In fact, compression and decompression are very fast and compression ratios achieved are better than those of the Ziv-Lempel family [848, 849]. In practice byte processing is much faster than bit processing because bit shifts and masking operations are not necessary at decoding time or at searching time.

One important consequence of using byte Huffman coding is the possibility of performing direct searching on compressed text. The searching algorithm is explained in Chapter 8. The exact search can be done on the compressed text directly, using any known sequential pattern matching algorithm. Moreover, it allows a large number of variations of the exact and approximate compressed pattern matching problem, such as phrases, ranges, complements, wild cards, and arbitrary regular expressions. The algorithm is based on a word-oriented shift-or algorithm and on a fast Boyer-Moore-type filter. For approximate searching on the compressed text it is eight times faster than an equivalent approximate searching on the uncompressed text, thanks to the use of the vocabulary by the algorithm [577, 576]. This technique is not only useful in speeding up sequential search. It can also be used to improve indexed schemes that combine inverted files and sequential search, like Glimpse [540].

7.4.4   Dictionary Methods

Dictionary methods achieve compression by replacing groups of consecutive symbols (or phrases) with a pointer to an entry in a dictionary. Thus, the central decision in the design of a dictionary method is the selection of entries in the dictionary. The choice of phrases can be made by static, semi-adaptive, or adaptive algorithms. The simplest dictionary schemes use static dictionaries containing short phrases. Static dictionary encoders are fast as they demand little effort for achieving a small amount of compression. One example that has been proposed several times in different forms is the digram coding, where selected pairs of letters are replaced with codewords. At each step the next two characters are inspected and verified if they correspond to a digram in the dictionary. If so, they are coded together and the coding position is shifted by two characters; otherwise, the single character is represented by its normal code and the coding position is shifted by one character.

The main problem with static dictionary encoders is that the dictionary might be suitable for one text and unsuitable for another. One way to avoid this problem is to use a semi-static dictionary scheme, constructing a new dictionary for each text to be compressed. However, the problem of deciding which phrases should be put in the dictionary is not an easy task at all. One elegant solution to this problem is to use an adaptive dictionary scheme, such as the one proposed in the 1970s by Ziv and Lempel.

The Ziv-Lempel type of adaptive dictionary scheme uses the idea of replacing strings of characters with a reference to a previous occurrence of the string. This approach is effective because most characters can be coded as part of a string that has occurred earlier in the text. If the pointer to an earlier occurrence of a string is stored in fewer bits than the string it replaces then compression is achieved.

Adaptive dictionary methods present some disadvantages over the statistical word-based Huffman method. First, they do not allow decoding to start in the middle of a compressed file. As a consequence direct access to a position in the compressed text is not possible, unless the entire text is decoded from the beginning until the desired position is reached. Second, dictionary schemes are still popular for their speed and economy of memory, but the new results in statistical methods make them the method of choice in an IR environment. Moreover, the improvement of computing technology will soon make statistical methods feasible for general use, and the interest in dictionary methods will eventually decrease.

7.4.5 Inverted File Compression

As already discussed, an inverted file is typically composed of (a) a vector containing all the distinct words in the text collection (which is called the *vocabulary*) and (b) for each word in the vocabulary, a list of all documents in which that word occurs. Inverted files are widely used to index large text files. The size of an inverted file can be reduced by compressing the inverted lists. Because the list of document numbers within the inverted list is in ascending order, it can also be considered as a sequence of *gaps* between document numbers. Since processing is usually done sequentially starting from the beginning of the list, the original document numbers can always be recomputed through sums of the gaps.

By observing that these gaps are small for frequent words and large for infrequent words, compression can be obtained by encoding small values with shorter codes. One possible coding scheme for this case is the *unary code*, in which an integer x is coded as $(x-1)$ one bits followed by a zero bit, so the code for the integer 3 is 110. The second column of Table 7.1 shows unary codes for integers between 1 and 10.

Elias [235] presented two other variable-length coding schemes for integers. One is Elias-γ code, which represents the number x by a concatenation of two

Gap x	Unary	Elias-γ	Elias-δ	Golomb $b = 3$
1	0	0	0	00
2	10	100	1000	010
3	110	101	1001	011
4	1110	11000	10100	100
5	11110	11001	10101	1010
6	111110	11010	10110	1011
7	1111110	11011	10111	1100
8	11111110	1110000	11000000	11010
9	111111110	1110001	11000001	11011
10	1111111110	1110010	11000010	11100

Table 7.1   Example codes for integers.

parts: (1) a unary code for $1 + \lfloor \log x \rfloor$ and (2) a code of $\lfloor \log x \rfloor$ bits that represents the value of $x - 2^{\lfloor \log x \rfloor}$ in binary. For $x = 5$, we have that $1 + \lfloor \log x \rfloor = 3$ and that $x - 2^{\lfloor \log x \rfloor} = 1$. Thus, the Elias-$\gamma$ code for $x = 5$ is generated by combining the unary code for 3 (code 110) with the 2-bits binary number for 1 (code 01) which yields the codeword 11001. Other examples of Elias-γ codes are shown in Table 7.1.

The other coding scheme introduced by Elias is the Elias-δ code, which represents the prefix indicating the number of binary bits by the Elias-γ code rather than the unary code. For $x = 5$, the first part is then 101 instead of 110. Thus, the Elias-δ codeword for $x = 5$ is 10101. In general, the Elias-δ code for an arbitrary integer x requires $1 + 2\lfloor \log \log 2x \rfloor + \lfloor \log x \rfloor$ bits. Table 7.1 shows other examples of Elias-δ codes. In general, for small values of x the Elias-γ codes are shorter than the Elias-δ codes. However, in the limit, as x becomes large, the situation is reversed.

Golomb [307] presented another run-length coding method for positive integers. The Golomb code is very effective when the probability distribution is geometric. With inverted files, the likelihood of a gap being of size x can be computed as the probability of having $x - 1$ non-occurrences (within consecutively numbered documents) of that particular word followed by one occurrence. If a word occurs within a document with a probability p, the probability of a gap of size x is then

$$Pr[x] = (1 - p)^{x-1} p$$

which is the *geometric distribution*. In this case, the model is parameterized and makes use of the actual density of pointers in the inverted file. Let N be the number of documents in the system and V be the size of the vocabulary. Then, the probability p that any randomly selected document contains any randomly chosen term can be estimated as

$$p = \frac{number\ of\ pointers}{N \times V}$$

where the number of pointers represent the 'size' of the index.

The Golomb method works as follows. For some parameter b, a gap $x > 0$ is coded as $q + 1$ in unary, where $q = \lfloor (x-1)/b \rfloor$, followed by $r = (x-1) - q \times b$ coded in binary, requiring either $\lfloor \log b \rfloor$ or $\lceil \log b \rceil$ bits. That is, if $r < 2^{\lceil \log b \rceil - 1}$ then the number coded in binary requires $\lfloor \log b \rfloor$ bits, otherwise it requires $\lceil \log b \rceil$ bits where the first bit is 1 and the remaining bits assume the value $r - 2^{\lceil \log b \rceil - 1}$ coded in $\lfloor \log b \rfloor$ binary digits. For example, with $b = 3$ there are three possible remainders, and those are coded as 0, 10, and 11, for $r = 0$, $r = 1$, and $r = 2$, respectively. Similarly, for $b = 5$ there are five possible remainders r, 0 through 4, and these are assigned codes 00, 01, 100, 101, and 110. Then, if the value $x = 9$ is to be coded relative to $b = 3$, calculation yields $q = 2$ and $r = 2$, because $9 - 1 = 2 \times 3 + 2$. Thus, the encoding is 110 followed by 11. Relative to $b = 5$, the values calculated are $q = 1$ and $r = 1$, resulting in a code of 10 followed by 101.

To operate with the Golomb compression method, it is first necessary to establish the parameter b for each term. For gap compression, an appropriate value is $b \approx 0.69(N/f_t)$, where N is the total number of documents and f_t is the number of documents that contain term t. Witten, Moffat and Bell [825] present a detailed study of different text collections. For all of their practical work on compression of inverted lists, they use Golomb code for the list of gaps. In this case Golomb code gives better compression than either Elias-γ or Elias-δ. However, it has the disadvantage of requiring two passes to be generated, since it requires knowledge of f_t, the number of documents containing term t.

Moffat and Bell [572] show that the index for the 2 gigabytes TREC-3 collection, which contains 162,187,989 pointers and 894,406 distinct terms, when coded with Golomb code, occupies 132 megabytes. Considering the average number of bits per pointer, they obtained 5.73, 6.19, and 6.43 using Golomb, Elias-δ, and Elias-γ, respectively.

7.5 Comparing Text Compression Techniques

Table 7.2 presents a comparison between arithmetic coding, character-based Huffman coding, word-based Huffman coding, and Ziv-Lempel coding, considering the aspects of compression ratio, compression speed, decompression speed, memory space overhead, compressed pattern matching capability, and random access capability.

One important objective of any compression method is to be able to obtain good compression ratios. It seems that two bits per character (or 25% compression ratio) is a very good result for natural language texts. Thus, 'very good' in the context of Table 7.2 means a compression ratio under 30%, 'good' means a compression ratio between 30% and 45%, and 'poor' means a compression ratio over 45%.

	Arithmetic	Character Huffman	Word Huffman	Ziv-Lempel
Compression ratio	very good	poor	very good	good
Compression speed	slow	fast	fast	very fast
Decompression speed	slow	fast	very fast	very fast
Memory space	low	low	high	moderate
Compressed pat. matching	no	yes	yes	yes
Random access	no	yes	yes	no

Table 7.2   Comparison of the main techniques.

Two other important characteristics of a compression method are compression and decompression speeds. Measuring the speed of various compression methods is difficult because it depends on the implementation details of each method, the compiler used, the computer architecture of the machine used to run the program, and so on. Considering compression speed, the LZ78 methods (Unix *compress* is an example) are among the fastest. Considering decompression speed, the LZ77 methods (*gzip* is an example) from the Ziv-Lempel are among the fastest.

For statistical methods (e.g., arithmetic and semi-static Huffman) the compression time includes the cost of the first pass during which the probability distribution of the symbols are obtained. With two passes over the text to compress, the Huffman-based methods are slower than some Ziv-Lempel methods, but not very far behind. On the other hand, arithmetic methods are slower than Huffman methods because of the complexity of arithmetic coding compared with canonical Huffman coding. Considering decompression speed, word-based Huffman methods are as fast as Ziv-Lempel methods, while character-based Huffman methods are slower than word-based Huffman methods. Again, the complexity of arithmetic coding make them slower than Huffman coding during decompression.

All Ziv-Lempel compression methods require a moderate amount of memory during encoding and decoding to store tables containing previously occurring strings. In general, more detailed tables that require more memory for storage yield better compression. Statistical methods store the probability distribution of the symbols of the text during the modeling phase, and the model during both compression and decompression phases. Consequently, the amount of memory depends on the size of the vocabulary of the text in each case, which is high for word-based models and low for character-based models.

In an IR environment, two important considerations are whether the compression method allows efficient random access and direct searching on compressed text (or compressed pattern matching). Huffman methods allow random access and decompression can start anywhere in the middle of a compressed file, while arithmetic coding and Ziv-Lempel methods cannot. More recently, practical, efficient, and flexible direct searching methods on compressed texts have been discovered for word-based Huffman compression [575, 576, 577].

Direct searching has also been proposed for Ziv-Lempel methods, but only on a theoretical basis, with no implementation of the algorithms [250, 19].

More recently, Navarro and Raffinot [592] presented some preliminary implementations of algorithms to search directly Ziv-Lempel compressed text. Their algorithms are twice as fast as decompressing and searching, but slower than searching the decompressed text. They are also able to extract data from the middle of the compressed text without necessarily decompressing everything, and although some previous text has to be decompressed (i.e., it is not really 'direct access'), the amount of work is proportional to the size of the text to be decompressed (and not to its position in the compressed text).

7.6   Trends and Research Issues

In this chapter we covered various text transformation techniques which we call simply text operations. We first discussed five distinct text operations for pre-processing a document text and generating a set of index terms for searching and querying purposes. These five text operations were here called lexical analysis, elimination of stopwords, stemming, selection of index terms, and thesauri. The first four are directly related to the generation of a good set of index terms. The fifth, construction of a thesaurus, is more related to the building of categorization hierarchies which are used for capturing term relationships. These relationships can then be used for expanding the user query (manually or automatically) towards a formulation which better suits the user information need.

Nowadays, there is controversy regarding the potential improvements to retrieval performance generated by stopwords elimination, stemming, and index terms selection. In fact, there is no conclusive evidence that such text operations yield consistent improvements in retrieval performance. As a result, modern retrieval systems might not use these text operations at all. A good example of this trend is the fact that some Web search engines index all the words in the text regardless of their syntactic nature or their role in the text.

Furthermore, it is also not clear that automatic query expansion using thesaurus-based techniques can yield improved retrieval performance. The same cannot be said of the use of a thesaurus to directly assist the user with the query formation process. In fact, the success of the 'Yahoo!' Web search engine, which uses a term categorization hierarchy to show term relationships to the user, is an indication that thesaurus-based techniques might be quite useful with the highly interactive interfaces being developed for modern digital library systems.

We also briefly discussed the operation of clustering. Since clustering is more an operation of grouping documents than an operation of text transformation, we did not cover it thoroughly here. For a more complete coverage of clustering the reader is referred to Chapter 5.

One text operation rather distinct from the previous ones is compression. While the previous text operations aim, in one form or another, at improving the quality of the answer set, the operation of compressing text aims at reducing space, I/O, communication costs, and searching faster in the compressed text (exactly or approximately). In fact, the gain obtained from compressing text is that it requires less storage space, takes less time to be transmitted, and permits efficient direct and sequential access to compressed text.

For effective operation in an IR environment, a compression method should satisfy the following requirements: good compression ratio, fast coding, fast decoding, fast random access without the need to decode from the beginning, and direct searching without the need to decompress the compressed text. A good compression ratio saves space in secondary storage and reduces communication costs. Fast coding reduces processing overhead due to the introduction of compression into the system. Sometimes, fast decoding is more important than fast coding, as in documentation systems in which a document is compressed once and decompressed many times from disk. Fast random access allows efficient processing of multiple queries submitted by the users of the information system. We compared various compression schemes using these requirements as parameters. We have seen that it is much faster to search sequentially a text compressed by a word-based byte Huffman encoding scheme than to search the uncompressed version of the text. Our discussion suggests that word-based byte Huffman compression (which has been introduced only very recently) shows great promise as an effective compression scheme for modern information retrieval systems.

We also discussed the application of compression to index structures such as inverted files. Inverted files are composed of several inverted lists which are themselves formed by document numbers organized in ascending order. By coding the difference between these document numbers, efficient compression can be attained.

The main trends in text compression today are the use of semi-static word-based modeling and Huffman coding. The new results in statistical methods, such as byte-Huffman coding, suggest that they are preferable methods for use in an IR environment. Further, with the possibility now of directly searching the compressed text, and the recent work [790] of Vo and Moffat on efficient manipulation of compressed indices, the trend is towards maintaining both the index and the text compressed at all times, unless the user wants to visualize the uncompressed text.

7.7   Bibliographic Discussion

Our discussion on lexical analysis and elimination of stopwords is based on the work of Fox [263]. For stemming, we based our discussion on the work of Frakes [274]. The Porter stemming algorithm detailed in the appendix is from [648], while our coverage of thesauri is based on the work of Foskett [261]. Here, however, we did not cover automatic generation of thesauri. Such discussion can be found in Chapter 5 and in [739, 735]. Additional discussion on the usefulness of thesauri is presented in [419, 735].

Regarding text compression, several books are available. Most of the topics discussed here are covered in more detail by Witten, Moffat and Bell [825]. They also present implementations of text compression methods, such as Huffman and arithmetic coding, as part of a fully operational retrieval system written in ANSI

C. Bell, Cleary and Witten [78] cover statistical and dictionary methods, laying particular stress on adaptive methods as well as theoretical aspects of compression, with estimates on the entropy of several natural languages. Storer [747] covers the main compression techniques, with emphasis on dictionary methods.

Huffman coding was originally presented in [386]. Adaptive versions of Huffman coding appear in [291, 446, 789]. Word-based compression is considered in [81, 571, 377, 77]. Bounds on the inefficiency of Huffman coding have been presented by [291]. Canonical codes were first presented in [713]. Many properties of the canonical codes are mentioned in [374]. Byte Huffman coding was proposed in [577]. Sequential searching on byte Huffman compressed text is described in [577, 576].

Sequential searching on Ziv-Lempel compressed data is presented in [250, 19]. More recently, implementations of sequential searching on Ziv-Lempel compressed text are presented in [593]. One of the first papers on arithmetic coding is in [675]. Other references are [823, 78].

A variety of compression methods for inverted lists are studied in [573]. The most effective compression methods for inverted lists are based on the sequence of gaps between document numbers, as considered in [77] and in [572]. Their results are based on run-length encodings proposed by Elias [235] and Golomb [307]. A comprehensive study of inverted file compression can be found in [825]. More recently Vo and Moffat [790] have presented algorithms to process the index with no need to fully decode the compressed index.

Chapter 8
Indexing and Searching

with Gonzalo Navarro

8.1 Introduction

Chapter 4 describes the query operations that can be performed on text databases. In this chapter we cover the main techniques we need to implement those query operations.

We first concentrate on searching queries composed of words and on reporting the documents where they are found. The number of occurrences of a query in each document and even its exact positions in the text may also be required. Following that, we concentrate on algorithms dealing with Boolean operations. We then consider sequential search algorithms and pattern matching. Finally, we consider structured text and compression techniques.

An obvious option in searching for a basic query is to scan the text sequentially. Sequential or online text searching involves finding the occurrences of a pattern in a text when the text is not preprocessed. Online searching is appropriate when the text is small (i.e., a few megabytes), and it is the only choice if the text collection is very volatile (i.e., undergoes modifications very frequently) or the index space overhead cannot be afforded.

A second option is to build data structures over the text (called *indices*) to speed up the search. It is worthwhile building and maintaining an index when the text collection is large and *semi-static*. Semi-static collections can be updated at reasonably regular intervals (e.g., daily) but they are not deemed to support thousands of insertions of single words per second, say. This is the case for most real text databases, not only dictionaries or other slow growing literary works. For instance, it is the case for Web search engines or journal archives.

Nowadays, the most successful techniques for medium size databases (say up to 200Mb) combine online and indexed searching.

We cover three main indexing techniques: inverted files, suffix arrays, and signature files. Keyword-based search is discussed first. We emphasize inverted files, which are currently the best choice for most applications. Suffix trees

191

and arrays are faster for phrase searches and other less common queries, but are harder to build and maintain. Finally, signature files were popular in the 1980s, but nowadays inverted files outperform them. For all the structures we pay attention not only to their search cost and space overhead, but also to the cost of building and updating them.

We assume that the reader is familiar with basic data structures, such as sorted arrays, binary search trees, B-trees, hash tables, and tries. Since tries are heavily used we give a brief and simplified reminder here. Tries, or digital search trees, are multiway trees that store sets of strings and are able to retrieve any string in time proportional to its length (independent of the number of strings stored). A special character is added to the end of the string to ensure that no string is a prefix of another. Every edge of the tree is labeled with a letter. To search a string in a trie, one starts at the root and scans the string character-wise, descending by the appropriate edge of the trie. This continues until a leaf is found (which represents the searched string) or the appropriate edge to follow does not exist at some point (i.e., the string is not in the set). See Figure 8.3 for an example of a text and a trie built on its words.

Although an index must be built prior to searching it, we present these tasks in the reverse order. We think that understanding first how a data structure is used makes it clear how it is organized, and therefore eases the understanding of the construction algorithm, which is usually more complex.

Throughout this chapter we make the following assumptions. We call n the size of the text database. Whenever a pattern is searched, we assume that it is of length m, which is much smaller than n. We call M the amount of main memory available. We assume that the modifications which a text database undergoes are additions, deletions, and replacements (which are normally made by a deletion plus an addition) of pieces of text of size $n' < n$.

We give experimental measures for many algorithms to give the reader a grasp of the real times involved. To do this we use a reference architecture throughout the chapter, which is representative of the power of today's computers. We use a 32-bit Sun UltraSparc-1 of 167 MHz with 64 Mb of RAM, running Solaris. The code is written in C and compiled with all optimization options. For the text data, we use collections from TREC-2, specifically WSJ, DOE, FR, ZIFF and AP. These are described in more detail in Chapter 3.

8.2   Inverted Files

An inverted file (or inverted index) is a word-oriented mechanism for indexing a text collection in order to speed up the searching task. The inverted file structure is composed of two elements: the *vocabulary* and the *occurrences*. The vocabulary is the set of all different words in the text. For each such word a list of all the text positions where the word appears is stored. The set of all those lists is called the 'occurrences' (Figure 8.1 shows an example). These positions can refer to words or characters. Word positions (i.e., position i refers to the i-th word) simplify

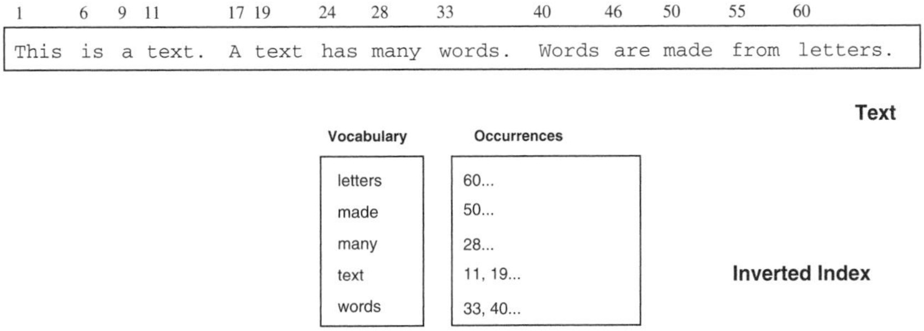

| 1 | 6 | 9 | 11 | | 17 | 19 | | 24 | 28 | | 33 | | 40 | | 46 | 50 | | 55 | | 60 |

```
This  is  a  text.  A  text  has  many  words.   Words  are  made  from  letters.
```

Text

Vocabulary	Occurrences
letters	60...
made	50...
many	28...
text	11, 19...
words	33, 40...

Inverted Index

Figure 8.1 A sample text and an inverted index built on it. The words are converted to lower-case and some are not indexed. The occurrences point to character positions in the text.

phrase and proximity queries, while character positions (i.e., the position i is the i-th character) facilitate direct access to the matching text positions.

Some authors make the distinction between inverted files and inverted lists. In an inverted file, each element of a list points to a document or file name, while inverted lists match our definition. We prefer not to make such a distinction because, as we will see later, this is a matter of the *addressing granularity*, which can range from text positions to logical blocks.

The space required for the vocabulary is rather small. According to Heaps' law (see Chapter 6) the vocabulary grows as $O(n^\beta)$, where β is a constant between 0 and 1 dependent on the text, being between 0.4 and 0.6 in practice. For instance, for 1 Gb of the TREC-2 collection the vocabulary has a size of only 5 Mb. This may be further reduced by stemming and other normalization techniques as described in Chapter 7.

The occurrences demand much more space. Since each word appearing in the text is referenced once in that structure, the extra space is $O(n)$. Even omitting stopwords (which is the default practice when words are indexed), in practice the space overhead of the occurrences is between 30% and 40% of the text size.

To reduce space requirements, a technique called *block addressing* is used. The text is divided in blocks, and the occurrences point to the blocks where the word appears (instead of the exact positions). The classical indices which point to the exact occurrences are called 'full inverted indices.' By using block addressing not only can the pointers be smaller because there are fewer blocks than positions, but also all the occurrences of a word inside a single block are collapsed to one reference (see Figure 8.2). Indices of only 5% overhead over the text size are obtained with this technique. The price to pay is that, if the exact occurrence positions are required (for instance, for a proximity query), then an online search over the qualifying blocks has to be performed. For instance, block addressing indices with 256 blocks stop working well with texts of 200 Mb.

Table 8.1 presents the projected space taken by inverted indices for texts of

Block 1	Block 2	Block 3	Block 4
This is a text.	A text has many	words. Words are	made from letters.

Text

Vocabulary	Occurrences
letters	4...
made	4...
many	2...
text	1, 2...
words	3...

Inverted Index

Figure 8.2   The sample text split into four blocks, and an inverted index using block addressing built on it.   The occurrences denote block numbers.   Notice that both occurrences of 'words' collapsed into one.

different sizes, with and without the use of stopwords. The full inversion stands for inverting all the words and storing their exact positions, using four bytes per pointer. The document addressing index assumes that we point to documents which are of size 10 Kb (and the necessary number of bytes per pointer, i.e. one, two, and three bytes, depending on text size). The block addressing index assumes that we use 256 or 64K blocks (one or two bytes per pointer) independently of the text size. The space taken by the pointers can be significantly reduced by using compression. We assume that 45% of all the words are stopwords, and that there is one non-stopword each 11.5 characters. Our estimation for the vocabulary is based on Heaps' law with parameters $V = 30n^{0.5}$. All these decisions were taken according to our experience and experimentally validated.

The blocks can be of fixed size (imposing a logical block structure over the text database) or they can be defined using the natural division of the text collection into files, documents, Web pages, or others. The division into blocks of fixed size improves efficiency at retrieval time, i.e. the more variance in the block sizes, the more amount of text sequentially traversed on average. This is because larger blocks match queries more frequently and are more expensive to traverse.

Alternatively, the division using natural cuts may eliminate the need for online traversal. For example, if one block per retrieval unit is used and the exact match positions are not required, there is no need to traverse the text for single-word queries, since it is enough to know which retrieval units to report. But if, on the other hand, many retrieval units are packed into a single block, the block has to be traversed to determine which units to retrieve.

It is important to notice that in order to use block addressing, the text must be readily available at search time. This is not the case for remote text (as in Web search engines), or if the text is in a CD-ROM that has to be mounted, for instance. Some restricted queries not needing exact positions can still be solved if the blocks are retrieval units.

Index	Small collection (1 Mb)		Medium collection (200 Mb)		Large collection (2 Gb)	
Addressing words	45%	73%	36%	64%	35%	63%
Addressing documents	19%	26%	18%	32%	26%	47%
Addressing 64K blocks	27%	41%	18%	32%	5%	9%
Addressing 256 blocks	18%	25%	1.7%	2.4%	0.5%	0.7%

Table 8.1   Sizes of an inverted file as approximate percentages of the size the whole text collection. Four granularities and three collections are considered. For each collection, the right column considers that stopwords are not indexed while the left column considers that all words are indexed.

8.2.1   Searching

The search algorithm on an inverted index follows three general steps (some may be absent for specific queries):

- **Vocabulary search** The words and patterns present in the query are isolated and searched in the vocabulary. Notice that phrases and proximity queries are split into single words.
- **Retrieval of occurrences** The lists of the occurrences of all the words found are retrieved.
- **Manipulation of occurrences** The occurrences are processed to solve phrases, proximity, or Boolean operations. If block addressing is used it may be necessary to directly search the text to find the information missing from the occurrences (e.g., exact word positions to form phrases).

Hence, searching on an inverted index always starts in the vocabulary. Because of this it is a good idea to have it in a separate file. It is possible that this file fits in main memory even for large text collections.

Single-word queries can be searched using any suitable data structure to speed up the search, such as hashing, tries, or B-trees. The first two give $O(m)$ search cost (independent of the text size). However, simply storing the words in lexicographical order is cheaper in space and very competitive in performance, since the word can be binary searched at $O(\log n)$ cost. Prefix and range queries can also be solved with binary search, tries, or B-trees, but not with hashing. If the query is formed by single words, then the process ends by delivering the list of occurrences (we may need to make a union of many lists if the pattern matches many words).

Context queries are more difficult to solve with inverted indices. Each element must be searched separately and a list (in increasing positional order) generated for each one. Then, the lists of all elements are traversed in synchronization to find places where all the words appear in sequence (for a phrase) or appear close enough (for proximity). If one list is much shorter than the others, it may be better to binary search its elements into the longer lists instead of performing a linear merge. It is possible to prove using Zipf's law that this is normally the case. This is important because the most time-demanding operation on inverted indices is the merging or intersection of the lists of occurrences.

If the index stores character positions the phrase query cannot allow the separators to be disregarded, and the proximity has to be defined in terms of character distance.

Finally, note that if block addressing is used it is necessary to traverse the blocks for these queries, since the position information is needed. It is then better to intersect the lists to obtain the blocks which contain all the searched words and then sequentially search the context query in those blocks as explained in section 8.5. Some care has to be exercised at block boundaries, since they can split a match. This part of the search, if present, is also quite time consuming.

Using Heaps' and the generalized Zipf's laws, it has been demonstrated that the cost of solving queries is sublinear in the text size, even for complex queries involving list merging. The time complexity is $O(n^\alpha)$, where α depends on the query and is close to 0.4..0.8 for queries with reasonable selectivity.

Even if block addressing is used and the blocks have to be traversed, it is possible to select the block size as an increasing function of n, so that not only does the space requirement keep sublinear but also the amount of text traversed in all useful queries is also sublinear.

Practical figures show, for instance, that both the space requirement and the amount of text traversed can be close to $O(n^{0.85})$. Hence, inverted indices allow us to have sublinear search time at sublinear space requirements. This is not possible on the other indices.

Search times on our reference machine for a full inverted index built on 250 Mb of text give the following results: searching a simple word took 0.08 seconds, while searching a phrase took 0.25 to 0.35 seconds (from two to five words).

8.2.2   Construction

Building and maintaining an inverted index is a relatively low cost task. In principle, an inverted index on a text of n characters can be built in $O(n)$ time. All the vocabulary known up to now is kept in a trie data structure, storing for each word a list of its occurrences (text positions). Each word of the text is read and searched in the trie. If it is not found, it is added to the trie with an empty list of occurrences. Once it is in the trie, the new position is added to the end of its list of occurrences. Figure 8.3 illustrates this process.

Once the text is exhausted, the trie is written to disk together with the list of occurrences. It is good practice to split the index into two files. In the

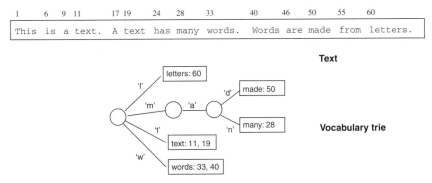

Figure 8.3 Building an inverted index for the sample text.

first file, the lists of occurrences are stored contiguously. In this scheme, the file
is typically called a 'posting file'. In the second file, the vocabulary is stored in
lexicographical order and, for each word, a pointer to its list in the first file is
also included. This allows the vocabulary to be kept in memory at search time
in many cases. Further, the number of occurrences of a word can be immediately
known from the vocabulary with little or no space overhead.

We analyze now the construction time under this scheme. Since in the
trie $O(1)$ operations are performed per text character, and the positions can be
inserted at the end of the lists of occurrences in $O(1)$ time, the overall process
is $O(n)$ worst-case time.

However, the above algorithm is not practical for large texts where the
index does not fit in main memory. A paging mechanism will severely degrade
the performance of the algorithm. We describe an alternative which is faster in
practice.

The algorithm already described is used until the main memory is exhausted (if the trie takes up too much space it can be replaced by a hash table
or other structure). When no more memory is available, the *partial* index I_i
obtained up to now is written to disk and erased from main memory before
continuing with the rest of the text.

Finally, a number of partial indices I_i exist on disk. These indices are then
merged in a hierarchical fashion. Indices I_1 and I_2 are merged to obtain the
index $I_{1..2}$; I_3 and I_4 produce $I_{3..4}$; and so on. The resulting partial indices are
now approximately twice the size. When all the indices at this level have been
merged in this way, the merging proceeds at the next level, joining the index
$I_{1..2}$ with the index $I_{3..4}$ to form $I_{1..4}$. This is continued until there is just one
index comprising the whole text, as illustrated in Figure 8.4.

Merging two indices consists of merging the sorted vocabularies, and whenever the same word appears in both indices, merging both lists of occurrences.
By construction, the occurrences of the smaller-numbered index are before those
of the larger-numbered index, and therefore the lists are just concatenated. This
is a very fast process in practice, and its complexity is $O(n_1 + n_2)$, where n_1 and
n_2 are the sizes of the indices.

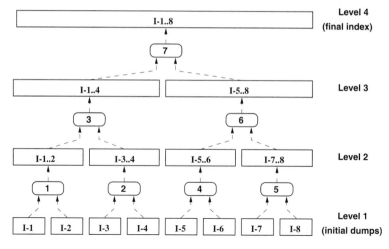

Figure 8.4 Merging the partial indices in a binary fashion. Rectangles represent partial indices, while rounded rectangles represent merging operations. The numbers inside the merging operations show a possible merging order.

The total time to generate the partial indices is $O(n)$ as before. The number of partial indices is $O(n/M)$. Each level of merging performs a linear process over the whole index (no matter how it is split into partial indices at this level) and thus its cost is $O(n)$. To merge the $O(n/M)$ partial indices, $\log_2(n/M)$ merging levels are necessary, and therefore the cost of this algorithm is $O(n\log(n/M))$.

More than two indices can be merged at once. Although this does not change the complexity, it improves efficiency since fewer merging levels exist. On the other hand, the memory buffers for each partial index to merge will be smaller and hence more disk seeks will be performed. In practice it is a good idea to merge even 20 partial indices at once.

Real times to build inverted indices on the reference machine are between 4-8 Mb/min for collections of up to 1 Gb (the slowdown factor as the text grows is barely noticeable). Of this time, 20-30% is spent on merging the partial indices.

To reduce build-time space requirements, it is possible to perform the merging in-place. That is, when two or more indices are merged, write the result in the same disk blocks of the original indices instead of on a new file. It is also a good idea to perform the hierarchical merging as soon as the files are generated (e.g., collapse I_1 and I_2 into $I_{1..2}$ as soon as I_2 is produced). This also reduces space requirements because the vocabularies are merged and redundant words are eliminated (there is no redundancy in the occurrences). The vocabulary can be a significative part of the smaller partial indices, since they represent a small text.

This algorithm changes very little if block addressing is used. Index maintenance is also cheap. Assume that a new text of size n' is added to the database. The inverted index for the new text is built and then both indices are merged as is done for partial indices. This takes $O(n + n' \log(n'/M))$. Deleting text can be done by an $O(n)$ pass over the index eliminating the occurrences that point inside eliminated text areas (and eliminating words if their lists of occurrences disappear in the process).

8.3   Other Indices for Text

8.3.1   Suffix Trees and Suffix Arrays

Inverted indices assume that the text can be seen as a sequence of words. This restricts somewhat the kinds of queries that can be answered. Other queries such as phrases are expensive to solve. Moreover, the concept of word does not exist in some applications such as genetic databases.

In this section we present suffix arrays. Suffix arrays are a space efficient implementation of suffix trees. This type of index allows us to answer efficiently more complex queries. Its main drawbacks are its costly construction process, that the text must be readily available at query time, and that the results are not delivered in text position order. This structure can be used to index only words (without stopwords) as the inverted index as well as to index any text character. This makes it suitable for a wider spectrum of applications, such as genetic databases. However, for word-based applications, inverted files perform better unless complex queries are an important issue.

This index sees the text as one long string. Each position in the text is considered as a text *suffix* (i.e., a string that goes from that text position to the end of the text). It is not difficult to see that two suffixes starting at different positions are lexicographically different (assume that a character smaller than all the rest is placed at the end of the text). Each suffix is thus uniquely identified by its position.

Not all text positions need to be indexed. *Index points* are selected from the text, which point to the *beginning* of the text positions which will be retrievable. For instance, it is possible to index only word beginnings to have a functionality similar to inverted indices. Those elements which are not index points are not retrievable (as in an inverted index it is not possible to retrieve the middle of a word). Figure 8.5 illustrates this.

Structure

In essence, a suffix tree is a trie data structure built over all the suffixes of the text. The pointers to the suffixes are stored at the leaf nodes. To improve space utilization, this trie is compacted into a Patricia tree.   This involves compressing unary paths, i.e. paths where each node has just one child. An indication of the next character position to consider is stored at the nodes which root a compressed path. Once unary paths are not present the tree has $O(n)$ nodes instead of the worst-case $O(n^2)$ of the trie (see Figure 8.6).

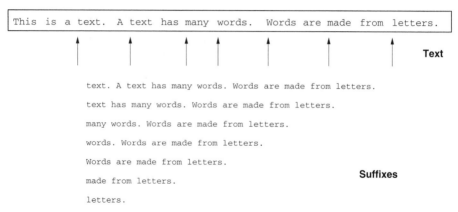

Figure 8.5 The sample text with the index points of interest marked. Below, the suffixes corresponding to those index points.

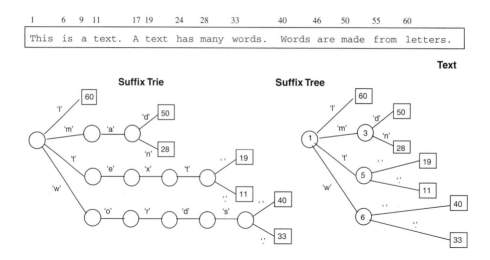

Figure 8.6 The suffix trie and suffix tree for the sample text.

The problem with this structure is its space. Depending on the implementation, each node of the trie takes 12 to 24 bytes, and therefore even if only word beginnings are indexed, a space overhead of 120% to 240% over the text size is produced.

Suffix arrays provide essentially the same functionality as suffix trees with much less space requirements. If the leaves of the suffix tree are traversed in left-to-right order (top to bottom in our figures), all the suffixes of the text are retrieved in lexicographical order. A suffix array is simply an array containing all the pointers to the text suffixes listed in lexicographical order, as shown in Figure 8.7. Since they store one pointer per indexed suffix, the space requirements

Figure 8.7 The suffix array for the sample text.

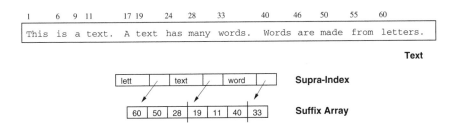

Figure 8.8 A supra-index over our suffix array. One out of three entries are sampled, keeping their first four characters. The pointers (arrows) are in fact unnecessary.

are almost the same as those for inverted indices (disregarding compression techniques), i.e. close to 40% overhead over the text size.

Suffix arrays are designed to allow binary searches done by comparing the contents of each pointer. If the suffix array is large (the usual case), this binary search can perform poorly because of the number of random disk accesses. To remedy this situation, the use of *supra-indices* over the suffix array has been proposed. The simplest supra-index is no more than a sampling of one out of b suffix array entries, where for each sample the first ℓ suffix characters are stored in the supra-index. This supra-index is then used as a first step of the search to reduce external accesses. Figure 8.8 shows an example.

This supra-index does not in fact need to take samples at fixed intervals, nor to take samples of the same length. For word-indexing suffix arrays it has been suggested that a new sample could be taken each time the first word of the suffix changes, and to store the word instead of ℓ characters. This is exactly the same as having a vocabulary of the text plus pointers to the array. In fact, the only important difference between this structure and an inverted index is that the occurrences of each word in an inverted index are sorted by text position, while in a suffix array they are sorted lexicographically by the text following the word. Figure 8.9 illustrates this relationship.

The extra space requirements of supra-indices are modest. In particular, it is clear that the space requirements of the suffix array with a vocabulary supra-index are exactly the same as for inverted indices (except for compression, as we see later).

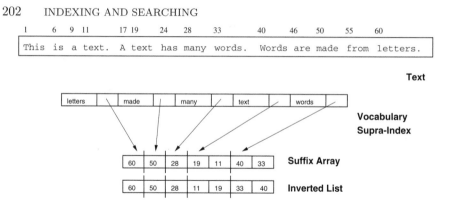

Figure 8.9   Relationship between our inverted list and suffix array with vocabulary supra-index.

Searching

If a suffix tree on the text can be afforded, many basic patterns such as words, prefixes, and phrases can be searched in $O(m)$ time by a simple trie search. However, suffix trees are not practical for large texts, as explained. Suffix arrays, on the other hand, can perform the same search operations in $O(\log n)$ time by doing a binary search instead of a trie search.

This is achieved as follows: the search pattern originates two 'limiting patterns' P_1 and P_2, so that we want any suffix S such that $P_1 \leq S < P_2$. We binary search both limiting patterns in the suffix array. Then, all the elements lying between both positions point to exactly those suffixes that start like the original pattern (i.e., to the pattern positions in the text). For instance, in our example of figure 8.9, in order to find the word 'text' we search for 'text' and 'texu', obtaining the portion of the array that contains the pointers 19 and 11.

All these queries retrieve a subtree of the suffix tree or an interval of the suffix array. The results have to be collected later, which may imply sorting them in ascending text order. This is a complication of suffix trees or arrays with respect to inverted indices.

Simple phrase searching is a good case for these indices. A simple phrase of words can be searched as if it was a simple pattern. This is because the suffix tree/array sorts with respect to the complete suffixes and not only their first word. A proximity search, on the other hand, has to be solved element-wise. The matches for each element must be collected and sorted and then they have to be intersected as for inverted files.

The binary search performed on suffix arrays, unfortunately, is done on disk, where the accesses to (random) text positions force a seek operation which spans the disk tracks containing the text. Since a random seek is $O(n)$ in size, this makes the search cost $O(n \log n)$ time. Supra-indices are used as a first step in any binary search operation to alleviate this problem. To avoid performing $O(\log n)$ random accesses to the text on disk (and to the suffix array on disk), the search starts in the supra-index, which usually fits in main memory (text samples included). After this search is completed, the suffix array block which is between the two selected samples is brought into memory and the binary search is completed (performing random accesses to the text on disk). This reduces disk search times to close to 25% of the original time. Modified binary search techniques that sacrifice the exact partition in the middle of the array taking into account the current disk head position allow a further reduction from 40% to 60%.

Search times in a 250 Mb text in our reference machine are close to 1 second for a simple word or phrase, while the part corresponding to the accesses to the text sums up 0.6 seconds. The use of supra-indices should put the total time close to 0.3 seconds. Note that the times, although high for simple words, do not degrade for long phrases as with inverted indices.

Construction in Main Memory

A suffix tree for a text of n characters can be built in $O(n)$ time. The algorithm, however, performs poorly if the suffix tree does not fit in main memory, which is especially stringent because of the large space requirements of the suffix trees. We do not cover the linear algorithm here because it is quite complex and only of theoretical interest.

We concentrate on direct suffix array construction. Since the suffix array is no more than the set of pointers lexicographically sorted, the pointers are collected in ascending text order and then just sorted by the text they point to. Note that in order to compare two suffix array entries the corresponding text positions must be accessed. These accesses are basically random. Hence, both the suffix array and the text must be in main memory. This algorithm costs $O(n \log n)$ string comparisons.

An algorithm to build the suffix array in $O(n \log n)$ character comparisons follows. All the suffixes are bucket-sorted in $O(n)$ time according to the first letter only. Then, each bucket is bucket-sorted again, now according to their first two letters. At iteration i, the suffixes begin already sorted by their 2^{i-1} first letters and end up sorted by their first 2^i letters. As at each iteration the total cost of all the bucket sorts is $O(n)$, the total time is $O(n \log n)$, and the average is $O(n \log \log n)$ (since $O(\log n)$ comparisons are necessary on average to distinguish two suffixes of a text). This algorithm accesses the text only in the first stage (bucket sort for the first letter).

In order to sort the strings in the i-th iteration, notice that since *all* suffixes are sorted by their first 2^{i-1} letters, to sort the text positions $T_{a...}$ and $T_{b...}$ in the suffix array (assuming that they are in the same bucket, i.e., they share their first 2^{i-1} letters), it is enough to determine the relative order between text positions $T_{a+2^{i-1}}$ and $T_{b+2^{i-1}}$ in the current stage of the search. This can be done in constant time by storing the reverse permutation. We do not enter here into further detail.

Construction of Suffix Arrays for Large Texts

There is still the problem that large text databases will not fit in main memory. It could be possible to apply an external memory sorting algorithm. However, each comparison involves accessing the text at random positions on the disk. This will severely degrade the performance of the sorting process.

We explain an algorithm especially designed for large texts. Split the text into blocks that can be sorted in main memory. Then, for each block, build its suffix array in main memory and merge it with the rest of the array already built for the previous text. That is:

- build the suffix array for the first block,

- build the suffix array for the second block,

- merge both suffix arrays,

- build the suffix array for the third block,

- merge the new suffix array with the previous one,

- build the suffix array for the fourth block,

- merge the new suffix array with the previous one,

- ... and so on.

The difficult part is how to merge a large suffix array (already built) with the small suffix array (just built). The merge needs to compare text positions which are spread in a large text, so the problem persists. The solution is to first determine how many elements of the large array are to be placed between each pair of elements in the small array, and later use that information to merge the arrays without accessing the text. Hence, the information that we need is how many suffixes of the large text lie between each pair of positions of the small suffix array. We compute counters that store this information.

The counters are computed without using the large suffix array. The text corresponding to the large array is sequentially read into main memory. Each suffix of that text is *searched* in the small suffix array (in main memory). Once we find the inter-element position where the suffix lies, we just increment the appropriate counter. Figure 8.10 illustrates this process.

We analyze this algorithm now. If there is $O(M)$ main memory to index, then there will be $O(n/M)$ text blocks. Each block is merged against an array of size $O(n)$, where all the $O(n)$ suffixes of the large text are binary searched in the small suffix array. This gives a total CPU complexity of $O(n^2 \log(M)/M)$.

Notice that this same algorithm can be used for index maintenance. If a new text of size n' is added to the database, it can be split into blocks as before and merged block-wise into the current suffix array. This will take $O(nn' \log(M)/M)$. To delete some text it suffices to perform an $O(n)$ pass over the array eliminating all the text positions which lie in the deleted areas.

As can be seen, the construction process is in practice more costly for suffix arrays than for inverted files. The construction of the supra-index consists of a fast final sequential pass over the suffix array.

Indexing times for 250 Mb of text are close to 0.8 Mb/min on the reference machine. This is five to ten times slower than the construction of inverted indices.

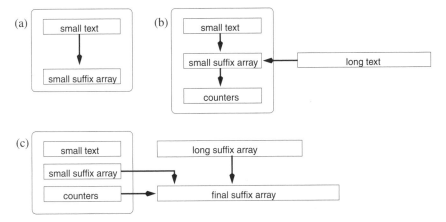

Figure 8.10   A step of the suffix array construction for large texts: (*a*) the local suffix array is built, (*b*) the counters are computed, (*c*) the suffix arrays are merged.

8.3.2   Signature Files

Signature files are word-oriented index structures based on hashing. They pose a low overhead (10% to 20% over the text size), at the cost of forcing a sequential search over the index. However, although their search complexity is linear (instead of sublinear as with the previous approaches), its constant is rather low, which makes the technique suitable for not very large texts. Nevertheless, inverted files outperform signature files for most applications.

Structure

A signature file uses a hash function (or 'signature') that maps words to bit masks of B bits. It divides the text in blocks of b words each. To each text block of size b, a bit mask of size B will be assigned. This mask is obtained by bitwise ORing the signatures of all the words in the text block. Hence, the signature file is no more than the sequence of bit masks of all blocks (plus a pointer to each block). The main idea is that if a word is present in a text block, then all the bits set in its signature are also set in the bit mask of the text block. Hence, whenever a bit is set in the mask of the query word and not in the mask of the text block, then the word is not present in the text block. Figure 8.11 shows an example.

However, it is possible that all the corresponding bits are set even though the word is not there. This is called a *false drop*. The most delicate part of the design of a signature file is to ensure that the probability of a false drop is low enough while keeping the signature file as short as possible.

The hash function is forced to deliver bit masks which have at least ℓ bits set. A good model assumes that ℓ bits are randomly set in the mask (with possible repetition). Let $\alpha = \ell/B$. Since each of the b words sets ℓ bits at

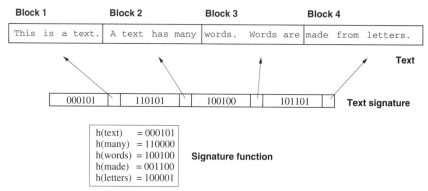

Figure 8.11 A signature file for our sample text cut into blocks.

random, the probability that a given bit of the mask is set in a word signature is $1 - (1 - 1/B)^{b\ell} \approx 1 - e^{-b\alpha}$. Hence, the probability that the ℓ random bits set in the query are also set in the mask of the text block is

$$(1 - e^{-b\alpha})^{\alpha B}$$

which is minimized for $\alpha = \ln(2)/b$. The false drop probability under the optimal selection $\ell = B \ln(2)/b$ is $(1/2^{\ln(2)})^{B/b} = 1/2^{\ell}$.

Hence, a reasonable proportion B/b must be determined. The space overhead of the index is approximately $(1/80) \times (B/b)$ because B is measured in bits and b in words. Then, the false drop probability is a function of the overhead to pay. For instance, a 10% overhead implies a false drop probability close to 2%, while a 20% overhead errs with probability 0.046%. This error probability corresponds to the expected amount of sequential searching to perform while checking if a match is a false drop or not.

Searching

Searching a single word is carried out by hashing it to a bit mask W, and then comparing the bit masks B_i of all the text blocks. Whenever $(W \& B_i = W)$, where & is the bitwise AND, all the bits set in W are also set in B_i and therefore the text block *may* contain the word. Hence, for all candidate text blocks, an online traversal must be performed to verify if the word is actually there. This traversal cannot be avoided as in inverted files (except if the risk of a false drop is accepted).

No other types of patterns can be searched in this scheme. On the other hand, the scheme is more efficient to search phrases and reasonable proximity queries. This is because *all* the words must be present in a block in order for that block to hold the phrase or the proximity query. Hence, the bitwise OR of all the query masks is searched, so that *all* their bits must be present. This reduces the probability of false drops. This is the only indexing scheme which improves in phrase searching.

Some care has to be exercised at block boundaries, however, to avoid missing a phrase which crosses a block limit. To allow searching phrases of j words or proximities of up to j words, consecutive blocks must overlap in j words.

If the blocks correspond to retrieval units, simple Boolean conjunctions involving words or phrases can also be improved by forcing all the relevant words to be in the block.

We were only able to find real performance estimates from 1992, run on a Sun 3/50 with local disk. Queries on a small 2.8 Mb database took 0.42 seconds. Extrapolating to today's technology, we find that the performance should be close to 20 Mb/sec (recall that it is linear time), and hence the example of 250 Mb of text would take 12 seconds, which is quite slow.

Construction

The construction of a signature file is rather easy. The text is simply cut in blocks, and for each block an entry of the signature file is generated. This entry is the bitwise OR of the signatures of all the words in the block.

Adding text is also easy, since it is only necessary to keep adding records to the signature file. Text deletion is carried out by deleting the appropriate bit masks.

Other storage proposals exist apart from storing all the bit masks in sequence. For instance, it is possible to make a different file for each bit of the mask, i.e. one file holding all the first bits, another file for all the second bits, etc. This reduces the disk times to search for a query, since only the files corresponding to the ℓ bits which are set in the query have to be traversed.

8.4   Boolean Queries

We now cover set manipulation algorithms. These algorithms are used when operating on sets of results, which is the case in Boolean queries. Boolean queries are described in Chapter 4, where the concept of *query syntax tree* is defined.

Once the leaves of the query syntax tree are solved (using the algorithms to find the documents containing the basic queries given), the relevant documents must be worked on by composition operators. Normally the search proceeds in three phases: the first phase determines which documents classify, the second determines the relevance of the classifying documents so as to present them appropriately to the user, and the final phase retrieves the exact positions of the matches to highlight them in those documents that the user actually wants to see.

This scheme avoids doing unnecessary work on documents which will not classify at last (first phase), or will not be read at last (second phase). However, some phases can be merged if doing the extra operations is not expensive. Some phases may not be present at all in some scenarios.

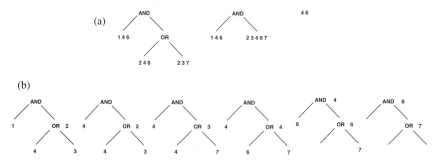

Figure 8.12 Processing the internal nodes of the query syntax tree. In (a) full evaluation is used. In (b) we show lazy evaluation in more detail.

Once the leaves of the query syntax tree find the classifying sets of documents, these sets are further operated by the internal nodes of the tree. It is possible to algebraically optimize the tree using identities such as $a\ OR\ (a\ AND\ b) = a$, for instance, or sharing common subexpressions, but we do not cover this issue here.

As all operations need to pair the same document in both their operands, it is good practice to keep the sets sorted, so that operations like intersection, union, etc. can proceed sequentially on both lists and also generate a sorted list. Other representations for sets not consisting of the list of matching documents (such as bit vectors) are also possible.

Under this scheme, it is possible to evaluate the syntax tree in *full* or *lazy* form. In the full evaluation form, both operands are first completely obtained and then the complete result is generated. In lazy evaluation, results are delivered only when required, and to obtain that result some data is recursively required to both operands.

Full evaluation allows some optimizations to be performed because the sizes of the results are known in advance (for instance, merging a very short list against a very long one can proceed by binary searching the elements of the short list in the long one). Lazy evaluation, on the other hand, allows the application to control when to do the work of obtaining new results, instead of blocking it for a long time. Hybrid schemes are possible, for example obtain all the leaves at once and then proceed in lazy form. This may be useful, for instance, to implement some optimizations or to ensure that all the accesses to the index are sequential (thus reducing disk seek times). Figure 8.12 illustrates this.

The complexity of solving these types of queries, apart from the cost of obtaining the results at the leaves, is normally linear in the total size of all the intermediate results. This is why this time may dominate the others, when there are huge intermediate results. This is more noticeable to the user when the final result is small.

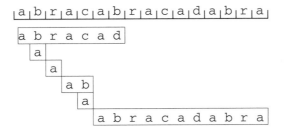

Figure 8.13 Brute-force search algorithm for the pattern 'abracadabra.' Squared areas show the comparisons performed.

8.5   Sequential Searching

We now cover the algorithms for text searching when no data structure has been built on the text. As shown, this is a basic part of some indexing techniques as well as the only option in some cases. We cover exact string matching in this section. Later we cover matching of more complex patterns. Our exposition is mainly conceptual and the implementation details are not shown (see the Bibliographic Discussion at the end of this chapter for more information).

The problem of exact string matching is: given a short pattern P of length m and a long text T of length n, find all the text positions where the pattern occurs. With minimal changes this problem subsumes many basic queries, such as word, prefix, suffix, and substring search.

This is a classical problem for which a wealth of solutions exists. We sketch the main algorithms, and leave aside a lot of the theoretical work that is not competitive in practice. For example, we do not include the Karp-Rabin algorithm, which is a nice application of hashing to string searching, but is not practical. We also briefly cover multipattern algorithms (that search many patterns at once), since a query may have many patterns and it may be more efficient to retrieve them all at once. Finally, we also mention how to do phrases and proximity searches.

We assume that the text and the pattern are sequences of characters drawn from an alphabet of size σ, whose first character is at position 1. The average-case analysis assumes random text and patterns.

8.5.1   Brute Force

The brute-force (BF) algorithm is the simplest possible one. It consists of merely trying all possible pattern positions in the text. For each such position, it verifies whether the pattern matches at that position. See Figure 8.13.

Since there are $O(n)$ text positions and each one is examined at $O(m)$ worst-case cost, the worst-case of brute-force searching is $O(mn)$. However, its average case is $O(n)$ (since on random text a mismatch is found after $O(1)$ comparisons on average). This algorithm does not need any pattern preprocessing.

Many algorithms use a modification of this scheme. There is a *window* of length m which is slid over the text. It is *checked* whether the text in the window is equal to the pattern (if it is, the window position is reported as a match). Then, the window is *shifted* forward. The algorithms mainly differ in the way they check and shift the window.

8.5.2   Knuth-Morris-Pratt

The KMP algorithm was the first with linear worst-case behavior, although on average it is not much faster than BF. This algorithm also slides a window over the text. However, it does not try all window positions as BF does. Instead, it reuses information from previous checks.

After the window is checked, whether it matched the pattern or not, a number of pattern letters were compared to the text window, and they all matched except possibly the last one compared. Hence, when the window has to be shifted, there is a *prefix* of the pattern that matched the text. The algorithm takes advantage of this information to avoid trying window positions which can be deduced not to match.

The pattern is preprocessed in $O(m)$ time and space to build a table called *next*. The *next* table at position j says which is the longest proper prefix of $P_{1..j-1}$ which is also a suffix and the characters following prefix and suffix are different. Hence $j - next[j] + 1$ window positions can be safely skipped if the characters up to $j - 1$ matched, and the j-th did not. For instance, when searching the word 'abracadabra,' if a text window matched up to 'abracab,' five positions can be safely skipped since $next[7] = 1$. Figure 8.14 shows an example.

The crucial observation is that this information depends only on the pattern, because if the text in the window matched up to position $j - 1$, then that text is equal to the pattern.

The algorithm moves a window over the text and a pointer inside the window. Each time a character matches, the pointer is advanced (a match is reported if the pointer reaches the end of the window). Each time a character is not matched, the window is shifted forward in the text, to the position given by *next*, but the pointer position in the text does not change. Since at each text comparison the window or the pointer advance by at least one position, the algorithm performs at most $2n$ comparisons (and at least n).

The Aho-Corasick algorithm can be regarded as an extension of KMP in matching a set of patterns. The patterns are arranged in a trie-like data structure. Each trie node represents having matched a prefix of some pattern(s). The *next* function is replaced by a more general set of *failure* transitions. Those transitions go between nodes of the trie. A transition leaving from a node representing the prefix x leads to a node representing a prefix y, such that y is the longest prefix in the set of patterns which is also a proper suffix of x. Figure 8.15 illustrates this.

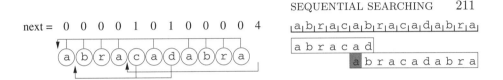

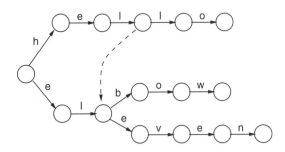

Figure 8.14   KMP algorithm searching 'abracadabra.' On the left, an illustration of the *next* function. Notice that after matching 'abracada' we do not try to match the last 'a' with the first one since what follows cannot be a 'b.' On the right, a search example. Grayed areas show the prefix information reused.

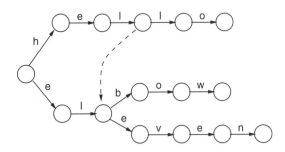

Figure 8.15   Aho-Corasick trie example for the set 'hello,' 'elbow' and 'eleven' showing only one of all the failure transitions.

This trie, together with its failure transitions, is built in $O(m)$ time and space (where m is the total length of all the patterns). Its search time is $O(n)$ no matter how many patterns are searched. Much as KMP, it makes at most $2n$ inspections.

8.5.3   Boyer-Moore Family

BM algorithms are based on the fact that the check inside the window can proceed backwards. When a match or mismatch is determined, a *suffix* of the pattern has been compared and found equal to the text in the window. This can be used in a way very similar to the *next* table of KMP, i.e. compute for every pattern position j the next-to-last occurrence of $P_{j..m}$ inside P. This is called the 'match heuristic.'

This is combined with what is called the 'occurrence heuristic.' It states that the text character that produced the mismatch (if a mismatch occurred) has to be aligned with the same character in the pattern after the shift. The heuristic which gives the longest shift is selected.

For instance, assume that 'abracadabra' is searched in a text which starts with 'abracababra.' After matching the suffix 'abra' the underlined text character 'b' will cause a mismatch. The match heuristic states that since 'abra' was matched a shift of 7 is safe. The occurrence heuristic states that since the underlined 'b' must match the pattern, a shift of 5 is safe. Hence, the pattern is

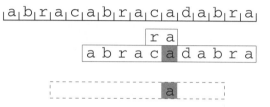

Figure 8.16 BM algorithm searching 'abracadabra.' Squared areas show the comparisons performed. Grayed areas have already been compared (but the algorithm compares them again). The dashed box shows the match heuristic, which was not chosen.

shifted by 7. See Figure 8.16.

The preprocessing time and space of this algorithm is $O(m + \sigma)$. Its search time is $O(n \log(m)/m)$ on average, which is 'sublinear' in the sense that not all characters are inspected. On the other hand, its worst case is $O(mn)$ (unlike KMP, the old suffix information is not kept to avoid further comparisons).

Further simplifications of the BM algorithm lead to some of the fastest algorithms on average. The Simplified BM algorithm uses only the occurrence heuristic. This obtains almost the same shifts in practice. The BM-Horspool (BMH) algorithm does the same, but it notices that it is not important any more that the check proceeds backwards, and uses the occurrence heuristic on the *last* character of the window instead of the one that caused the mismatch. This gives longer shifts on average. Finally, the BM-Sunday (BMS) algorithm modifies BMH by using the character *following* the last one, which improves the shift especially on short patterns.

The Commentz-Walter algorithm is an extension of BM to multipattern search. It builds a trie on the reversed patterns, and instead of a backward window check, it enters into the trie with the window characters read backwards. A shift function is computed by a natural extension of BM. In general this algorithm improves over Aho-Corasick for not too many patterns.

8.5.4 Shift-Or

Shift-Or is based on *bit-parallelism*. This technique involves taking advantage of the intrinsic parallelism of the bit operations inside a computer word (of w bits). By cleverly using this fact, the number of operations that an algorithm performs can be cut by a factor of at most w. Since in current architectures w is 32 or 64, the speedup is very significant in practice.

The Shift-Or algorithm uses bit-parallelism to simulate the operation of a non-deterministic automaton that searches the pattern in the text (see Figure 8.17). As this automaton is simulated in time $O(mn)$, the Shift-Or algorithm achieves $O(mn/w)$ worst-case time (optimal speedup).

The algorithm first builds a table B which for each character stores a bit mask $b_m...b_1$. The mask in $B[c]$ has the i-th bit set to zero if and only if

$B[a] =$	1	0	0	1	0	1	0	1	0	0	1
$B[b] =$	0	1	0	0	0	0	0	0	1	0	0
$B[r] =$	0	0	1	0	0	0	0	0	0	1	0
$B[c] =$	0	0	0	0	1	0	0	0	0	0	0
$B[d] =$	0	0	0	0	0	0	1	0	0	0	0
$B[*] =$	0	0	0	0	0	0	0	0	0	0	0

Figure 8.17   Non-deterministic automaton that searches 'abracadabra,' and the associated B table.   The initial self-loop matches any character.   Each table column corresponds to an edge of the automaton.

$p_i = c$ (see Figure 8.17).   The state of the search is kept in a machine word $D = d_m...d_1$, where d_i is zero whenever the state numbered i in Figure 8.17 is active.   Therefore, a match is reported whenever d_m is zero.   In the following, we use '|' to denote the bitwise OR and '&' to denote the bitwise AND.

D is set to all ones originally, and for each new text character T_j, D is updated using the formula

$$D' \leftarrow (D << 1) \mid B[T_j]$$

(where '$<<$' means shifting all the bits in D one position to the left and setting the rightmost bit to zero).   It is not hard to relate the formula to the movement that occurs in the non-deterministic automaton for each new text character.

For patterns longer than the computer word (i.e., $m > w$), the algorithm uses $\lceil m/w \rceil$ computer words for the simulation (not all them are active all the time).   The algorithm is $O(n)$ on average and the preprocessing is $O(m+\sigma)$ time and $O(\sigma)$ space.

It is easy to extend Shift-Or to handle classes of characters by manipulating the B table and keeping the search algorithm unchanged.

This paradigm also can search a large set of extended patterns, as well as multiple patterns (where the complexity is the same as before if we consider that m is the total length of all the patterns).

8.5.5   Suffix Automaton

The Backward DAWG matching   (BDM) algorithm is based on a suffix automaton.   A *suffix automaton*   on a pattern P is an automaton that recognizes all the suffixes of P.   The non-deterministic version of this automaton has a very regular structure and is shown in Figure 8.18.

The BDM algorithm converts this automaton to deterministic.   The size and construction time of this automaton is $O(m)$.   This is basically the preprocessing effort of the algorithm.   Each path from the initial node to any internal

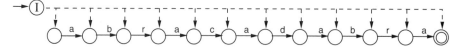

Figure 8.18 A non-deterministic suffix automaton.   Dashed lines represent ε-transitions (i.e., they occur without consuming any input). I is the initial state of the automaton.

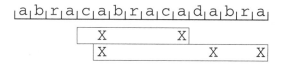

Figure 8.19 The BDM algorithm for the pattern 'abracadabra.' The rectangles represent elements compared to the text window. The Xs show the positions where a pattern prefix was recognized.

node represents a substring of the pattern. The final nodes represent pattern suffixes.

To search a pattern P, the suffix automaton of P^r (the reversed pattern) is built. The algorithm searches backwards inside the text window for a substring of the pattern P using the suffix automaton. Each time a terminal state is reached before hitting the beginning of the window, the position inside the window is remembered. This corresponds to finding a *prefix* of the pattern equal to a suffix of the window (since the reverse suffixes of P^r are the prefixes of P). The last prefix recognized backwards is the *longest* prefix of P in the window. A match is found if the complete window is read, while the check is abandoned when there is no transition to follow in the automaton. In either case, the window is shifted to align with the longest prefix recognized. See Figure 8.19.

This algorithm is $O(mn)$ time in the worst case and $O(n \log(m)/m)$ on average. There exists also a multipattern version of this algorithm called MultiBDM, which is the fastest for many patterns or very long patterns.

BDM rarely beats the best BM algorithms. However, a recent bit-parallel implementation called BNDM improves over BM in a wide range of cases. This algorithm simulates the non-deterministic suffix automaton using bit-parallelism. The algorithm supports some extended patterns and other applications mentioned in Shift-Or, while keeping more efficient than Shift-Or.

8.5.6 Practical Comparison

Figure 8.20 shows a practical comparison between string matching algorithms run on our reference machine. The values are correct within 5% of accuracy with a 95% confidence interval. We tested English text from the TREC collection, DNA (corresponding to 'h.influenzae') and random text uniformly generated over 64 letters. The patterns were randomly selected from the text except for random text, where they were randomly generated. We tested over 10 Mb of text and measured CPU time. We tested short patterns on English and random text and long patterns on DNA, which are the typical cases.

We first analyze the case of random text, where except for very short patterns the clear winners are BNDM (the bit-parallel implementation of BDM) and the BMS (Sunday) algorithm. The more classical Boyer-Moore and BDM algorithms are also very close. Among the algorithms that do not improve with the pattern length, Shift-Or is the fastest, and KMP is much slower than the naive algorithm.

The picture is similar for English text, except that we have included the Agrep software in this comparison, which worked well only on English text. Agrep turns out to be much faster than others. This is not because of using a special algorithm (it uses a BM-family algorithm) but because the code is carefully optimized. This shows the importance of careful coding as well as using good algorithms, especially in text searching where a few operations per text character are performed.

Longer patterns are shown for a DNA text. BNDM is the fastest for moderate patterns, but since it does not improve with the length after $m > w$, the classical BDM finally obtains better times. They are much better than the Boyer-Moore family because the alphabet is small and the suffix automaton technique makes better use of the information on the pattern.

We have not shown the case of extended patterns, that is, where flexibility plays a role. For this case, BNDM is normally the fastest when it can be applied (e.g., it supports classes of characters but not wild cards), otherwise Shift-Or is the best option. Shift-Or is also the best option when the text must be accessed sequentially and it is not possible to skip characters.

8.5.7   Phrases and Proximity

If a sequence of words is searched to appear in the text exactly as in the pattern (i.e., with the same separators) the problem is similar to that of exact search of a single pattern, by just forgetting the fact that there are many words. If any separator between words is to be allowed, it is possible to arrange it using an extended pattern or regular expression search.

The best way to search a phrase element-wise is to search for the element which is less frequent or can be searched faster (both criteria normally match). For instance, longer patterns are better than shorter ones; allowing fewer errors is better than allowing more errors. Once such an element is found, the neighboring words are checked to see if a complete match is found.

A similar algorithm can be used to search a proximity query.

8.6   Pattern Matching

We present in this section the main techniques to deal with complex patterns. We divide it into two main groups: searching allowing errors and searching for extended patterns.

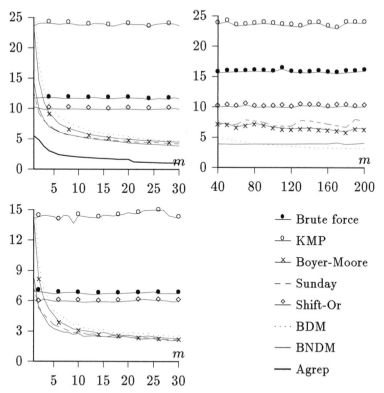

Figure 8.20 Practical comparison among algorithms. The upper left plot is for short patterns on English text. The upper right one is for long patterns on DNA. The lower plot is for short patterns on random text (on 64 letters). Times are in tenths of seconds per megabyte.

8.6.1   String Matching Allowing Errors

This problem (called 'approximate string matching') can be stated as follows: given a short pattern P of length m, a long text T of length n, and a maximum allowed number of errors k, find all the text positions where the pattern occurs with at most k errors. This statement corresponds to the Levenshtein distance. With minimal modifications it is adapted to searching whole words matching the pattern with k errors.

This problem is newer than exact string matching, although there are already a number of solutions. We sketch the main approaches.

Dynamic Programming

The classical solution to approximate string matching is based on dynamic programming. A matrix $C[0..m, 0..n]$ is filled column by column, where $C[i, j]$

represents the minimum number of errors needed to match $P_{1..i}$ to a suffix of $T_{1..j}$. This is computed as follows

$$
\begin{aligned}
C[0,j] &= 0 \\
C[i,0] &= i \\
C[i,j] &= \text{if } (P_i = T_j) \text{ then } C[i-1,j-1] \\
&\quad \text{else } 1 + \min(C[i-1,j], C[i,j-1], C[i-1,j-1])
\end{aligned}
$$

where a match is reported at text positions j such that $C[m,j] \leq k$ (the final positions of the occurrences are reported).

Therefore, the algorithm is $O(mn)$ time. Since only the previous column of the matrix is needed, it can be implemented in $O(m)$ space. Its preprocessing time is $O(m)$. Figure 8.21 illustrates this algorithm.

In recent years several algorithms have been presented that achieve $O(kn)$ time in the worst case or even less in the average case, by taking advantage of the properties of the dynamic programming matrix (e.g., values in neighbor cells differ at most by one).

Automaton

It is interesting to note that the problem can be reduced to a non-deterministic finite automaton (NFA). Consider the NFA for $k = 2$ errors shown in Figure 8.22. Each row denotes the number of errors seen. The first one 0, the second one 1, and so on. Every column represents matching the pattern up to a given position. At each iteration, a new text character is read and the automaton changes its states. Horizontal arrows represent matching a character, vertical arrows represent insertions into the pattern, solid diagonal arrows represent replacements, and dashed diagonal arrows represent deletions in the pattern (they are ε-transitions). The automaton accepts a text position as the end of a match

		s	u	r	g	e	r	y
	0	0	0	0	0	0	0	0
s	1	0	1	1	1	1	1	1
u	2	1	0	1	2	2	2	2
r	3	2	1	0	1	2	2	3
v	4	3	2	1	1	2	3	3
e	5	4	3	2	2	1	2	3
y	6	5	4	3	3	2	2	2

Figure 8.21 The dynamic programming algorithm search 'survey' in the text 'surgery' with two errors. Bold entries indicate matching positions.

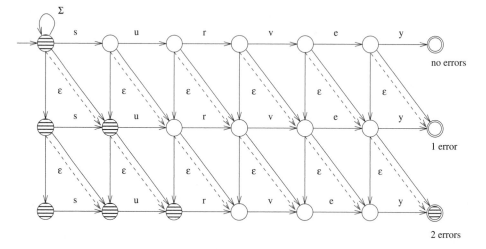

Figure 8.22   An NFA for approximate string matching of the pattern 'survey' with two errors. The shaded states are those active after reading the text 'surgery'. Unlabelled transitions match any character.

with k errors whenever the $(k+1)$-th rightmost state is active.

It is not hard to see that once a state in the automaton is active, all the states of the same column and higher rows are active too. Moreover, at a given text character, if we collect the smallest active rows at each column, we obtain the current column of the dynamic programming algorithm. Figure 8.22 illustrates this (compare the figure with Figure 8.21).

One solution is to make this automaton deterministic (DFA). Although the search phase is $O(n)$, the DFA can be huge. An alternative solution is based on bit-parallelism and is explained next.

Bit-Parallelism

Bit-parallelism has been used to parallelize the computation of the dynamic programming matrix (achieving average complexity $O(kn/w)$) and to parallelize the computation of the NFA (without converting it to deterministic), obtaining $O(kmn/w)$ time in the worst case. Such algorithms achieve $O(n)$ search time for short patterns and are currently the fastest ones in many cases, running at 6 to 10 Mb per second on our reference machine.

Filtering

Finally, other approaches first filter the text, reducing the area where dynamic programming needs to be used. These algorithms achieve 'sublinear' expected time in many cases for low error ratios (i.e., not all text characters are inspected,

$O(kn\log_\sigma(m)/m)$ is a typical figure), although the filtration is not effective for more errors. Filtration is based on the fact that some portions of the pattern must appear with no errors even in an approximate occurrence.

The fastest algorithm for low error levels is based on filtering: if the pattern is split into $k+1$ pieces, any approximate occurrence must contain at least one of the pieces with no errors, since k errors cannot alter all the $k+1$ pieces. Hence, the search begins with a multipattern exact search for the pieces and it later verifies the areas that may contain a match (using another algorithm).

8.6.2   Regular Expressions and Extended Patterns

General regular expressions are searched by building an automaton which finds all their occurrences in a text. This process first builds a non-deterministic finite automaton of size $O(m)$, where m is the length of the regular expression. The classical solution is to convert this automaton to deterministic form. A deterministic automaton can search any regular expression in $O(n)$ time. However, its size and construction time can be exponential in m, i.e. $O(m2^m)$. See Figure 8.23. Excluding preprocessing, this algorithm runs at 6 Mb/sec in the reference machine.

Recently the use of bit-parallelism has been proposed to avoid the construction of the deterministic automaton. The non-deterministic automaton is simulated instead. One bit per automaton state is used to represent whether the state is active or not. Due to the algorithm used to build the non-deterministic automaton, all the transitions move forward except for ε-transitions. The idea is that for each text character two steps are carried out. The first one moves forward, and the second one takes care of all the ε-transitions. A function E from bit masks to bit masks is precomputed so that all the corresponding bits are moved according to the ε-transitions. Since this function is very large (i.e., 2^m entries) its domain is split in many functions from 8- or 16-bit submasks to m-bit masks. This is possible because $E(B_1...B_j) = E(B_1)|...|E(B_j)$, where B_i

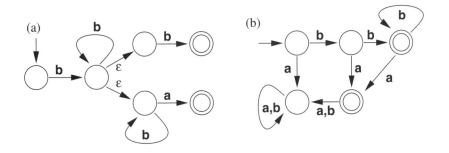

Figure 8.23   The non-deterministic (a) and deterministic (b) automata for the regular expression b b* (b | b*a).

are the submasks. Hence, the scheme performs $\lceil m/8 \rceil$ or $\lceil m/16 \rceil$ operations per text character and needs $\lceil m/8 \rceil 2^8 \lceil m/w \rceil$ or $\lceil m/16 \rceil 2^{16} \lceil m/w \rceil$ machine words of memory.

Extended patterns can be rephrased as regular expressions and solved as before. However, in many cases it is more efficient to give them a specialized solution, as we saw for the extensions of exact searching (bit-parallel algorithms). Moreover, extended patterns can be combined with approximate search for maximum flexibility. In general, the bit-parallel approach is the best equipped to deal with extended patterns.

Real times for regular expressions and extended pattern searching using this technique are between 2–8 Mb/sec.

8.6.3   Pattern Matching Using Indices

We end this section by explaining how the indexing techniques we presented for simple searching of words can in fact be extended to search for more complex patterns.

Inverted Files

As inverted files are word-oriented, other types of queries such as suffix or substring queries, searching allowing errors and regular expressions, are solved by a *sequential* (i.e., online) search over the vocabulary. This is not too bad since the size of the vocabulary is small with respect to the text size.

After either type of search, a list of vocabulary words that matched the query is obtained. All their lists of occurrences are now *merged* to retrieve a list of documents and (if required) the matching text positions. If block addressing is used and the positions are required or the blocks do not coincide with the retrieval unit, the search must be completed with a sequential search over the blocks.

Notice that an inverted index is word-oriented. Because of that it is not surprising that it is not able to efficiently find approximate matches or regular expressions that span many words. This is a restriction of this scheme. Variations that are not subject to this restriction have been proposed for languages which do not have a clear concept of word, like Finnish. They collect text *samples* or *n-grams*, which are fixed-length strings picked at regular text intervals. Searching is in general more powerful but more expensive.

In a full-inverted index, search times for simple words allowing errors on 250 Mb of text took our reference machine from 0.6 to 0.85 seconds, while very complex expressions on extended patterns took from 0.8 to 3 seconds. As a comparison, the same collection cut in blocks of 1 Mb size takes more than 8 seconds for an approximate search with one error and more than 20 for two errors.

Suffix Trees and Suffix Arrays

If the suffix tree indexes all text positions it can search for words, prefixes, suffixes and substrings with the same search algorithm and cost described for word search. However, indexing all positions makes the index 10 to 20 times the text size for suffix trees.

Range queries are easily solved too, by just searching both extremes in the trie and then collecting all the leaves which lie in the middle. In this case the cost is the height of the tree, which is $O(\log n)$ on average (excluding the tasks of collecting and sorting the leaves).

Regular expressions can be searched in the suffix tree. The algorithm simply simulates sequential searching of the regular expression. It begins at the root, since any possible match starts there too. For each child of the current node labeled by the character c, it assumes that the next text character is c and recursively enters into that subtree. This is done for each of the children of the current node. The search stops only when the automaton has no transition to follow. It has been shown that for random text only $O(n^\alpha \text{polylog}(n))$ nodes are traversed (for $0 < \alpha < 1$ dependent on the regular expression). Hence, the search time is sublinear for regular expressions *without* the restriction that they must occur inside a word. Extended patterns can be searched in the same way by taking them as regular expressions.

Unrestricted approximate string matching is also possible using the same idea. We present a simplified version here. Imagine that the search is online and traverse the tree recursively as before. Since all suffixes start at the root, any match starts at the root too, and therefore do not allow the match to start later. The search will automatically stop at depth $m + k$ at most (since at that point more than k errors have occurred). This implies constant search time if n is large enough (albeit exponential on m and k). Other problems such as approximate search of extended patterns can be solved in the same way, using the appropriate online algorithm.

Suffix trees are able to perform other complex searches that we have not considered in our query language (see Chapter 4). These are specialized operations which are useful in specific areas. Some examples are: find the longest substring in the text that appears more than once, find the most common substring of a fixed size, etc.

If a suffix array indexes all text positions, *any* algorithm that works on suffix trees at $C(n)$ cost will work on suffix arrays at $O(C(n) \log n)$ cost. This is because the operations performed on the suffix tree consist of descending to a child node, which is done in $O(1)$ time. This operation can be simulated in the suffix array in $O(\log n)$ time by binary searching the new boundaries (each suffix tree node corresponds to a string, which can be mapped to the suffix array interval holding all suffixes starting with that string). Some patterns can be searched directly in the suffix array in $O(\log n)$ total search time without simulating the suffix tree. These are: word, prefix, suffix and subword search, as well as range search.

However, again, indexing all text positions normally makes the suffix array size four times or more the text size. A different alternative for suffix arrays is to index only word beginnings and to use a vocabulary supra-index, using the same search algorithms used for the inverted lists.

8.7   Structural Queries

The algorithms to search on structured text (see Chapter 4) are largely dependent on each model. We extract their common features in this section.

A first concern about this problem is how to store the structural information. Some implementations build an ad hoc index to store the structure. This is potentially more efficient and independent of any consideration about the text. However, it requires extra development and maintenance effort.

Other techniques assume that the structure is marked in the text using 'tags' (i.e., strings that identify the structural elements). This is the case with HTML text but not the case with C code where the marks are implicit and are inherent to C. The technique relies on the same index to query content (such as inverted files), using it to index and search those tags as if they were words. In many cases this is as efficient as an ad hoc index, and its integration into an existing text database is simpler. Moreover, it is possible to define the structure dynamically, since the appropriate tags can be selected at search time. For that goal, inverted files are better since they naturally deliver the results in text order, which makes the structure information easier to obtain. On the other hand, some queries such as direct ancestry are hard to answer without an ad hoc index.

Once the content and structural elements have been found by using some index, a set of answers is generated. The models allow further operations to be applied on those answers, such as 'select all areas in the left-hand argument which contain an area of the right-hand argument.' This is in general solved in a way very similar to the set manipulation techniques already explained in section 8.4. However, the operations tend to be more complex, and it is not always possible to find an evaluation algorithm which has linear time with respect to the size of the intermediate results.

It is worth mentioning that some models use completely different algorithms, such as exhaustive search techniques for tree pattern matching. Those problems are NP-complete in many cases.

8.8   Compression

In this section we discuss the issues of searching compressed text directly and of searching compressed indices. Compression is important when available storage is a limiting factor, as is the case of indexing the Web.

Searching and compression were traditionally regarded as exclusive operations. Texts which were not to be searched could be compressed, and to search a compressed text it had to be decompressed first. In recent years, very efficient compression techniques have appeared that allow searching directly in the compressed text. Moreover, the search performance is *improved*, since the CPU times are similar but the disk times are largely reduced. This leads to a win-win situation.

Discussion on how common text and lists of numbers can be compressed has been covered in Chapter 7.

8.8.1   Sequential Searching

A few approaches to directly searching compressed text exist. One of the most successful techniques in practice relies on Huffman coding taking words as symbols. That is, consider each different text word as a symbol, count their frequencies, and generate a Huffman codefor the words. Then, compress the text by replacing each word with its code. To improve compression/decompression efficiency, the Huffman code uses an alphabet of bytes instead of bits. This scheme compresses faster and better than known commercial systems, even those based on Ziv-Lempel coding.

Since Huffman coding needs to store the codes of each symbol, this scheme has to store the whole vocabulary of the text, i.e. the list of all different text words. This is fully exploited to efficiently search complex queries. Although according to Heaps' law the vocabulary (i.e., the alphabet) grows as $O(n^\beta)$ for $0 < \beta < 1$, the generalized Zipf's law shows that the distribution is skewed enough so that the entropy remains constant (i.e., the compression ratio will not degrade as the text grows). Those laws are explained in Chapter 6.

Any single-word or pattern query is first searched in the vocabulary. Some queries can be binary searched, while others such as approximate searching or regular expression searching must traverse sequentially all the vocabulary. This vocabulary is rather small compared to the text size, thanks to Heaps' law. Notice that this process is exactly the same as the vocabulary searching performed by inverted indices, either for simple or complex pattern matching.

Once that search is complete, the list of different words that match the query is obtained. The Huffman codes of all those words are collected and they are searched in the compressed text. One alternative is to traverse byte-wise the compressed text and traverse the Huffman decoding tree in synchronization, so that each time that a leaf is reached, it is checked whether the leaf (i.e., word) was marked as 'matching' the query or not. This is illustrated in Figure 8.24. Boyer-Moore filtering can be used to speed up the search.

Solving phrases is a little more difficult. Each element is searched in the vocabulary. For each word of the vocabulary we define a bit mask. We set the i-th bit in the mask of all words which match with the i-th element of the phrase query. This is used together with the Shift-Or algorithm. The text is traversed byte-wise, and only when a leaf is reached, does the Shift-Or algorithm consider that a new text symbol has been read, whose bit mask is that of the leaf (see Figure 8.24). This algorithm is surprisingly simple and efficient.

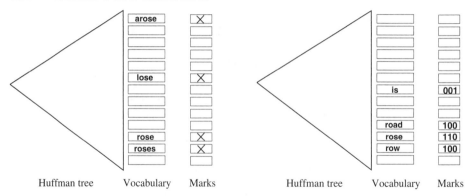

Figure 8.24   On the left, searching for the simple pattern 'rose' allowing one error. On the right, searching for the phrase 'ro* rose is,' where 'ro*' represents a prefix search.

This scheme is especially fast when it comes to solving a complex query (regular expression, extended pattern, approximate search, etc.) that would be slow with a normal algorithm. This is because the complex search is done only in the small vocabulary, after which the algorithm is largely insensitive to the complexity of the originating query. Its CPU times for a simple pattern are slightly higher than those of Agrep (briefly described in section 8.5.6). However, if the I/O times are considered, compressed searching is faster than all the online algorithms. For complex queries, this scheme is unbeaten by far.

On the reference machine, the CPU times are 14 Mb/sec for any query, while for simple queries this improves to 18 Mb/sec if the speedup technique is used. Agrep, on the other hand, runs at 15 Mb/sec on simple searches and at 1–4 Mb/sec for complex ones. Moreover, I/O times are reduced to one third on the compressed text.

8.8.2   Compressed Indices

Inverted Files

Inverted files are quite amenable to compression. This is because the lists of occurrences are in increasing order of text position. Therefore, an obvious choice is to represent the differences between the previous position and the current one. These differences can be represented using less space by using techniques that favor small numbers (see Chapter 7). Notice that, the longer the lists, the smaller the differences. Reductions in 90% for block-addressing indices with blocks of 1 Kb size have been reported.

It is important to notice that compression does not necessarily degrade time performance. Most of the time spent in answering a query is in the disk transfer. Keeping the index compressed allows the transference of less data, and it may be worth the CPU work of decompressing. Notice also that the lists of occurrences are normally traversed in a sequential manner, which is not affected by a differential compression. Query times on compressed or decompressed indices are reported to be roughly similar.

The text can also be compressed independently of the index. The text will be decompressed only to display it, or to traverse it in case of block addressing. Notice in particular that the online search technique described for compressed text in section 8.8.1 uses a vocabulary. It is possible to integrate both techniques (compression and indexing) such that they share the same vocabulary for both tasks and they do not decompress the text to index or to search.

Suffix Trees and Suffix Arrays

Some efforts to compress suffix trees have been pursued. Important reductions of the space requirements have been obtained at the cost of more expensive searching. However, the reduced space requirements happen to be similar to those of uncompressed suffix arrays, which impose much smaller performance penalties.

Suffix arrays are very hard to compress further. This is because they represent an almost perfectly random permutation of the pointers to the text.

However, the subject of building suffix arrays on compressed text has been pursued. Apart from reduced space requirements (the index plus the compressed text take less space than the uncompressed text), the main advantage is that both index construction and querying almost double their performance. Construction is faster because more compressed text fits in the same memory space, and therefore fewer text blocks are needed. Searching is faster because a large part of the search time is spent in disk seek operations over the text area to compare suffixes. If the text is smaller, the seeks reduce proportionally.

A compression technique very similar to that shown in section 8.8.1 is used. However, the Huffman code on words is replaced by a Hu-Tucker coding. The Hu-Tucker code respects the lexicographical relationships between the words, and therefore direct binary search over the compressed text is possible (this is necessary at construction and search time). This code is suboptimal by a very small percentage (2–3% in practice, with an analytical upper bound of 5%).

Indexing times for 250 Mb of text on the reference machine are close to 1.6 Mb/min if compression is used, while query times are reduced to 0.5 seconds in total and 0.3 seconds for the text alone. Supra-indices should reduce the total search time to 0.15 seconds.

Signature Files

There are many alternative ways to compress signature files. All of them are based on the fact that only a few bits are set in the whole file. It is then possible to use efficient methods to code the bits which are not set, for instance run-length encoding. Different considerations arise if the file is stored as a sequence of bit masks or with one file per bit of the mask. They allow us to reduce space and hence disk times, or alternatively to increase B (so as to reduce the false drop probability) keeping the same space overhead. Compression ratios near 70% are reported.

8.9   Trends and Research Issues

In this chapter we covered extensively the current techniques of dealing with text retrieval. We first covered indices and then online searching. We then reviewed set manipulation, complex pattern matching and finally considered compression techniques. Figure 8.25 summarizes the tradeoff between the space needed for the index and the time to search one single word.

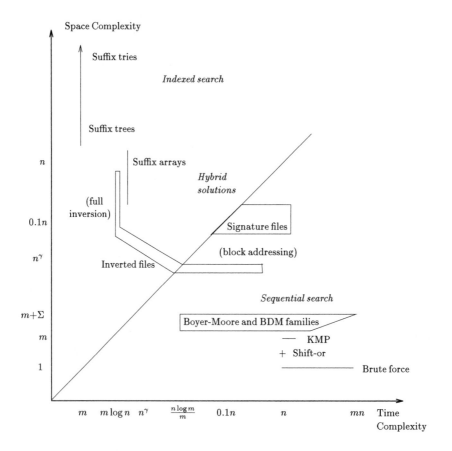

Figure 8.25   Tradeoff of index space versus word searching time.

Probably the most adequate indexing technique in practice is the inverted file. As we have shown throughout the chapter, many hidden details in other structures make them harder to use and less efficient in practice, as well as less flexible for dealing with new types of queries. These structures, however, still find application in restricted areas such as genetic databases (for suffix trees and arrays, for the relatively small texts used and their need to pose specialized queries) or some office systems (for signature files, because the text is rarely queried in fact).

The main trends in indexing and searching textual databases today are

- **Text collections are becoming huge**. This poses more demanding requirements at all levels, and solutions previously affordable are not any more. On the other hand, the speed of the processors and the relative slowness of external devices have changed what a few years ago were reasonable options (e.g., it is better to keep a text compressed because reading less text from disk and decompressing in main memory pays off).

- **Searching is becoming more complex**. As the text databases grow and become more heterogeneous and error-prone, enhanced query facilities are required, such as exploiting the text structure or allowing errors in the text. Good support for extended queries is becoming important in the evaluation of a text retrieval system.

- **Compression is becoming a star in the field**. Because of the changes mentioned in the time cost of processors and external devices, and because of new developments in the area, text retrieval and compression are no longer regarded as disjoint activities. Direct indexing and searching on compressed text provides better (sometimes much better) time performance and less space overhead at the same time. Other techniques such as block addressing trade space for processor time.

8.10 Bibliographic Discussion

A detailed explanation of a full inverted index and its construction and querying process can be found in [26]. This work also includes an analysis of the algorithms on inverted lists using the distribution of natural language. The in-place construction is described in [572]. Another construction algorithm is presented in [341].

The idea of block addressing inverted indices was first presented in a system called Glimpse [540], which also first exposed the idea of performing complex pattern matching using the vocabulary of the inverted index. Block addressing indices are analyzed in [42], where some performance improvements are proposed. The variant that indexes sequences instead of words has been implemented in a system called Grampse, which is described in [497].

Suffix arrays were presented in [538] together with the algorithm to build them in $O(n \log n)$ character comparisons. They were independently discovered by [309] under the name of 'PAT arrays.' The algorithm to build large suffix arrays is presented in [311]. The use of supra-indices over suffix array is proposed in [37], while the modified binary search techniques to reduce disk seek time are presented in [56]. The linear-time construction of suffix trees is described in [780].

The material on signature files is based on [243]. The different alternative ways of storing the signature file are explained in [242].

The original references for the sequential search algorithms are: KMP [447], BM [110], BMH [376], BMS [751], Shift-Or [39], BDM [205] and BNDM [592]. The multipattern versions are found in [9, 179], and MultiBDM in [196]. Many enhancements of bit-parallelism to support extended patterns and allow errors are presented in [837]. Many ideas from that paper were implemented in a widely distributed software for online searching called Agrep [836].

The reader interested in more details about sequential searching algorithms may look for the original references or in good books on algorithms such as [310, 196].

One source for the classical solution to approximate string matching is [716]. An $O(kn)$ worst-case algorithm is described in [480]. The use of a DFA is proposed in [781]. The bit-parallel approach to this problem started in [837], although currently the fastest bit-parallel algorithms are [583] and [43]. Among all the filtering algorithms, the fastest one in practice is based on an idea presented in [837], later enhanced in [45], and finally implemented in [43].

A good source from which to learn about regular expressions and building a DFA is [375]. The bit-parallel implementation of the NFA is explained in [837]. Regular expression searching on suffix trees is described in [40], while searching allowing errors is presented in [779].

The Huffman coding was first presented in [386], while the word-oriented alternative is proposed in [571]. Sequential searching on text compressed using that technique is described in [577]. Compression used in combination with inverted files is described in [850], with suffix trees in [430], with suffix arrays in [575], and with signature files in [243, 242]. A good general reference on compression is [78].

Chapter 9
Parallel and Distributed IR

by Eric Brown

9.1 Introduction

The volume of electronic text available online today is staggering. By many accounts, the World Wide Web alone contains over 200 million pages of text, comprising nearly 500 gigabytes of data. Moreover, the Web (see Chapter 13) has been growing at an exponential rate, nearly doubling in size every six months. Large information service providers, such as LEXIS-NEXIS (see Chapter 14), have amassed document databases that reach into the terabytes. On a slightly smaller scale, the largest corporate intranets now contain over a million Web pages. Even private collections of online documents stored on personal computers are growing larger as disk space becomes cheaper and electronic content becomes easier to produce, download, and store.

As document collections grow larger, they become more expensive to manage with an information retrieval system. Searching and indexing costs grow with the size of the underlying document collection; larger document collections invariably result in longer response times. As more documents are added to the system, performance may deteriorate to the point where the system is no longer usable. Furthermore, the economic survival of commercial systems and Web search engines depends on their ability to provide high query processing rates. In fact, most of a Web search company's gross income comes from selling 'advertising impressions' (advertising banners displayed at the user's screen) whose number is proportional to the number of query requests attended.

To support the demanding requirements of modern search environments, we must turn to alternative architectures and algorithms. In this chapter we explore parallel and distributed information retrieval techniques. The application of parallelism can greatly enhance our ability to scale traditional information retrieval algorithms and support larger and larger document collections.

We continue this introduction with a review of parallel computing and parallel program performance measures. In section 9.2 we explore techniques for implementing information retrieval algorithms on parallel platforms, including inverted file and signature file methods. In section 9.3, we turn to distributed information retrieval and approaches to collection partitioning, source selection, and distributed results merging (often called collection fusion). We discuss future trends in section 9.4, and conclude with a bibliographic discussion in section 9.5.

9.1.1   Parallel Computing

Parallel computing is the simultaneous application of multiple processors to solve a single problem, where each processor works on a different part of the problem. With parallel computing, the overall time required to solve the problem can be reduced to the amount of time required by the longest running part. As long as the problem can be further decomposed into more parts that will run in parallel, we can add more processors to the system, reduce the time required to solve the problem, and scale up to larger problems.

Processors can be combined in a variety of ways to form parallel architectures. Flynn [259] has defined a commonly used taxonomy of parallel architectures based on the number of the instruction and data streams in the architecture. The taxonomy includes four classes:

- **SISD** single instruction stream, single data stream
- **SIMD** single instruction stream, multiple data stream
- **MISD** multiple instruction stream, single data stream
- **MIMD** multiple instruction stream, multiple data stream.

The SISD class includes the traditional von Neumann [134] computer running sequential programs, e.g., uniprocessor personal computers. SIMD computers consist of N processors operating on N data streams, with each processor executing the same instruction at the same time. Machines in this class are often massively parallel computers with many relatively simple processors, a communication network between the processors, and a control unit that supervises the synchronous operation of the processors, e.g., the Thinking Machines CM-2. The processors may use shared memory, or each processor may have its own local memory. Sequential programs require significant modification to make effective use of a SIMD architecture, and not all problems lend themselves to a SIMD implementation.

MISD computers use N processors operating on a single data stream in shared memory. Each processor executes its own instruction stream, such that multiple operations are performed simultaneously on the same data item. MISD architectures are relatively rare. Systolic arrays are the best known example.

MIMD is the most general and most popular class of parallel architectures. A MIMD computer contains N processors, N instruction streams, and N data streams. The processors are similar to those used in a SISD computer; each processor has its own control unit, processing unit, and local memory.† MIMD systems usually include shared memory or a communication network that connects the processors to each other. The processors can work on separate, unrelated tasks, or they can cooperate to solve a single task, providing a great deal of flexibility. MIMD systems with a high degree of processor interaction are called *tightly coupled*, while systems with a low degree of processor interaction are *loosely coupled*. Examples of MIMD systems include multiprocessor PC servers, symmetric multiprocessors (SMPs) such as the Sun HPC Server, and scalable parallel processors such as the IBM SP2.

Although MIMD typically refers to a single, self-contained parallel computer using two or more of the same kind of processor, MIMD also characterizes *distributed computing* architectures. In distributed computing, multiple computers connected by a local or wide area network cooperate to solve a single problem. Even though the coupling between processors is very loose in a distributed computing environment, the basic components of the MIMD architecture remain. Each computer contains a processor, control unit, and local memory, and the local or wide area network forms the communication network between the processors.

The main difference between a MIMD parallel computer and a distributed computing environment is the cost of interprocessor communication, which is considerably higher in a distributed computing environment. As such, distributed programs are usually coarse grained, while programs running on a single parallel computer tend to be finer grained. Granularity refers to the amount of computation relative to the amount of communication performed by the program. Coarse-grained programs perform large amounts of computation relative to communication; fine-grained programs perform large amounts of communication relative to computation. Of course, an application may use different levels of granularity at different times to solve a given problem.

9.1.2 Performance Measures

When we employ parallel computing, we usually want to know what sort of performance improvement we are obtaining over a comparable sequential program running on a uniprocessor. A number of metrics are available to measure the performance of a parallel algorithm. One such measure is the speedup obtained with the parallel algorithm relative to the best available sequential algorithm for solving the same problem, defined as:

$$S = \frac{\text{Running time of best available sequential algorithm}}{\text{Running time of parallel algorithm}}$$

---

† The processors used in a MIMD system may be identical to those used in SISD systems, or they may provide additional functionality, such as hardware cache coherence for shared memory.

Ideally, when running a parallel algorithm on N processors, we would obtain perfect speedup, or $S = N$. In practice, perfect speedup is unattainable either because the problem cannot be decomposed into N equal subtasks, the parallel architecture imposes control overheads (e.g., scheduling or synchronization), or the problem contains an inherently sequential component. Amdahl's law [18] states that the maximal speedup obtainable for a given problem is related to f, the fraction of the problem that must be computed sequentially. The relationship is given by:

$$S \leq \frac{1}{f + (1 - f)/N} \leq \frac{1}{f}$$

Another measure of parallel algorithm performance is efficiency, given by:

$$\phi = \frac{S}{N}$$

where S is speedup and N is the number of processors. Ideal efficiency occurs when $\phi = 1$ and no processor is ever idle or performs unnecessary work. As with perfect speedup, ideal efficiency is unattainable in practice.

Ultimately, the performance improvement of a parallel program over a sequential program should be viewed in terms of the reduction in real time required to complete the processing task combined with the additional monetary cost associated with the parallel hardware required to run the parallel program. This gives the best overall picture of parallel program performance and cost effectiveness.

9.2   Parallel IR

9.2.1   Introduction

We can approach the development of parallel information retrieval algorithms from two different directions. One possibility is to develop new retrieval strategies that directly lend themselves to parallel implementation. For example, a text search procedure can be built on top of a neural network. Neural networks (see Chapter 2) are modeled after the human brain and solve problems using a large number of nodes (neurons), each of which has a set of inputs, a threshold, and an output. The output of one node is connected to the input of one or more other nodes, with the boundaries of the network defining the initial input and final output of the system. A node's output value is determined by a weighted function of the node's inputs and threshold. A training procedure is used to learn appropriate settings for the weights and thresholds in the network. Computation proceeds by applying input values to the network, computing each active node's output value, and conditioning these values through the network until the final output values are obtained. Neural networks naturally lend themselves to parallel implementation on SIMD hardware. The challenge with this approach is to define the retrieval task in such a way that it maps well onto the computational paradigm.

The other possibility is to adapt existing, well studied information retrieval algorithms to parallel processing. This is the approach that we will consider throughout the rest of this chapter. The modifications required to adapt an existing algorithm to parallel implementation depend on the target parallel platform. We will investigate techniques for applying a number of retrieval algorithms to both MIMD and SIMD architectures. Since parallel information retrieval is still very much an active research area, few approaches have fallen out as accepted standard techniques. We will, therefore, present a sampling of the work that has been done and avoid preferring one technique over another.

9.2.2   MIMD Architectures

MIMD architectures offer a great deal of flexibility in how parallelism is defined and exploited to solve a problem. The simplest way in which a retrieval system can exploit a MIMD computer is through the use of *multitasking*. Each of the processors in the parallel computer runs a separate, independent search engine. The search engines do not cooperate to process individual queries, but they may share code libraries and data cached by the file system or loaded into shared memory. The submission of user queries to the search engines is managed by a broker, which accepts search requests from the end users and distributes the requests among the available search engines. This is depicted in Figure 9.1. As more processors are added to the system, more search engines may be run and more search requests may be processed in parallel, increasing the throughput of the system. Note, however, that the response time of individual queries remains unchanged.

In spite of the simplicity of this approach, care must be taken to properly balance the hardware resources on the system. In particular, as the number of processors grows, so must the number of disks and I/O channels. Unless the entire retrieval index fits in main memory, the search processes running on the different processors will perform I/O and compete for disk access. A bottleneck at the disk will be disastrous for performance and could eliminate the throughput gains anticipated from the addition of more processors.

In addition to adding more disks to the computer, the system administrator must properly distribute the index data over the disks. Disk contention will remain as long as two search processes need to access index data stored on the same disk. At one extreme, replicating the entire index on each disk eliminates disk contention at the cost of increased storage requirements and update complexity. Alternatively, the system administrator may partition and replicate index data across the disks according to profile information; heavily accessed data is replicated while less frequently accessed data is distributed randomly. Yet another approach is to install a disk array, or RAID [165], and let the operating system handle partitioning the index. Disk arrays can provide low latency and high throughput disk access by striping files across many disks.

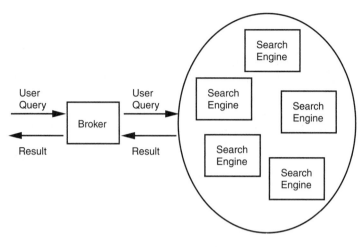

Figure 9.1   Parallel multitasking on a MIMD machine.

To move beyond multitasking and improve query response time, the computation required to evaluate a single query must be partitioned into subtasks and distributed among the multiple processors, as shown in Figure 9.2. In this configuration the broker and search processes run in parallel on separate processors as before, but now they all cooperate to evaluate the same query. High level processing in this system proceeds as follows. The broker accepts a query from the end user and distributes it among the search processes. Each of the search processes then evaluates a portion of the query and transmits an intermediate result back to the broker. Finally, the broker combines the intermediate results into a final result for presentation to the end user.

Since IR computation is typically characterized by a small amount of processing per datum applied to a large amount of data, how to partition the computation boils down to a question of how to partition the *data*. Figure 9.3 presents a high level view of the data processed by typical search algorithms (see Chapter 8). Each row represents a document, d_j, and each column represents an indexing item, k_i. Here, k_i may be a term, phrase, concept, or a more abstract indexing item such as a dimension in an LSI vector or a bit in a document signature. The entries in the matrix, $w_{i,j}$, are (possibly binary) weights, indicating if and to what degree indexing item i is assigned to document j. The indexing item weights associated with a particular document form a vector, $\vec{d_j} = (w_{1,j}, \ldots, w_{t,j})$. During search, a query is also represented as a vector of indexing item weights, $\vec{q} = (w_{1,q}, \ldots, w_{t,q})$, and the search algorithm scores each document by applying a matching function $F(\vec{d_j}, \vec{q}) = sim(d_j, q)$.

This high level data representation reveals two possible methods for partitioning the data. The first method, *document partitioning*, slices the data matrix horizontally, dividing the documents among the subtasks. The N documents in the collection are distributed across the P processors in the system,

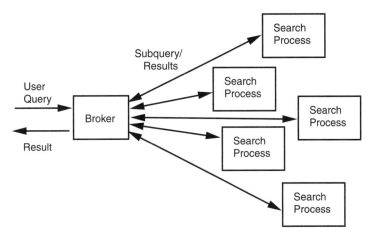

Figure 9.2   Partitioned parallel processing on a MIMD machine.

Indexing Items

		k_1	k_2	...	k_i	...	k_t
D	d_1	$w_{1,1}$	$w_{2,1}$	...	$w_{i,1}$	...	$w_{t,1}$
o	d_2	$w_{1,2}$	$w_{2,2}$	...	$w_{i,2}$	...	$w_{t,2}$
c	...	...	...	...	...	...	...
u							
m	d_j	$w_{1,j}$	$w_{2,j}$	...	$w_{i,j}$	...	$w_{t,j}$
e	...	...	...	...	...	...	...
n							
t	d_N	$w_{1,N}$	$w_{2,N}$	...	$w_{i,N}$	...	$w_{t,N}$
s							

Figure 9.3   Basic data elements processed by a search algorithm.

creating P subcollections of approximately N/P documents each. During query processing, each parallel process (one for each processor) evaluates the query on the subcollection of N/P documents assigned to it, and the results from each of the subcollections are combined into a final result list. The second method, *term partitioning*, slices the data matrix vertically, dividing the indexing items among the P processors such that the evaluation procedure for each document is spread over multiple processors in the system. Below we consider both of these partitioning schemes for each of the three main index structures.

Inverted Files

We first discuss inverted files for systems that employ document partitioning. Following that, we cover systems that employ term partitioning. There are two approaches to document partitioning in systems that use inverted files, namely, logical document partitioning and physical document partitioning.

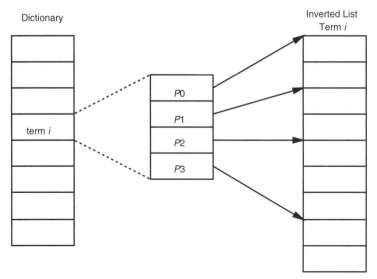

Figure 9.4   Extended dictionary entry for document partitioning.

Logical Document Partitioning

In this case, the data partitioning is done logically using essentially the same basic underlying inverted file index as in the original sequential algorithm (see Chapter 8). The inverted file is extended to give each parallel process (one for each processor) direct access to that portion of the index related to the processor's subcollection of documents. Each term dictionary entry is extended to include P pointers into the corresponding inverted list, where the j-th pointer indexes the block of document entries in the inverted list associated with the subcollection in the j-th processor. This is shown in Figure 9.4, where the dictionary entry for term i contains four pointers into term i's inverted list, one for each parallel process ($P = 4$).

When a query is submitted to the system, the broker (from Figure 9.2) first ensures that the necessary term dictionary and inverted file entries are loaded into shared memory, where all of the parallel processes can access a single shared copy. The broker then initiates P parallel processes to evaluate the query. Each process executes the same document scoring algorithm on its document subcollection, using the extended dictionary to access the appropriate entries in the inverted file. Since all of the index operations during query processing are read-only, there is no lock contention among the processes for access to the shared term dictionary and inverted file. The search processes record document scores in a single shared array of document score accumulators and notify the broker when they have completed. Updates to the accumulator array do not produce lock contention either since the subcollections scored by the different search processes are mutually exclusive. After all of the search processes have finished, the broker sorts the array of document score accumulators and produces the final ranked list of documents.

At inverted file construction time, the indexing process for logically partitioned documents can exploit the parallel processors using a variant of the indexing scheme described by Brown [123] (see Chapter 8). First, the indexer partitions the documents among the processors. Next, it assigns document identifiers such that all identifiers in partition i are less than all identifiers in partition $i + 1$. The indexer then runs a separate indexing process on each processor in parallel. Each indexing process generates a batch of inverted lists, sorted by indexing item. After all of the batches have been generated, a merge step is performed to create the final inverted file. Since the inverted lists in each batch are sorted the same way, a binary heap-based priority queue is used to assemble the inverted list components from each batch that correspond to the current indexing item. The components are concatenated in partition number order to produce a final inverted list and a dictionary entry for the indexing item is created that includes the additional indexing pointers shown in Figure 9.4.

Physical Document Partitioning
In this second approach to document partitioning, the documents are physically partitioned into separate, self-contained subcollections, one for each parallel processor. Each subcollection has its own inverted file and the search processes share nothing during query evaluation. When a query is submitted to the system, the broker distributes the query to all of the parallel search processes. Each parallel search process evaluates the query on its portion of the document collection, producing a local, intermediate hit-list. The broker then collects the intermediate hit-lists from all of the parallel search processes and merges them into a final hit-list.

The P intermediate hit-lists can be merged efficiently using a binary heap-based priority queue [188]. A priority queue of n elements has the property that element i is greater than elements $2i$ and $2i + 1$, where i ranges from 1 to n. A priority queue is not fully sorted, but the maximal element is always immediately available (i.e., in $\Theta(1)$ time) and can be extracted in $O(\log n)$ time. Inserting an element into a priority queue can be done in $O(\log n)$ time as well. To merge the intermediate hit-lists, a priority queue of P elements is created with the first entry from each intermediate hit-list inserted into the queue in $O(P \log P)$ time. To generate the final (and global) hit-list with the top k retrieved documents (in a global ranking), k elements are extracted from the priority queue. As each element is extracted from the priority queue, the intermediate hit-list from which the element was originally drawn inserts a new element into the priority queue. The P intermediate hit-lists can be merged into a final hit-list of k elements in $O((P + k) \log P)$ time.

The merge procedure just described assumes that the parallel search processes produce globally consistent document scores, i.e., document scores that can be merged directly. Depending on the ranking algorithm in use, each parallel search process may require global term statistics in order to produce globally consistent document scores. There are two basic approaches to collect information on global term statistics. The first approach is to compute global term statistics at indexing time and store these statistics with each of the subcollections. The second approach is for the query processing to proceed in two phases. During the first phase, the broker collects subcollection term statistics from each of the search processes and combines them into global term statistics. During the second phase, the broker distributes the query and global term statistics to the search processes and query evaluation proceeds as before. The first solution offers better query processing performance at the expense of more complex indexing, while the second solution allows subcollections to be built and maintained independently at the expense of doubling communication costs during query evaluation.

To build the inverted files for physically partitioned documents, each processor creates, in parallel, its own complete index corresponding to its document partition. If global collection statistics are stored in the separate term dictionaries, then a merge step must be performed that accumulates the global statistics for all of the partitions and distributes them to each of the partition dictionaries.

Logical document partitioning requires less communication than physical document partitioning with similar parallelization, and so is likely to provide better overall performance. Physical document partitioning, on the other hand, offers more flexibility (e.g., document partitions may be searched individually) and conversion of an existing IR system into a parallel IR system is simpler using physical document partitioning. For either document partitioning scheme, threads provide a convenient programming paradigm for creating the search processes, controlling their operation, and communicating between them. Threads are natively supported in some modern programming languages (e.g., Java [491]) and well supported in a standard way in others (e.g., POSIX threads in C/C++). Thread packages allow programmers to develop parallel programs using high level abstractions of concurrent execution, communication, and synchronization. The compiler and runtime system then map these abstractions to efficient operating system services and shared memory operations.

Term Partitioning

When term partitioning is used with an inverted file-based system, a single inverted file is created for the document collection (using the parallel construction technique described above for logical document partitioning) and the inverted lists are spread across the processors. During query evaluation, the query is decomposed into indexing items and each indexing item is sent to the processor that holds the corresponding inverted list. The processors create hit-lists with partial document scores and return them to the broker. The broker then combines the hit-lists according to the semantics of the query. For Boolean queries, the hit-lists are unioned, intersected, or subtracted as appropriate. For ranked free text queries, the hit-lists contain term scores that must be combined according to the semantics of the ranking formula.

In comparison, document partitioning affords simpler inverted index construction and maintenance than term partitioning. Their relative performance during query processing was shown by Jeong and Omiecinski [404] to depend on term distributions. Assuming each processor has its own I/O channel and disks, when term distributions in the documents and the queries are more skewed, document partitioning performs better. When terms are uniformly distributed in user queries, term partitioning performs better. For instance, using TREC data, Ribeiro-Neto and Barbosa [673, 57] have shown that term partitioning might be twice as fast with long queries and 5–10 times faster with very short (Web-like) queries.

Suffix Arrays

We can apply document partitioning to suffix arrays in a straightforward fashion. As with physical document partitioning for inverted files, the document collection is divided among the P processors and each partition is treated as an independent, self-contained collection. The system can then apply the suffix array construction techniques described in Chapter 8 to each of the partitions, with the enhancement that all of the partitions are indexed concurrently. During search, the broker broadcasts the query to all of the search processes, collects the intermediate results, and merges the intermediate results into a final hit-list.

If all of the documents will be kept in a single collection, we can still exploit the parallel processors to reduce indexing time. An interesting property of the suffix array construction algorithm for large texts (described in Chapter 8) is that each of the merges of partial indices is independent. Therefore all of the $O((n/M)^2)$ merges may be run in parallel on separate processors. After all merges are complete, the counters for each partial index must be accumulated and the final index merge may be performed.

Term partitioning for a suffix array amounts to distributing a single suffix array over multiple processors such that each processor is responsible for a lexicographical interval of the array. During query processing, the broker distributes the query to the processors that contain the relevant portions of the suffix array and merges the results. Note that when searching the suffix array, all of the processors require access to the entire text. On a single parallel computer with shared memory (e.g., an SMP system), this is not a problem since the text may be cached in shared memory. This may be a problem, however, if shared memory is not available and communication costs are high, as is the case in a distributed system (e.g., a network of workstations).

Signature Files

To implement document partitioning in a system that uses signature files, the documents are divided among the processors as before and each processor generates signatures for its document partition. At query time, the broker generates a signature for the query and distributes it to all of the parallel processors. Each processor evaluates the query signature locally as if its document partition was a separate, self-contained collection. Then the results are sent to the broker, which combines them into a final hit-list for the user. For Boolean queries, the final result is simply a union of the results returned from each processor. For ranked queries, the ranked hit-lists are merged as described above for inverted file implementations.

To apply term partitioning in a signature file-based system, we would have to use a bit-sliced signature file [627] and partition the bit slices across the processors. The amount of sequential work required to merge the intermediate results from each of the processors and eliminate false drops, however, severely limits the speedup S available with this organization. Accordingly, this organization is not recommended.

9.2.3 SIMD Architectures

SIMD architectures lend themselves to a more restricted domain of problems than MIMD architectures. As such, SIMD computers are less common than MIMD computers. Perhaps the best known example of the SIMD architecture is the Thinking Machines CM-2, which has been used to support both signature file- and inverted file-based information retrieval algorithms. Each processing element in the CM-2 has a 1 bit arithmetic logic unit (ALU) and a small amount of local memory. The processing elements execute local and non-local parallel instructions. A local parallel instruction causes each processing element to perform the same operation in unison on data stored in the element's local memory. A non-local parallel instruction involves communication between the processing elements and includes operations such as summing the components of a vector or finding a global maximum.

The CM-2 uses a separate front-end host computer to provide an interface to the back-end parallel processing elements. The front-end controls the loading and unloading of data in the back-end and executes serial program instructions, such as condition and iteration statements. Parallel macro instructions are sent from the front-end to a back-end microcontroller, which controls the simultaneous execution of the instruction on a set of back-end processing elements.

The CM-2 provides a layer of abstraction over the back-end processors, called *virtual processors*. One or more virtual processors map to a single physical processor. Programs express their processing needs in terms of virtual processors, and the hardware maps virtual processor operations onto physical processors. A physical processor must sequentially perform the operations for each of its virtual processors. The ratio of virtual to physical processors is called the *virtual processing ratio*, *VP*. As *VP* increases, an approximately linear increase in running time occurs.

Signature Files

The most natural application of a SIMD computer in IR is to support signature files. Recall from Chapter 8 the basic search process for signature files. First, the search system constructs a signature for the query terms. Next, the system compares the query signature with the signature of every document in the collection and marks documents with matching signatures as potentially relevant.

```
probe_doc (P_bit Doc_sig[], char *term)
{
   int    i;
   P_int Doc_match;

   Doc_match = 1;
   for (i = 0; i < num_hashes; i++) {
      Doc_match &= Doc_sig[hash (i, term)];
   }
   return Doc_match;
}
```

Figure 9.5 probe_doc.

Finally, the system scans the full text of potentially relevant documents to eliminate false drops, ranks the matching documents, and returns the hit-list to the
user. If the probability of false drops is acceptably low, the full text scan may
be eliminated. Also, if the system is processing Boolean queries, it may need to
generate more than one signature for the query and combine the intermediate
results of each signature according to the operators used in the query.

Stanfill [741] shows how this procedure can be adapted to the CM-2 (or any
similar SIMD machine). The core of the procedure is the subroutine shown in
Figure 9.5.‡ This routine probes the document signature Doc_sig for the given
query word term by applying each of the signature hash functions to term and
ANDing together the corresponding bits in Doc_sig. The result of the AND
operation is stored in Doc_match. If Doc_match is 1, term is present in Doc_sig;
if Doc_match is 0, term is absent. Both Doc_sig and Doc_match are parallel
variables, such that each virtual processor operates in parallel on its own copy
of the variables. By loading the entire signature file onto the back-end virtual
processors, all of the document signatures can be searched in parallel.

This procedure must be enhanced under the following condition. If the
number of words in a document $|d|$ exceeds the number of words W that can
be inserted into a document signature, then the document must be segmented
into $|d|/W$ segments and represented by $|d|/W$ signatures. In this case, the
probe_doc routine is applied to all signatures for a document and an OR is taken
over the individual signature results to obtain the final result for the document.
If the false drop probability warrants scanning the full text of the documents,
only those segments with matching signatures need be scanned. As soon as a
qualifying segment is found, the entire document is marked as a match for the
query.

---

‡ The algorithms shown in this chapter are presented using a C-like pseudo-code. Parallel
data type names begin with a capital 'P'.

```
bool_search (P_bit Doc_sig[], bquery_t query)
{
  switch (query.op) {
    case AND:
      return (bool_search (Doc_sig, query.arg1)
              && bool_search (Doc_sig, query.arg2));
    case OR:
      return (bool_search (Doc_sig, query.arg1)
              || bool_search (Doc_sig, query.arg2));
    case NOT:
      return (!bool_search (Doc_sig, query.arg1));
    case WORD:
      return (probe_doc (Doc_sig, query.arg1));
  }
}
```

Figure 9.6 `bool_search`.

A general Boolean retrieval system can be implemented on top of `probe_doc` with the recursive procedure shown in Figure 9.6. Here `bquery_t` is a recursive data type that contains two arguments and an operator. If the operator is `NOT` or `WORD`, then the second argument in the `bquery_t` is empty. The final return value is stored in a parallel Boolean variable, which indicates for each document whether or not that document satisfies the Boolean query. Again, if the probability of false drops associated with the signature scheme is acceptably low, the set of matching documents may be returned immediately. Otherwise, the system must perform further processing on the text of each matching document to eliminate false drops.

If weights are available for the query terms, it is possible to build a ranking retrieval system on top of the parallel signature file search process. Query term weights could be supplied by the end-user when the query is created, or they could be assigned by the system using a collection statistic such as *idf* (see Chapter 2). The algorithm in Figure 9.7 shows how to use `probe_doc` to build a ranking system.

In `rank_search`, the `wquery_t` data type contains an array of query terms and an array of weights associated with those terms. First, all documents that contain the current term are identified with `probe_doc`. Next, the score for each of those documents is updated by adding the weight associated with the current query term (the `where` clause tests a parallel variable expression and activates only those processors that satisfy the expression). After all query terms have been processed, the parallel variable `Doc_score` contains the rank scores for all of the documents.

The final step in the processing of a weighted query is to rank the scored documents by sorting and returning the top k hits. This can be accomplished in

```
rank_search (P_bit Doc_sig[], wquery_t query)
{
   int      i;
   P_float Doc_score;
   P_bool  Doc_match;

   Doc_score = 0;
   for (i = 0; i < query.num_terms; i++) {
      Doc_match = probe_doc (Doc_sig, query.terms[i]);
      where (Doc_match) {
         Doc_score += query.weights[i];
      }
   }
   return (Doc_score);
}
```

Figure 9.7 rank_search.

a number of ways. One possibility is to use the global ranking routine provided by the CM-2, which takes a parallel variable and returns 0 for the largest value, 1 for the next largest value, etc. Applying this routine to Doc_score yields the ranked documents directly. If the number of hits returned is much less than the number of documents in the collection ($k \ll N$), the global ranking function performs more work than necessary. An alternative is for the retrieval system to use the global maximum routine in an iterative process of identification and extraction. During each iteration, the system applies the global maximum routine to Doc_score to identify the current top ranked document. The document is added to the hit-list and its score in Doc_score is set to -1. After k iterations, the top k hits will have been entered on the hit-list.

The techniques just described assume that the entire signature file fits in main memory. If this is not the case, additional steps must be taken to process the entire document collection. A straightforward approach is to process the collection in batches. A batch consists of as many document signatures as will fit in main memory at one time. Each batch is read into memory and scored using one of the above algorithms. The intermediate results are saved in an array of document scores. After all batches have been processed, the array of document scores is ranked and the final hit-list is generated.

In general, processing the collection in batches performs poorly due to the I/O required to read in each batch. The performance penalty imposed by the I/O can be reduced by processing multiple queries on each batch, such that the I/O costs are amortized over multiple queries. This helps query processing throughput, but does nothing to improve query processing response time.

An alternative to processing in batches is to use a parallel *bit-sliced sig-nature file*, proposed by Panagopoulos and Faloutsos [627] (see Chapter 8).

$$
\begin{array}{c|cccccc}
doc_1 & 0 & 1 & 1 & 0 & 1 & 1 \\
doc_2 & 1 & 0 & 0 & 1 & 0 & 0 \\
doc_3 & 1 & 1 & 1 & 0 & 1 & 0 \\
doc_4 & 0 & 1 & 0 & 0 & 0 & 0 \\
doc_5 & 1 & 1 & 0 & 0 & 0 & 1
\end{array}
$$

Figure 9.8   Document signatures.

Figure 9.8 shows a matrix representation of the signatures for a small document collection ($N = 5$). In a traditional signature file, each row of the matrix, or document signature, is stored contiguously. In a bit-sliced signature file, each column of the matrix, or bit-slice, is stored contiguously. A bit-slice is a vertical slice through the matrix, such that bit-slice i contains the i-th bit from every document signature. With this organization, the retrieval system can load just those bit-slices required by the query terms in question. Note that the file offset of bit-slice i (starting with 0) is $i*N$ bits, and the length of each bit-slice is N bits.

When using a bit-sliced signature file, each virtual processor is still responsible for scoring a single document. A virtual processor's local memory is used to store the bits from each bit-slice that correspond to the processor's document. A bit-slice, therefore, is distributed across the virtual processors with one bit at each processor. The set of bits across the virtual processors that corresponds to a single bit-slice is called a *frame*. The total number of frames is $F = M/N$, where M is the size of memory in bits available for storing bit-slices. When $F < W$ (W is the number of bit-slices in the file), the system employs a frame replacement policy to determine which bit-slices must be resident to process the query. The frame replacement policy may simply fetch all of the bit-slices that correspond to the query terms, or it may analyze the query and identify a subset of bit-slices that, when evaluated, still provides an acceptably low false drop probability.

To search the bit-sliced signature file, we must make a few modifications to our basic query processing procedures. First, the frame replacement routine must be run at the start of processing a query to insure that the required bit-slices are resident. Second, the signature hash functions must be updated to return a frame index rather than a signature bit index. The frame index is the index of the frame that contains the bit-slice corresponding to the previously computed signature bit index. Finally, the parallel bit array, Doc_sig, passed into probe_doc is replaced with the parallel bit array Frames, which provides each virtual processor access to its frames.

Panagopoulos and Faloutsos [627] analyze the performance of the parallel bit-sliced signature file and show that query response times of under 2 seconds can be achieved on a 128 Gb database on the CM-2. Although this technique addresses the issue of query response time on large document collections, it defeats one of the often claimed advantages of the signature file organization, namely, that indexing new documents is straightforward. In a traditional signature file organization, new document signatures may simply be appended to the signature file. With a bit-sliced signature file, the signature file must be inverted, resulting in update costs similar to that of an inverted file.

Inverted Files

While the adaptation of signature file techniques to SIMD architectures is rather natural, inverted files are somewhat awkward to implement on SIMD machines. Nevertheless, Stanfill *et al.* [744, 740] have proposed two adaptations of inverted files for the CM-2. Recall from Chapter 8 the structure of an inverted list. In its simplest form, an inverted list contains a *posting* for each document in which the associated term appears. A posting is a tuple of the form $\langle k_i, d_j \rangle$, where k_i is a term identifier and d_j is a document identifier. Depending on the retrieval model, postings may additionally contain weights or positional information. If positional information is stored, then a posting is created for each occurrence of k_i in d_j.

The first parallel inverted file implementation for the CM-2 uses two data structures to store the inverted file: a postings table and an index. The postings table contains the document identifiers from the postings and the index maps terms to their corresponding entries in the postings table. Before the postings are loaded into these structures, they are sorted by term identifier. The document identifiers are then loaded into the postings table in this sorted order, filling in a series of rows of length P, where P is the number of processors in use. The postings table is treated as a parallel array, where the array subscript selects a particular row, and each row is spread across the P processors. For each term, the index stores the locations of the first and last entries in the postings table for the set of document identifiers associated with the term. Figure 9.9 shows a small document collection, the raw postings, and the resulting postings table and index. For example, to find the documents that contain the term 'piggy,' we look up 'piggy' in the index and determine that the postings table entries from row 1, position 3, to row 2, position 1, contain the corresponding document identifiers, or 0, 1, and 2.

At search time these data structures are used to rank documents as follows. First, the retrieval system loads the postings table onto the back-end processors. Next, the system iterates over the query terms. For each query term, an index lookup returns the range of postings table entries that must be processed. The search system then iterates over the rows included in this range. For each row, the processors that contain entries for the current term are activated and the associated document identifiers are used to update the scores of the corresponding documents.

Document scores are built up in accumulators (called *mailboxes* by Stanfill), which are allocated in a parallel array similar to the postings table. To update the accumulator for a particular document, we must determine the accumulator's row and position within the row. For convenience, we'll assume that this information (rather than document identifiers) is stored in the postings table. Furthermore,

Documents

This little piggy went to market.	This little piggy stayed home.	This little piggy had roast beef.

Postings

beef	2
had	2
home	1
little	0
little	1
little	2
market	0
piggy	0
piggy	1
piggy	2
roast	2
stayed	1
this	0
this	1
this	2
to	0
went	0

Index

Term	First Row	First Pos.	Last Row	Last Pos.
beef	0	0	0	0
had	0	1	0	1
home	0	2	0	2
little	0	3	1	1
market	1	2	1	2
piggy	1	3	2	1
roast	2	2	2	2
stayed	2	3	2	3
this	3	0	3	2
to	3	3	3	3
went	4	0	4	0

Postings Table

2	2	1	0
1	2	0	0
1	2	2	1
0	1	2	0
0			

Figure 9.9   Parallel inverted file.

we'll assume that weights have been associated with each posting and stored in the postings table. The complete algorithm for scoring a weighted term is shown in Figure 9.10.

The `score_term` routine assumes that the index lookup for the query term has been done and the results were stored in `term`. The routine iterates over each row of postings associated with the term and determines which positions to process within the current row. `Position` is a parallel integer constant where the first instance contains 0, the second instance contains 1, etc., and the last instance contains $N\_PROCS - 1$. It is used in the `where` clause to activate the appropriate processors based on the positions of interest in the current row. The left-indexing performed on `Doc_score` at the end of the routine provides access to a particular instance of the parallel variable. This operation is significant because it involves communication between the processors. Posting weights must be shipped from the processor containing the posting to the processor containing the accumulator for the corresponding document. After the system has processed all of the query terms with `score_term`, it ranks the documents based on their scores and returns the top k documents.

It is expensive to send posting weights to accumulators on different processors. To address this problem, Stanfill [740] proposed the *partitioned postings*

```
score_term (P_float Doc_score[], P_posting Posting[],
           term_t term)
{
   int     i;
   int     first_pos;
   int     last_pos;
   P_int   Doc_row;
   P_int   Doc_pos;
   P_float Weight;

   for (i = term.first_row; i <= term.last_row; i++) {
     first_pos = (i == term.first_row ?
                     term.first_pos : 0);
     last_pos = (i == term.last_row ?
                     term.last_pos : N_PROCS - 1);
     where (Position >= first_pos
             && Position <= last_pos) {
       Doc_row = Posting[i].row;
       Doc_pos = Posting[i].pos;
       Weight = term.weight * Posting[i].weight;
       [Doc_pos]Doc_score[Doc_row] += Weight;
     }
   }
}
```

Figure 9.10   score_term.

file, which eliminates the communication required in the previous algorithm by storing the postings and accumulator for a given document on the same processor. There are two tricks to accomplishing this. First, as the postings are loaded into the postings table, rather than working left to right across the rows and filling each row before starting with the next one, the postings are added to the column that corresponds to the processor where the associated document will be scored. This ensures that all of the postings associated with a document will be loaded onto the same processor as the document's accumulator. Figure 9.11(a) shows how the postings from Figure 9.9 would be loaded into a table for two processors, with documents 0 and 1 assigned to processor 0 and document 2 assigned to processor 1.

Figure 9.11(a) also demonstrates a problem with this scheme. The postings for the term *this* are skewed and no longer span consecutive rows. To handle this situation, we apply the second trick of the partitioned postings file, which is to segment the postings such that every term in segment i is lexicographically less than or equal to every term in segment $i + 1$. This is shown in Figure 9.11(b) using segments of three rows. Note how some segments may need to be padded with blank space in order to satisfy the partitioning constraints.

home	1	beef	2
little	0	had	2
little	1	little	2
market	0	piggy	2
piggy	0	roast	2
piggy	1	this	2
stayed	1		
this	0		
this	1		
to	0		
went	0		

(a)

home	1	beef	2
little	0	had	2
little	1	little	2
market	0	piggy	2
piggy	0	roast	2
piggy	1		
stayed	1	this	2
this	0		
this	1		
to	0		
went	0		

(b)

Figure 9.11   Skewed and partitioned postings.

Index

Term	First Partition	Last Partition	Tag
beef	0	0	0
had	0	0	1
home	0	0	2
little	0	0	3
market	1	1	0
piggy	1	1	1
roast	1	1	2
stayed	2	2	0
this	2	2	1
to	3	3	0
went	3	3	1

Postings Table

2	1	0	0
3	0	1	0
3	1	3	0
0	0	1	0
1	0	2	0
1	1		
0	1	1	0
1	0		
1	1		
0	0		
1	0		

Figure 9.12   Partitioned postings file.

The postings table and index undergo a few more modifications before reaching their final form, shown in Figure 9.12. First, term identifiers in the postings are replaced by term tags. The system assigns tags to terms such that no two terms in the same partition share the same tag. Second, document identifiers in the postings are replaced by document row numbers, where the row number identifies which row contains the accumulator for the document. Since the accumulator is at the same position (i.e., processor) as the posting, the row number is sufficient to identify the document. Finally, the index is modified to record the starting partition, ending partition, and tag for each term.

```
ppf_score_term (P_float Doc_score[], P_posting Posting[],
                term_t term)
{
  int     i;
  P_int   Doc_row;
  P_float Weight;

  for (i = term.first_part * N_ROWS;
       i < (term.last_part + 1) * N_ROWS; i++) {
    where (Posting[i].tag == term.tag) {
      Doc_row = Posting[i].row;
      Weight = term.weight * Posting[i].weight;
      Doc_score[Doc_row] += Weight;
    }
  }
}
```

Figure 9.13 ppf_score_term.

The modified term scoring algorithm is shown in Figure 9.13.

Here N_ROWS is the number of rows per partition. The algorithm iterates over the rows of postings that span the term's partitions and activates the processors with matching postings. Each active processor extracts the document row from the posting, calculates the term weight, and updates the document's score. After all query terms have been processed, the system ranks the documents and returns the top k. Stanfill [740] shows that the partitioned postings file imposes a space overhead of approximately 1/3 the original text (of which 10–20% is wasted partition padding) and can support sub 2-second query response times on a terabyte of text using a 64K processor CM-2.

9.3   Distributed IR

9.3.1   Introduction

Distributed computing is the application of multiple computers connected by a network to solve a single problem. A distributed computing system can be viewed as a MIMD parallel processor with a relatively slow inter-processor communication channel and the freedom to employ a heterogeneous collection of processors in the system. In fact, a single processing node in the distributed system could be a parallel computer in its own right. Moreover, if they all support the same public interface and protocol for invoking their services, the computers in the system may be owned and operated by different parties.

Distributed systems typically consist of a set of server processes, each running on a separate processing node, and a designated broker process responsible for accepting client requests, distributing the requests to the servers, collecting intermediate results from the servers, and combining the intermediate results into a final result for the client. This computation model is very similar to the MIMD parallel processing model shown in Figure 9.2. The main difference here is that the subtasks run on different computers and the communication between the subtasks is performed using a network protocol such as TCP/IP [176] (rather than, for example, shared memory-based inter-process communication mechanisms). Another significant difference is that in a distributed system it is more common to employ a procedure for selecting a subset of the distributed servers for processing a particular request rather than broadcasting every request to every server in the system.

Applications that lend themselves well to a distributed implementation usually involve computation and data that can be split into coarse-grained operations with relatively little communication required between the operations. Parallel information retrieval based on *document partitioning* fits this profile well. In section 9.2.2 we saw how document partitioning can be used to divide the search task up into multiple, self-contained subtasks that each involve extensive computation and data processing with little communication between them. Moreover, documents are almost always grouped into collections, either for administrative purposes or to combine related documents into a single source. Collections, therefore, provide a natural granularity for distributing data across servers and partitioning the computation. Note that since term partitioning imposes greater communication overhead during query processing, it is rarely employed in a distributed system.

To build a distributed IR system, we need to consider both engineering issues common to many distributed systems and algorithmic issues specific to information retrieval. The critical engineering issues involve defining a search protocol for transmitting requests and results; designing a server that can efficiently accept a request, initiate a subprocess or thread to service the request, and exploit any locality inherent in the processing using appropriate caching techniques; and designing a broker that can submit asynchronous search requests to multiple servers in parallel and combine the intermediate results into a final end user response. The algorithmic issues include how to distribute documents across the distributed search servers, how to select which servers should receive a particular search request, and how to combine the results from the different servers.

The search protocol specifies the syntax and semantics of messages transmitted between clients and servers, the sequence of messages required to establish a connection and carry out a search operation, and the underlying transport mechanism for sending messages (e.g., TCP/IP). At a minimum, the protocol should allow a client to:

- obtain information about a search server, e.g., a list of databases available for searching at the server and possibly statistics associated with the databases;

- submit a search request for one or more databases using a well defined query language;
- receive search results in a well defined format;
- retrieve items identified in the search results.

For closed systems consisting of homogeneous search servers, a custom search protocol may be most appropriate, particularly if special functionality (e.g., encryption of requests and results) is required. Alternatively, a standard protocol may be used, allowing the system to interoperate more easily with other search servers. The Z39.50 [606] standard (see Chapter 4) for client/server information retrieval defines a widely used protocol with enough functionality to support most search applications. Another proposed protocol for distributed, heterogeneous search, called STARTS (Stanford Proposal for Internet Meta-Searching) [317], was developed at Stanford University in cooperation with a consortium of search product and service vendors. STARTS was designed from scratch to support distributed information retrieval and includes features intended to solve the algorithmic issues related to distributed IR, such as merging results from heterogeneous sources.

The other engineering issues related to building efficient client/server systems have been covered extensively in the literature (see, for example, Comer and Stevens [176] and Zomaya [852]). Rather than review them here, we continue with a more detailed look at the algorithmic issues involved in distributed IR.

9.3.2 Collection Partitioning

The procedure used to assign documents to search servers in a distributed IR system depends on a number of factors. First, we must consider whether or not the system is centrally administered. In a system comprising independently administered, heterogeneous search servers, the distributed document collections will be built and maintained independently. In this case, there is no central control of the document partitioning procedure and the question of how to partition the documents is essentially moot. It may be the case, however, that each independent search server is focused on a particular subject area, resulting in a semantic partitioning of the documents into distributed collections focused on particular subject areas. This situation is common in *meta* search systems that provide centralized access to a variety of back-end search service providers.

When the distributed system is centrally administered, more options are available. The first option is simple replication of the collection across all of the search servers. This is appropriate when the collection is small enough to fit on a single search server, but high availability and query processing throughput are required. In this scenario, the parallelism in the system is being exploited via multitasking (see Figure 9.1) and the broker's job is to route queries to the search servers and balance the loads on the servers.

Indexing the documents is handled in one of two ways. In the first method, each search server separately indexes its replica of the documents. In the second method, each server is assigned a mutually exclusive subset of documents to index and the index subsets are replicated across the search servers. A merge of the subsets is required at each search server to create the final indexes (which can be accomplished using the technique described under Document Partitioning in section 9.2.2). In either case, document updates and deletions must be broadcast to all servers in the system. Document additions may be broadcast, or they may be batched and partitioned depending on their frequency and how quickly updates must be reflected by the system.

The second option is random distribution of the documents. This is appropriate when a large document collection must be distributed for performance reasons but the documents will always be viewed and searched as if they are part of a single, logical collection. The broker broadcasts every query to all of the search servers and combines the results for the user.

The final option is explicit semantic partitioning of the documents. Here the documents are either already organized into semantically meaningful collections, such as by technical discipline, or an automatic clustering or categorization procedure is used to partition the documents into subject specific collections.

9.3.3   Source Selection

Source selection is the process of determining which of the distributed document collections are most likely to contain relevant documents for the current query, and therefore should receive the query for processing. One approach is to always assume that every collection is equally likely to contain relevant documents and simply broadcast the query to all collections. This approach is appropriate when documents are randomly partitioned or there is significant semantic overlap between the collections.

When document collections are partitioned into semantically meaningful collections or it is prohibitively expensive to search every collection every time, the collections can be ranked according to their likelihood of containing relevant documents. The basic technique is to treat each collection as if it were a single large document, index the collections, and evaluate the query against the collections to produce a ranked listing of collections. We can apply a standard cosine similarity measure using a query vector and collection vectors. To calculate a term weight in the collection vector using tf-idf style weighting (see Chapter 2), term frequency $tf_{i,j}$ is the total number of occurrences of term i in collection j, and the inverse document frequency idf_i for term i is $\log(N/n_i)$, where N is the total number of collections and n_i is the number of collections in which term i appears.

A danger of this approach is that although a particular collection may receive a high query relevance score, there may not be individual documents within the collection that receive a high query relevance score, essentially resulting in a false drop and unnecessary work to score the collection. Moffat and Zobel [574] propose avoiding this problem by indexing each collection as a series of blocks, where each block contains B documents. When B equals 1, this is equivalent to indexing all of the documents as a single, monolithic collection. When B equals the number of documents in each collection, this is equivalent to the original solution. By varying B, a tradeoff is made between collection index size and likelihood of false drops.

An alternative to searching a collection index was proposed by Voorhees [792], who proposes using training queries to build a content model for the distributed collections. When a new query is submitted to the system, its similarity to the training queries is computed and the content model is used to determine which collections should be searched and how many hits from each collection should be returned.

9.3.4 Query Processing

Query processing in a distributed IR system proceeds as follows:

(1) Select collections to search.

(2) Distribute query to selected collections.

(3) Evaluate query at distributed collections in parallel.

(4) Combine results from distributed collections into final result.

As described in the previous section, Step 1 may be eliminated if the query is always broadcast to every document collection in the system. Otherwise, one of the previously described selection algorithms is used and the query is distributed to the selected collections. Each of the participating search servers then evaluates the query on the selected collections using its own local search algorithm. Finally, the results are merged.

At this point we have covered everything except how to merge the results. There are a number of scenarios. First, if the query is Boolean and the search servers return Boolean result sets, all of the sets are simply unioned to create the final result set. If the query involves free-text ranking, a number of techniques are available ranging from simple/naive to complex/accurate.

The simplest approach is to combine the ranked hit-lists using round robin interleaving. This is likely to produce poor quality results since hits from irrelevant collections are given status equal to that of hits from highly relevant collections. An improvement on this process is to merge the hit-lists based on relevance score. As with the parallel process described for Document Partitioning in section 9.2.2, unless proper global term statistics are used to compute the document scores, we may get incorrect results. If documents are randomly distributed such that global term statistics are consistent across all of the distributed collections, the merging based on relevance score is sufficient to maintain retrieval effectiveness. If, however, the distributed document collections are semantically partitioned or maintained by independent parties, then reranking must be performed.

Callan [139] proposes reranking documents by weighting document scores based on their collection similarity computed during the source selection step. The weight for a collection is computed as $w = 1+ \mid C \mid \cdot(s - \bar{s})/\bar{s}$, where $\mid C \mid$ is the number of collections searched, s is the collection's score, and $\bar{s}$ is the mean of the collection scores.

The most accurate technique for merging ranked hit-lists is to use accurate global term statistics. This can be accomplished in one of a variety of ways. First, if the collections have been indexed for source selection, that index will contain global term statistics across all of the distributed collections. The broker can include these statistics in the query when it distributes the query to the remote search servers. The servers can then account for these statistics in their processing and produce relevance scores that can be merged directly. If a collection index is unavailable, query distribution can proceed in two rounds of communication. In the first round, the broker distributes the query and gathers collection statistics from each of the search servers. These statistics are combined by the broker and distributed back to the search servers in the second round.

Finally, the search protocol can require that search servers return global query term statistics and per-document query term statistics [317, 441]. The broker is then free to rerank every document using the query term statistics and a ranking algorithm of its choice. The end result is a hit-list that contains documents from the distributed collections ranked in the same order as if all of the documents had been indexed in a single collection.

9.3.5   Web Issues

Information retrieval on the World Wide Web is covered extensively in Chapter 13. For completeness, we briefly mention here how parallel and distributed information retrieval applies to the Web. The most direct application is to gather all of the documents on the Web into a single, large document collection. The parallel and distributed techniques described above can then be used directly as if the Web were any other large document collection. This is the approach currently taken by most of the popular Web search services.

Alternatively, we can exploit the distributed system of computers that make up the Web and spread the work of collecting, organizing, and searching all of the documents. This is the approach taken by the Harvest system [108]. Harvest comprises a number of components for gathering, summarizing, replicating, distributing, and searching documents. User queries are processed by *brokers*, which collect and refine information from *gatherers* and other brokers. The information at a particular broker is typically related to a restricted set of topics, allowing users to direct their queries to the most appropriate brokers. A central broker registry helps users find the best brokers for their queries (see Figure 13.4).

9.4   Trends and Research Issues

Parallel computing holds great potential for tackling the performance and scale issues associated with the large and growing document collections currently available online. In this chapter we have surveyed a number of techniques for exploiting modern parallel architectures. The trend in parallel hardware is the development of general MIMD machines. Coincident with this trend is the availability of features in modern programming languages, such as threads and associated synchronization constructs, that greatly facilitate the task of developing programs for these architectures. In spite of this trend, research in parallel IR algorithms on MIMD machines is relatively young, with few standard results to draw on.

Much of the early work in parallel IR was aimed at supporting signature files on SIMD architectures. Although SIMD machines are well suited to processing signature files, both SIMD machines and signature files have fallen out of favor in their respective communities. SIMD machines are difficult to program and are well suited to a relatively small class of problems. As Chapter 8 points out, signature files provide poor support for document ranking and hold few, if any, advantages over inverted files in terms of functionality, index size, and processing speed [851].

Distributed computing can be viewed as a form of MIMD computing with relatively high interprocessor communication costs. Most of the parallel IR algorithms discussed in this chapter, however, have a high ratio of computation to communication, and are well suited to both symmetric multiprocessor and distributed implementations. In fact, by using an appropriate abstraction layer for inter-process communication, we can easily implement a parallel system that works well on both multiprocessor and distributed architectures with relatively little modification.

Many challenges remain in the area of parallel and distributed text retrieval. While we have presented a number of approaches in this chapter, none stand out as the definitive solution for building parallel or distributed information retrieval systems. In addition to the continued development and investigation of parallel indexing and search techniques for systems based on inverted files and suffix arrays, two specific challenges stand out.

The first challenge is measuring retrieval effectiveness on large text collections. Although we can easily measure the speedup achieved by a given parallel system, measuring the quality of the results produced by that system is another story. This challenge, of course, is not unique to parallel IR systems. Large collections pose problems particularly when it comes to generating relevance judgments for queries. The pooling techniques used in TREC (see Chapter 3) may not work. There, ranked result lists are combined from multiple systems to produce a relatively small set of documents for human evaluation. The assumption is that most, if not all, of the relevant documents will be included in the pool. With large collections, this assumption may not hold. Moreover, it is unclear how important recall is in this context.

The second significant challenge is interoperability, or building distributed IR systems from heterogeneous components. The need for distributed systems comprising heterogeneous back-end search servers is clear from the popularity of meta search services on the Web. The functionality of these systems is limited, however, due to the lack of term statistics from the back-end search servers, which would otherwise allow for accurate reranking and result list merging. Moreover, each search server employs its own, custom query language, opening up the possibility that the original intent of the query is lost when it is translated to the back-end query languages. Protocol standardization efforts, such as STARTS [317], attempt to address these problems, but commitment to these standards by the entire community of search providers is required.

9.5   Bibliographic Discussion

A thorough overview of parallel and distributed computing can be found in the *Parallel and Distributed Computing Handbook* [852], edited by Albert Zomaya. Many interesting research papers specific to parallel and distributed information systems can be found in the proceedings of the IEEE *International Conference on Parallel and Distributed Information Systems*.

Stanfill *et al.* [742, 744, 740] are responsible for much of the early work using massively parallel hardware (in particular, the Thinking Machines Connection Machine) to solve IR problems. Pogue and Willet [645] also explored massively parallel IR using the ICL Distributed Array Processor. Salton and Buckley [701] provide some interesting comments on the early implementations of parallel IR, challenging both their speed and effectiveness.

Lu *et al.* [524] analyze how to properly scale SMP hardware for parallel IR and emphasize the importance of proper hardware balance. Investigations into parallel and distributed inverted file implementations have been performed by Tomasic and García-Molina [762, 763, 764], Jeong and Omiecinski [404], and Ribeiro-Neto and Barbosa [673]. Parallel and distributed algorithms for suffix array construction and search have been explored by Navarro *et al.* [591]. Given P processors and total text of size n, they obtain average indexing times that are $O(n/P \log n)$ CPU time and $O(n/P)$ communication time.

Macleod *et al.* [535] offer a number of strategies and tips for building distributed information retrieval systems. Cahoon and McKinley [137] analyze the performance of the Inquery distributed information retrieval system.

Source selection and collection fusion issues have been investigated by Gravano *et al.* using the GlOSS system [318], Voorhees *et al.* [792], Callan *et al.* [139], Moffat and Zobel [574], Viles and French [787], and others.

Acknowledgements

The author gratefully acknowledges the support of IBM.

Chapter 10
User Interfaces and Visualization

by Marti A. Hearst

10.1 Introduction

This chapter discusses user interfaces for communication between human information seekers and information retrieval systems. Information seeking is an imprecise process. When users approach an information access system they often have only a fuzzy understanding of how they can achieve their goals. Thus the user interface should aid in the understanding and expression of information needs. It should also help users formulate their queries, select among available information sources, understand search results, and keep track of the progress of their search.

The human-computer interface is less well understood than other aspects of information retrieval, in part because humans are more complex than computer systems, and their motivations and behaviors are more difficult to measure and characterize. The area is also undergoing rapid change, and so the discussion in this chapter will emphasize recent developments rather than established wisdom.

The chapter will first outline the human side of the information seeking process and then focus on the aspects of this process that can best be supported by the user interface. Discussion will encompass current practice and technology, recently proposed innovative ideas, and suggestions for future areas of development.

Section 10.2 outlines design principles for human-computer interaction and introduces notions related to information visualization. section 10.3 describes information seeking models, past and present. The next four sections describe user interface support for starting the search process, for query specification, for viewing retrieval results in context, and for interactive relevance feedback. The last major section, section 10.8, describes user interface techniques to support the information access process as a whole. Section 10.9 speculates on future developments and Section 10.10 provides suggestions for further reading. Figure 10.1 presents the flow of the chapter contents.

Figure 10.1   The flow of this chapter's contents.

10.2 Human-Computer Interaction

What makes an effective human-computer interface? Ben Shneiderman, an expert in the field, writes [725, p.10]:

> Well designed, effective computer systems generate positive feelings of success, competence, mastery, and clarity in the user community. When an interactive system is well-designed, the interface almost disappears, enabling users to concentrate on their work, exploration, or pleasure.

As steps towards achieving these goals, Shneiderman lists principles for design of user interfaces. Those which are particularly important for information access include (slightly restated): provide informative feedback, permit easy reversal of actions, support an internal locus of control, reduce working memory load, and provide alternative interfaces for novice and expert users. Each of these principles should be instantiated differently depending on the particular interface application. Below we discuss those principles that are of special interest to information access systems.

10.2.1 Design Principles

Offer informative feedback. This principle is especially important for information access interfaces. In this chapter we will see current ideas about how to provide users with feedback about the relationship between their query specification and documents retrieved, about relationships among retrieved documents, and about relationships between retrieved documents and metadata describing collections. If the user has control of how and when feedback is provided, then the system provides an *internal locus of control.*

Reduce working memory load. Information access is an iterative process, the goals of which shift and change as information is encountered. One key way information access interfaces can help with memory load is to provide mechanisms for keeping track of choices made during the search process, allowing users to return to temporarily abandoned strategies, jump from one strategy to the next, and retain information and context across search sessions. Another memory-aiding device is to provide browsable information that is relevant to the current stage of the information access process. This includes suggestions of related terms or metadata, and search starting points including lists of sources and topic lists.

Provide alternative interfaces for novice and expert users. An important tradeoff in all user interface design is that of simplicity versus power. Simple interfaces are easier to learn, at the expense of less flexibility and sometimes less efficient use. Powerful interfaces allow a knowledgeable user to do more and have more control over the operation of the interface, but can be time-consuming to learn and impose a memory burden on people who use the system only intermittently. A common solution is to use a 'scaffolding' technique [684]. The novice user is presented with a simple interface that can be learned quickly and that provides the basic functionality of the application, but is restricted in power and flexibility. Alternative interfaces are offered for more experienced users, giving them more control, more options, and more features, or potentially even entirely different interaction models. Good user interface design provides intuitive bridges between the simple and the advanced interfaces.

Information access interfaces must contend with special kinds of simplicity/power tradeoffs. One such tradeoff is the amount of information shown about the workings of the search system itself. Users who are new to a system or to a particular collection may not know enough about the system or the domain associated with the collection to make choices among complex features. They may not know how best to weight terms, or in the case of relevance feedback, not know what the effects of reweighting terms would be. On the other hand, users that have worked with a system and gotten a feeling for a topic are likely to be able to choose among suggested terms to add to their query in an informed manner. Determining how much information to show the user of the system is a major design choice in information access interfaces.

10.2.2 The Role of Visualization

The tools of computer interface design are familiar to most computer users today: windows, menus, icons, dialog boxes, and so on. These make use of bit-mapped display and computer graphics to provide a more accessible interface than command-line-based displays. A less familiar but growing area is that of *information visualization*, which attempts to provide visual depictions of very large information spaces.

Humans are highly attuned to images and visual information [769, 456, 483]. Pictures and graphics can be captivating and appealing, especially if well designed. A visual representation can communicate some kinds of information much more rapidly and effectively than any other method. Consider the difference between a written description of a person's face and a photograph of it, or the difference between a table of numbers containing a correlation and a scatter plot showing the same information.

The growing prevalence of fast graphics processors and high resolution color monitors is increasing interest in information visualization. Scientific visualization, a rapidly advancing branch of this field, maps physical phenomena onto two- or three-dimensional representations [433]. An example of scientific visualization is a colorful image of the pattern of peaks and valleys on the ocean floor; this provides a view of physical phenomena for which a photograph cannot (currently) be taken. Instead, the image is constructed from data that represent the underlying phenomena.

Visualization of inherently abstract information is more difficult, and visualization of textually represented information is especially challenging. Language is our main means of communicating abstract ideas for which there is no obvious physical manifestation. What does a picture look like that describes negotiations over a trade agreement in which one party demands concessions on environmental policies while the other requires help in strengthening its currency?

Despite the difficulties, researchers are attempting to represent aspects of the information access process using information visualization techniques. Some of these will be described later in this chapter. Aside from using *icons* and *color highlighting*, the main information visualization techniques include *brushing and linking* [233, 773], *panning and zooming* [71], *focus-plus-context* [502], *magic lenses* [95], and the use of *animation* to retain context and help make occluded information visible [676, 143]. These techniques support dynamic, interactive use. Interactivity seems to be an especially important property for visualizing abstract information, although it has not played as large a role within scientific visualization.

Brushing and linking refers to the connecting of two or more views of the same data, such that a change to the representation in one view affects the representation in the other views as well. For example, say a display consists of two parts: a histogram and a list of titles. The histogram shows, for a set of documents, how many documents were published each year. The title list shows the titles for the corresponding documents. Brushing and linking would allow the user to assign a color, say red, to one bar of the histogram, thus causing the titles in the list display that were published during the corresponding year to also be highlighted in red.

Panning and zooming refers to the actions of a movie camera that can scan sideways across a scene (panning) or move in for a closeup or back away to get a wider view (zooming). For example, text clustering can be used to show a top-level view of the main themes in a document collection (see Figures 10.7 and 10.8). Zooming can be used to move 'closer,' showing individual documents as icons, and then zoom in closer still to see the text associated with an individual document.

When zooming is used, the more detail that is visible about a particular item, the less can be seen about the surrounding items. Focus-plus-context is used to partly alleviate this effect. The idea is to make one portion of the view — the focus of attention — larger, while simultaneously shrinking the surrounding objects. The farther an object is from the focus of attention, the smaller it is made to appear, like the effect seen in a fisheye camera lens (also in some door peepholes).

Magic lenses are directly manipulable transparent windows that, when overlapped on some other data type, cause a transformation to be applied to the underlying data, thus changing its appearance (see Figure 10.13). The most straightforward application of magic lenses is for drawing tasks, and it is especially useful if used as a two-handed interface. For example, the left hand can be used to position a color lens over a drawing of an object. The right hand is used to mouse-click on the lens, thus causing the appearance of the underlying object to be transformed to the color specified by the lens.

Additionally, there are a large number of graphical methods for depicting trees and hierarchies, some of which make use of animation to show nodes that would otherwise be occluded (hidden from view by other nodes) [286, 364, 407, 478, 676].

It is often useful to combine these techniques into an interface layout consisting of an *overview plus details* [321, 644]. An overview, such as a table-of-contents of a large manual, is shown in one window. A mouse-click on the title of the chapter causes the text of the chapter itself to appear in another window, in a linking action (see Figure 10.19). Panning and zooming or focus-plus-context can be used to change the view of the contents within the overview window.

10.2.3   Evaluating Interactive Systems

From the viewpoint of user interface design, people have widely differing abilities, preferences, and predilections. Important differences for information access interfaces include relative spatial ability and memory, reasoning abilities, verbal aptitude, and (potentially) personality differences [227, 725]. Age and cultural differences can contribute to acceptance or rejection of interface techniques [557]. An interface innovation can be useful and pleasing for some users, and foreign and cumbersome for others. Thus software design should allow for flexibility in interaction style, and new features should not be expected to be equally helpful for all users.

An important aspect of human-computer interaction is the methodology for evaluation of user interface techniques. Precision and recall measures have been widely used for comparing the ranking results of non-interactive systems, but are less appropriate for assessing interactive systems [470]. The standard evaluations emphasize high recall levels; in the TREC tasks systems are compared to see how well they return the top 1000 documents (see chapter 3). However, in many interactive settings, users require only a few relevant documents and do not care about high recall to evaluate highly interactive information access systems, useful metrics beyond precision and recall include: time required to learn the system, time required to achieve goals on benchmark tasks, error rates, and retention of the use of the interface over time. Throughout this chapter, empirical results of user studies are presented whenever they are available.

Empirical data involving human users is time consuming to gather and difficult to draw conclusions from. This is due in part to variation in users' characteristics and motivations, and in part to the broad scope of information access activities. Formal psychological studies usually only uncover narrow conclusions within restricted contexts. For example, quantities such as the length of time it takes for a user to select an item from a fixed menu under various conditions have been characterized empirically [142], but variations in interaction behavior for complex tasks like information access are difficult to account for accurately. Nielsen [605] advocates a more informal evaluation approach (called heuristic evaluation) in which user interface affordances are assessed in terms of more general properties and without concern about statistically significant results.

10.3   The Information Access Process

A person engaged in an information seeking process has one or more *goals* in mind and uses a search system as a tool to help achieve those goals. Goals requiring information access can range quite widely, from finding a plumber to keeping informed about a business competitor, from writing a publishable scholarly article to investigating an allegation of fraud.

Information access *tasks* are used to achieve these goals. These tasks span the spectrum from asking specific questions to exhaustively researching a topic. Other tasks fall between these two extremes. A study of business analysts [614] found three main kinds of information seeking tasks: monitoring a well known topic over time (such as researching competitors' activities each quarter), following a plan or stereotyped series of searches to achieve a particular goal (such as keeping up to date on good business practices), and exploring a topic in an undirected fashion (as when getting to know an unfamiliar industry). Although the goals differ, there is a common core revolving around the information seeking component, which is our focus here.

10.3.1   Models of Interaction

Most accounts of the information access process assume an interaction cycle consisting of query specification, receipt and examination of retrieval results, and then either stopping or reformulating the query and repeating the process until a perfect result set is found [700, 726]. In more detail, the standard process can be described according to the following sequence of steps (see Figure 10.2):

(1) Start with an information need.

(2) Select a system and collections to search on.

(3) Formulate a query.

(4) Send the query to the system.

(5) Receive the results in the form of information items.

(6) Scan, evaluate, and interpret the results.

(7) Either stop, or,

(8) Reformulate the query and go to step 4.

This simple interaction model (used by Web search engines) is the only model that most information seekers see today. This model does not take into account the fact that many users dislike being confronted with a long disorganized list of retrieval results that do not directly address their information needs. It also contains an underlying assumption that the user's information need is static and the information seeking process is one of successively refining a query until it retrieves all and only those documents relevant to the original information need.

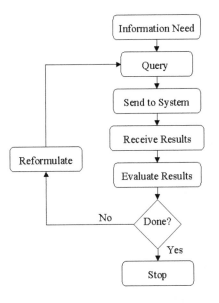

Figure 10.2   A simplified diagram of the standard model of the information access processes.

In actuality, users learn during the search process. They scan information, read the titles in result sets, read the retrieved documents themselves, viewing lists of topics related to their query terms, and navigating within hyperlinked Web sites. The recent advent of hyperlinks as a pivotal part of the information seeking process makes it no longer feasible to ignore the role of scanning and navigation within the search process itself. In particular, today a near-miss is much more acceptable than it was with bibliographic search, since an information seeker using the Web can navigate hyperlinks from a near-miss in the hopes that a useful page will be a few links away.

The standard model also downplays the interaction that takes place when the user scans terms suggested as a result of relevance feedback, scans thesaurus structures, or views thematic overviews of document collections. It de-emphasizes the role of source selection, which is increasingly important now that, for the first time, tens of thousands of information collections are immediately reachable for millions of people.

Thus, while useful for describing the basics of information access systems, this simple interaction model is being challenged on many fronts [65, 614, 105, 365, 192]. Bates [65] proposes the 'berry-picking' model of information seeking, which has two main points. The first is that, as a result of reading and learning from the information encountered throughout the search process, the users' information needs, and consequently their queries, continually shift. Information encountered at one point in a search may lead in a new, unanticipated direction. The original goal may become partly fulfilled, thus lowering the priority of one goal in favor of another. This is posed in contrast to the assumption of 'standard' information retrieval that the user's information need remains the same throughout the search process. The second point is that users' information needs are not satisfied by a single, final retrieved set of documents, but rather by a series of selections and bits of information found along the way. This is in contrast to the assumption that the main goal of the search process is to hone down the set of retrieved documents into a perfect match of the original information need.

The berry-picking model is supported by a number of observational studies [236, 105], including that of O'Day and Jeffries [614]. They found that the information seeking process consisted of a series of interconnected but diverse searches on one problem-based theme. They also found that search results for a goal tended to trigger new goals, and hence search in new directions, but that the context of the problem and the previous searches was carried from one stage of search to the next. They also found that the main value of the search resided in the accumulated learning and acquisition of information that occurred during the search process, rather than in the final results set.

Thus, a user interface for information access should allow users to reassess their goals and adjust their search strategy accordingly. A related situation occurs when users encounter a 'trigger' that causes them to pursue a different strategy temporarily, perhaps to return to the current unfinished activity at a later time. An implication of these observations is that the user interface should support search strategies by making it easy to follow trails with unanticipated results. This can be accomplished in part by supplying ways to record the progress of the current strategy and to store, find, and reload intermediate results, and by supporting pursuit of multiple strategies simultaneously.

The user interface should also support methods for monitoring the status of the current strategy in relation to the user's current task and high-level goals. One way to cast the activity of monitoring the progress of a search strategy relative to a goal or subgoal is in terms of a cost/benefit analysis, or an analysis of diminishing returns [690]. This kind of analysis assumes that at any point in the search process, the user is pursuing the strategy that has the highest expected utility. If, as a consequence of some local tactical choices, another strategy presents itself as being of higher utility than the current one, the current one is (temporarily or permanently) abandoned in favor of the new strategy.

There are a number of theories and frameworks that contrast *browsing*, *querying, navigating,* and *scanning* along several dimensions [75, 159, 542, 804]. Here we assume that users scan information structure, be it titles, thesaurus terms, hyperlinks, category labels, or the results of clustering, and then either select a displayed item for some purpose (to read in detail, to use as input to a query, to navigate to a new page of information) or formulate a query (either by recalling potential words or by selecting categories or suggested terms that have been scanned). In both cases, a new set of information is then made viewable for scanning. Queries tend to produce new, ad hoc collections of information that have not been gathered together before, whereas selection retrieves information that has already been composed or organized. Navigation refers to following a chain of links, switching from one view to another, toward some goal, in a sequence of scan and select operations. Browsing refers to the casual, mainly undirected exploration of information structures, and is usually done in tandem with selection, although queries can also be used to create subcollections to browse through. An important aspect of the interaction process is that the output of one action should be easily used as the input to the next.

10.3.2   Non-Search Parts of the Information Access Process

The O'Day and Jeffries study [614] found that information seeking is only one part of the full work process their subjects were engaged in. In between searching sessions many different kinds of work was done with the retrieved information, including reading and annotating [617] and analysis. O'Day and Jeffries examined the analysis steps in more detail, finding that 80% of this work fell into six main types: finding trends, making comparisons, aggregating information, identifying a critical subset, assessing, and interpreting. The remaining 20% consisted of cross-referencing, summarizing, finding evocative visualizations for reports, and miscellaneous activities. The Sensemaking work of Russell *et al.* [690] also discusses information work as a process in which information retrieval plays only a small part. They observe that most of the effort made in Sensemaking is in the synthesis of a good representation, or ways of thinking about, the problem at hand. They describe the process of formulating and crystallizing the important concepts for a given task.

From these observations it is convenient to divide the entire information access process into two main components: search/retrieval, and analysis/synthesis of results. User interfaces should allow both kinds of activity to be tightly interwoven. However, analysis/synthesis are activities that can be done independently of information seeking, and for our purposes it is useful to make a distinction between the two types of activities.

10.3.3   Earlier Interface Studies

The bulk of the literature on studies of human-computer information seeking behavior concerns information intermediaries using online systems consisting of bibliographic records (e.g., [546, 707, 104]), sometimes with costs assessed per time unit. Unfortunately, many of the assumptions behind those studies do not reflect the conditions of modern information access [335, 222]. The differences include the following:

- The text being searched now is often full text rather than bibliographic citations. Because users have access to full text, rather than document surrogates, it is more likely that simple queries will find relevant answers directly as part of the search process.

- Modern systems use statistical ranking (which is more effective when abstracts and full text are available than when only titles and citations are available) whereas most studies were performed on Boolean systems.

- Much of modern searching is done by end users, many new to online searching, rather than professional intermediaries, which were the focus of many of the earlier studies.

- Tens of thousands of sources are now available online on networked information systems, and many are tightly coupled via hyperlinks, as opposed to being stored in separate collections owned by separate services. Earlier studies generally used systems in which moving from one collection to another required prior knowledge of the collections and considerable time and effort to switch. A near miss is much more useful in this hyperlinked environment than in earlier systems, since hyperlinks allow users to navigate from the near miss directly to the source containing information of interest. In a card catalog environment, where documents are represented as isolated units, a near miss consists of finding a book in the general area of interest and then going to the bookshelf in the library to look for related books, or obtaining copies of many issues of a journal and scanning for related articles.

- Finally, most users have access to bit-mapped displays allowing for direct manipulation, or at least form fillin. Most earlier studies and bibliographic systems were implemented on TTY displays, which require command-line based syntax and do a poor job of retaining context.

Despite these significant differences, some general information seeking strategies have been identified that seem to transfer across systems. Additionally, although modern systems have remedied many of the problems of earlier online public access catalogs, they also introduce new problems of their own.

10.4   Starting Points

Search interfaces must provide users with good ways to get started. An empty screen or a blank entry form does not provide clues to help a user decide how to start the search process. Users usually do not begin by creating a long, detailed expression of their information need. Studies show that users tend to start out with very short queries, inspect the results, and then modify those queries in an incremental feedback cycle [22]. The initial query can be seen as a kind of 'testing the water' to see what kinds of results are returned and get an idea of how to reformulate the query [804, 65]. Thus, one task of an information access interface is to help users select the sources and collections to search on.

For example, there are many different information sources associated with cancer, and there are many different kinds of information a user might like to know about cancer. Guiding the user to the right set of starting points can help with the initial problem formulation. Traditional bibliographic search assumes that the user begins by looking through a list of names of sources and choosing which collections to search on, while Web search engines obliterate the distinctions between sources and plunge the user into the middle of a Web site with little information about the relationship of the search hit to the rest of the collection. In neither case is the interface to the available sources particularly helpful.

In this section we will discuss four main types of starting points: *lists*, *overviews*, *examples*, and *automated source selection*.

10.4.1   Lists of Collections

Typical online systems such as LEXIS-NEXIS require users to begin any inquiry with a scan through a long list of source names and guess which ones will be of interest. Usually little information beyond the name of the collection is provided online for these sources (see Figure 10.3). If the user is not satisfied with the results on one collection, they must reissue the query on another collection.

Frequent searchers eventually learn a set of sources that are useful for their domains of interest, either through experience, formal training, or recommendations from friends and colleagues. Often-used sources can be stored on a 'favorites' list, also known as a *bookmark* list or a *hotlist* on the Web. Recent research explores the maintenance of a personalized information profile for users or work groups, based on the kinds of information they've used in the past [277].

However, when users want to search outside their domains of expertise, a list of familiar sources is not sufficient. Professional searchers such as librarians

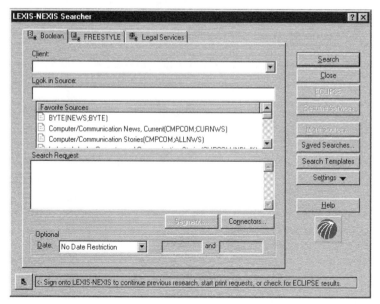

Figure 10.3   The LEXIS-NEXIS source selection screen.

learn through experience and years of training which sources are appropriate for various information needs. The restricted nature of traditional interfaces to information collections discourages exploration and discovery of new useful sources. However, recently researchers have devised a number of mechanisms to help users understand the contents of collections as a way of getting started in their search.

10.4.2   Overviews

Faced with a large set of text collections, how can a user choose which to begin with? One approach is to study an overview of the contents of the collections. An overview can show the topic domains represented within the collections, to help users select or eliminate sources from consideration. An overview can help users get started, directing them into general neighborhoods, after which they can navigate using more detailed descriptions. Shneiderman [724] advocates an interaction model in which the user begins with an overview of the information to be worked with, then pans and zooms to find areas of potential interest, and then view details. The process is repeated as often as necessary.

Three types of overviews are discussed in this subsection. The first is display and navigation of large topical *category hierarchies* associated with the documents of a collection. The second is automatically derived overviews, usually created by unsupervised *clustering techniques* on the text of documents, that attempt to extract overall characterizing themes from collections. The third type of overview is that created by applying a variant of *co-citation analysis* on connections or links between different entities within a collection. Other kinds of overviews are possible, for example, showing graphical depictions of bookshelves or piles of books [681, 46].

Category or Directory Overviews

There exist today many large online text collections to which category labels have been assigned. Traditional online bibliographic systems have for decades assigned subject headings to books and other documents [752]. MEDLINE, a large collection of biomedical articles, has associated with it Medical Subject Headings (MeSH) consisting of approximately 18,000 categories [523]. The Association for Computing Machinery (ACM) has developed a hierarchy of approximately 1200 category (keyword) labels.† Yahoo![839], one of the most popular search sites on the World Wide Web, organizes Web pages into a hierarchy consisting of thousands of category labels.

The popularity of Yahoo! and other Web directories suggests that hierarchically structured categories are useful starting points for users seeking information on the Web. This popularity may reflect a preference to begin at a logical starting point, such as the home page for a set of information, or it may reflect a desire to avoid having to guess which words will retrieve the desired information. (It may also reflect the fact that directory services attempt to cull out low quality Web sites.)

The meanings of category labels differ somewhat among collections. Most are designed to help organize the documents and to aid in query specification. Unfortunately, users of online bibliographic catalogs rarely use the available subject headings [335, 222]. Hancock-Beaulieu and Drabenstott and Weller, among others, put much of the blame on poor (command line-based) user interfaces which provide little aid for selecting subject labels and require users to scroll through long alphabetic lists. Even with graphical Web interfaces, finding the appropriate place within a category hierarchy can be a time-consuming task, and once a collection has been found using such a representation, an alternative means is required for searching within the site itself.

Most interfaces that depict category hierarchies graphically do so by associating a document directly with the node of the category hierarchy to which it has been assigned. For example, clicking on a category link in Yahoo! brings up a list of documents that have been assigned that category label. Conceptually, the document is stored within the category label. When navigating the results of a search in Yahoo!, the user must look through a list of category labels and guess which one is most likely to contain references to the topic of interest. A wrong path requires backing up and trying again, and remembering which pages contain which information. If the desired information is deep in the hierarchy, or

---

† http://www.acm.org/class

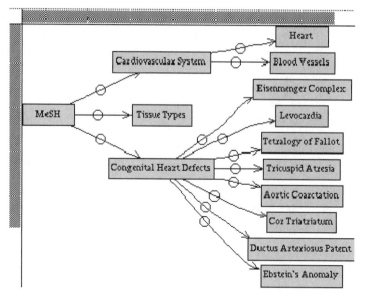

Figure 10.4   The MeSHBrowse interface for viewing category labels hierarchically [453].

not available at all, this can be a time-consuming and frustrating process. Because documents are conceptually stored 'inside' categories, users cannot create queries based on combinations of categories using this interface.

It is difficult to design a good interface to integrate category selection into query specification, in part because display of category hierarchies takes up large amounts of screen space. For example, Internet Grateful Med‡ is a Web-based service that allows an integration of search with display and selection of MeSH category labels. After the user types in the name of a potential category label, a long list of choices is shown in a page. To see more information about a given label, the user selects a link (e.g., Radiation Injuries). The causes the context of the query to disappear because a new Web page appears showing the ancestors of the term and its immediate descendants. If the user attempts to see the siblings of the parent term (Wounds and Injuries) then a new page appears that changes the context again. Radiation Injuries appears as one of many siblings and its children can no long be seen. To go back to the query, the illustration of the category hierarchy disappears.

The MeSHBrowse system [453] allows users to interactively browse a subset of semantically associated links in the MeSH hierarchy. From a given starting point, clicking on a category causes the associated categories to be displayed in a two-dimensional tree representation. Thus only the relevant subset of the

---

‡ http://igm.nlm.nih.gov:80/

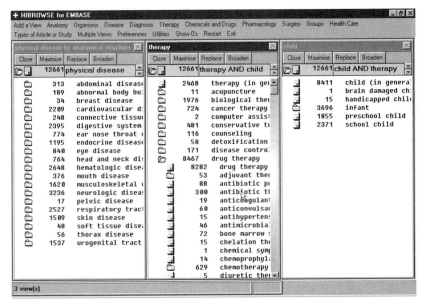

Figure 10.5   The HiBrowse interface for viewing category labels hierarchically and according to facets [646].

hierarchy is shown at one time, making browsing of this very large hierarchy a more tractable endeavor. The interface has the space limitations inherent in a two-dimensional hierarchy display and does not provide mechanisms for search over an underlying document collection. See Figure 10.4.

The HiBrowse system [646] represents category metadata more efficiently by allowing users to display several different subsets of category metadata simultaneously. The user first selects which attribute type (or facet, as attributes are called in this system) to display. For example, the user may first choose the 'physical disease' value for the Disease facet. The categories that appear one level below this are shown along with the number of documents that contain each category. The user can then select other attribute types, such as Therapy and Groups (by age). The number of documents that contain attributes from all three types are shown. If the user now selects a refinement of one of the categories, such as the 'child' value for the Groups attribute, then the number of documents that contain all three selected facet types are shown. At the same time, the number of documents containing the subcategories found below 'physical disease' and 'therapy (general)' are updated to reflect this more restricted specification. See Figure 10.5. A problem with the HiBrowse system is that it requires users to navigate through the category hierarchy, rather than specify queries directly. In other words, query specification is not tightly coupled with display of category metadata. As a solution to some of these problems, the Cat-a-Cone interface [358] will be described in section 10.8.

Automatically Derived Collection Overviews

Many attempts to display overview information have focused on automatically extracting the most common general themes that occur within the collection. These themes are derived via the use of unsupervised analysis methods, usually variants of document clustering. Clustering organizes documents into groups based on similarity to one another; the centroids of the clusters determine the themes in the collections.

The Scatter/Gather browsing paradigm [203, 202] clusters documents into topically-coherent groups, and presents descriptive textual summaries to the user. The summaries consist of topical terms that characterize each cluster generally, and a set of typical titles that hint at the contents of the cluster. Informed by the summaries, the user may select a subset of clusters that seem to be of most interest, and recluster their contents. Thus the user can examine the contents of each subcollection at progressively finer granularity of detail. The reclustering is computed on-the-fly; different themes are produced depending on the documents contained in the subcollection to which clustering is applied. The choice of clustering algorithm influences what clusters are produced, but no one algorithm has been shown to be particularly better than the rest when producing the same number of clusters [816].

A user study [640] showed that the use of Scatter/Gather on a large text collection successfully conveys some of the content and structure of the corpus. However, that study also showed that Scatter/Gather without a search facility was less effective than a standard similarity search for finding relevant documents for a query. That is, subjects allowed only to navigate, not to search over, a hierarchical structure of clusters covering the entire collection were less able to find documents relevant to the supplied query than subjects allowed to write queries and scan through retrieval results.

It is possible to integrate Scatter/Gather with conventional search technology by applying clustering on the results of a query to organize the retrieved documents (see Figure 10.6). An offline experiment [359] suggests that clustering may be more effective if used in this manner. The study found that documents relevant to the query tend to fall mainly into one or two out of five clusters, if the clusters are generated from the top-ranked documents retrieved in response to the query. The study also showed that precision and recall were higher within the best cluster than within the retrieval results as a whole. The implication is that a user might save time by looking at the contents of the cluster with the highest proportion of relevant documents and at the same time avoiding those clusters with mainly non-relevant documents. Thus, clustering of retrieval results may be useful for helping direct users to a subset of the retrieval results that contain a large proportion of the relevant documents.

General themes do seem to arise from document clustering, but the themes are highly dependent on the makeup of the documents within the clusters [359, 357]. The unsupervised nature of clustering can result in a display of topics at varying levels of description. For example, clustering a collection of documents about computer science might result in clusters containing documents about

☐ Cluster 1 Size: 8   key army war francis spangle banner air song scott word poem british
○ Star–Spangled Banner, The
○ Key, Francis Scott
○ Fort McHenry
○ Arnold, Henry Harley
○ Nikisch, Arthur

☐ Cluster 2 Size: 68   film play career win television role record award york popular stage p
○ Burstyn, Ellen
○ Stanwyck, Barbara
○ Berle, Milton
○ Zukor, Adolph
○ Bankhead, Tallulah

☐ Cluster 3 Size: 97   bright magnitude cluster constellation line type contain period spectr
○ star
○ Galaxy, The
○ extragalactic systems
○ interstellar matter
○ cluster star

Figure 10.6   Display of Scatter/Gather clustering retrieval results [203].

artificial intelligence, computer theory, computer graphics, computer architecture, programming languages, government, and legal issues. The latter two themes are more general than the others, because they are about topics outside the general scope of computer science. Thus clustering can results in the juxtaposition of very different levels of description within a single display.

Scatter/Gather shows a textual representation of document clusters. Researchers have developed several approaches to map documents from their high dimensional representation in document space into a 2D representation in which each document is represented as a small glyph or icon on a map or within an abstract 2D space. The functions for transforming the data into the lower dimensional space differ, but the net effect is that each document is placed at one point in a scatter-plot-like representation of the space. Users are meant to detect themes or clusters in the arrangement of the glyphs. Systems employing such graphical displays include BEAD [156], the Galaxy of News [671], and ThemeScapes [821]. The ThemeScapes view imposes a three-dimensional representation on the results of clustering (see Figure 10.7). The layout makes use of 'negative space' to help emphasize the areas of concentration where the clusters occur. Other systems display inter-document similarity hierarchically [529, 14], while still others display retrieved documents in networks based on inter-document similarity [262, 761].

Kohonen's feature map algorithm has been used to create maps that graphically characterize the overall content of a document collection or subcollection [520, 163] (see Figure 10.8). The regions of the 2D map vary in size and shape corresponding to how frequently documents assigned to the corresponding themes occur within the collection. Regions are characterized by single words or phrases,

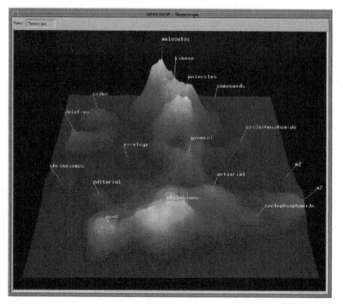

Figure 10.7   A three-dimensional overview based on document clustering [821].

and adjacency of regions is meant to reflect semantic relatedness of the themes within the collection. A cursor moved over a document region causes the titles of the documents most strongly associated with that region to be displayed in a pop-up window. Documents can be associated with more than one region.

Evaluations of Graphical Overviews

Although intuitively appealing, graphical overviews of large document spaces have yet to be shown to be useful and understandable for users. In fact, evaluations that have been conducted so far provide negative evidence as to their usefulness. One study found that for non-expert users the results of clustering were difficult to use, and that graphical depictions (for example, representing clusters with circles and lines connecting documents) were much harder to use than textual representations (for example, showing titles and topical words, as in Scatter/Gather), because documents' contents are difficult to discern without actually reading some text [443].

Another recent study compared the Kohonen feature map overview representation on a browsing task to that of Yahoo! [163]. For one of the tasks, subjects were asked to find an 'interesting' Web page within the entertainment category of Yahoo! and of an organization of the same Web pages into a Kohonen map layout. The experiment varied whether subjects started in Yahoo! or in the graphical map. After completion of the browing task, subjects were asked to attempt to repeat the browse using the other tool. For the subjects that

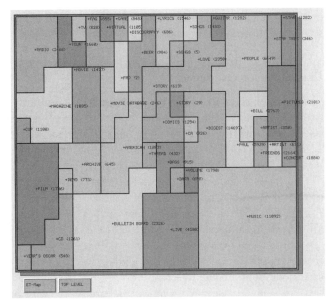

Figure 10.8   A two-dimensional overview created using a Kohonen feature map learning algorithm on Web pages having to do with the topic Entertainment [163].

began with the Kohonen map visualization, 11 out of 15 found an interesting page within ten minutes. Eight of these were able to find the same page using Yahoo!. Of the subjects who started with Yahoo!, 14 out of 16 were able to find interesting home pages. However, only two of the 14 were able to find the page in the graphical map display! This is strong evidence against the navigability of the display and certainly suggests that the simple label view provided by Yahoo! is more useful. However, the map display may be more useful if the system is modified to tightly integrate querying with browsing.

The subjects did prefer some aspects of the map representation. In particular, some liked the ease of being able to jump from one area to another without having to back up as is required in Yahoo!, and some liked the fact that the maps have varying levels of granularity. The subjects disliked several aspects of the display. The experimenters found that some subjects expressed a desire for a visible hierarchical organization, others wanted an ability to zoom in on a sub-area to get more detail, and some users disliked having to look through the entire map to find a theme, desiring an alphabetical ordering instead. Many found the single-term labels to be misleading, in part because they were ambiguous (one region called 'BILL' was thought to correspond to a person's name rather than counting money).

The authors concluded that this interface is more appropriate for casual browsing than for search. In general, unsupervised thematic overviews are perhaps most useful for giving users a 'gist' of the kinds of information that can be found within the document collection, but generally have not been shown to be helpful for use in the information access process.

Co-citation Clustering for Overviews

Citation analysis has long been recognized as a way to show an overview of the contents of a collection [812]. The main idea is to determine 'centrally-located' documents based on co-citation patterns. There are different ways to determine citation patterns: one method is to measure how often two articles are cited together by a third. Another alternative is to pair articles that cite the same third article. In both cases the assumption is that the paired articles share some commonalities. After a matrix of co-citations is built, documents are clustered based on the similarity of their co-citation patterns. The resulting clusters are interpreted to indicate dominant themes within the collection. Clustering can focus on the authors of the documents rather than the contents, to attempt to identify central authors within a field. This idea has recently been implemented using Web-based documents in the Referral Web project [432]. The idea has also been applied to Web pages, using Web link structure to identify major topical themes among Web pages [485, 639]. A similar idea, but computed a different way, is used to explicitly identify pages that act as good starting points for particular topics (called 'authority pages' by Kleinberg [444]).

10.4.3   Examples, Dialogs, and Wizards

Another way to help users get started is to start them off with an example of interaction with the system. This technique is also known as *retrieval by reformulation*. An early version of this idea is embodied in the Rabbit system [818] which provides graphical representations of example database queries. A general framework for a query is shown to the user who then modifies it to construct a partially complete description of what they want. The system then shows an example of the kind of information available that matches this partial description. For instance, if a user searching a computer products database indicates an interest in disks, an example item is retrieved with its disk descriptors filled in. The user can use or modify the displayed descriptors, and iterate the procedure.

The idea of retrieval by reformulation has been developed further and extended to the domains of user interface development [581] and software engineering [669]. The Helgon system [255] is a modern variant of this idea applied to bibliographic database information. In Helgon, users begin by navigating a hierarchy of topics from which they select structured examples, according to their interests. If a feature of an example is inappropriately set, the user can modify the feature to indicate how it would appear in the desired information. Unfortunately, in tests with users, the system was found to be problematic. Users had problems with the organization of the hierarchy, and found that searching for a useful example by critiquing an existing one to be tedious. This result underscores an unfortunate difficulty with examples and dialogues: that of getting the user to the right starting dialogue or the right example strategy becomes a search problem in itself. (How to index prior examples is studied extensively in the case-based reasoning (CBR) literature [492, 449].)

A more dynamic variation on this theme is the interactive dialog. Dialog-based interfaces have been explored since the early days of information retrieval research, in an attempt to mimic the interaction provided by a human search intermediary (e.g., a reference librarian). Oddy did early work in the THOMAS system, which provided a question and answer session within a command-line-based interface [615]. More recently, Belkin *et al.* have defined quite elaborate dialog interaction models [75] although these have not been assessed empirically to date.

The DLITE system interface [192] uses an animated focus-plus-context dialog as a way to acquaint users with standard sequences of operations within the system. Initially an outline of all of the steps of the dialog is shown as a list. The user can expand the explanation of any individual step by clicking on its description. The user can expand out the entire dialog to see what questions are coming next, and then collapse it again in order to focus on the current tactic.

A more restricted form of dialog that has become widely used in commercial products is that of the *wizard*. This tool helps users in time-limited tasks, but does not attempt to overtly teach the processes required to complete the tasks. The wizard presents a step-by-step shortcut through the sequence of menu choices (or tactics) that a user would normally perform in order to get a job done, reducing user input to just a few choices with default settings [636]. A recent study [145] found wizards to be useful for goals that require many steps, for users who lack necessary domain knowledge (for example, a restaurant owner installing accounting software), and when steps must be completed in a fixed sequence (for example, a procedure for hiring personnel). Properties of successful wizards included allowing users to rerun a wizard and modify their previous work, showing an overview of the supported functions, and providing lucid descriptions and understandable outcomes for choices. Wizards were found not to be helpful when the interface did not solve a problem effectively (for example, a commercial wizard for setting up a desktop search index requests users to specify how large to make the index, but supplies no information about how to make this decision). Wizards were also found not to be helpful when the goal was to teach the user how to use the interface, and when the wizard was not user-tested. It maybe the case that information access is too variable a process for the use of wizards.

A *guided tour* leads a user through a sequence of navigational choices through hypertext links, presenting the nodes in a logical order for some goal. In a dynamic tour, only relevant nodes are displayed, as opposed to the static case where the author decides what is relevant before the users have even formulated their queries [329]. A recent application is the Walden Paths project which enables teachers to define instructionally useful paths through pages found on the Web [289]. This approach has not been commonly used to date for information access but could be a promising direction for acquainting users with search strategies in large hyperlinked systems.

10.4.4 Automated Source Selection

Human-computer interfaces for helping guide users to appropriate sources is a wide open area for research. It requires both eliciting the information need from users and understanding which needs can be satisfied by which sources. An ambitious approach is to build a model of the source and of the information need of the user and try to determine which fit together best. User modeling systems and intelligent tutoring systems attempt to do this both for general domains [204, 814] and for online help systems [378].

A simpler alternative is to create a representation of the contents of information sources and match this representation against the query specification. This approach is taken by GlOSS, a system which tries to determine in advance the best bibliographic database to send a search request to, based on the terms in the query [765]. The system uses a simple analysis of the combined frequencies of the query words within the individual collections. The SavvySearch system [383] takes this idea a step further, using actions taken by users after a query to decide how to decrease or increase the ranking of a search engine for a particular query (see also Chapter 13).

The flip side to automatically selecting the best source for a query is to automatically send a query to multiple sources and then combine the results from the various systems in some way. Many metasearch engines exist on the Web. How to combine the results effectively is an active area of research, sometimes known as collection fusion [63, 767, 388].

10.5 Query Specification

To formulate a query, a user must select collections, metadata descriptions, or information sets against which the query is to be matched, and must specify words, phrases, descriptors, or other kinds of information that can be compared to or matched against the information in the collections. As a result, the system creates a set of documents, metadata, or other information type that match the query specification in some sense and displays the results to the user in some form.

Shneiderman [725] identifies five primary human-computer interaction styles. These are: *command language, form fillin, menu selection, direct manipulation*, and *natural language*.§ Each technique has been used in query specification interfaces and each has advantages and disadvantages. These are described below in the context of Boolean query specification.

---

§ This list omits non-visual modalities, such as audio.

10.5.1 Boolean Queries

In modern information access systems the matching process usually employs a statistical ranking algorithm. However, until recently most commercial full-text systems and most bibliographic systems supported only Boolean queries. Thus the focus of many information access studies has been on the problems users have in specifying Boolean queries. Unfortunately, studies have shown time and again that most users have great difficulty specifying queries in Boolean format and often misjudge what the results will be [111, 322, 558, 841].

Boolean queries are problematic for several reasons. Foremost among these is that most people find the basic syntax counter-intuitive. Many English-speaking users assume everyday semantics are associated with Boolean operators when expressed using the English words AND and OR, rather than their logical equivalents. To inexperienced users, using AND implies the widening of the scope of the query, because more kinds of information are being requested. For instance, 'dogs and cats' may imply a request for documents about dogs and documents about cats, rather than documents about both topics at once. 'Tea or coffee' can imply a mutually exclusive choice in everyday language. This kind of conceptual problem is well documented [111, 322, 558, 841]. In addition, most query languages that incorporate Boolean operators also require the user to specify complex syntax for other kinds of connectors and for descriptive metadata. Most users are not familiar with the use of parentheses for nested evaluation, nor with the notions associated with operator precedence.

By serving a massive audience possessing little query-specification experience, the designers of World Wide Web search engines have had to come up with more intuitive approaches to query specification. Rather than forcing users to specify complex combinations of ANDs and ORs, they allow users to choose from a selection of common simple ways of combining query terms, including 'all the words' (place all terms in a conjunction) and 'any of the words' (place all terms in a disjunction).

Another Web-based solution is to allow syntactically-based query specification, but to provide a simpler or more intuitive syntax. The '+' prefix operator gained widespread use with the advent of its use as a mandatory specifier in the Altavista Web search engine. Unfortunately, users can be misled to think it is an infix AND rather than a prefix mandatory operator, and thus assume that 'cat + dog' will only retrieve articles containing both terms (where in fact this query requires dog but allows cat to be optional).

Another problem with pure Boolean systems is they do not rank the retrieved documents according to their degree of match to the query. In the pure Boolean framework a document either satisfies the query or it does not. Commercial systems usually resort to ordering documents according to some kind of descriptive metadata, usually in reverse chronological order. (Since these systems usually index timely data corresponding to newspaper and news wires, date of publication is often one of the most salient features of the document.) Web-based systems usually rank order the results of Boolean queries using statistical algorithms and Web-specific heuristics.

10.5.2   From Command Lines to Forms and Menus

Aside from conceptual misunderstandings of the logical meaning of AND and OR, another part of the problem with pure Boolean query specification in online bibliographic systems is the arbitrariness of the syntax and the contextlessness nature of the TTY-based interface in which they are predominantly available. Typically input is typed at a prompt and is of a form something like the following:

> COMMAND ATTRIBUTE value {BOOLEAN-OPERATOR AT-TRIBUTE value}*
> e.g.,
> FIND PA darwin AND TW species OR TW descent
> or
> FIND TW Mt St. Helens AND DATE 1981

(These examples are derived from the syntax of the telnet interface to the University of California Melvyl system [526].) The user must remember the commands and attribute names, which are easily forgotten between usages of the system [553]. Compounding this problem, despite the fact that the command languages for the two main online bibliographic systems at UC Berkeley have different but very similar syntaxes, after more than ten years one of the systems still reports an error if the author field is specified as PA instead of PN, as is done in the other system. This lack of flexibility in the syntax is characteristic of interfaces designed to suit the system rather than its users.

The new Web-based version of Melvyl‖ provides form fillin and menu selection so the user no longer has to remember the names and types of attributes available. Users select metadata types from listboxes and attributes are shown explicitly, allowing selection as an alternative to specification. For example, the 'search type' field is adjacent to an entry form in which users can enter keywords, and a choice between AND and NOT is provided adjacent to a list of the available document types (editorial, feature, etc.). Only the metadata associated with a given collection is shown in the context of search over that collection. (Unfortunately the system is restricted to searching over only one database at a time. It does however provide a mechanism for applying a previously executed search to a new database.) See Figure 10.9.

The Web-based version of Melvyl also allows retention of context between searches, storing prior results in tables and hyperlinking these results to lists containing the retrieved bibliographic information. Users can also modify any of the previously submitted queries by selecting a checkbox beside the record of the query. The graphical display makes explicit and immediate many of the powerful options of the system that most users would not learn using the command-line version of the interface.

Bit-mapped displays are an improvement over command-line interface, but do not solve all the problems. For example, a blank entry form is in some ways

---

‖ http://www.melvyl.ucop.edu/

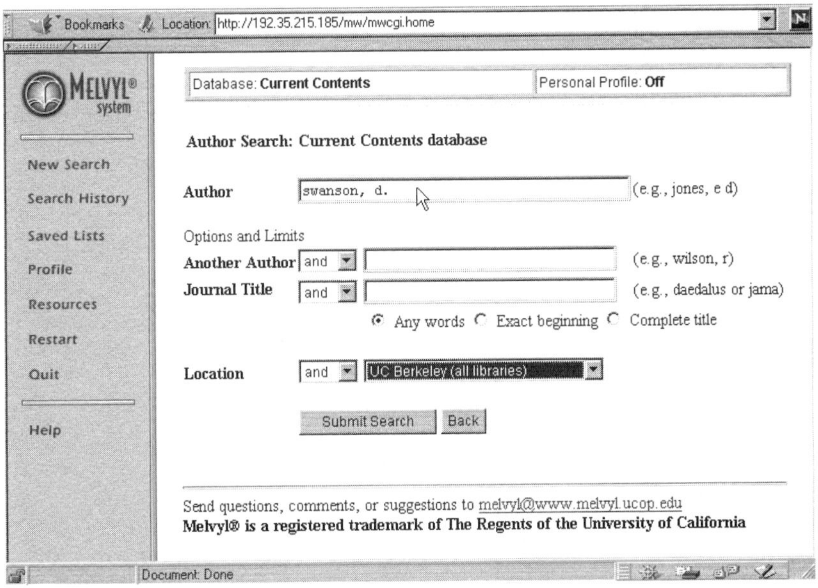

Figure 10.9   A view of query specification in the Web-based version of the Melvyl bibliographic catalog. Copyright © 1998, The Regents of the University of California.

not much better than a TTY prompt, because it does not provide the user with clues about what kinds of terms should be entered.

10.5.3 Faceted Queries

Yet another problem with Boolean queries is that their strict interpretation tends to yield result sets that are either too large, because the user includes many terms in a disjunct, or are empty, because the user conjoins terms in an effort to reduce the result set. This problem occurs in large part because the user does not know the contents of the collection or the role of terms within the collection.

A common strategy for dealing with this problem, employed in systems with command-line-based interfaces like DIALOG's, is to create a series of short queries, view the number of documents returned for each, and combine those queries that produce a reasonable number of results. For example, in DIALOG, each query produces a resulting set of documents that is assigned an identifying name. Rather than returning a list of titles themselves, DIALOG shows the set number with a listing of the number of matched documents. Titles can be shown by specifying the set number and issuing a command to show the titles. Document sets that are not empty can be referred to by a set name and combined with AND operations to produce new sets. If this set in turn is too small, the user can back up and try a different combination of sets, and this process is repeated in pursuit of producing a reasonably sized document set.

This kind of query formulation is often called a *faceted* query, to indicate that the user's query is divided into topics or facets, each of which should be present in the retrieved documents [553, 348]. For example, a query on drugs for the prevention of osteoporosis might consist of three facets, indicated by the disjuncts

(osteoporosis OR 'bone loss')
(drugs OR pharmaceuticals)
(prevention OR cure)

This query implies that the user would like to view documents that contain all three topics.

A technique to impose an ordering on the results of Boolean queries is what is known as *post-coordinate* or *quorum-level* ranking [700, Ch. 8]. In this approach, documents are ranked according to the size of the subset of the query terms they contain. So given a query consisting of 'cats,' 'dogs,' 'fish,' and 'mice,' the system would rank a document with at least one instance of 'cats,' 'dogs,' and 'fish' higher than a document containing 30 occurrences of 'cats' but no occurrences of the other terms.

Combining faceted queries with quorum ranking yields a situation intermediate between full Boolean syntax and free-form natural language queries. An interface for specifying this kind of interaction can consist of a list of entry lines. The user enters one topic per entry line, where each topic consists of a list of semantically related terms that are combined in a disjunct. Documents that contain at least one term from each facet are ranked higher than documents containing terms only from one or a few facets. This helps ensure that documents which contain discussions of several of the user's topics are ranked higher than those that contain only one topic. By only requiring that one term from each facet be matched, the user can specify the same concept in several different ways in the hopes of increasing the likelihood of a match. If combined with graphical feedback about which subsets of terms matched the document, the user can see the results of a quorum ranking by topic rather than by word. Section 10.6 describes the TileBars interface which provides this type of feedback.

This idea can be extended yet another step by allowing users to weight each facet. More likely to be readily usable, however, is a default weighting in which the facet listed highest is assigned the most weight, the second facet is assigned less weight, and so on, according to some distribution over weights.

10.5.4 Graphical Approaches to Query Specification

Direct manipulation interfaces provide an alternative to command-line syntax. The properties of direct manipulation are [725, p.205]: (1) continuous representation of the object of interest, (2) physical actions or button presses instead of complex syntax, and (3) rapid incremental reversible operations whose impact on the object of interest is immediately visible. Direct manipulation interfaces often evoke enthusiasm from users, and for this reason alone it is worth exploring their use. Although they are not without drawbacks, they are easier to use than other methods for many users in many contexts.

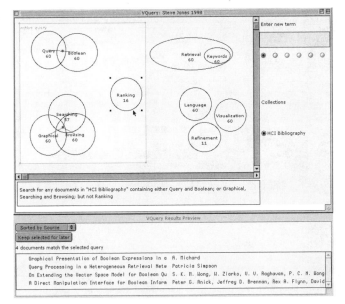

Figure 10.10   The VQuery Venn diagram visualization for Boolean query specification [417].

Several variations of graphical interfaces, both directly manipulable and static, have been developed for simplifying the specification of Boolean syntax. User studies tend to reveal that these graphical interfaces are more effective in terms of accuracy and speed than command-language counterparts. Three such approaches are described below.

Graphical depictions of *Venn diagrams* have been proposed several times as a way to improve Boolean query specification. A query term is associated with a ring or circle and intersection of rings indicates conjunction of terms. Typically the number of documents that satisfy the various conjuncts are displayed within the appropriate segments of the diagram. Several studies have found such interfaces more effective than their command-language-based syntax [417, 368, 558]. Hertzum and Frokjaer found that a simple Venn diagram representation produced faster and more accurate results than a Boolean query syntax. However, a problem with this format is the limitations on the complexity of the expression. For example, a maximum of three query terms can be ANDed together in a standard Venn diagram. Innovations have been designed to get around this problem, as seen in the VQuery system [417] (see Figure 10.10). In VQuery, a direct manipulation interface allows users to assign any number of query terms to ovals. If two or more ovals are placed such that they overlap with one another, and if the user selects the area of their intersection, an AND is implied among those terms. (In Figure 10.10, the term 'Query' is conjoined with 'Boolean'.) If the user selects outside the area of intersection but within the ovals, an OR is implied among the corresponding terms. A NOT operation

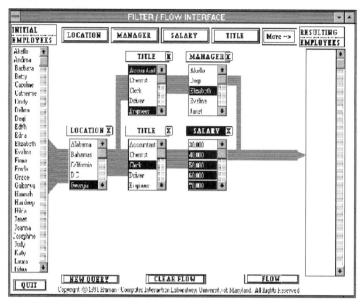

Figure 10.11   The filter-flow visualization for Boolean query specification [841].

is associated with any term whose oval appears in the active area of the display but which remains unselected (in the figure, NOT 'Ranking' has been specified). An active area indicates the current query; all groups of ovals within the active area are considered part of a conjunction. Ovals containing query terms can be moved out of the active area for later use.

Young and Shneiderman [841] found improvements over standard Boolean syntax by providing users with a direct manipulation *filter-flow* model. The user is shown a scrollable list of attribute types on the left-hand side and selects attributes from another list of attribute types shown across the top of the screen. Clicking on an attribute name causes a listbox containing values for those attributes to be displayed in the main portion of the screen. The user then selects which values of the attributes to let the flow go through. Placing two or more of these attributes in sequence creates the semantics of a conjunct over the selected values. Placing two or more of these in parallel creates the semantics of a disjunct. The number of documents that match the query at each point is indicated by the width of the 'water' flowing from one attribute to the next. (See Figure 10.11.) A conjunct can reduce the amount of flow. The items that match the full query are shown on the far right-hand side. A user study found that fewer errors were made using the filter flow model than a standard SQL database query. However, the examples and study pertain only to database querying rather than information access, since the possible query terms for information access cannot be represented realistically in a scrollable list. This interface could perhaps be modified to better suit information access applications by having the user supply initial query terms, and using the attribute selection facility to show those terms

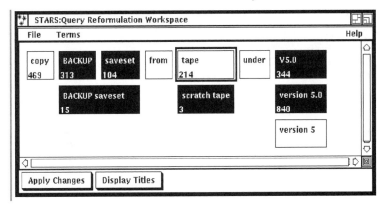

Figure 10.12   A block-oriented diagram visualization for Boolean query specification [21].

that are conceptually related to the query terms. Another alternative is to use this display as a category metadata selection interface (see Section 10.4).

Anick *et al.* [21] describe another innovative direct manipulation interface for Boolean queries. Initially the user types a natural language query which is automatically converted to a representation in which each query term is represented within a block. The blocks are arranged into rows and columns (See Figure 10.12). If two or more blocks appear along the same row they are considered to be ANDed together. Two or more blocks within the same column are ORed. Thus the user can represent a technical term in multiple ways within the same query, providing a kind of faceted query interface. For example, the terms 'version 5', 'version 5.0', and 'v5' might be shown in the same column. Users can quickly experiment with different combinations of terms within Boolean queries simply by activating and deactivating blocks. This facility also allows users to have multiple representations of the same term in different places throughout the display, thus allowing rapid feedback on the consequences of specifying various combinations of query terms. Informal evaluation of the system found that users were able to learn to manipulate the interface quickly and enjoyed using it. It was not formally compared to other interaction techniques [21].

This interface provides a kind of *query preview*: a low cost, rapid turnaround visualization of the results of many variations on a query [643]. Another example of query previewing can be found in some help systems, which show all the words in the index whose first letters match the characters that the user has typed so far. The more characters typed, the fewer possible matches become available. The HiBrowse system described above [646] also provides a kind of preview for viewing category hierarchies and facets, showing how many documents would be matched if a category one level below the current one were selected. It perhaps could be improved by showing the consequences of more combinations of categories in an animated manner. If based on prior action and interests of the user, query previewing may become more generally applicable for information access interfaces.

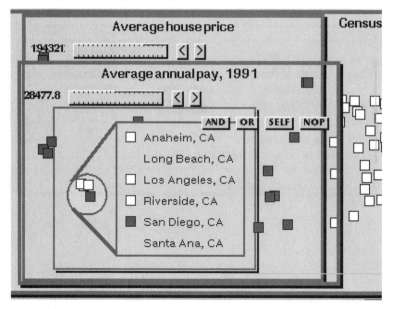

Figure 10.13   A magic lens interface for query specification (courtesy of Ken Fishkin).

A final example of a graphical approach to query specification is the use of magic lenses. Fishkin and Stone have suggested an extension to the usage of this visualization tool for the specification of Boolean queries [256]. Information is represented as lists or icons within a 2D space. Lenses act as filters on the document set. (See Figure 10.13.) For example, a word can be associated with a transparent lens. When this lens is placed over an iconic representation of a set of documents, it can cause all documents that do not contain a given word to disappear. If a second lens representing another word is then laid over the first, the lenses combine to act as a conjunction of the two words with the document set, hiding any documents that do not contain both words. Additional information can be adjusted dynamically, such as a minimum threshold for how often the term occurs in the documents, or an on-off switch for word stemming. For example, Figure 10.13 shows a disjunctive query that finds cities with relatively low housing prices or high annual salaries. One lens 'calls out' a clump of southern California cities, labeling each. Above that is a lens screening for cities with average house price below $194,321 (the data is from 1990), and above this one is a lens screening for cities with average annual pay above $28,477. This approach, while promising, has not been evaluated in an information access setting.

10.5.5 Phrases and Proximity

In general, proximity information can be quite effective at improving precision of searches. On the Web, the difference between a single-word query and a two-word exact phrase match can mean the difference between an unmanageable mess of retrieved documents and a short list with mainly relevant documents.

A large number of methods for specifying phrases have been developed. The syntax in LEXIS-NEXIS requires the proximity range to be specified with an infix operator. For example, 'white w/3 house' means 'white within 3 words of house, independent of order.' Exact proximity of phrases is specified by simply listing one word beside the other, separated by a space. A popular method used by Web search engines is the enclosure of the terms between quotation marks. Shneiderman *et al.* [726] suggest providing a list of entry labels, as suggested above for specifying facets. The difference is, instead of a disjunction, the terms on each line are treated as a phrase. This is suggested as a way to guide users to more precise query specification.

The disadvantage of these methods is that they require exact match of phrases, when it is often the case (in English) that one or a few words comes between the terms of interest. For example, in most cases the user probably wants 'president' and 'lincoln' to be adjacent, but still wants to catch cases of the sort 'President Abraham Lincoln.' Another consideration is whether or not stemming is performed on the terms included in the phrase. The best solution may be to allow users to specify exact phrases but treat them as small proximity ranges, with perhaps an exponential fall-off in weight in terms of distance of the terms. This has been shown to be a successful strategy in non-interactive ranking algorithms [174]. It has also been shown that a combination of quorum ranking of faceted queries with the restriction that the facets occur within a small proximity range can dramatically improve precision of results [356, 566].

10.5.6   Natural Language and Free Text Queries

Statistical ranking algorithms have the advantage of allowing users to specify queries naturally, without having to think about Boolean or other operators. But they have the drawback of giving the user less feedback about and control over the results. Usually the result of a statistical ranking is the listing of documents and the association of a score, probability, or percentage beside the title. Users are given little feedback about why the document received the ranking it did and what the roles of the query terms are. This can be especially problematic if the user is particularly interested in one of the query terms being present.

One search strategy that can help with this particular problem with statistical ranking algorithms is the specification of 'mandatory' terms within the natural language query. This in effect helps the user control which terms are considered important, rather than relying on the ranking algorithm to correctly weight the query terms. But knowing to include a mandatory specification requires the user to know about a particular command and how it works.

The preceding discussion assumes that a natural language query entered by the user is treated as a bag of words, with stopwords removed, for the purposes of document match. However, some systems attempt to parse natural language queries in order to extract concepts to match against concepts in the text collection [399, 552, 748].

Alternatively, the natural language syntax of a question can be used to attempt to answer the question. (Question answering in information access is different than that of database management systems, since the information desired is encoded within the text of documents rather than specified by the database schema.) The Murax system [463] determines from the syntax of a question if the user is asking for a person, place, or date. It then attempts to find sentences within encyclopedia articles that contain noun phrases that appear in the question, since these sentences are likely to contain the answer to the question. For example, given the question 'Who was the Pulitzer Prize-winning novelist that ran for mayor of New York City?,' the system extracts the noun phrases 'Pulitzer Prize,' 'winning novelist,' 'mayor,' and 'New York City.' It then looks for proper nouns representing people's names (since this is a 'who' question) and finds, among others, the following sentences:

The Armies of the Night (1968), a personal narrative of the 1967 peace march on the Pentagon, won **Mailer** the **Pulitzer Prize** and the National Book Award.

In 1969 **Mailer** ran unsuccessfully as an independent candidate for **mayor** of **New York City**.

Thus the two sentences link together the relevant noun phrases and the system hypothesizes (correctly) from the title of the article in which the sentences appear that Norman Mailer is the answer.

Another approach to automated question answering is the FAQ finder system which matches question-style queries against question-answer pairs on various topics [130]. The system uses a standard IR search to find the most likely FAQ (frequently asked questions) files for the question and then matches the terms in the question against the question portion of the question-answer pairs.

A less automated approach to question answering can be found in the Ask Jeeves system [34]. This system makes use of hand-picked Web sites and matches these to a predefined set of question types. A user's query is first matched against the question types. The user selects the most accurate rephrase of their question and this in turn is linked to suggested Web sites. For example, the question 'Who is the leader of Sudan?' is mapped into the question type 'Who is the head of state of X (Sudan)?' where the variable is replaced by a listbox of choices, with Sudan the selected choice in this case. This is linked to a Web page that lists current heads of state. The system also automatically substitutes in the name 'Sudan' in a query against that Web page, thus bringing the answer directly to the user's attention. The question is also sent to standard Web search engines. However, a system is only as good as its question templates. For example a question 'Where can I find reviews of spas in Calistoga?' matches the question 'Where can I find X (reviews) of activities for children aged Y (1)?' and 'Where can I find a concise encyclopedia article on X (hot springs)?'

10.6   Context

This section discusses interface techniques for placing the current document set in the *context* of other information types, in order to make the document set more understandable. This includes showing the relationship of the document set to query terms, collection overviews, descriptive metadata, hyperlink structure, document structure, and to other documents within the set.

10.6.1   Document Surrogates

The most common way to show results for a query is to list information about documents in order of their computed relevance to the query. Alternatively, for pure Boolean ranking, documents are listed according to a metadata attribute, such as date. Typically the document list consists of the document's title and a subset of important metadata, such as date, source, and length of the article. In systems with statistical ranking, a numerical score or percentage is also often shown alongside the title, where the score indicates a computed degree of match or probability of relevance. This kind of information is sometimes referred to as a *document surrogate*. See Figure 10.14 from [824].

Some systems provide users with a choice between a short and a detailed view. The detailed view typically contains a summary or abstract. In bibliographic systems, the author-written or service-written abstract is shown. Web search engines automatically generate excerpts, usually extracting the first few lines of non-markup text in the Web page.

In most interfaces, clicking on the document's title or an iconic representation of the document shown beside the title will bring up a view of the document itself, either in another window on the screen, or replacing the listing of search results. (In traditional bibliographic systems, the full text was unavailable online, and only bibliographic records could be readily viewed.)

10.6.2   Query Term Hits Within Document Content

In systems in which the user can view the full text of a retrieved document, it is often useful to *highlight* the occurrences of the terms or descriptors that match those of the user's query. It can also be useful for the system to scroll the view of the document to the first passage that contains one or more of the query terms, and highlight the matched terms in a contrasting color or reverse video. This display is thought to help draw the user's attention to the parts of the document most likely to be relevant to the query. Highlighting of query terms has been found time and again to be a useful feature for information access interfaces [481],[542, p.31]. Color highlighting has also recently been found to be useful for scanning lists of bibliographic records [52].

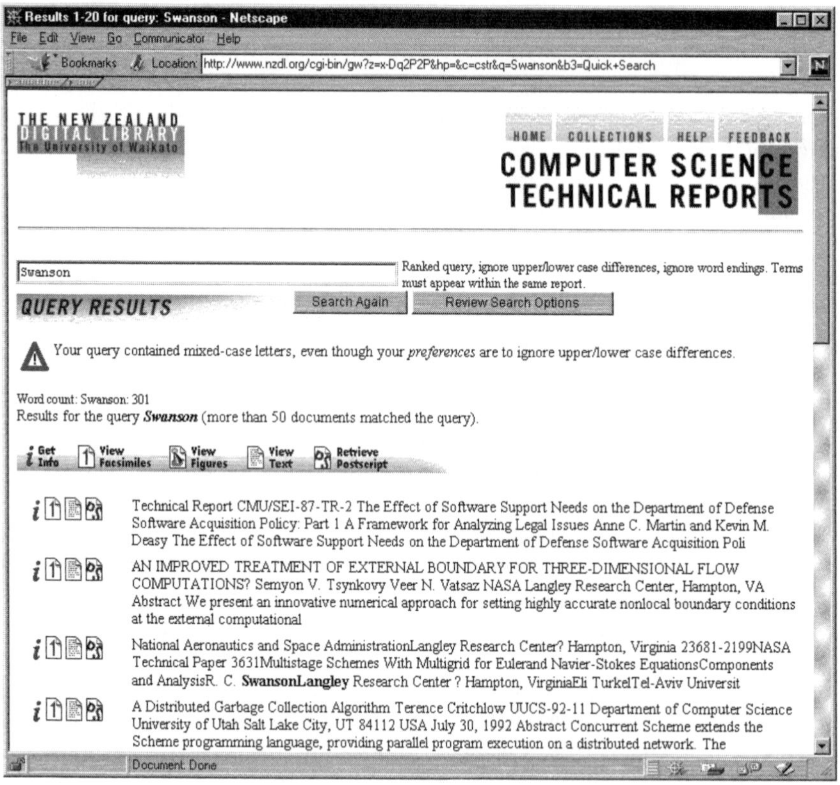

Figure 10.14   An example of a ranked list of titles and other document surrogate information [824].

KWIC

A facility related to highlighting is the *keyword-in-context* (KWIC) document surrogate. Sentence fragments, full sentences, or groups of sentences that contain query terms are extracted from the full text and presented for viewing along with other kinds of surrogate information (such as document title and abstract). Note that a KWIC listing is different than an abstract. An abstract summarizes the main topics of the document but might not contain references to the terms within the query. A KWIC extract shows sentences that summarize the ways the query terms are used within the document. This display can show not only which subsets of query terms occur in the retrieved documents, but also the context they appear in with respect to one another.

Tradeoff decisions must be made between how many lines of text to show and which lines to display. It is not known which contexts are best selected for viewing but results from text summarization research suggest that the best fragments to show are those that appear near the beginning of the document and that contain the largest subset of query terms [464]. If users have specified which

terms are more important than others, then those fragments containing important terms should be shown before those that contain only less important terms.
However, to help retain coherence of the excerpts, selected sentences should be
shown in order of their occurrence in the original document, independent of how
many search terms they contain.

The KWIC facility is usually not shown in Web search result display, most
likely because the system must have a copy of the original document available
from which to extract the sentences containing the search terms. Web search engines typically only retain the index without term position information. Systems
that index individual Web sites can show KWIC information in the document
list display.

TileBars

A more compact form of query term hit display is made available through the
TileBars interface. The user enters a query in a faceted format, with one topic
per line. After the system retrieves documents (using a quorum or statistical
ranking algorithm), a graphical bar is displayed next to the title of each document showing the degree of match for each facet. TileBars thus illustrate at
a glance which passages in each article contain which topics – and moreover,
how frequently each topic is mentioned (darker squares represent more frequent
matches).

Each document is represented by a rectangular bar. Figure 10.15 shows an
example. The bar is subdivided into rows that correspond to the query facets.
The top row of each TileBar corresponds to 'osteoporosis,' the second row to
'prevention,' and the third row to 'research.' The bar is also subdivided into
columns, where each column refers to a passage within the document. Hits that
overlap within the same passage are more likely to indicate a relevant document
than hits that are widely dispersed throughout the document [356]. The patterns are meant to indicate whether terms from a facet occur as a main topic
throughout the document, as a subtopic, or are just mentioned in passing.

The darkness of each square corresponds to the number of times the query
occurs in that segment of text; the darker the square the greater the number of
hits. White indicates no hits on the query term. Thus, the user can quickly see
if some subset of the terms overlap in the same segment of the document. (The
segments for this version of the interface are fixed blocks of 100 tokens each.)

The first document can be seen to have considerable overlap among the
topics of interest towards the middle, but not at the beginning or the end (the
actual end is cut off). Thus it most likely discusses topics in addition to research
into osteoporosis. The second through fourth documents, which are considerably
shorter, also have overlap among all terms of interest, and so are also probably of
interest to the user. (The titles help to verify this.) The next three documents are
all long, and from the TileBars we can tell they discuss research and prevention,
but do not even touch on osteoporosis, and so probably are not of interest.

Because the TileBars interface allows the user to specify the query in terms

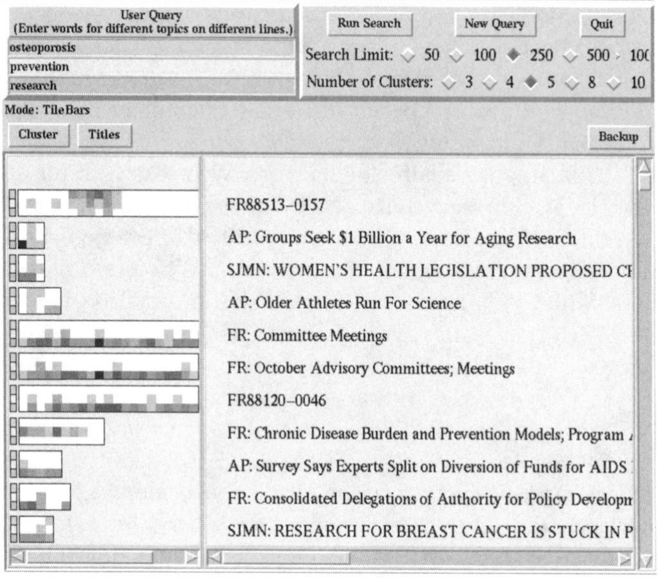

Figure 10.15   An example of the TileBars retrieval results visualization [355].

of facets, where the terms for each facet are listed on an entry line, a color can be assigned to each facet. When the user displays a document with query term hits, the user can quickly ascertain what proportion of search topics appear in a passage based only on how many different highlight colors are visible. Most systems that use highlighting use only a single color to bring attention to all of the search terms.

It would be difficult for users to specify in advance which patterns of term hits they are interested in. Instead, TileBars allows users to scan graphic representations and recognize which documents are and are not of interest. It may be the case that TileBars may be most useful for helping users discard misleadingly interesting documents, but only preliminary studies have been conducted to date. Passages can correspond to paragraphs or sections, fixed sized units of arbitrary length, or to automatically determined multiparagraph segments [355].

SeeSoft

The SeeSoft visualization [232] represents text in a manner resembling columns of newspaper text, with one 'line' of text on each horizontal line of the strip. (See Figure 10.16.) The representation is compact and aesthetically pleasing. Graphics are used to abstract away the details, providing an overview showing the amount and shape of the text. Color highlighting is used to pick out various attributes, such as where a particular word appears in the text. Details of a smaller portion of the display can be viewed via a pop-up window; the overview shows more of the text but in less detail.

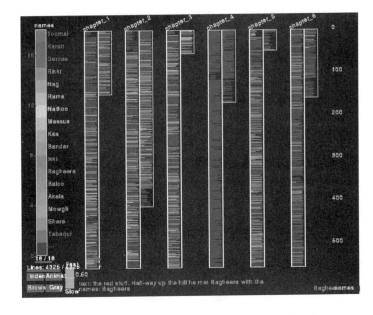

Figure 10.16   An example of the SeeSoft visualization for showing locations of characters within a text [232].

SeeSoft was originally designed for software development, in which a line of text is a meaningful unit of information. (Programmers tend to place each individual programming statement on one line of text.) Thus SeeSoft shows attributes relevant to the programming domain, such as which lines of code were modified by which programmer, and how often particular lines have been modified, and how many days have elapsed since the lines were last modified. The SeeSoft developers then experimented with applying this idea to the display of text, although this has not been integrated into an information access system. Color highlighting is used to show which characters appear where in a book of fiction, and which passages of the Bible contain references to particular people and items. Note the use of the abstraction of an entire line to stand for a single word such as a character's name (even though though this might obscure a tightly interwoven conversation between two characters).

10.6.3   Query Term Hits Between Documents

Other visualization ideas have been developed to show a different kind of information about the relationship between query terms and retrieved documents. Rather than showing how query terms appear within individual documents, as is done in KWIC interfaces and TileBars, these systems display an overview or summary of the retrieved documents according to which subset of query terms they contain. The following subsections describe variations on this idea.

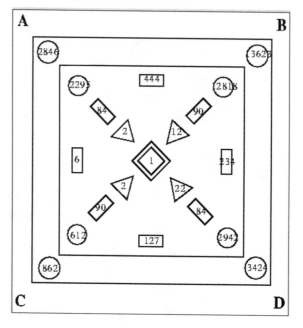

Figure 10.17   A sketch of the InfoCrystal retrieval results display [738].

InfoCrystal

The InfoCrystal shows how many documents contain each subset of query terms [738]. This relieves the user from the need to specify Boolean ANDs and ORs in their query, while still showing which combinations of terms actually appear in documents that were ordered by a statistical ranking (although beyond four terms the interface becomes difficult to understand). The InfoCrystal allows visualization of all possible relations among N user-specified 'concepts' (or Boolean keywords). The InfoCrystal displays, in a clever extension of the Venn diagram paradigm, the number of documents retrieved that have each possible subset of the N concepts. Figure 10.17 shows a sketch of what the InfoCrystal might display as the result of a query against four keywords or Boolean phrases, labeled A, B, C, and D. The diamond in the center indicates that one document was discovered that contains all four keywords. The triangle marked with '12' indicates that 12 documents were found containing attributes A, B, and D, and so on.

The InfoCrystal does not show proximity among the terms within the documents, nor their relative frequency. So a document that contains dozens of hits on 'volcano' and 'lava' and one hit on 'Mars' will be grouped with documents that contain mainly hits on 'Mars' but just one mention each of 'volcano' and 'lava.'

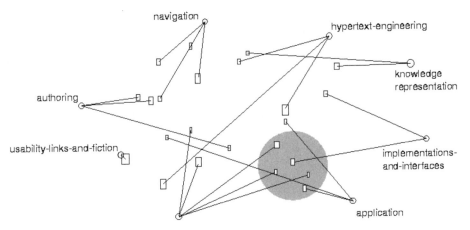

Figure 10.18   An example of the VIBE retrieval results display [452].

VIBE and Lyberworld

Graphical presentations that operate on similar principles are VIBE [452] and Lyberworld [363]. In these displays, query terms are placed in an abstract graphical space. After the search, icons are created that indicate how many documents contain each subset of query terms. The subset status of each group of documents is indicated by the placement of the icon. For example, in VIBE a set of documents that contain three out of five query terms are shown on an axis connecting these three terms, at a point midway between the representations of the three query terms in question. (See Figure 10.18.) Lyberworld presents a 3D version of this idea.

Lattices

Several researchers have employed a graphical depiction of a mathematical lattice for the purposes of query formulation, where the query consists of a set of constraints on a hierarchy of categories (actually, semantic attributes in these systems) [631, 147]. This is one solution to the problem of displaying documents in terms of multiple attributes; a document containing terms A, B, C, and D could be placed at a point in the lattice with these four categories as parents. However, if such a representation were to be applied to retrieval results instead of query formulation, the lattice layout would in most cases be too complex to allow for readability.

None of the displays discussed in this subsection have been evaluated for effectiveness at improving query specification or understanding of retrieval results, but they are intriguing ideas and perhaps are useful in conjunction with other displays.

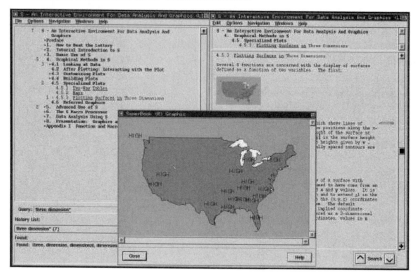

Figure 10.19   The SuperBook interface for showing retrieval results on a large manual in context [481].

10.6.4   SuperBook: Context via Table of Contents

The SuperBook system [481, 229, 230] makes use of the structure of a large document to display query term hits in context. The table of contents (TOC) for a book or manual are shown in a hierarchy on the left-hand side of the display, and full text of a page or section is shown on the right-hand side. The user can manipulate the table of contents to expand or contract the view of sections and subsections. A focus-plus-context mechanism is used to expand the viewing area of the sections currently being looked at and compress the remaining sections. When the user moves the cursor to another part of the TOC, the display changes dynamically, making the new focus larger and shrinking down the previously observed sections.

After the user specifies a query on the book, the search results are shown in the context of the table of contents hierarchy. (See Figure 10.19.) Those sections that contain search hits are made larger and the others are compressed. The query terms that appear in chapter or section names are highlighted in reverse video. When the user selects a page from the table of contents view, the page itself is displayed on the right-hand side and the query terms within the page are highlighted in reverse video.

The SuperBook designers created innovative techniques for evaluating its special features. Subjects were compared using this system against using paper documentation and against a more standard online information access system. Subjects were also compared on different kinds of carefully selected tasks: browsing topics of interest, citation searching, searching to answer questions, and searching and browsing to write summary essays. For most of the tasks

SuperBook subjects were faster and more accurate or equivalent in speed and accuracy to a standard system. When differences arose between SuperBook and the standard system, the investigators examined the logs carefully and hypothesized plausible explanations. After the initial studies, they modified SuperBook according to these hypotheses and usually saw improvements as a result [481].

The user studies on the improved system showed that users were faster and more accurate at answering questions in which some of the relevant terms were within the section titles themselves, but they were also faster and more accurate at answering questions in which the query terms fell within the full text of the document only, as compared both to a paper manual and to an interface that did not provide such contextualizing information. SuperBook was not faster than paper when the query terms did not appear in the document text or the table of contents. This and other evidence from the SuperBook studies suggests that query term highlighting is at least partially responsible for improvements seen in the system.

10.6.5   Categories for Results Set Context

In section 10.4 we saw the use of category or directory information for providing overviews of text collection content. Category metadata can also be used to place the results of a query in context.

For example, the original formulation of SuperBook allowed navigation within a highly structured document, a computer manual. The CORE project extended the main idea to a collection of over 1000 full-text chemistry articles. A study of this representation demonstrated its superiority to a standard search system on a variety of task types [228]. Since a table of contents is not available for this collection, context is provided by placing documents within a category hierarchy containing terms relevant to chemistry. Documents assigned a category are listed when that category is selected for more detailed viewing, and the categories themselves are organized into a hierarchy, thus providing a hierarchical view on the collection.

Another approach to using predefined categories to provide context for retrieval results is demonstrated by the DynaCat system [650]. The DynaCat system organizes retrieved documents according to which types of categories, selected from the large MeSH taxonomy, are known in advance to be important for a given query type. DynaCat begins with a set of query types known to be useful for a given user population and collection. One query type can encompass many different queries. For example, the query type 'Treatment-Adverse Effects' covers queries such as 'What are the complications of a mastectomy?' as well as 'What are the side-effects of aspirin?' Documents are organized according to a set of criteria associated with each query type. These criteria specify which types of categories that are acceptable to use for organizing the documents and consequently, which categories should be omitted from the display. Once categories have been assigned to the retrieved documents, a hierarchy is formed based on where the categories exist within MeSH. The algorithm selects only a subset of the category

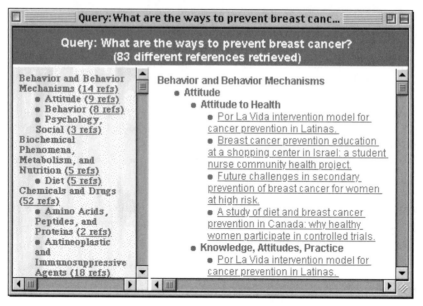

Figure 10.20 The DynaCat interface for viewing category labels that correspond to query types [650].

labels that might be assigned to the document to be used in the organization.

Figure 10.20 shows the results for a query on breast cancer prevention. The interface is tiled into three windows. The top window displays the user's query and the number of documents found. The left window shows the categories in the first two levels of the hierarchy, providing a table of contents view of the organization of search results. The right pane displays all the categories in the hierarchy and the titles of the documents that belong in those categories.

An obstacle to using category labels to organize retrieval results is the requirement of precompiled knowledge about which categories are of interest for a particular user or a particular query type. The SONIA system [692] circumvents this problem by using a combination of unsupervised and supervised methods to organize a set of documents. The unsupervised method (document clustering similar to Scatter/Gather) imposes an initial organization on a user's personal information collection or on a set of documents retrieved as the result of a query. The user can then invoke a direct manipulation interface to make adjustments to this initial clustering, causing it to align more closely with their preferences (because unsupervised methods do not usually produce an organization that corresponds to a human-derived category structure [357]). The resulting organization is then used to train a supervised text categorization algorithm which automatically classifies any new documents that are added to the collection. As the collection grows it can be periodically reorganized by rerunning the clustering algorithm and redoing the manual adjustments.

10.6.6   Using Hyperlinks to Organize Retrieval Results

Although the SuperBook authors describe it as a hypertext system, it is actually better thought of as a means of showing search results in the context of a structure that users can understand and view all at once. The hypertext component was not analyzed separately to assess its importance, but it usually is not mentioned by the authors when describing what is successful about their design. In fact, it seems to be responsible for one of the main problems seen with the revised version of the system — that users tend to wander off (often unintentionally) from the pages they are reading, thus causing the time spent on a given topic to be longer for SuperBook in some cases. (Using completion time to evaluate users on browsing tasks can be problematic, however, since by definition browsing is a casual, unhurried process [804].)

This wandering may occur in part because SuperBook uses a non-standard kind of hypertext, in which any word is automatically linked to occurrences of the same word in other parts of the document. This has not turned out to be how hypertext links are created in practice. Today, hyperlinked help systems and hyperlinks on the Web make much more discriminating use of hyperlink connections (in part since they are usually generated by an author rather than automatically). These links tend to be labeled in a somewhat meaningful manner by their surrounding context. Back-of-the-book indexes often do not contain listings of every occurrence of a word, but rather to the more important uses or the beginnings of series of uses. Automated hypertext linking should perhaps be based on similar principles. Additionally, at least one study showed that users formed better mental models of a small hypertext system that was organized hierarchically than one that allowed more flexible access [226]. Problems relating to navigation of hypertext structure have long been suspected and investigated in the hypertext literature [181, 551, 440, 334].

More recent work has made better use of hyperlink information for providing context for retrieval results. Some of this work is described below.

Cha-Cha: SuperBook on the Web

The Cha-Cha intranet search system [164] extends the SuperBook idea to a large heterogeneous Web site such as might be found in an organization's intranet. Figure 10.21 shows an example. This system differs from SuperBook in several ways. On most Web sites there is no existing real table of contents or category structure, and an intranet like those found at large universities or large corporations is usually not organized by one central unit. Cha-Cha uses link structure present within the site to create what is intended to be a meaningful organization on top of the underlying chaos. After the user issues a query, the shortest paths from the root page to each of the search hits are recorded and a subset of these are selected to be shown as a hierarchy, so that each hit is shown only once. (Users can begin with a query, rather than with a table of contents view.) If a user does not know to use the term 'health center' but instead queries on 'medical center,' if 'medical' appears as a term in a document within

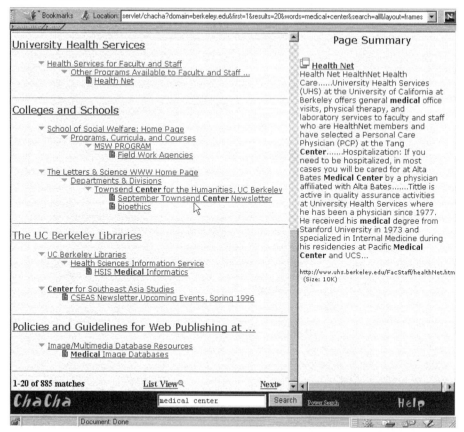

Figure 10.21   The Cha-Cha interface for showing Web intranet search results in context displaying results on the query 'medical centre'[164].

the health center part of the Web, the home page (or starting point) of this center will be presented as well as the more specific hits. Users can then either query or navigate within a subset of sites if they wish. The organization produced by this simple method is surprisingly comprehensible on the UC Berkeley site. It seems especially useful for providing the information about the sources (the Web server) associated with the search hits, whose titles are often cryptic.

The AMIT system [826] also applies the basic ideas behind SuperBook to the Web, but focuses on a single-topic Web site, which is likely to have a more reasonable topic structure than a complex intranet. The link structure of the Web site is used as contextualizing information but all of the paths to a given document are shown and focus-plus-context is used to emphasize subsets of the document space. The WebTOC system [585] is similar to AMIT but focuses on showing the structure and number of documents within each Web subhierarchy, and is not tightly coupled with search.

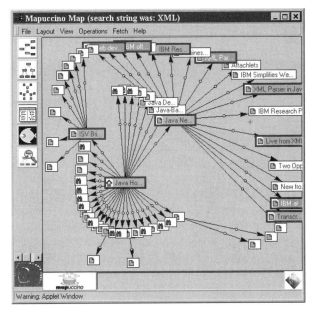

Figure 10.22 Example of a Web subset visualized by Mapuccino (courtesy of M. Jacovi, B. Shaul and Y. Maarek).

Mapuccino: Graphical Depiction of Link Structure

The Mapuccino system (formerly WebCutter) [527] allows the user to issue a query on a particular Web site. The system crawls the site in real-time, checking each encountered page for relevance to the query. When a relevant page is found, the weights on that page's outlinks are increased. Thus, the search is based partly on an assumption that relevant pages will occur near one another in the Web site. The subset of the Web site that has been crawled is depicted graphically in a nodes-and-links view (see Figure 10.22). This kind of display does not provide the user with information about what the *contents* of the pages are, but rather only shows their link structure. Other researchers have also investigated spreading activation among hypertext links as a way to guide an information retrieval system, e.g., [278, 555].

10.6.7 Tables

Tabular display is another approach for showing relationships among retrieval documents. The Envision system [273] allows the user to organize results according to metadata such as author or date along the X and Y-axes, and uses graphics to show values for attributes associated with retrieved documents within each cell (see Figure 10.23). Color, shape, and size of an iconic representation of a document are used to show the computed relevance, the type of document, or

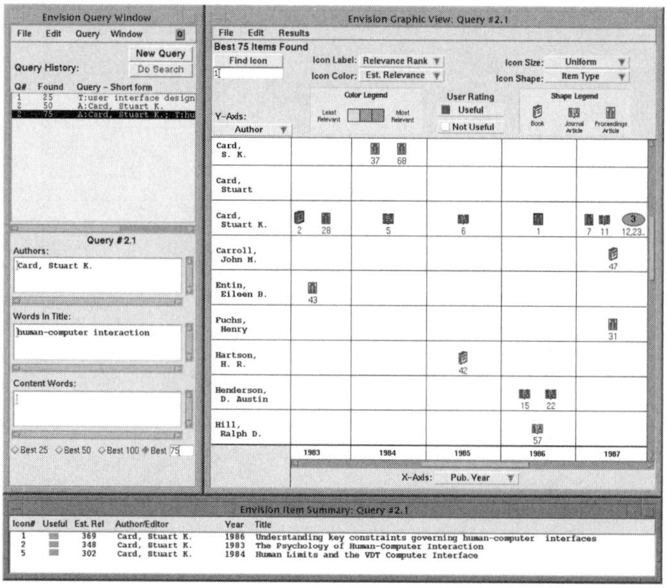

Figure 10.23   The Envision tabular display for graphically organizing retrieved documents [270].

other attributes. Clicking on an icon brings up more information about the document in another window. Like the WebCutter system, this view provides few cues about how the documents are related to one another in terms of their content or meaning. The SenseMaker system also allows users to group documents into different views via a table-like display [51], including a Scatter/Gather [203] style view. Although tables are appealing, they cannot show the intersections of many different attributes; rather they are better for pairwise comparisons. Another problem with tables for display of textual information is that very little information can be fitted on a screen at a time, making comparisons difficult.

The Table Lens [666] is an innovative interface for viewing and interactively reorganizing very large tables of information (see Figure 10.24). It uses focus-plus-context to fit hundreds of rows of information in a space occupied by at most two dozen rows in standard spreadsheets. And because it allows for rapid reorganization via sorting of columns, users can quickly switch from a view focused around one kind of metadata to another. For example, first sorting documents by rank and then by author name can show the relative ranks of different articles by the same author. A re-sort by date can show patterns in relevance scores with respect to date of publication. This rapid re-sorting capability helps circumvent the problems associated with the fact that tables cannot show many simultaneous intersections.

Another variation on the table theme is that seen in the Perspective Wall [530] in which a focus-plus-context display is used to center information currently

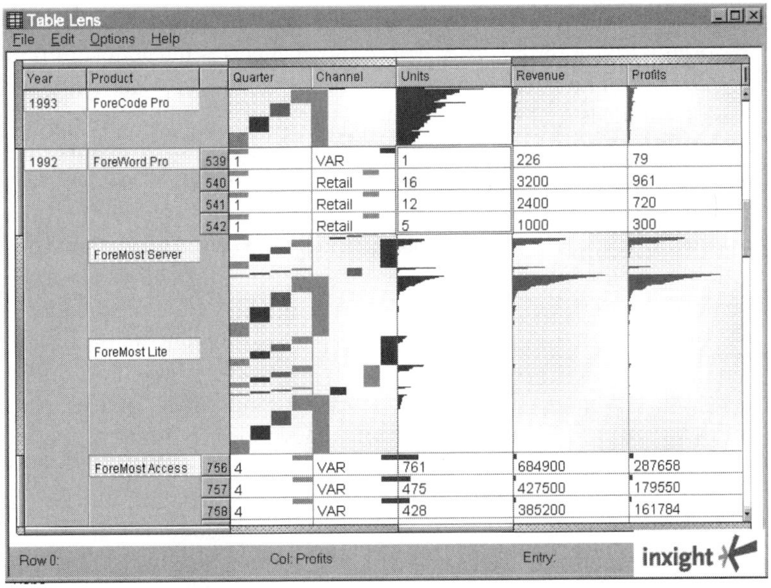

Figure 10.24   The TableLens visualization [666].

of interest in the middle of the display, compressing less important information into the periphery on the sides of the wall. The idea is to show in detail the currently most important information while at the same time retaining the context of the rest of the information. For example, if viewing documents in chronological order, the user can easily tell if they are currently looking at documents in the beginning, middle, or end of the time range.

These interfaces have not been applied to information access tasks. The problem with such displays when applied to text is that they require an attribute that can be shown according to an underlying order, such as date. Unfortunately, information useful for organizing text content, such as topic labels, does not have an inherent meaningful order. Alphabetical order is useful for looking up individual items, but not for seeing patterns across items according to adjacency, as in the case for ordered data types like dates and size.

10.7   Using Relevance Judgements

An important part of the information access process is query reformulation, and a proven effective technique for query reformulation is *relevance feedback*. In its original form, relevance feedback refers to an interaction cycle in which the user selects a small set of documents that appear to be relevant to the query, and the system then uses features derived from these selected relevant documents to revise the original query. This revised query is then executed and a new set of documents is returned. Documents from the original set can appear in the new results list, although they are likely to appear in a different rank order. Relevance feedback in its original form has been shown to be an effective mechanism for improving retrieval results in a variety of studies and settings [702, 343, 127]. In recent years the scope of ideas that can be classified under this term has widened greatly.

Relevance feedback introduces important design choices, including which operations should be performed automatically by the system and which should be user initiated and controlled. Bates discusses this issue in detail [66], asserting that despite the emphasis in modern systems to try to automate the entire process, an intermediate approach in which the system helps automate search at a *strategic* level is preferable. Bates suggests an analogy of an automatic camera versus one with adjustable lenses and shutter speeds. On many occasions, a quick, easy method that requires little training or thought is appropriate. At other times the user needs more control over the operation of the machinery, while still not wanting to know about the low level details of its operation.

A related idea is that, for any interface, control should be described in terms of the task being done, not in terms of how the machine can be made to accomplish the task [607]. Continuing the camera analogy, the user should be able to control the mood created by the photograph, rather than the adjustment of the lens. In information access systems, control should be over the kind of information returned, not over which terms are used to modify the query. Unfortunately it is often quite difficult to build interfaces to complex systems that behave in this manner.

10.7.1 Interfaces for Standard Relevance Feedback

A standard interface for relevance feedback consists of a list of titles with checkboxes beside the titles that allow the user to mark relevant documents. This can imply either that unmarked documents are not relevant or that no opinion has been made about unmarked documents, depending on the system. Another option is to provide a choice among several checkboxes indicating relevant or not relevant (with no selection implying no opinion). In some cases users are allowed to indicate a value on a relevance scale [73]. Standard relevance feedback algorithms usually do not perform better given negative relevance judgement evidence [225], but machine learning algorithms can take advantage of negative feedback [629, 460].

After the user has made a set of relevance judgements and issued a search command, the system can either automatically reweight the query and re-execute the search, or generate a list of terms for the user to select from in order to augment the original query. (See Figure 10.25, taken from [448].) Systems usually do not suggest terms to remove from the query.

After the query is re-executed, a new list of titles is shown. It can be helpful to retain an indicator such as a marked checkbox beside the documents that the user has already judged. A difficult design decision concerns whether or not to show documents that the user has already viewed towards the top of the ranked list [1]. Repeatedly showing the same set of documents at the top may inconvenience a user who is trying to create a large set of relevant documents,

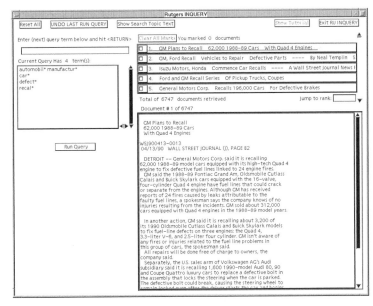

Figure 10.25   An example of an interface for relevance feedback [448].

but at the same time, this can serve as feedback indicating that the revised query does not downgrade the ranking of those documents that have been found especially important. One solution is to retain a separate window that shows the rankings of only the documents that have not been retrieved or ranked highly previously. Another solution is to use smaller fonts or gray-out color for the titles of documents already seen.

Creating multiple relevance judgements is an effortful task, and the notion of relevance feedback is unfamiliar to most users. To circumvent these problems, Web-based search engines have adopted the terminology of 'more like this' as a simpler way to indicate that the user is requesting documents similar to the selected one. This 'one-click' interaction method is simpler than standard relevance feedback dialog which requires users to rate a small number of documents and then request a reranking. Unfortunately, in most cases relevance feedback requires many relevance judgements in order to work well. To partly alleviate this problem, Aalbersberg [1] proposes incremental relevance feedback which works well given only one relevant document at a time and thus can be used to hide the two-step procedure from the user.

10.7.2   Studies of User Interaction with Relevance Feedback Systems

Standard relevance feedback assumes the user is involved in the interaction by specifying the relevant documents. In some interfaces users are also able to select which terms to add to the query. However, most ranking and reweighting algorithms are difficult to understand or predict (even for the creators of the algorithms!) and so it might be the case that users have difficulties controlling a relevance feedback system explicitly.

A recent study was conducted to investigate directly to what degree user control of the feedback process is beneficial. Koenemann and Belkin [448] measured the benefits of letting users 'under the hood' during relevance feedback. They tested four cases using the Inquery system [772]:

- **Control** No relevance feedback; the subjects could only reformulate the query by hand.

- **Opaque** The subjects simply selected relevant documents and saw the revised rankings.

- **Transparent** The subjects could see how the system reformulated the queries (that is, see which terms were added — the system did not reweight the subjects' query terms) and the revised rankings.

- **Penetrable** The system is stopped midway through the reranking process. The subjects are shown the terms that the system would have used for opaque and transparent query reformulation. The subjects then select which, if any, of the new terms to add to the query. The system then presents the revised rankings.

The 64 subjects were much more effective (measuring precision at a cutoff of top 5, top 10, top 30, and top 100 documents) with relevance feedback than without it. The penetrable group performed significantly better than the control, with the opaque and transparent performances falling between the two in effectiveness. Search times did not differ significantly among the conditions, but there were significant differences in the number of feedback iterations. The subjects in the penetrable group required significantly fewer iterations to achieve better queries (an average of 5.8 cycles in the penetrable group, 8.2 cycles in the control group, 7.7 cycles in the opaque group, and surprisingly, the transparent group required more cycles, 8.8 on average). The average number of documents marked relevant ranged between 11 and 14 for the three conditions. All subjects preferred relevance feedback over the baseline system, and several remarked that they preferred the 'lazy' approach of selecting suggested terms over having to think up their own.

An observational study on a TTY-based version of an online catalog system [338] also found that users performed better using a relevance feedback mechanism that allowed manual selection of terms. However, a later observational study did not find overall success with this form of relevance feedback [337]. The authors attribute these results to a poor design of a new graphical interface. These results may also be due to the fact that users often selected only one relevant document before performing the feedback operation, although they were using a system optimized from multiple document selection.

10.7.3 Fetching Relevant Information in the Background

Standard relevance feedback is predicated on the goal of improving an ad hoc query or building a profile for a routing query. More recently researchers have begun developing systems that monitor users' progress and behavior over long interaction periods in an attempt to predict which documents or actions the user is likely to want in future. These systems are called semi-automated *assistants* or recommender 'agents,' and often make use of machine learning techniques [565]. Some of these systems require explicit user input in the form of a goal statement [406] or relevance judgements [629], while others quietly record users' actions and try to make inferences based on these actions.

A system developed by Kozierok and Maes [460, 536] makes predictions about how users will handle email messages (what order to read them in, where to file them) and how users will schedule meetings in a calendar manager application. The system 'looks over the shoulder' of the users, recording every relevant action into a database. After enough data has been accumulated, the system uses a nearest-neighbors method [743] to predict a user's action based on the similarity of the current situation to situations already encountered. For example, if the user almost always saves email messages from a particular person into a particular file, the system can offer to automate this action the next time a message from that person arrives [536]. This system integrates learning from both implicit and explicit user feedback. If a user ignores the system's suggestion, the system treats this as negative feedback, and accordingly adds the overriding action to the action database. After certain types of incorrect predictions, the system asks the user questions that allow it to adjust the weight of the feature that caused the error. Finally, the user can explicitly train the system by presenting it with hypothetical examples of input-action pairs.

Another system, Syskill and Webert [629], attempts to learn a user profile based on explicit relevance judgements of pages explored while browsing the Web. In a sense this is akin to standard relevance feedback, except the user judgements are retained across sessions and the interaction model differs: as the user browses a new Web page, the links on the page are automatically annotated as to whether or not they should be relevant to the user's interest.

A related system is Letizia [518], whose goal is to bring to the user's attention a percentage of the available next moves that are most likely to be of interest, given the user's earlier actions. Upon request, Letizia provides recommendations for further action on the user's part, usually in the form of suggestions of links to follow when the user is unsure what to do next. The system monitors the user's behavior while navigating and reading Web pages, and concurrently evaluates the links reachable from the current page. The system uses only implicit feedback. Thus, saving a page as a bookmark is taken as strong positive evidence for the terms in the corresponding Web page. Links skipped are taken as negative support for the information reachable from the link. Selected links can indicate positive or negative evidence, depending on how much time the user spends on the resulting page and whether or not the decision to leave a page quickly is later reversed. Additionally, the evidence for user interest remains persistent across browsing sessions. Thus, a user who often reads kayaking pages is at another time reading the home page of a professional contact and may be alerted to the fact that the colleague's personal interests page contains a link to a shared hobby. The system uses a best-first search strategy and heuristics to determine which pages to recommend most strongly.

A more user-directed approach to prefetching potentially relevant information is seen in the Butterfly system [531]. This interface helps the user follow a series of citation links from a given reference, an important information seeking strategy [66]. The system automatically examines the document the user is currently reading and prefetches the bibliographic citations it refers to. It also retrieves lists of articles that cite the focus document. The underlying assumption is that the services from which the citations are requested do not respond immediately. Rather than making the user wait during the delay associated with each request, the system handles many requests in parallel and the interface uses graphics and animations to show the incrementally growing list of available citations. The system does not try to be clever about which cites to bring first; rather the user can watch the 'organically' growing visualization of the document and its citations, and based on what looks relevant, direct the system as to which parts of the citation space to spend more time on.

10.7.4   Group Relevance Judgements

Recently there has been much interest in using relevance judgements from a large number of different users to rate or rank information of general interest [672]. Some variations of this *social recommendation* approach use only similarity among relevance judgements by people with similar tastes, ignoring the representation of the information being judged altogether. This has been found highly effective for rating information in which taste plays a major role, such as movie and music recommendations [720]. More recent work has combined group relevance judgements with content information [64].

10.7.5   Pseudo-Relevance Feedback

At the far end of the system versus user feedback spectrum is what is informally known as pseudo-relevance feedback. In this method, rather than relying on the user to choose the top k relevant documents, the system simply assumes that its top-ranked documents are relevant, and uses these documents to augment the query with a relevance feedback ranking algorithm. This procedure has been found to be highly effective in some settings [760, 465, 12], most likely those in which the original query statement is long and precise. An intriguing extension to this idea is to use the output of clustering of retrieval results as the input to a relevance feedback mechanism, either by having the user or the system select the cluster to be used [359], but this idea has not yet been evaluated.

10.8   Interface Support for the Search Process

The user interface designer must make decisions about how to arrange various kinds of information on the computer screen and how to structure the possible sequences of interactions. This design problem is especially daunting for a complex activity like information access. In this section we discuss design choices surrounding the layout of information within complex information systems, and illustrate the ideas with examples of existing interfaces. We begin with a discussion of very simple search interfaces, those used for string search in 'find' operations, and then progress to multiwindow interfaces and sophisticated workspaces. This is followed by a discussion of the integration of scanning, selecting, and querying within information access interfaces and concludes with interface support for retaining the history of the search process.

10.8.1   Interfaces for String Matching

A common simple search need is that of the 'find' operation, typically run over the contents of a document that is currently being viewed. Usually this function does not produce ranked output, nor allow Boolean combinations of terms; the main operation is a simple string match (without regular expression capabilities). Typically a special purpose search window is created, containing a few simple controls (e.g., case-sensitivity, search forward or backward). The user types the query string into an entry form and string matches are highlighted in the target document (see Figure 10.26).

The next degree of complexity is the 'find' function for searching across small collections, such as the files on a personal computer's hard disk, or the history list of a Web browser. This type of function is also usually implemented as a simple string match. Again, the controls and parameter settings are shown at the top of a special purpose search window and the various options are set via checkboxes and entry forms. The difference from the previous example is that a results list is shown within the search interface itself (see Figure 10.27).

A common problem arises even in these very simple interfaces. An ambiguous state occurs in which the results for an earlier search are shown while the user is entering a new query or modifying the previous one. If the user types in

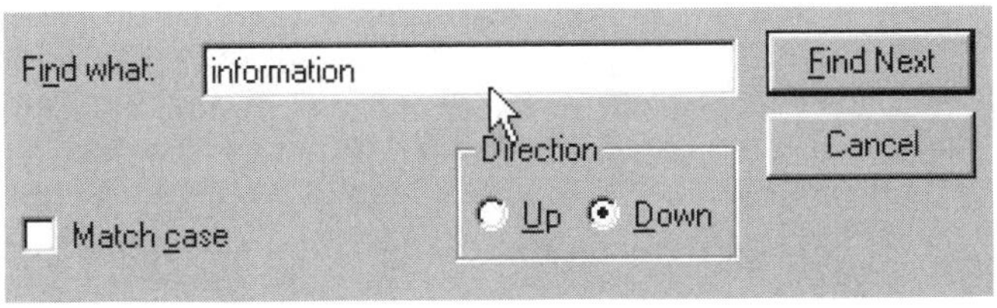

Figure 10.26   An example of a simple interface for string matching, from Netscape Communicator 4.05.

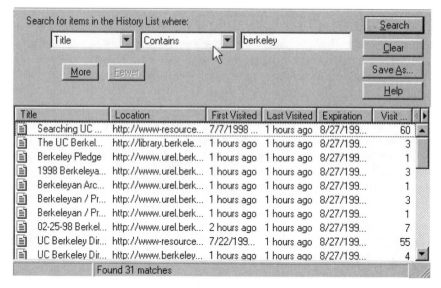

Figure 10.27   An example of an string matching over a list, in this case, a history of recently viewed Web pages, from Netscape Communicator 4.05.

new terms and but then does not activate the search, the interface takes on a potentially misleading state, since a user could erroneously assume that the old search hits shown correspond to the newly typed-in query. One solution for this problem is to clear the results list as soon as the user begins to type in a new query.

However, the user may want to refer to terms shown in the search results to help reformulate the query, or may decide not to issue the new query and instead continue with the previous results. These goals would be hampered by erasing the current result set as soon as the new query is typed. Another solution is to bring up a new window for every new query. However, this requires the user to execute an additional command and can lead to a proliferation of windows. A third, probably more workable solution, is to automatically 'stack' the queries and results lists in a compact format and allow the user to move back and forth among the stacked up prior searches.

Simple interfaces like these can be augmented with functionality that can greatly aid initial query formulation. Spelling errors are a major cause of void result sets. A spell-checking function that suggests alternatives for query terms that have low frequency in the collection might be useful at this stage. Another option is to suggest thesaurus terms associated with the query terms at the time the query terms are entered. Usually these kinds of information are shown after the query is entered and documents have been retrieved, but an alternative is to provide this information as the user enters the query, in a form of query preview.

10.8.2 Window Management

For search tasks more complex than the simple string matching find operations described above, the interface designer must decide how to lay out the various choices and information displays within the interface.

As discussed above, traditional bibliographic search systems use TTY-based command-line interfaces or menus. When the system responds to a command, the new results screen obliterates the contents of the one before it, requiring the user to remember the context. For example, the user can usually see only one level of a subject hierarchy at a time, and must leave the subject view in order to see query view or the document view. The main design choices in such a system are in the command or menu structure, and the order of presentation of the available options.

In modern graphical interfaces, the windowing system can be used to divide functionality into different, simultaneously displayed views [582]. In information access systems, it is often useful to link the information from one window to the information in another, for example, linking documents to their position in a table of contents, as seen in SuperBook. Users can also use the selection to cut and paste information from one window into another, for example, copy a word from a display of thesaurus terms and paste the word into the query specification form.

When arranging information within windows, the designer must choose between a *monolithic* display, in which all the windows are laid out in predefined positions and are all simultaneously viewable, *tiled windows*, and *overlapping windows*. User studies have been conducted comparing these options when applied to various tasks [725, 96]. Usually the results of these studies depend on the domain in which the interface is used, and no clear guidelines have yet emerged for information access interfaces.

The monolithic interface has several advantages. It allows the designer to control the organization of the various options, makes all the information simultaneously viewable, and places the features in familiar positions, making them easier to find. But monolithic interfaces have disadvantages as well. They often work best if occupying the full viewing screen, and the number of views is inherently limited by the amount of room available on the screen (as opposed to overlapping windows which allow display of more information than can fit on the screen at once). Many modern work-intensive applications adopt a monolithic design, but this can hamper the integration of information access with other work processes such as text editing and data analysis. Plaisant *et al.* [644] discuss issues relating to coordinating information across different windows to providing overview plus details.

A problem for any information access interface is an inherent limit in how many kinds of information can be shown at once. Information access systems must always reserve room for a text display area, and this must take up a significant proportion of screen space in order for the text to be legible. A tool within a paint program, for example, can be made quite small while nevertheless remaining recognizable and usable. For legibility reasons, it is difficult to compress many of the information displays needed for an information access system (such as lists of thesaurus terms, query specifications, and lists of saved titles) in this manner. Good layout, graphics, and font design can improve the situation; for example, Web search results can look radically different depending on spacing, font, and other small touches [580].

Overlapping windows provide flexibility in arrangement, but can quickly lead to a crowded, disorganized display. Researchers have observed that much user activity is characterized by movement from one set of functionally related windows to another. Bannon *et al.* [54] define the notion of a *workspace* — the grouping together of sets of windows known to be functionally related to some activity or goal — arguing that this kind of organization more closely matches users' goal structure than individual windows [96]. Card *et al.* [140] also found that window usage could be categorized according to a 'working set' model. They looked at the relationship between the demands of the task and the number of windows in use, and found the largest number of individual windows were in use when users transitioned from one task to another.

Based on these and other observations, Henderson and Card [420] built a system intended to make it easier for users to move between 'multiple virtual workspaces' [96]. The system uses a 3D spatial metaphor, where each workspace is a 'room,' and users transition between workspaces by 'moving' through virtual doors. By 'traveling' from one room to the next, users can change from one work context to another. In each work context, the application programs and data files that are associated with that work context are visible and readily available for reopening and perusal. The workspace notion as developed by Card *et al.* also emphasizes the importance of having sessions persist across time. The user should be able to leave a room dedicated to some task, work on another task, and three days later return to the first room and see all of the applications still in the same state as before. This notion of bundling applications and data together for each task has since been widely adopted by window manager software in workstation operating system interfaces.

Elastic windows [428] is an extension to the workspace or rooms notion to the organization of 2D tiled windows. The main idea is to make the transition easier from one role or task to another, by adjusting how much of the screen real estate is consumed by the current role. The user can enlarge an entire group of windows with a simple gesture, and this resizing automatically causes the rest of the workspaces to reduce in size so they all still fit on the screen without overlap.

10.8.3 Example Systems

The following sections describe the information layout and management approaches taken by several modern information access interfaces.

The InfoGrid Layout

The InfoGrid system [667] is a typical example of a monolithic layout for an information access interface. The layout assumes a large display is available

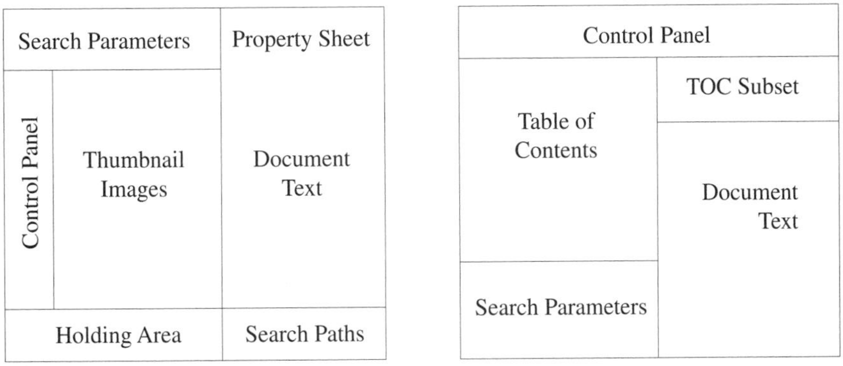

Search Parameters	Property Sheet
Thumbnail Images	Document Text
Holding Area	Search Paths

(Control Panel — vertical label on left side of left diagram)

Control Panel	
Table of Contents	TOC Subset
	Document Text
Search Parameters	

Figure 10.28   Diagrams of monolithic layouts for information access interfaces.

and is divided into a left-hand and right-hand side (see Figure 10.28). The left-hand side is further subdivided into an area at the top that contains structured entry forms for specifying the properties of a query, a column of iconic controls lining the left side, and an area for retaining documents of interest along the bottom. The main central area is used for the viewing of retrieval results, either as thumbnail representations of the original documents, or derived organizations of the documents, such as Scatter/Gather-style cluster results. Users can select documents from this area and store them in the holding area below or view them in the right-hand side. Most of the right-hand side of the display is used for viewing selected documents, with the upper portion showing metadata associated with the selected document. The area below the document display is intended to show a graphical history of earlier interactions.

Designers must make decisions about which kinds of information to show in the primary view(s). If InfoGrid were used on a smaller display, either the document viewing area or the retrieval results viewing area would probably have to be shown via a pop-up overlapping window; otherwise the user would have to toggle between the two views. If the system were to suggest terms for relevance feedback, one of the existing views would have to be supplanted with this information or a pop-up window would have to be used to display the candidate terms. The system does not provide detailed information for source selection, although this could be achieved in a very simple way with a pop-up menu of choices from the control panel.

The SuperBook Layout

The layout of the InfoGrid is quite similar to that of SuperBook (see section 10.6). The main difference is that SuperBook retains the table of contents-like display in the main left-hand pane, along with indicators of how many documents containing search hits occur in each level of the outline. Like InfoGrid, the main pane of the right-hand side is used to display selected documents. Query formulation is done just below the table of contents view (although in earlier versions this appeared in a separate window). Terms related to the user's query are shown in this window as well. Large images appear in pop-up overlapping windows.

The SuperBook layout is the result of several cycles of iterative design [481]. Earlier versions used overlapping windows instead of a monolithic layout, allowing users to sweep out a rectangular area on the screen in order to create a new text box. This new text box had its own set of buttons that allowed users to jump to occurrences of highlighted words in other documents or to the table of contents. SuperBook was redesigned after noting results of experimental studies [350, 532] showing that users can be more efficient if given fewer, well chosen interaction paths, rather than allowing wide latitude (A recent study of auditory interfaces found that although users were more efficient with a more flexible interface, they nevertheless preferred the more rigid, predictable interface [801]). The designers also took careful note of log files of user interactions. Before the redesign, users had to choose to view the overall frequency of a hit, move the mouse to the table of contents window, click the button and wait for the results to be updated. Since this pattern was observed to occur quite frequently, in the next version of the interface, the system was redesigned to automatically perform this sequence of actions immediately after a search was run.

The SuperBook designers also attempted a redesign to allow the interface to fit into smaller displays. The redesign made use of small, overlapping windows. Some of the interaction sequences that were found useful in this more constrained environment were integrated into later designs for large monolithic displays.

The DLITE Interface

The DLITE system [193, 192] makes a number of interesting design choices. It splits functionality into two parts: control of the search process and display of results . The control portion is a graphical direct manipulation display with animation (see Figure10.29). Queries, sources, documents, and groups of retrieved documents are represented as graphical objects. The user creates a query by filling out the editable fields within a query constructor object. The system manufactures a query object, which is represented by a small icon which can be dragged and dropped onto iconic representations of collections or search services. If a service is active, it responds by creating an empty results set object and attaching the query to this. A set of retrieval results is represented as a circular pool, and documents within the result set are represented as icons distributed along the perimeter of the pool. Documents can be dragged out of the results set pool and dropped into other services, such as a document summarizer or a language translator. Meanwhile, the user can make a copy of the query icon and drop it onto another search service. Placing the mouse over the iconic representation of the query causes a 'tool-tips' window to pop up to show the contents of the underlying query. Queries can be stored and reused at a later time, thus facilitating retention of previously successful search strategies.

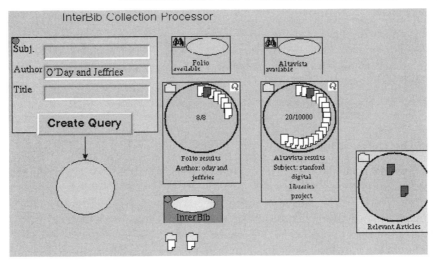

Figure 10.29   The DLITE interface [193].

A flexible interface architecture frees the user from the restriction of a rigid order of commands. On the other hand, as seen in the SuperBook discussion, such an architecture must provide guidelines, to help get the user started, give hints about valid ways to proceed, and prevent the user from making errors. The graphical portion of the DLITE interface makes liberal use of animation to help guide the user. For example, if the user attempts to drop a query in the document summarizer icon — an illegal operation — rather than failing and giving the user an accusatory error message [185], the system takes control of the object being dropped, refusing to let it be placed on the representation for the target application, and moves the object left, right, and left again, mimicking a 'shake-the-head-no' gesture. Animation is also used to help the user understand the state of the system, for example, in showing the progress of the retrieval of search results by moving the result set object away from the service from which it was invoked.

DLITE uses a separate Web browser window for the display of detailed information about the retrieved documents, such as their bibliographic citations and their full text. The browser window is also used to show Scatter/Gather-style cluster results and to allow users to select documents for relevance feedback. Earlier designs of the system attempted to incorporate text display into the direct manipulation portion, but this was found to be infeasible because of the space required [192]. Thus, DLITE separates the control portion of the information access process from the scanning and reading portion. This separation allows for reusable query construction and service selection, while at the same time allowing for a legible view of documents and relationships among retrieved documents. The selection in the display view is linked to the graphical control portion, so a document viewed in the display could be used as part of a query in a query constructor.

DLITE also incorporates the notion of a workspace, or 'workcenter,' as it is known in this system. Different workspaces are created for different kinds of tasks. For example, a workspace for buying computer software can be equipped with source icons representing good sources of reviews of computer software, good Web sites to search for price information and link to the user's online credit service.

The SketchTrieve Interface

The guiding principle behind the SketchTrieve interface [365] is the depiction of information access as an informal process, in which half-finished ideas and partly explored paths can be retained for later use, saved and brought back to compare to later interactions, and the results can be combined via operations on graphical objects and connectors between them. It has been observed [584, 722] that users use the physical layout of information within a spreadsheet to organize information. This idea motivates the design of SketchTrieve, which allows users to arrange retrieval results in a side-by-side manner to facilitate comparison and recombination (see Figure 10.30).

The notion of a canvas or workspace for the retention of the previous context should be adopted more widely in future. Many issues are not easily solved, such as how to show the results of a set of interrelated queries, with minor modifications based on query expansion, relevance feedback, and other forms of modification. One idea is to show sets of related retrieval results as a stack of

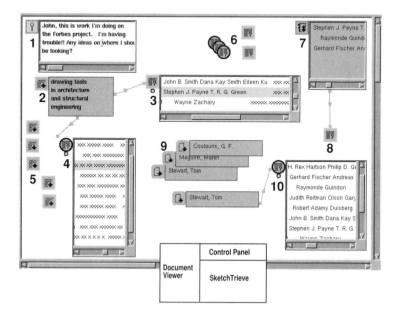

Figure 10.30   The SketchTrieve interface [365].

cards within a folder and allow the user to extract subsets of the cards and view them side by side, as is done in SketchTrieve, or compare them via a difference operation.

10.8.4   Examples of Poor Use of Overlapping Windows

Sometimes conversion from a command-line-based interface to a graphical display can cause problems. Hancock-Beaulieu *et al.* [337] describe poor design decisions made in an overlapping windows display for a bibliographic system. (An improvement was found with a later redesign of the system that used a monolithic interface [336].) Problems can also occur when designers make a 'literal' transformation from a TTY interface to a graphical interface. The consequences can be seen in the current LEXIS-NEXIS interface, which does not make use of the fact that window systems allow the user to view different kinds of information simultaneously. Instead, despite the fact that it occupies the entire screen, the interface does not retain window context when the user switches from one function to another. For example, viewing a small amount of metadata about a list of retrieved titles causes the list of results to disappear, rather than overlaying the information with a pop-up window or rearranging the available space with resizable tiles. Furthermore, this metadata is rendered in poorly-formatted ASCII instead of using the bit-map capabilities of a graphical interface. When a user opts to see the full text view of a document, it is shown in a small space, a few paragraphs at a time, instead of expanding to fill the entire available space.

10.8.5   Retaining Search History

Section 10.3 discusses information seeking strategies and behaviors that have been observed by researchers in the field. This discussion suggests that the user interface should show what the available choices are at any given point, as well as what moves have been made in the past, short-term tactics as well as longer-term strategies, and allow the user to annotate the choices made and information found along the way. Users should be able to bundle search sessions as well as save individual portions of a given search session, and flexibly access and modify each. There is also increasing interest in incorporating personal preference and usage information both into formulation of queries and use of the results of search [277].

   For the most part these strategies are not supported well in current user interfaces; however some mechanisms have been introduced that begin to address these needs. In particular, mechanisms to retain prior history of the search are useful for these tasks. Some kind of history mechanism has been made available in most search systems in the past. Usually these consist of a list of the commands executed earlier. More recently, graphical history has been introduced, that allows tracking of commands and results as well. Kim and Hirtle

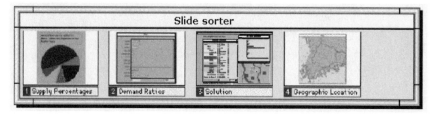

Figure 10.31   The VISAGE interaction history visualization [685].

[440] present a summary of graphical history presentation mechanisms. Recently, a graphical interface that displays Web page access history in a hierarchical structure was found to require fewer page accesses and require less time when returning to pages already visited [370].

An innovation of particular interest for information access interfaces is exemplified by the saving of state in miniature form in a 'slide sorter' view as exercised by the VISAGE system for information visualization [685] (see Figure 10.31). The VISAGE application has the added advantage of being visual in nature and so individual states are easier to recognize. Although intended to be used as a presentation creation facility, this interface should also be useful for retaining search action history.

10.8.6   Integrating Scanning, Selection, and Querying

User interfaces for information access in general do not do a good job of supporting strategies, or even of sequences of movements from one operation to the next. Even something as simple as taking the output of retrieval results from one query and using them as input to another query executed in a later search session is not well supported in most interfaces.

Hertzum and Frokjaer [368] found that users preferred an integration of scanning and query specification in their user interfaces. They did not, however, observe better results with such interactions. They hypothesized that if interactions are too unrestricted this can lead to erroneous or wasteful behavior, and interaction between two different modes requires more guidance. This suggests that more flexibility is needed, but within constraints (this argument was also made in the discussion of the SuperBook system in section 10.6).

There are exceptions. The new Web version of the Melyvl system provides ways to take the output of one query and modify it later for re-execution (see Figure 10.32). The workspace-based systems such as DLITE and Rooms allow storage and reuse of previous state. However, these systems do not integrate the general search process well with scanning and selection of information from auxiliary structures. Scanning, selection, and querying needs to be better integrated in general. This discussion will conclude with an example of an interface that does attempt to tightly couple querying and browsing.

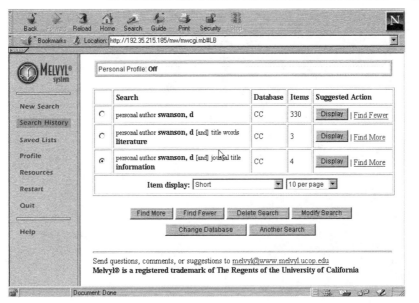

Figure 10.32   A view of query history revision in the Web-based version of the Melvyl bibliographic catalog. Copyright ©, The Regents of the University of California.

The Cat-a-Cone interface integrates querying and browsing of very large category hierarchies with their associated text collections. The prototype system uses 3D+animation interface components from the Information Visualizer [144], applied in a novel way, to support browsing and search of text collections and their category hierarchies. See Figure 10.33. A key component of the interface is the separation of the graphical representation of the category hierarchy from the graphical representation of the documents. This separation allows for a fluid, flexible interaction between browsing and search, and between categories and documents. It also provides a mechanism by which a *set* of categories associated with a document can be viewed along with their hierarchical context.

Another key component of the design is assignment of first-class status to the representation of text content. The retrieved documents are stored in a 3D+animation book representation [144] that allows for compact display of moderate numbers of documents. Associated with each retrieved document is a page of links to the category hierarchy and a page of text showing the document contents. The user can 'ruffle' the pages of the book of retrieval results and see corresponding changes in the category hierarchy, which is also represented in 3D+animation. All and only those parts of the category space that reflect the semantics of the retrieved document are shown with the document.

The system allows for several different kinds of starting points. Users can start by typing in a name of a category and seeing which parts of the category hierarchy match it. For example, Figure 10.34 shows the results of searching on

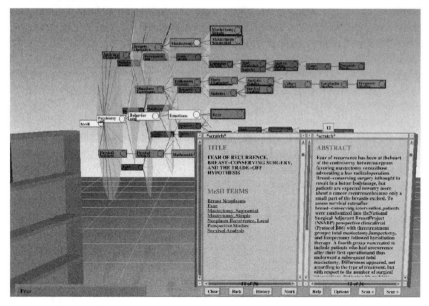

Figure 10.33   The Cat-a-Cone interface for integrating category and text scanning and search [358].

'Radiation' over the MeSH terms in this subcollection. The word appears under four main headings (*Physical Sciences, Diseases, Diagnostics,* and *Biological Sciences*). The hierarchy immediately shows why 'Radiation' appears under *Diseases* — as part of a subtree on occupational hazards. Now the user can select one or more of these category labels as input to a query specification.

Another way the user can start is by simply typing in a free text query into an entry label. This query is matched against the collection. Relevant documents are retrieved and placed in the book format. When the user 'opens' the book to a retrieved document, the parts of the category hierarchy that correspond to the retrieved documents are shown in the hierarchical representation. Thus, multiple intersecting categories can be shown simultaneously, in their hierarchical context. Thus, this interface fluidly combines large, complex metadata, starting points, scanning, and querying into one interface. The interface allows for a kind of relevance feedback, by suggesting additional categories that are related to the documents that have been retrieved. This interaction model is similar to that proposed by [5].

Recall the evaluation of the Kohonen feature map representation discussed in section 10.4. The experimenters found that some users expressed a desire for a visible hierarchical organization, others wanted an ability to zoom in on a subarea to get more detail, and some users disliked having to look through the entire map to find a theme, desiring an alphabetical ordering instead. The subjects liked the ease of being able to jump from one area to another without

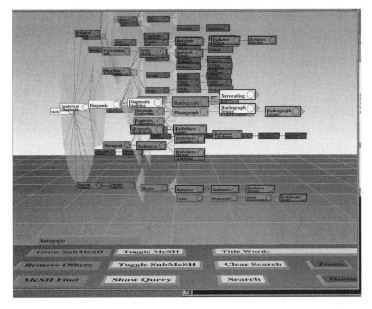

Figure 10.34   An interface for a starting point for searching over category labels [358].

having to back up (as is required in Yahoo!) and liked the fact that the maps have varying levels of granularity.

These results all support the design decisions made in the Cat-a-Cone. Hierarchical representation of term meanings is supported, so users can choose which level of description is meaningful to them. Furthermore, different levels of description can be viewed simultaneously, so more familiar concepts can be viewed in more detail, and less familiar at a more general level. An alphabetical ordering of the categories coupled with a regular expression search mechanism allows for straightforward location of category labels. Retrieved documents are represented as first-class objects, so full text is visible, but in a compact form. Category labels are disambiguated by their ancestor/descendant/sibling representation. Users can jump easily from one category to another and can in addition query on multiple categories simultaneously (something that is not a natural feature of the maps). The Cat-a-Cone has several additional advantages as well, such as allowing a document to be placed at the intersection of several categories, and explicitly linking document contents with the category representation.

10.9   Trends and Research Issues

The importance of human computer interaction is receiving increasing recognition within the field of computer science [587]. As should be evident from the contents of this chapter, the role of the user interface in the information access process has only recently begun to receive the attention it deserves. Research in this area can be expected to increase rapidly, primarily because of the rise of the Web. The Web has suddenly made vast quantities of information available globally, leading to an increase in interest in the problem of information access. This has lead to the creation of new information access paradigms, such as the innovative use of relevance feedback seen in the Amazon.com interface. Because the Web provides a platform-independent user interface, investment in better user interface design can have an impact on a larger user population than before.

Another trend that can be anticipated is an amplified interest in organization and search over personal information collections. Many researchers are proposing that in future a person's entire life will be recorded using various media, from birth to death. One motivation for this scenario is to enable searching over everything a person has ever read or written. Another motivation is to allow for searching using contextual clues, such as 'find the article I was reading in the meeting I had on May 1st with Pam and Hal'. If this idea is pursued, it will require new, more sophisticated interfaces for searching and organizing a huge collection of personal information.

There is also increasing interest in leveraging the behavior of individuals and groups, both for rating and assessing the quality of information items, and for suggesting starting points for search within information spaces. Recommender systems can be expected to increase in prevalence and diversity. User interfaces will be needed to guide users to appropriate recommended items based on their information needs.

The field of information visualization needs some new ideas about how to display large, abstract information spaces intuitively. Until this happens, the role of visualization in information access will probably be primarily confined to providing thematic overviews of topic collections and displaying large category hierarchies dynamically. Breakthroughs in information visualization can be expected to have a strong impact on information access systems.

10.10   Bibliographic Discussion

The field of human-computer interaction is a broad one, and this chapter touches on only a small subset of pertinent issues. For further information, see the excellent texts on user interface design by Shneiderman [725], information seeking behavior by Marchionini [542], and digital libraries by Lesk [501]. An excellent book on visual design is that of Mullet and Sano [580]. Tufte has written thought-provoking and visually engaging books on the power of information visualization [769, 770] and a collection of papers on information visualization has been edited by Card *et al.* [141].

This chapter has discussed many ideas for improving the human-computer interaction experience for information seekers. This is the most rapidly developing area of information access today, and improvements in the interface are likely to lead the way toward better search results and better-enabled information creators and users. Research in the area of human-computer interaction is difficult because the field is relatively new, and because it can be difficult to obtain strong results when running user studies. These challenges should simply encourage those who really want to influence the information access systems of tomorrow.

Acknowledgements

The author gratefully acknowledges the generous and helpful comments on the contents of this chapter by Gary Marchionini and Ben Shneiderman, the excellent administrative assistance of Barbara Goto, and the great faith and patience of Ricardo Baeza-Yates and Berthier Ribeiro-Neto.

Chapter 11
Multimedia IR: Models and Languages

by Elisa Bertino, Barbara Catania, and Elena Ferrari

11.1   Introduction

The need for an integrated management for multimedia data is rapidly growing in several application environments such as offices, CAD/CAM applications, and medical applications. For this reason, multimedia information systems are widely recognized to be one of the most promising fields in the area of information management.

The most important characteristic of a multimedia information system is the variety of data it must be able to support. Multimedia systems must have the capability to store, retrieve, transport, and present data with very heterogeneous characteristics such as text, images (both still and moving), graphs, and sound. For this reason, the development of a multimedia system is considerably more complex than a traditional information system. Conventional systems only deal with simple data types, such as strings or integers. On the contrary, the underlying data model, the query language, and the access and storage mechanisms of a multimedia system must be able to support objects with a very complex structure. The need then arises for developing *Multimedia Information Retrieval* (Multimedia IR for short) systems specifically for handling multimedia data. Traditional IR systems (see Chapter 2) only deal with textual, unstructured data; therefore, they are unable to support the mix of structured and unstructured data, and different kinds of media, typical of a Multimedia IR system. For instance, a traditional IR system does not support metadata information such as that provided by database schema, which is a fundamental component in a database management system (DBMS). On the other hand, Multimedia IR systems require some form of database schema because several multimedia applications need to structure their data at least partially. However, the notion of schema may need to be weakened with respect to the traditional notion to ensure a higher degree of flexibility in structuring data. Moreover, a Multimedia IR system requires handling metadata which is crucial for data retrieval, whereas traditional IR systems do not have such requirement.

The architecture of a Multimedia IR system depends on two main factors: first, the peculiar characteristics of multimedia data, and second, the kinds of operations to be performed on such data. In what follows, we briefly deal with both these aspects.

Data Modeling

A Multimedia IR system should be able to represent and store multimedia objects in a way that ensures their fast retrieval. The system should be therefore able to deal with different kinds of media and with *semi-structured data*, i.e., data whose structure may not match, or only partially match, the structure prescribed by the data schema. In order to represent semi-structured data, the system must typically extract some features from the multimedia objects. A related issue is how these features are extracted and efficiently maintained by the system.

Data Retrieval

The main goal of a Multimedia IR system is to efficiently perform *retrieval*, based on user requests, exploiting not only data attributes, as in traditional DBMSs, but also the *content* of multimedia objects. This poses several interesting challenges, due to the heterogeneity of data, the fuzziness of information, the loss of information in the creation of indexes, and the need of an interactive refinement of the query result. Data retrieval relies on the following basic steps:

(1) **Query specification**. In this step, the user specifies the request. The query interface should allow the user to express fuzzy predicates for proximity searches (for example, 'Find all images similar to a car'), content-based predicates (for example, 'Find multimedia objects containing an apple'), conventional predicates on the object attributes (for example, conditions on the attribute 'color' of an image, such as 'Find all red images'), and structural predicates (for example, 'Find all multimedia objects containing a video clip').

(2) **Query processing and optimization**. Similarly to traditional systems, the query is parsed and compiled into an internal form. In generating this internal representation, the query is also optimized, choosing the best evaluation plan. Note that, due to the presence of fuzzy terms, content-based predicates, and structural predicates, query processing is a very complex activity. A great amount of work has been done on query processing both in traditional [402] and spatial databases [247, 82, 118, 361, 623]. However, little work has been done on query processing strategies for multimedia databases. The main problem is the heterogeneity of data: different query processing strategies, one for each data type, should be combined together in some way.

(3) **Query answer**. The retrieved objects are returned to the user in decreasing order of relevance. Relevance is measured as a distance function from the query object to the stored ones.

(4) **Query iteration**. In traditional DBMSs, the query process ends when the system returns the answer to the user. In a Multimedia IR system, due to the inevitable lack of precision in the user request, the query execution is iterated until the user is satisfied. At each iteration the user supplies the system with additional information by which the request is refined, reducing or increasing the number of returned answers.

From the previous discussion it follows that a Multimedia IR system differs from a traditional IR system in two main aspects. First, the structure of multimedia objects is more complex than the structure of typical textual data, handled by traditional IR systems. This complexity requires the integration of traditional IR technology with the technology of multimedia database management systems to adequately represent, manage, and store multimedia objects. Note that the use of a DBMS also provides update functionalities and transaction management which are in general not covered by typical IR systems. Second, object retrieval is mainly based on a similarity approach. Moreover, the objects retrieved by a query are usually returned to the user in a ranked form. These aspects are successfully handled by IR techniques (see Chapter 2). However, IR systems have initially been developed to support libraries of articles, journals, and encyclopedic knowledge bases (see Chapter 2). In those systems, the fundamental unit is the *textual document*. Thus, the techniques developed for traditional IR systems should be extended to deal with documents containing other media.

Multimedia IR systems should therefore combine both the DBMS and the IR technology, to integrate the data modeling capabilities of DBMSs with the advanced and similarity-based query capabilities of IR systems. The resulting system will be able to answer attribute-based queries as well as content-based queries. The whole architecture of the resulting system, in particular the query optimizer, must take this aspect into account in order to efficiently support user requests.

In this chapter, we discuss modeling and query language issues for multimedia objects, pointing out the differences and the analogies between a traditional IR system and a multimedia one. Problems related to feature extraction and searching are covered by Chapter 12.

The first part of the chapter is devoted to the presentation of the most relevant models proposed in the literature for multimedia data, with particular attention to commercial proposals.

The second part of the chapter investigates the peculiarities of multimedia query languages with respect to traditional ones. Then, as an example, two different language proposals are presented. Also in this case, we focus on commercial proposals and we discuss how the new standard SQL3 could be used to deal with multimedia data retrieval.

11.2   Data Modeling

As we have already remarked, the complex nature of multimedia data may benefit from the use of DBMS functions for data representation and querying. However, the integration of multimedia data in a traditional DBMS is not an easy task. Indeed, traditional DBMSs are mainly targeted to support conventional data. Multimedia data is inherently different from conventional data. The main difference is that information about the content of multimedia data are usually not encoded into attributes provided by the data schema (*structured data*). Rather, text, image, video, and audio data are typically *unstructured*. Therefore, specific methods to identify and represent content features and semantic structures of multimedia data are needed. Another distinguishing feature of multimedia data is its large storage requirements. One single image usually requires several Kbytes of storage, whereas a single second of video can require several Mbytes of storage. Moreover, the content of multimedia data is difficult to analyze and compare, in order to be actively used during query processing.

Addressing data modeling issues in the framework of Multimedia IR systems entails two main tasks. First, a data model should be defined by which the user can specify the data to be stored into the system. Such a data model should have the ability of an integrated support for both conventional and multimedia data types and should provide methods to analyze, retrieve, and query such data. Second, the system should provide a model for the internal representation of multimedia data. The definition of such a model is crucial for the efficiency of query processing.

As far as the first aspect is concerned, a promising technology with respect to the modeling requirements of multimedia data is the object-oriented one [89]. The richness of the data model provided by OODBMSs makes them more suitable than relational DBMSs for modeling both multimedia data types and their semantic relationships. Moreover, the concept of class can be naturally used to define ad hoc data types for multimedia data in that a class is characterized by both a set of attributes and a set of operations that can be performed on these attributes. Classes can, moreover, be related into inheritance hierarchies, thus allowing the definition of a multimedia class as a specialization of one or more superclasses. However, the performance of OODBMs in terms of storage techniques, query processing, and transaction management is not comparable to that of relational DBMSs. Another drawback of OODBMs is that they are highly non-standard. Indeed, even though a standard language has been defined by the Object Database Management Group (ODMG), very few systems support it.

For all the above reasons, a lot of effort has been devoted to the extension of the relational model with capabilities for modeling complex objects, typical of the object-oriented context. The goal of the so-called *object-relational* technology is to extend the relational model with the ability of representing complex data types by maintaining, at the same time, the performance and the simplicity of relational DBMSs and related query languages. The possibility of defining abstract data types inside the relational model allows one to define ad hoc data types for multimedia data. For instance, such data types can provide support for content-dependent queries. In the following section, we will give some examples of such extensions.

The second problem related to data modeling is how multimedia data are represented inside the system. Due to the particular nature of multimedia data, it is not sufficient to describe it through a set of attributes as usually done with traditional data. Rather, some information should be extracted from the objects and used during query processing. The extracted information is typically represented as a set of *features*; each multimedia object is therefore internally represented as a list of features, each of which represents a point in a multi-dimensional space. Multi-attribute access methods can then be used to index and search for them (see Chapter 12). Features can be assigned to multimedia objects either manually by the user, or automatically by the system. In general, a hybrid approach is used, by which the system determines some of the values and the user corrects or augments them. In both cases, values assigned to some specific features, such as the shape of an image or the style of an audio object, are assigned to the object by comparing the object with some previously classified objects. For instance, to establish whether an image represents a car or a house, the shape of the image is compared with the shapes of already classified cars and houses before taking a decision. Finally, it is important to recall that feature extraction cannot be precise. Therefore, a weight is usually assigned to each feature value representing the uncertainty of assigning such a value to that feature. For example, if we are 80% sure that a shape is a square, we can store this value together with the recognized shape.

From the previous discussion, it follows that data modeling in a Multimedia IR system is an articulated activity that must take into account both the complex structure of data and the need of representing features extracted from multimedia objects.

In the following, we give a brief overview of some proposals to model multimedia data. We start by reviewing the support for multimedia data provided by commercial DBMSs. Then, as an example of a research proposal, we survey the data model developed in the context of the MULTOS project.

11.2.1   Multimedia Data Support in Commercial DBMSs

Most current relational DBMSs support variable-length data types which can be used to represent multimedia data. The way these data are supported by commercial DBMSs is mostly non-standard in that each DBMS vendor uses different names for such data types and provides support for different operations on them.

For example, the Oracle DBMS provides the VARCHAR2 data type to represent variable length character strings. The maximum length of VARCHAR2 data is 4000 bytes. The RAW and LONG RAW data types are used for data that is not to be interpreted by Oracle. These data types can be used to store graphics, sounds, or unstructured objects. LOB data types can be used to store Large unstructured data OBjects up to four gigabytes in size. BLOBs are used to store unstructured Binary Large OBjects, whereas CLOBs are used to store Character Large OBject data.

The Sybase SQL server supports IMAGE and TEXT data types to store images and unstructured text, respectively, and provides a limited set of functions for their searching and manipulation.

However, the support provided by the above mentioned data types is very limited in that the DBMS does not provide any interpretation of the data content. Moreover, operations that can be performed on such data by means of the built-in functions provided by the DBMS are very simple.

As we have already remarked, most commercial relational DBMSs vendors are investing a lot of effort in extending the relational model with the capability of modeling complex objects, typical of the object-oriented context. Such efforts have given rise to the upcoming SQL3 standard. From a data modeling point of view, the major improvement provided by SQL3 with respect to its predecessor SQL-92, is the support for an *extensible type system*. Extensibility of the type system is achieved by providing constructs to define user-dependent abstract data types, in an object-oriented like manner. In SQL3, each type specification consists of both attribute and function specifications. A strong form of encapsulation is provided, in that attribute values can only be accessed by using some system functions. Moreover, user-defined functions can be either visible from any object or only visible in the object they refer to. Both single and multiple inheritance can be defined among user-defined types and dynamic late binding is provided [89].

SQL3 also provides three types of collection data types: sets, multisets, and lists. The elements of a collection must have compatible types. Several system-defined operations are provided to deal with collections. Besides the definition of user-dependent abstract data types, SQL3 provides a restricted form of object identifier that supports sharing and avoids data duplication.

Although SQL3 has not yet been officially published, most commercial products have already implemented their proprietary versions of SQL3. An example in such direction is the *data cartridges* provided by Oracle for multimedia data handling, or the *data blades* supported by Illustra.†

Oracle provides data cartridges for text, spatial data, image, audio and video data. To give a concrete example, Oracle8 provides a ConText cartridge, which is a text management solution combining data management capabilities of a traditional DBMS with advanced text retrieval and natural-language process technology. The ConText cartridge supports the most popular document formats, including ASCII, MS Word, and HTML. One of the most relevant feature of the ConText cartridge is its ability to find documents about a specific topic (thus providing a form of content-based retrieval). Content-based queries on text documents can be combined with traditional queries in the same SQL statement and can be efficiently executed due to the use of indexing techniques specific for texts. Such techniques are based on the notion of *inverted files* (see Chapter 8) which map a given word to the documents containing it, thus allowing a fast retrieval of all the documents containing a particular word.

---

† Illustra was acquired by Informix in 1995.

Illustra provides 3D and 2D spatial data blades for modeling spatial data. The supported data types include boxes, vectors, quadrangles, etc., and examples of supported operations are INTERSECT, CONTAINS, OVERLAPS, CENTER, and so on. Spatial data blades also implement R-trees for performing efficient spatial queries [330, 717]. The text data blade provides data types for representing unstructured text and performing content-based queries. For example, the method *ContainWords* can be used to search for all the documents containing a particular word. Moreover, Illustra supports a data blade which can be used to query images by content.

The object-relational technology and its extensive type system is now starting to be widely used both in industrial and research projects. An example of this trend is the La Scala archive project, currently under development at the Laboratorio di Informatica Musicale of the University of Milano [254]. The goal of this project is the development of the multimedia archive of Teatro alla Scala, one of the best known musical temples of the world, using the Oracle technology and the related data cartridges. The system is organized around La Scala *nights*. Each night encompasses the phonic items, score, and other graphical and video items related to the performance. When a new performance has to be prepared, the musicians can easily access all the materials (such as CD-ROMs, video, photos, and scores) of previous editions of the same performance. Accessing such information has required the development of ad hoc cartridges to represent and query non-conventional data. For instance, we are currently developing a data cartridge that allows content-based queries on music scores. We apply pattern matching techniques to music scores to enable the user to sing a few bars into a microphone linked to the computer and see all the music scores containing a piece of music close to the one being sung. Users can then view the retrieved musical graphic scores, or excerpts from them, and simultaneously play the corresponding music.

As an example of a data model suitable for a multimedia environment, in the following we consider the data model developed in the context of the MULTOS project [759].

11.2.2   The MULTOS Data Model

MULTOS (MULTimedia Office Server) is a multimedia document‡ server with advanced document retrieval capabilities, developed in the context of an ESPRIT project in the area of Office Systems [759].

MULTOS is based on a *client/server* architecture. Three different types of document servers are supported: *current servers*, *dynamic servers*, and *archive servers*, which differ in storage capacity and document retrieval speed. Such servers support filing and retrieval of multimedia objects based on document collections, document types, document attributes, document text, and images.

---

‡ As MULTOS deals with office services, in the following we use the words *object* and *document* as synonymous.

The MULTOS data model allows the representation of high level concepts present in the documents contained in the database, the grouping of documents into classes of documents having similar content and structure, and the expression of conditions on free text.

Each document is described by a logical structure, a layout structure, and a conceptual structure. The *logical* structure determines arrangements of logical document components (e.g., title, introduction, chapter, section, etc.). The *layout* structure deals with the layout of the document content and it contains components such as pages, frames, etc. The *conceptual* structure allows a semantic-oriented description of the document content as opposed to the syntax-oriented description provided by the logical and layout structure. The conceptual structure has been added to provide support for document retrieval by content. MULTOS provides a formal model, based on a data structuring tool available in semantic data models, to define the document conceptual structure. The logical and layout structures are defined according to the ODA document representation [398].

Documents having similar conceptual structures are grouped into *conceptual types*. In order to handle types in an effective manner, conceptual types are maintained in a hierarchy of generalization, where a subtype inherits from its supertypes the conceptual structure and can then refine it. Types can be *strong* or *weak*. A strong type completely specifies the structure of its instances. A weak type, on the other hand, partially specifies the structure of its instances. Moreover, components of unspecified type (called *spring component types*) can appear in a document definition.

Example 1 *The conceptual structure of the type* Generic_Letter *is shown in Figure 11.1. The node* Letter_Body *is a spring conceptual component. The complete conceptual structure in Figure 11.2 corresponds to the type* Business_Product_Letter. *This type has been obtained from* Generic_Letter *by specialization of* Letter_Body *into a complex conceptual component, defined as an aggregation of five conceptual components. According to the conceptual model, the document type* Business_Product_Letter *is linked to the document type* Generic_Letter *by an 'is-a' relationship. In this example, the '+' symbol attached to the* Receiver *component means that it is multivalued. Notice also that the* Name *and the* Address *appear in two subtrees having as roots the conceptual components* Receiver *and* Sender, *respectively.*

For document retrieval, conceptual types play the role of the database schema which enables the use of efficient access structures. Moreover, conceptual types are the basis for formulating queries at an abstract level.

MULTOS also provides a sophisticated approach to deal with image data. First, an image analysis process is performed, consisting of two phases: *low level image analysis* and *high level image analysis*. During the low level image analysis phase, the basic objects composing a given image and their relative positions are identified. The high level image analysis phase deals with image interpretation according to the Dempster-Shafter theory of evidence [60, 312].

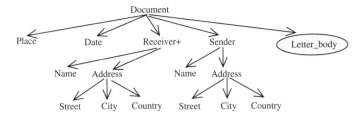

Figure 11.1   Conceptual structure of the type `Generic_Letter`.

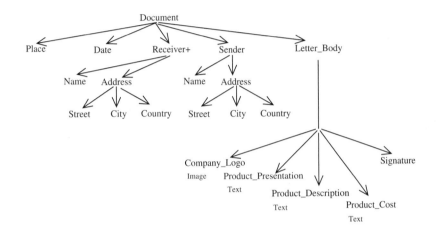

Figure 11.2   Complete conceptual structure of the type `Business_Product_Letter`.

At the end of the image analysis process, images are described in terms of the objects recognized, with associated belief and plausibility values, and the classes to which they belong. The information is then exploited in image access.

Image access information is stored in an *image header*, associated with the image file. Access structures are then built for a fast access to image headers. Two types of index are constructed:

- **Object index**. For each object a list is maintained. Each element of the lists is a pair (BI,IMH), where IMH is a pointer to the header of the image containing the object, and BI is the associated belief interval, representing the probability that the image considered really contains the object.

- **Cluster index**. For each image class, a list of pairs (MF,IMH) is maintained. IMH is a pointer to an image header corresponding to an image with a non-null degree of membership to the class, and MF is the value of the membership degree. The membership degree of an image to a given class is computed by comparing the image interpretation resulting from the analysis phase, with the class description, using techniques analogous to the ones used in text IR systems [698] (see Chapter 6).

11.3   Query Languages

Queries in relational or object-oriented database systems are based on an *exact match* mechanism, by which the system is able to return exactly those tuples or objects satisfying some well specified criteria given in the query expression and nothing more. In general, query predicates specify which values the object attributes must contain.

Because of the semi-structured nature of multimedia objects, the previous approach is no longer adequate in a Multimedia IR system. In this context, the user should still be able to query the content of multimedia objects by specifying values of semantic attributes but he/she should also be able to specify additional conditions about the content of multimedia data. Thus, the exact match is only one of the possible ways of querying multimedia objects. More often, a similarity-based approach is applied that considers both the structure and the content of the objects. Queries of the latter type are called *content-based* queries since they retrieve multimedia objects depending on their global content. Information on the global content of an object is not represented as attribute values in the database system. Rather, as we have already remarked in section 11.2, a set of information, called features, is extracted and maintained for each object. When the query is submitted, the features of the query object are matched with respect to the features of the objects stored in the database and only the objects that are *more similar* to the query one are returned to the user (see Chapter 12).

The characteristics of content-based query processing impacts the definition of a multimedia query language and, in general, of the user interface. In particular, in designing a multimedia query language, three main aspects require attention:

- How the user enters his/her request to the system, i.e., which interfaces are provided to the user for query formulation.

- Which conditions on multimedia objects can be specified in the user request. The conditions that can be expressed depend on the support the system provides for content-based retrieval (see Chapter 12).

- How uncertainty, proximity, and weights impact the design of the query language.

In the following, we discuss the above aspects in detail. Then, we present two examples of multimedia query languages. First, we illustrate how traditional relational query languages can be extended to deal with multimedia data, discussing the main characteristics of the upcoming SQL3 query language. Then, as an example of a research proposal, we introduce the query language supported by MULTOS (see section 11.2.2).

11.3.1   Request Specification

Two different interfaces can be presented to the user for querying multimedia objects. The first type of interface is based on *browsing and navigation*. Usually, due to the complex structure of multimedia objects, it may be useful to let users browse and navigate inside the structure of multimedia objects to locate the desired objects. Such an approach is typically used in CAD/CAM/CASE environments due to the complex structure of the objects under consideration.

Navigation, however, is not always the best way to find multimedia objects, in that it may be heavily time consuming when the object desired is deeply nested. The second approach for selecting objects is therefore based, as traditionally in DBMSs, on specifying the conditions the objects of interest must satisfy, by means of queries.

Queries, in turn, can be specified in two different ways: the first, typical of a traditional database context, is to enter the query by using a specific query language. However, in some cases (especially when images and audio data are considered), a *query by example* approach is preferred. Under this approach, queries are specified by using actual data inside a visual environment; the user provides the system with an object example that is then used to retrieve all the stored objects similar to the given one. For example, the user may choose a house and pose the query: 'Retrieve all houses of similar shape and different color.' This approach requires the use of a GUI environment where the user can pick examples and compose the query object. In order to pick examples, the system must supply some *domains*, i.e., sets of typical values, one for each object feature (see section 11.2).

11.3.2   Conditions on Multimedia Data

Multimedia query languages should provide predicates for expressing conditions on the attributes, the content, and the structure of multimedia objects. In general, query predicates can be classified into three different groups:

- **Attribute predicates** concern the attributes (i.e., the structured content) of multimedia objects.

- **Structural predicates** concern the structure of the data being considered.

- **Semantic predicates** concern the semantic and unstructured content of the data involved.

By the term *attribute predicates* we mean predicates against traditional attributes, i.e., attributes for which an exact value is supplied for each object. Examples of attributes are the speaker of an audio object, the size of an object, or its type. By querying these predicates, the system applies an exact-match retrieval, using the same techniques as traditional DBMSs.

Structural predicates concern the structure of multimedia objects. Such predicates can be answered by using some form of metadata [99, 442] and information about the database schema. With respect to traditional databases, structural queries play a fundamental role in multimedia query processing, due to the complex structure of multimedia objects. An example of use of a structural predicate is the query: 'Find all multimedia objects containing at least one image and a video clip.'

On the other hand, *semantic predicates* concern the semantic content of the queried data, depending on the features that have been extracted and stored for each multimedia object. An example of a semantic query is 'Find all the objects containing the word OFFICE.' Note that the word 'OFFICE' may appear either in a textual component of the object or as a text attribute of some image components. The query 'Find all the red houses' is a query on the image content. This query can be executed only if color and shape are features that have been previously extracted from images.

Current systems support semantic predicates only with respect to specific features, such as the color, the shape, the texture, and sometimes the motion. For example, QBIC allows the retrieval of images with similar shapes or similar textures with respect to the object example specified in the query [257]. More innovative approaches include the Name-it project, whose aim is to process a video clip and automatically associate spoken or typed names with their corresponding faces [708].

The main difference between attribute predicates and semantic predicates is that, in the latter case, an exact match cannot be applied. This means that there is no guarantee that the objects retrieved by this type of predicate are 100% correct or precise. In general, the result of a query involving semantic predicates is a set of objects, each of which has an associated degree of relevance with respect to the query. The user can subsequently select the better matches and submit the query again.

Structural and semantic predicates can also refer to spatial or temporal properties of multimedia objects. Spatial semantic predicates specify conditions about the relative positions of a set of objects in an image or a video. Examples of spatial semantic predicates are: `contain`, `intersect`, `is contained in`, `is adjacent to`. Temporal semantic predicates are mainly related to continuous media, like audio and video. They allow one to express temporal relationships among the various frames of a single audio or video. For example, the query 'Find all the objects that contain an audio component, where the hint of the discussion is first policy, and then economy' is a temporal audio query.

From the point of view of structural predicates, spatial and temporal predicates can be used to specify temporal synchronization properties and spatial layout properties for the presentation of multimedia objects [87, 88]. For instance, in the query: 'Find all the objects containing an image overlapping the associated text', a spatial structural predicate is used to impose a condition on the spatial layout of the retrieved objects. Analogously, the query: 'Find all the objects in which a jingle is played for the duration of an image display' is an example of a structural temporal query. Note, moreover, that temporal and spatial predicates can be combined to express more articulated requirements. An example is the query: 'Find all the objects in which the logo of a car company is displayed and, when it disappears, a graphic showing the increases in the company sales is shown in the same position where the logo was.'

Due to the complex structure of multimedia objects, all the previous types of predicates can refer either to the whole object or, if the underlying data model supports complex object representation, to some subcomponents of the object. In the last case, the query language must also be able to navigate the object structure. A typical example in this direction is represented by path expressions in object-oriented systems [89].

11.3.3   Uncertainty, Proximity, and Weights in Query Expressions

As we have already remarked, the execution of a content-dependent query returns a set of relevant objects. An interesting aspect in designing a multimedia query language is how it is possible to specify the degree of relevance of the retrieved objects. In general, this can be done in three different ways:

- By using some imprecise terms and predicates, such as `normal`, `unacceptable`, `typical`. Each of those terms does not represent a precise value but a set of possible acceptable values with respect to which the attribute or the feature has to be matched.

- By specifying particular proximity predicates. In this case, the predicate does not represent a precise relationship between objects or between attributes/features and values. Rather, the relationship represented is based on the computation of a semantic *distance* between the query object and the stored ones, on the basis of the extracted features. The *Nearest object search* is an example of proximity predicate, by which the user requests all the objects which are closest or within a certain distance of a given object. Indexing support for this kind of query is discussed in Chapter 12.

- By assigning each condition or term a given *weight*, specifying the degree of precision by which a condition must be verified by an object. For example, the query 'Find all the objects containing an image representing a screen (HIGH) and a keyboard (LOW)' [657], can be used to retrieve all the objects containing an image representing a screen and a keyboard. However, the objects containing only a screen are also retrieved and returned to the user, after the ones containing both the screen and the keyboard, since the condition imposing the containment of a keyboard is weaker than the condition imposing the containment of a screen.

The use of imprecise terms and relationships, as well as the use of weights, allows the user to drive the similarity-based selection of relevant objects. The corresponding query is executed by assigning some importance and preference values to each predicate and term. Then, objects are retrieved and presented to the user as an ordered list. This ordering is given by a score associated with each object, giving a measure of the matching degree between the object and the query. The computation of the score is based on probabilistic models, using the preference values assigned to each predicate.

11.3.4   Some Proposals

In the following we briefly survey some query languages supporting retrieval of multimedia objects. In order to describe how standard languages are evolving to support multimedia applications, we first describe the facilities provided by the upcoming standard SQL3 to support such kinds of applications. Then, we present the query language supported by the MULTOS system [90], introduced in section 11.2.2.

The SQL3 Query Language

As we have seen in section 11.2.1, the extensible type system and in general the ability to deal with complex objects make SQL3 suitable for modeling multimedia data. From the query language point of view, the major improvements of SQL3 with respect to SQL-92 can be summarized as follows:

- **Functions and stored procedures**. SQL3 allows the user to integrate external functionalities with data manipulation. This means that functions of an external library can be introduced into a database system as *external functions*. Such functions can be either implemented by using an external language, and in this case SQL3 only specifies which is the language and where the function can be found, or can be directly implemented by using SQL3 itself. In this way, impedance mismatch between two different programming languages and type systems is avoided. Of course, this approach requires an extension of SQL with imperative programming languages constructs.

- **Active database facilities**. Another important property of SQL3 is the support of active rules, by which the database is able to react to some system- or user-dependent events by executing specific actions. Active rules, or triggers, are very useful to enforce integrity constraints.

From the multimedia perspective point of view, the aspects described make SQL3 suitable for being used as an interface language for multimedia applications. In particular, the ability to deal with external functions and user-defined data types enables the language to deal with objects with a complex structure, as multimedia objects. Note that, without this characteristic, the ability to deal with BLOB would have been useless since it reduces the view of multimedia data to single large uninterpreted data values, which are not adequate for the rich semantics of multimedia data. By the use of triggers, spatial and temporal constraints can be enforced, thus preserving the database consistency. Finally, as SQL3 is a widespread standard, it allows one to model multimedia objects in the framework of a well understood technology.

Though the above facilities make SQL3 suitable for use as an interface for multimedia applications, there are also some limitations. The main drawback is related to retrieval support and, as a consequence, optimization. Indeed, no IR techniques are integrated into the SQL3 query processor. This means that the ability to perform content-based search is application dependent. As a consequence, objects are not ranked and are therefore returned to the application as a unique set. Moreover, specialized indexing techniques can be used but they are not transparent to the user.

Bearing in mind the previous limitations, several projects have already been started with the aim of integrating SQL3 with IR facilities. An example of such a project is represented by SQL/MM Full Text [190]. Text is in this case considered as a nested sequence of words, sentences, and paragraphs. In order to precisely capture the structure and the meaning of the words, SQL/MM Full Text is also able to view the text as a tree structure entity. The structure of this entity is controlled by a grammar. These facilities allow one to easily express queries to perform selection on the basis of the text content and/or text structure.

There have also been several proposals for introducing spatial data types and predicates into the SQL framework. Among them, we recall Probe [623], Spatial SQL [231], Pictorial SQL [687], and QBE [418].

The MULTOS Query Language

The development of the MULTOS query language has been driven by a number of requirements: first, it should be possible to easily navigate through the document structure. *Path-names* can be used for this purpose. Path-names can be total, if the path identifies only one component, or partial, if several components are identified by the path. Path-names are similar to object-oriented path expressions. Queries both on the content and on document structure must be supported.

Query predicates on complex components must be supported. In this case, the predicate applies to all the document subcomponents that have a type compatible with the type required by the query. This possibility is very useful when a user does not recall the structure of a complex component.

In general, a MULTOS query has the form:

```
FIND DOCUMENTS VERSION  version-clause
SCOPE  scope-clause
TYPE  type-clause
WHERE  condition-clause
WITH  component
```

where:

- The *version-clause* specifies which versions of the documents should be considered by the query.

- The *scope-clause* restricts the query to a particular set of documents. This set of documents is either a user-defined document collection or a set of documents retrieved by a previous query.

- The *type-clause* allows the restriction of a query to documents belonging to a prespecified set of types. The conditions expressed by the *condition-clause* only apply to the documents belonging to these types and their subtypes. When no type is specified, the query is applied to all document types.

- The *condition-clause* is a Boolean combination of simple conditions (i.e., predicates) on documents components. Predicates are expressed on conceptual components of documents. Conceptual components are referenced by path-names. The general form of a predicate is:

  component restriction

  where *component* is a path-name and *restriction* is an operator followed by an expression.

- The *with-clause* allows one to express structural predicates. *Component* is a path-name and the clause looks for all documents structurally containing such a component.

Different types of conditions can be specified in order to query different types of media. In particular, MULTOS supports three main classes of predicates: predicates on data attributes, on which an exact match search is performed; predicates on textual components, determining all objects containing some specific strings; and predicates on images, specifying conditions on the image content. Image predicates allow one to specify conditions on the class to which an image should belong or conditions on the existence of a specified object within an image and on the number of occurrences of an object within an image. The following example illustrates the basic features of the MULTOS query language.

Example 2 *Consider the conceptual structure* Generic_letter, *presented in example 1. The following is an example of query:*

```
FIND DOCUMENT VERSIONS LAST WHERE
Document.Date > 1/1/1998 AND
(*Sender.Name = "Olivetti" OR
*Product_Presentation CONTAINS "Olivetti") AND
*Product_Description CONTAINS "Personal Computer" AND
(*Address.Country = "Italy" OR TEXT CONTAINS "Italy") AND
WITH *Company_Logo.
```

According to this query, the user looks for the last version of all documents, dated after January 1998, containing a company logo, having the word 'Olivetti' either as sender name or in the product presentation (which is a textual component), with the word 'Personal Computer' in the product description section *(which is another textual component) and with the word 'Italy' either constitut-ing the country in the address or contained in any part of the entire document. Symbol '*' indicates that the path-name is not complete, that is, it could identify more than one component.*

The query language provided by MULTOS also supports the specification of imprecise queries that can be used when the user has an uncertain knowledge about the content of the documents he/she is seeking [657]. Such uncertainty is expressed by associating both a *preference* and an *importance* value with the attributes in the query. Such values are then used for ranking the retrieved documents. The following example illustrates the discussion.

Example 3 *The query:*

```
FIND DOCUMENT VERSIONS LAST WHERE
(Document.Date BETWEEN (12/31/1998,1/31/98) PREFERRED
BETWEEN (2/1/1998,2/15/98) ACCEPTABLE) HIGH AND
(*Sender.Name = "Olivetti" OR
*Product_Presentation CONTAINS "Olivetti") HIGH AND
(*Product_Description CONTAINS "Personal Computer") HIGH AND
(*Product_Description CONTAINS "good ergonomics") LOW AND
(*Address.Country = "Italy" OR TEXT CONTAINS "Italy") HIGH
AND
WITH *Company_Logo HIGH
(IMAGE MATCHES
screen HIGH
keyboard HIGH
AT LEAST 2 floppy_drives LOW) HIGH
```

finds the last versions of all documents written in January, but possibly even at the beginning of February 1998, containing a company logo, having the word 'Olivetti' either as sender name or in the product presentation, with the word 'Personal Computer' in the product description section, and with the word 'Italy' either constituting the country in the address or contained in any part of the entire document. Personal Computers are described in the product description section as products having good ergonomics. Moreover, the document should contain a picture of the Personal Computer, complete with screen and keyboard, with at least two floppy drives. The value 'LOW' associated with the condition on 'good ergonomics' indicates that the user formulating the query is not completely sure about this description of PC. By contrast, he/she is sure of all the conditions whose associated value is 'HIGH.'

11.4   Trends and Research Issues

In this chapter we have discussed the main issues in developing a Multimedia IR system. We have observed that only the integration of DBMS and IR tech-nologies provides the ability to represent, store, and manipulate multimedia data and, at the same time, to retrieve those data by applying content-based searches.

We then discussed the main issues arising in defining a data model for multimedia data. Since multimedia data has, in general, a complex structure, the data model must be able to reflect and manage this complexity. Object-oriented or object-relational data models represent the right technology for multimedia data representation. Additional relevant requirements include the support of semi-structured data and metadata. Another important requirement is the ability to internally represent the content of multimedia data in a way that ensures fast retrieval of the stored data and efficient processing of content-based queries. To achieve this goal, semantic features can be extracted from the data, stored inside the system, and used during query processing.

The second topic discussed in this chapter is related to multimedia query languages. We observed that a multimedia query language is characterized by the type of interface presented to the user and the types of predicates it allows in a query. Such predicates are used to perform content-based searches and to let the user drive the selection of relevant objects.

Examples of commercial and prototype systems have been discussed, with respect to the data modeling and query language capabilities.

Several aspects require further investigation. For example, even though SQL3 supports multimedia data representation, it cannot be taken as the basis for the definition of a Multimedia IR system. Additional research is needed to integrate SQL3 with specific language constructs and underlying techniques to perform information retrieval and query optimization.

Another topic is related to XML (see Chapter 6), the new standard format for data on the Web [304]. XML is a text-based format, providing a standard data model to encode the content, the semantics, and the schema of ordinary documents, structured records, and metacontent information about a Web site. The extension of such a standard to support multimedia data and content-based queries is an important research direction.

A further direction concerns the techniques for ranking the objects returned by a partial-match query. Such ranking usually only takes into account the degree of similarity of the objects retrieved with the query request. However, other factors can be considered, such as the profile of the user submitting the query, or the history of the previous queries specified by the user. Taking into account these aspects is very important, since it gives rise to a *customized ranking* which is closer to the user needs.

11.5   Bibiographic Discussion

As we have seen, due to their complex nature, the object-oriented paradigm seems the right approach to model multimedia data. Details about object-oriented database models and architectures can be found in [89]. The object database standard, as defined by the Object Database Management Group, is presented in [150].

On the research side, several models have been proposed for multimedia data. Such proposals range from data models suitable for a particular media type, like data models for videos [211, 238, 297, 621], data models for images [170] or models for spatial data [623], to general-purpose multimedia data models [169, 296, 397, 545, 759, 827].

Issues related to the definition and the classification of metadata in the multimedia context are extensively discussed in [99, 442]. Among the systems supporting similarity-based queries, we recall QBIC [257], Name-It [708], QBE [418], Probe [623], and PICQUERY [418]. For additional details about video and image multimedia databases we refer the reader to [405] and [438], respectively. Details about modeling and architectural aspects of the MULTOS system can be found in [759].

Chapter 12
Multimedia IR: Indexing and Searching

by Christos Faloutsos

12.1 Introduction

The problem we focus on here is the design of fast searching methods that will search a database of multimedia objects to locate objects that match a query object, exactly or approximately. Objects can be two-dimensional color images, gray-scale medical images in 2D or 3D (e.g., MRI brain scans), one-dimensional time series, digitized voice or music, video clips, etc. A typical query by content would be, e.g., '*in a collection of color photographs, find ones with the same color distribution as a sunset photograph.*'

Specific applications include image databases; financial, marketing and production time series; scientific databases with vector fields; audio and video databases; DNA/Genome databases; etc. In such databases, typical queries would be '*find companies whose stock prices move similarly,*' or '*find images that look like a sunset,*' or '*find medical X-rays that contain something that has the texture of a tumor.*' Searching for similar patterns in such databases as the above is essential, because it helps in predictions, computer-aided medical diagnosis and teaching, hypothesis testing and, in general, in 'data mining' [8] and rule discovery.

Of course, the distance of two objects has to be quantified. We rely on a domain expert to supply such a distance function $\mathcal{D}()$:

Definition *Given two objects, O_1 and O_2, the distance (= dissimilarity) of the two objects is denoted by*

$$\mathcal{D}(O_1, O_2) \tag{12.1}$$

For example, if the objects are two (equal-length) time series, the distance $\mathcal{D}()$ could be their Euclidean distance (the root of the sum of squared differences).

Similarity queries can been classified into two categories:

- **Whole match** Given a collection of N objects $O_1, O_2, \ldots, O_N$ and a query object Q, we want to find those data objects that are within distance ε from Q. Notice that the query and the objects are of the same type: for example, if the objects are 512×512 gray-scale images, so is the query.

- **Sub-pattern match** Here the query is allowed to specify only part of the object. Specifically, given N data objects (e.g., images) $O_1, O_2, \ldots, O_N$, a query (sub-)object Q and a tolerance ε, we want to identify the parts of the data objects that match the query. If the objects are, e.g., 512×512 gray-scale images (like medical X-rays), in this case the query could be, e.g., a 16×16 subpattern (e.g., a typical X-ray of a tumor).

Additional types of queries include the '*nearest neighbors*' queries (e.g., '*find the five most similar stocks to IBM's stock*') and the '*all pairs*' queries or '*spatial joins*' (e.g., '*report all the pairs of stocks that are within distance ε from each other*'). Both the above types of queries can be supported by the approach we describe next. As we shall see, we reduce the problem into searching for multi-dimensional points, which will be organized in R-trees; in this case, nearest-neighbor search can be handled with a branch-and-bound algorithm and the spatial join query can be handled with recent, highly fine-tuned algorithms, as discussed in section 12.8. Thus, we do not focus on nearest-neighbor and 'all-pairs' queries.

For all the above types of queries, the ideal method should fulfill the following requirements:

- It should be *fast*. Sequential scanning and distance calculation with each and every object will be too slow for large databases.

- It should be '*correct*.' In other words, it should return all the qualifying objects, without missing any (i.e., no 'false dismissals'). Notice that 'false alarms' are acceptable, since they can be discarded easily through a post-processing step. Of course, as we see, e.g. in Figure 12.5, we try to keep their number low (but not necessarily minimal), so that the total response time is minimized.

- The ideal method should require a small space overhead.

- The method should be dynamic. It should be easy to insert, delete, and update objects.

As we see next, the heart of the presented 'GEMINI' approach is to use f feature extraction functions to map objects into points in f-dimensional space; thus, we can use highly fine-tuned database spatial access methods to accelerate the search.

The remainder of the chapter is organized as follows. Section 12.2 gives some background material on past related work on spatial access methods. Section 12.3 describes the main ideas for GEMINI, a generic approach to indexing multimedia objects. Section 12.4 shows the application of the approach for 1D time series indexing. Section 12.5 gives another case study, for color images, within the QBIC project. Section 12.6 presents 'FastMap', a method to do automatic feature extraction. Section 12.7 summarizes the conclusions and lists problems for future research and section 12.8 provides pointers to the related bibliography.

12.2 Background — Spatial Access Methods

As mentioned earlier, the idea is to map objects into points in f-D space, and to use multiattribute access methods (also referred to as *spatial access methods* or SAMs) to cluster them and to search for them.

Thus, a brief introduction to multidimensional indexing methods (or spatial access methods) is in order. The prevailing methods form three classes: (1) R^*-trees and the rest of the R-tree family, (2) linear quadtrees, and (3) grid-files.

Several of these methods explode exponentially with the dimensionality, eventually reducing to sequential scanning. For linear quadtrees, the effort is proportional to the hypersurface of the query region [244]; the hypersurface grows exponentially with the dimensionality. Grid files face similar problems, since they require a directory that grows exponentially with the dimensionality. The R-tree-based methods seem to be most robust for higher dimensions, provided that the fanout of the R-tree nodes remains > 2. Below, we give a brief description of the R-tree method and its variants, since it is one of the typical representatives of spatial access methods.

The R-tree represents a spatial object by its minimum bounding rectangle (MBR). Data rectangles are grouped to form parent nodes, which are recursively grouped, to form grandparent nodes and, eventually, a tree hierarchy. The MBR of a parent node completely contains the MBRs of its children; MBRs are allowed to overlap. Nodes of the tree correspond to disk pages. Disk pages, or 'disk blocks', are consecutive byte positions on the surface of the disk that are typically fetched with one disk access. The goal of the insertion, split, and deletion routines is to give trees that will have good clustering, with few, tight parent MBRs. Figure 12.1 illustrates data rectangles (in black), organized in an R-tree with fanout 3. Figure 12.2 shows the file structure for the same R-tree, where nodes correspond to disk pages.

A range query specifies a region of interest, requiring all the data regions that intersect it. To answer this query, we first retrieve a superset of the qualifying data regions: we compute the MBR of the query region, and then we recursively descend the R-tree, excluding the branches whose MBRs do not intersect the query MBR. Thus, the R-tree will give us quickly the data regions whose MBR intersects the MBR of the query region. The retrieved data regions will be further examined for intersection with the query region.

Algorithms for additional operations (nearest neighbor queries, spatial joins, insertions, and deletions) are more complicated and are still under research (see the Bibliographic Discussion).

The original R-tree paper inspired much follow-up work, as described in

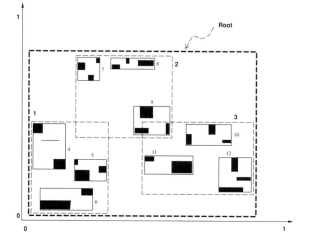

Figure 12.1 Data (dark rectangles) organized in an R-tree with fanout = 3. Solid, light-dashed, and heavy-dashed lines indicate parents, grandparents and great-grandparent (the root, in this example).

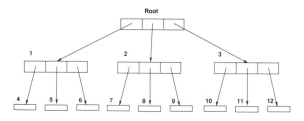

Figure 12.2 The file structure for the R-tree of the previous figure (fanout = 3).

section 12.8. It is important to highlight, however, that *any* spatial access method can be used (like R^*-trees, X-trees, SR-trees, and so on).

12.3   A Generic Multimedia Indexing Approach

To illustrate the basic idea, we shall focus on 'whole match' queries. For such queries the problem is defined as follows:

- We have a collection of N objects: O_1, O_2, ..., O_N.
- The distance/dissimilarity between two objects (O_i, O_j) is given by the function $\mathcal{D}(O_i, O_j)$, which can be implemented as a (possibly, slow) program.
- The user specifies a query object Q, and a tolerance ε.

Our goal is to find the objects in the collection that are within distance ε from the query object. An obvious solution is to apply sequential scanning: For each and every object O_i ($1 \leq i \leq N$), we can compute its distance from Q and report the objects with distance $\mathcal{D}(Q, O_i) \leq \varepsilon$.

However, sequential scanning may be slow, for two reasons:

(1) The distance computation might be expensive. For example, as discussed in Chapter 8, the editing distance in DNA strings requires a dynamic programming algorithm, which grows like the product of the string lengths (typically, in the hundreds or thousands, for DNA databases).

(2) The database size N might be huge.

Thus, we are looking for a faster alternative. The GEMINI (GEneric Multimedia object INdexIng) approach we present next, is based on two ideas, each of which tries to avoid each of the two disadvantages of sequential scanning:

- a 'quick-and-dirty' test, to discard quickly the vast majority of non-qualifying objects (possibly, allowing some false alarms);
- the use of spatial access methods, to achieve faster-than-sequential searching.

The case is best illustrated with an example. Consider a database of time series, such as yearly stock price movements, with one price per day. Assume that the distance function between two such series S and Q is the Euclidean distance

$$\mathcal{D}(S, Q) \equiv \left(\sum_{i=1}^{} (S[i] - Q[i])^2 \right)^{1/2} \qquad (12.2)$$

where $S[i]$ stands for the value of stock S on the i-th day. Clearly, computing the distance of two stocks will take 365 subtractions and 365 squarings in our example.

The idea behind the quick-and-dirty test is to characterize a sequence with a single number, which will help us discard many non-qualifying sequences. Such a number could be, e.g., the average stock price over the year. Clearly, if two stocks differ in their averages by a large margin, it is impossible that they will be similar. The converse is not true, which is exactly the reason we may have false alarms. Numbers that contain some information about a sequence (or a multimedia object, in general), will be referred to as 'features' for the rest of this chapter. Using a good feature (like the 'average,' in the stock prices example), we can have a quick test, which will discard many stocks, with a single numerical comparison for each sequence (a big gain over the 365 subtractions and squarings that the original distance function requires).

If using one feature is good, using two or more features might be even better, because they may reduce the number of false alarms (at the cost of making the quick-and-dirty test a bit more elaborate and expensive). In our stock prices example, additional features might be, e.g., the standard deviation, or, even better, some of the discrete Fourier transform (DFT) coefficients, as we shall see in section 12.4.

The end result of using f features for each of our objects is that we can map each object into a point in f-dimensional space. We shall refer to this mapping as $\mathcal{F}()$ (for 'F'eature):

Definition   *Let $\mathcal{F}()$ be the mapping of objects to f-dimensional points, that is, $\mathcal{F}(O)$ will be the f-D point that corresponds to object O.*

This mapping provides the key to improve on the second drawback of sequential scanning: by organizing these f-D points into a spatial access method, we can cluster them in a hierarchical structure, like the R^*-trees. Upon a query, we can exploit the R^*-tree, to prune out large portions of the database that are not promising. Thus, we do not even *have* to do the quick-and-dirty test on all of the f-D points!

Figure 12.3 illustrates the basic idea: Objects (e.g., time series that are 365 points long) are mapped into 2D points (e.g., using the average and the standard deviation as features). Consider the 'whole match' query that requires all the objects that are similar to S_n within tolerance ε: this query becomes an f-D sphere in feature space, centered on the image $\mathcal{F}(S_n)$ of S_n. Such queries on multidimensional points is exactly what R-trees and other SAMs are designed to answer efficiently. More specifically, the search algorithm for a whole match query is as follows:

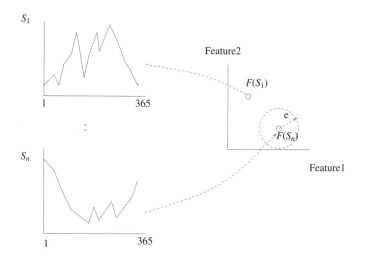

Figure 12.3   Illustration of the basic idea: a database of sequences $S_1, \ldots, S_N$; each sequence is mapped to a point in feature space; a query with tolerance ε becomes a sphere of radius ε.

Algorithm 1 *Search:*

(1) Map the query object Q into a point $\mathcal{F}(Q)$ in feature space.

(2) Using a spatial access method, retrieve all points within the desired tolerance ε from $\mathcal{F}(Q)$.

(3) Retrieve the corresponding objects, compute their actual distance from Q and discard the false alarms.

Intuitively, the method has the potential to relieve both problems of the sequential scan, presumably resulting in much faster searches. The only step that we have to be careful with is that the mapping $\mathcal{F}()$ from objects to f-D points does not distort the distances. Let $\mathcal{D}()$ be the distance function of two objects, and $\mathcal{D}_{feature}()$ be the (say, Euclidean) distance of the corresponding feature vectors. Ideally, the mapping should preserve the distances exactly, in which case the SAM will have neither false alarms nor false dismissals. However, requiring perfect distance preservation might be difficult. For example, it is not obvious which features we have to use to match the editing distance between two DNA strings. Even if the features are obvious, there might be practical problems: for example, in the stock price example, we could treat every sequence as a 365-dimensional vector; although in theory a SAM can support an arbitrary number of dimensions, in practice they all suffer from the 'dimensionality curse,' as discussed earlier.

The crucial observation is that we can guarantee that there will be no false dismissals if the distance in feature space matches or underestimates the distance between two objects. Intuitively, this means that our mapping $\mathcal{F}()$ from objects to points *should make things look closer* (i.e., it should be a contractive mapping).

Mathematically, let O_1 and O_2 be two objects (e.g., same-length sequences) with distance function $\mathcal{D}()$ (e.g., the Euclidean distance) and $\mathcal{F}(O_1)$, $\mathcal{F}(O_2)$ be their feature vectors (e.g., their first few Fourier coefficients), with distance function $\mathcal{D}_{feature}()$ (e.g., the Euclidean distance, again). Then we have:

Lemma 12.1 (Lower Bounding) *To guarantee no false dismissals for whole-match queries, the feature extraction function $\mathcal{F}()$ should satisfy the following formula:*

$$\mathcal{D}_{feature}(\mathcal{F}(O_1), \mathcal{F}(O_2)) \leq \mathcal{D}(O_1, O_2) \qquad \textbf{(12.3)}$$

As proved in [249], lower-bounding the distance works correctly for range queries. Will it work for the other queries of interest, like 'all pairs' and 'nearest neighbor' ones? The answer is affirmative in both cases. An 'all pairs' query can easily be handled by a 'spatial join' on the points of the feature space: using a similar reasoning as before, we see that the resulting set of pairs will be a superset of the qualifying pairs. For the nearest neighbor query, the following algorithm guarantees no false dismissals: (1) find the point $\mathcal{F}(P)$ that is the nearest neighbor to the query point $\mathcal{F}(Q)$, (2) issue a range query, with query object Q and radius $\varepsilon = \mathcal{D}(Q, P)$ (i.e., the actual distance between the query object Q and data object P).

In conclusion, the GEMINI approach to indexing multimedia objects for fast similarity searching is as follows:

Algorithm 2 *(GEMINI) GEneric Multimedia object INdexIng approach:*

(1) Determine the distance function $\mathcal{D}()$ between two objects.

(2) Find one or more numerical feature-extraction functions, to provide a 'quick-and-dirty' test.

(3) Prove that the distance in feature space lower-bounds *the actual distance $\mathcal{D}()$, to guarantee correctness.*

(4) Use a SAM (e.g., an R-tree), to store and retrieve the f-D feature vectors.

The first two steps of GEMINI deserve some more discussion: the first step involves a domain expert. The methodology focuses on the *speed* of search only; the quality of the results is completely relying on the distance function that the expert will provide. Thus, GEMINI will return *exactly the same* response set (and therefore, the same quality of output, in terms of precision-recall) that would be returned by a sequential scanning of the database; the only difference is that GEMINI will be faster.

The second step of GEMINI requires intuition and imagination. It starts by trying to answer the question (referred to as the '*feature-extracting*' question for the rest of this chapter):

> **'Feature-extracting' question:** *If we are allowed to use only one numerical feature to describe each data object, what should this feature be?*

The successful answers to the above question should meet two goals: first, they should facilitate step 3 (the distance lower-bounding), and second, they should capture most of the characteristics of the objects.

We give case studies of steps 2 and 3 of the GEMINI algorithm in the following sections. The first involves 1D time series, and the second focuses on 2D color images. We shall see that the philosophy of the quick-and-dirty filter, in conjunction with the lower-bounding lemma, can lead to solutions to two problems:

- the dimensionality curse (time series)
- the 'cross-talk' of features (color images).

For each case study, we first describe the objects and the distance function, then show how to apply the lower-bounding lemma, and finally give experimental results, on real or realistic data.

12.4   One-dimensional Time Series

Here the goal is to search a collection of (equal-length) time series, to find the ones that are similar to a desirable series. For example, '*in a collection of yearly stock price movements, find the ones that are similar to IBM.*'

12.4.1   Distance Function

According to GEMINI (algorithm 2), the first step is to determine the distance measure between two time series. A typical distance function is the Euclidean distance (equation 12.2), which is routinely used in financial and forecasting applications. Additional, more elaborate distance functions, that, for example, include time-warping, are discussed in section 12.8.

12.4.2   Feature Extraction and Lower-bounding

Having decided on the Euclidean distance as the dissimilarity measure, the next step is to find some features that can lower-bound it. We would like a set of features that first, preserve/lower-bound the distance, and second, carry much information about the corresponding time series (so that the false alarms are few). The second requirement suggests that we use 'good' features, that have much discriminatory power. In the stock price example, a 'bad' feature would be, e.g., the first day's value: the reason being that two stocks might have similar first-day values, yet they may differ significantly from then on. Conversely, two otherwise similar sequences may agree everywhere, except for the first day's values. At the other extreme, we could use the values of *all* 365 days as features. However, although this would perfectly match the actual distance, it would lead to the 'dimensionality curse' problem.

Clearly, we need some better features. Applying the second step of the GEMINI algorithm, we ask the feature-extracting question: '*If we are allowed to use only one feature from each sequence, what would this feature be?*' A natural answer is the average. By the same token, additional features could be the average of the first half, of the second half, of the first quarter, etc. Or, in a more systematic way, we could use the coefficients of the Fourier transform, and, for our case, the Discrete Fourier Transform (DFT). For a signal $\vec{x} = [x_i]$, $i = 0, \ldots, n-1$, let X_F denote the n-point DFT coefficient at the F-th frequency ($F = 0, \ldots, n-1$).

The third step of the GEMINI methodology is to show that the distance in feature space lower-bounds the actual distance. The solution is provided by Parseval's theorem, which states that the DFT preserves the energy of a signal, as well as the distances between two signals:

$$\mathcal{D}(\vec{x}, \vec{y}) = \mathcal{D}(\vec{X}, \vec{Y}) \tag{12.4}$$

where $\vec{X}$ and $\vec{Y}$ are Fourier transforms of $\vec{x}$ and $\vec{y}$ respectively.

Thus, if we keep the first $f (f \leq n)$ coefficients of the DFT as the features, we lower-bound the actual distance:

$$
\begin{aligned}
\mathcal{D}_{feature}(\mathcal{F}(\vec{x}), \mathcal{F}(\vec{y})) &= \sum_{F=0}^{f-1} |X_F - Y_F|^2 \\
&\leq \sum_{F=0}^{n-1} |X_F - Y_F|^2 \\
&= \sum_{i=0}^{n-1} |x_i - y_i|^2
\end{aligned}
$$

and finally

$$
\mathcal{D}_{feature}(\mathcal{F}(\vec{x}), \mathcal{F}(\vec{y})) \leq \mathcal{D}(\vec{x}, \vec{y}) \tag{12.5}
$$

because we ignore positive terms from equation 12.2. Thus, there will be *no false dismissals*, according to lemma 12.1.

Notice that the GEMINI approach can be applied with *any* orthonormal transform, such as, the Discrete Cosine Transform (DCT), the wavelet transform etc., because they all preserve the distance between the original and the transformed space. In fact, our response time will improve with the ability of the transform to concentrate the energy: the fewer the coefficients that contain most of the energy, the more accurate our estimate for the actual distance, the fewer the false alarms, and the faster our response time. Thus, the performance results presented next are just pessimistic bounds; better transforms will achieve even better response times.

In addition to being readily available, (e.g., in 'Mathematica,' 'S,' 'maple,' 'matlab' etc.), the DFT concentrates the energy in the first few coefficients, for a large class of signals, the *colored noises*. These signals have a skewed energy spectrum ($O(F^{-b})$, as follows:

- For $b = 2$, we have the so-called *random walks* or *brown noise*, which model successfully stock movements and exchange rates (e.g., [541]).

- With even more skewed spectrum ($b > 2$), we have the *black noises* [712]. Such signals model successfully, for example, the water level of rivers and the rainfall patterns as they vary over time [541].

- With $b = 1$, we have the *pink noise*. Birkhoff's theory [712] claims that 'interesting' signals, such as musical scores and other works of art, consist of *pink noise*, whose energy spectrum follows $O(F^{-1})$. The argument of the theory is that white noise with $O(F^0)$ energy spectrum is completely unpredictable, while brown noise with $O(F^{-2})$ energy spectrum is too predictable and therefore 'boring.' The energy spectrum of pink noise lies in between.

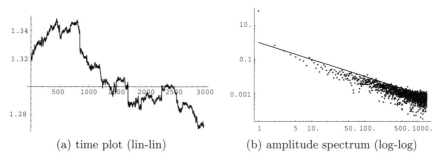

(a) time plot (lin-lin)   (b) amplitude spectrum (log-log)

Figure 12.4   (a) The Swiss-franc exchange rate (7 August 1990 to 18 April 1991 – first 3000 values out of 30,000) and (b) log-log amplitude of its Fourier transform, along with the $1/F$ line.

As an illustration of the above observations, Figure 12.4(a) plots the movement of the exchange rate between the Swiss franc and the US dollar starting 7 August 1990 (3000 measurements); Figure 12.4(b) shows the amplitude of the Fourier coefficients as a function of the frequency F, as well as the $1/F$ line, in a logarithmic-logarithmic plot. Notice that, since it is successfully modeled as a random walk, the amplitude of the Fourier coefficients follow the $1/F$ line. The above data set is available through anonymous ftp from `sfi.santafe.edu`.

In addition to 1D signals (stock price movements and exchange rates), it is believed that several families of real n-D signals belong to the family of 'colored noises', with skewed spectrum. For example, 2D signals, like photographs, are far from white noise, exhibiting a few strong coefficients in the lower spatial frequencies. The JPEG image compression standard exploits this phenomenon, effectively ignoring the high frequency components of the discrete cosine transform, which is closely related to the Fourier transform. If the image consisted of white noise, no compression would be possible at all.

12.4.3   Experiments

Performance results with the GEMINI approach on time series are reported in [6]. There, the method is compared to a *sequential scanning* method. The R^*-tree was used for the spatial access method within GEMINI. The sequences were artificially generated random walks, with length $n = 1024$; their number N varied from 50 to 400.

Figure 12.5 shows the break-up of the response time, as a function of the number f of DFT coefficients kept. The diamonds, triangles, and squares indicate total time, post-processing time, and R^*-tree time, respectively. Notice that, as we keep more features f, the R^*-tree becomes bigger and slower, but more accurate (fewer false alarms, and therefore shorter post-processing time). This tradeoff reaches an equilibrium for $f = 2$ or 3. For the rest of the experiments, the $f = 2$ Fourier coefficients were kept for indexing, resulting in a four-dimensional R^*-tree (two real numbers for each complex DFT coefficient).

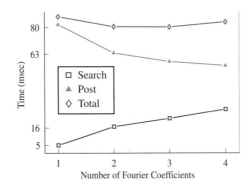

Figure 12.5 Breakup of the execution time, for range query (db size $N = 400$ sequences).

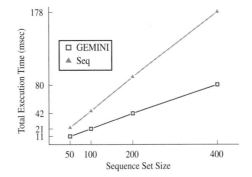

Figure 12.6 Search time per query vs. number N of sequences, for whole-match queries; GEMINI (black line) and sequential scanning (gray line).

Figure 12.6 shows the response time for the two methods (GEMINI and sequential scan), as a function of the number of sequences N. Clearly, GEMINI outperforms the sequential scanning.

The major conclusions from the application of GEMINI on time series are the following:

(1) GEMINI can be successfully applied to time series, and specifically to the ones that behave like 'colored noises' (stock prices movements, currency exchange rates, water level in rivers etc.).

(2) For signals with skewed spectrum like the above ones, the minimum in the response time is achieved for a small number of Fourier coefficients ($f = 1, 2, 3$). Moreover, the minimum is rather flat, which implies that

a suboptimal choice for f will give search time that is close to the minimum. Thus, with the help of the lower-bounding lemma and the energy-concentrating properties of the DFT, we managed to avoid the 'dimensionality curse.'

(3) The success in 1D series suggests that GEMINI is promising for 2D or higher-dimensionality signals, if those signals also have skewed spectrum. The success of JPEG (that uses DCT) indicates that real images indeed have a skewed spectrum.

Finally, the method has been extended to handle subpattern matching; for time sequences, the details are in [249]. We only mention the main idea here. Assuming that query patterns have length of at least w, we preprocess every sequence of the database, by allowing a sliding window of length w at each and every possible position, and by extracting the f features for a given positioning of the window. Thus, every sequence becomes a trail in the f-dimensional feature space, which can be further approximated by a set of few MBRs that cover it. Representing each sequence by a few MBRs in feature space may allow false alarms, but no false dismissals. The approach can be generalized for subpattern matching in 2D signals (and, in general, in n-dimensional vector fields).

12.5   Two-dimensional Color Images

GEMINI has also been applied for color images, within the QBIC project of IBM. The QBIC (Query By Image Content) project studies methods to query large online image databases using the images' content as the basis of the queries. Examples of the content include color, texture, shape, position, and dominant edges of image items and regions. Potential applications include medical ('*Give me other images that contain a tumor with a texture like this one*'), photo-journalism ('*Give me images that have blue at the top and red at the bottom*'), and many others in art, fashion, cataloging, retailing, and industry.

Here we will discuss methods on databases of still images, with two main datatypes: 'images' ($\equiv$ 'scenes') and 'items.' A scene is a (color) image, and an item is a part of a scene, for example, a person, a piece of outlined texture, or an apple. Each scene has zero or more items. The identification and extraction of items is beyond the scope of this discussion (see [603] for more details).

In this section we give an overview of the indexing aspects of QBIC, and specifically the distance functions and the application of the GEMINI approach. More details about the algorithms and the implementation of QBIC are in [257].

12.5.1   Image Features and Distance Functions

We mainly focus on the color features, because color presents an interesting problem (namely, the '*cross-talk*' of features), which can be resolved by the GEMINI

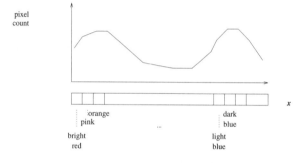

Figure 12.7   An example of a color histogram of a fictitious sunset photograph: many red, pink, orange, purple, and blue-ish pixels; few yellow, white, and green-ish ones.

approach (algorithm 2). For color, we compute a k-element color histogram for each item and scene, where $k = 256$ or 64 colors. Each component in the color histogram is the percentage of pixels that are most similar to that color. Figure 12.7 gives an example of such a histogram of a fictitious photograph of a sunset: there are many red, pink, orange, and purple pixels, but only a few white and green ones.

Once these histograms are computed, one method to measure the distance between two histograms ($k \times 1$ vectors) $\vec{x}$ and $\vec{y}$ is given by

$$d_{hist}^2(\vec{x}, \vec{y}) = (\vec{x} - \vec{y})^t \mathcal{A}(\vec{x} - \vec{y}) = \sum_i^k \sum_j^k a_{ij}(x_i - y_i)(x_j - y_j) \qquad (\textbf{12.6})$$

where the superscript t indicates matrix transposition, and the color-to-color similarity matrix $\mathcal{A}$ has entries a_{ij} which describe the similarity between color i and color j.

12.5.2   Lower-bounding

In applying the GEMINI method for color indexing, there are two obstacles: first, the *'dimensionality curse'* (k may be large, e.g. 64 or 256 for color features) and, most importantly, the *quadratic nature of the distance function*. The distance function in the feature space involves cross-talk among the features (see equation 12.6), and thus it is a full quadratic form involving all cross terms. Not only is such a function much more expensive to compute than a Euclidean (or any L_p) distance, but it also precludes efficient implementation of commonly used spatial access methods. Figure 12.8 illustrates the situation. To compute the distance between the two color histograms $\vec{x}$ and $\vec{q}$, the, e.g., bright-red component of $\vec{x}$ has to be compared not only to the bright-red component of $\vec{q}$, but also to the pink, orange, etc. components of $\vec{q}$.

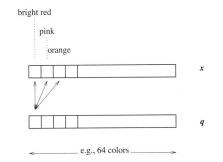

Figure 12.8   Illustration of the 'cross-talk' between two color histograms.

To resolve the cross-talk problem, we try to apply the GEMINI approach (algorithm 2). The first step of the algorithm has been done: the distance function between two color images is given by equation 12.6, that is, $\mathcal{D}() = d_{hist}()$. The second step is to find one or more numerical features, whose Euclidean distance would lower-bound $d_{hist}()$. Thus, we ask the feature-extracting question again: *If we are allowed to use only one numerical feature to describe each color image, what should this feature be?* Taking a cue from the previous section on time series, we can consider some average value, or the first few coefficients of the two-dimensional DFT transform. Since we have three color components, (e.g., Red, Green, and Blue), we could consider the average amount of red, green, and blue in a given color image.

Notice that different color spaces (such as Munsell) can be used, with absolutely no change in our indexing algorithms. Thus, we continue the discussion with the RGB color space. This means that the color of an individual pixel is described by the triplet (R,G,B) (for 'R'ed, 'G'reen, 'B'lue). The average color vector of an image or item $\bar{x} = (R_{avg}, G_{avg}, B_{avg})^t$, is defined in the obvious way, with

$$R_{avg} = (1/P) \sum_{p=1}^{P} R(p),$$

$$G_{avg} = (1/P) \sum_{p=1}^{P} G(p),$$

$$B_{avg} = (1/P) \sum_{p=1}^{P} B(p)$$

where P is the number of pixels in the item, and $R(p)$, $G(p)$, and $B(p)$ are the red, green and blue components (intensities, typically in the range 0–255) respectively of the p-th pixel. Given the average colors $\bar{x}$ and $\bar{y}$ of two items, we define $d_{avg}()$ as the Euclidean distance between the three-dimensional average color vectors,

$$d^2_{avg}(\bar{x}, \bar{y}) = (\bar{x} - \bar{y})^t (\bar{x} - \bar{y}) \tag{12.7}$$

The third step of the GEMINI algorithm is to prove that our simplified distance $d_{avg}()$ lower-bounds the actual distance $d_{hist}()$. Indeed, this is true, as an application of the so-called Quadratic Distance Bounding or QDB Theorem (see [244]).

The result is that, given a color query, our retrieval proceeds by first filtering the set of images based on their average (R, G, B) color, then doing a final, more accurate matching using their full k-element histogram. The resulting speedup is discussed next.

12.5.3   Experiments

We now present experimental results [244] with GEMINI on color, using the bounding theorem, The experiments compare the relative performance (in terms of CPU time and disk accesses) between first, simple sequential evaluation of d_{hist} for all database vectors (referred to as 'naive'), and second, GEMINI.

The experiments report the total and the CPU times required by the methods, by performing simulations on a database of $N = 924$ color image histograms, each of $k = 256$ colors, of assorted natural images.

Results are shown in Figure 12.9, which presents the total response time as a function of the selectivity (ratio of actual hits over the database size N). The figure also shows the CPU time for each method. Notice that, even for a selectivity of 5% (which would return ≈ 50 images to the user), the GEMINI method is much faster than the straightforward, sequential computation of the histogram distances. In fact, it requires from a fraction of a second up to ≈ 4 seconds, while the naive method requires consistently ≈ 10 seconds. Moreover, notice that for larger databases, the naive method will have a linearly increasing response time.

Thus, the conclusions are the following:

- The GEMINI approach (i.e., the idea to extract some features for a quick-and-dirty test) motivated a fast method, using the average RGB distance; it also motivated a strong theorem (the so-called QDB theorem [244]) which guarantees the correctness in our case.

- In addition to resolving the cross-talk problem, GEMINI solved the 'dimensionality curse' problem at no extra cost, requiring only $f = 3$ features, as opposed to $k = 64$ or 256 that $d_{hist}()$ required.

12.6   Automatic Feature Extraction

GEMINI is useful for any setting that we can extract features from. In fact, algorithms for automatic feature extraction methods exist, like the 'Multidimen-

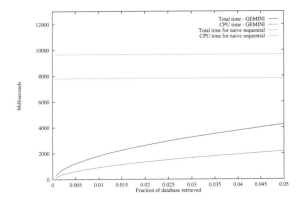

Figure 12.9 Response time vs. selectivity, for the sequential ('naive') retrieval and for GEMINI.

sional Scaling' (MDS)   and 'FastMap.' Extracting features not only facilitates the use of off-the-shelf spatial access methods, but it also allows for visual data mining: we can plot a 2D or 3D projection of the data set, and inspect it for clusters, correlations, and other patterns.

Figure 12.10 shows the results of FastMap on 35 documents of seven classes, after deriving $k = 3$ features/dimensions. The classes include basketball reports ('Bbr'), abstracts of computer science technical reports ('Abs'), cooking recipes ('Rec'), and so on. The distance function was a decreasing function of the cosine similarity. The figure shows the 3D scatter-plot, (a) in its entirety and (b) after zooming into the center, to highlight the clustering abilities of FastMap. Notice that the seven classes are separated well, in only $k = 3$ dimensions.

12.7 Trends and Research Issues

In this chapter we focused on how to accelerate queries by content on image databases and, more general, on multimedia databases. Target queries are, e.g., '*find images with a color distribution of a sunset photograph;*' or, '*find companies whose stock price moves similarly to a given company's stock.*'

The method expects a distance function $\mathcal{D}()$ (given by domain experts), which should measure the dissimilarity between two images or objects O_1, O_2. We mainly examined *whole match, range* queries (that is, '*queries by example*' where the user specifies the ideal object and asks for all objects that are within distance ε from the ideal object). Extensions to other types of queries (nearest neighbors, all pairs and subpattern match) are briefly discussed. We focused on the GEMINI approach, which combines two ideas:

- The first is to devise a '*quick-and-dirty*' test, which will eliminate several

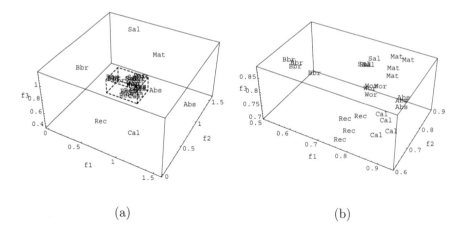

(a)   (b)

Figure 12.10 A collection of documents, after FastMap in 3-D space: (*a*) the whole collection and (*b*) magnification of the dashed box.

non-qualifying objects. To achieve that, we should extract f numerical features from each object, which should somehow describe the object (for example, the first few DFT coefficients for a time sequence, or for a gray-scale image). The key question to ask is *'If we are allowed to use only one numerical feature to describe each data object, what should this feature be?'*

- The second idea is to further accelerate the search, by organizing these f-dimensional points using state-of-the art spatial access methods [400], like the R^*-trees. These methods typically group neighboring points together, thus managing to discard large unpromising portions of the address space early.

The above two ideas achieve fast searching. Moreover, we need to consider the condition under which the above method will be not only fast, but also *correct*, in the sense that it will not miss any qualifying object. Notice that false alarms are acceptable, because they can be discarded, in the obvious way. The answer is provided by the *lower-bounding* lemma, which intuitively states that the mapping $\mathcal{F}()$ of objects to f-D points should *make things look closer*.

In the rest of the chapter, we discussed how to apply GEMINI for a variety of environments, like 1D time sequences and 2D color images. As discussed in the bibliographic notes, GEMINI has been applied to multiple other settings, like tumor-like shapes, time sequences with the time-warping distance function, 2D medical images, and so on. Moreover, it is one of the main reasons behind a strong recent interest on high-dimensionality index structures.

With respect to future trends, probably the most notable and most challenging trend is data mining in multimedia and mixed-media data sets. For example, given a collection of medical records, with demographic data, text data (like history), 2D images (like X-rays), and 1D signals (electrocardiograms), we want to find correlations, clusters, patterns, and outliers. Successful detection of such patterns is the basis for forecasting, for hypothesis formation, anomaly detection, and several other knowledge discovery operations. GEMINI, insisting on turning every data type into a feature vector, should prove extremely useful: the reason is that it opens the door for off-the-shelf statistical and machine learning packages, which typically expect a set of vectors as input. Typical such packages are the 'Principal Component Analysis' (PCA, also known as 'Latent Semantic Indexing' (LSI), 'Karhunen-Loeve Transform' (KLT), and 'Singular Value Decomposition' (SVD)), Artificial Neural Networks, tree classifiers, to name a few.

12.8 Bibliographic Discussion

Spatial Access Methods

Structures and Algorithms
For a recent, very thorough survey of spatial access methods, see [290]. For the introduction of R-trees, see the seminal paper by Guttman [330]. Among the numerous follow-up variations, the R^*-tree [69] seems to be one of the best performing methods, using the idea of deferred splitting with 'forced-reinsert,' thus achieving higher space utilization, and therefore more compact, shorter, and faster trees. Another strong contender is the Hilbert R-tree [427], which achieves even higher space utilization and often outperforms the R^*-tree. A generalized framework and implementation for all these methods is the GiST tree [362] which is available, at the time of writing, at `http://gist.cs.berkeley.edu:8000/gist`.

With respect to algorithms, the range search is trivial in R-trees. Nearest neighbors queries require more careful record keeping, with a branch-and-bound algorithm (e.g., [686]). Spatial joins (e.g., 'find all pairs of points within distance ε') have also attracted a lot of interest: see the filtering algorithms in [119] and the methods in [521] and [458].

Indexing high-dimensional address spaces has attracted a lot of recent interest: the TV-trees [519] adaptively use only a few of the available dimensions. The SR-trees [431] use spheres in conjunction to rectangles, as bounding regions. The more recent X-trees [83] gracefully switch to sequential scanning for extremely high dimensionalities.

For the analysis of spatial access methods and selectivity estimation, the concept of 'fractal dimension' has given very accurate results in every case it was tried: range queries [247], nearest neighbor queries [628], spatial joins [79], quadtrees [245]. The idea behind the fractal dimension is to consider the intrinsic dimensionality of the given set of points. For example, consider the points on the diagonal of a 3D cube: their 'embedding' dimensionality is $E = 3$; however, their intrinsic dimensionality is $D = 1$. Using the appropriate definition for the dimensionality, like the Hausdorff fractal dimension, or the correlation fractal dimension [712], it turns out that real data sets have a fractional dimensionality: the value is 1.1–1.2 for coastlines, ≈ 2.7 for the brain surface of mammals, ≈ 1.3 for the periphery of rain patches, ≈ 1.7 for the end-points of road segments, to name but a few [247].

Metric Trees

Finally, a class of access methods that operate on the distance function directly seems promising. These methods require only a distance function, and they typically build a cluster hierarchy, that is, a tree structure of 'spheres', which include the children spheres, and so on, recursively. This class includes the Burkhard-Keller methods [131], the Fixed-query trees [47], the GNAT trees [116], the MVP trees [112], and the M-trees [172]. The technology is still young: most of the above methods are designed for static data sets. On the positive side, they don't need feature extraction; on the negative side, they don't provide for visualization and data mining, like GEMINI and FastMap do (see Figure 12.10).

Multimedia Indexing, DSP and Feature Extraction

GEMINI — Feature Extraction

Probably the earliest paper that suggested feature extraction for fast indexing is [400], for approximate matching in shapes. The proof of the lower bounding lemma is in [249].

Algorithms for automatic feature extraction include the traditional, Multidimensional Scaling (MDS), see, e.g., [462]. MDS has attracted tremendous interest, but it is $O(N^2)$, quadratic on the number of database objects N. Thus, it is impractical for large data sets. An $O(N)$ alternative is the so-called FastMap [248], which was used to produce Figure 12.10.

Time Sequences

For additional, more elaborate distance functions, that include time-warping, see Chapter 8 or [706]. An indexing method with the time-warping distance function has recently been developed [840], using FastMap.

For linear time sequence forecasting, see the classic book on the Box-Jenkins methodology [109]. For more recent, non-linear forecasting methods, see the intriguing volumes from the Santa-Fe Institute [149, 808].

Digital Signal Processing (DSP)

Powerful tools for the analysis of time sequences and n-D signals in general include the traditional Fourier transform (see, e.g., [622]), the popular discrete cosine transform, which is the basis for the JPEG image compression standard [802], and the more recent, and even more effective, wavelet transform (DWT) [689]. An excellent introduction to all these methods, as well as source code, is available in [651].

Image Features and Similarity Functions

There is a lot of work in machine vision on feature extraction and similarity measures. Classic references are e.g., [53, 224, 285]. A recent survey on image registration and image comparison methods is in [125]. The proof for quadratic distance bounding theorem of section 12.5 is in [244].

Other Applications of Multimedia Indexing

There are numerous papers on indexing in multimedia databases. A small sample of them include the following: for time sequences allowing scaling or subpattern matching, see [305], [7], [246]. For voice and video see, e.g., [800]. For shapes see, e.g., [244]. For medical image databases see, e.g., [381], [454], [635]. For multimedia searching on the Web, see, e.g., [4, 733, 80, 714].

Data Mining

Finally, there is a lot of work on traditional machine learning [565] and statistics (e.g., [408]).

Chapter 13
Searching the Web

13.1   Introduction

The World Wide Web dates from the end of the 1980s [85] and no one could have imagined its current impact. The boom in the use of the Web and its exponential growth are now well known. Just the amount of textual data available is estimated to be in the order of one terabyte. In addition, other media, such as images, audio, and video, are also available. Thus, the Web can be seen as a very large, unstructured but ubiquitous database. This triggers the need for efficient tools to manage, retrieve, and filter information from this database. This problem is also becoming important in large intranets, where we want to extract or infer new information to support a decision process, a task called data mining. As mentioned in Chapter 1, we make the important distinction between data and information retrieval. We are interested in the latter case, in which the user searches for data that fulfills his information need.

We focus on text, because although there are techniques to search for images and other non-textual data, they cannot be applied (yet) on a large scale. We also emphasize syntactic search. That is, we search for Web documents that have user-specified words or patterns in their text. As discussed in Chapter 2, such words or patterns may or may not reflect the intrinsic semantics of the text. An alternative approach to syntactic search is to do a natural language analysis of the text. Although the techniques to preprocess natural language and extract the text semantics are not new, they are not yet very effective and they are also too costly for large amounts of data. In addition, in most cases they are only effective with well structured text, a thesaurus, and other contextual information.

There are basically three different forms of searching the Web. Two of them are well known and are frequently used. The first is to use search engines that index a portion of the Web documents as a full-text database. The second is to use Web directories, which classify selected Web documents by subject. The third and not yet fully available, is to search the Web exploiting its hyperlink†

---

† We will use hyperlink or link to denote a pointer (anchor) from a Web page to another Web page.

structure. We cover all three forms of Web search here.

We first discuss the challenges of searching the Web, followed by some Web statistics and models which can be used to understand the complexity of the problem. Next, we discuss in detail the main tools used today to search the Web. The discussion includes search engines, Web directories, hybrid systems, user interfaces, and searching examples. We continue with new query languages that exploit the graphical structure of the Web. Finally, we survey current trends and research issues. As Web research is a very dynamic field, we may have missed some important work, for which we apologize in advance.

13.2   Challenges

We now mention the main problems posed by the Web. We can divide them in two classes: problems with the data itself and problems regarding the user and his interaction with the retrieval system. The problems related to the data are:

- **Distributed data**: due to the intrinsic nature of the Web, data spans over many computers and platforms. These computers are interconnected with no predefined topology and the available bandwidth and reliability on the network interconnections varies widely.

- **High percentage of volatile data**: due to Internet dynamics, new computers and data can be added or removed easily (it is estimated that 40% of the Web changes every month [424]). We also have dangling links and relocation problems when domain or file names change or disappear.

- **Large volume**: the exponential growth of the Web poses scaling issues that are difficult to cope with.

- **Unstructured and redundant data**: most people say that the Web is a distributed hypertext. However, this is not exactly so. Any hypertext has a conceptual model behind it, which organizes and adds consistency to the data and the hyperlinks. That is hardly true in the Web, even for individual documents. In addition, each HTML page is not well structured and some people use the term *semi-structured data*. Moreover, much Web data is repeated (mirrored or copied) or very similar. Approximately 30% of Web pages are (near) duplicates [120, 723]. Semantic redundancy can be even larger.

- **Quality of data**: the Web can be considered as a new publishing medium. However, there is, in most cases, no editorial process. So, data can be false, invalid (for example, because it is too old), poorly written or, typically, with many errors from different sources (typos, grammatical mistakes, OCR errors, etc.). Preliminary studies show that the number of words with typos can range from 1 in 200 for common words to 1 in 3 for foreign surnames [588].

- **Heterogeneous data**: in addition to having to deal with multiple media types and hence with multiple formats, we also have different languages and, what is worse, different alphabets, some of them very large (for example, Chinese or Japanese Kanji).

Most of these problems (such as the variety of data types and poor data quality) are not solvable simply by software improvements. In fact, many of them will not change (and they should not, as in the case of language diversity!) because they are problems (also features) intrinsic to human nature.

The second class of problems are those faced by the user during the interaction with the retrieval system. There are basically two problems: (1) how to specify a query and (2) how to interpret the answer provided by the system. Without taking into account the semantic content of a document, it is not easy to precisely specify a query, unless it is very simple. Further, even if the user is able to pose the query, the answer might be a thousand Web pages. How do we handle a large answer? How do we rank the documents? How do we select the documents that really are of interest to the user? In addition, a single document could be large. How do we browse efficiently in large documents?

So, the overall challenge, in spite of the intrinsic problems posed by the Web, is to submit a good query to the search system, and obtain a manageable and relevant answer. Moreover, in practice we should try to achieve the latter goal even for poorly formulated queries. In the rest of this chapter, we use the term Web pages for HTML documents (HTML is described in Chapter 6). To denote all possible data types available on the Web, we use the term Web documents.

13.3   Characterizing the Web

13.3.1   Measuring the Web

Measuring the Internet and in particular the Web, is a difficult task due to its highly dynamic nature. Nowadays, there are more than 40 million computers in more than 200 countries connected to the Internet, many of them hosting Web servers. The estimated number of Web servers ranges from 2.4 million according to NetSizer [597] (November 1998) to over three million according to the Netcraft Web survey [596] (October 1998). This wide range might be explained when we consider that there are many Web sites that share the same Web server using virtual hosts, that not all of them are fully accessible, that many of them are provisional, etc. Other estimations were made by sampling 0.1% of all Internet numeric addresses obtaining about 2 million unique Web sites [619] or by counting domain names starting with www which in July 1998 were 780,000 according to the Internet Domain survey [599]. However, since not all Web servers have this prefix, the real number is even higher. Considering that in July 1998 the number of Internet hosts was estimated at 36.7 million [599], there is about one Web server per every ten computers connected to the

Internet. The characterization of the Web is a new task of the Web Consortium [797].

In two interesting articles, already (sadly) outdated, Bray [114] and Woodruff *et al.* [834] studied different statistical measures of the Web. The first study uses 11 million pages while the second uses 2.6 million pages, with both sets gathered in November 1995. Their characterization of Web pages is partially reproduced in the following paragraphs. A first question is how many different institutions (not Web servers) maintain Web data. This number is smaller than the number of servers, because many places have multiple servers. The exact number is unknown, but should be more than 40% of the number of Web servers (this percentage was the value back in 1995). The exact number of Web pages is also not known. Estimates at the beginning of 1998 ranged from 200 to 320 million, with 350 million as the best current estimate (July 1998 [91]). The latter study used 20,000 random queries based on a lexicon of 400,000 words extracted from Yahoo!. Those queries were submitted to four search engines and the union of all the answers covered about 70% of the Web. Figure 13.1 gives an approximation of how the number of Web servers and the number of pages have changed in recent years. Between 1997 and 1998, the size of the Web doubled in nine months and is currently growing at a rate of 20 million pages per month. On the other hand, it is estimated that the 30,000 largest Web sites (about 1% of the Web) account for approximately 50% of all Web pages [619].

The most popular formats for Web documents are HTML, followed by GIF and JPG (both for images), ASCII text, and Postscript, in that order. The most popular compression tools used are GNU zip, Zip, and Compress. What is a typical HTML page? First, most HTML pages are not standard, meaning that they do not comply with all the HTML specifications. In ad-

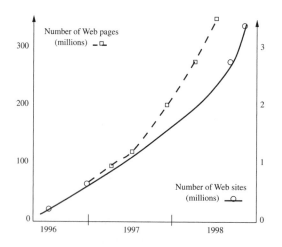

Figure 13.1   Approximate growth of the Web.

dition, although HTML is an instance of SGML, HTML documents seldom start with a formal document type definition. Second, they are small (around 5 Kbs on average with a median of 2 Kbs) and usually contain few images (between one and two on average with an average size of 14 Kb). The pages that have images use them for presentation issues such as colored bullets and lines. An average page has between five and 15 hyperlinks (more than eight links on average) and most of them are local (that is, they point to pages in their own Web server hierarchy). On average, no external server points to any given page (typically, there are only local links pointing to a given page). This is true even for home pages of Web sites. In fact, in 1995, around 80% of these home pages had fewer than ten external links pointing to each of them.

The top ten most referenced sites are Microsoft, Netscape, Yahoo!, and top US universities. In these cases we are talking about sites which are referenced by at least 100,000 places. On the other hand, the site with most links to outside sites is Yahoo!. In some sense, Yahoo! and other directories are the glue of the Web. Without them we would have many isolated portions (which is the case with many personal Web pages). If we assume that the average HTML page has 5 Kb and that there are 300 million Web pages, we have at least 1.5 terabytes of text. This is consistent with other measures obtained from search engines. Note that this volume does not include non-textual documents.

Regarding the languages used in Web pages, there have been three studies made. The first study was done by Funredes [637] from 1996 to 1998. It uses the AltaVista search engine and is based on searching different words in different languages. This technique might not be significant statistically, but the results are consistent with the second study which was carried out by Alis Technology [11] and is based on automatic software that can detect the language used. One of the goals of the study was to test such software (done in 8000 Web servers). The last study was done by OCLC in June of 1998 [619] by sampling Internet numeric addresses and using the SILC language identification software. Table 13.1 gives the percentages of Web pages written in each language (with the exception of the OCLC data that counts Web sites), as well as the number of people (millions) who speak the language. The variations for Japanese might be due to an inability to detect pages written in Kanji. Some languages, in particular Spanish and Portuguese, are growing fast and will surpass French in the near future. The total number of languages exceeds 100.

13.3.2   Modeling the Web

Can we model the document characteristics of the whole Web? Yes, as has already been discussed partially in Chapter 6. The Heaps' and Zipf's laws are also valid in the Web. In particular, the vocabulary grows faster (larger β) and the word distribution should be more biased (larger θ). However, there are no experiments on large Web collections to measure these parameters.

Language	Funredes (1998, %)	Alis Tech. (June 1997, %)	OCLC (June 1998, %)	Spoken by (millions)
English	76.4	82.3	71	450
Japanese	4.8	1.6	4	126
German	4.4	4.0	7	118
French	2.9	1.5	3	122
Spanish	2.6	1.1	3	266
Italian	1.5	0.8	1	63
Portuguese	0.8	0.7	2	175

Table 13.1   Languages of the Web.

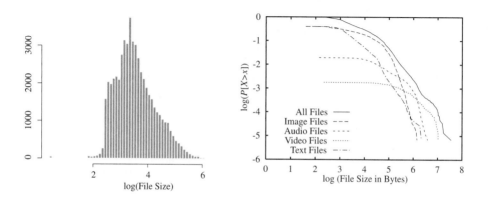

Figure 13.2   Left: Distribution for all file sizes (courtesy of M. Crovella, 1998). Right: Right tail distribution for different file types (from Crovella and Bestavros, 1996). All logarithms are in base 10.

An additional model is related to the distribution of document sizes. According to this model, the document sizes are self-similar [201], that is, they have a large variance (a similar behavior appears in Web traffic). This can be modeled by two different distributions. The main body of the distribution follows a logarithmic normal distribution, such that the probability of finding a document of size x bytes is given by

$$p(x) = \frac{1}{x\sigma\sqrt{2\pi}} \exp -(\ln x - \mu)^2/2\sigma^2$$

where the average (μ) and standard deviation (σ) are 9.357 and 1.318, respectively [59]. Figure 13.2 (left) shows the size distribution of the experimental data.

The right tail of the distribution is 'heavy-tailed.' That is, the majority of documents are small, but there is a non-trivial number of large documents. This is intuitive for image or video files, but it is also true for HTML pages. A good fit is obtained with the Pareto distribution

$$p(x) = \frac{\alpha k^\alpha}{x^{1+\alpha}}$$

where x is measured in bytes and k and α are parameters of the distribution [59] (see Figure 13.2 (right)). For text files, α is about 1.36, being smaller for images and other binary formats [201, 819]. Taking all Web documents into account, we get $\alpha = 1.1$ and $k = 9.3$ Kb [58]. That is, 9.3 Kb is the cut point between both distributions, and 93% of all the files have a size below this value. In fact, for less than 50 Kb, images are the typical files, from 50 to 300 Kb we have an increasing number of audio files, and over that to several megabytes, video files are more frequent. The parameters of these distributions were obtained from a sample of more than 54,000 Web pages requested by several users in a period of two months of 1995. Recent data collected in 1998 show that the size distributions have the same form, but parameters change [58]. Related information can be found on Web benchmarks such as WebSpec96 and the Sun/Inktomi Inkbench [395].

13.4   Search Engines

In this section we cover different architectures of retrieval systems that model the Web as a full-text database. One main difference between standard IR systems and the Web is that, in the Web, all queries must be answered without accessing the text (that is, only the indices are available). Otherwise, that would require either storing locally a copy of the Web pages (too expensive) or accessing remote pages through the network at query time (too slow). This difference has an impact on the indexing and searching algorithms, as well as on the query languages made available.

13.4.1   Centralized Architecture

Most search engines use a centralized crawler-indexer architecture. Crawlers are programs (software agents) that traverse the Web sending new or updated pages to a main server where they are indexed. Crawlers are also called robots, spiders, wanderers, walkers, and knowbots. In spite of their name, a crawler does not actually move to and run on remote machines, rather the crawler runs on a local system and sends requests to remote Web servers. The index is used in a centralized fashion to answer queries submitted from different places in the Web. Figure 13.3 shows the software architecture of a search engine based on the AltaVista architecture [17]. It has two parts: one that deals with the users,

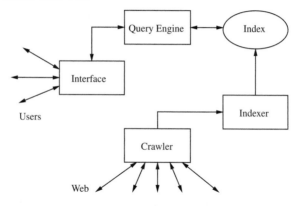

Figure 13.3 Typical crawler-indexer architecture.

consisting of the user interface and the query engine and another that consists of the crawler and indexer modules. In 1998, the overall AltaVista system was running on 20 multi-processor machines, all of them having more than 130 Gb of RAM and over 500 Gb of disk space. Only the query engine uses more than 75% of these resources.

The main problem faced by this architecture is the gathering of the data, because of the highly dynamic nature of the Web, the saturated communication links, and the high load at Web servers. Another important problem is the volume of the data. In fact, the crawler-indexer architecture may not be able to cope with Web growth in the near future. Particularly important is good load balancing between the different activities of a search engine, internally (answering queries and indexing) and externally (crawling).

The largest search engines, considering Web coverage in June 1998, were AltaVista [17], HotBot [380], Northern Light [608], and Excite [240], in that order. According to recent studies, these engines cover 28–55% [749] or 14–34% [490] of all Web pages, whose number was estimated at over 300 million in 1998. Table 13.2 lists the most important search engines and their estimated sizes along with their corresponding URLs. Beware that some search engines are powered by the same internal engine. For example, HotBot, GoTo, and Microsoft are powered by Inktomi [395] and Magellan by Excite's internal engine. Up to date information can be found in [749, 609].

Most search engines are based in the United States and focus on documents in English. Nevertheless, there are search engines specialized in different countries and/or languages, which are able, for instance, to query and retrieve documents written in Kanji (Chinese, Japanese, and Korean). Also there are search engines that take other approaches, like Ask Jeeves! which simulates an interview [34] or DirectHit [215] which ranks the Web pages in the answer in order of their popularity. We should also mention those search engines aimed at specific topics, for example the Search Broker [537] which allows us to search in many specific topics and DejaNews [212] which searches the USENET archives.

Search engine	URL	Web pages indexed
AltaVista	`www.altavista.com`	140
AOL Netfind	`www.aol.com/netfind/`	–
Excite	`www.excite.com`	55
Google	`google.stanford.edu`	25
GoTo	`goto.com`	–
HotBot	`www.hotbot.com`	110
Infoseek	`www.infoseek.com`	30
Lycos	`www.lycos.com`	30
Magellan	`www.mckinley.com`	55
Microsoft	`search.msn.com`	–
NorthernLight	`www.nlsearch.com`	67
WebCrawler	`www.webcrawler.com`	2

Table 13.2 URLs and estimated size (millions) of the largest search engines (May 1998).

There are also engines to retrieve specific Web pages such as personal or institutional home pages or specific objects such as electronic mail addresses, images, or software applets.

13.4.2 Distributed Architecture

There are several variants of the crawler-indexer architecture. Among them, the most important is Harvest [108]. Harvest uses a distributed architecture to gather and distribute data, which is more efficient than the crawler architecture. The main drawback is that Harvest requires the coordination of several Web servers.

The Harvest distributed approach addresses several of the problems of the crawler-indexer architecture, such as: (1) Web servers receive requests from different crawlers, increasing their load; (2) Web traffic increases because crawlers retrieve entire objects, but most of their content is discarded; and (3) information is gathered independently by each crawler, without coordination between all the search engines.

To solve these problems, Harvest introduces two main elements: gatherers and brokers. A gatherer collects and extracts indexing information from one or more Web servers. Gathering times are defined by the system and are periodic (i.e. there are harvesting times as the name of the system suggests). A broker provides the indexing mechanism and the query interface to the data gathered. Brokers retrieve information from one or more gatherers or other brokers, updating incrementally their indices. Depending on the configuration of gatherers and brokers, different improvements on server load and network traffic can be

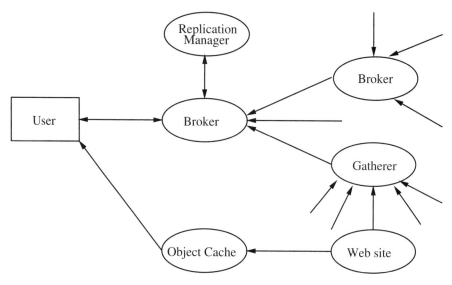

Figure 13.4   Harvest architecture.

achieved. For example, a gatherer can run on a Web server, generating no external traffic for that server. Also, a gatherer can send information to several brokers, avoiding work repetition. Brokers can also filter information and send it to other brokers. This design allows the sharing of work and information in a very flexible and generic manner. An example of the Harvest architecture is shown in Figure 13.4 [108].

One of the goals of Harvest is to build topic-specific brokers, focusing the index contents and avoiding many of the vocabulary and scaling problems of generic indices. Harvest includes a distinguished broker that allows other brokers to register information about gatherers and brokers. This is useful to search for an appropriate broker or gatherer when building a new system. The Harvest architecture also provides replicators and object caches. A replicator can be used to replicate servers, enhancing user-base scalability. For example, the registration broker can be replicated in different geographic regions to allow faster access. Replication can also be used to divide the gathering process between many Web servers. Finally, the object cache reduces network and server load, as well as response latency when accessing Web pages. More details on the system can be found in [108].

Currently, there are hundreds of Harvest applications on the Web (for example, the CIA, NASA, the US National Academy of Sciences, and the US Government Printing Office), as this software is on the public domain.‡ Netscape's Catalog Server is a commercial version of Harvest and Network Appliances' cache is a commercial version of the Harvest Cache.

---

‡ Information is available at `harvest.transarc.com`.

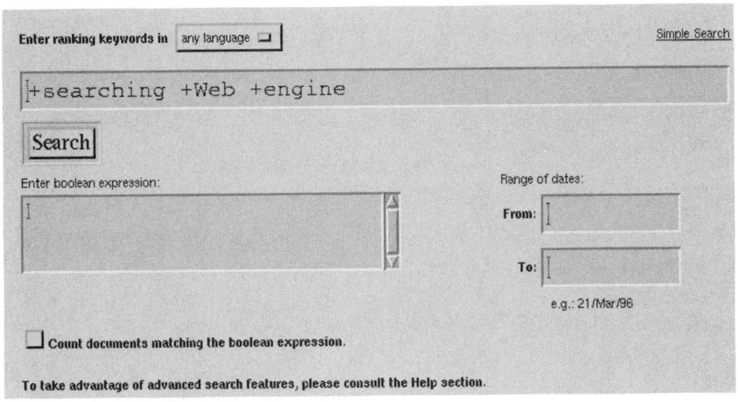

Figure 13.5   Query interface for complex queries in AltaVista.

13.4.3   User Interfaces

There are two important aspects of the user interface of search engines: the query interface and the answer interface (see also Chapter 10). The basic query interface is a box where one or more words can be typed. Although a user would expect that a given sequence of words represents the same query in all search engines, it does not. For example, in AltaVista a sequence of words is a reference to the union of all the Web pages having at least one of those words, while in HotBot it is a reference to the Web pages having all the words. Another problem is that the logical view of the text is not known, that is, some search engines use stopwords, some do stemming, and some are not case sensitive (see Chapter 7).

All search engines also provide a query interface for complex queries as well as a command language including Boolean operators and other features, such as phrase search, proximity search, and wild cards. Figures 13.5 and 13.6 show the query interfaces for complex queries for the three largest search engines. They provide several filtering functions. The results can be filtered by additional words that must be present or absent from the answer or in a particular field such as the URL or title, language, geographic region or Internet domain, date range, or inclusion of specific data types such as images or audio.

The answer usually consists of a list of the ten top ranked Web pages. Figure 13.7 shows the three top documents for the main four search engines for the query **searching and Web and engine**. Each entry in this list includes some information about the document it represents. Typically, the information includes the URL, size, the date when the page was indexed, and a couple of lines with its content (title plus first lines or selected headings or sentences). Some search engines allow the user to change the number of pages returned in the list and the amount of information per page, but in most cases this is fixed or limited to a few choices. The order of the list is typically by relevance, but sorting by URL or date is also available in some engines. In addition, most search engines also have an option to find documents similar to each Web page in the answer.

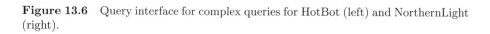

Figure 13.6 Query interface for complex queries for HotBot (left) and NorthernLight (right).

▶ **AltaVista found 3,156,580 Web pages for you.**   <u>**Refine your search**</u>

1. <u>**Welcome to PCfriend USA Searching Engine Web Site**</u>
  URL: www.pcfriend.net/menu1.htm
  Last modified 23–Feb–98 – page size 626 bytes – in English [<u>Translate</u>]

2. <u>**Searching Engine**</u>
  Home| TYP Databank| TYP Homepages| Net Trade Center| Fair News| Leading
  Firms. Business & Finance Database| New Media Database| World Trade
  Promotion...
  URL: top1.twn–online.com.tw/search/eindex.htm
  Last modified 22–Sep–98 – page size 4K – in English [<u>Translate</u>]

3. <u>**Searching Engine**</u>
  Welcome] ~ [Contact] ~ [Map] ~ [Search] Searching Engine – Here are some popu
  complete. substring. Infoseek. the...
  URL: violet.tele.pitt.edu/search.html
  Last modified 23–Jun–97 – page size 12K – in English [<u>Translate</u>]

Web Matches: 49,690   1 - 10 <u>next</u> ▶

Get the **Top 10 Most Visited Sites for "Searching Web Engine"**

1. <u>s y b i l w e b</u>
welcome to sybilweb overview | about sybilweb | site map | search
| help | contact Search Tips Answers to Frequently Asked
Questions (FAQ) Search Corner Web Compass Canada Sybil's
Search Engine overview sybilweb, the Web component of Sybil's
Search.
99% http://www.sybilweb.com/
See results from <u>this site only</u>.

2. <u>Welcome to CompLatinos S.A., Costa Rica, Webdesign,</u>
<u>Maintenance, Computers</u>
Aha, you have found the CompLatinos S.A., Costa Rica, Design,
Submitting, Hosting, Maintenance, Translation, Links, Logo
99% http://www.complatinos.com/
See results from <u>this site only</u>.

3. <u>Yu Search Engine – Yu Internet Pretrazivac</u>
Srpski . Info . Add URL . Add E–mail . Business . Open Site . Daily
News . Guide YuSearch Promo: Advertising . Web Hosting Click!
Web Search Enter keywords for searching Yu Web: E–mail Search
Enter keywords for searching E–mail: Web Index Arts ...
97% http://www.yusearch.com/
See results from <u>this site only</u>.

Power Search found 113,731 items for:

searching Web engine   SEARCH   HELP/HI

◇ Special Collection   ◇ World Wide Web   ◉ All Sources

📄 **Documents that best match your search**

1. <u>Internet Search Mechanisms</u>
   79% – Directories & Lists: Internet Search Mechanisms Internet
   Search Mechanisms Harold Goldstein – dcbiker@goldray.... – Visit
   the Goldpages See Fossilized Insects, get your beading supplies and   www
   help save the... Date Not Available
   Commercial site: http://goldray.i95.net/searches.htm

2. <u>Internet Search Mechanisms</u>
   79% – Directories & Lists: Internet Search Mechanisms Internet
   Search Mechanisms Harold Goldstein – dcbiker@goldray.... – Visit
   the Goldpages See Fossilized Insects, get your beading supplies and   www
   help save the... Date Not Available
   Commercial site: http://goldray.com/searches.htm

3. <u>NetVet Web Searching Web Picks</u>
   79% – Directories & Lists: NetVet Web Searching Web Picks
   Search Tools This Site Other Veterinary WWW Search Forms Other
   Search Engines Search NetVet and the Electronic Zoo! Other   www
   Veterinary...01/07/98
   Educational site: http://netvet.wustl.edu/search.htm

Top 10 matches. [12760 hits. About Your Results]   **Show Titles only   List by Web site**

74% <u>W3 Search Engines</u> – This documents collects some of the most useful search engines available on the
WWW. Omissions are the fault of the maintainer. Suggestions for additions are welcome! Some interesting
information sources are available only through specialized software.
http://cuiwww.unige.ch/meta–index.html
<u>Search for more documents like this one</u>

73% <u>webtaxi.com : the search engine and database navigation interface/guid...</u> – webtaxi.com is a breakthrough
navigation service designed to help Internet users conveniently search the World Wide Web. webtaxi.com
enhances the existing capabilities of current versions of Netscape Navigator (2.0 and higher). This free service
was developed to offer efficient point and click access to search engines, newsgroups and thousands of
hard–to–reach databases. webtaxi.com provides...
http://www.webtaxi.com/
<u>Search for more documents like this one</u>

71% <u>Free Software from AOL and PLS</u> – The industry's leading search software products are now free! nbsp;
PLS's powerful search engine and products, accompanied by complete documentation, are available for
download from this Web site free of charge. Check it out. And check back frequently for updates on product and
service offerings.
http://www.pls.com/

Figure 13.7   Output for the query `searching and Web and engine` for the four main
search engines; from top to bottom: AltaVista, HotBot, NorthernLight, and Excite.

The user can also refine the query by constructing more complex queries based on the previous answer.

The Web pages retrieved by the search engine in response to a user query are ranked, usually using statistics related to the terms in the query. In some cases this may not have any meaning, because relevance is not fully correlated with statistics about term occurrence within the collection. Some search engines also taking into account terms included in metatags or the title, or the popularity of a Web page to improve the ranking. This topic is covered next.

13.4.4 Ranking

Most search engines use variations of the Boolean or vector model (see Chapter 2) to do ranking. As with searching, ranking has to be performed without accessing the text, just the index. There is not much public information about the specific ranking algorithms used by current search engines. Further, it is difficult to compare fairly different search engines given their differences, and continuous improvements. More important, it is almost impossible to measure recall, as the number of relevant pages can be quite large for simple queries. Some inconclusive studies include [327, 498].

Yuwono and Lee [844] propose three ranking algorithms in addition to the classical tf-idf scheme (see Chapter 2). They are called Boolean spread, vector spread, and most-cited. The first two are the normal ranking algorithms of the Boolean and vector model extended to include pages pointed to by a page in the answer or pages that point to a page in the answer. The third, most-cited, is based only on the terms included in pages having a link to the pages in the answer. A comparison of these techniques considering 56 queries over a collection of 2400 Web pages indicates that the vector model yields a better recall-precision curve, with an average precision of 75%.

Some of the new ranking algorithms also use hyperlink information. This is an important difference between the Web and normal IR databases. The number of hyperlinks that point to a page provides a measure of its popularity and quality. Also, many links in common between pages or pages referenced by the same page often indicates a relationship between those pages. We now present three examples of ranking techniques that exploit these facts, but they differ in that two of them depend on the query and the last does not.

The first is WebQuery [148], which also allows visual browsing of Web pages. WebQuery takes a set of Web pages (for example, the answer to a query) and ranks them based on how connected each Web page is. Additionally, it extends the set by finding Web pages that are highly connected to the original set. A related approach is presented by Li [512].

A better idea is due to Kleinberg [444] and used in HITS (Hypertext Induced Topic Search). This ranking scheme depends on the query and considers the set of pages S that point to or are pointed by pages in the answer. Pages that have many links pointing to them in S are called authorities (that is, they should have relevant content). Pages that have many outgoing links are called hubs (they should point to similar content). A positive two-way feedback exists:

better authority pages come from incoming edges from good hubs and better hub pages come from outgoing edges to good authorities. Let $H(p)$ and $A(p)$ be the hub and authority value of page p. These values are defined such that the following equations are satisfied for all pages p:

$$H(p) = \sum_{u \in S \mid p \rightarrow u} A(u) , \qquad A(p) = \sum_{v \in S \mid v \rightarrow p} H(v)$$

where $H(p)$ and $A(p)$ for all pages are normalized (in the original paper, the sum of the squares of each measure is set to one). These values can be determined through an iterative algorithm, and they converge to the principal eigenvector of the link matrix of S. In the case of the Web, to avoid an explosion of the size of S, a maximal number of pages pointing to the answer can be defined. This technique does not work with non-existent, repeated, or automatically generated links. One solution is to weight each link based on the surrounding content. A second problem is that the topic of the result can become diffused. For example, a particular query is enlarged by a more general topic that contains the original answer. One solution to this problem is to analyze the content of each page and assign a score to it, as in traditional IR ranking. The link weight and the page score can be included on the previous formula multiplying each term of the summation [154, 93, 153]. Experiments show that the recall and precision on the first ten answers increases significantly [93]. The order of the links can also be used by dividing the links into subgroups and using the HITS algorithm on those subgroups instead of the original Web pages [153].

The last example is PageRank, which is part of the ranking algorithm used by Google [117]. PageRank simulates a user navigating randomly in the Web who jumps to a random page with probability q or follows a random hyperlink (on the current page) with probability $1 - q$. It is further assumed that this user never goes back to a previously visited page following an already traversed hyperlink backwards. This process can be modeled with a Markov chain, from where the stationary probability of being in each page can be computed. This value is then used as part of the ranking mechanism of Google. Let $C(a)$ be the number of outgoing links of page a and suppose that page a is pointed to by pages p_1 to p_n. Then, the PageRank, $PR(a)$ of a is defined as

$$PR(a) = q + (1 - q) \sum_{i=1}^{n} PR(p_i)/C(p_i)$$

where q must be set by the system (a typical value is 0.15). Notice that the ranking (weight) of other pages is normalized by the number of links in the page. PageRank can be computed using an iterative algorithm, and corresponds to the principal eigenvector of the normalized link matrix of the Web (which is the transition matrix of the Markov chain). Crawling the Web using this ordering has been shown to be better than other crawling schemes [168] (see next section).

Therefore, to help ranking algorithms, page designers should include informative titles, headings, and meta fields, as well as good links. However, keywords should not be repeated as some search engines penalize repeating words (spamming). Using full terms instead of indirect ways to refer to subjects should also be considered.

13.4.5   Crawling the Web

In this section we discuss how to crawl the Web, as there are several techniques. The simplest is to start with a set of URLs and from there extract other URLs which are followed recursively in a breadth-first or depth-first fashion. For that reason, search engines allow users to submit top Web sites that will be added to the URL set. A variation is to start with a set of populars URLs, because we can expect that they have information frequently requested. Both cases work well for one crawler, but it is difficult to coordinate several crawlers to avoid visiting the same page more than once. Another technique is to partition the Web using country codes or Internet names, and assign one or more robots to each partition, and explore each partition exhaustively.

Considering how the Web is traversed, the index of a search engine can be thought of as analogous to the stars in an sky. What we see has never existed, as the light has traveled different distances to reach our eye. Similarly, Web pages referenced in an index were also explored at different dates and they may not exist any more. Nevertheless, when we retrieve a page, we obtain its actual content. How fresh are the Web pages referenced in an index? The pages will be from one day to two months old. For that reason, most search engines show in the answer the date when the page was indexed. The percentage of invalid links stored in search engines vary from 2 to 9%. User submitted pages are usually crawled after a few days or weeks. Starting there, some engines traverse the whole Web site, while others select just a sample of pages or pages up to a certain depth. Non-submitted pages will wait from weeks up to a couple of months to be detected. There are some engines that learn the change frequency of a page and visit it accordingly [175]. They may also crawl more frequently popular pages (for example, pages having many links pointing to them). Overall, the current fastest crawlers are able to traverse up to 10 million Web pages per day.

The order in which the URLs are traversed is important. As already mentioned, the links in a Web page can be traversed breadth first or depth first. Using a breadth first policy, we first look at all the pages linked by the current page, and so on. This matches well Web sites that are structured by related topics. On the other hand, the coverage will be wide but shallow and a Web server can be bombarded with many rapid requests. In the depth first case, we follow the first link of a page and we do the same on that page until we cannot go deeper, returning recursively. This provides a narrow but deep traversal. Only recently, some research on this problem has appeared [168], showing that good ordering schemes can make a difference if crawling better pages first (using the PageRank scheme mentioned above).

Due to the fact that robots can overwhelm a server with rapid requests and can use significant Internet bandwidth (in particular the whole bandwidth of small domains can be saturated), a set of guidelines for robot behavior has been developed [457]. For this purpose, a special file is placed at the root of every Web server indicating the restrictions at that site, in particular the pages that should not be indexed. Crawlers can also have problems with HTML pages that use frames (a mechanism to divide a page in two or more parts) or image maps (hyperlinks associated to images). In addition, dynamically generated pages cannot be indexed as well as password protected pages.

13.4.6 Indices

Most indices use variants of the inverted file (see Chapter 8). In short, an inverted file is a list of sorted words (vocabulary), each one having a set of pointers to the pages where it occurs. Some search engines use elimination of stopwords to reduce the size of the index. Also, it is important to remember that a logical view of the text is indexed. Normalization operations may include removal of punctuation and multiple spaces to just one space between each word, uppercase to lowercase letters, etc. (see Chapter 7). To give the user some idea about each document retrieved, the index is complemented with a short description of each Web page (creation date, size, the title and the first lines or a few headings are typical). Assuming that 500 bytes are required to store the URL and the description of each Web page, we need 50 Gb to store the description for 100 million pages. As the user initially receives only a subset of the complete answer to each query, the search engine usually keeps the whole answer set in memory, to avoid having to recompute it if the user asks for more documents.

State of the art indexing techniques can reduce the size of an inverted file to about 30% of the size of the text (less if stopwords are used). For 100 million pages, this implies about 150 Gb of disk space. By using compression techniques, the index size can be reduced to 10% of the text [825]. A query is answered by doing a binary search on the sorted list of words of the inverted file. If we are searching multiple words, the results have to be combined to generate the final answer. This step will be efficient if each word is not too frequent. Another possibility is to compute the complete answer while the user requests more Web pages, using a lazy evaluation scheme. More details on searching over an inverted file can be found in Chapter 8.

Inverted files can also point to the actual occurrences of a word within a document (full inversion). However, that is too costly in space for the Web, because each pointer has to specify a page and a position inside the page (word numbers can be used instead of actual bytes). On the other hand, having the positions of the words in a page, we can answer phrase searches or proximity queries by finding words that are near each other in a page. Currently, some search engines are providing phrase searches, but the actual implementation is not known.

Finding words which start with a given prefix requires two binary searches in the sorted list of words. More complex searches, like words with errors, arbitrary wild cards or, in general, any regular expression on a word, can be performed by doing a sequential scan over the vocabulary (see Chapter 8). This may seem slow, but the best sequential algorithms for this type of query can search around 20 Mb of text stored in RAM in one second (5 Mb is more or less the vocabulary size for 1 Gb of text). Thus, for several gigabytes we can answer those queries in a few seconds. For the Web this is still too slow but not completely out of the question. In fact, using Heaps' law and assuming $\beta = 0.7$ for the Web, the vocabulary size for 1 Tb is 630 Mb which implies a searching time of half a minute.

Pointing to pages or to word positions is an indication of the granularity of the index. The index can be less dense if we point to logical blocks instead of pages. In this way we reduce the variance of the different document sizes, by making all blocks roughly the same size. This not only reduces the size of the pointers (because there are fewer blocks than documents) but also reduces the number of pointers because words have locality of reference (that is, all the occurrences of a non-frequent word will tend to be clustered in the same block). This idea was used in Glimpse [540] which is at the core of Harvest [108]. Queries are resolved as for inverted files, obtaining a list of blocks that are then searched sequentially (exact sequential search can be done over 30 Mb per second in RAM). Glimpse originally used only 256 blocks, which was efficient up to 200 Mb for searching words that were not too frequent, obtaining an index of only 2% of the text. By tuning the number of blocks and the block size, reasonable space-time trade-offs can be achieved for larger document collections (for more details see Chapter 8). These ideas cannot be used (yet) for the Web because sequential search cannot be afforded, as it implies a network access. However, in a distributed architecture where the index is also distributed, logical blocks make sense.

13.5   Browsing

In this section we cover Web tools which are based on browsing and searching, in particular Web directories. Although the Web coverage provided by directories is very low (less than 1% of all Web pages), the answers returned to the user are usually much more relevant.

13.5.1   Web Directories

The best and oldest example of a Web directory is Yahoo! [839], which is likely the most used searching tool. Other large Web directories include eBLAST, LookSmart, Magellan, and NewHoo. Some of them are hybrids, because they also provide searches in the whole Web. Most search engines also provide subject categories nowadays, including AltaVista Categories, AOL Netfind, Excite Channels, HotBot, Infoseek, Lycos Subjects, and WebCrawler Select. are specific to some areas. For example, there are Web sites focused on business, news,

Web directory	URL	Web sites	Categories
eBLAST	`www.eblast.com`	125	–
LookSmart	`www.looksmart.com`	300	24
Lycos Subjects	`a2z.lycos.com`	50	–
Magellan	`www.mckinley.com`	60	–
NewHoo	`www.newhoo.com`	100	23
Netscape	`www.netscape.com`	–	–
Search.com	`www.search.com`	–	–
Snap	`www.snap.com`	–	–
Yahoo!	`www.yahoo.com`	750	–

Table 13.3 URLs, Web pages indexed and categories (both in thousands) of some Web directories (beginning of 1998).

Arts & Humanities	Local
Automotive	News
Business & Economy	Oddities
Computers & Internet	People
Education	Philosophy & Religion
Employment	Politics
Entertainment & Leisure	Recreation
Games	Reference
Government	Regional
Health & Fitness	Science & Technology
Hobbies & Interests	Shopping & Services
Home	Social Science
Investing	Society & Culture
Kids & Family	Sports
Life & Style	Travel & Tourism
Living	World

Table 13.4 The first level categories in Web directories.

and, in particular, research bibliography. Web directories are also called catalogs, yellow pages, or subject directories. Table 13.3 gives the URLs of the most important Web directories (not including the search engines already listed in section 13.4).

Directories are hierarchical taxonomies that classify human knowledge. Table 13.4 shows the first level of the taxonomies used by Web directories (the number of first level categories ranges from 12 to 26). Some subcategories are also available in the main page of Web directories, adding around 70 more topics. The largest directory, Yahoo!, has close to one million pages classified, followed by LookSmart, which has about 24,000 categories in total. Yahoo! also offers

14 regional or country specialized directories in other languages including Chinese, Danish, French, German, Italian, Japanese, Korean, Norwegian, Spanish, and Swedish. In most cases, pages have to be submitted to the Web directory, where they are reviewed, and, if accepted, classified in one or more categories of the hierarchy. Although the taxonomy can be seen as a tree, there are cross references, so it is really a directed acyclic graph.

The main advantage of this technique is that if we find what we are looking for, the answer will be useful in most cases. On the other hand, the main disadvantage is that the classification is not specialized enough and that not all Web pages are classified. The last problem becomes worse every day as the Web grows. The efforts to do automatic classification, by using clustering or other techniques, are very old. However, up to now, natural language processing is not 100% effective in extracting relevant terms from a document. Thus, classification is done manually by a limited number of people. This is a potential problem with users having a different notion of categories than the manmade categorization.

Web directories also allow the user to perform a search on the taxonomy descriptors or in the Web pages pointed to by the taxonomy. In fact, as the number of classified Web pages is small, we can even afford to have a copy of all pages. In that case they must be updated frequently, which may pose performance and temporal validity problems. In addition, most Web directories also send the query to a search engine (through a strategic alliance) and allow the whole Web to be searched.

13.5.2 Combining Searching with Browsing

Usually, users either browse following hypertext links or they search a Web site (or the whole Web). Currently, in Web directories, a search can be reduced to a subtree of the taxonomy. However, the search may miss related pages that are not in that part of the taxonomy. Some search engines find similar pages using common words, but often this is not effective.

WebGlimpse is a tool that tries to solve these problems by combining browsing with searching [539]. WebGlimpse attaches a small search box to the bottom of every HTML page, and allows the search to cover the neighborhood of that page or the whole site, without having to stop browsing. This is equivalent to following hypertext links that are constructed on the fly through a neighborhood search. WebGlimpse can be useful in building indices for personal Web pages or collections of favorite URLs.

First, WebGlimpse indexes a Web site (or a collection of specific documents) and computes neighborhoods according to user specifications. As a result, WebGlimpse adds the search boxes to selected pages, collects remote pages that are relevant, and caches those pages locally. Later, the users can search in the neighborhood of a page using the search boxes. As the name suggests, WebGlimpse uses Glimpse as its search engine [540].

The neighborhood of a Web page is defined as the set of Web pages that are reachable by a path of hypertext links within a maximum predefined distance. This distance can be set differently for local and remote pages. For example, it can be unlimited locally, but be only three at any remote site. The neighborhood can also include all the subdirectories of the directory where the Web page is. The result is a graph of all the neighborhoods of the Web site or collection, and for each Web page, a file with all the Web pages in its neighborhood. When searching, any query in the whole index can be intersected with a neighborhood list, obtaining the relevant Web pages. A nice addition to WebGlimpse would be to visualize the neighborhoods. This problem is the topic of the next section.

13.5.3   Helpful Tools

There are many software tools to help browsing and searching. Some of them are add-ons to browsers, such as Alexa [10]. Alexa is a free Web navigation service that can be attached as a toolbar at the bottom of any browser and accompanies the user in his surfing. It provides useful information about the sites that are visited, including their popularity, speed of access, freshness, and overall quality (obtained from votes of Alexa users). Alexa also suggests related sites helping one's navigation. Another navigation service and searching guide is WebTaxi [805].

There are other tools that use visual metaphors, which can be broadly classified into two types: tools designed to visualize a subset of the Web and tools designed to visualize large answers. Both cases need to represent a large graph in a meaningful way. Specific commercial examples of tools to visualize Web subsets are Microsoft's SiteAnalyst (formerly from NetCarta), MAPA from Dynamic Diagrams, IBM's Mapuccino (formerly WebCutter [527], shown in Figure 10.22), SurfSerf, Merzscope from Merzcom, CLEARweb, Astra SiteManager, WebAnalyzer from InContext, HistoryTree from SmartBrowser, etc. Non-commercial works include WebMap [220], Sitemap, Ptolomeaus, and many earlier research [234, 578, 564, 20]. We have not included more generic visualization software, where Web visualization is just a particular case, or other related visualization tools such as Web usage analysis [642, 294, 737].

Metaphors to visualize large answers are covered in Chapter 10. Visual tools are not yet deployed in the whole Web because there is no standard way of communicating visualizers and search engines. One possible approach is to use a markup language based on XML (see Chapter 6), as proposed in [15].

13.6   Metasearchers

Metasearchers are Web servers that send a given query to several search engines, Web directories and other databases, collect the answers and unify them. Examples are Metacrawler [715] and SavvySearch [383, 223]. The main advantages of metasearchers are the ability to combine the results of many sources and the fact that the user can pose the same query to various sources through a single common interface. Metasearchers differ from each other in how ranking

Metasearcher	URL	Sources used
Cyber 411	www.cyber411.com	14
Dogpile	www.dogpile.com	25
Highway61	www.highway61.com	5
Inference Find	www.infind.com	6
Mamma	www.mamma.com	7
MetaCrawler	www.metacrawler.com	7
MetaFind	www.metafind.com	7
MetaMiner	www.miner.uol.com.br	13
MetaSearch	www.metasearch.com	—
SavvySearch	savvy.cs.colostate.edu:2000	>13

Table 13.5   URLs of metasearchers and number of sources that they use (October 1998).

is performed in the unified result (in some cases no ranking is done), and how well they translate the user query to the specific query language of each search engine or Web directory (the query language common to all of them could be small). Table 13.5 shows the URLs of the main metasearch engines as well as the number of search engines, Web directories and other databases that they search. Metasearchers can also run on the client, for example, Copernic, EchoSearch, WebFerret, WebCompass, and WebSeeker. There are others that search several sources and show the different answers in separate windows, such as All4One, OneSeek, Proteus, and Search Spaniel.

The advantages of metasearchers are that the results can be sorted by different attributes such as host, keyword, date, etc; which can be more informative than the output of a single search engine. Therefore browsing the results should be simpler. On the other hand, the result is not necessarily all the Web pages matching the query, as the number of results per search engine retrieved by the metasearcher is limited (it can be changed by the user, but there is an upper limit). Nevertheless, pages returned by more than one search engine should be more relevant.

We expect that new metasearchers will do better ranking. A first step in this direction is the NEC Research Institute metasearch engine, Inquirus [488, 489]. The main difference is that Inquirus actually downloads and analyzes each Web page obtained and then displays each page, highlighting the places where the query terms were found. The results are displayed as soon as they are available in a progressive manner, otherwise the waiting time would be too long. This technique also allows non-existent pages or pages that have changed and do not contain the query any more to be discarded, and, more important, provides for better ranking than normal search engines. On the other hand, this metasearcher is not available to the general public.

Measure	Average value	Range
Number of words	2.35	0 to 393
Number of operators	0.41	0 to 958
Repetitions of each query	3.97	1–1.5 million
Queries per user session	2.02	1–173,325
Screens per query	1.39	1–78,496

Table 13.6   Queries on the Web: average values.

The use of metasearchers is justified by coverage studies that show that a small percentage of Web pages are in all search engines [91]. In fact, fewer than 1% of the Web pages indexed by AltaVista, HotBot, Excite, and Infoseek are in all of those search engines. This fact is quite surprising and has not been explained (yet). Metasearchers for specific topics can be considered as software agents and are covered in section 13.8.2.

13.7   Finding the Needle in the Haystack

13.7.1   User Problems

We have already glanced at some of the problems faced by the user when interacting with the query interfaces currently provided by search engines. First, the user does not exactly understand the meaning of searching using a set of words, as discussed in Chapter 10. Second, the user may get unexpected answers because he is not aware of the logical view of the text adopted by the system. An example is the use of uppercase letters when the search engine is not case sensitive. Hence, a word like 'Bank' loses part of its semantics if we search for 'bank.' Simple experiments also show that due to typos or variations of a word, even if correctly capitalized, 10–20% of the matches can be lost. Similarly, foreign names or words that are difficult to spell may appear incorrectly which may result in a loss of up to 50% of the relevant answers, as mentioned in section 13.2.

Another problem is that most users have trouble with Boolean logic. In natural language, sometimes we use 'and' and 'or' with different meaning depending on the context. For example, when choosing between two things, we use an exclusive 'or,' which does not match the Boolean interpretation. Because of this, several studies show that around 80% of the queries do not use any Boolean or other operation. For these reasons many people have trouble using command query languages, and query forms should clearly specify which words must or must not be contained in a document that belongs to the answer.

There are a few surveys and analyses of query logs with respect to the usage of search engines [647, 403, 728]. The latter reference is based on 285 million user sessions containing 575 million queries. Table 13.6 gives the main results of that study, carried out in September 1998. Some of the strange results might be due to queries done by mechanized search agents. The number of queries submitted per day to AltaVista is over 13 million. Users select a search engine mainly based on ease of use, speed, coverage, relevance of the answer, and habit. The main purposes are research, leisure, business, and education. The main problems found are that novice users do not know how to start and lack the general knowledge that would help in finding better answers. Other problems are that search engines are slow, that the answer is too large, not very relevant, and not always up to date. Also, most people do not care about advertising, which is one of the main sources of funding for search engines. When searching, 25% of the users use a single keyword, and on average their queries have only two or three terms. In addition, about 15% of the users restrict the search to a predefined topic and most of them (nearly 80%) do not modify the query. In addition, most users (about 85%) only look at the first screen with results and 64% of the queries are unique. Also, many words appear in the same sentence, suggesting that proximity search should be used. There are also studies about users' demographics and software and hardware used.

13.7.2   Some Examples

Now we give a couple of search examples. One problem with full-text retrieval is that although many queries can be effective, many others are a total deception. The main reason is that a set of words does not capture all the semantics of a document. There is too much contextual information (that can be explicit or even implicit) lost at indexing time, which is essential for proper understanding. For example, suppose that we want to learn an oriental game such as Shogi or Go. For the first case, searching for Shogi will quickly give us good Web pages where we can find what Shogi is (a variant of chess) and its rules. However, for Go the task is complicated, because unlike Shogi, Go is not a unique word in English (in particular, because uppercase letters are converted to lowercase letters, see Chapter 7). The problem of having more than one meaning for a word is called *polysemy*. We can add more terms to the query, such as `game` and `Japanese` but still we are out of luck, as the pages found are almost all about Japanese games written in English where the common verb go is used. Another common problem comes from synonyms. If we are searching for a certain word, but a relevant page uses a synonym, we will not find it.

The following example (taken from [152]) better explains the polysemy problem, where the ambiguity comes from the same language. Suppose that we want to find the running speed of the jaguar, a big South American cat. A first naive search in AltaVista would be `jaguar speed`. The results are pages that talk about the Jaguar car, an Atari video game, a US football team, a local network server, etc. The first page about the animal is ranked 183 and is a fable, without information about the speed. In a second try, we add the term `cat`. The answers are about the Clans Nova Cat and Smoke Jaguar, LMG Enterprises, fine cars, etc. Only the page ranked

25 has some information on jaguars but not the speed. Suppose we try Yahoo!. We look at 'Science:Biology:Zoology:Animals:Cats:Wild_Cats' and 'Science:Biology:Animal_Behavior.' No information about jaguars there.

13.7.3   Teaching the User

Interfaces are slowly improving in assisting the user with the task of acquiring a better grasp of what Web pages are being retrieved. Query forms must specify clearly if one or all the words must be in a page, which words should not be in a page, etc., without using a written Boolean query language. Second, users should try to give as many terms as possible, in particular terms that must be or should not be in the pages. In particular, a user should include all possible synonyms of a word. If the user can restrict the search to a field (for example, the page title) or limit some attribute (date, country), this will certainly reduce the size of the answer. In case of doubt, the user should remember to look at the help information provided by the search engine. If he cannot find where one of the relevant terms is in a page, he can use the Find option of the browser.

Even if we are able to pose a good query, the answer can still be quite large. Considering that the visual tools mentioned before are not yet available for the general public, the user must learn from experience. There are many strategies for quickly finding relevant answers. If the user is looking for an institution, he can always try to guess the corresponding URL by using the www prefix followed by a guessed institution acronym or brief name and ending with a top level domain (country code or com, edu, org, gov for the US). If this does not work, the user can search the institution name in a Web directory.

If we are looking for work related to a specific topic, a possible strategy is: (1) select an article relevant to the topic, if possible with non-common author surnames or title keywords (if it is not available, try any bibliographic database or a Web directory search for a first reference); and (2) use a search engine to find all Web pages that have all those surnames and keywords. Many of the results are likely to be relevant, because we can find: (a) newer papers that reference the initial reference, (b) personal Web pages of the authors, and most important, (c) pages about the topic that already contain many relevant references. This strategy can be iterated by changing the reference used as better references appear during the search.

As mentioned at the beginning of this chapter, the Web poses so many problems, that it is easier and more effective to teach the user how to properly profit from search engines and Web directories, rather than trying to guess what the user really wants. Given that the coverage of the search engines is low, use several engines or a metasearcher. Also, remember that you have to evaluate the quality of each answer, even if it appears to be relevant. Remember that anybody can publish in the Web, and that does not mean that the data is correct or still valid. The lessons learned in the examples shown above are: (1) search engines still return too much hay together with the needle; and (2) Web directories do not have enough depth to find the needle. So, we can use the following rules of thumb:

- **Specific queries** Look in an encyclopedia, that is the reason that they exist. In other words, do not forget libraries.

- **Broad queries** Use Web directories to find good starting points.

- **Vague queries** Use Web search engines and improve the query formulation based on relevant answers.

13.8   Searching using Hyperlinks

In this section we cover other paradigms to search the Web, which are based on exploiting its hyperlinks. They include Web query languages and dynamic searching. These ideas are still not widely used due to several reasons, including performance limitations and lack of commercial products.

13.8.1   Web Query Languages

Up to this point, queries have been based on the content of each page. However, queries can also include the link structure connecting Web pages. For example, we would like to search for all the Web pages that contain at least one image and are reachable from a given site following at most three links. To be able to pose this type of query, different data models have been used. The most important are a labeled graph model to represent Web pages (nodes) and hyperlinks (edges) between Web pages, and a semi-structured data model to represent the content of Web pages. In the latter model, the data schema is not usually known, may change over time, may be large and descriptive, etc. [2, 129].

Although some models and languages for querying hypertext were proposed before the Web appeared [563, 72, 184], the first generation of Web query languages were aimed at combining content with structure (see also Chapter 4). These languages combine patterns that appear within the documents with graph queries describing link structure (using path regular expressions). They include W3QL [450], WebSQL [556, 33], WebLog [476], and WQL [511]. The second generation of languages, called Web data manipulation languages, maintain the emphasis on semi-structured data. However, they extend the previous languages by providing access to the structure of Web pages (the model also includes the internal structure) and by allowing the creation of new structures as a result of a query. Languages in this category include STRUQL [253], FLORID [373], and WebOQL [32]. All the languages mentioned are meant to be used by programs, not final users. Nevertheless, there are some examples of query interfaces for these languages.

Web query languages have been extended to other Web tasks, such as extracting and integrating information from Web pages, and constructing and restructuring Web sites. More details about Web query languages can be found in the excellent survey by Florescu, Levy, and Mendelzon [258].

13.8.2 Dynamic Search and Software Agents

Dynamic search in the Web is equivalent to sequential text searching. The idea is to use an online search to discover relevant information by following links. The main advantage is that you are searching in the current structure of the Web, and not in what is stored in the index of a search engine. While this approach is slow for the entire Web, it might be used in small and dynamic subsets of the Web. The first heuristic devised was the *fish search* [113], which exploits the intuition that relevant documents often have neighbors that are relevant. Hence, the search is guided by following links in relevant documents. This was improved by *shark search* [366], which does a better relevance assessment of neighboring pages. This algorithm has been embedded in Mapuccino (see section 13.5.3), and Figure 10.22 shows a Web subset generated by this type of search. The main idea of these algorithms is to follow links in some priority, starting from a single page and a given query. At each step, the page with highest priority is analyzed. If it is found to be relevant, a heuristic decides to follow or not to follow the links on that page. If so, new pages are added to the priority list in the appropriate positions.

Related work includes software agents for searching specific information on the Web [602, 477]. This implies dealing with heterogeneous sources of information which have to be combined. Important issues in this case are how to determine relevant sources (see also Chapters 9 and 15, as well as section 10.4.4) and and how to merge the results retrieved (the fusion problem). Examples are shopping robots such as Jango [401], Junglee [180], and Express [241].

13.9 Trends and Research Issues

The future of the Web might surprise us, considering that its massive use started less than five years ago. There are many distinct trends and each one opens up new and particular research problems. What follows is a compilation of the major trends as we have perceived them.

- **Modeling:** Special IR models tailored for the Web are needed [308, 155, 652]. As we have seen, Web user queries are different. We also have the pull/push dichotomy: Will we search for information or will the information reach us? In both cases we need better search paradigms and better information filtering [782].

- **Querying:** Further work on combining structure and content in the queries is needed as well as new visual metaphors to pose those queries and visualize the answers [44]. Future query languages may include concept-based search and natural language processing, as well as searching by example (this implies document clustering and categorization on the Web [810, 120, 157]).

- **Distributed architectures:** New distributed schemes to traverse and search the Web must be devised to cope with its growth. This will have an impact on current crawling and indexing techniques, as well as caching techniques for the Web. Which will be the bottleneck in the future? Server capacity or network bandwidth?

- **Ranking:** Better ranking schemes are needed, exploiting both content and structure (internal to a page and hyperlinks); in particular, combining and comparing query-dependent and independent techniques. One problem related to advertisements is that search engines may rank some pages higher due to reasons that are not based on the real relevance of a page (this is called the search engine persuasion problem in [543]).

- **Indexing:** Which is the best logical view for the text? What should be indexed? How to exploit better text compression schemes to achieve fast searching and get lower network traffic? How to compress efficiently word lists, URL tables, etc. and update them without significant run-time penalty? Many implementation details must be improved.

- **Dynamic pages:** A large number of Web pages are created on demand and current techniques are not able to search on those dynamic pages. This is called the hidden Web.

- **Duplicated data:** Better mechanisms to detect and eliminate repeated Web pages (or pages that are syntactically very similar) are needed. Initial approaches are based on resemblance measures using document fingerprints [121, 120]. This is related to an important problem in databases: finding similar objects.

- **Multimedia:** Searching for non-textual objects will gain importance in the near future. There are already some research results in the literature [579, 80, 136].

- **User interfaces:** Better user interfaces are clearly needed. The output should also be improved, for example allowing better extraction of the main content of a page or the formulation of content-based queries [766].

- **Browsing:** More tools will appear, exploiting links, popularity of Web pages, content similarity, collaboration, 3D, and virtual reality [384, 638, 385, 421]. An important trend would be to unify further searching with browsing.

An important issue to be settled in the future is a standard protocol to query search engines. One proposal for such a protocol is STARTS [316], which could allow us to choose the best sources for querying, evaluate the query at these sources, and merge the query results. This protocol would make it easier to build metasearchers, but at the same time that is one of the reasons for not having a standard. In that way, metasearchers cannot profit from the work done by search engines and Web directories. This is a particular case of the federated searching problem from heterogeneous sources as it is called in the database community [656]. This is a problem already studied in the case of the Web, including discovery and ranking of sources [161, 845, 319]. These issues are also very important for digital libraries [649] (see also Chapter 15) and visualization issues [15]. A related topic is metadata standards for the Web (see Chapter 6) and their limitations [544]. XML helps [436, 213, 306], but semantic integration is still needed.

Hyperlinks can also be used to infer information about the Web. Although this is not exactly searching the Web, this is an important trend called Web mining. Traditionally, Web mining had been focused on text mining, that is, extracting information from Web pages. However, the hyperlink structure can be exploited to obtain useful information. For example, the ParaSite system [736] uses hyperlink information to find pages that have moved, related pages, and personal Web pages. HITS, already mentioned in Section 13.4.4, has also been used to find communities and similar pages [444, 298]. Other results on exploiting hyperlink structure can be found in [639, 543, 154]. Further improvements in this problem include Web document clustering [810, 120, 162] (already mentioned), connectivity services (for example, asking which Web pages point to a given page [92]), automatic link generation [320], extracting information [100, 115], etc.

Another trend is intranet applications. Many companies do not want their private networks to be public. However, for business reasons they want to allow Web users to search inside their intranets obtaining partial information. This idea leads to the concept of *portals* for which there are already several commercial products. New models to see Web sites as databases and/or information systems are also important.

13.10   Bibliographic Discussion

There are hundreds of books about the Web. Many of them include some information about searching the Web and tips for users. A recent book edited by Abrams includes a chapter on searching the Web [3]. Other sources are [682], the special numbers of *Scientific American* on the Internet (March 1997) and IEEE's *Internet Computing on Search Technologies* (July/August 1998). For details about crawlers and other software agents see [166, 817].

In addition, the best source for references to the Web is the Web itself. To start with, there are many Web sites devoted to inform and rate search engines and Web directories. Among them we can distinguish Search Engine Watch [749] and Search Engine Showdown [609]. A survey about Web characterizations is given by Pitkow [641] and a good directory to Web characteristics is [217]. Other Web pages provide pointers and references related to searching the Web, in particular the World Wide Web Consortium (`www.w3.org`), the World Wide Web journal (`w3j.com`) and WWW conferences. These and other pointers are available in the Web page of this book (see Chapter 1).

Acknowledgements

We would like to thank the following for their helpful comments: Omar Alonso, Eric Brown, Pablo de la Fuente, Monika Henzinger and Gonzalo Navarro.

Chapter 14
Libraries and Bibliographical Systems

by Edie M. Rasmussen

14.1 Introduction

Despite the image sometimes presented of libraries as archaic collections of dusty books accessed through a card catalog, libraries were among the earliest institutions to make use of information retrieval systems. This early adoption took two main forms: searching remote electronic databases provided by commercial vendors in order to provide reference services to patrons, and the creation and searching of catalog records for materials held within the library. Each of these applications followed different developmental paths resulting in different products and functionality. According to Hildreth [372],

> Proceeding along different paths, the developmental histories of online public access catalogs (OPACs) and conventional information retrieval (IR) systems differed in three respects: origins of systems development, file and database content, and intended users. (p.10)

Initial development of information retrieval systems was carried out by government laboratories in support of research in science and technology, based on bibliographic databases containing largely textual information, with trained search intermediaries as the intended users. OPACs were developed initially inhouse by large, usually academic, library systems, and later by commercial vendors of turnkey systems.† They used standardized record formats, generally the MARC record with minimal subject information (title, a few subject headings, and a classification number); and unlike commercial IR systems, they were intended from the outset for end users (library patrons). These factors led to significant differences between commercial IR systems and OPACs.

---

† 'Turnkey systems' include software (and often hardware) and are usually developed with a specific library type and size in mind; within the constraints of the system, some customizing to suit the particular library is often possible.

Developed independently of each other, information retrieval systems and OPACs are quite different in character and use, and will be treated separately in this chapter. For these applications, a brief history, overview of current trends, some sample records and search examples will be given, and profiles of well-known systems will be presented. (Topics related to the *use* of IR systems in libraries, through Reference and Technical Services departments, and the techniques by which reference librarians perform the reference function, are beyond the scope of this chapter.) An important recent phenomenon, the digital library (see Chapter 15), has the potential to integrate information retrieval functions in the library under a common interface, eliminating the distinction between locally held and remote resources. Some examples of libraries which have attempted this integration will be discussed.

14.2   Online IR Systems and Document Databases

A synergistic relationship exists between the producers and vendors of document databases‡ (see Figure 14.1). In general, database producers create a product which they license to the database vendors. These vendors or search services provide search software and access to their customers, who benefit from the ability to search multiple databases from a single source.

It is common to speak of the online database industry, since production of databases has usually been undertaken by corporations, organizations, or government on a for-profit or cost-recovery basis. These database producers have seen databases as products for sale or lease, often to libraries, and usually by a third party or database vendor. The role of database vendor is to license databases from their producers and add value by making them available to users. Database vendors provide some degree of standardization to the record formats, create indexes (usually in the form of inverted files), and provide a common interface for searching multiple databases. Examples of well known database vendors are DIALOG, LEXIS-NEXIS, OCLC, and H.W. Wilson; profiles are given in Figure 14.2. Some database producers choose to serve as their own search service providers, leading to a degree of vertical integration within the database industry; examples are the National Library of Medicine (NLM), which provides free access to its Medline database through the Web, and the H.W. Wilson Company, which markets its own series of databases.

A significant aspect of these major commercial services is the very large size of their databases and the need for rapid, reliable service for many simultaneous users. In a description of their computing complex, LEXIS-NEXIS [510] give their database size as 1.3 billion documents, with 1.3 million subscribers, and 120 million annual searches. They return an answer set within six to ten seconds,

---

‡ 'Database' is commonly used by producers and vendors of document databases when referring to their product. These databases lack the tabular structure of relational databases and contain bibliographic information and/or the full-text of documents. This usage will be followed in this chapter.

Database Producers:

- design database structure
- collect in-scope literature
- enter bibliographic information in standard form
- abstract (or edit authors' abstracts)
- index with (usually) controlled vocabulary
- generate file updates at regular intervals
- market backfile and updates to vendors

Database Vendors:

- create search software
- license databases from producers
- standardize (as possible) record structure
- mount databases, creating inverted indexes
- update databases as appropriate (daily, weekly, monthly)
- provide documentation for searchers
- market to clients
- provide service and training to client base

Figure 14.1   Role of database producers and vendors.

with a claimed availability above 99.99% and reliability of 99.83%. Similarly, DIALOG claims to be over 50 times the size of the Web.

14.2.1   Databases

The history of commercial online retrieval systems begins with the creation of databases of bibliographic information in electronic form. In fact, Neufeld and Cornog claim 'databases can almost be said to have created the information industry as we now know it' [600]. Abstracting and indexing tools in printed form were available in the nineteenth century and became increasingly available in the twentieth century. Professional organizations, commercial firms, and government bodies served as publishers, selecting relevant materials from the world's literature, creating bibliographic records for them, and providing abstracts and indexing information. These databases were concentrated in the sciences, with titles such as *Chemical Abstracts*, *Biological Abstracts*, and *Engineering Index*, but humanities (*Historical Abstracts*) and social sciences (*PsycINFO*) products soon became available.

As publishers of abstracts and indexes turned to computer-assisted typesetting and printing for their products, the resulting magnetic tapes of information began to be used for information retrieval purposes. Today virtually all print abstracting and indexing products are also available in electronic form, and many new products are available solely in electronic form, without a print equivalent. As storage costs have dropped dramatically, many of these electronic databases

- **The DIALOG Corporation**

  DIALOG, 'the world's largest online information company,' contains about 500 databases covering a full range of subjects, including science, technology and medicine, humanities, business, and electronic newspapers. Bibliographic and full-text databases are included. Some databases are also available in CD-ROM versions for onsite searching.
  URL: `http://www.dialog.com`

- **LEXIS-NEXIS**

  LEXIS-NEXIS markets full-text databases to the legal and business community. LEXIS provides access to 4800 legal research products including state and federal case law, statutes, and regulations. NEXIS covers over 18,000 news and business sources.
  URL: `http://www.lexis-nexis.com`

- **OCLC**

  OCLC (the Online Computer Library Center, Inc.), which began as a bibliographic utility for cooperative cataloging of library materials, now offers access to over 70 databases and 1.5 million full-text articles. Features include an interface oriented to end-users and links to documents as well as to an inter-library loan module.
  URL: `http://www.oclc.org/oclc/menu/fs.html`

- **H.W. Wilson**

  H.W. Wilson began producing print indexes in 1898, and now offers 40 databases to the public, school, and college library market. Wilson has electronic, CD-ROM, magnetic tape, and Web-based versions of its databases.
  URL: `http://www.hwwilson.com/default.htm`

Figure 14.2 Profiles of database vendors.

have expanded to include not only bibliographic information about documents, but the text of the documents themselves. These are referred to as full-text databases, and include databases of journal articles and newspapers as well as reference materials such as encyclopedias and directories. Characteristics of some common databases (as available on DIALOG) are given in Figure 14.3.

Databases and Indexing

In general, bibliographic databases are expensive to produce, because they require rigorous selection and analysis of the documents that they cover. Some databases cover materials in a specific group of journals, others attempt to be comprehensive, collecting the world's literature within the defined subject scope. Every item must be examined for relevance to the database's goals, indexed,

- **CA SEARCH: Chemical Abstracts**

  Coverage: bibliographical records for worldwide literature of chemistry and its applications

  File size: 14 million records; weekly updates of 11,000 records

- **MEDLINE**

  Coverage: the broad field of biomedicine, including clinical and experimental medicine, dentistry, nursing, pharmacology, psychiatry, etc. It indexes articles from 3,700 journals worldwide

  File size: about 9.5 million records; weekly updates of 7700 records

- **New York Times - Fulltext**

  Coverage: full-text of *New York Times* from 1981 to the present

  File size: 1.8 million records; daily updates

- **PsycINFO: Psychological Abstracts**

  Coverage: bibliographic records for materials in psychology and related behavioral and social sciences, including psychiatry, sociology, anthropology, education, pharmacology, and linguistics; 1887 to the present

  File size: 1.5 million records; monthly updates of 5000 records

Figure 14.3   Characteristics of some well known databases on DIALOG.

abstracted, and entered in the system. Despite the promise of SGML tagging of materials by primary producers, most of this work is still done by the database producer, with a clerical staff to handle data input and subject specialists to abstract (more commonly, edit the author's abstract) and index the material.

Each bibliographic database is a unique product designed to meet the information needs of a particular user group. Therefore, there is no single standard for the content of a database record. Typically, it contains tagged information that includes a record key, bibliographic data such as author, title, and source of the document, an abstract, and subject indicators such as indexing terms or category codes. In full-text databases (see Chapters 2 and 4), the text of the document is also included. Sample database records from *BIOSIS PREVIEWS* (*Biological Abstracts*) and *Historical Abstracts* are shown in Figures 14.4 and 14.5. Note that the vocabulary (descriptors and codes) used for subject description is very dependent on the field of study (in this case, biology and history).

As these database records show, the subject information they contain is of two types: so-called 'natural language' or 'free text' information found in the title or abstract field, and terms from an indexing or controlled vocabulary which are assigned by human indexers. Most databases include indexing terms in a descriptor field, usually taken from a database-specific thesaurus (e.g., for *PsycINFO*, the *Thesaurus of Psychological Index Terms*). Other types of codes or indexing may be applied as relevant to the database (for instance, biosystematic

DIALOG(R)File 5:BIOSIS PREVIEWS(R)

(c) 1998 BIOSIS. All rts. reserv.

13165209 BIOSIS Number: 99165209

Population genetics of the Komodo dragon Varanus komodoensis

Ciofi C; Bruford M; Swingland I R

D.I.C.E., Univ. Kent, Kent, UK

Bulletin of the Ecological Society of America 77 (3 SUPPL. PART 2). 1996. 81.

Full Journal Title: 1996 Annual Combined Meeting of the Ecological Society of America on Ecologists/Biologists as Problem Solvers, Providence, Rhode Island, USA, August 10-14, 1996. Bulletin of the Ecological Society of America

ISSN: 0012-9623

Language: ENGLISH

Document Type: CONFERENCE PAPER

Print Number: Biological Abstracts/RRM Vol. 048 Iss. 010 Ref. 171812

Descriptors/Keywords: MEETING ABSTRACT; VARANUS KOMODOENSIS; KOMODO DRAGON; MONITOR LIZARD; GENETIC DIVERGENCE; GENE FLOW; EVOLUTION; GENETIC DIVERSITY; SPECIES RANGE; POPULATION SIZE; POPULATION GENETICS; LESSER SUNDA REGION; INDONESIAN ISLANDS; ORIENTAL REGION; KOMODO; RINCA; FLORES; GILI MOTANG; INDONESIA

Concept Codes:

03506 Genetics and Cytogenetics-Animal

03509 Genetics and Cytogenetics-Population Genetics (1972-)

07508 Ecology; Environmental Biology-Animal

62800 Animal Distribution (1971-)

00520 General Biology-Symposia, Transactions and Proceedings of Conferences, Congresses, Review Annuals

Biosystematic Codes:

85408 Sauria

Super Taxa:

Animals; Chordates; Vertebrates; Nonhuman Vertebrates; Reptiles

Figure 14.4 Sample record: *BIOSIS PREVIEWS*.§

codes in *BIOSIS PREVIEWS*, historical time periods in *Historical Abstracts*). The assignment of these subject terms contributes significantly to the cost of database production. Obviously an automated indexing system would be of interest to database producers, though production systems currently in use are best described as performing 'machine-assisted' rather than automatic indexing.

§ With permission of BIOSIS UK. The format of this record has now changed as BIOSIS now use New Relational Indexing

---

DIALOG(R)File 39: Historical Abstracts
(c) 1998 ABC-CLIO. All rts. reserv.
1488625 47A-9910
THE U.S.S. KEARSARGE, SIXTEEN IRISHMEN, AND A DARK AND
STORMY NIGHT.
Sloan, Edward W
American Neptune 1994 54(4): 259-264.
NOTE: Based on primary sources, including the Official Records of the Union
and Confederate Navies in the War of the Rebellion, Series I and II (1894-1927);
28 notes.
DOCUMENT TYPE: ARTICLE
ABSTRACT: Tells the story of the Union navy's Kearsarge, a sloop-of-war that
patrolled English seas looking for Confederate commerce raiders. Upon dock-
ing at the Irish port of Cobh (Queenstown) in November 1863, 16 locals stowed
away. They were subsequently returned to Cobh, but in the meantime Captain
John Winslow temporarily enlisted the men in order, he said, that they be jus-
tifiably clothed and fed, although other ship diaries indicate that the ship was
short-handed and Winslow intended a real enlistment. Whatever the reality, the
captain inadvertently created an international crisis since his action technically
violated the British Foreign Enlistments Act. It is unclear whether Confederates
plotted the incident to embarrass the Union in Britain because there are dispar-
ities between official accounts and the diaries of individual crewmen. (S)
DESCRIPTORS: USA ; Civil War ; Ireland -(Cobh) ; Kearsarge -(vessel) ; Political Crisis ; Military Service ; Stowaways ; 1862-1864
HISTORICAL PERIOD: 1860D 1800H
HISTORICAL PERIOD (Starting): 1862
HISTORICAL PERIOD (Ending): 1864

Figure 14.5 Sample record: *Historical Abstracts.* From ABC-CLIO,CA,USA.

A subject of early (and ongoing) research has been the relative value of 'free
text' and controlled vocabulary terms in contributing to retrieval performance.
This subject was addressed in the Cranfield studies in the 1960s [415], and has
continued to be examined by researchers up to the present time; good reviews
of this research have been presented by Svenonius [752], Lancaster [479], and
Rowley [688]. No definitive answer has been found, though later studies seem
to suggest a complementarity between the two types of indexing in promoting
good retrieval.

14.2.2 Online Retrieval Systems

The use of the computer for bibliographic information retrieval was first demonstrated in the 1950s, and initiated by the National Library of Medicine in 1964
using batch processing [107]. Also in the 1960s, federally funded projects were
carried out to develop prototype online systems which were then implemented
in government research laboratories. The first production service, Lockheed's

DIALOG system, was implemented for NASA and subsequently made available to other government locations before becoming a commercial activity in the early 1970s and undergoing several changes in ownership. Today DIALOG operates worldwide with databases offered via the Internet to libraries and other organizations as well as individuals.

With a few exceptions, database vendors do not produce information but rather make it available to searchers via a common search interface. Database vendors license databases from the producers, process the databases to introduce as much standardization as is feasible (e.g., standard field names), mount the database through the creation of inverted indexes, create database descriptions and aids to searchers in a standard format, and conduct training sessions for clients (see Figure 14.1). These organizations offer a value-added service by providing a common gateway to multiple databases. A database vendor may offer cross-database searches; for example, DIALOG allows the searcher to search simultaneously a predetermined or searcher-selected grouping of databases to create a merged set of references, then process the set to remove duplicates.

14.2.3   IR in Online Retrieval Systems

Since the inception of these online retrieval services, their retrieval functionality has been based primarily on the Boolean model for retrieval, in contrast to research in the IR field which has focused on improving retrieval performance through non-Boolean models, such as the vector space model (see Chapter 2). A number of factors guided the choice of the Boolean model as the basis for these services. Research in indexing and retrieval at the time, particularly the Cranfield studies, a series of experiments comparing natural and controlled vocabulary indexing, suggested that 'natural language' retrieval provided a level of retrieval performance comparable to manual indexing. Boolean logic was already being used in some libraries for manual retrieval systems, such as edge-notched cards and optical coincidence cards, and seemed to offer a natural mechanism for implementing retrieval based on combinations of words in documents. Research on alternate retrieval models was in its infancy, and the effectiveness of these models had not been proven for large databases. Most significantly, perhaps, the limited processing and storage capability of the computers of the time, while enough to support the inverted file structures and logical operations required for Boolean retrieval in an online environment, could not provide real time retrieval performance for other retrieval models which were more computationally intensive.

Despite developments in IR research which suggested that alternative models might provide improved retrieval performance, Boolean retrieval has remained the commonest access method offered by database vendors, although in recent years some systems have added a form of natural language input with ranked output processing as an alternative access method. Reasons that have been suggested for the predominance of Boolean searching include financial considerations (cost of major changes in search software and database structures), service issues (a client community trained on existing systems), and lack of evidence in support of viable alternatives in operational environments [662].

In general, database vendors use proprietary search software which is specific to their system, so that information professionals who search multiple systems are required to learn a different command vocabulary for each. A standard has been developed for a Common Command Language, NISO Z39.58 or ISO 8777, as described in Chapter 4, but it does not substitute for the advanced search features which are unique to individual search systems. The basic functionality for an IR search system is the ability to search for single terms or phrases, or Boolean combinations of them, to create sets of documents that can be further manipulated, then printed or displayed. Typically the system will also offer the option of using proximity operators to specify term relationships (A adjacent to B, A within n words of B, etc.) as discussed in Chapter 5, and to specify the location of the search term within the record (A occurring in title field, B occurring in the descriptor field, etc.). Of course, these capabilities require the storage of a significant amount of positional information within the inverted index. Other functions that may be available are the ability to browse the database index to select search terms (see Chapter 10) or to follow the term relationships within a database thesaurus to find candidate search terms (see Chapter 7). Other, more sophisticated functions, perhaps associated with a specific category of database, are also available, such as the ability to conduct structural searches for compounds in a chemistry database.

As a term is entered by a searcher, the system creates a 'set' corresponding to all documents containing that term, and assigns a set number for the searcher's use. Multiple sets of retrieved documents are maintained in temporary storage. These set numbers serve as surrogates for the document set when issuing search commands, and Boolean logic can be used to manipulate existing sets. A display command allows the searcher to review the search history and return to previous sets. Based on data about the size of a set retrieved with search term or expression, and a review of the associated documents and their indexing, searchers continually revise a search until they feel they have achieved the best possible outcome. This iterative process is as much art as science, and its success is highly dependent on the skill and subject knowledge of the searcher.

A typical Boolean search on DIALOG is shown in Figure 14.6. In this search, the user requests a specific database (file 61, *Library and Information Science Abstracts*) and then uses the 'Select Steps' or `ss` command to create sets of records. The '(w)' represents a proximity operator, so set 5 (S5) will contain all records containing the phrases 'document retrieval' or 'text retrieval' or 'information retrieval.' Set 13 (S13) will contain all records containing the term 'OPAC' or the phrase 'online public access catalog.' The '?' is a truncation operator, and '? ?' limits truncation to one letter, so alternate spellings and plural of 'catalog' and the singular or plural of 'OPAC' will be retrieved. The two sets are combined with a Boolean AND operator, and finally the set is further limited to records that contain the terms in the title (`ti`) or descriptor (`de`) field, resulting in 100 records for review.

```
begin 61
File  61:LISA(LIBRARY&INFOSCI)  1969-1998/May
      (c) 1998 Reed Reference Publishing

      Set  Items  Description
      ---  -----  -----------
? ss (document or information or text)(w)retrieval
      S1    7363  DOCUMENT
      S2   92299  INFORMATION
      S3    6219  TEXT
      S4   29302  RETRIEVAL
      S5   15338  (DOCUMENT OR INFORMATION OR TEXT)(W)RETRIEVAL
? ss opac? ? or online(w)public(w)access(w)catalog?
      S6    1111  OPAC? ?
      S7   20922  ONLINE
      S8   32238  PUBLIC
      S9   16388  ACCESS
     S10   18798  CATALOG?
     S11     424  ONLINE(W)PUBLIC(W)ACCESS(W)CATALOG?
     S12    1246  OPAC? ? OR ONLINE(W)PUBLIC(W)ACCESS(W)CATALOG?
? s s5 and s12
           15338  S5
            1246  S12
     S13     146  S5 AND S12
? s s13/ti,de
     S14     100  S13/TI,DE
```

Figure 14.6   A DIALOG search.

14.2.4 'Natural Language' Searching

To ensure their place in the market, database vendors continually develop new features that they feel will be of value to their client group, as well as add new database products. In general, these new features are augmentations to the existing Boolean search engine — removal of duplicates, sophisticated ranking or sorting within the retrieved set. However, about five years ago several of the major database vendors announced they were adding 'natural language' search functionality to their systems. WESTLAW (a legal resources vendor) introduced its WIN system, DIALOG offered TARGET, and LEXIS-NEXIS announced a system called FREESTYLE [758, 653]. WIN and FREESTYLE accept a natural language query; TARGET requires the searcher to eliminate terms that are not useful for searching. All three systems provide ranked lists of retrieved documents. The 'natural language' systems are offered as auxiliary modules to standard Boolean searching, and are not intended to replace it. A sample TARGET search is shown in Figure 14.7.

In this search in BIOSIS, the searcher is first provided with a series of instructions on dealing with phrases, synonyms, etc. The searcher enters a series of search terms (up to 25) at the '?' prompt, in this case 'komodo dragon food

```
? target
Input search terms separated by spaces (e.g., DOG CAT FOOD). You
can enhance your TARGET search with the following options:
   - PHRASES are enclosed in single quotes
       (e.g., 'DOG FOOD')
   - SYNONYMS are enclosed in parentheses
       (e.g., (DOG CANINE))
   - SPELLING variations are indicated with a ?
       (e.g., DOG?  to search DOG, DOGS)
   - Terms that MUST be present are flagged with an asterisk
       (e.g., DOG *FOOD)
Q = QUIT   H = HELP
? komodo dragon food diet nutrition
Your TARGET search request will retrieve up to 50 of the
statistically most relevant records.
Searching 1997-1998 records only
...Processing Complete
     Your search retrieved 50 records.
Press ENTER to browse results  C = Customize display  Q = QUIT
H = HELP
```

Figure 14.7   A TARGET search on DIALOG.

diet nutrition'. By default the search is limited to the most recent two years of the file, and the 50 highest scoring records are available for display in ranked order. In this example no restrictions are made on the search terms but as the on-screen instructions indicate, Boolean logic can be imposed on the search terms, resulting in a Boolean search with ranked output.

14.3   Online Public Access Catalogs (OPACs)

Library catalogs serve as lists of the library's holdings, organized as finding tools for the collection. For many years the card catalog served this function, and later computer-produced catalogs in book, microfilm, and microfiche form. Online catalogs were implemented in libraries during the 1970s, although these first catalogs were usually modules linked to the automated circulation system and had brief catalog records and very limited functionality. (The circulation system was the first component of what are now called library management systems (LMSs) or integrated library systems (ILSs) to be introduced). By the 1980s, true online public access catalogs had been implemented.

Hildreth [372] has described the history of online catalogs by classifying them according to three generations. In the first generation, OPACs were largely known-item finding tools, typically searchable by author, title, and control number, and contained relatively short, non-standard bibliographic records. As is typical of technologies in their infancy, they were basically an old technology (the card catalog) in an automated form. In the second generation, increased search functionality included access by subject headings and, latterly, keyword, some basic Boolean search capability, and ability to browse subject headings. Second generation catalogs also offered a choice of display formats (e.g., short, medium, long) and improved usability (for instance, different dialogs for novices and experts, more informative error messages, etc.). According to Hildreth, problems with second generation systems included failed searches, navigational confusion, problems with the subject indexing vocabulary and excessively large, badly organized retrieval sets.

Needed enhancements for third generation systems, as delineated by Hildreth, included search strategy assistance, integrated free text/controlled vocabulary approaches, augmented cataloging records, cross-database access, natural language input, individualized displays and context-sensitive error correction. For many years library catalogs remained on what Hildreth referred to as the 'second generation plateau.' One of the barriers to innovation in OPAC development has been the cost of developing new systems and the need for a reliable customer base. From the perspective of the library, selecting and migrating to a new system is a costly process, and with library budgets traditionally squeezed, libraries have been cautious in selecting new and untried systems. They have learned to be wary of the *'it's in the next release'* syndrome, while system developers have required a stable customer base to fund new systems.

Third generation systems are now appearing, and with features not envisioned by Hildreth, who was speaking in a pre-Web environment. The availability of electronic resources on the Web has blurred the distinction between local and global resources, and between cataloging information and other electronic databases. According to a recent vendor survey [632],

> Automated system vendors have a vested interest in the transition of libraries to a mixed digital/print environment. Many see their own survival dependent upon their ability to help libraries thrive in this mixed arena. (p.47)

Therefore, much of the emphasis in recent library systems development has been on the deployment of functionality for library management systems within new open systems architectures [351]. Features appearing in these new systems include improved graphical user interfaces (GUIs), support for Z39.50, electronic forms, hypertext links and Dublin Core (a developing metadata standard for multimedia materials), and incorporation of Java programming. Systems are also beginning to move beyond the basic Boolean search functionality, and some, like EOSi's Q series (described in section 14.3.3) have advanced search features.

14.3.1 OPACs and Their Content

Libraries use standardized systems for cataloging and classifying the materials (texts and other media) they hold. Typically, they follow the Anglo-American Cataloging Rules to describe these materials, an organizational scheme (such as Library of Congress or the Dewey Decimal Classification) to assign subject codes, and use a subject heading list (such as the Library of Congress Subject

```
00723cam  22002418a 45000010013000000080041000130050017000054
01000180007102000330008904000130012205000026001350820017001610
10000200017824500740019825000120027226000052002843000034003360
50400640037065000041000434
001   0013   97002718
008   0041   970417s1997    ilua    b    001 0 eng
005   0017   19971128134653.1
010   0018    $a    97002718
020   0033    $a0838907075 (acid-free paper)
040   0013    $aDLC$cDLC
050   0026   00$aZ699.35.M28$bH34 1997
082   0017   00$a025.3/16$221
100   0020   1 $aHagler, Ronald.
245   0074   14$aThe bibliographic record and information
             technology / $cRonald Hagler.
250   0012    $a3rd ed.
260   0052    $aChicago :$bAmerican Library Association,$c1997.
300   0034    $axvi, 394 p. :$bill. ;$c24 cm.
504   0064    $aIncludes bibliographical references (p.375-380)
             and index.
650   0041    0$aMachine-readable bibliographic data.#
```

Figure 14.8   Sample MARC record.

Headings) to assign a series of subject descriptors. Given this standardization, cooperative cataloging ventures by library consortia have the potential to lower the cost per unit to catalog library materials, broaden access through shared databases, and facilitate the sharing of materials. Thus library cataloging relies on centralized and shared information through bibliographic utilities such as the Online Computer Library Center (OCLC). (OCLC is also a database vendor with characteristics shown in Figure 14.2.)

The structure that underlies this cooperation among many libraries supporting distinct online catalogs is the MARC Record. MARC (Machine Readable Cataloging Record) is a data format that implements national and international standards, such as the Information Interchange Format (ANSI Z39.2) and the Format for Information Exchange (ISO 2709). With some variations (USMARC, UKMARC, etc.) it is used worldwide. A sample MARC record is shown in Figure 14.8.

The MARC record has three parts: a fixed length (24 character) leader; a record directory showing the 3-digit tag for each field contained in the record with the length of that field in characters; and the data-containing fields and subfields themselves. Subfields are indicated by codes (e.g., '$a') within the field and are specific to each field. For instance, field 260 contains publication information and may have subfields for place, publisher, and date. (To improve readability the record here has been reformatted slightly, so that the field tag (e.g., 001) and field length (e.g., 0013) from the directory are repeated with the data for each field). A recent innovation is the adoption of the 856 field for holdings information to include URLs, allowing the specification of Web hyperlinks.

14.3.2   OPACs and End Users

Probably the greatest challenge for designers of OPACs is to create usable systems. OPACs are found in every type of library, and while users of research libraries might be expected to be knowledgeable about library practices in organizing and accessing information, elsewhere the end user could as easily be a schoolchild, college undergraduate, or patron of a local public library with little or no formal training in library use (what Borgman calls 'perpetual novices' [105]). The underlying record structure (the MARC record) is detailed and complex, and the organizational structures (LCSH, LC classification scheme) are far from intuitive.

The most common type of searching in OPACs is subject searching, and failures by users in topical searching are well documented [484]. Common failures are null sets ('zero results'), or at the other extreme, information overload in which more references are retrieved than can easily be examined [484]. According to one study of transaction logs for the MELVYL catalog [252], 82% of in-library users had a zero retrieval for one or more searches. Interestingly, over 25% of users continued their search through ten or more tries, and another 25% did not appear to retrieve any useful information. Writing in 1986, Borgman [104] raised the question, 'Why are online catalogs hard to use?,' and in 1996, revisited the problem with 'Why are online catalogs *still* hard to use?' [105]. She argues the reason is that they do not incorporate knowledge about user behavior, and place too heavy a burden on the searcher for query specification. Greater contextual assistance for searchers has been suggested by a number of researchers [105, 252, 371].

14.3.3   OPACs: Vendors and Products

The OPAC market is a specialized one, and products are developed and marketed by a limited number of vendors who compete for market position. While it is rare to find a library of any size that does not have a library management system, libraries are constantly in a state of flux, upgrading their systems as old ones become obsolete or unsupported, and introducing new systems. For example, many academic libraries had OPACs based on the venerable mainframe-based NOTIS software, and have undertaken to identify a suitable replacement. Most of the vendors target niche markets: academic libraries, public libraries, and school and special libraries. Profiles of three such vendors are found in Figure 14.9. Fuller details of these and other systems can be found in [351] and [61].

14.3.4   Alternatives to Vendor OPACs

While early OPACs were developed inhouse, sometimes by enthusiastic amateurs at considerable expenditure of time and money, and a significant risk of failure,

- **Endeavor Information Systems, Inc.**

  With a significant academic library clientele, Endeavor has replaced a number of NOTIS systems. Its system, Voyager, is based on a multi-tier architecture with Oracle as the DBMS. The public access client and server are Z39.50 compliant. The search engine supports natural language queries and relevance ranking to display results.
  URL: `http://www.endinfosys.com`

- **Innovative Interfaces, Inc. (III)**

  A large company for this industry, III has an academic library customer base, and also a public library presence. Its newest system, Millennium, is based on its INNOPAC library management system but adds a thin client architecture with modules developed in Java. In addition to its own search engine, INNOPAC uses one licensed from Fulcrum Technologies. In Millennium, relevance ranking is available for full-text searching.
  URL: `http://www.iii.com`

- **EOS International (EOSi)**

  EOSi markets to smaller libraries; it has a large special library clientele plus a significant academic, public, and school library customer base. Its Q series of library management system tools uses a three-tier, client/server architecture. The search engine is Excalibur RetrievalWare, on license from Excalibur Technologies. Standard Boolean searching is available but greater functionality is supplied by natural language entry, dictionary-based query expansion, fuzzy search for bad data, and relevance ranked output.
  URL: `http://www.eosintl.com`

Figure 14.9 Library management system vendors.

today's environment supports turnkey systems developed by a third party. However, there are some instances of systems developed with a research focus for implementation in academic libraries. Notable examples are the Okapi system [416] at City University, London, MARIAN [264] at Virginia Tech, the MELVYL system at the University of California [526], and the Cheshire II system [486] for a UC Berkeley branch library.

The Cheshire II system was designed for the UC Berkeley Mathematics, Statistics and Astronomy library using standards such as Z39.50 and SGML. It provides integrated access to bibliographic, full-text and multimedia resources. The search engine offers both probabilistic ranking and Boolean searches, which can be combined in a single search. Cheshire II was designed as a research as well as an operational environment, and issues such as combining probabilistic and

Boolean models, and design of the client interface to support searching with a variety of Z39.50 servers while minimizing cognitive overload on searchers [486].

14.4   Libraries and Digital Library Projects

Libraries are concerned with enhanced, seamless access to electronic information from all sources. These libraries [351]

> see the library's Web pages, not the OPAC, as the entry point for library users. Through the web pages the user gains access to the library catalog, networked information resources, and locally created information. (p.5)

Through the Web, a single interface can provide access to the local OPAC and reference materials, as well as to remotely accessible databases in the sciences, humanities, and business, including full-text journals, newspapers, and directories. Special collections, in multimedia as well as text formats, become available to the user through the same gateway. Many libraries, particularly academic and large public libraries, have undertaken digital library projects to achieve interoperability, ease of use, and equity of access (see Chapter 15). Two such projects, the Los Angeles Public Library's Virtual Electronic Library project (http://www.lapl.org), and University of Pennsylvania's Digital Library (http://www.library.upenn.edu) are described in [351].

The Web not only provides integration in terms of resources and collections, but the accompanying standards which support interoperability lead to a uniform search architecture. With this approach, the traditional distinction between information retrieval from OPACs and from remote electronic databases is beginning to disappear.

14.5   Trends and Research Issues

With a few exceptions, librarians are consumers of information systems, whether information retrieval systems provided by database vendors, or turnkey OPACs. Even in the digital library environment, their emphasis is on providing integrated access to a diversity of modules for information retrieval. Their interest therefore is in obtaining and using systems which offer ease of integration in their automated environment, and ease of use for themselves and their patrons. The former goal is approached through standards such as SGML and Z39.50, and the development and application of these standards is an important trend in the design of IR systems for libraries. For the latter goal, ease of use, the trend toward user-centered research and design is significant because it offers the potential to answer Borgman's query, 'Why are online catalogs *still* hard to use?' [105]. Much of the recent research interest is in cognitive and behavioral issues (as reviewed in [482]). Developing an understanding of information need, either in general or for a specific client group, has been an important component of this work.

Researchers are also interested in the searching behavior of users. Obviously, there is no single 'user' group, and studies have focused on groups such as trained intermediaries, children, and subject specialists, in both the search service and OPAC environment. One such project conducted over two years is the Getty Online Search Project which studied the end user search behavior of humanities scholars [67]. The interest in end user behavior also extends to an examination of relevance, since an understanding of the criteria by which users determine if retrieved information meets their information need is critical to achieving user-centered design.

14.6   Bibliographic Discussion

The early history of online databases and systems makes interesting reading, and Hahn's 'Pioneers of the Online Age' is a good place to start [331]. The early history of online systems is also described by Bourne [107], and the history of electronic databases by Neufeld and Cornog [600]. The current status of the online industry is profiled annually in the May 1 issue of *Library Journal* (see, for example, [757]).

An overview of research issues in OPACs is provided by Large and Beheshti [482]. A 1996 issue of the *Journal of the American Society for Information Science* was a special topic issue on 'Current Research in Online Public Access Systems' [68]. Comparative information on OPACs (and other library management system software) is readily available. A Council on Library and Information Resources report profiles 12 major vendors and their products [351]. The April 1 issue of *Library Journal* each year includes an 'Automated System Marketplace' update which discusses trends in library management systems, provides company and product information, and tabulates sales. *Library Technology Reports* frequently publishes 'consumer reports' of online systems; for instance, one issue was devoted to a survey of Z39.50 clients [813].

Recent monographs by Allen [13] and Marchionini [542] address the issues of user-centered design and electronic information seeking behavior.

Chapter 15
Digital Libraries

by Edward A. Fox and Ohm Sornil

The benefits of digital libraries will not be appreciated unless they are easy to use effectively. [525]

15.1   Introduction

Information retrieval is essential for the success of digital libraries (DLs), so they can achieve high levels of effectiveness while at the same time affording ease of use to a diverse community. Accordingly, a significant portion of the research and development efforts related to DLs has been in the IR area. This chapter reviews some of these efforts, organizes them into a simple framework, and highlights needs for the future.

Those interested in a broader overview of the field are encouraged to refer to the excellent book by Lesk [501] and the high quality papers in proceedings of the ACM Digital Libraries Conferences. Those more comfortable with online information should refer to *D-Lib Magazine* [280]; the publications of the National Science Foundation (NSF), Defense Advanced Research Projects Agency (DARPA), and National Aeronautics and Space Administration (NASA) 'Research on Digital Libraries Initiative' (DLI) [349]; or online courseware [268]. There also have been special issues of journals devoted to the topic [265, 267, 710]. Recently, it has become clear that a global focus is needed [270] to extend beyond publications that have a regional [55] or national emphasis [221].

Many people's views of DLs are built from the foundation of current libraries [683]. Capture and conversion (digitization) are key concerns [160], but DLs are more than digital collections [634]. It is very important to understand the assumptions adopted in this movement towards DLs [509] and, in some cases, to relax them [29].

Futuristic perspectives of libraries have been a key part of the science fiction literature [811] as well as rooted in visionary statements that led to much of the work in IR and hypertext [135]. DLs have been envisaged since the earliest days of the IR field. Thus, in *Libraries of the Future*, Licklider lays out many of the challenges, suggests a number of solutions, and clearly calls for IR-related efforts [516]. He describes and predicts a vast expansion of the world of publishing, indicating the critical need to manage the record of knowledge, including search, retrieval, and all the related supporting activities. He notes that to handle this problem we have no underlying theory, no coherent representation scheme, no unification of the varied approaches of different computing specialties — and so must tackle it from a number of directions.

After more than 30 years of progress in computing, we still face these challenges and work in this field as a segmented community, viewing DLs from one or another perspective: database management, human-computer interaction (HCI), information science, library science, multimedia information and systems, natural language processing, or networking and communications. As can be seen in the discussion that follows, this practice has led to progress in a large number of separate projects, but has also made interoperability one of the most important problems to solve [624].

Since one of the threads leading to the current interest in DLs came out of discussions of the future of IR [264], since people's needs still leave a rich research agenda for the IR community [197], and since the important role of Web search systems demonstrates the potential value of IR in DLs [711], it is appropriate to see how IR may expand its horizons to deal with the key problems of DLs and how it can provide a unifying and integrating framework for the DL field. Unfortunately, there is little agreement even regarding attempts at integrating database management and text processing approaches [325]. Sometimes, though, it is easier to solve a hard problem if one takes a broader perspective and solves a larger problem. Accordingly we briefly and informally introduce the '5S' model as a candidate solution and a way to provide some theoretical and practical unification for DLs.

We argue that DLs in particular, as well as many other types of information systems, can be described, modeled, designed, implemented, used, and evaluated if we move to the foreground five key abstractions: streams, structures, spaces, scenarios, and societies. 'Streams' have often been used to describe texts, multimedia content, and other sequences of abstract items, including protocols, interactive dialogs, server logs, and human discussions. 'Structures' cover data structures, databases, hypertext networks, and all of the IR constructs such as inverted files, signature files, MARC records (see Chapter 8 for more details), and thesauri. 'Spaces' cover not only 1D, 2D, 3D, virtual reality, and other multidimensional forms, some including time, but also vector spaces, probability spaces, concept spaces, and results of multidimensional scaling or latent-semantic indexing. 'Scenarios' not only cover stories, HCI designs and specifications, and requirements statements, but also describe processes, procedures, functions, services, and transformations — the active and time-spanning aspects of DLs. Scenarios have been essential to our understanding of different DL user communities' needs [525], and are particularly important in connection with social issues [48]. 'Societies' cover these concerns especially regarding authors, librarians, annotators, and other stakeholders. For the sake of brevity we omit further direct discussion of this abstraction, especially since anthropologists, communication researchers, psychologists, sociologists, and others are now engaging in DL research.

Since the 5S model can be used to describe work on databases, HCI, hyperbases, multimedia systems, and networks, as well as other fields related to library and information science, we refer to it below to help unify our coverage and make sure that it encompasses all aspects of DLs. For example, the 5S model in general, and scenarios in particular, may help us move from a paper-centered framework for publishing and communicating knowledge [195] to a hybrid paper/electronic one with a variety of streams and spaces. The 5S model is a simple way to organize our thinking and understand some of the changes that DLs will facilitate:

> The boundaries between authors, publishers, libraries, and readers evolved partly in response to technology, particularly the difficulty and expense of creating and storing paper documents. New technologies can shift the balance and blur the boundaries. [525]

To ground these and other subsequent discussions, then, we explore a number of definitions of DLs, using 5S to help us see what is missing or emphasized in each.

15.2   Definitions

Since DL is a relatively new field, many workshops and conferences continue to have sessions and discussions to define a 'digital library' [266, 347]. Yet, defining DLs truly should occur in the context of other related entities and practices [315]. Thus, a 'digital archive' is like a DL, but often suggests a particular combination of space and structure, and emphasizes the scenario of preservation, as in 'digital preservation' that is based upon digitization of artifacts. Similarly, 'electronic preservation' calls for media migration and format conversions to make DLs immune to degradation and technological obsolescence. Maintaining 'integrity' in a DL requires ensuring authenticity, handled by most regular libraries, as well as consistency, which is a concern whenever one must address replication and versioning, as occurs in database systems and in distributed information systems.

While these concerns are important, we argue that 'DL' is a broader concept. Because it is true that the 'social, economic, and legal questions are too important to be ignored in the research agenda in digital libraries' [525], we really prefer definitions that have communities of users (societies) as part of a DL:

> DLs are constructed — collected and organized — by a community of users. Their functional capabilities support the information needs and uses of that community. DL is an extension, enhancement, and integration of a variety of information institutions as physical places where resources are selected, collected, organized, preserved, and accessed in support of a user community. [48]

This definition has many aspects relating to 5S, but largely omits streams, and only indirectly deals with spaces by calling for extensions beyond physical places. Its coverage of scenarios is weak, too, only giving vague allusion to user support. In contrast, definitions that emphasize functions and services are of particular importance to the development community [299], as are definitions concerned with distributed multimedia information systems:

> The generic name for federated structures that provide humans both intellectual and physical access to the huge and growing worldwide networks of information encoded in multimedia digital formats. [97]

While brief, this definition does tie closely with 5S, though it is weak on scenarios, only mentioning the vague and limited concept of 'access.'

To the IR community a DL can be viewed as an extended IR system, in the context of federation and media variations [48]. Also, DLs must support (large) collections of documents, searching, and cataloging/indexing. They bring together in one place all aspects of 5S, and many of the concerns now faced by IR researchers: multilingual processing, search on multimedia content, information visualization, handling large distributed collections of complex documents, usability, standards, and architectures, all of which are explored in the following sections.

15.3   Architectural Issues

Since DLs are part of the global information infrastructure, many discussions of them focus on high level architectural issues [611]. On the one hand, DLs can be just part of the 'middleware' of the Internet, providing various services that can be embedded in other task-support systems. In this regard they can be treated separately from their content, allowing development to proceed without entanglement in problems of economics, censorship, or other social concerns.

On the other hand, DLs can be independent systems and so must have an architecture of their own in order to be built. Thus, many current DLs are cobbled together from pre-existing pieces, such as search engines, Web browsers, database management systems, and tools for handling multimedia documents.

From either perspective, it is helpful to extend definitions into more operational forms that can lead to specification of protocols when various components are involved. Such has been one of the goals of efforts at the Corporation for National Research Initiatives (CNRI), as illustrated in Figure 15.1.

Thus, Kahn and Wilensky proposed one important framework [426]. Arms *et al.* have extended this work into DL architectures [28, 31]. One element is a digital object, which has content (bits) and a handle (a type of name or identifier) [189], and also may have properties, a signature, and a log of transactions that involve it. Digital objects have associated metadata, that can be managed in sets [472]. Repositories of digital objects can provide security and can respond to a repository access protocol [30]. Significant progress has been made toward adopting a scheme of digital object identifiers, first illustrated by the Online

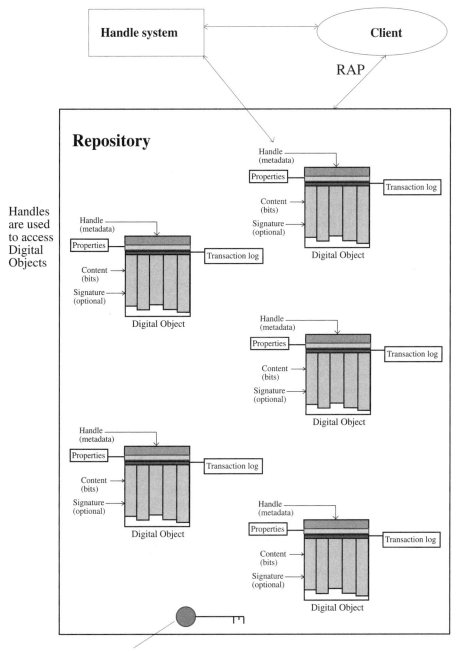

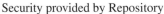

Figure 15.1 Digital objects, handles, and repositories (adapted from [426, 28, 31, 30]).

Computer Library Center, Inc. (OCLCs) Persistent URLs (PURLs) [654], and agreement seems likely on a standard for Digital Object Identifiers (DOIs) [396].

Other implementation efforts have focused more on services [473] and security [475]. A useful testbed for this work has been computer science reports [210], most recently through the Networked Computer Science Technical Reference Library, NCSTRL [471].

Two large Digital Libraries Initiative (DLI) projects have devoted a good deal of attention to architecture, taking radically different approaches. At Stanford, the key concern has been interoperability [624]. Their 'InfoBus' [625] allows a variety of information resources to be connected through suitable mediators and then used via the shared bus through diverse interfaces. At the University of Michigan, the emphasis has been on agent technologies [97]. This approach can have a number of classes of entities involved in far-flung distributed processing. It is still unknown how efficiently an agent-based DL can operate or even be built.

Ultimately, software to use in DLs will be selected as a result of comparisons. One basis for such comparisons is the underlying conceptual model [820]. Another basis is the use of metrics, which is the subject of recent efforts towards definition and consensus building [499]. In addition to metrics traditionally used in IR, dealing with efficiency, effectiveness, and usability, a variety of others must be selected, according to agreed-upon scenarios. Also important to understand is the ability of DLs to handle a variety of document types (combinations of streams and structures), to accurately and economically represent their content and relationships (structures), and to support a range of access approaches and constraints (scenarios).

15.4   Document Models, Representations, and Access

Without documents there would be no IR or DLs. Hence, it is appropriate to consider definitions of 'document' [709], and to develop suitable formalizations [508], as well as to articulate research concerns [505]. For efficiency purposes, especially when handling millions of documents and gigabytes, terabytes, or petabytes of space, compression is crucial [825]. While that is becoming more manageable, converting very large numbers of documents using high quality representations [151] can be prohibitively expensive, especially relative to the costs of retrieval, unless items are popular. All of these matters relate to the view of a document as a stream (along with one or more organizing structures); alternatively one can use scenarios to provide focus on the usage of documents. These problems shift, and sometimes partially disappear, when one considers the entire life cycle and social context of a document [124, 353] or when DLs become an integral part of automation efforts that deal with workflow and task support for one or more document collections.

15.4.1   Multilingual Documents

One social issue with documents relates to culture and language [633]. Whereas there are many causes of the movement toward English as a basis for global scientific and technical interchange, DLs may actually lead to an increase in availability of non-English content. Because DLs can be constructed for a particular institution or nation, it is likely that the expansion of DLs will increase access to documents in a variety of languages. Some of that may occur since many users of information desire it from all appropriate sources, regardless of origin, and so will wish to carry out a parallel (federated) search across a (distributed) multilingual collection.

The key aspects of this matter are surveyed in [613]. At the foundation, there are issues of character encoding. Unicode provides a single 16-bit coding scheme suitable for all natural languages [783]. However, a less costly implementation may result from downloading fonts as needed from a special server or gateway, or from a collection of such gateways, one for each special collection [208].

The next crucial problem is searching multilingual collections. The simplest approach is to locate words or phrases in dictionaries and to use the translated terms to search in collections in other languages [387]. However, properly serving many users in many languages calls for more sophisticated processing [612]. It is likely that research in this area will continue to be of great importance to both the IR and DL communities.

15.4.2 Multimedia Documents

From the 5S perspective, we see that documents are made up of one or more streams, often with a structure imposed (e.g., a raster organization of a pixel stream represents a color image). Multimedia documents' streams usually must be synchronized in some way, and so it is promising that a new standard for handling this over the Web has been adopted [379].

At the same time, as discussed in Chapters 11 and 12, IR has been applied to various types of multimedia content. Thus, at Columbia University, a large image collection from the Web can be searched on content using visual queries [158]. IBM developed the *Query By Image Content* (QBIC) system for images and video [257] and has generously helped build a number of important image collections to preserve and increase access to key antiquities [300].

Similarly, the Carnegie Mellon University DLI project, Informedia [146], has focused on video content analysis, word spotting, summarization, search, and in-context results presentation [146]. Better handling of multimedia is at the heart of future research on many types of documents in DLs [354]. Indeed, to properly handle the complexity of multimedia collections, very powerful representation, description, query and retrieval systems, such as those built upon logical inference [283], may be required.

15.4.3 Structured Documents

While multimedia depends on the stream abstraction, structured documents require both the abstractions of streams and structures. Indeed, structured documents in their essence are streams with one or more structures imposed, often by the insertion of markup in the stream, but sometimes through a separate external structure, like pointers in hypertext.

Since Chapter 6 of this book covers many of the key issues of document structure, we focus in this section on issues of particular relevance to DLs [288]. For example, since DLs typically include both documents and metadata describing them, it is important to realize that metadata as in MARC records can be represented as an SGML document (see Chapter 6 for more details) and that SGML content can be included in the base document and/or be kept separately [293].

Structure is often important in documents when one wants to add value or make texts 'smart' [167]. It can help identify important concepts [626]. SGML is often used to describe structure since most documents fall into one or more common logical structures [750], that can be formally described using a Document Type Definition (DTD). Another type of structure that is important in DLs, as well as earlier paper forms, results from annotation [548]. In this case stream and structure are supplemented by scenarios since annotations result from users interacting with a document collection, as well as collaborating with each other through these shared artifacts [680].

Structure is also important in retrieval. Macleod was one of the first to describe special concerns related to IR involving structured documents [533]. Searching on structure as well as content remains one of the distinguishing advantages of IR systems like OpenText (formerly 'PAT' [38]). Ongoing work considers retrieval with structured documents, such as with patterns and hierarchical texts [439]. An alternative approach, at the heart of much of the work in the Berkeley DLI project [775], shifts the burden of handling structure in documents to the user, by allowing multiple layers of filters and tools to operate on so-called 'multivalent documents' [774]. Thus, a page image including a table can be analyzed with a table tool that understands the table structure and sorts it by considering the values in a user-selected column.

Structure at the level above documents, that is, of collections of documents, is what makes searching necessary and possible. It also is a defining characteristic of DLs, especially when the collections are distributed.

15.4.4   Distributed Collections

Though our view of DLs encompasses even those that are small, self-contained, and constrained to a personal collection with a suitable system and services, most DLs are spread across computers, that is spanning physical and/or logical spaces. Dealing with collections of information that are distributed in nature is one of the common requirements for DL technology. Yet, proper handling of such collections is a challenging problem, possibly since many computer scientists are poorly equipped to think about situations involving spaces as well as the other aspects of 5S.

Of particular concern is working with a number of DLs, each separately constructed, so the information systems are truly heterogeneous. Integration requires support for at least some popular scenarios (often a simple search that

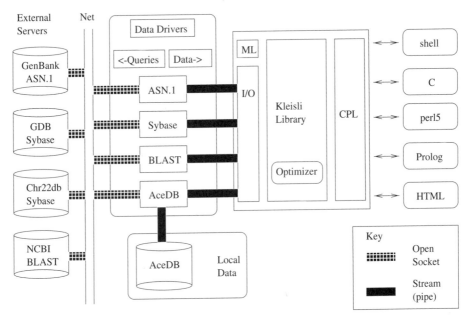

Figure 15.2 Architecture of the BioKleisli system (adapted from [829, 128]).

is a type of least common denominator) by systems that expect differing types of communication streams (e.g., respond to different protocols and query languages), have varying types of streams and structures, and combine these two differently in terms of representations of data and metadata. To tackle this problem, one approach has been to develop a description language for each DL and to build federated search systems that can interpret that description language [161].

However, when DL content is highly complex (e.g., when there are 'unstructured' collections, meaning that the structure is complex and not well described), there is need for richer description languages and more powerful systems to interpret and support highly expressive queries/operations [828, 209, 128]. An architecture of this type is illustrated in Figure 15.2 for the BioKleisli system [829].

In addition to these two approaches – namely reducing functionality for end users in order to give DL developers more freedom and increasing functionality by making the federated system smarter and able to use more computational resources on both servers and clients – there is the third approach of making each DL support a powerful protocol aimed at effective retrieval. This third course is supported by the Computer Interchange of Museum Information (CIMI) effort [570], wherein a Z39.50 interface exists on a number of museum information servers and clients [570]. While Z39.50 was aimed at the needs of libraries desiring interoperability among library catalogs, it does support many of the needs for DLs. Thus, the CIMI interoperability demonstration, with its support for multimedia content, is of great import, but does leave open further improvement in supporting richer DL interaction scenarios, involving more powerful federated searchers.

15.4.5 Federated Search

Federated search work has often been prompted by challenging application requirements. For example, to allow computer science technical reports from around the world to become accessible with minimal investment and maximal local control, the NSF-funded Wide Area TEchnical Report Service (WATERS)initiative was launched [279]. This was then integrated with an effort begun earlier with DARPA funding, the Computer Science Technical Report (CSTR) project [260], leading to a hybrid effort, the Networked CS Technical Reference (previously, Report) Library (NCSTRL) [471]. At the heart of NCSTRL is a simple search system, a well-thought-out open federated DL protocol and the Dienst reference implementation, developed at Cornell University [210]. While this system was custom-built with little dependence on other software, its type of operation could be constructed more rapidly atop various supports like CORBA [788].

Federated search has had an interesting history, with workers adopting a variety of approaches. First, there are those interested in collecting the required information, often through Web crawling of various sorts [715]. Second, there are those focusing on intelligent search [27]. One example is work emphasizing picking the best sites to search [126]. These efforts often assume some integrated information organization across the distributed Internet information space [393].

Third, there is work on fusion of results. This can be viewed in the abstract, regardless of whether the various collections are nearby or distributed, with the target of improving retrieval by culling from a number of good sources [76]. One approach adopts a probabilistic inference network model [139]. Another views the problem as database merging [791]. Alternatively, one can assume that there are a number of search engines distributed to cover the collection, that must be used intelligently [292].

Fourth, there are commercial solutions, including through special Web services [223]. Probably the most visible is the patented, powerful yet elegant, approach by Infoseek Corporation [394].

Finally, there is a new line of work to develop comprehensive and realistic architectures for federated search [219, 218]. The long-term challenge is to segment the collection and/or its indexes so that most searches only look at a small number of the most useful sources of information, yet recall is kept high. Ultimately, however, there are rich types of use of DL content, once one of these approaches to search is carried out.

15.4.6 Access

When priceless objects are described by DL image collections [300], when collections are large and/or well organized so as to appear of value to communities of users, or when there are valuable services in information manipulation (searching, ordering, reporting, summarizing, etc.) afforded by a DL, some method of payment is often required [194, 191, 49, 251]. Though previously access to scientific literature was not viewed as a commodity as it is today [328], DLs clearly must manage intellectual property [559]. These services must support agreed-upon principles [586], copyright practices [705], as well as contracts and other agreements and laws [346].

Though technology is only part of the picture [822], a key to the implementation of policies for access management [30] is having trusted systems [746]. Security is one topic often ignored by the IR community. However, many aspects of security can be of fundamental importance in DLs [302, 301]. Just as encryption is essential to support electronic commerce, watermarking and stronger mechanisms are crucial in DLs to protect intellectual property rights and to control the types of access afforded to different user groups. Scenarios are important here, to ensure that suitable constraints are imposed on processing, all the way from input to output. For example, secret documents may not even be made visible in searches through metadata. On the other hand, advertising full documents as well as allowing locating and viewing metadata records is appropriate when the purpose of security is to enforce payment in 'pay by the drink' document downloading systems. Inference systems can be used for complicated rights management situations [16]. A deeper understanding of these requirements and services can be obtained by considering representative DL projects, such as those mentioned in the next section.

15.5   Prototypes, Projects, and Interfaces

Though numerous efforts in the IR, hypertext, multimedia, and library automation areas have been underway for years as precursors of today's DL systems, one of the first new efforts aimed at understanding the requirements for DLs and constructing a prototype from scratch was the ENVISION project, launched in 1991 [269]. Based on discussions with experts in the field and a careful study of prospective users of the computer science collection to be built with the assistance of ACM, the ENVISION system was designed to extend the MARIAN search system [264] with novel visualization techniques [273, 360]. Careful analysis has shown its 2D approach to management of search results is easy to use and effective for a number of DL activities [610].

The CORE project, another early effort, is an electronic library prototype on chemical journal articles. Its collection included, for each article, both scanned images and an SGML marked-up version, as well as indexes for full-text Boolean searching. It was undertaken by the American Chemical Society, Chemical Abstracts Service, OCLC, Bellcore, and Cornell University, along with other partners [237]. This project also was concerned with collection building as well as testing of a variety of interfaces that were designed based on user studies.

One of the most visible project efforts is the Digital Libraries Initiative, initially supported by NSF, DARPA, and NASA [349]. Phase 1 provided funding for six large projects over the period 1994–1998. These projects spanned a wide range of major topics in developing the National Information Infrastructure (NII) and addressed future technological problems. The Illinois project [777] focused on manually structured text documents in full systems with many users; the Berkeley project [775] emphasized automatically recognized image documents, also with large systems. The Santa Barbara [776] and Carnegie Mellon [146] projects investigated the ability to manipulate new media; Carnegie Mellon focused on segmenting and indexing video using speech recognition and program structure, and Santa Barbara concentrated on indexing maps using image processing and region metadata. Stanford [745] and Michigan [784] investigated the intermediaries to perform operations on large digital libraries; Stanford investigated interoperability of different search services, and Michigan concentrated on interacting software agents to provide services to users [710].

Since these projects have been described elsewhere in depth, it should suffice here to highlight some of the connections of those projects with the IR community. First, each project has included a component dealing with document collections. The Illinois project produced SGML versions of a number of journals while the Berkeley project concentrated on page images and other image classes. Santa Barbara adopted a spatial perspective, including satellite imagery, while Carnegie Mellon University (CMU) focused on video. Stanford built no collections, but rather afforded access to a number of information sources to demonstrate interoperability. At the University of Michigan, some of the emphasis was on having agents dynamically select documents from a distributed set of resources.

Second, the DLI projects all worked on search. Text retrieval, and using automatically constructed cross-vocabulary thesauri to help find search terms, was emphasized in Illinois. Image searching was studied at Berkeley and Santa Barbara while video searching was investigated at CMU. Michigan worked with agents for distributed search while Stanford explored the coupling of a variety of architectures and interfaces for retrieval.

Finally, it is important to note that the DLI efforts all spent time on interface issues. Stanford used animation and data flows to provide flexible manipulation and integration of services [192]. At Michigan, there were studies of the PAD++ approach to 2D visualization [70]. Further discussion of interfaces can be found below in subsection 15.5.2.

It should be noted that these projects only partially covered the 5S issues. Structures were not well studied, except slightly in connection with the Illinois work on SGML and the Berkeley work on databases. Scenarios were largely ignored, except in some of the interface investigations. Similarly, spaces were not investigated much, except in connection with the vocabulary transfer work at Illinois and the spatial collection and browsing work at Santa Barbara. Other projects in the broader international scene, some of which are discussed in the next section, may afford more thorough 5S coverage.

Since the announcement of DLI, activities and interest related to digital libraries have increased dramatically. The six DLI projects were highly visible and grew in scope; however, it was quickly realized that DLI still needed additional direction and coherence. During the initial funding period of the DLI program, additional workshops were created to develop consensus on the directions and boundaries with discussions from various communities. An important aspect that many people realized from the workshops is the importance of efforts in domains outside computer and information science to the advances in digital libraries research [324].

A follow-on program, Digital Libraries Initiative – Phase 2 (DLI-2), jointly supported by NSF, DARPA, NASA, the National Library of Medicine (NLM), the Library of Congress (LoC), the National Endowment for the Humanities (NEH), and others, was announced in the spring of 1998 focus less on technology research than DLI, but, more importantly, supporting research across the information life cycle, from content creation, access, and use to preservation and archiving, moving towards the concept of digital libraries as human-centered systems. DLI-2 will emphasize the study of interactions between digital libraries and humans, fuller understanding of and improving access to digital content and collections, and interoperability and integration toward flexible information environments at the level of individual, group, and institution [324, 216]. The program will involve people not only from science and engineering but also from arts and humanities.

15.5.1 International Range of Efforts

DL efforts, accessible over the Internet, can now lead to worldwide access. Since each nation wishes to share the highlights of its history, culture, and accomplishments with the rest of the world, developing a DL can be very helpful [86]. Indeed, we see many nations with active DL programs [270], and there are many others underway or emerging.

One of the largest efforts is the European ERCIM program [239]. This is enhanced by the large eLib initiative in the UK [778]. There are good results from activities in New Zealand [601] and Australia [389]. In Singapore, billions are being invested in developing networked connectivity and digital libraries as part of educational innovation programs [729]. For information on other nations, see the online table pointing to various national projects associated with a recent special issue on this topic [270].

As mentioned briefly above, many nations around the world have priceless antiquities that can be more widely appreciated through DLs [300]. Whether in pilot mode or as a commercial product, *IBM Digital Library* [390], with its emphasis on rights management, has been designed and used to help in this regard.

These projects all require multimedia and multilingual support, as discussed earlier. Different scenarios of use are appropriate in different cultures, and different structures and spaces are needed for various types of collections. Indeed, many international collections aim for global coverage, but with other criteria defining their focus. Thus, the Networked Digital Library of Theses and Dissertations (NDLTD) [594] is open to all universities, as well as other supporting organizations, with the aim of providing increased access to scholarly resources as a direct result of improving the skills and education of graduate students, who directly submit their works to the DL.

15.5.2 Usability

Key to the success of DL projects is having usable systems. This is a serious challenge! Simple library catalog systems were observed in 1986 to be difficult to use [104], and still remain so after a further decade of research and development [105].

The above mentioned ENVISION project's title began with the expression 'User-Centered' and concentrated most of its resources on work with the interface [360]. A 1997 study at Virginia Tech of four digital library systems concluded that many have serious usability problems [434], though the design of the Illinois DLI system seemed promising. The Virginia Tech study uncovered an important aspect of the situation, and suggested that it will be years before DL systems are properly understood and used. A pre-test asked about user expectations for a DL, and found that very few had worked with a DL. The post-test showed that user expectations and priorities for various features changed dramatically over the short test period. Thus, it is likely that in general, as DL usage spreads, there will be an increase in understanding, a shift in what capabilities users expect, and a variety of extensions to the interfaces now considered.

Early in the DLI work, DL use was perceived as a research focus [98], and understanding and assessing user needs became a key concern [382]. For two years, a workshop was held at the Allerton conference center of the University of Illinois on this topic. Since the 1995 event [313] had a diverse group of researchers, it was necessary to understand the various perspectives and terminologies. There were discussions of fundamental issues, such as information, from a human factors perspective [214], as well as specific explorations of tasks like document browsing [528].

The 1996 event was more focused due to greater progress in building and studying usability of DLs [314]. Thus, there was discussion of Stanford's Sense-Maker system which supports rapid shifting between contexts that reflect stages of user exploration [51]. Social concerns that broaden the traditional IR perspective were highlighted [367]. In addition, there was movement towards metrics (see discussion earlier about DL metrics) and factors for adopting DLs [429].

DL interfaces and usability concerns have been central to many efforts at Xerox PARC. Some of the research considers social issues related to documents [354] while other research bridges the gap between paper and digital documents [353]. There are many issues about documents, especially their stability and how multimedia components as well as active elements affect retrieval, preservation, and other DL activities [506]. Some insight into DL use may result from actual user observation as well as other measures of what (parts of) documents are read [507]. There also has been collaboration between PARC and the UCB DLI team, which has extended the Xerox magic filter work into multivalent documents (discussed earlier) as well as having developed results visualization methods like

TileBars where it is easy to spot the location of term matches in long documents [355].

Further work is clearly needed in DL projects to improve the systems and their usability. But for these systems to work together, there also must be some emphasis on standards.

15.6   Standards

Since there are many DL projects worldwide, involving diverse research, development, and commercial approaches, it is imperative that standards are employed so as to make interoperability and data exchange possible. Since by tradition any library can buy any book, and any library patron can read anything in the library, DLs must make differences in representation transparent to their users. In online searching as well, data that can be understood by clients as well as other DLs should be what is transferred from each information source. At the heart of supporting federated DLs, especially, is agreement on protocols for computer-computer communication.

15.6.1   Protocols and Federation

In the 1980s it became clear that as library catalog systems proliferated, and library patrons sought support for finding items not locally available through inter-library loan or remote cataloging search, some protocol was needed for searching remote bibliographic collections. The national standard Z39.50, which later became an international standard as well, led to intensive development of implementations and subsequent extensive utilization [515]. One example of widespread utilization was the WAIS system (based on Z39.50), very popular before the World Wide Web emerged. Ongoing development of Z39.50 has continued, including its application to DLs, as demonstrated in the CIMI project described earlier, where a number of different clients and server implementations all worked together.

Also mentioned earlier is the NCSTRL effort, starting with CS technical reports, in which the Dienst protocol was developed [210]. This is a 'lighter' protocol than Z39.50, designed to support federated searching of DLs, but also connected to the centralized preprint service (CoRR) at Los Alamos National Laboratory. Dienst seems suitable for electronic theses and dissertations as well as technical reports, and so it has been considered in regard to NDLTD.

These protocols assume that each server and client will be changed to use the protocol. A less intrusive approach, but one harder to implement and enforce, is to have some mechanism to translate from a special server or gateway system to/from each of the information sources of interest. The STARTS protocol [316] was proposed to move in this direction, but competition among search services on the Internet is so severe that acceptance seems unlikely. Though this is unfortunate, simple federated schemes have been implemented in the DLI projects at Stanford and Illinois, and a simple one is in use in NDLTD. Yet, even more important than new protocols for DL federated search is agreement on metadata schemes, which does seem feasible.

15.6.2 Metadata

In the broadest sense, metadata can describe not only documents but also collections and whole DLs along with their services [50]. In a sense, this reflects movement toward holistic treatment like 5S. Yet in most DL discussions, metadata just refers to a description of a digital object. This is precisely the role played by library catalog records. Hence, cataloging schemes like MARC are a starting point for many metadata descriptions [514].

While MARC has been widely used, it usually involves working with binary records which must be converted for interchange. One alternative is to encode MARC records using some readable coding scheme, like SGML [293]. Another concern with MARC is that there are a number of national versions with slight differences, as well as differences in cataloging practices that yield the MARC records. USMARC is one such version. It is very important in the DL field, and can be encoded using SGML, or easily converted to simpler metadata schemes like the 'Dublin Core' [513]. Other 'crosswalks' exist between Dublin Core (DC), MARC, and schemes like GILS, proposed for a Government Information Locator Service [598]. A mapping also exists between DC and the Z39.50 protocol discussed in the previous section [503].

DC is a simple scheme, with 15 core elements that can be used to describe any digital object. What is of real import is that it has been widely accepted. That is because there have been years of discussion and development, focused around international workshops [806, 620, 560, 833, 333]. The core elements include seven that describe content (Title, Subject, Description, Source, Language, Relation, and Coverage). There are four elements that deal with intellectual property issues (Creator, Publisher, Contributor, and Rights). Finally, to deal with instances of abstract digital objects, there are four other types (Data, Type, Format, and Identifier).

Since digital objects and their metadata often have to be interchanged across systems, the problem of packaging arises. The Warwick Framework, which evolved out of the same type of discussions leading to DC, deals with packages and connections between packages [472]. In general, such discussion about metadata is crucial to allow the move from traditional libraries (with their complex and expensive cataloging), past the Web (with its general lack of cataloging and metadata), to a reasonable environment wherein metadata is available for all sorts of digital objects (suitable to allow the organization of vast collections in DLs [734]).

Because the Web has need of such organization, this has become an interest of its coordinating body, the WWW Consortium [84]. In 1996, as concern increased about protecting children from exposure to objectionable materials, metadata schemes became connected with censoring and filtering requirements. The problem was renamed for the more general case, in keeping with Harvest's treatment of 'resource discovery,' to 'resource description.' The Resource Description Framework (RDF) thus became an area of study for the Consortium [753]. It should be noted that RDF can lead to header information inside digital objects, including those coded in SGML or HTML, as well as XML (see Chapter 6 for more details). In the more general case, however, RDF is essentially a scheme for annotating digital objects, so alternatively the descriptions can be stored separately from those objects. These options bring us back to the Warwick Framework where there may be multiple containers, sometimes connected through indirection, of packages of metadata, like MARC or DC.

We see that DLs can be complex collections with various structuring mechanisms for managing data and descriptions of that data, the so-called metadata. However, coding may combine data with metadata, as is specified in the guidelines of the Text Encoding Initiative (TEI) [670]. This reminds us of the complexities that arise when combining streams and structures, where there are many equivalent representations. We also see that for DL standards to be useful, such as appears to be the case for DC, the structures involved must be relatively simple, and have well understood related scenarios of use. While this now appears to work for data interchange, further work is required for interoperability, i.e., interchange through the streams involved in protocols.

15.7   Trends and Research Issues

There are many remaining challenges in the DL field. While TEI provides guidance in complex encoding situations, and has been advocated by the University of Michigan for electronic theses and dissertations, it is unclear how far the rest of the scholarly community will move towards the thorough markup and description of digital objects that characterize humanistic study [670]. Though such markup is valuable to support context-dependent queries as well as electronic document preservation, it will only be generally feasible when there are less expensive tools and more efficient methods for adding in such markup and description, which may occur as XML usage expands. Then, too, the IR community must provide guidance regarding automatic indexing of marked up documents, metadata, full-text, multimedia streams, and complex hypermedia networks so that the rich and varied content of DLs can be searched.

On a grander scale are the problems of handling worldwide DLs, in the context of varying collection principles, enormous difference in response time between local and remote servers, and the needs of users for different views [474]. Thus, one type of scenario might deal with searching all dissertations worldwide, another might be concerned with finding recent results from a particular research group, a third might consider only freely available works in a particular specialty area, a fourth might deal with seeking the new works recently highly rated by a distributed group of close friends, and yet another might involve the most readable overviews in an unknown area.

Other key research challenges have been highlighted in various workshops aimed at establishing an agenda for investigation [525]. Of central concern is covering the range from personal to global DLs, the so-called 'scaling' problem. At the same time, the problem of interoperability must be faced [624]. As argued earlier, we view the solution to these problems to be the acknowledgement of the role of 5S in the DL arena and the focus of research and development on treating streams, structures, spaces, scenarios, and societies as first class objects and building blocks for DLs. We will continue to explore this approach in future work, and believe that, to the extent that integrated support for 5S is developed, real progress will be made towards the next generation of digital libraries.

15.8   Bibliographical Discussion

As explained in section 15.1, there are many good sources of information about digital libraries. The best pair are the book by Lesk [501] and the online *D-Lib Magazine* [280]. Pointers to the latest information and sources can be found through online courseware [268]. New books will appear from MIT Press and other publishers. Large funding initiatives, programs, and projects (e.g., [216, 778, 349]) involving the US National Science Foundation (see e.g., the call for Digital Libraries Initiative - Phase 2, NSF 98-63, http://www.dli2.nsf.gov) and other sponsors, and becoming more and more international in nature (e.g., International Digital Libraries Collaborative, NSF 99-6, will lead to a continuing stream of reports on workshops (e.g., [266, 313, 314, 333, 833, 525]) and high quality research presentations at premiere events like the ACM Digital Libraries conferences (e.g. [50, 192, 382, 507, 548, 705, 791]).

Acknowledgements

The preparation of this chapter and work described therein was supported in part by US Department of Education grant P116B61190 and by NSF grants CDA-9303152, CDA-9308259, CDA-9312611, DUE-9752190, DUE-975240, and IRI-9116991.

Appendix
Porter's Algorithm

The rules in the Porter algorithm are separated into five distinct phases numbered from 1 to 5. They are applied to the words in the text starting from phase 1 and moving on to phase 5. Further, they are applied sequentially one after the other as commands in a program. Thus, in what follows, we specify the Porter algorithm in a pseudo programming language whose commands take the form of rules for suffix substitution (as above). This pseudo language adopts the following (semi-formal) conventions:

- A consonant variable is represented by the symbol C which is used to refer to any letter other than a,e,i,o,u and other than the letter y preceded by a consonant.

- A vowel variable is represented by the symbol V which is used to refer to any letter which is not a consonant.

- A generic letter (consonant or vowel) is represented by the symbol L.

- The symbol ϕ is used to refer to an empty string (i.e., one with no letters).

- Combinations of C, V, and L are used to define *patterns*.

- The symbol * is used to refer to zero or more repetitions of a given pattern.

- The symbol + is used to refer to one or more repetitions of a given pattern.

- Matched parentheses are used to subordinate a sequence of variables to the operators * and +.

- A generic pattern is a combination of symbols, matched parentheses, and the operators * and +.

- The substitution rules are treated as commands which are separated by a semicolon punctuation mark.

- The substitution rules are applied to the suffixes in the current word.

- A conditional *if* statement is expressed as *'if (pattern) rule'* and the rule is executed only if the pattern in the condition matches the current word.

- A line which starts with a % is treated as a comment.

- Curly brackets (braces) are used to form compound commands.

- A 'select rule with longest suffix' statement selects a single rule for execution among all the rules in a compound command. The rule selected is the one with the largest matching suffix.

Thus, the expression $(C)^*$ refers to a sequence of zero or more consonants while the expression $((V)^*(C)^*)^*$ refers to a sequence of zero or more vowels followed by zero or more consonants which can appear zero or more times. It is important to distinguish the above from the sequence $(V * C)$ which states that a sequence must be present and that this sequence necessarily starts with a vowel, followed by a subsequence of zero or more letters, and finished by a consonant. Finally, the command

$$\text{if } (*V * L) \text{ then ed} \longrightarrow \phi$$

states that the substitution of the suffix ed by nil (i.e., the removal of the suffix ed) only occurs if the current word contains a vowel and at least one additional letter.

The Porter algorithm is applied to each word in the text (simple formulation) and is given by the following procedure.

% *Phase 1: Plurals and past participles.*

select rule with longest suffix {

        sses $\longrightarrow$ ss;
        ies $\longrightarrow$ i;
        ss $\longrightarrow$ ss;
        s $\longrightarrow$ ϕ; }

select rule with longest suffix {

        if $((C)^*((V)^+(C)^+)^+(V)^*\text{eed})$ then eed $\longrightarrow$ ee;
        if $(*V^*\text{ed or } *V^*\text{ing})$ then {

```
select rule with longest suffix {

        ed ⟶ φ;
        ing ⟶ φ; }

    select rule with longest suffix {

            at ⟶ ate;
            bl ⟶ ble;
            iz ⟶ ize;
```

if $((*C_1C_2)$ and $(C_1 = C_2)$ and $(C_1 \notin \{l,s,z\}))$ then $C_1C_2 \longrightarrow C_1$; if $(((C)^*((V)^+(C)^+)C_1V_1C_2)$ and $(C_2 \notin \{w,x,y\}))$ then $C_1V_1C_2 \longrightarrow C_1V_1C_2e$; }

```
        }

    }
```

if $(*V*y)$ then y $\longrightarrow$ i;
if $((C)^*((V)^+(C)^+)^+(V)^*)$ then
select rule with longest suffix {

```
        ational ⟶ ate;
        tional ⟶ tion;
        enci ⟶ ence;
        anci ⟶ ance;
        izer ⟶ ize;
        abli ⟶ able;
        alli ⟶ al;
        entli ⟶ ent;
        eli ⟶ e;
        ousli ⟶ ous;
        ization ⟶ ize;
        ation ⟶ ate;
        ator ⟶ ate;
        alism ⟶ al;
        iveness ⟶ ive;
        fulness ⟶ ful;
        ousness ⟶ ous;
        aliti ⟶ al;
        iviti ⟶ ive;
        biliti ⟶ ble; }
```

if $((C)^*((V)^+(C)^+)^+(V)^*)$ then
select rule with longest suffix {

```
        icate ⟶ ic;
        ative ⟶ φ;
```

alize $\longrightarrow$ al;
iciti $\longrightarrow$ ic;
ical $\longrightarrow$ ic;
ful $\longrightarrow$ ϕ;
ness $\longrightarrow$ ϕ; }

if $((C)^*((V)^+(C)^+)((V)^+(C)^+)^+(V)^*)$ then
select rule with longest suffix {

al $\longrightarrow$ ϕ;
ance $\longrightarrow$ ϕ;
ence $\longrightarrow$ ϕ;
er $\longrightarrow$ ϕ;
ic $\longrightarrow$ ϕ;
able $\longrightarrow$ ϕ;
ible $\longrightarrow$ ϕ;
ant $\longrightarrow$ ϕ;
ement $\longrightarrow$ ϕ;
ment $\longrightarrow$ ϕ;
ent $\longrightarrow$ ϕ;
ou $\longrightarrow$ ϕ;
ism $\longrightarrow$ ϕ;
ate $\longrightarrow$ ϕ;
iti $\longrightarrow$ ϕ;
ous $\longrightarrow$ ϕ;
ive $\longrightarrow$ ϕ;
ize $\longrightarrow$ ϕ;
if (*s or *t) then ion $\longrightarrow$ ϕ; }

select rule with longest suffix {

if $((C)^*((V)^+(C)^+)((V)^+(C)^+)^+(V)^*)$ then e $\longrightarrow$ ϕ;
if $(((C)^*((V)^+(C)^+)(V)^*)$ and not $((*C_1V_1C_2)$ and $(C_2 \notin \{w,x,y\})))$ then e $\longrightarrow$ nil; }

if $((C)^*((V)^+(C)^+)((V)^+(C)^+)^+V^*ll)$ then ll $\longrightarrow$ l;

Glossary

Ad hoc retrieval:

standard retrieval task in which the user specifies his information need through a query which initiates a search (executed by the information system) for documents which are likely to be relevant to the user.

All-pairs or spatial-join query:

a query that requests all the *pairs* of objects that are within the specified distance from their partner.

Amdahl's law:

Using N processors, the maximal speedup S obtainable for a given problem is related to f, the fraction of the problem that must be computed sequentially. The relationship is given by: $S_N \leq \frac{1}{f+(1-f)/N} \leq \frac{1}{f}$

ASCII:

Standard binary codes to represent characters in one byte for most European languages.

Belief network:

a probabilistic model of document retrieval based on interpreting documents, user queries, and index terms as nodes of a Bayesian network. This model is distinct from the inference network model.

Bit-parallelism:

a speed-up technique based on exploiting the fact that the processor performs some operations in parallel over all the bits of the computer word.

Block addressing:

a technique used to reduce the size of the lists of occurrences by pointing to text blocks instead of exact positions.

Boolean model:

a classic model of document retrieval based on classic set theory.

Browsing:

interactive task in which the user is more interested in exploring the document collection than in retrieving documents which satisfy a specific information need.

CACM collection:

a reference collection composed of all the 3204 articles published in the Communications of the ACM from 1958 to 1979.

CISI collection:

a reference collection composed of 1460 documents selected from previous collections assembled at ISI (Institute of Scientific Information).

Clustering:

the grouping of documents which satisfy a set of common properties. The aim is to assemble together documents which are related among themselves. Clustering can be used, for instance, to expand a user query with new and related index terms.

Coding:

the substitution of text symbols by numeric codes with the aim of encrypting or compressing text.

Collection:

a group of items, often documents. In (digital) libraries this designates all the works included, usually selected based on a collection management plan.

Compression of text:

the study of techniques for representing text in fewer bytes or bits.

Content-based query:

query exploiting data content.

Conversion:

changing from one form to another, as in converting from analog to digital (also called 'digitization'), or paper to online (as in 'retrospective conversion' of a card catalog to an online catalog, or old books to scanned images).

Cystic Fibrosis collection:

a reference collection composed of 1239 documents indexed with the term *cystic fibrosis* in the National Library of Medicine's MEDLINE database.

Data cartridge:

data structure and associated methods to represent and query a particular multimedia data type.

Data mining:

extraction of new data, relations, or partial information from any type of data.

Data retrieval:

the retrieval of items (tuples, objects, Web pages, documents) whose contents satisfy the conditions specified in a (regular expression like) user query.

Database industry:

the organizations, including commercial, government, and not-for-profit sectors, who produce, provide access to, and market databases of bibliographic, reference, and full-text information.

Database producers:

the organizations, including commercial, government, and not-for-profit sectors, who create electronic abstracting and indexing tools as well as other reference and full-text databases.

Database vendors:

the organizations, primarily in the commercial and not-for-profit sectors, who license databases from their producers and provide search software and a front end for consumer access to the information contained.

Digital library:

the combination of a collection of digital objects (repository); descriptions of those objects (metadata); a set of users (patrons or target audience or users); and systems that offer a variety of services such as capture, indexing, cataloging, search, browsing, retrieval, delivery, archiving, and preservation.

Digital object:

a string of bits that is viewed as an entity in its own right (e.g., a full-text document) though it may be a part of another digital object (e.g., an image that is part of a book), often with associated 'metadata' and sometimes with terms and conditions (especially on access).

Digital preservation:

ensuring that a digital object continues to be accessible and useful over a long period of time, which usually requires both media conversion (copying from one old tape format to a new tape format before the old tapes are no longer readable) and format conversion (changing from some file structure or encoding to a newer one that will continue to be used and understood).

Directory:

a usually hierarchical categorization of concepts in a domain of knowledge.

Distributed computing:

the application of multiple computers connected by a network to solve a single problem.

Distributed information retrieval:

the application of distributed computing techniques to solve information retrieval problems.

DLI:

Digital Libraries Initiative, a program of the US National Science Foundation, for research and development related to digital libraries, which began with $24M of funding split across six universities for 1994-98, and which will continue from 1998 onward with roughly double that amount of support

Document:

a unit of retrieval. It might be a paragraph, a section, a chapter, a Web page, an article, or a whole book.

Document surrogate:

a representation of a document such as the title and a short summary. Surrogates are commonly used to display the answers to a user query.

DTD:

Document Type Definition: SGML definition for a markup language.

E measure:

an information retrieval performance measure, distinct from the harmonic mean, which combines recall and precision.

Edit distance:

(between two strings): minimum number of insertions, deletions, and replacements of characters necessary to make two strings equal.

Efficiency:

a measure of parallel algorithm performance given by: $\phi = \frac{S}{N}$, where S is speedup and N is the number of processors.

Entropy:

measure of information defined on the statistics on the characters of a text.

Exact match:

mechanism by which only the objects satisfying some well specified criteria, against object attributes, are returned to the user as a query answer.

Extended Boolean model:

a set theoretic model of document retrieval based on an extension of the classic Boolean model. The idea is to interpret partial matches as Euclidean distances represented in a vectorial space of index terms.

Extended pattern:

a general pattern allowing rich expressions such as wild cards, classes of characters, and others.

Faceted query:

a query which is divided into topics and/or facets, each of which should be present in documents in the answer.

Feature:

information extracted from an object and used during query processing.

Federated search:

support for finding items that are scattered among a distributed collection of information sources or services, typically involving sending queries to a number of servers and then merging the results to present in an integrated, consistent, coordinated format.

Filtering:

retrieval task in which the information need of the user is relatively static while *new* documents constantly enter the system. Typical examples are news wire services and electronic mail lists.

Full text:

a logical view of the documents in which all the words which compose the text of the document are used as indexing terms.

Fuzzy model:

a set theoretic model of document retrieval based on fuzzy theory.

Generalized vector space model:

a generalization of the classic vector model based on a less restrictive interpretation of term-to-term independence.

Global analysis:

a reference to techniques of identifying document and term relationships through the analysis of all the documents in a collection. Global analysis is used, for instance, to build thesauri.

Granularity:

the amount of computation relative to the amount of communication performed by a parallel program.

Guided tour:

a sequence of navigational choices (usually in a hypertext) aimed at presenting the nodes in a logical order for some goal.

Harmonic mean:

an information retrieval performance measure which combines recall and precision.

Heaps' Law:

an empirical rule which describes the vocabulary growth as a function of the text size. It establishes that a text of n words has a vocabulary of size $O(n^\beta)$ for $0 < \beta < 1$.

HTML:

hypertext markup language of the Web, based on SGML.

Huffman coding:

an algorithm for coding text in which the most frequent symbols are represented by the shortest codes.

Human-Computer Interfaces (HCI):

the study of interfaces which assist the user with information seeking related tasks such as: query formulation, selection of information sources, understanding of search results, and tracking of the retrieval task.

Hypertext model:

a model of information retrieval based on representing document relationships as edges of a generic graph in which the documents are the nodes.

Independence of index terms:

see *Term-to-term independence.*

Index:

a data structure built on the text to speed up searching.

Index point:

the initial position of a text element which can be searched for, for example a word.

Index term (or keyword):

a pre-selected term which can be used to refer to the content of a document. Usually, index terms are nouns or noun groups. In the Web, however, some search engines use all the words in a document as index terms.

Inference network:

a probabilistic model of document retrieval based on interpreting documents, user queries, and index terms as nodes of a Bayesian network.

Information retrieval (IR):

part of computer science which studies the retrieval of information (not data) from a collection of written documents. The retrieved documents aim at satisfying a *user information need* usually expressed in natural language.

Information retrieval performance:

an evaluation of an information system in terms of the quality of the answers it generates with regard to a set of test queries. The quality of the answer set is evaluated by comparing the documents in it with those in a set of documents (provided by specialists) known to be relevant to the test query in focus.

Informative feedback:

information to the user about the relationship between the query specification and the documents retrieved.

Interoperability:

the working together of a number of computer systems, typically for a common purpose, such as when a number of digital libraries 'support federated searching,' often enabled by standards and agreed-upon conventions including data formats and protocols.

Intranet:

an Internet type network built inside an organization, which may or may not be connected to the Internet itself.

Inverted file:

a text index composed of a vocabulary and a list of occurrences.

Keyword:

see *Index term.*

Kohonen's feature map:

a bi-dimensional map whose regions represent the main themes in a document or in a collection.

KWIC:

KeyWords In Context, a technique that displays the occurrences of query terms within the context of the documents retrieved.

Latent semantic indexing:

an algebraic model of document retrieval based on a singular value decomposition of the vectorial space of index terms.

Levenshtein distance:

see *Edit distance.*

Lexicographical order:

order in which the words are listed in a dictionary or telephone guide.

Local analysis:

a reference to techniques of identifying document and term relationships through the analysis of the documents retrieved by a given user query.

Local context analysis:

a technique of query expansion which combines local and global analysis.

Logical view of documents:

the representation of documents and Web pages adopted by the system. The most common form is to represent the text of the document by a set of indexing terms or keywords.

MARC:

a standardized record format used by libraries and bibliographic utilities for sharing and storing cataloging information about bibliographic materials.

Metasearch:

a search technique common on the World Wide Web where a single point of entry is provided to multiple heterogeneous back-end search engines. A meta search system sends a user's query to the back-end search engines, combines the results, and returns a single, unified hit-list to the user.

Metadata:

attributes of data or a document, usually descriptive as author or content, often broken up into categories or facets, typically maintained in a catalog, sometimes recorded according to a scheme like the Dublin Core or MARC.

MIMD:

a parallel computer architecture consisting of multiple instruction streams and multiple data streams.

MISD:

a parallel computer architecture consisting of multiple instruction streams and a single data stream.

Model for IR:

a set of premisses and an algorithm for ranking documents with regard to a user query. More formally, an IR model is a quadruple $[\mathbf{D}, \mathbf{Q}, \mathcal{F}, R(q_i, d_j)]$ where $\mathbf{D}$ is a set of logical views of documents, $\mathbf{Q}$ is a set of user queries, $\mathcal{F}$ is a framework for modeling documents and queries, and $R(q_i, d_j)$ is a ranking function which associates a numeric ranking to the query q_i and the document d_j.

Modeling:

the part of IR which studies the algorithms (or *models*) used for ranking documents according to a system assigned likelihood of relevance to a given user query.

Multidimensional Scaling (MDS):

a method to map objects into points, trying to preserve distances.

Multimedia data:

data combining several different media, such as text, images, sound, and video.

Multimedia Database Management System:

system able to represent, manage, and store multimedia data.

Multimedia Information Retrieval System:

Information Retrieval system handling multimedia data.

Multitasking:

the simultaneous execution of multiple, independent tasks. On a single processor machine the tasks share the processor and their execution is interleaved sequentially. On a machine with multiple processors the tasks may execute concurrently.

Nearest-neighbor query:

a query that requests the spatial object closest to the specified object.

Neural networks:

an algebraic model of document retrieval based on representing query, index terms, and documents as a neural network.

n-gram:

any substring of length n.

Non-overlapping lists model:

a model of retrieving structured documents through indexing structures implemented as non-overlapping lists.

Object-relational database technology:

technology that extends the relational model with the main features of the object-oriented one.

Occurrence list:

a data structure which assigns to each text word the list of its positions in the text.

OCR (Optical Character Recognition):

software that takes as input a bit-mapped image (for example, produced by a scanner) and outputs any text present in the image as ASCII text. The quality of the result depends on the text type and fonts and can be as high as 99%.

Online Public Access Catalog:

see *OPAC*.

OPAC (Online Public Access Catalog):

library management system software which provides user access to information contained in a library collection.

Optical Character Recognition:

see *OCR*.

Panning (see also *zooming*):

action of a movie camera that scans sideways across a scene. This effect can be simulated in a screen window even in the absence of the camera.

Parallel computing:

the simultaneous application of multiple processors to solve a single problem. Each processor works on a different part of the problem.

Parallel information retrieval:

the application of parallel computing to solve information retrieval problems.

Pattern:

set of syntactic features that describe the text segments to be matched, ranging from simple words to regular expressions.

Precision:

an information retrieval performance measure that quantifies the fraction of retrieved documents which are known to be relevant.

Probabilistic model:

a classic model of document retrieval based on a probabilistic interpretation of document relevance (to a given user query).

Proximal nodes model:

a model of retrieving structured documents through a hierarchical indexing structure.

Query:

the expression of the user information need in the input language provided by the information system. The most common type of input language simply allows the specification of keywords and of a few Boolean connectives.

Query expansion:

a process of adding new terms to a given user query in an attempt to provide better contextualization (and hopefully retrieve documents which are more useful to the user).

Query preview:

a low-cost, rapid-turnaround visualization of what the results of many variations on a query might be.

Range query:

a query that requests all the spatial objects that intersect the given range.

Recall:

an information retrieval performance measure that quantifies the fraction of known relevant documents which were effectively retrieved.

Reference collection:

a collection of documents used for testing information retrieval models and algorithms. A reference collection usually includes a set of documents, a set of test queries, and a set of documents known to be relevant to each query.

Regular expression:

general pattern that allows the expression of alternative strings, repetitions and concatenations of substrings.

Repository:

a physical or digital place where objects are stored for a period of time, from which individual objects can be obtained if they are requested and their terms and conditions are satisfied.

Retrieval task:

the task executed by the information system in response to a user request. It is basically of two types: *ad hoc* and *filtering*.

Retrieval unit:

the type of objects returned by an information retrieval system as the response to a query, e.g. documents, files, Web pages, etc.

Scatter/Gather:

a browsing strategy which clusters the local documents in the answer set dynamically into topically-coherent groups and presents the user with descriptions of such groups.

Search history:

a mechanism for tracking the history of a user session or of a collection of user sessions. The search history should show what the available choices are at any given point, what moves have been made in the past, short-term tactics, and annotations on choices made along the way.

Search starting point:

'where' or 'how' an information-seeking task is initiated. Search interfaces should provide the users with good ways to get started.

Semi-static text:

a text collection which does not change too frequently.

Semi-structured data:

data whose structure may not match, or only partially match, the structure prescribed by the data schema.

Sequential or on-line text searching:

the problem of finding a pattern in a text without using any precomputed information on the text.

SGML:

standard markup metalanguage. HTML is a markup language based on SGML.

Signature file:

a text index based on storing a signature for each text block to be able to filter out some blocks quickly.

SIMD:

a parallel computer architecture consisting of a single instruction stream and multiple data streams.

SISD:

a traditional sequential computer architecture consisting of a single instruction stream and a single data stream.

SMP (Symmetric Multiprocessor):

a common MIMD computer architecture where all of the parallel processors have equal access to the same system resources, and any processor can execute any task. The processors may operate independently, or they may cooperate to execute a parallel task concurrently.

Source selection:

the process of selecting one or more document collections from a set of document collections where the selected collections are most likely to contain documents relevant to the query. Commonly used in distributed IR systems.

SQL3:

the upcoming SQL standard for relational databases.

Spatial Access Methods:

file structures for fast storage and retrieval of spatial objects like points, lines, polygons.

Speedup:

a measure of parallel algorithm performance, defined as:

$$S = \frac{\text{Running time of best available sequential algorithm}}{\text{Running time of parallel algorithm}}$$

STARTS (Stanford Proposal for Internet Meta-Searching):

a protocol for distributed, heterogeneous search developed at Stanford University in cooperation with a consortium of search product and search service vendors.

Statistical text compression:

a reference to techniques and methods of text compression based on probability estimates for the rates of occurrence of each symbol.

Stemming:

a technique for reducing words to their grammatical roots.

Stopwords:

words which occur frequently in the text of a document. Examples of stopwords are articles, prepositions, and conjunctions.

Suffix tree and suffix array:

text indices based on a lexicographical arrangement of all the text suffixes.

Syntax tree:

structural interpretation of a query, where the nodes are the operators and the subtrees are the operands.

Tag:

a string which is used to mark the beginning or ending of structural elements in the text.

Term-to-term independence:

a fundamental assumption underlying the classic vector model which states that the vectors used for representing index terms form an orthonormal basis. Such an assumption is usually interpreted to mean pairwise orthogonality (but not in the generalized vector space model).

Text structure:

information present in a text apart from its content, which relates its different portions in a semantically meaningful way.

Textual Image:

image that is mostly text and then can be compressed more than conventional images. In addition, by using OCR, keywords can be extracted and used for retrieving the image.

Thesaurus:

a data structure composed of (1) a pre-compiled list of important words in a given domain of knowledge and (2) for each word in this list, a list of related (synonym) words.

TREC collection:

a reference collection which contains over a million documents and which has been used extensively in the TREC conferences. The TREC collection has been organized by NIST and is becoming a standard for comparing IR models and algorithms.

User information need:

a natural language declaration of the informational need of a user. For instance, *'find documents which discuss the political implications of the Monica Lewinsky scandal in the results of the 1998 elections for the U.S. Congress'*.

User relevance feedback:

an interactive process of obtaining information from the user about the relevance and the non-relevance of retrieved documents.

URL:

stands for Uniform Resource Locator and is used to address any Internet resource, including Web pages.

Vector model:

a classic model of document retrieval based on representing documents and queries as vectors of index terms. The model adopts as its foundation the notion of term-to-term independence.

Vocabulary:

the set of all the different words in a text.

WAIS:

(Wide Area Information Service): suite of protocols designed to publish information and to allow querying of databases in the Internet.

Working memory load:

information about the decisions and choices made during an interactive user session. A system with a well designed interface should keep this information around to facilitate the task of the user (for instance, allowing the user to easily resume temporarily abandoned strategies).

XML:

a subset of SGML, defined for the Web. In XML it is easier to define new markup languages.

Z39.50:

a national standard that has become an international standard. It is a protocol for client/server communication with retrieval systems, allowing a single client to interact with one or more systems, or retrieval systems (or gateways) to communicate with other retrieval systems. It supports connection-oriented sessions, having a system EXPLAIN itself, submission of queries, obtaining information, the results lists, and obtaining retrieved documents.

Zipf's Law:

an empirical rule that describes the frequency of the text words. It states that the i-th most frequent word appears as many times as the most frequent one divided by i^θ, for some $\theta \geq 1$.

Zooming (see also *panning*):

action of a movie camera that can either move in for a close-up or back away to get a wider view. This effect can be simulated in a screen window even in the absence of the camera.

References

[1] Ijsbrand Jan Aalbersberg. Incremental relevance feedback. In *Proc. of the 15th Annual International ACM SIGIR Conference on Research and Development in Information Retrieval*, pages 11–22, Copenhagen, Denmark, 1992.

[2] Serge Abiteboul. Querying semi-structured data. In Foto N. Afrati and Phokion Kolaitis, editors, *Int. Conf. on Database Theory (ICDT)*, number 1186 in LNCS, pages 1–18, Delphi, Greece, 1997. Springer-Verlag.

[3] Marc Abrams, editor. *World Wide Web: Beyond the Basics*. Prentice Hall, 1998.

[4] Brent Agnew, Christos Faloutsos, Zhengyu Wang, Don Welch, and Xiaogang Xue. Multimedia indexing over the Web. In *Proc. of the SPIE Conference on Storage and Retrieval for Image and Video Databases*, pages 72–83, San Jose, CA, Feb 1997.

[5] M. Agosti, G. Gradenigo, and P. G. Marchetti. A hypertext environment for interacting with large textual databases. *Information Processing & Management*, 28(3):371–387, 1992.

[6] Rakesh Agrawal, Christos Faloutsos, and Arun Swami. Efficient similarity search in sequence databases. In *Fourth Int. Conf. on Foundations of Data Organization and Algorithms*, pages 69–84, Evanston, Illinois, Oct 1993. ftp://olympos.cs.umd.edu/pub/TechReports/fodo.ps.

[7] Rakesh Agrawal, King-Ip Lin, Harpreet S. Sawhney, and Kyuseok Shim. Fast similarity search in the presence of noise, scaling and translation in time-series databases. In *Proc. of VLDB Conf.*, pages 490–501, Zurich, Switzerland, September 1995.

[8] Rakesh Agrawal and Ramakrishnan Srikant. Fast algorithms for mining association rules in large databases. In *Proc. of VLDB Conf.*, pages 487–499, Santiago, Chile, Sept 1994.

[9] A. Aho and M. Corasick. Efficient string matching: an aid to bibliographic search. *Communications of the ACM*, 18(6):333–340, June 1975.

[10] Alexa: Main Page. http://www.alexa.com, 1998.

[11] Alis Technologies, Web languages hit parade. http://babel.alis.com:8080/palmares.html, 1997.

[12] James Allan. Relevance feedback with too much data. In *Proc. of the 18th Annual International ACM SIGIR Conference on Research and Development in Information Retrieval*, pages 337–343, Seattle, WA, USA, 1995.

[13] Bryce L. Allen. *Information Tasks: Toward a User-Centered Approach to Information Systems*. Academic Press, San Diego, CA, 1996.

[14] Robert B. Allen, Pascal Obry, and Michael Littman. An interface for navigating clustered document sets returned by queries. In *Proc. of ACM COCS: Conference on Organizational Computing Systems*, pages 66–171, Milpitis, CA, November 1993.

[15] O. Alonso and R. Baeza-Yates. A model for visualizing large answers in WWW. In *XVIII Int. Conf. of the Chilean CS Society*, pages 2–7, Antofagasta, Chile, 1998. IEEE CS Press.

[16] T. M. Alrashid, J. A. Barker, B. S. Christian, S. C. Cox, M. W. Rabne, E. A. Slotta, and L. R. Upthegrove. Safeguarding Copyrighted Contents, Digital Libraries and Intellectual Property Management, CWRU's Rights Management System. *D-Lib Magazine*, April 1998. http://www.dlib.org/dlib/april98/04barker.html.

[17] AltaVista: Main page. http://www.altavista.com, 1996.

[18] G. M. Amdahl. Validity of the single-processor approach to achieving large scale computing capabilities. In *Proc. AFIPS 1967 Spring Joint Computer Conf.*, volume 30, pages 483–485, Atlantic City, N.J., April 1967.

[19] A. Amir, G. Benson, and M. Farach. Let sleeping files lie: pattern matching in z-compressed files. *Journal of Computer and Systems Sciences*, 52(2):299–307, 1996.

[20] Keith Andrews. Visualizing cyberspace: Information visualization in the Harmony Internet browser. In *Proceedings '95 Information Visualization*, pages 97–104, Atlanta, USA, October 1995.

[21] P. Anick, J. Brennan, R. Flynn, D. Hanssen, B. Alvey, and J. Robbins. A direct manipulation interface for Boolean information retrieval via natural language query. In *Proc. of the 13th Annual International ACM/SIGIR Conference*, pages 135–150, Brussels, Belgium, 1990.

[22] Peter G. Anick. Adapting a full-text information retrieval system to the computer troubleshooting domain. In *Proc. of the 17th Annual International ACM SIGIR Conference on Research and Development in Information Retrieval*, pages 349–358, 1994.

[23] ANSI/NISO Standards, Z39.50-Information Retrieval: Application Service Definition and Protocol Specification, 1995. See http://lcweb.loc.gov/z3950/agency.

[24] P. Apers, H. Blanken, and M. Houtsma. *Multimedia Databases in Perspective*. Springer-Verlag, 1997.

[25] A. Apostolico and Z. Galil. *Combinatorial Algorithms on Words*. Springer-Verlag, New York, 1985.

[26] M. Araújo, G. Navarro, and N. Ziviani. Large text searching allowing errors. In *Proc. WSP'97*, pages 2–20, Valparaíso, Chile, 1997. Carleton University Press.

[27] Y. Arens, C. Chee, C. Hsu, and C. Knoblock. Retrieving and integrating data from multiple information sources. *Journal on Intelligent and Cooperative Information Systems*, 2(2):127–158, 1993.

[28] W. Y. Arms. Key concepts in the architecture of the digital library. *D-Lib Magazine*, July 1995. http://www.dlib.org/dlib/July95/07arms.html.

[29] W. Y. Arms. Relaxing assumptions about the future of digital libraries: The hare and the tortoise. *D-Lib Magazine*, April 1997. http://www.dlib.org/dlib/april97/04arms.html.

[30] W. Y. Arms. Implementing Policies for Access Management. *D-Lib Magazine*, February 1998. http://www.dlib.org/dlib/february98/arms/02arms.html.

[31] W. Y. Arms, C. Blanchi, and E. A. Overly. An Architecture for Information in digital libraries. *D-Lib Magazine*, February 1997. http://www.dlib.org/dlib/february97/cnri/02arms1.html.

[32] Gustavo Arocena and Alberto Mendelzon.   WebOQL: Restructuring documents, databases and Webs. In *Int. Conf. on Data Engineering*, pages 24–33, Orlando Florida, 1998.

[33] Gustavo O. Arocena, Alberto O. Mendelzon, and George A. Mihaila. Applications of a Web query language. In *6th Int. WWW Conference*, Santa Clara, CA, USA, April 1997.

[34] AskJeeves: Main Page. http://www.askjeeves.com, 1998.

[35] R. Attar and A. S. Fraenkel. Local feedback in full-text retrieval systems. *Journal of the ACM*, 24(3):397–417, 1977.

[36] R. Baeza-Yates. An extended model for full-text databases. *Journal of Brazilian CS Society*, 3(2):57–64, April 1996.

[37] R. Baeza-Yates, E. Barbosa, and N. Ziviani. Hierarchies of indices for text searching. In *Proceedings of RIAO'94 Intelligent Multimedia Information Retrieval Systems and Management*, pages 11–13, 1994.

[38] R. Baeza-Yates and G. Gonnet. Efficient Text Searching of Regular Expressions. In G. Ausiello, M. Dezani-Ciancaglini, and S. Ronchi Della Rocca, editors, *ICALP'89*, number 372 in LNCS, pages 46–62, Stresa, Italy, 1989. Springer-Verlag.

[39] R. Baeza-Yates and G. Gonnet. A new approach to text searching. *Communications of the ACM*, 35(10):74–82, October 1992.

[40] R. Baeza-Yates and G. Gonnet. Fast text searching for regular expressions or automaton searching on a trie. *J. of the ACM*, 43(6):915–936, Nov 1996.

[41] R. Baeza-Yates and G. Navarro. Integrating contents and structure in text retrieval. *ACM SIGMOD Record*, 25(1):67–79, March 1996.

[42] R. Baeza-Yates and G. Navarro. Block-addressing indices for approximate text retrieval. In *Proc. of the 6th CIKM Conference*, pages 1–8, Las Vegas, Nevada, 1997.

[43] R. Baeza-Yates and G. Navarro. Faster approximate string matching. *Algorithmica*, 23(2):127–158, 1999.

[44] R. Baeza-Yates, G. Navarro, J. Vegas, and P. de la Fuente. A model and a visual query language for structured text. In Berthier Ribeiro-Neto, editor, *Proc. of the 5th Symposium on String Processing and Information Retrieval*, pages 7–13, Santa Cruz, Bolivia, Sept 1998. IEEE CS Press.

[45] R. Baeza-Yates and C. Perleberg. Fast and practical approximate pattern matching. *Information Processing Letters*, 59:21–27, 1996.

[46] Ricardo Baeza-Yates. Visualizing large answers in text databases. In *Int. Workshop on Advanced User Interfaces*, pages 101–107, Gubbio, Italy, May 1996. ACM Press.

[47] Ricardo A. Baeza-Yates, Walter Cunto, Udi Manber, and Sun Wu. Proximity matching using fixed queries trees. In M. Crochemore and D. Gusfield, editors, *5th Combinatorial Pattern Matching*, number 807 in LNCS, pages 198–212. Springer-Verlag, Asilomar, CA, June 1994.

[48] J. Baker. UCLA-NSF Social Aspects of Digital Libraries Workshop, January 1996. http://www.gslis.ucla.edu/DL/.

[49] Y. Bakos and E. Brynjolfsson. Bundling Information Goods: Pricing, Profits, and Efficiency. Technical report, MIT Center for Coordination Science, 1997.

[50] M. Q. W. Baldonado, C.-C. K. Chang, L. Gravano, and A. Paepcke. Metadata for digital libraries: architecture and design rationale. In *Proc. of the 2nd ACM International Conference on Digital Libraries*, pages 47–56, Philadelphia, PA, USA, 1997.

[51] Michelle Q. Wang Baldonado and Terry Winograd. Sensemaker: An information-exploration interface supporting the contextual evolution of a user's interests. In *Proc. of*

the ACM SIGCHI Conference on Human Factors in Computing Systems, pages 11–18, Atlanta, GA, USA, May 1997.

[52] Michelle Q. Wang Baldonado and Terry Winograd. Hi-cites: Dynamically-created citations with active highlighting. In *Proc. of the ACM SIGCHI Conference on Human Factors in Computing Systems*, pages 408–415, Los Angeles, CA, March 1998.

[53] D. Ballard and C. Brown. *Computer Vision*. Prentice Hall, 1982.

[54] Liam Bannon, Allen Cypher, Steven Greenspan, and Melissa L. Monty. Evaluation and analysis of users' activity organization. In *Proc. of the ACM SIGCHI Conference on Human Factors in Computing Systems*, pages 54–57, 1983.

[55] D. Barber. OhioLINK: A Consortial Approach to Digital Library Management. *D-Lib Magazine*, April 1997. http://www.dlib.org/dlib/april97/04barber.html.

[56] E. Barbosa, G. Navarro, R. Baeza-Yates, C. Perleberg, and N. Ziviani. Optimized binary search and text retrieval. In P. Spirakis, editor, *Proc. of European Symposium on Algorithms*, number 979 in LNCS, pages 311–326. Springer-Verlag, 1995. Improved version to appear in *Algorithmica* including W. Cunto as author.

[57] R. Barbosa. *Query Performance on Distributed Digital Libraries*. CS Department, Federal University of Minas Gerais, Brazil, 1998. Master Thesis. In Portuguese.

[58] P. Barford, A. Bestavros, A. Bradley, and M. E. Crovella. Changes in web client access patterns: Characteristics and caching implications. *World Wide Web*, 1999. Special Issue on Characterization and Performance Evaluation, to appear.

[59] P. Barford and M. Crovella. Generating representative Web workloads for network and server performance evaluation. In *ACM Sigmetrics Conference on Measurement and Modeling of Computer Systems*, pages 151–160, July 1998.

[60] J. Barnett. Computational methods for a mathematical theory of evidence. In *Proc. of the 7th Int. Joint Conference on Artificial Intelligence*, pages 868–875, Vancouver, Canada, 1981.

[61] Jeff Barry, Dania Bilal, and W. David Penniman. Automated system marketplace: the competitive struggle. *Library Journal*, 123(6):43–52, 1998.

[62] Brian T. Bartell, Garrison W. Cottrell, and Richard K. Belew. Latent semantic indexing is an optimal special case of multidimensional scaling. In *Proc. of the 15th Annual International ACM SIGIR Conference on Research and Development in Information Retrieval*, pages 161–167, Copenhagen, Denmark, 1992.

[63] Brian T. Bartell, Garrison W. Cottrell, and Richard K. Belew. Automatic combination of multiple ranked retrieval systems. In *Proc. of the 17th Annual International ACM SIGIR Conference on Research and Development in Information Retrieval*, pages 173–181, Dublin, Ireland, 1994.

[64] Chumki Basu, Haym Hirsh, and William Cohen. Recommendation as classification: Using social and content-based information in recommendation. In *Proc. of AAAI*, pages 714–720, Madison, WI, July 1998.

[65] Marcia J. Bates. The design of browsing and berrypicking techniques for the on-line search interface. *Online Review*, 13(5):407–431, 1989.

[66] Marcia J. Bates. Where should the person stop and the information search interfaces start? *Information Processing & Management*, 26(5):575–591, 1990.

[67] Marcia J. Bates. Document familiarity, relevance, and bradford's law: The Getty online searching project report no. 5. *Information Processing & Management*, 32:697–707, 1996.

[68] Micheline Beaulieu and Christine L. Borgman, editors. *Journal of the American Society for Information Science*, volume 47(7). John Wiley & Sons, 1996.

[69] N. Beckmann, H.-P. Kriegel, R. Schneider, and B. Seeger. The R*-tree: An efficient and robust access method for points and rectangles. *ACM SIGMOD*, pages 322–331, May 1990.

[70] B. Bederson, L. Stead, and J. Hollan. Pad++: Advances in multiscale interfaces. In *Proc. of ACM SIGCHI Conference on Human Factors in Computing Systems*, pages 315–316, Boston, MA, USA, 1994. See this and other papers at http://www.cs.umd.edu/hcil/pad++/papers/ .

[71] Benjamin B. Bederson, James D. Hollan, Ken Perlin, Jonathan Meyer, David Bacon, and George Furnas. Pad++: A zoomable graphical sketchpad for exploring alternate interface physics. *Journal of Visual Languages and Computing*, 7(1):3–31, 1996.

[72] C. Beeri and Y. Kornatzky. A logical query language for hypertext systems. In *Proc. of the European Conference on Hypertext*, pages 67–80. Cambridge University Press, 1990.

[73] Rick Belew. Rave reviews: Acquiring relevance assessments from multiple users. In Marti A. Hearst and Haym Hirsh, editors, *Working Notes of the AAAI Spring Symposium on Machine Learning in Information Access*, Stanford, CA, March 1996.

[74] N. Belkin and B. Croft. Information filtering and information retrieval: Two sides of a same coin? *Communications of the ACM*, 35(12):29–38, December 1992.

[75] N. Belkin, P. G. Marchetti, and C. Cool. Braque – design of an interface to support user interaction in information retrieval. *Information Processing and Management*, 29(3):325–344, 1993.

[76] N. J. Belkin, P. Kantor, E. A. Fox, and J. A. Shaw. Combining the evidence of multiple query representations for information retrieval. *Information Processing & Management*, 31(3):431–448, May–June 1995.

[77] T. C. Bell, A. Moffat, C. Nevill-Manning, I. H. Witten, and J. Zobel. Data compression in full-text retrieval systems. *Journal of the American Society for Information Science*, 44:508–531, 1993.

[78] T. C. Bell, J. Cleary, and I. H. Witten. *Text Compression*. Prentice-Hall, 1990.

[79] Alberto Belussi and Christos Faloutsos. Estimating the selectivity of spatial queries using the 'correlation' fractal dimension. In *Proc. of VLDB Conf.*, pages 299–310, Zurich, Switzerland, September 1995.

[80] A. B. Benítez, M. Beigi, and S-F. Chang. Using relevance feedback in content-based image metasearch. *IEEE Internet Computing*, 2(4):59–69, 1998.

[81] J. Bentley, D. Sleator, R. Tarjan, and V. Wei. A locally adaptive data compression scheme. *Communications of the ACM*, 29:320–330, 1986.

[82] S. Berchtold, C. Boehm, B. Braunmueller, D. A. Keim, and H. P. Kriegel. Fast similarity search in multimedia databases. In *Proc. of the ACM SIGMOD Int'l Conf. on Management of Data*, pages 1–12, 1997.

[83] Stefan Berchtold, Daniel A. Keim, and Hans-Peter Kriegel. The X-tree : An index structure for high-dimensional data. *VLDB*, pages 28–39, 1996.

[84] T. Berners-Lee. The World Wide Web Consortium. http://www.w3.org.

[85] Tim Berners-Lee, Robert Cailliau, Ari Luotonen, Henrik Frystyk Nielsen, and Arthur Secret. The World-Wide Web. *Communication of the ACM*, 37(8):76–82, 1994.

[86] J. W. Berry. Digital libraries: new initiatives with world wide implications. *IFLA Journal*, 22(1):9–17, 1995. http://www.nlc-bnc.ca/ifla/IV/ifla61/61-berjo.htm.

[87] E. Bertino and E. Ferrari. Temporal synchronization models for multimedia data. *IEEE Trans. on Knowledge and Data Eng.*, 10(4):612–631, July/August 1998.

[88] E. Bertino, E. Ferrari, and M. Stolf. MPGS: An interactive tool for the specification and generation of multimedia presentations. *IEEE Transactions on Multimedia Systems*, 1999. To appear.

[89] E. Bertino and L. D. Martino. *Object-Oriented Database Systems — Concepts and Architecture*. Addison-Wesley, 1993.

[90] E. Bertino and F. Rabitti. Query Processing in MULTOS. In C. Thanos, editor, *Multimedia Office Filing: The MULTOS Approach*, pages 273–295. Elsevier Science Publishers B.V. (North Holland), 1990.

[91] K. Bharat and A. Z. Broder. A technique for measuring the relative size and overlap of public Web search engines. In *7th WWW Conference*, pages 379–388, Brisbane, Australia, 1998.

[92] Krishna Bharat, Andrei Broder, Monika Henzinger, Puneet Kumar, and Suresh Venkatasubramanian. The connectivity server: fast access to linkage information on the Web. In *7th WWW Conf.*, Brisbane, Australia, April 1998.

[93] Krishna Bharat and Monika Henzinger. Improved algorithms for topic distillation in hyperlinked environments. In B. Croft, A. Moffat, C. J. van Rijsbergen, R. Wilkinson, and J. Zobel, editors, *21st ACM SIGIR*, pages 104–111, Melbourne, Australia, 1998.

[94] J. Bichteler and E. A. Eaton III. The combined use of bibliographic coupling and co-citation for document retrieval. *Journal of the American Society for Information Science*, 31(4), July 1980.

[95] Eric A. Bier, Maureen C. Stone, Ken Pier, Ken Fishkin, Thomas Baudel, Matt Conway, William Buxton, and Tony DeRose. Toolglass and magic lenses: The see-through interface. In *Proc. of ACM Conference on Human Factors in Computing Systems*, volume 2 of *Videos: Part II*, pages 445–446, Boston, MA, USA, 1994.

[96] Patricia A. Billingsley. Taking panes: Issues in the design of windowing systems. In Martin Helander, editor, *Handbook of Human-Computer Interaction*, pages 413–436. Springer Verlag, 1988.

[97] W. P. Birmingham, E. H. Durfee, T. Mullen, and M. P. Wellman. The distributed agent architecture of the University of Michigan Digital Library. *AAAI Spring Symposium on Information Gathering from Heterogeneous, Distributed Environments*, 1995. Stanford, CA, AAAI Press.

[98] A. P. Bishop. Working towards an understanding of digital library use: A report on the user research efforts of the NSF/ARPA/NASA DLI projects. *D-Lib Magazine*, October 1995. http://www.dlib.org/dlib/october95/10bishop.html.

[99] K. Bohm and T. C. Rakov. Metadata for multimedia documents. In *Proc. of the ACM SIGMOD Int. Conf. on Management of Data*, pages 21–26, Minneapolis, MN, USA, May 1994.

[100] Philippe Bonnet and Anthony Tomasic. Partial answers for unavailable data sources. In *Workshop on Flexible Query-Answering Systems*, pages 43–54, 1998.

[101] A. Bookstein. On the perils of merging Boolean and weighted retrieval systems. *Journal of the American Society for Information Sciences*, 29(3):156–158, 1978.

[102] A. Bookstein. Fuzzy requests: An approach to weighted Boolean searches. *Journal of the American Society for Information Sciences*, 31:240–247, 1980.

[103] A. Bookstein. Implication of Boolean structure for probabilistic retrieval. In *Proc. of the 8th Annual International ACM/SIGIR Conference on Research and Development in Information Retrieval*, pages 11–17, Montreal, Canada, 1985.

[104] Christine L. Borgman. Why are online catalogs hard to use? Lessons learned from information retrieval studies. *Journal of the American Society for Information Science*, 37(6):387–400, 1986.

[105] Christine L. Borgman. Why are online catalogs *still* hard to use? *Journal of the American Society for Information Science*, 47(7):493–503, 1996.

[106] J. Bosak. XML, Java, and the future of the Web. Technical report, Sun Microsystems, 1997. http://sunsite.unc.edu/pub/sun-info/standards/xml/why/xmlapps.htm.

[107] Charles P. Bourne. On-line systems: history, technology, and economics. *Journal of the American Society for Information Science*, 31:155–160, 1980.

[108] C. Mic Bowman, Peter B. Danzig, Darren R. Hardy, Udi Manber, and Michael F. Schwartz. The Harvest information discovery and access system. In *Proc. 2nd Int. WWW Conf.*, pages 763–771, October 1994.

[109] George E. P. Box, Gwilym M. Jenkins, and Gregory C. Reinsel. *Time Series Analysis: Forecasting and Control.* Prentice Hall, Englewood Cliffs, NJ, USA, 3rd edition, 1994.

[110] R. S. Boyer and J. S. Moore. A fast string searching algorithm. *Communications of the ACM*, 20(10):762–772, 1977.

[111] James Boyle, William Ogden, Steven Uhlir, and Patricia Wilson. QMF usability: How it really happened. In *Proc. of IFIP INTERACT'84: Human-Computer Interaction*, pages 877–882, 1984.

[112] Tolga Bozkaya and Z. Meral Ozsoyoglu. Distance-based indexing for high-dimensional metric spaces. In *Proc. of ACM SIGMOD Conference*, pages 357–368, Tucson, AZ, USA, 1997.

[113] P. M. E. De Bra and R. D. J. Post. Searching for arbitrary information in the WWW: The fish search for Mosaic. In *Proc. of the 2nd Int. WWW Conference*, Chicago, October 1994. http://www.ncsa.uiuc.edu/SDG/IT94/Proceedings/www-fall94.html.

[114] T. Bray. Measuring the web. In *Proc. of the 5th Int. WWW Conference*, Paris, May 1996. http://www5conf.inria.fr/fich_html/papers/P9/Overview.html.

[115] S. Brin. Extracting patterns and relations from the World Wide Web. In *Workshop on Web Databases*, Valencia, Spain, March 1998.

[116] Sergei Brin. Near neighbor search in large metric spaces. In *Proc. of VLDB Conf.*, pages 574–584, Zurich, Switzerland, Sept 1995.

[117] Sergey Brin and Lawrence Page. The anatomy of a large-scale hypertextual Web search engine. In *Proc. of the 7th Int. WWW Conference*, Brisbane, Australia, April 1998.

[118] T. Brinkhoff, H. P. Kriegel, and R. Schneider. Comparison of approximations of complex objects used for approximation-based query processing in spatial database systems. In *Proc. of the IEEE Conference on Data Engineering*, pages 40–49, Vienna, Austria, 1993.

[119] Thomas Brinkhoff, Hans-Peter Kriegel, Ralf Schneider, and Bernhard Seeger. Multi-step processing of spatial joins. In *Proc. of ACM SIGMOD*, pages 197–208, Minneapolis, MN, USA, May 1994.

[120] A. Broder, S. Glassman, M. Manasse, and G. Zweig. Syntactic clustering of the Web. In *6th Int. WWW Conference*, pages 391–404, Santa Clara, CA, USA, April 1997.

[121] A. Z. Broder. On the resemblance and containment of documents. In *Conf. on Compression and Complexity of Sequences*, pages 21–29, Salerno, Italy, 1997. IEEE Computer Society.

[122] J. Broglio, J. P. Callan, W. B. Croft, and D. W. Nachbar. Document retrieval and routing using the INQUERY system. In D. K. Harman, editor, *Overview of the Third Retrieval Conference (TREC-3)*, pages 29–38. NIST Special Publication 500-225, 1995.

[123] Eric W. Brown. *Execution Performance Issues in Full-Text Information Retrieval.* PhD thesis, University of Massachusetts, Amherst, 1996. Available as UMass Comp. Sci. Tech. Rep. TR95-81.

[124] J. S. Brown and P. Duguid. The social life of documents. *First Monday*, May 1996. http://www.firstmonday.dk/issues/issue1/documents/.

[125] Lisa Gottesfeld Brown. A survey of image registration techniques. *ACM Computing Surveys*, 24(4):325–376, December 1992.

[126] M. Buckland and C. Plaunt. On the Construction of Selection Systems. *Library Hi Tech*, 12:15–28, 1994.

[127] Chris Buckley, Gerard Salton, and James Allan. The effect of adding relevance information in a relevance feedback environment. In *Proc. of the 17th Annual International ACM SIGIR Conference on Research and Development in Information Retrieval*, pages 292–300, Dublin, Ireland, 1994.

[128] P. Buneman, S. B. Davidson, K. Hart, C. Overton, and L. Wong. A data transformation system for biological data sources. In *Proc. of the 21st International Conference on Very Large Data Bases*, pages 158–169, Zurich, Switzerland, September 1995.

[129] Peter Buneman. Semistructured data. In *ACM SIGACT-SIGMOD-SIGART Symposium on Principles of Database Systems*, pages 117–121, Tucson, Arizona, 1997.

[130] Robin Burke, Kristian Hammond, Vladimir Kulukin, Steven Lytinen, Noriko Tomuro, and Scott Schoenberg. Experiences with the FAQ system. *AI Magazine*, 18(2):57–66, 1997.

[131] W. A. Burkhard and R. M. Keller. Some approaches to best-match file searching. *Communications of the ACM*, 16(4):230–236, April 1973.

[132] F. Burkowski. An algebra for hierarchically organized text-dominated databases. *Information Processing & Management*, 28(3):333–348, 1992.

[133] F. Burkowski. Retrieval activities in a database consisting of heterogeneous collections of structured text. In *Proc. of the 15th Annual International ACM/SIGIR Conference on Research and Development in Information Retrieval*, pages 112–125, Copenhagen, Denmark, 1992.

[134] Arthur W. Burks, Herman H. Goldstine, and John von Neumann. Preliminary discussion of the logical design of an electronic computing instrument. In William Aspray and Arthur Burks, editors, *Papers of John von Neumann on Computers and Computer Theory*, pages 97–142. The MIT Press, Cambridge, MA, 1987 (originally appeared in 1946).

[135] V. Bush. As we may think. *The Atlantic Monthly*, 176(1):101–108, July 1945.

[136] D. Byers. Full-text indexing of non-textual resources. In *7th WWW Conf.*, Brisbane, Australia, April 1998.

[137] Brendon Cahoon and Kathryn McKinley. Performance evaluation of a distributed architecture for information retrieval. In *Proc. 19th Int. ACM SIGIR Conference on Research and Development in Information Retrieval*, pages 110–118, Zurich, Switzerland, August 1996.

[138] J. Callan. Document filtering with inference networks. In *Proc. of the 19th ACM SIGIR Conference*, pages 262–269, Zurich, Switzerland, August 1996.

[139] J. P. Callan, Z. Lu, and W. Bruce Croft. Searching Distributed Collections with Inference Networks. In E. A. Fox, P. Ingwersen, and R. Fidel, editors, *Proc. of the 18th Annual International ACM SIGIR Conference on Research and Development in Information Retrieval*, pages 21–28, Seattle, Washington, July 1995. ACM Press.

[140] S. K. Card, M. Pavel, and J. E. Farrell. Window-based computer dialogues. In *Proc. of Interact '84, First IFIP Conference on Human-Computer Interaction*, pages 355–359, 1984.

[141] Stuart K. Card, Jock D. MacKinlay, and Ben Shneiderman. *Readings in Information Visualization: Using Vision to Think*. Morgan Kaufmann Publishers, 1998.

[142] Stuart K. Card, Thomas P. Moran, and Allen Newell. *The Psychology of Human-Computer Interaction*. L. Erlbaum Associates, 1983.

[143] Stuart K. Card, George G. Robertson, and Jock D. Mackinlay. The information visualizer, an information workspace. In *Proc. of the ACM SIGCHI Conference on Human Factors in Computing Systems*, pages 181–188, 1991.

[144] Stuart K. Card, George G. Robertson, and William York. The WebBook and the Web Forager: An information workspace for the World-Wide Web. In *Proc. of the ACM SIGCHI Conference on Human Factors in Computing Systems*, pages 111–117, Zurich, Switzerland, April 1996.

[145] S. Carliner. Designing wizards. *Training & Development*, 52(7):62–63, 1998.

[146] Carnegie Mellon University DLI Team, Informedia.   http://www.informedia. cs.cmu.edu/.

[147] Claudio Carpineto and Giovanni Romano. Information retrieval through hybrid navigation of lattice representations. *International Journal of Human-Computer Studies*, 45(5):553–578, 1996.

[148] J. Carriere and R. Kazman. WebQuery: Searching and visualizing the Web through connectivity. In *6th Int. WWW Conf.*, Santa Clara, CA, USA, April 1997.

[149] M. Castagli and S. Eubank. *Nonlinear Modeling and Forecasting*. Addison-Wesley, 1992.

[150] R. Cattel. *The Object Database Standard: ODMG-93*. Morgan Kauffman, 1993.

[151] W. B. Cavnar and A. M. Gillies. Data retrieval and the realities of document donversion. In *Proc. of the 1st Annual Conference on the Theory and Practice of Digital Libraries*, College Station, TX, USA, June 1994.

[152] S. Chakrabarti, B. Dom, R. Agrawal, and P. Raghavan. Scalable feature selection, classification and signature generation for organizing large text databases into hierarchical topic taxonomies. *VLDB Journal*, 7(3):163–178, 1998.

[153] S. Chakrabarti, B. Dom, D. Gibson, S. Kumar, P. Raghavan, S. Rajagopalan, and A. Tomkins. Experiments in topic distillation. In *ACM-SIGIR'98 Post Conference Workshop on Hypertext Information Retrieval for the Web*, Melbourne, Australia, 1998.

[154] S. Chakrabarti, B. Dom, P. Raghavan, S. Rajagopalan, D. Gibson, and J. Kleinberg. Automatic resource compilation by analyzing hyperlink structure and associated text. In *7th Int. WWW Conference*, pages 65–74, Brisbane, Australia, April 1998.

[155] M. Chalmers, K. Rodden, and D. Brodbeck. The order of things: activity-centred information access. In *7th Int. WWW Conference*, Brisbane, Australia, April 1998.

[156] Matthew Chalmers and Paul Chitson. Bead: Exploration in information visualization. In *Proc. of the 15th Annual International ACM/SIGIR Conference*, pages 330–337, Copenhagen, Denmark, 1992.

[157] C-H. Chang and C-C. Hsu. Customizable multi-engine search tool with clustering. In *6th. Int. WWW Conference*, Santa Clara, CA, USA, April 1997.

[158] S.-F. Chang, J. R. Smith, H. J. Meng, H. Wang, and D. Zhong. Finding Images/Video in Large Archives: Columbia's Content-Based Visual Query Project. *D-Lib Magazine*, February 1997. http://www.dlib.org/dlib/february97/columbia/02chang.html.

[159] Shan-Ju Chang and Ronald E. Rice. Browsing: A multidimensional framework. *Annual Review of Information Science and Technology*, 28:231–276, 1993.

[160] S. Chapman and A. R. Kenney.   Digital conversion of library research materials: A case for full informational capture.   *D-Lib Magazine*, October 1996. http://www.dlib.org/dlib/october96/cornell/10chapman.html.

[161] S. Chawathe, H. García-Molina, J. Hammer, K. Ireland, Y. Papakonstantinou, J. Ullman, and J. Widom. The TSIMMIS project: Integration of heterogeneous information sources. In *Proc. of IPSJ Conference*, pages 7–18, October 1994.

[162] C. Chen. Structuring and visualizing the WWW by generalized similarity analysis. In *Proc. of the 8th ACM Conference on Hypertext and Hypermedia*, pages 177–186, Southampton, England, 1997.

[163] Hsinchun Chen, Andrea L. Houston, Robin R. Sewell, and Bruce R. Schatz. Internet browsing and searching: User evaluations of category map and concept space techniques. *Journal of the American Society for Information Science*, 49(7):582–608, 1998.

[164] Michael Chen and Marti A. Hearst. Presenting Web site search results in context: A demonstration. In *Proc. of the 20th Annual International ACM/SIGIR Conference*, page 381, Melbourne, Australia, 1998.

[165] Peter M. Chen, Edward K. Lee, Garth A. Gibson, Randy H. Katz, and David A. Paterson. RAID: High-performance, reliable secondary storage. *ACM Computing Surveys*, 26(2):145–185, June 1994.

[166] F. Cheong. *Internet Agents, Spiders, Wanderers, Brokers and Bots*. New Riders, 1996.

[167] D. R. Chestnutt. The model editions partnership: 'Smart Text' and beyond. *D-Lib Magazine*, July/August 1997. http://www.dlib.org/dlib/july97/07chesnutt.html.

[168] J. Cho, H. García-Molina, and L. Page. Efficient crawling through URL ordering. In *7th WWW Conference*, Brisbane, Australia, April 1998.

[169] S. Christodoulakis, M. Theodoridou, F. Ho, M. Papa, and A. Pathria. Multimedia document presentation, information extraction, and document formation in MINOS: a model and a system. *IEEE Transactions on Office Information Systems*, 4(4):345–383, October 1986.

[170] W. W. Chu, I. T. Ieong, R. K. Taira, and C. M. Breant. A Temporal Evolutionary Object-Oriented Model and its Query Languages for Medical Image Management. In *Proc. of the Int. Conference on Very Large Data Bases*, pages 53–64, Vancouver, Canada, Aug 1992.

[171] K. Church and W. Gale. Poisson mixtures. *Natural Language Engineering*, 1(2):163–190, 1995.

[172] Paolo Ciaccia, Marco Patella, and Pavel Zezula. M-tree: An efficient access method for similarity search in metric spaces. In *Proc. of VLDB Conf.*, pages 426–435, Athens, Greece, August 1997.

[173] C. Clarke, G. Cormack, and F. Burkowski. An algebra for structured text search and a framework for its implementation. *The Computer Journal*, 38(1):43–56, 1995.

[174] Charles L. A. Clarke, Gordon V. Cormack, and Forbes J. Burkowski. Shortest substring ranking (multitext experiments for TREC-4). In Donna Harman, editor, *Proc. of the Fourth Text Retrieval Conference TREC-4*. National Institute of Standards and Technology Special Publication, 1996.

[175] E. G. Coffman, Z. Liu, and R. R. Weber. Optimal robot scheduling for Web search engines. Technical Report 3317, INRIA, France, December 1997.

[176] Douglas E. Comer and David L. Stevens. *Internetworking with TCP/IP Vol III: Client-Server Programming and Applications*. Prentice-Hall, Inc., Englewood Cliffs, NJ, USA, 1993.

[177] *Communications of the ACM*, 37(2), February 1994.

[178] *Communications of the ACM*, 38(8), August 1995.

[179] B. Commentz-Walter. A string matching algorithm fast on the average. In *Proc. ICALP'79*, pages 118–132. Springer-Verlag, 1979.

[180] Compaq: Junglee shopping guide. http://www.compaq.junglee/compaq/top.html, 1998.

[181] Jeff Conklin. Hypertext: An introduction and survey. *IEEE Computer*, 20(9):17–41, September 1987.

[182] Dan Connolly on the architecture of the Web: Let a thousand flowers bloom. *IEEE Internet Computing*, 2(2):22–31, 1998.

[183] M. Consens and T. Milo. Algebras for querying text regions. In *Proc. of the ACM Conference on Principles of Distributed Systems*, pages 11–22, San Jose, California, USA, 1995.

[184] M. P. Consens and A. O. Mendelzon. Expressing structural hypertext queries in Graphlog. In *Hypertext'89*, pages 269–292, 1989.

[185] Alan Cooper. *About Face: The Essentials of User Interface Design*. IDG Books, 1995.

[186] William S. Cooper, Fredric C. Gey, and Daniel P. Dabney. Probabilistic retrieval based on staged logistic regression. In *Proc. of the 15th Annual International ACM SIGIR Conference on Research and Development in Information Retrieval*, pages 198–210, Copenhagen, Denmark, 1992.

[187] Wm. S. Cooper. The formalism of probability theory in IR: A foundation or an encumbrance? In *Proc. of the 17th Annual International ACM SIGIR Conference on Research and Development in Information Retrieval*, pages 242–247, Dublin, Ireland, 1994. Triennial ACM-SIGIR Award Paper.

[188] Thomas H. Cormen, Charles E. Leiserson, and Ronald L. Rivest. *Introduction to Algorithms*. The MIT Press/McGraw-Hill, Cambridge, MA, 1990.

[189] Corporation for National Research Initiatives, The Handle System, May 1998. http://www.handle.net/.

[190] P. Cotton, editor. *ISO Working Draft SQL Multimedia and Application Packages (SQL/MM), Part II Full text*. ISO/IEC, 1993. SC21/WG3 N1631, SQL/MM MUN-004.

[191] S. B. Cousins, S. P. Ketchpel, A. Paepcke, H. García-Molina, S. W. Hassan, and M. Roscheisen. InterPay: Managing multiple payment mechanisms in digital libraries. In *Proc. of the 2nd Annual Conference on the Theory and Practice of Digital Libraries*, Austin, Texas, June 1995.

[192] S. B. Cousins, A. Paepcke, T. Winograd, E. A. Bier, and K. Pier. The digital library integrated task environment (DLITE). In *Proc. of the 2nd ACM International Conference on Digital Libraries*, pages 142–151, Philadelphia, PA, USA, July 1997.

[193] Steve B. Cousins. *Reification and Affordances in a User Interface for Interacting with Heterogeneous Distributed Applications*. PhD thesis, Stanford University, May 1997.

[194] B. Cox, J. D. Tygar, and M. Sirbu. NetBill Security and Transaction Protocol. In *Proc. of the 1st USENIX Workshop on Electronic Commerce*, New York, USA, July 1995.

[195] S. Y. Crawford, J. M. Hurd, and A. C. Weller. *From Print to Electronic: the Transformation of Scientific Communication*. American Society for Information Science Monograph Series, Medford, New Jersey, 1996.

[196] M. Crochemore and W. Rytter. *Text Algorithms*. Oxford University Press, Oxford, UK, 1994.

[197] W. B. Croft. What do people want from information retrieval? (The top 10 research issues for companies that use and sell IR systems). *D-Lib Magazine*, November 1995. http://www.dlib.org/dlib/november95/11croft.html.

[198] W. B. Croft. Experiments with representation in a document retrieval system. *Information Technology: Research and Development*, 2(1):1–21, 1983.

[199] W. B. Croft and D. J. Harper. Using probabilistic models of retrieval without relevance information. *Journal of Documentation*, 35(4):285–295, 1979.

[200] Carolyn J. Crouch and Bokyung Yang. Experiments in automatic statistical thesaurus construction. In *Proc. of the ACM-SIGIR Conference on Research and Development in Information Retrieval*, pages 77–88, Copenhagen, Denmark, 1992.

[201] M. Crovella and A. Bestavros. Self-similarity in World Wide Web traffic: Evidence and possible causes. In *ACM Sigmetrics Conference on Measurement and Modeling of Computer Systems*, pages 160–169, May 1996.

[202] Douglass R. Cutting, David Karger, and Jan Pedersen. Constant interaction-time Scatter/Gather browsing of very large document collections. In *Proc. of the 16th Annual International ACM/SIGIR Conference*, pages 126–135, Pittsburgh, PA, 1993.

[203] Douglass R. Cutting, Jan O. Pedersen, David Karger, and John W. Tukey. Scatter/Gather: A cluster-based approach to browsing large document collections. In *Proc. of the 15th Annual International ACM/SIGIR Conference*, pages 318–329, Copenhagen, Denmark, 1992.

[204] Allen Cypher, editor. *Watch What I Do: Programming by Demonstration*. MIT Press, Cambridge, 1993.

[205] A. Czumaj, M. Crochemore, L. Gasieniec, S. Jarominek, Thierry Lecroq, W. Plandowski, and W. Rytter. Speeding up two string-matching algorithms. *Algorithmica*, 12:247–267, 1994.

[206] T. Dao, R. Sacks-Davis, and J. Thom. Indexing structured text for queries on containment relationships. In *Proc. of 7th Australasian Database Conference*, Melbourne, Australia, Jan/Feb 1996.

[207] Rick Darnell. *HTML 4.0 Unleashed, Professional Reference Edition*. Samms.net Publishing, 1998.

[208] M. Dartois, A. Maeda, T. Sakaguchi, T. Fujita, S. Sugimoto, and K. Tabata. A multilingual electronic text collection of folk tales for casual users using off-the-shelf browsers. *D-Lib Magazine*, October 1997. http://www.dlib.org/dlib/october97/sugimoto/10sugimoto.html.

[209] S. Davidson, C. Overton, V. Tannen, and L. Wong. BioKleisli: A digital library for biomedical researchers. *International Journal of Digital Libraries*, 1(1):35–53, April 1997.

[210] J. R. Davis and C. Lagoze. A protocol and server for a distributed technical report library. Technical report, Cornell University Computer Science Department, June 1994.

[211] Y. F. Day, S. Dagtas, M. Iino, A. Khokhar, and A. Ghafoor. Object-oriented conceptual modeling of video data. In *Proc. of the IEEE Conference on Data Engineering*, pages 401–405, Taipei, Taiwan, 1995.

[212] DejaNews: Main Page. http://www.dejanews.com, 1998.

[213] Alin Deutsch, Mary Fernández, Daniela Florescu, Alon Levy, and Dan Suciu. A query language for XML. http://www.research.att.com/~mff/xml/w3cnote.html, 1998.

[214] A. Dillon. What is the shape of information? Human factors in the development and use of digital libraries. Allerton discussion document submitted for the 1995 Allerton Institute. http://edfu.lis.uiuc.edu/allerton/95/s4/dillon.html.

[215] DirectHit: Main Page. http://www.directhit.com, 1998.

[216] Division of Information and Intelligent Systems, National Science Foundation. Digital Libraries Initiative – Phase 2. Announcement Number NSF 98-63, 1998. http://www.nsf.gov/pubs/1998/nsf9863/nsf9863.htm.

[217] M. Dodge. The geography of cyberspace directory: Main page. http://www.geog.ucl.ac.uk/casa/martin/geography_of_cyberspace.html, 1997.

[218] R. Dolin, D. Agrawal, A. El Abbadi, and J. Pearlman. Using automated classification for summarizing and selecting heterogeneous information sources. *D-Lib Magazine*, January 1998. http://www.dlib.org/dlib/january98/dolin/01dolin.html.

[219] R. Dolin, D. Agrawal, L. Dillon, and A. El Abbadi. Pharos: a scalable distributed architecture for locating heterogeneous information sources. In *Proc. of the 6th CIKM Conference*, pages 348–355, Las Vegas, Nevada, 1997.

[220] P. Dömel. Webmap: A graphical hypertext navigation tool. In *Proc. of the 2nd. WWW Conference*, 1994. http://www.ncsa.uiuc.edu/SDG/IT94/Proceedings/-WWW2_Proceedings.html.

[221] P. Doty and A. P. Bishop. The national information infrastructure and electronic publishing: A reflective essay. *Journal of the American Society for Information Science*, 45(10):785–799, 1994.

[222] Karen M. Drabenstott and Marjorie S. Weller. The exact-display approach for online catalog subject searching. *Information Processing and Management*, 32(6):719–745, 1996.

[223] D. Dreilinger. Savvy Search, 1996. http://savvy.cs.colostate.edu:2000/form?beta.

[224] R. O. Duda and P. E. Hart. *Pattern Classification and Scene Analysis*. Wiley, New York, 1973.

[225] Mark D. Dunlop. The effect of accessing nonmatching documents on relevance feedback. *ACM Transactions on Information Systems*, 15(2):137–153, 1997.

[226] Deborah M. Edwards and Lynda Hardman. 'Lost in hyperspace': Cognitive mapping and navigation in a hypertext environment. In Ray McAleese, editor, *Hypertext I: Theory into Practice*, pages 105–125. Ablex Publishing Corporation, 1988.

[227] Dennis E. Egan. Individual differences in human-computer interaction. In Martin Helander, editor, *Handbook of Human-Computer Interaction*, pages 543–568. Springer Verlag, 1988.

[228] Dennis E. Egan, Michael E. Lesk, R. Daniel Ketchum, Carol C. Lochbaum, Joel R. Remde, Louis M. Gómez, and Thomas K. Landauer. Hypertext for the electronic library? CORE sample results. In *Proc. of the ACM Hypertext Conference*, pages 299–312, May 1991.

[229] Dennis E. Egan, Joel R. Remde, Louis M. Gomez, Thomas K. Landauer, Jennifer Eberhardt, and Carol C. Lochbaum. Formative design evaluation of SuperBook. *Transactions on Information Systems*, 7(1):30–57, 1989.

[230] Dennis E. Egan, Joel R. Remde, Thomas K. Landauer, Carol C. Lochbaum, and Louis M. Gomez. Behavioral evaluation and analysis of a hypertext browser. In *Proc. of the ACM SIGCHI Conference on Human Factors in Computing Systems*, pages 205–210, May 1989.

[231] M. J. Egenhofer. Extending SQL for Graphical Display. *Cartography and Geographic Information Systems*, 18(4):230–245, 1991.

[232] Stephen G. Eick. Graphically displaying text. *Journal of Computational and Graphical Statistics*, 3(2):127–142, June 1994.

[233] Stephen G. Eick and Graham J. Wills. High interaction graphics. *European Journal of Operations Research*, 81(3):445–459, March 1995.

[234] Stephen G. Eick and Graham J. Wills. Navigating large networks with hierarchies. In *Proc. of the Conference on Visualization '93*, pages 204–209, San Jose, October 1993.

[235] P. Elias. Universal codeword sets and representations of the integers. *IEEE Transactions on Information Theory*, 21:194–203, 1975.

[236] D. Ellis. A behavioural model for information retrieval system design. *Journal of Information Science*, 15:237–247, 1989.

[237] R. Entlich, L. Garson, M. Lesk, L. Normore, J. Olsen, and S. Weibel. Making a digital library: The Chemistry Online Retrieval Experiment – A summary of the CORE project (1991-1995). *D-Lib Magazine*, December 1995. http://www.dlib.org/dlib/december95/briefings/12core.html.

[238] M. L. Escobar-Molano and S. Ghandeharizadeh. A Framework for Conceptualizing Structured Video. In *Proc. First Int. Workshop on Multimedia Information Systems*, pages 95–110, Arlington,Virginia, September 1995.

[239] ERCIM Digital Library Working Group, European Research Consortium for Informatics and Mathematics, June 1998. http://www.area.pi.cnr.it/ErcimDL/.

[240] Excite: Main page. http://www.excite.com, 1995.

[241] Express: Main Page. http://www.express.infoseek.com, 1998.

[242] C. Faloutsos and R. Chan. Text access methods for optical and large magnetic disks: design and performance comparison. In *Proc. of VLDB'88*, pages 280–293, Los Angeles, CA, USA, 1988.

[243] C. Faloutsos and S. Christodoulakis. Description and performance analysis of signature file methods. *ACM TOIS*, 5(3):237–257, 1987.

[244] Christos Faloutsos, Ron Barber, Myron Flickner, J. Hafner, Wayne Niblack, Dragutin Petkovic, and William Equitz. Efficient and effective querying by image content. *J. of Intelligent Information Systems*, 3(3/4):231–262, July 1994.

[245] Christos Faloutsos and Volker Gaede. Analysis of n-dimensional quadtrees using the Hausdorff fractal dimension. In *Proc. of VLDB Conf.*, pages 40–50, Bombay, India, September 1996.

[246] Christos Faloutsos, H. V. Jagadish, Alberto O. Mendelzon, and Tova Milo. A signature technique for similarity-based queries. In *SEQUENCES'97*, Salerno, Italy, June 1997.

[247] Christos Faloutsos and Ibrahim Kamel. Beyond uniformity and independence: Analysis of R-trees using the concept of fractal dimension. In *Proc. ACM SIGACT-SIGMOD-SIGART PODS*, pages 4–13, Minneapolis, MN, May 1994.

[248] Christos Faloutsos and King-Ip (David) Lin. FastMap: A fast algorithm for indexing, data-mining and visualization of traditional and multimedia datasets. *Proc. of ACM SIGMOD*, pages 163–174, May 1995.

[249] Christos Faloutsos, M. Ranganathan, and Yannis Manolopoulos. Fast subsequence matching in time-series databases. In *Proc. ACM SIGMOD*, pages 419–429, Minneapolis, MN, USA, May 1994. 'Best Paper' award.

[250] M. Farach and M. Thorup. String matching in Lempel-Ziv compressed strings. In *Proc. 27th ACM Annual Symposium on the Theory of Computing*, pages 703–712, Las Vegas, NE, USA, 1995.

[251] I. A. Ferguson and M. J. Wooldridge. Paying their way: Commercial digital libraries for the 21st century. *D-Lib Magazine*, June 1997. http://www.dlib.org/dlib/june97/zuno/06ferguson.html.

[252] Terry Ellen Ferl and Larry Millsap. The knuckle-cracker's dilemma: a transaction log study of OPAC subject searching. *Information Technology and Libraries*, 15:81–98, 1996.

[253] Mary Fernandez, Daniela Florescu, Alon Levy, and Dan Suciu. A query language for a Web-site management system. *SIGMOD Record*, 26(3):4–11, September 1997.

[254] E. Ferrari and G. Haus. Designing music objects for a multimedia database. In *Proc. 12th Colloquium on Musical Informatics*, pages 135–138, Gorizia, Italy, September 1998.

[255] Gerhard Fischer and Helga Nieper-Lemke. Helgon: Extending the retrieval reformulation paradigm. In *Proc. of ACM CHI Conference on Human Factors in Computing Systems*, pages 357–362, 1989.

[256] Ken Fishkin and Maureen C. Stone. Enhanced dynamic queries via movable filters. In *Proc. of ACM CHI Conference on Human Factors in Computing Systems*, volume 1 of *Papers: Information Visualization*, pages 415–420, Denver, CO, USA, 1995.

[257] Myron Flickner, Harpreet Sawhney, Wayne Niblack, Jon Ashley, Qian Huang, Byron Dom, Monika Gorkani, Jim Hafner, Denis Lee, Dragutin Petkovic, David Steele, and Peter Yanker. Query by image and video content: The QBIC system. *IEEE Computer*, 28(9):23–32, September 1995.

[258] D. Florescu, A. Levy, and A. Mendelzon. Database techniques for the World-Wide Web: A survey. *SIGMOD Record*, 27(3):59–74, 1998.

[259] M. J. Flynn. Very high-speed computing systems. In *Proc. IEEE*, volume 54, pages 1901–1909, 1966.

[260] Corporation for National Research Initiatives. Computer Science Technical Reports Project (CSTR), May 1996. http://www.cnri.reston.va.us/home/cstr.html.

[261] D. J. Foskett. Thesaurus. In K. Sparck Jones and P. Willet, editors, *Readings in Information Retrieval*, pages 111–134. Morgan Kaufmann Publishers, Inc., 1997.

[262] Richard H. Fowler, Wendy A. L. Fowler, and Bradley A. Wilson. Integrating query, thesaurus, and documents through a common visual representation. In *Proc. of the 14th Annual International ACM/SIGIR Conference*, pages 142–151, Chicago, 1991.

[263] C. Fox. Lexical analysis and stoplists. In W. Frakes and R. Baeza-Yates, editors, *Information Retrieval: Data Structures & Algorithms*, pages 102–130. Prentice Hall, Englewood Cliffs, NJ, USA, 1992.

[264] E. Fox, R. France, E. Sahle, A. Daoud, and B. Cline. Development of a Modern OPAC: From REVTOLC to MARIAN. In *Proc. of the 16th Annual International ACM SIGIR Conference on Research and Development in Information Retrieval*, pages 248–259, Pittsburgh, PA, June/July 1993.

[265] E. Fox and L. Lunin. Introduction and overview to perspectives on digital libraries: Guest editor's introduction to special issue. *Journal of the American Society for Information Science*, 44(8):441–443, 1993.

[266] E. A. Fox. Source book on digital libraries. Technical Report TR-93-35, Virginia Polytechnic Institute and State University, 1993.

[267] E. A. Fox, R. M. Akscyn, R. K. Furuta, and J. J. Leggett. Digital libraries. *Communications of the ACM*, 38(4):22–28, April 1995.

[268] E. A. Fox and R. Gupta. Courseware on Digital Libraries. http://ei.cs.vt.edu/~dlib/.

[269] E. A. Fox, L. S. Heath, and D. Hix. Project Envision Final Report: A user-centered database from the computer science literature, July 1995. http://ei.cs.vt.edu/papers/ENVreport/final.html.

[270] E. A. Fox and G. Marchionini. Toward a worldwide digital library. *Communications of the ACM*, 41(4):29–32, April 1998. http://purl.lib.vt.edu/dlib/pubs/CACM199804.

[271] E. A. Fox. *Extending the Boolean and Vector Space Models of Information Retrieval with P-Norm Queries and Multiple Concept Types*. PhD thesis, Cornell University, Ithaca, New York, Http://www.ncstrl.org, 1983.

[272] Edward A. Fox. Characterization of two new experimental collections in computer and information science containing textual and bibliographical concepts. *Technical Report*, 83-561, 1983. Http://www.ncstrl.org.

[273] Edward A. Fox, Deborah Hix, Lucy T. Nowell, Dennis J. Brueni, William C. Wake, Lenwood S. Heath, and Durgesh Rao. Users, user interfaces, and objects: Envision, a digital library. *Journal of the American Society for Information Science*, 44(8):480–491, 1993.

[274] W. Frakes. Stemming algorithms. In W. Frakes and R. Baeza-Yates, editors, *Information Retrieval: Data Structures & Algorithms*, pages 131–160. Prentice Hall, Englewood Cliffs, NJ, USA, 1992.

[275] W. B. Frakes and R. Baeza-Yates. *Information Retrieval: Data Structures & Algorithms*. Prentice Hall, Englewood Cliffs, NJ, USA, 1992.

[276] W. Francis and H. Kucera. *Frequency Analysis of English Usage*. Houghton Mifflin Co., 1982.

[277] Eric Freeman and Scott Fertig. Lifestreams: Organizing your electronic life. In Robin Burke, editor, *Working Notes of the AAAI Fall Symposium on AI Applications in Knowledge Navigation and Retrieval*, Cambridge, MA, November 1995.

[278] H. P. Frei and D. Stieger. The use of semantic links in hypertext information retrieval. *Information Processing & Management*, 31(1):1–13, 1994.

[279] J. French, E. Fox, K. Maly, and A. Selman. Wide Area Technical Report Service: Technical Reports Online. *Communications of the ACM*, 38(4):47, April 1995.

[280] A. Friedlander. D-lib Program: Research in Digital Libraries, May 1998. http://www.dlib.org/.

[281] N. Fuhr. Models for retrieval with probabilistic indexing. *Information Processing & Management*, 25:55–72, 1989.

[282] N. Fuhr. Probabilistic models in information retrieval. *The Computer Journal*, 35(3):243–255, 1992.

[283] N. Fuhr. DOLORES: A System for Logic-Based Retrieval of Multimedia Objects. In B. Croft, A. Moffat, C. J. van Rijsbergen, R. Wilkinson, and J. Zobel, editors, *Proc. of the 21st Annual International ACM SIGIR Conference on Research and Development in Information Retrieval*, pages 257–265, Melbourne, Australia, 1998.

[284] Norbert Fuhr. Optimal polynomial retrieval functions based on the probability ranking principle. *ACM Transactions on Information Systems*, 7(3):183–204, 1989.

[285] Keinosuke Fukunaga. *Introduction to Statistical Pattern Recognition*. Academic Press, 2nd edition, 1990.

[286] George W. Furnas and Jeff Zacks. Multitrees: Enriching and reusing hierarchical structure. In *Proc. of ACM CHI Conference on Human Factors in Computing Systems*, volume 2, pages 330–336, 1994.

[287] G. W. Furnas, S. Deerwester, S. T. Dumais, T. K. Landauer, R. A. Harshman, L. A. Streeter, and K. E. Lochbaum. Information retrieval using a singular value decomposition model of latent semantic structure. In *Proc. of the 11th Annual International ACM SIGIR Conference on Research and Development in Information Retrieval*, pages 465–480, 1988.

[288] R. Furuta. Defining and Using Structure in Digital Documents. In *Proc. of the 1st Annual Conference on the Theory and Practice of Digital Libraries*, College Station, TX, USA, 1994.

[289] Richard Furuta, Frank M. Shipman III, Catherine C. Marshall, Donald Brenner, and Hao wei Hsieh. Hypertext paths and the World-Wide Web: Experiences with Walden's paths. In *Proc. of the Eighth ACM Conference on Hypertext*, pages 167–176, Southampton, England, 1997.

[290] Volker Gaede and Oliver Günther. Multidimensional access methods. *ACM Computing Surveys*, 30(2):170–231, 1998.

[291] R. G. Gallager. Variations on a theme by Huffman. *IEEE Transactions on Information Theory*, 24:668–674, 1978.

[292] S. Gauch, G. Wang, and M. Gómez. ProFusion: Intelligent fusion from multiple, distributed search engines. *Journal of Universal Computing*, 2(9):637–649, September 1996.

[293] E. Gaynor. From MARC to Markup: SGML and Online Library Systems. *ALCTS Newsletter*, 7(2), 1996.

[294] Naum Gershon, Joshua LeVasseur, Joel Winstead, James Croall, Ari Pernick, and William Ruh. Visualizing Internet resources. In *Proc. of the '95 Information Visualization*, pages 122–128, Atlanta, October 1995.

[295] Fredric C. Gey. Inferring probability of relevance using the method of logistic regression. In *Proc. of the 17th Annual International ACM SIGIR Conference on Research and Development in Information Retrieval*, pages 222–231, Dublin, Ireland, 1994.

[296] S. Gibbs. Composite Multimedia and Active Objects. In *Proc. Int. Conf. on Object-Oriented Programming: Systems, Languages, and Applications*, pages 97–112, October 1991.

[297] S. Gibbs, C. Breiteneder, and D. Tsichritzis. Audio/video databases: an object-oriented approach. In *Proc. 9th Int. Conf. on Data Engineering*, pages 381–390, 1993.

[298] D. Gibson, J. Kleinberg, and P. Raghavan. Inferring Web communities from link topologies. In *9th ACM Conference on Hypertext and Hypermedia*, Pittsburgh, USA, 1998.

[299] H. Gladney, E. Fox, Z. Ahmed, R. Ashany, N. Belkin, and M. Zemankova. Digital library: Gross structure and requirements: Report from a March 1994 workshop. In *Proc. of the 1st Annual Conference on the Theory and Practice of Digital Libraries*, pages 101–107, College Station, TX, USA, 1994.

[300] H. Gladney, F. Mintzer, F. Schiattarella, J. Bescós, and M. Treu. Digital access to antiquities. *Communications of the ACM*, 41(4):49–57, April 1998.

[301] H. M. Gladney. Safeguarding digital library contents and users: document access control. *D-Lib Magazine*, June 1997. http://www.dlib.org/dlib/june97/ibm/06gladney.html.

[302] H. M. Gladney and J. B. Lotspiech. Safeguarding digital library contents and users: Assuring convenient security and data quality. *D-Lib Magazine*, May 1997. http://www.dlib.org/dlib/may97/ibm/05gladney.html.

[303] Charles Goldfarb. *The SGML Handbook*. Oxford University Press, Oxford, 1990.

[304] Charles Goldfarb and Paul Prescod. *The XML Handbook*. Prentice Hall, Oxford, 1998.

[305] Dina Q. Goldin and Paris C. Kanellakis. On similarity queries for time-series data: Constraint specification and implementation. *Int. Conf. on Principles and Practice of Constraint Programming*, pages 137–153, Sept 1995.

[306] R. Goldman, J. McHugh, and J. Widom. Lore: A database management system for XML. Technical report, Stanford University Database Group, 1998.

[307] S. W. Golomb. Run-length encodings. *IEEE Transactions on Information Theory*, 12(3):399–401, 1966.

[308] G. Golovchinsky. What the query told the link: the integration of Hypertext and Information Retrieval. In *8th ACM Conference on Hypertext and Hypermedia*, pages 67–74, Southampton, England, 1997.

[309] G. Gonnet. Examples of PAT applied to the Oxford English Dictionary. Technical Report OED-87-02, UW Centre for the New OED and Text Research, Univ. of Waterloo, 1987.

[310] G. Gonnet and R. Baeza-Yates. *Handbook of Algorithms and Data Structures*. Addison-Wesley, Wokingham, England, 2nd edition, 1991.

[311] G. Gonnet, R. Baeza-Yates, and T. Snider. New indices for text: Pat trees and Pat arrays. In William Frakes and Ricardo Baeza-Yates, editors, *Information Retrieval: Data Structures and Algorithms*, pages 66–82. Prentice Hall, Englewood Cliffs, NJ, USA, 1992.

[312] J. Gordon and E. Shortliffe. The Dempster-Shafer Theory of Evidence. In *Rule-Based Expert Systems*, pages 113–138. Addison-Wesley Publishing Company, 1984.

[313] Graduate School of Library and Information Science, University of Illinois at Urbana-Champaign, 37th Allerton Institute 1995, January 1996. http://edfu.lis.uiuc.edu/allerton/95/.

[314] Graduate School of Library and Information Science, University of Illinois at Urbana-Champaign, 38th Allerton Institute, January 1997. http://edfu.lis.uiuc.edu/allerton/96/.

[315] P. Graham. Glossary on Digital Library Terminology, 1997. Informal file sent by electronic mail for comments, available with permission of the author if suitable attribution is made.

[316] L. Gravano, K. Chang, H. García-Molina, C. Lagoze, and A. Paepcke. STARTS: Stanford protocol proposal for Internet retrieval and search. Technical report, Stanford University, Digital Library Project, 1997. http://www-db.stanford.edu/~gravano/starts.html.

[317] Luis Gravano, Chen-Chuan K. Chang, and Hector García-Molina. STARTS: Stanford proposal for Internet meta-searching. In *Proc. ACM SIGMOD Int. Conf. on Management of Data*, pages 207–218, Tucson, AZ, May 1997.

[318] Luis Gravano, Hector García-Molina, and Anthony Tomasic. The effectiveness of GlOSS for the text-database discovery problem. In *Proc. ACM SIGMOD Int. Conf. on Management of Data*, pages 126–137, Minneapolis, MN, May 1994.

[319] Luis Gravano, Hector García-Molina, and Anthony Tomasic. GlOSS: Text-source discovery over the Internet. *ACM Transactions on Database Systems*, 1999. To appear.

[320] S. J. Green. Automated link generation: can we do better than term repetition. In *7th WWW Conference*, Brisbane, Australia, 1998.

[321] Stephan Green, Gary Marchionini, Catherine Plaisant, and Ben Shneiderman. Previews and overviews in digital libraries: Designing surrogates to support visual information seeking. Technical Report Department of Computer Science CS-TR-3838, University of Maryland, 1997.

[322] Sharon L. Greene, Susan J. Devlin, Philip E. Cannata, and Louis M. Gomez. No IFs, ANDs, or ORs: A study of database querying. *International Journal of Man-Machine Studies*, 32(3):303–326, 1990.

[323] Gregory Grefenstette. *Cross-Language Information Retrieval*. Kluwer Academic Publishers, Boston, USA, 1998.

[324] S. M. Griffin. NSF/DARPA/NASA Digital Libraries Initiative: A program manager's perspective. *D-Lib Magazine*, July/August 1998. http://www.dlib.org/dlib/july98/07griffin.html.

[325] D. A. Grossman, O. Frieder, D. O. Holmes, and D. C. Roberts. Integrating structured data and text: A relational approach. *Journal of the American Society for Information Science*, 48:122–132, 1997.

[326] David A. Grossman and Ophir Frieder. *Information Retrieval: Algorithms and Heuristics*. Kluwer Academic Publishers, 1998.

[327] V. Gudivada, V. Raghavan, W. Grosky, and R. Kasanagottu. Information retrieval on the World Wide Web. *IEEE Internet Computing*, Oct-Nov:58–68, 1997.

[328] J.-C. Guédon. The virtual library: An oxymoron? NLM and MLA 1998 Leiter Lecture, National Library of Medicine, Bethesda, MD, May 1998.

[329] Catherine Guinan and Alan F. Smeaton. Information retrieval from hypertext using dynamically planned guided tours. In *Proc. of the 4th ACM Conference on Hypertext*, pages 122–130, 1992.

[330] A. Guttman. R-trees: A dynamic index structure for spatial searching. In *Proc. ACM SIGMOD*, pages 47–57, Boston, Mass, June 1984.

[331] Trudi Bellardo Hahn. Pioneers of the online age. *Information Processing & Management*, 32:33–48, 1996.

[332] David Haines and W. Bruce Croft. Relevance feedback and inference networks. In *Proc. of the 16th Annual International ACM SIGIR Conference on Research and Development in Information Retrieval*, pages 2–11, Pittsburgh, PA, USA, 1993.

[333] J. Hakala. The 5th Dublin Core Metadata Workshop, October 1997. http://linnea.helsinki.fi/meta/DC5.html.

[334] Frank G. Halasz, Thomas P. Moran, and Randall H. Trigg. Notecards in a nutshell. In *Proc. of ACM CHI+GI Conference on Human Factors in Computing Systems and Graphics Interface*, pages 45–52, 1987.

[335] Micheline Hancock-Beaulieu. User friendliness and human-computer interaction in on-line library catalogs. *Program*, 46(1):29–37, 1992.

[336] Micheline Hancock-Beaulieu. Experiments on interfaces to support query expansion. *Journal of Documentation*, 53(1):8–19, 1997.

[337] Micheline Hancock-Beaulieu, Margaret Fieldhouse, and Thien Do. An evaluation of interactive query expansion in an online library catalogue with a graphical user interface. *Journal of Documentation*, 51(3):225–243, 1995.

[338] Micheline Hancock-Beaulieu and Stephen Walker. An evaluation of automatic query expansion in an online library catalogue. *Journal of Documentation*, 48(4):406–421, 1992.

[339] D. Harman. Ranking algorithms. In W. B. Frakes and R. Baeza-Yates, editors, *Information Retrieval: Data Structures & Algorithms*, pages 363–392. Prentice Hall, Englewood Cliffs, NJ, USA, 1992.

[340] D. Harman. Relevance feedback and other query modification techniques. In W. B. Frakes and R. Baeza-Yates, editors, *Information Retrieval: Data Structures & Algorithms*, pages 241–263. Prentice Hall, Englewood Cliffs, NJ, USA, 1992.

[341] D. Harman, E. Fox, R. Baeza-Yates, and W. Lee. Inverted files. In W. Frakes and R. Baeza-Yates, editors, *Information Retrieval: Algorithms and Data Structures*, chapter 3, pages 28–43. Prentice Hall, Englewood Cliffs, NJ, USA, 1992.

[342] D. K. Harman. Overview of the third text retrieval conference. In *Proc. of the 3rd Text REtrieval Conference (TREC-3)*, pages 1–19, Gaithersburg, USA, 1995. National Institute of Standards and Technology Special Publication.

[343] Donna Harman. Relevance feedback revisited. In *Proc. of the 5th Annual International ACM SIGIR Conference on Research and Development in Information Retrieval*, pages 1–10, Copenhagen, Denmark, 1992.

[344] D. J. Harper. *Relevance Feedback in Document Retrieval Systems: An Evaluation of Probabilistic Strategies*. PhD thesis, Jesus College, Cambridge, England, 1980.

[345] D. J. Harper and C. J. van Rijsbergen. An evaluation of feedback in document retrieval using co-occurrence data. *Journal of Documentation*, 34(3):189–216, 1978.

[346] G. Harper. The Conference on Fair Use (CONFU), September 1997. http://www.utsystem.edu/ogc/intellectualproperty/confu.htm.

[347] S. P. Harter. What is a digital library? Definitions, content, and issues. In *Proc. of KOLISS DL '96: International Conference on Digital Libraries and Information Services for the 21st Century*, Seoul, Korea, September 1996. http://php.indiana.edu/~harter/korea-paper.htm.

[348] Stephen P. Harter. *Online Information Retrieval*. Academic Press, 1986.

[349] S. Harum. Digital Library Initiative, January 1998. http://dli.grainger.uiuc.edu/national.htm.

[350] Alexander G. Hauptmann and Bert F. Green. A comparison of command, menu-selection and natural-language computer programs. *Behaviour and Information Technology*, 2(2):163–178, 1983.

[351] Leigh Watson Healy. *Library Systems: Current Developments and Future Directions*. Council on Library and Information Resources, Washington DC, 1998.

[352] J. Heaps. *Information Retrieval — Computational and Theoretical Aspects*. Academic Press, 1978.

[353] M. Hearst, G. Kopec, and D. Brotsky. Research in support of digital libraries at Xerox PARC, Part II: Paper and digital documents. *D-Lib Magazine*, June 1996. http://www.dlib.org/dlib/june96/hearst/06hearst.html.

[354] M. A. Hearst. Research in Support of Digital Libraries at Xerox PARC, Part I: The changing social roles of documents. *D-Lib Magazine*, May 1996. http://www.dlib.org/dlib/may96/05hearst.html.

[355] Marti A. Hearst. TileBars: Visualization of term distribution information in full text information access. In *Proc. of the ACM SIGCHI Conference on Human Factors in Computing Systems*, pages 59–66, Denver, CO, May 1995.

[356] Marti A. Hearst. Improving full-text precision using simple query constraints. In *Proc. of the 5th Annual Symposium on Document Analysis and Information Retrieval*, Las Vegas, NV, 1996.

[357] Marti A. Hearst. The use of categories and clusters in organizing retrieval results. In Tomek Strzalkowski, editor, *Natural Language Information Retrieval*. Kluwer Academic Publishers, 1999. To appear.

[358] Marti A. Hearst and Chandu Karadi. Cat-a-cone: An interactive interface for specifying searches and viewing retrieval results using a large category hierarchy. In *Proc. of the 20th Annual International ACM SIGIR Conference*, pages 246–255, Philadelphia, PA, 1997.

[359] Marti A. Hearst and Jan O. Pedersen. Reexamining the cluster hypothesis: Scatter/gather on retrieval results. In *Proc. of the 19th Annual International ACM SIGIR Conference*, pages 76–84, Zurich, Switzerland, 1996.

[360] L. Heath, D. Hix, L. Nowell, W. Wake, G. Averboch, and E. Fox. Envision: A user-centered database from the computer science literature. *Communications of the ACM*, 38(4):52–53, April 1995.

[361] J. H. Hellerstein and M. Stonebraker. Predicate migration: Optimizing queries with expensive predicates. In *Proc. of the ACM SIGMOD Int. Conf. on Management of Data*, pages 267–276, Washington, DC, USA, 1993.

[362] Joseph M. Hellerstein, Jeffrey F. Naughton, and Avi Pfeffer. Generalized search trees for database systems. In *Proc. of VLDB Conf.*, pages 562–573, Zurich, Switzerland, Sept 1995.

[363] Matthias Hemmje, Clemens Kunkel, and Alexander Willett. LyberWorld – a visualization user interface supporting fulltext retrieval. In *Proc. of the 17th Annual International ACM SIGIR Conference*, pages 249–259, Dublin, Ireland, July 1994.

[364] R. Hendly, N. Drew, A. Wood, and R. Beale. Narcissus: Visualizing information. In *Proc. of the IEEE Information Visualization Symposium*, pages 90–96, Atlanta, GA, USA, Oct 1995.

[365] David G. Hendry and David J. Harper. An informal information-seeking environment. *Journal of the American Society for Information Science*, 48(11):1036–1048, 1997.

[366] M. Hersovici, M. Jacobi, Y. S. Maarek, D. Pelleg, M. Shtalhaim, and S. Ur. The shark-search algorithm. An application: tailored Web site mapping. In *7th WWW Conference*, Brisbane, Australia, April 1998.

[367] C. Hert. Information retrieval: A social informatics perspective. Allerton discussion document submitted for the 1996 Allerton Institute, 1996.

[368] Morten Hertzum and Erik Frokjaer. Browsing and querying in online documentation: A study of user interfaces and the interaction process. *ACM Transactions on Computer-Human Interaction*, 3(2):136–161, 1996.

[369] Eric van Herwijnen. *Practical SGML*. Kluwer Academic Publishers, 2nd edition, 1994.

[370] Ron R. Hightower, Laura T. Ring, Jonathan I. Helfman, Benjamin B. Bederson, and James D. Hollan. Graphical multiscale Web histories: A study of padprints. In *Proc. of the Ninth ACM Conference on Hypertext*, pages 58–65, Pittsburgh, PA, USA, 1998.

[371] Charles R. Hildreth. The use and understanding of keyword searching in an university online catalog. *Information Technology and Libraries*, 16:52–62, 1997.

[372] C. R. Hildreth. Online library catalogues as IR systems: what can we learn from research? In P. A. Yates Mercer, editor, *Future Trends in Information Science and Technology*, pages 9–25. Taylor-Graham, Los Angeles, 1988.

[373] Rainer Himmeroder, Georg Lausen, Bertram Ludascher, and Christian Schlepphorst. On a declarative semantics for Web queries. In *Proc. of the Int. Conf. on Deductive and Object-Oriented Database (DOOD)*, pages 386–398, Singapore, December 1997.

[374] D. S. Hirschberg and D. A. Lelewer. Efficient decoding of prefix codes. *Communications of the ACM*, 33(4), 1990.

[375] J. Hopcroft and J. Ullman. *Introduction to Automata Theory, Languages and Computation*. Addison-Wesley Publishing Company, 1979.

[376] R. N. Horspool. Practical fast searching in strings. *Software Practice and Experience*, 10:501–506, 1980.

[377] R. N. Horspool and G. V. Cormack. Constructing word-based text compression algorithms. In *Proc. of IEEE Second Data Compression Conference*, pages 62–81, 1992.

[378] E. Horvitz, J. Breese, D. Heckerman, D. Hovel, and K. Rommelse. The Lumiere project: Bayesian user modeling for inferring the goals and needs of software users. In *Proc. of AAAI 98*, Madison, WI, July 1998.

[379] P. Hoschka. Synchronized multimedia integration language. W3C Working Draft, February 1998. http://www.w3.org/TR/WD-smil.

[380] Hotbot: Main page. http://www.hotbot.com, 1996.

[381] T. Y. Hou, A. Hsu, P. Liu, and M. Y. Chiu. A content-based indexing technique using relative geometry features. In *Proc. of SPIE'92*, volume 1662, pages 59–68, 1992.

[382] N. Van House, D. Levy, A. Bishop, and B. Buttenfield. User needs assessment and evaluation: issues and methods (workshop). In *Proc. of the 1st ACM International Conference on Digital Libraries*, page 186, College Station, TX, USA, 1996.

[383] Adele Howe and Danielle Dreilinger. Savvysearch: A metasearch engine that learns which search engines to query. *AI Magazine*, 18(2):19–25, 1997.

[384] J-Y. Huang, C-T. Fang-Tsou, and J-L. Chang. Multiuser 3D Web browsing system. *IEEE Internet Computing*, 2(5):70–73, 1998.

[385] M. L. Huang, P. Eades, and R. F. Cohen. WebOFDAV — navigating and visualizing the Web on-line with animated context swapping. In *7th WWW Conference*, Brisbane, Australia, April 1998.

[386] D. Huffman. A method for the construction of minimum-redundancy codes. *Proc. of the I.R.E.*, 40(9):1090–1101, 1952.

[387] D. A. Hull and G. Grefenstette. Querying across languages: A dictionary-based approach to multilingual information retrieval. In *Proc. of the 19th Annual Int. ACM SIGIR Conference on Research and Development in Information Retrieval*, pages 49–57, Zurich, Switzerland, 1996.

[388] David A. Hull, Jan O. Pedersen, and Hinrich Schütze. Method combination for document filtering. In *Proc. of the 19th Annual Int. ACM SIGIR Conference*, pages 279–287, Zurich, Switzerland, 1996.

[389] R. Iannella. Australian digital library initiatives. *D-Lib Magazine*, December 1996. http://www.dlib.org/dlib/december96/12iannella.html.

[390] IBM Corporation, IBM Digital Library, 1998. http://www.software.ibm.com/is/dig-lib/.

[391] E. Ide. New experiments in relevance feedback. In G. Salton, editor, *The SMART Retrieval System*, pages 337–354. Prentice Hall, 1971.

[392] IEEE Standards Committee on Optical Disk and Multimedia Platforms (SC ODMP), IEEE SFQL. Technical report, IEEE, Washington, USA, 1992.

[393] G. H. Brett II. An integrated system for distributed information services. *D-Lib Magazine*, December 1996. http://www.dlib.org/dlib/december96/dipps/12brett.html.

[394] Infoseek Corporation, Distributed Search Patent. http://software.infoseek.com/-patents/dist_search/Default.htm.

[395] Inktomi: Main Page. http://www.inktomi.com, 1998.

[396] International DOI Foundation, Digital Object Identifier System, June 1998. http://www.doi.org/index.html.

[397] H. Ishikawa, F. Suzuki, F. Kozakura, A. Makinouchi, M. Miyagishima, M. Aoshima Y. Izumida, and Y. Yamane. The model, language and implementation of an object-oriented multimedia knowledge base management system. *ACM Transactions on Database Systems*, 18:1–50, 1993.

[398] ISO. *Office Document Architecture (ODA) an Interchange Format*, 1986.

[399] Paul S. Jacobs and Lisa F. Rau. Innovations in text interpretation. *Artificial Intelligence*, 63(1-2):143–191, 1993.

[400] H. V. Jagadish. A retrieval technique for similar shapes. In *Proc. ACM SIGMOD Conf.*, pages 208–217, Denver, Colorado, May 1991.

[401] Jango: Main Page. http://www.jango.com, 1998.

[402] M. Jarke and J. Koch. Query optimization in database systems. *ACM Computing Surveys*, 16(2):111–152, June 1984.

[403] B. J. Jensen, A. Spink, J. Bateman, and T. Saracevic. Real life information retrieval: A study of user queries on the Web. *ACM SIGIR Forum*, 32(1):5–17, 1998.

[404] Byeong-Soo Jeong and Edward Omiecinski. Inverted file partitioning schemes in multiple disk systems. *IEEE Trans. Par. and Dist. Syst.*, 6(2):142–153, February 1995.

[405] H. Jiang, A. K. Elmagarmid, A. A. Helal, A. Joshi, and M. Ahmed. *Video Database Systems*. Kluwer Academic, San Francisco, CA, 1997.

[406] Thorsten Joachims, Dayne Freitag, and Tom Mitchell. WebWatcher: A tour guide for the World Wide Web. In *Proc. of the 15th Int. Joint Conference on Artificial Intelligence*, Nagoya, Japan, August 1997.

[407] Brian Johnson and Ben Shneiderman. Tree-maps: a space-filling approach to the visualization of hierarchical information structures. In *Proc. of the 2nd Int. IEEE Visualization Conference*, pages 284–291, San Diego, USA, 1991.

[408] I. T. Jolliffe. *Principal Component Analysis*. Springer Verlag, 1986.

[409] K. Sparck Jones. A statistical interpretation of term specificity and its application to retrieval. *Journal of Documentation*, 28(1):11–20, 1972.

[410] K. Sparck Jones. A statistical interpretation of term specificity and its application to retrieval. *Information Storage and Retrieval*, 9(11):619–633, 1973.

[411] K. Sparck Jones. Experiments in relevance weighting of search terms. *Information Processing & Management*, 15(13):133–144, 1979.

[412] K. Sparck Jones. Search term relevance weighting given little relevance information. *Journal of Documentation*, 35(1):30–48, 1979.

[413] K. Sparck Jones and E. O. Barber. What makes an automatic keyword classification effective. *Journal of the American Society for Information Sciences*, 22(3):166–175, 1971.

[414] K. Sparck Jones and P. Willet. *Readings in Information Retrieval*. Morgan Kaufmann Publishers, Inc., 1997.

[415] Karen Sparck Jones. The Cranfield tests. In Karen Sparck Jones, editor, *Information Retrieval Experiment*, pages 256–284. Butterworths, London, 1981.

[416] S. Jones, S. Walker, M. Gatford, and T. Do. Peeling the onion: Okapi system architecture and software design issues. *Journal of Documentation*, 53:58–68, 1997.

[417] Steve Jones. Graphical query specification and dynamic result previews for a digital library. In *Proc. of UIST'98, ACM Symposium on User Interface Software and Technology*, San Francisco, USA, November 1998.

[418] T. Joseph and A. F. Cárdenas. PICQUERY: A high level language for pictorial database management. *IEEE Transactions on Software Engineering*, 14(5):630–638, 1988.

[419] T. Joyce and R. M. Needham. The thesaurus approach to information retrieval. In K. Sparck Jones and P. Willet, editors, *Readings in Information Retrieval*, pages 15–20. Morgan Kaufmann Publishers, Inc., 1997.

[420] D. Austin Henderson Jr and Stuart K. Card. Rooms: The use of multiple virtual workspaces to reduce space contention in a window-based graphical user interface. *ACM Transactions on Graphics*, 5(3):211–243, 1986.

[421] E. J. Whitehead Jr and M. Wiggins. WebDAV: IETF standard for collaborative authoring on the Web. *IEEE Internet Computing*, 2(5):34–40, 1998.

[422] W. M. Shaw Jr, R. Burgin, and P. Howell. Performance standards and evaluations in IR test collections: Cluster-based retrieval models. *Information Processing & Management*, 33(1):1–14, 1997.

[423] W. M. Shaw Jr., R. Burgin, and P. Howell. Performance standards and evaluations in IR test collections: Vector-space and other retrieval models. *Information Processing & Management*, 33(1):15–36, 1997.

[424] B. Kahle. Archiving the Internet. http://www.alexa.com/~brewster/essays/sciam_article.html, 1997.

[425] B. Kahle and A. Medlar. An information server for corporate users: Wide Area Information Servers. *ConneXions — The Interoperability Report*, 5(11):2–9, 1991. ftp://think.com/wais/wais-corporate-paper.text.

[426] R. Kahn and R. Wilensky. A framework for distributed digital object services. Technical Report cnri.dlib/tn95-01, CNRI, May 1995. http://www.cnri.reston.va.us/k-w.html.

[427] Ibrahim Kamel and Christos Faloutsos. Hilbert R-tree: An improved R-tree using fractals. In *Proc. of VLDB Conference*, pages 500–509, Santiago, Chile, Sept 1994.

[428] Eser Kandogan and Ben Shneiderman. Elastic windows: Evaluation of multi-window operations. In *Proc. of ACM Conference on Human Factors in Computing Systems*, volume 1, pages 250–257, Atlanta, GA, USA, March 1997.

[429] P. B. Kantor. Assessing the factors leading to adoption of digital libraries, and growth in their impacts: the Goldilocks principle. Allerton discussion document submitted for the 1996 Allerton Institute. http://edfu.lis.uiuc.edu/allerton/96/kantor.html.

[430] J. Karkkäinen and E. Ukkonen. Two and higher dimensional pattern matching in optimal expected time. In *Proc. of ACM-SIAM Symposium on Discrete Algorithms*, pages 715–723, San Francisco, USA, 1994.

[431] Norio Katayama and Shin'ichi Satoh. The SR-tree: An index structure for high-dimensional nearest neighbor queries. In *Proc. of ACM SIGMOD*, pages 369–380, Tucson, AZ, 1997.

[432] Henry Kautz, Bart Selman, and Mehul Shah. The hidden Web. *AI Magazine*, 18(2):27–36, 1997.

[433] P. R. Keller and M. M. Keller. *Visual Cues: Practical Data Visualization*. IEEE Computer Society Press, 1993.

[434] R. Kengeri, C. D. Seals, H. P. Reddy, H. D. Harley, and E. A. Fox. Usability study of digital libraries: ACM, IEEE-CS, NCSTRL, NDLTD, December 1997. http://fox.cs.vt.edu/~fox/u/Usability.pdf.

[435] M. M. Kessler. Comparison of results of bibliographic coupling and analytic subject indexing. *American Documentation*, 16(3):223–233, July 1965.

[436] R. Khare and A. Rifkin. XML: A door to automated Web applications. *IEEE Internet Computing*, 1(4):78–86, 1977.

[437] R. Khare and A. Rifkin. The origin of (document) species. In *7th WWW Conference*, Brisbane, Australia, April 1998.

[438] S. Khoshafian and A. B. Baker. *Multimedia and Imaging Databases*. Morgan Kauffman, 1996.

[439] P. Kilpelainen and H. Mannila. Retrieval from hierarchical texts by partial patterns. In *Proc. of the 16th Annual Int. ACM SIGIR Conference on Research and Development in Information Retrieval*, pages 214–222, Pittsburgh, USA, 1993.

[440] Hanhwe Kim and Stephen C. Hirtle. Spatial metaphors and disorientation in hypertext browsing. *Behaviour and Information Technology*, 14(4):239–250, 1995.

[441] Steven T. Kirsch. Document retrieval over networks wherein ranking and relevance scores are computed at the client for multiple database documents. US Patent 5,659,732, August 1997.

[442] W. Klas and A. Sheth. Special issue on meta-data for digital media. *SIGMOD Record*, 23(4):19–20, 1994.

[443] Adrienee J. Kleiboemer, Manette B. Lazear, and Jan O. Pedersen. Tailoring a retrieval system for naive users. In *Proc. of the 5th Annual Symposium on Document Analysis and Information Retrieval*, Las Vegas, NV, USA, 1996.

[444] Jon Kleinberg. Authoritative sources in a hyperlinked environment. In *Proc. of the 9th ACM-SIAM Symposium on Discrete Algorithms*, pages 668–677, San Francisco, USA, Jan 1998.

[445] D. E. Knuth. *The Art of Computer Programming*, volume 3: Searching and Sorting. Addison-Wesley, 1973.

[446] D. E. Knuth. Dynamic Huffman coding. *Journal of Algorithms*, 6:163–180, 1985.

[447] D. E. Knuth, J. H. Morris, Jr, and V. R. Pratt. Fast pattern matching in strings. *SIAM Journal on Computing*, 6(1):323–350, 1977.

[448] Jurgen Koenemann and Nicholas J. Belkin. A case for interaction: A study of interactive information retrieval behavior and effectiveness. In *Proc. of ACM Conference on Human Factors in Computing Systems*, volume 1 of *Papers*, pages 205–212, Zurich, Switzerland, 1996.

[449] Janet L. Kolodner. *Case-based Reasoning*. Morgan Kaufmann Publishers, 1993.

[450] D. Konopnicki and O. Shmueli. W3QS: A query system for the World Wide Web. In *Proc. of VLDB'95*, pages 54–65, Zurich, Switzerland, September 1995.

[451] Robert Korfhage. *Information Storage and Retrieval*. John Wiley & Sons, Inc., 1997.

[452] Robert R. Korfhage. To see or not to see – is that the query? In *Proc. of the 14th Annual Int. ACM SIGIR Conference*, pages 134–141, Chicago, USA, 1991.

[453] Flip Korn and Ben Shneiderman. Navigating terminology hierarchies to access a digital library of medical images. Technical Report HCIL-TR-94-03, University of Maryland, USA, Korn & Shneiderman, 1995.

[454] Flip Korn, Nikolaos Sidiropoulos, Christos Faloutsos, Eliot Siegel, and Zenon Protopapas. Fast nearest-neighbor search in medical image databases. *Proc. Conf. on Very Large Data Bases*, pages 215–226, September 1996.

[455] J. Korpela. Lurching toward Babel: HTML, CSS, and XML. *IEEE Computer*, 31(7):103–106, 1998.

[456] S. M. Kosslyn. Understanding charts and graphs. *Applied Cognitive Psychology*, 3:185–226, 1989.

[457] M. Koster. Guidelines for robot writers, 1993. http://info.webcrawler.com/mak/-projects/robots/guidelines.html.

[458] Nick Koudas, Christos Faloutsos, and Ibrahim Kamel. Declustering spatial databases on a multi-computer architecture. *EDBT Conf. Proc.*, pages 592–614, March 1996.

[459] Gerald Kowalski. *Information Retrieval Systems, Theory and Implementation*. Kluwer Academic Publishers, Boston, USA, 1997.

[460] Robyn Kozierok and Pattie Maes. A learning interface agent for scheduling meetings. In *Proc. of the 1993 Int. Workshop on Intelligent User Interfaces*, pages 81–88, New York, NY, 1993.

[461] D. Kraft and D. A. Buel. Fuzzy sets and generalized Boolean retrieval systems. *International Journal of Man-Machine Studies*, 19:45–56, 1983.

[462] Joseph B. Kruskal and Myron Wish. *Multidimensional scaling*. SAGE publications, Beverly Hills, 1978.

[463] Julian Kupiec. MURAX: A robust linguistic approach for question answering using an on-line encyclopedia. In *Proc. of the 16th Annual Int. ACM SIGIR Conference*, pages 181–190, Pittsburgh, PA, 1993.

[464] Julian Kupiec, Jan Pedersen, and Francine Chen. A trainable document summarizer. In *Proc. of the 18th Annual Int. ACM SIGIR Conference*, pages 68–73, Seattle, WA, 1995.

[465] K. L. Kwok, L. Grunfeld, and D. D. Lewis. TREC-3 ad-hoc, routing retrieval and thresholding experiments using PIRCS. In *Proc. of the Text REtrieval Conference*, pages 247–256, Gaithersburg, MD, USA, 1995.

[466] K. L. Kwok. A neural network for probabilistic information retrieval. In *Proc. of the ACM SIGIR Conference on Research and Development in Information Retrieval*, pages 21–30, Cambridge, USA, June 1989.

[467] K. L. Kwok. Experiments with a component theory of probabilistic information retrieval based on single terms as document components. *ACM Transactions on Information Systems*, 8(4):363–386, October 1990.

[468] K. L. Kwok. A network approach to probabilistic information retrieval. *ACM Transactions on Information Systems*, 13(3):324–353, July 1995.

[469] K. L. Kwok, L. Papadopolous, and Y. Y. Kwan. Retrieval experiments with a large collection using PIRCS. In *Proc. of the 1st TExt Retrieval Conference*, pages 153–172, Gaithersburg, MD, USA, 1993. Special Publication 500-267, National Institute of Standards and Technology (NIST).

[470] Eric Lagergren and Paul Over. Comparing interactive information retrieval systems across sites: The TREC-6 interactive track matrix experiment. In *Proc. of the 21st Annual Int. ACM SIGIR Conference*, pages 164–172, Melbourne, Australia, 1998.

[471] C. Lagoze. Networked Computer Science Technical Reference Library. http://www.ncstrl.org.

[472] C. Lagoze. The Warwick framework: a container architecture for diverse sets of metadata. *D-Lib Magazine*, July/August 1996. http://www.dlib.org/dlib/july96/lagoze/07lagoze.html.

[473] C. Lagoze and D. Ely. Implementation issues in an open architecture framework for digital object services. Technical Report TR95-1540, Cornell University Computer Science Department, 1995.

[474] C. Lagoze, D. Fielding, and S. Payette. Making global digital libraries work: collection services, connectivity regions, and collection views. In *Proc. of the 3rd ACM International Conference on Digital Libraries*, 1998.

[475] C. Lagoze, R. McGrath, E. Overly, and N. Yeager. A design for inter-operable secure object stores (ISOS). Technical Report TR95-1558, Cornell University Computer Science Department, 1995.

[476] Laks V. S. Lakshmanan, Fereidoon Sadri, and Iyer N. Subramanian. A declarative language for querying and restructuring the Web. In *6th Int. Workshop on Research Issues in Data Engineering, RIDE '96*, New Orleans, February 1996.

[477] B. LaMacchia. The Internet fish construction kit. In *6th. Int'l. WWW Conference*, Santa Clara, CA, USA, April 1997.

[478] John Lamping, Ramana Rao, and Peter Pirolli. A focus+context technique based on hyperbolic geometry for visualizing large hierarchies. In *Proc. of the ACM Conference on Human Factors in Computing Systems*, pages 401–408, Denver, CO, USA, May 1995.

[479] F. W. Lancaster. Natural language in information retrieval. In *Indexing and Abstracting in Theory and Practice*, pages 193–218. University of Illinois, Champaign, IL, 1991.

[480] G. Landau and U. Vishkin. Fast string matching with k differences. *Journal of Computer Systems Science*, 37:63–78, 1988.

[481] Thomas K. Landauer, Dennis E. Egan, Joel R. Remde, Michael Lesk, Carol C. Lochbaum, and Daniel Ketchum. Enhancing the usability of text through computer delivery and formative evaluation: the SuperBook project. In C. McKnight, A. Dillon, and J. Richardson, editors, *Hypertext: A Psychological Perspective*, pages 71–136. Ellis Horwood, 1993.

[482] Andrew Large and Jamshid Beheshti. OPACS: a research review. *LISR*, 19:111–133, 1997.

[483] Jill H. Larkin and Herbert A. Simon. Why a diagram is (sometimes) worth ten thousand words. *Cognitive Science*, 11:65–99, 1987.

[484] Ray R. Larson. Between Scylla and Charybdis: Subject searching in the online catalog. *Advances in Librarianship*, 15:175–236, 1991.

[485] Ray R. Larson. Bibliometrics of the World Wide Web: An exploratory analysis of the intellectual structure of cyberspace. In *Proc. of the 1996 Annual ASIS Meeting*, pages 71–78, 1996.

[486] Ray R. Larson, Jerome McDonough, Paul O'Leary, and Lucy Kuntz. Cheshire II: Designing a next-generation online catalog. *Journal of the American Society for Information Science*, 47(7):555–567, 1996.

[487] Ora Lassila. Web metadata: A matter of semantics. *IEEE Internet Computing*, 2(4):30–37, 1998.

[488] S. Lawrence and C. L. Giles. Inquirus, the NECI meta search engine. In *7th WWW Conference*, pages 95–105, Brisbane, Australia, 1998.

[489] S. Lawrence and C. Lee Giles. Context and page analysis for improved Web search. *IEEE Internet Computing*, 2(4):38–46, 1998.

[490] S. Lawrence and C. L. Giles. Searching the World Wide Web (in reports). *Science*, 280(5360):98, April 3 1998.

[491] Doug Lea. *Concurrent Programming in Java: Design Principles and Patterns*. The Java Series. Addison-Wesley, Reading, MA, 1997.

[492] David B. Leake, editor. *Case-based Reasoning: Experiences, Lessons, and Future Directions*. AAAI Press, Menlo Park, CA, 1996.

[493] J. H. Lee, W. Y. Kim, and Y. H. Lee. Ranking documents in thesaurus-based Boolean retrieval systems. *Information Processing & Management*, 30(1):79–91, 1993.

[494] J. J. Lee and P. Kantor. A study of probabilistic information retrieval systems in the case of inconsistent expert judgements. *Journal of the American Society for Information Sciences*, 42(3):166–172, 1991.

[495] Joon Ho Lee. Properties of extended Boolean models in information retrieval. In *Proc. of the Seventeenth Annual International ACM SIGIR Conference on Research and Development in Information Retrieval*, pages 182–190, Dublin, Ireland, 1994.

[496] Joon Ho Lee, Won Yong Kim, Myoung Ho Kim, and Yoon Joon Lee. On the evaluation of Boolean operators in the extended Boolean retrieval framework. In *Proc. of the 16th Annual Int. ACM SIGIR Conference on Research and Development in Information Retrieval*, pages 291–297, Pittsburgh, PA, USA, 1993.

[497] O. Lehtinen, E. Sutinen, and J. Tarhio. Experiments on block indexing. In *Proc. of WSP'96*, pages 183–193, Recife, Brazil, 1996. Carleton University Press.

[498] H. V. Leighton and J. Srivastava. Precision among World Wide Web search engines: AltaVista, Excite, Hotbot, Infoseek, and Lycos. http://www.winona.msus.edu/library/webind2/webind2.htm, 1997.

[499] B. Leiner. D-Lib Working Group on Digital Library Metrics, May 1998. http://www.dlib.org/metrics/public/metrics-home.html.

[500] M. E. Lesk. Word-word associations in document retrieval systems. *American Documentation*, 20(1):8–36, 1969.

[501] Michael Lesk. *Practical Digital Libraries; Books, Bytes, and Bucks*. Morgan Kaufmann, 1997.

[502] Y. K. Leung and M. D. Apperley. A review and taxonomy of distortion-oriented presentation techniques. *ACM Transactions on Computer-Human Interaction*, 1(2):126–160, 1994.

[503] R. LeVan. Dublin Core and Z39.50. Draft version 1.2, February 1998. http://cypress.dev.oclc.org:12345/~rrl/docs/dublincoreandz3950.html.

[504] V. Levenshtein. Binary codes capable of correcting deletions, insertions and reversals. *Soviet Physics Doklady*, 10(8):707–710, 1966. Original in Russian in *Doklady Akademii Nauk SSSR, 163(4):8 45–848, 1965.*

[505] D. M. Levy. Topics in document research. In *Proc. of the ACM Conference on Document Processing Systems (SIGDOC '88)*, pages 187–193, 1988.

[506] D. M. Levy. Fixed or fluid?: document stability and new media. In *Proc. of the 1994 ACM European Conference on Hypermedia Technology*, pages 24–31, 1994.

[507] D. M. Levy. I read the news today, oh boy: reading and attention in digital libraries. In *Proc. of the 2nd ACM Int. Conference on Digital Libraries*, pages 202–211, Philadelphia, PA, USA, July 1997.

[508] D. M. Levy, D. C. Brotsky, and K. R. Olson. Formalizing the figural: aspects of a foundation for document manipulation. In *Proc. of the ACM Conference on Document Processing Systems (SIGDOC '88)*, pages 145–151, 1988.

[509] D. M. Levy and C. C. Marshall. Going digital: a look at assumptions underlying digital libraries. *Communications of the ACM*, 38:77–84, April 1995.

[510] The LEXIS-NEXIS Computing Complex. http://www.lexis-nexis.com/lncc/about/datacenter.html.

[511] W-S. Li, J. Shim, K. S. Candan, and Y. Hara. WebDB: A Web query system and its modeling, language, and implementation. In *Proc. of Advances in Digital Libraries*, Santa Barbara, CA, USA, April 1998.

[512] Y. Li. Toward a qualitative search engine. *IEEE Internet Computing*, 2(4):24–29, 1998.

[513] Library of Congress, Metadata, Dublin Core and USMARC: A Review of Current Efforts, January 1997. gopher://marvel.loc.gov/00/.listarch/usmarc/dp99.doc.

[514] Library of Congress, MARC Standards, June 1998. http://lcweb.loc.gov/marc/marc.html.

[515] Library of Congress, Z39.50 Maintenance Agency, June 1998. http://lcweb.loc.gov/z3950/agency/.

[516] J. C. R. Licklider. *Libraries of the Future*. Cambridge, MA.: M.I.T. Press, 1965.

[517] H. W. Lie and B. Bos. *Cascading Style Sheets: Designing for the Web*. Addison-Wesley, 1997.

[518] Henry Lieberman. Letizia: an agent that assists Web browsing. In *Proc. of the 14th Int. Joint Conference on Artificial Intelligence*, pages 924–929, 1995.

[519] King-Ip Lin, H. V. Jagadish, and Christos Faloutsos. The TV-tree — an index structure for high-dimensional data. *VLDB Journal*, 3:517–542, October 1994.

[520] Xia Lin, Dagobert Soergel, and Gary Marchionini. A self-organizing semantic map for information retrieval. In *Proc. of the 14th Annual Int. ACM SIGIR Conference*, pages 262–269, Chicago, 1991.

[521] Ming-Ling Lo and Chinya V. Ravishankar. Spatial joins using seeded trees. In *Proc. of ACM SIGMOD*, pages 209–220, Minneapolis, MN, USA, May 1994.

[522] R. M. Losee and A. Bookstein. Integrating Boolean queries in conjunctive normal form with probabilistic retrieval models. *Information Processing & Management*, 24(3):315–321, 1988.

[523] Henry J. Lowe and G. Octo Barnett. Understanding and using the medical subject headings (MeSH) vocabulary to perform literature searches. *Journal of the American Medical Association*, 271(4):1103–1108, 1994.

[524] Zhihong Lu, Kathryn S. McKinley, and Brendon Cahoon. The hardware/software balancing act for information retrieval on symmetric multiprocessors. Technical Report TR98-25, Dept. of Comp. Sci., Univ. of Mass., Amherst, MA, 1998.

[525] C. Lynch and H. García-Molina. Interoperability, scaling, and the digital libraries research agenda: A report on the May 18-19, 1995, IITA Digital Libraries Workshop, August 1995. http://www-diglib.stanford.edu/diglib/pub/reports/iita-dlw/main.html.

[526] Clifford Lynch. The next generation of public access information retrieval systems for research libraries: lessons from ten years of the MELVYL system. *Information Technology and Libraries*, 11(4):405–415, 1992.

[527] Y. Maarek, M. Jacovi, M. Shtalhaim, S. Ur, D. Zernik, and I. Z. Ben Shaul. WebCutter: A system for dynamic and tailorable site mapping. In *6th WWW Conference*, pages 713–722, Santa Clara, CA, USA, 1997.

[528] Y. S. Maarek. Organizing documents to support browsing in digital libraries. Allerton discussion document submitted for the 1995 Allerton Institute. http://edfu.lis.uiuc.edu/allerton/95/s4/maarek.html.

[529] Y. S. Maarek and A. J. Wecker. The librarian's assistant: Automatically assembling books into dynamic bookshelves. In *Proc. of RIAO '94: Intelligent Multimedia Information Retrieval Systems and Management*, New York, USA, October 1994.

[530] Jock Mackinlay, George Robertson, and Stuart K. Card. The perspective wall: Detail and context smoothly integrated. In *Proc. of the ACM Conference on Human Factors in Computing Systems*, pages 173–179, 1991.

[531] Jock D. Mackinlay, Ramana Rao, and Stuart K. Card. An organic user interface for searching citation links. In *Proc. of ACM Conference on Human Factors in Computing Systems*, volume 1 of *Papers*, pages 67–73, Denver, CO, USA, 1995.

[532] A. MacLean, P. J. Barnard, and M. D. Wilson. Evaluating the human interface of a data entry system: User choice and performance measures yield different tradeoff functions. In *Proc. of the HCI'85 Conference on People and Computers: Designing the Interface*, pages 172–185, 1985.

[533] I. A. MacLeod. Storage and retrieval of structured documents. *Information Processing & Management*, 26(2):197–208, 1990.

[534] I. A. MacLeod. A query language for retrieving information from hierarchic text structures. *The Computer Journal*, 34(3):254–264, 1991.

[535] Ian A. Macleod, T. Patrick Martin, Brent Nordin, and John R. Phillips. Strategies for building distributed information retrieval systems. *Information Processing & Management*, 23(6):511–528, 1987.

[536] Pattie Maes and Robyn Kozierok. Learning interface agents. In *Proc. of AAAI 93*, pages 459–465, Washington, DC, July 1993.

[537] U. Manber and P. Bigot. Search Broker: Main page. http://debussy.cs.arizona.edu/sb/, 1997.

[538] U. Manber and G. Myers. Suffix arrays: a new method for on-line string searches. In *Proc. of ACM-SIAM Symposium on Discrete Algorithms*, pages 319–327, San Francisco, USA, 1990.

[539] U. Manber, M. Smith, and B. Gopal. WebGlimpse: combining browsing and searching. In *Proc. of USENIX Technical Conference*, pages 195–206, Anaheim, USA, Jan 1997.

[540] Udi Manber and Sun Wu. GLIMPSE: A tool to search through entire file systems. In *Proc. of USENIX Technical Conference*, pages 23–32, San Francisco, USA, January 1994. ftp://cs.arizona.edu/glimpse/glimpse.ps.Z.

[541] B. Mandelbrot. *Fractal Geometry of Nature*. W. H. Freeman, New York, 1977.

[542] Gary Marchionini. *Information Seeking in Electronic Environments*. Cambridge University Press, Cambridge, 1995.

[543] M. Marchiori. The quest for correct information on the Web: Hyper search engines. In *6th WWW Conf.*, pages 265–274, Santa Clara, CA, USA, 1997.

[544] M. Marchiori. The limits of Web metadata and beyond. In *7th WWW Conference*, Brisbane, Australia, April 1998.

[545] S. Marcus and V. S. Subrahmanian. Foundations of Multimedia Database Systems. *Journal of the ACM*, 4(3):474–505, 1996.

[546] Karen Markey, Pauline Atherton, and Claudia Newton. An analysis of controlled vocabulary and free text search statements in online searches. *Online Review*, 4:225–236, 1982.

[547] M. E. Maron and J. L. Kuhns. On relevance, probabilistic indexing and information retrieval. *Association for Computing Machinery*, 7(3):216–244, 1960.

[548] C. C. Marshall. Annotation: from paper books to the digital library. In *Proc. of the 2nd ACM Int. Conference on Digital Libraries*, pages 131–141, Philadelphia, PA, USA, 1997.

[549] Y. Masunaga. Design issues of OMEGA an object-oriented multimedia database management system. *Journal of Information Processing*, 14:60–74, 1991.

[550] Mark T. Maybury. *Intelligent Multimedia Information Retrieval*. MIT Press, 1997.

[551] Ray McAleese, editor. *Hypertext I: Theory into Practice*. Ablex Publishing Corporation, 1988.

[552] B. McCune, R. Tong, J. S. Dean, and D. Shapiro. Rubric: A system for rule-based information retrieval. *IEEE Transactions on Software Engineering*, 11(9), 1985.

[553] Charles T. Meadow, Barbara A. Cerny, Christine L. Borgman, and Donald O. Case. Online access to knowledge: System design. *Journal of the American Society for Information Science*, 40(2):86–98, 1989.

[554] Daniel A. Menasce and Virgilio A. F. Almeida. *Capacity Planning for Web Performance: Metrics, Models, and Methods*. Prentice Hall, 1998.

[555] Filippo Menczer and Richard K. Belew. Adaptive information agents in distributed textual environments. In Katia P. Sycara and Michael Wooldridge, editors, *Proc. of the 2nd Int. Conference on Autonomous Agents*, pages 157–164, May 1998.

[556] A. Mendelzon, G. Mihaila, and T. Milo. Querying the World Wide Web. *International Journal on Digital Libraries*, 1(1):54–67, April 1997.

[557] Beth Meyer, Richard A. Sit, Victoria A. Spaulding, Sherry E. Mead, and Neff Walker. Age group differences in World Wide Web navigation. In Katia P. Sycara and Michael Wooldridge, editors, *Proc. of ACM Conference on Human Factors in Computing Systems*, pages 157–164, Atlanta, GA, USA, March 1997.

[558] A. Michard. Graphical presentation of Boolean expressions in a database query language: design notes and an ergonomic evaluation. *Behaviour and Information Technology*, 1(3):279–288, 1982.

[559] F. Miksa and P. Doty. Intellectual Realities and the Digital Library. In *Proc. of the 1st Annual Conference on the Theory and Practice of Digital Libraries*, College Station, TX, USA, June 1994.

[560] E. J. Miller. CNI/OCLC Metadata Workshop: Workshop on Metadata for Networked Images, September 1996. http://purl.oclc.org/metadata/image.

[561] G. A. Miller, E. B. Newman, and E. A. Friedman. Length-frequency statistics for written english. *Information and Control*, 1:370–389, 1958.

[562] J. Minker, G. A. Wilson, and B. H. Zimmerman. An evaluation of query expansion by the addition of clustered terms for a document retrieval system. *Information Storage and Retrieval*, 8(6):329–348, 1972.

[563] T. Minohara and R. Watanabe. Queries on structure in hypertext. In D. Lomet, editor, *Proc. of Foundations of Data Organization and Algorithms*, number 730 in LNCS, pages 394–411, Chicago, IL, USA, 1993. Springer-Verlag.

[564] Richard Mitchell, David Day, and Lynette Hirschman. Fishing for information on the Internet. In *Proc. of the '95 Information Visualization*, pages 105–111, Atlanta, USA, October 1995.

[565] Tom M. Mitchell. *Machine Learning.* McGraw-Hill, 1997.

[566] Mandar Mitra, Amit Singhal, and Chris Buckley. Improving automatic query expansion. In B. Croft, A. Moffat, C. J. van Rijsbergen, R. Wilkinson, and J. Zobel, editors, *Proc. of 21st Annual Int. ACM SIGIR Conference on Research and Development in Information Retrieval*, pages 206–214, Melbourne, Australia, 1998.

[567] S. Miyamoto, T. Miyake, and K. Nakayama. Generation of a pseudothesaurus for information retrieval based on co-occurrences and fuzzy set operations. *IEEE Transactions on Systems and Man Cybernetics*, 13(1):62–70, 1983.

[568] S. Miyamoto and K. Nakayama. Fuzzy information retrieval based on a fuzzy pseudothesaurus. *IEEE Transactions on Systems and Man Cybernetics*, 16(2):278–282, 1986.

[569] S. Mizzaro. Relevance: The whole history. *Journal of the American Society for Information Science*, 48(9):810–832, 1997.

[570] W. E. Moen. Accessing distributed cultural heritage information. *Communications of the ACM*, 41(4):45–48, April 1998.

[571] A. Moffat. Word-based text compression. *Software Practice and Experience*, 19(2):185–198, 1989.

[572] A. Moffat and T. Bell. In situ generation of compressed inverted files. *Journal of the American Society for Information Science*, 46(7):537–550, 1995.

[573] A. Moffat and J. Zobel. Parameterized compression for sparse bitmaps. In *Proc. of the ACM SIGIR International Conference on Research and Development in Information Retrieval*, pages 274–285, Copenhagen, Denmark, 1992.

[574] Alistair Moffat and Justin Zobel. Information retrieval systems for large document collections. In Donna K. Harman, editor, *The Third Text REtrieval Conference (TREC-3)*, pages 85–94, Gaithersburg, MD, USA, 1995. Dept of Commerce, National Institute of Standards and Technology. Special Publication 500-226.

[575] E. S. Moura, G. Navarro, and N. Ziviani. Indexing compressed text. In R. Baeza-Yates, editor, *Proc. of the 4th South American Workshop on String Processing*, volume 8, pages 95–111, Valparaíso, Chile, 1997. Carleton University Press International Informatics Series.

[576] E. S. Moura, G. Navarro, N. Ziviani, and R. Baeza-Yates. Direct pattern matching on compressed text. In *Proc. of the 5th Symposium on String Processing and Information Retrieval*, pages 90–95, Santa Cruz, Bolivia, September 1998.

[577] E. S. Moura, G. Navarro, N. Ziviani, and R. Baeza-Yates. Fast searching on compressed text allowing errors. In *Proc. of the ACM-SIGIR International Conference on Research and Development in Information Retrieval*, pages 298–306, Melbourne, Australia, August 1998.

[578] S. Mukherjea and J. D. Foley. Visualizing the World Wide Web with the Navigational View Builder. *Computer Networks and ISDN Systems*, 27:1075–1087, 1995.

[579] S. Mukherjea, K. Hirata, and Y. Hara. Towards a multimedia World-Wide Web information retrieval engine. In *6th Int. WWW Conference*, Santa Clara, CA, USA, April 1997.

[580] Kevin Mullet and Darell Sano. *Designing Visual Interfaces: Communication-Oriented Techniques.* SunSoft Press, 1995.

[581] Brad Myers. *Creating User Interfaces by Demonstration.* Academic Press, New York, 1988.

[582] Brad Myers. A taxonomy of window manager user interfaces. *IEEE Computer Graphics and Applications*, pages 65–84, Sept 1988.

[583] G. Myers. A fast bit-vector algorithm for approximate pattern matching based on dynamic programming. In M. Farach-Colton, editor, *Proc. of Combinatorial Pattern Matching*, number 1448 in LNCS, pages 1–13, Rutgers, USA, 1998. Springer-Verlag.

[584] Bonnie A. Nardi. *A Small Matter of Programming: Perspectives on End User Computing*. MIT Press, 1993.

[585] A. Nation. Visualizing Websites using a hierarchical table of contents browser: WebTOC. In *Proc. of the 3rd Conference on Human Factors and the Web*, Denver, CO, 1997.

[586] National Humanities Alliance, Basic Principles for Managing Intellectual Property in the Digital Environment, March 1997. http://www-ninch.cni.org/ISSUES/COPYRIGHT/-PRINCIPLES/NHA_Complete.html.

[587] *Nation's Information Infrastructure Steering Committee, Computer Science, More than screen deep: toward every-citizen interfaces to the nation's information infrastructure.* National Academy Press, Washington, DC, USA, 1997.

[588] G. Navarro. *Approximate Text Searching.* PhD thesis, Dept. of Computer Science, Univ. of Chile, December 1998.

[589] G. Navarro and R. Baeza-Yates. A language for queries on structure and contents of textual databases. In *Proc. of the 18th Annual Int. ACM SIGIR Conference on Research and Development in Information Retrieval*, pages 93–101, Seattle, USA, July 1995.

[590] G. Navarro and R. Baeza-Yates. Proximal nodes: A model to query document databases by content and structure. *ACM Transactions on Office and Information Systems*, 15(4):401–435, 1997.

[591] G. Navarro, J. Kitajima, B. Ribeiro-Neto, and N. Ziviani. Distributed generation of suffix arrays. In A. Apostolico and J. Hein, editors, *Proc. of Combinatorial Pattern Matching*, number 1264 in LNCS, pages 102–115, Aarhus, Denmark, 1997. Springer-Verlag.

[592] G. Navarro and M. Raffinot. A bit-parallel approach to suffix automata: fast extended string matching. In M. Farach-Colton, editor, *Proc. of Combinatorial Pattern Matching*, number 1448 in LNCS, pages 14–33, Rutgers, USA, 1998. Springer-Verlag.

[593] G. Navarro and M. Raffinot. A general practical approach to pattern matching over Ziv-Lempel compressed text. Technical Report TR/DCC-98-12, Dept. of Computer Science, Univ. of Chile, 1998. ftp://ftp.dcc.uchile.cl/pub/users/gnavarro/lzsrch.ps.gz.

[594] NDLTD. Networked Digital Library of Theses and Dissertations, June 1998. http://www.ndltd.org/.

[595] J. Nesbit. The accuracy of approximate string matching algorithms. *Journal of Computer-Based Instruction*, 13(3):80–83, 1986.

[596] Netcraft Web Server Survey. http://www.netcraft.com/Survey/, 1998.

[597] NetSizer: Main Page. http://www.netsizer.com, 1998.

[598] Network Development and MARC Standards Office, Dublin Core/MARC/GILS Crosswalk, July 1997. http://www.loc.gov/marc/dccross.html.

[599] Network Wizards: Internet Domain Survey. http://www.nw.com, 1998.

[600] M. Lynne Neufeld and Martha Cornog. Database history: from dinosaurs to compact discs. *Journal of the American Society for Information Science*, 37(4):183–190, 1986.

[601] New Zealand DL Group, The New Zealand Digital Library Project. http://www.nzdl.org/.

[602] D. Ngu and X. Wu. SiteHelper: a localized agent that helps incremental exploration of the World Wide Web. In *6th. Int. WWW Conference*, Santa Clara, CA, USA, April 1997.

[603] Wayne Niblack, Ron Barber, Will Equitz, Myron Flickner, Eduardo Glasman, Dragutin Petkovic, Peter Yanker, Christos Faloutsos, and Gabriel Taubin. The QBIC project: Querying images by content using color, texture and shape. In *Int. Symposium on Electronic Imaging: Science and Technology, Conf. 1908, Storage and Retrieval for Image and Video Databases*, February 1993.

[604] Jakob Nielsen. *Hypertext and Hypermedia*. Academic Press, 1990.

[605] Jakob Nielsen. *Usability Engineering*. Academic Press, 1993.

[606] NISO Press, Bethesda, MD. *Information Retrieval (Z39.50): Application Service Definition and Protocol Specification (ANSI/NISO Z39.50-1995)*, 1995. Accessible at http://lcweb.loc.gov/z3950/agency/.

[607] D. A. Norman. *The Psychology of Everyday Things*. Basic Books, New York, 1988.

[608] Northern Light: Main page. http://www.northernlight.com, 1997.

[609] G. Notess. Search Engines Showdown. http://imt.net/~notess/search/, 1998.

[610] L. Nowell. *Graphical Encoding for Information Visualization: Using Icon Color, Shape, and Size to Convey Nominal and Quantitative Data*. PhD Thesis, Virginia Polytechnic and State University, Department of Computer Science, 1997.

[611] P. J. Nuernberg, R. Furuta, J. J. Leggett, C. C. Marshall, and F. M. Shipman III. Digital Libraries: Issues and Architectures. In *Proc. of the 2nd Annual Conference on the Theory and Practice of Digital Libraries*, Austin, Texas, 1995.

[612] D. W. Oard. Serving Users in Many Languages: Cross-Language Information Retrieval for Digital Libraries. *D-Lib Magazine*, December 1997. http://www.dlib.org/dlib/december97/oard/12oard.html.

[613] D. W. Oard and B. J. Dorr. A survey of multilingual text retrieval. Technical Report UMIACS-TR-96-19, University of Maryland, Institute for Advanced Computer Studies, 1996.

[614] Vicki L. O'Day and Robin Jeffries. Orienteering in an information landscape: how information seekers get from here to there. In *Proc. of the INTERCHI '93*, Amsterdam, Netherlands, April 1993. IOS Press.

[615] R. N. Oddy. Information retrieval through man-machine dialogue. *Journal of Documentation*, 33:1–14, 1977.

[616] Y. Ogawa, T. Morita, and K. Kobayashi. A fuzzy document retrieval system using the keyword connection matrix and a learning method. *Fuzzy Sets and Systems*, 39:163–179, 1991.

[617] Kenton O'Hara and Abigail Sellen. A comparison of reading paper and on-line documents. In *Proc. of ACM Conference on Human Factors in Computing Systems*, Atlanta, GA, USA, March 1997. http://www.acm.org/sigchi/chi97/proceedings/paper/koh.htm.

[618] K. Olsen, R. Korfhage, K. Sochats, M. Spring, and J. Williams. Visualization of a document collection with implicit and explicit links: The Vibe system. *Scandinavian Journal of Information Systems*, 5, 1993.

[619] Ed O'Neill, Brian Lavoie, and Pat McClain. OCLC Web characterization project (position paper). In *Web Characterization Workshop*, Boston, USA, Nov 1998. http://www.w3.org/1998/11/05/WC-workshop/Papers/oneill.htm.

[620] Online Computer Library Center, Inc. (OCLC). Metadata Workshop II, April 1996. http://www.oclc.org:5046/oclc/research/conferences/metadata2/ .

[621] E. Oomoto and K. Tanaka. OVID: Design and implementation of a video-object database system. *IEEE Trans. on Knowledge and Data Engineering.*, 5:629–641, 1993.

[622] Alan Victor Oppenheim and Ronald W. Schafer. *Digital Signal Processing*. Prentice Hall, Englewood Cliffs, NJ, 1975.

[623] J. A. Orenstein. A Comparison of Spatial Query Processing Techniques for Native and Parameter Spaces. In *Proc. of the ACM SIGMOD Int. Conf. on Management of Data*, pages 343–352, Atlantic City, New Jersey, 1988.

[624] A. Paepcke, C.-C. K. Chang, H. García-Molina, and T. Winograd. Interoperability for Digital Libraries Worldwide. *Communications of the ACM*, 41(4):33–43, April 1998.

[625] A. Paepcke, S. B. Cousins, H. García-Molina, S. W. Hassan, and S. P. Ketchpel. Using distributed objects for digital library interoperability. *IEEE Computer*, 29(5):61–68, May 1996.

[626] C. D. Paice and P. A. Jones. The identification of important concepts in highly structured technical papers. In *Proc. of the 16th Annual Int. ACM SIGIR Conference on Research and Development in Information Retrieval*, pages 69–78, Pittsburgh, USA, 1993.

[627] George Panagopoulos and Christos Faloutsos. Bit-sliced signature files for very large text databases on a parallel machine architecture. In *Proc. 4th Int. Conf. on Extending Database Technology (EDBT)*, number 779 in LNCS, pages 379–392, London, 1994. Springer-Verlag.

[628] Apostolos Papadopoulos and Yannis Manolopoulos. Performance of nearest neighbor queries in R-trees. In Foto N. Afrati and Phokion Kolaitis, editors, *Proc. of 6th Int. Conf. on Database Theory*, number 1186 in LNCS, pages 394–408, Delphi, Greece, Jan 1997.

[629] Michael Pazzani, Daniel Billsus, and Jack Muramatsu. Syskill & Webert: Identifying interesting Web sites. In *Proc. of the Thirteenth Annual National Conference on Artificial Intelligence*, pages 54–61, Portland, OR, USA, August 1996.

[630] Judea Pearl. *Probabilistic Reasoning in Intelligent Systems: Networks of Plausible Inference*. Morgan Kaufmann Publishers, Inc., 1988.

[631] Gert Schmeltz Pedersen. A browser for bibliographic information retrieval, based on an application of lattice theory. In *Proc. of the 16th Annual Int. ACM SIGIR Conference*, pages 270–279, Pittsburgh, PA, 1993.

[632] Theresa Pepin, Jeff Barry, and W. David Penniman. Automated system marketplace: the competitive edge: expanded access drives vendors. *Library Journal*, 122(6):47–56, 1997.

[633] C. Peters and E. Picchi. across languages, across cultures: Issues in multilinguality and digital libraries. *D-Lib Magazine*, May 1997. http://www.dlib.org/dlib/may97/peters/05peters.html.

[634] P. E. Peters. Digital libraries are much more than digitized collections. *EDUCOM Review*, 30(4), 1995.

[635] Euripides G. M. Petrakis and Christos Faloutsos. Similarity searching in medical image databases. *IEEE Trans. on Knowledge and Data Engineering*, 9(3):435–447, May 1997.

[636] Lori Phelps. Active documentation: Wizards as a medium for meeting user needs. In *Proc. of the ACM 15th International Conference on Systems Documentation*, pages 207–210, 1997.

[637] D. Pimienta. Languages, culture, and Internet (in French). http://funredes.org/, March 1998.

[638] Peter Pirolli and Stuart Card. Information foraging models of browsers for very large document spaces. In *Advanced Visual Interfaces*, L'Aquila, Italy, May 1998.

[639] Peter Pirolli, James Pitkow, and Ramana Rao. Silk from a sow's ear: Extracting usable structures from the Web. In *Proc. of the ACM SIGCHI Conference on Human Factors in Computing Systems*, pages 118–125, Zurich, Switzerland, May 1996. ACM Press.

[640] Peter Pirolli, Patricia Schank, Marti A. Hearst, and Christine Diehl. Scatter/gather browsing communicates the topic structure of a very large text collection. In *Proc. of the ACM SIGCHI Conference on Human Factors in Computing Systems*, pages 213–220, Zurich, Switzerland, May 1996.

[641] J. E. Pitkow. Summary of WWW characterizations. In *7th WWW Conference*, Brisbane, Australia, 1998.

[642] J. E. Pitkow and K. A. Bharat. WebViz: A tools for World Wide Web access log analysis. In *Proc. of the 1st Int. WWW Conference*, Geneva, Switzerland, May 1994. http://www1.cern.ch/PapersWWW94/pitkow-webvis.ps.

[643] Catherine Plaisant, Tom Bruns, Ben Shneiderman, and Khoa Doan. Query previews in networked information systems: the case of EOSDIS. In *Proc. of ACM Conference on Human Factors in Computing Systems*, volume 2 of *Formal Video Program*, pages 202–203, Atlanta, GA, USA, March 1997.

[644] Catherine Plaisant, David Carr, and Ben Shneiderman. Image-browser taxonomy and guidelines for designers. *IEEE Software*, 12(2):21–32, 1995.

[645] Christine A. Pogue and Peter Willet. Use of text signatures for document retrieval in a highly parallel environment. *Parallel Computing*, 4:259–268, 1987.

[646] Steven Pollitt. Interactive information retrieval based on faceted classification using views. In *Proc. of the 6th Int. Study Conference on Classification (FID/CR)*, University College, London, June 1997.

[647] A. Pollock and A. Hockley. What's wrong with Internet searching. *D-Lib Magazine*, March 1997.

[648] M. F. Porter. An algorithm for suffix stripping. In K. Sparck Jones and P. Willet, editors, *Readings in Information Retrieval*, pages 313–316. Morgan Kaufmann Publishers, Inc., 1997.

[649] J. Powell and E. Fox. Multilingual federated searching across heterogeneous collections. *D-Lib Magazine*, September 1998.

[650] Wanda Pratt. Dynamic organization of search results using the UMLS. In *American Medical Informatics Association Fall Symposium*, Nashville, TN, USA, October 1997.

[651] William H. Press, Saul A. Teukolsky, William T. Vetterling, and Brian P. Flannery. *Numerical Recipes in C*. Cambridge University Press, 2nd edition, 1992.

[652] G. Pringle, L. Allison, and D. L. Dowe. What is a tall poppy among Web pages? In *7th WWW Conference*, Brisbane, Australia, April 1998.

[653] Teresa Pritchard-Schoch. Comparing natural language retrieval: WIN & Freestyle. *Online*, 19(4):83–87, 1995.

[654] The PURL Team, Persistent Uniform Resource Locator (PURL). http://purl.oclc.org/.

[655] Yonggang Qiu and H. P. Frei. Concept based query expansion. In *Proc. of the 16th ACM SIGIR Conference on Research and Development in Information Retrieval*, pages 160–169, Pittsburgh, PA, USA, 1993.

[656] D. Quass, A. Rajaraman, Y. Sagiv, J. Ullman, and J. Widom. Querying semistructured heterogeneous information. In *Deductive and Object-Oriented Databases, Proc. of the DOOD '95 Conference*, pages 319–344, Singapore, December 1995. Springer-Verlag.

[657] F. Rabitti and P. Savino. Retrieval of multimedia document by imprecise query specification. In F. Bancilhon, C. Thanos, and D. Tsichritzis, editors, *Proc. of the Int. Conference on Extended Database Technologies*, number 416 in LNCS, pages 203–218, Venice, Italy, 1990.

[658] T. Radecki. Mathematical model of information retrieval system based on the concept of fuzzy thesaurus. *Information Processing & Management*, 12:313–318, 1976.

[659] T. Radecki. Mathematical model of time-effective information retrieval system based on the theory of fuzzy sets. *Information Processing & Management*, 13:109–116, 1977.

[660] T. Radecki. Fuzzy set theoretical approach to document retrieval. *Information Processing & Management*, 15:247–259, 1979.

[661] T. Radecki. On the inclusiveness of information retrieval systems with documents indexed by weighted descriptors. *Fuzzy Sets and Systems*, 5:159–176, 1981.

[662] Tadeusz Radecki. Trends in research on information retrieval—the potential for improvements in conventional Boolean retrieval systems. *Information Processing & Management*, 24:219–227, 1988.

[663] V. V. Raghavan, P. Bollmann, and G. S. Jung. Retrieval system evaluation using recall and precision: Problems and answers. In *Proc. of the 12th ACM SIGIR Conference*, pages 59–68, Cambridge, USA, June 1989.

[664] V. V. Raghavan, G. S. Jung, and P. Bollmann. A critical investigation of recall and precision as measures of retrieval system performance. *ACM Transactions on Office and Information Systems*, 7(3):205–229, 1989.

[665] V. V. Raghavan and S. K. M. Wong. A critical analysis of vector space model for information retrieval. *Journal of the American Society for Information Sciences*, 37(5):279–287, 1986.

[666] R. Rao and S. K. Card. The Table Lens: Merging graphical and symbolic representations in an interactive focus+context visualization for tabular information. In *Proc. of the ACM SIGCHI Conference on Human Factors in Computing Systems*, pages 318–322, Boston, MA, USA, April 1994.

[667] R. Rao, S. K. Card, H. D. Jellinek, J. D. Mackinlay, and G. G. Robertson. The Information Grid: A framework for building information retrieval and retrieval-centered applications. In *Proc. of the ACM Symposium on User Interface Software and Technology*, Monterey, CA, USA, Nov 1992.

[668] E. Rasmussen. Clustering algorithms. In W. B. Frakes and R. Baeza-Yates, editors, *Information Retrieval: Data Structures & Algorithms*, pages 419–442. Prentice Hall, Englewood Cliffs, NJ, USA, 1992.

[669] David F. Redmiles. Reducing the variability of programmers' performance through explained examples. In *Proc. of the ACM Conference on Human Factors in Computing Systems*, pages 67–73, 1993.

[670] A. Renear. The digital library research agenda: What's missing — and how humanities textbase projects can help. *D-Lib Magazine*, July/August 1997. http://www.dlib.org/dlib/july97/07renear.html.

[671] Earl Rennison. Galaxy of news: An approach to visualizing and understanding expansive news landscapes. In *Proc. of UIST'94, ACM Symposium on User Interface Software and Technology*, pages 3–12, New York, 1994.

[672] Paul Resnick and Hal Varian. Introduction: Special issue on collaborative filtering. *Communications of the ACM*, 40(3):56–58, March 1997.

[673] B. Ribeiro-Neto and R. Barbosa. Query performance in tightly coupled distributed digital libraries. In *Proc. of the 3rd Annual Int. ACM Conference on Digital Libraries*, Pittsburgh, PA, USA, 1998.

[674] Berthier A. Ribeiro-Neto and Richard Muntz. A belief network model for IR. In *Proc. of the 19th Annual Int. ACM SIGIR Conference on Research and Development in Information Retrieval*, pages 253–260, Zurich, Switzerland, 1996.

[675] J. Rissanen and G. G. Langdon. Arithmetic coding. *IBM Journal of Research and Development*, 23:149–162, 1979.

[676] George C. Robertson, Stuart K. Card, and Jock D. Mackinlay. Information visualization using 3D interactive animation. *Communications of the ACM*, 36(4):56–71, 1993.

[677] S. E. Robertson and K. Sparck Jones. Relevance weighting of search terms. *Journal of the American Society for Information Sciences*, 27(3):129–146, 1976.

[678] J. J. Rocchio. Relevance feedback in information retrieval. In G. Salton, editor, *The SMART Retrieval System — Experiments in Automatic Document Processing*. Prentice Hall Inc., Englewood Cliffs, NJ, 1971.

[679] Peter Roget. *Roget's II The New Thesaurus*. Houghton Mifflin Company, Boston, USA, 1988.

[680] M. Roscheisen, C. Mogensen, and T. Winograd. Interaction design for shared World-Wide Web annotations. Stanford Digital Library Project Working Paper, February 1995. http://walrus.stanford.edu/diglib/pub/reports/brio-chi95.html .

[681] David E. Rose, Richard Mander, Tim Oren, Dulce B. Ponceleón, Gitta Salomon, and Yin Yin Wong. Content awareness in a file system interface: Implementing the 'pile' metaphor for organizing information. In *Proc. of the 16th Annual Int. ACM SIGIR Conference on Research and Development in Information Retrieval*, pages 260–269, 1993.

[682] Louis Rosenfeld and Peter Morville. *Information Architecture for the World Wide Web*. O'Reilly & Associates, 1998.

[683] A. Ross. Library functions, scholarly communication, and the foundation of the digital library: Laying claim to the control zone. *The Library Quarterly*, 66:239–265, July 1996.

[684] Mary Beth Rosson, John M. Carroll, and Rachel K. E. Bellamy. Smalltalk Scaffolding: A case study of minimalist instruction. In *Proc. of the ACM Conference on Human Factors in Computing Systems*, pages 423–429, 1990.

[685] Steven F. Roth, Mei C. Chuah, Stephan Kerpedjiev, John A. Kolojejchick, and Peter Lucas. Towards an information visualization workspace: Combining multiple means of expression. *Human-Computer Interaction*, 12(1-2):131–185, 1997.

[686] Nick Roussopoulos, Steve Kelley, and F. Vincent. Nearest neighbor queries. In *Proc. of ACM-SIGMOD*, pages 71–79, San Jose, CA, May 1995.

[687] N. Roussopoulus, C. Faloutsos, and T. Sellis. An efficient pictorial database system for PSQL. *IEEE Transactions on Software Engineering*, 14(5):639–650, May 1988.

[688] Jennifer Rowley. The controlled versus natural indexing languages debate revisited: a perspective on information retrieval practice and research. *Journal of Information Science*, 20(2):108–119, 1994.

[689] Mary Beth Ruskai, Gregory Beylkin, Ronald Coifman, Ingrid Daubechies, Stephane Mallat, Yves Meyer, and Louise Raphael. *Wavelets and their Applications*. Jones and Bartlett Publishers, Boston, MA, 1992.

[690] Daniel M. Russell, Mark J. Stefik, Peter Pirolli, and Stuart K. Card. The cost structure of sensemaking. In *Proc. of ACM Conference on Human Factors in Computing Systems*, pages 269–276, 1993.

[691] W. M. Sachs. An approach to associative retrieval through the theory of fuzzy sets. *Journal of the American Society for Information Sciences*, pages 85–87, 1976.

[692] M. Sahami, S. Yusufali, and M. Q. W. Baldonado. SONIA: A service for organizing networked information autonomously. In *Proc. of the 3rd Annual Conference on Digital Libraries*, pages 200–209, New York, USA, 1998.

[693] A. Salminen and F. Tompa. PAT expressions: an algebra for text search. Technical Report OED-92-02, UW Centre for the New Oxford English Dictionary, July 1992.

[694] G. Salton. Associative document retrieval techniques using bibliographic information. *Journal of the ACM*, 10(4):440–457, October 1963.

[695] G. Salton. *The SMART Retrieval System — Experiments in Automatic Document Processing*. Prentice Hall Inc., Englewood Cliffs, NJ, 1971.

[696] G. Salton and C. Buckley. Term-weighting approaches in automatic retrieval. *Information Processing & Management*, 24(5):513–523, 1988.

[697] G. Salton and M. E. Lesk. Computer evaluation of indexing and text processing. *Journal of the ACM*, 15(1):8–36, January 1968.

[698] G. Salton and M. J. McGill. *Introduction to Modern Information Retrieval*. McGraw-Hill Book Co., New York, 1983.

[699] G. Salton, C. S. Yang, and C. T. Yu. A theory of term importance in automatic text analysis. *Journal of the American Society for Information Sciences*, 26(1):33–44, 1975.

[700] Gerard Salton. *Automatic Text Processing: the Transformation, Analysis, and Retrieval of Information by Computer*. Addison-Wesley, Reading, MA, 1989.

[701] Gerard Salton and Chris Buckley. Parallel text search methods. *Communications of the ACM*, 31(2):202–215, February 1988.

[702] Gerard Salton and Chris Buckley. Improving retrieval performance by relevance feedback. *J. of the American Society for Information Science*, 41(4):288–297, 1990.

[703] Gerard Salton, Edward A. Fox, and Harry Wu. Extended Boolean information retrieval. *Communications of the ACM*, 26(11):1022–1036, November 1983.

[704] Gerard Salton and C. S. Yang. On the specification of term values in automatic indexing. *Journal of Documentation*, 29:351–372, 1973.

[705] P. Samuelson. Copyright and digital libraries. In *Proc. of the 2nd ACM International Conference on Digital Libraries*, pages 113–114, Philadelphia, PA, USA, 1997.

[706] David Sankoff and Joseph B. Kruskal. *Time warps, string edits and macromolecules: The theory and practice of sequence comparisons*. Addison-Wesley, Reading, MA, 1983.

[707] Tefko Saracevic, Paul Kantor, Alice Y. Chamis, and Donna Trivison. A study of information seeking and retrieving. I. Background and methodology. *Journal of the American Society for Information Science*, 39(3):161–176, 1988.

[708] S. Sato and T. Kanade. Name-it: Association of Face and Name in Video. Technical Report CMU-CS-96-205, CMU School of Computer Science, 1996.

[709] L. Schamber. What is a document? Rethinking the concept in uneasy times. *Journal of the American Society for Information Science*, 47:669–671, September 1996.

[710] B. Schatz and H. Chen. Building large-scale digital libraries: Guest editors' introduction to theme issue on the US Digital Library Initiative. *IEEE Computer*, 29(5):22–26, May 1996. http://computer.org/computer/dli/.

[711] B. R. Schatz. Information retrieval in digital libraries: Bringing search to the Net. *Science*, 275:327–335, January 1997.

[712] Manfred Schroeder. *Fractals, Chaos, Power Laws: Minutes from an Infinite Paradise*. W. H. Freeman and Company, New York, 1991.

[713] E. S. Schwartz and B. Kallick. Generating a canonical prefix encoding. *Communications of the ACM*, 7:166–169, 1964.

[714] S. Sclaroff, L. Taycher, and M. La Cascia. ImageRover: A content-based image browser for the World Wide Web. In *Proc. IEEE Workshop on Content-based Access of Image and Video Libraries*, San Juan, Puerto Rico, June 1997.

[715] E. Selberg and O. Etzioni. Multi-service search and comparison using the MetaCrawler. *4th Int. WWW Conference*, December 1995.

[716] P. Sellers. The theory and computation of evolutionary distances: pattern recognition. *Journal of Algorithms*, 1:359–373, 1980.

[717] T. Sellis, N. Roussopoulos, and C. Faloutsos. The R$^+$-tree: A dynamic index for multi-dimensional objects. In *Proc. of the 13th Int. Conference on Very Large Data Bases*, pages 507–518, Brighton, England, 1987.

[718] C. E. Shannon. A mathematical theory of communication. *Bell System Technical Journal*, 27:398–403, 1948.

[719] Jacob Shapiro, Vladimir G. Voiskunskii, and Valery J. Frants. *Automated Information Retrieval : Theory and Text-Only Methods*. Academic Press, 1997.

[720] Upendra Shardanand and Pattie Maes. Social information filtering: Algorithms for automating Word of Mouth. In *Proc. of ACM Conference on Human Factors in Computing Systems*, pages 210–217, Denver, CO, USA, 1995.

[721] W. M. Shaw, J. B. Wood, R. E. Wood, and H. R. Tibbo. The cystic fibrosis database: Content and research opportunities. *Library and Information Science Research*, 13:347–366, 1991.

[722] Frank M. Shipman, III, Catherine C. Marshall, and Thomas P. Moran. Finding and using implicit structure in human-organized spatial layouts of information. In *Proc. of ACM Conference on Human Factors in Computing Systems*, volume 1, pages 346–353, Denver, CO, USA, 1995.

[723] N. Shivakumar and H. García-Molina. Finding near-replicas of documents on the Web. In *Workshop on Web Databases*, Valencia, Spain, March 1998.

[724] Ben Shneiderman. The eyes have it: A task by data type taxonomy. In *Proc. of IEEE Symp. Visual Languages 96*, pages 336–343, Boulder, CO, USA, 1996.

[725] Ben Shneiderman. *Designing the User Interface: Strategies for Effective Human-computer Interaction*. Addison-Wesley, Reading, MA, 1997.

[726] Ben Shneiderman, Donald Byrd, and W. Bruce Croft. Sorting out searching: A user-interface framework for text searches. *Communications of the ACM*, 41(4):95–98, 1998.

[727] Ben Shneiderman and Greg Kearsley. *Hypertext Hands-On! An Introduction to a New Way of Organizing and Accessing Information*. Addison-Wesley Publishing Co., Reading, MA, 1989.

[728] C. Silverstein, M. Henzinger, J. Marais, and M. Moricz. Analysis of a very large alta vista query log. Technical Report 1998-014, COMPAQ Systems Research Center, Palo Alto, CA, USA, 1998.

[729] Singapore advanced research and education network (singaren). http://www.singaren.net.sg/.

[730] H. Small. Co-citation in the scientific literature: A new measure of relationship between two documents. *Journal of the American Society for Information Science*, 24(4):265–269, 1973.

[731] H. Small. The relationship of information science to the social sciences: A co-citation analysis. *Information Processing & Management*, 17(1):39–50, 1981.

[732] H. Small and M. E. D. Koenig. Journal clustering using a bibliographic coupling method. *Information Processing & Management*, 13(5):277–288, 1977.

[733] D. C. Smith and S.-F. Chang. Searching for images and videos on the World-Wide Web. *IEEE Multimedia Magazine*, 4(3):12–20, 1997.

[734] T. R. Smith. The Meta-information environment of digital libraries. *D-Lib Magazine*, July/August 1996. http://www.dlib.org/dlib/july96/new/07smith.html.

[735] Dagobert Soergel. *Indexing Languages and Thesauri: Construction and Maintenance.* Melville Publishing Co., Los Angeles, CA, 1974.

[736] Ellen Spertus. ParaSite: Mining structural information on the Web. In *6th Int. WWW Conference*, Santa Clara, CA, USA, April 1997.

[737] M. Spiliopoulou and L. Faulstich. WUM — A tool for WWW utilization analysis. In *Workshop on Web Databases*, pages 109–115, Valencia, Spain, March 1998.

[738] Anselm Spoerri. InfoCrystal: A visual tool for information retrieval & management. In *Proc. of Information Knowledge and Management '93*, pages 11–20, Washington, DC, Nov 1993.

[739] P. Srinivasdan. Thesaurus construction. In W. Frakes and R. Baeza-Yates, editors, *Information Retrieval: Data Structures & Algorithms*, pages 161–218. Prentice Hall, Englewood Cliffs, NJ, USA, 1992.

[740] Craig Stanfill. Partitioned posting files: A parallel inverted file structure for information retrieval. In *Proc. 13th Int. ACM SIGIR Conference on Research and Development in Information Retrieval*, pages 413–428, Brussels, Belgium, 1990.

[741] Craig Stanfill. Parallel information retrieval algorithms. In William B. Frakes and Ricardo Baeza-Yates, editors, *Information Retrieval Data Structures & Algorithms*, pages 459–497. Prentice Hall, Englewood Cliffs, NJ, USA, 1992.

[742] Craig Stanfill and Brewster Kahle. Parallel free-text search on the Connection Machine system. *Communications of the ACM*, 29(12):1229–1239, December 1986.

[743] Craig Stanfill and Brewster Kahle. Toward memory-based reasoning. *Communications of the ACM*, 29(12):1213–1228, 1986.

[744] Craig Stanfill, Robert Thau, and David Waltz. A parallel indexed algorithm for information retrieval. In *Proc. 12th Int. ACM SIGIR Conf. on Research and Development in Information Retrieval*, pages 88–97, Cambridge, USA, June 1989.

[745] Stanford DLI Team, Stanford University Digital Libraries Project. http://www-diglib.stanford.edu/diglib/.

[746] M. Stefik. Trusted systems. *Scientific American*, March 1997. http://www.sciam.com/-0397issue/0397stefik.html.

[747] J. A. Storer. *Data Compression: Methods and Theory.* Computer Science Press, 1988.

[748] Tomek Strzalkowski, editor. *Natural Language Information Retrieval.* Kluwer Academic Publishers, 1999. To appear.

[749] D. Sullivan. Search Engine Watch: Main page. http://www.searchenginewatch.com, 1997.

[750] K. Summers. Toward a taxonomy of logical document structures. In *DAGS95: Electronic Publishing and the Information Superhighway, May 30–June 2, 1995*, 1995. http://www.cs.dartmouth.edu/~samr/DAGS95/Papers/summers.html .

[751] D. Sunday. A very fast substring search algorithm. *Communications of the ACM*, 33(8):132–142, August 1990.

[752] Elaine Svenonius. Unanswered questions in the design of controlled vocabularies. *Journal of the American Society for Information Science*, 37(5):331–340, 1986.

[753] R. Swick. Resource Description Framework (RDF), June 1998. http://www.w3.org/RDF.

[754] J. Tague-Sutcliffe. Measuring the informativeness of a retrieval process. In *Proc. of the 15th Annual Int. ACM SIGIR Conference on Research and Development in Information Retrieval*, pages 23–36, Copenhagen, Denmark, 1992.

[755] V. A. Tahani. A fuzzy model of document retrieval systems. *Information Processing & Management*, 12:177–187, 1976.

[756] TEI. A gentle introduction to SGML. Technical report, Text Encoding Initiative, 1996. http://www.sil.org/sgml/gentle.html.

[757] Carol Tenopir and Jeff Barry. Database marketplace: data dealers face stormy weather. *Library Journal*, 123(9):38–46, 1998.

[758] Carol Tenopir and Pamela Cahn. TARGET & FREESTYLE: DIALOG and Mead join the relevance ranks. *Online*, 18(3):31–47, 1994.

[759] C. Thanos, editor. *Multimedia Office Filing: The MULTOS Approach*. Elsevier Science Publishers B.V. (North Holland), 1990.

[760] P. Thompson, H. Turtle, B. Yang, and J. Flood. TREC-3 ad-hoc retrieval and routing experiments using the WIN system. In *Proc. of the Text REtrieval Conference*, pages 211–218, Gaithersburg, MD, USA, 1995.

[761] R. H. Thompson and B. W. Croft. Support for browsing in an intelligent text retrieval system. *International Journal of Man-Machine Studies*, 30(6):639–668, 1989.

[762] Anthony Tomasic and Hector García-Molina. Caching and database scaling in distributed shared-nothing information retrieval systems. In *Proc. of the ACM SIGMOD Int. Conf. on Management of Data*, pages 129–138, Washington, DC, USA, May 1993.

[763] Anthony Tomasic and Hector García-Molina. Performance of inverted indices in shared-nothing distributed text document information retrieval systems. In *Proc. of the 2nd Int. Conf. on Parallel and Distributed Information Systems*, pages 8–17, San Diego, USA, 1993.

[764] Anthony Tomasic and Hector García-Molina. Performance issues in distributed shared-nothing information retrieval systems. *Information Processing & Management*, 32(6):647–665, 1996.

[765] Anthony Tomasic, Luis Gravano, Calvin Lue, Peter Schwarz, and Laura Haas. Data structures for efficient broker implementation. *ACM Transactions on Information Systems*, 15(3):223–253, 1997.

[766] A. Tombros and M. Sanderson. Advantages of query biased summaries in Information Retrieval. In B. Croft, A. Moffat, C. J. van Rijsbergen, R. Wilkinson, and J. Zobel, editors, *Proc. of the 21st ACM SIGIR Conference on Reseach and Development in Information Retrieval*, pages 2–10, Melbourne, Australia, 1998.

[767] Geoffrey Towell, Ellen M. Voorhees, Narendra K. Gupta, and Ben Johnson-Laird. Learning collection fusion strategies for information retrieval. In *Proc. of the 12th Int. Conference on Machine Learning*, pages 540–548. Morgan Kaufmann, 1995.

[768] The TREC NIST site, 1998. http://trec.nist.gov.

[769] Edward Tufte. *The Visual Display of Quantitative Information*. Graphics Press, Chelshire, CT, 1983.

[770] Edward Tufte. *Envisioning Information*. Graphics Press, Chelshire, CT, 1990.

[771] H. Turtle and W. B. Croft. Evaluation of an inference network-based retrieval model. *ACM Transactions on Information Systems*, 9(3):187–222, July 1991.

[772] Howard Turtle and W. Bruce Croft. Inference networks for document retrieval. In *Proc. of the 13th Annual Int. ACM SIGIR Conference on Research and Development in Information Retrieval*, pages 1–24, Brussels, Belgium, 1990.

[773] L. A. Tweedie, R. Spence, D. Williams, and R. Bhogal. The attribute explorer. In *Proc. of the Video Track of the ACM Conference on Human Factors in Computing Systems*, pages 435–436, Boston, MA, USA, April 1994.

[774] UC Berkeley Digital Library Project, About MVD version 1.0alpha3. http://elib.cs.berkeley.edu/java/help/About.html.

[775] UC Berkeley DLI Team, UC Berkeley Digital Library Project. http://elib.cs.berkeley.edu/.

[776] UC Santa Barbara DLI Team, Alexandria Digital Library. http://alexandria.sdc.ucsb.edu/.

[777] UIUC DLI Team, University of Illinois at Urbana-Champaign Digital Libraries. http://dli.grainger.uiuc.edu/default.htm.

[778] The UK Office for Library and Information Networking, Electronic Libraries Programme, eLib, March 1998. http://www.ukoln.ac.uk/services/elib/.

[779] E. Ukkonen. Approximate string matching over suffix trees. In A. Apostolico, M. Crochemore, Z. Galil, and U. Manber, editors, *Proc. of Combinatorial Pattern Matching*, number 684 in LNCS, pages 228–242, Padova, Italy, 1993. Springer-Verlag.

[780] E. Ukkonen. Constructing suffix trees on-line in linear time. *Algorithmica*, 14(3):249–260, Sep 1995.

[781] Esko Ukkonen. Finding approximate patterns in strings. *Journal of Algorithms*, 6:132–137, 1985.

[782] G. M. Underwood, P. P. Maglio, and R. Barrett. User-centered push for timely information delivery. In *7th WWW Conference*, Brisbane, Australia, 1998.

[783] Unicode Consortium, Unicode. http://www.unicode.org/.

[784] University of Michigan DLI Team, Univ. of Michigan Digital Library Project. http://www.si.umich.edu/UMDL/.

[785] C. J. van Rijsbergen. *Information Retrieval*. Butterworths, 1979.

[786] J. Verhoeff, W. Goffmann, and Jack Belzer. Inefficiency of the use of Boolean functions for information retrieval systems. *Communications of the ACM*, 4(12):557–558, 594, December 1961.

[787] Charles L. Viles and James C. French. Dissemination of collection wide information in a distributed information retrieval system. In *Proc. 18th Int. ACM SIGIR Conference on Research and Development in Information Retrieval*, pages 12–20, Seattle, WA, USA, July 1995.

[788] S. Vinoski. CORBA: Integrating diverse applications within distributed heterogeneous environments. *IEEE Communications Magazine*, 14(2), February 1997.

[789] J. S. Vitter. Algorithm 673: Dynamic Huffman coding. *ACM Transactions on Mathematical Software*, 15:158–167, 1989.

[790] A. N. Vo and A. Moffat. Compressed inverted files with reduced decoding overhead. In *Proc. of the ACM-SIGIR Int. Conference on Research and Development in Information Retrieval*, pages 290–297, Melbourne, Australia, 1998.

[791] E. M. Voorhees and R. M. Tong. Multiple search engines in database merging. In *Proc. of the 2nd ACM International Conference on Digital Libraries*, pages 93–102, Philadelphia, PA, USA, 1997.

[792] Ellen M. Voorhees, Narendra K. Gupta, and Ben Johnson-Laird. The collection fusion problem. In Donna K. Harman, editor, *The Third Text REtrieval Conference (TREC-3)*, pages 95–104, Gaithersburg, MD, USA, 1995. Dept. of Commerce, National Institute of Standards and Technology. Special Publication 500-226.

[793] E. M. Voorhees. *The Effectiveness and Efficiency of Agglomerative Hierarchic Clustering in Document Retrieval*. PhD thesis, Cornell University, 1986.

[794] E. M. Voorhees and D. K. Harman. Overview of the 6th text retrieval conference (TREC-6). In E. M. Voorhees and D. K. Harman, editors, *Proc. of the Sixth Text REtrieval Conference*, pages 1–24. NIST Special Publication, Gaithersburg, MD, USA, 1997.

[795] W3C. Extensible markup language (XML) 1.0. Technical report, WWW Consortium (W3C), 1998. http://www.w3.org/TR/1998/REC-xml-19980210.

[796] W3C. HTML 4.0 specification. Technical report, WWW Consortium (W3C), 1998. http://www.w3.org/TR/1998/REC-html40-19980424/.

[797] W3C. Web characterization activity, 1998. http://www.w3.org/WCA/.

[798] W3C. XML linking language (XLink). Technical report, WWW Consortium (W3C), 1998. http://www.w3.org/TR/1998/WD-xlink-19980303.

[799] W3C. XSL requirements summary. Technical report, WWW Consortium (W3C), 1998. http://www.w3.org/TR/1998/WD-XSLReq-19980511.

[800] Howard D. Wactlar, Takeo Kanade, Michael A. Smith, and Scott M. Stevens. Intelligent access to digital video: Informedia project. *IEEE Computer*, 29(5):46–52, May 1996.

[801] Marilyn A. Walker, Jeanne Fromer, Giuseppe Di Fabbrizio, Craig Mestel, and Don Hindle. What can I say: Evaluating a spoken language interface to email. In *Proc. of the ACM SIGCHI Conference on Human Factors in Computing Systems*, pages 582–589, Los Angeles, CA, March 1998.

[802] Gregory K. Wallace. The JPEG still picture compression standard. *Communications of the ACM*, 34(4):31–44, April 1991.

[803] S. Wartick. Boolean operations. In W. B. Frakes and R. Baeza-Yates, editors, *Information Retrieval: Data Structures & Algorithms*, pages 264–292. Prentice Hall, Englewood Cliffs, NJ, USA, 1992.

[804] John A. Waterworth and Mark H. Chignell. A model of information exploration. *Hypermedia*, 3(1):35–58, 1991.

[805] WebTaxi: Main Page. http://www.webtaxi.com, 1998.

[806] S. Weibel, J. Godby, E. Miller, and R. Daniel. OCLC/NCSA Metadata Workshop Report: The Essential Elements of Network Object Description, March 1995. http://purl.oclc.org/oclc/rsch/metadataI.

[807] S. Weibel and E. Miller. Dublin Core Metadata, 1997. URL: http://purl.org/metadata/dublin_core.

[808] Andreas S. Weigend and Neil A. Gerschenfeld. *Time Series Prediction: Forecasting the Future and Understanding the Past*. Addison Wesley, 1994.

[809] Bella H. Weinberg. Bibliographic coupling: A review. *Information Storage and Retrieval*, 10(5-6):189–196, 1974.

[810] R. Weiss, B. Vélez, M. Sheldon, C. Nemprempre, P. Szilagyi, and D. K. Gifford. HyPursuit: A hierarchical network engine that exploits content-link hypertext clustering. In *Proc. of the 7th ACM Conference on Hypertext and Hypermedia*, pages 180–193, Washington, DC, USA, 1996.

[811] H. G. Wells. World Brain: The idea of a permanent world encyclopedia. Contribution to the New Encyclopedie Francaise, 1937. http://sherlock.berkeley.edu/wells/world_brain.html.

[812] H. D. White and K. W. McCain. Bibliometrics. *Annual Review of Information Science and Technology*, 24:119–186, 1989.

[813] Howard S. White, editor. *Library Technology Reports*, volume 33(5). American Library Association, Chicago, IL, September/October 1997.

[814] Robert Wilensky, Yigal Arens, and David N. Chin. Talking to UNIX in English: An overview of UC. *Communications of the ACM*, 27(6), 1984.

[815] R. Wilkinson and P. Hingston. Using the cosine measure in a neural network for document retrieval. In *Proc. of the ACM SIGIR Conference on Research and Development in Information Retrieval*, pages 202–210, Chicago, USA, Oct 1991.

[816] Peter Willet. Recent trends in hierarchical document clustering: A critical review. *Information Processing and Management*, 24(5):577–597, 1988.

[817] J. Williams. *Bots and other Internet Beasts*. Prentice Hall, Englewood Cliffs, NJ, 1996.

[818] Michael David Williams. What makes rabbit run? *International Journal of Man-Machine Studies*, 21(4):333–352, 1984.

[819] W. Willinger and V. Paxson. Where mathematics meets the Internet. *Notices of the AMS*, 45(8):961–970, 1998.

[820] T. Winograd. Conceptual models for comparison of digital library systems and approaches. Stanford Digital Library Project Working Paper, July 1995. http://www-diglib.stanford.edu/diglib/WP/PUBLIC/DOC13.html.

[821] James A. Wise, James J. Thomas, Kelly Pennock, David Lantrip, Marc Pottier, and Anne Schur. Visualizing the non-visual: Spatial analysis and interaction with information from text documents. In *Proc. of the Information Visualization Symposium 95*, pages 51–58. IEEE Computer Society Press, 1995.

[822] N. Wiseman. Implementing a national access management system for electronic services: Technology alone is not enough. *D-Lib Magazine*, March 1998. http://www.dlib.org/dlib/march98/wiseman/03wiseman.html.

[823] I. H. Witten, R. Neal, and J. G. Cleary. Arithmetic coding for data compression. *Communications of the ACM*, 30(6):520–541, 1987.

[824] Ian H. Witten, Craig Nevill-Manning, Roger McNab, and Sally Jo Cunningham. A public library based on full-text retrieval. *Communications of the ACM*, 41(4):71–75, 1998.

[825] I. H. Witten, A. Moffat, and T. C. Bell. *Managing Gigabytes: Compressing and Indexing Documents and Images*. Van Nostrand Reinhold, New York, 1994.

[826] Kent Wittenburg and Eric Sigman. Integration of browsing, searching, and filtering in an applet for Web information access. In *Proc. of the ACM Conference on Human Factors in Computing Systems, Late Breaking Track*, Atlanta, GA, USA, 1997. http://www1.acm.org:82/sigs/sigchi/chi97/proceedings/short-talk/kw.htm.

[827] D. Woelk, W. Kim, and W. Luther. An object-oriented approach to multimedia databases. In *Proc. of the ACM SIGMOD Int. Conf. on Management of Data*, pages 312–325, Washington, DC, USA, June 1986.

[828] L. Wong. BioKleisli. http://corona.iss.nus.sg:8080/biokleisli.html.

[829] L. Wong. BioKleisli Architecture. http://sdmc.krdl.org.sg/kleisli/kleisli/Architecture.html.

[830] S. K. M. Wong and Y. Y. Yao. On modeling information retrieval with probabilistic inference. *ACM Transactions on Information Systems*, 13(1):39–68, 1995.

[831] S. K. M. Wong, W. Ziarko, V. V. Raghavan, and P. C. N. Wong. On modeling of information retrieval concepts in vector spaces. *ACM Transactions on Database Systems*, 12(2):299–321, 1987.

[832] S. K. M. Wong, W. Ziarko, and P. C. N. Wong. Generalized vector space model in information retrieval. In *Proc. 8th ACM SIGIR Conference on Research and Development in Information Retrieval*, pages 18–25, New York, USA, 1985.

[833] A. Wood. DC-4: NLA/DSTC/OCLC Dublin Core Down Under / The 4th Dublin Core Metadata Workshop, March 1997. http://www.dstc.edu.au/DC4/.

[834] A. Woodruff, P. Aoki, E. Brewer, P. Gauthier, and L. Rowe. An investigation of documents from the World Wide Web. In *5th WWW Conference*, Paris, France, 1996.

[835] H. Wu and G. Salton. The estimation of term relevance weights using relevance feedback. *Journal of Documentation*, 37(4):194–214, 1981.

[836] S. Wu and U. Manber. Agrep — a fast approximate pattern-matching tool. In *Proc. of USENIX Technical Conference*, pages 153–162, San Francisco, CA, USA, 1992.

[837] S. Wu and U. Manber. Fast text searching allowing errors. *Communications of the ACM*, 35(10):83–91, October 1992.

[838] J. Xu and W. B. Croft. Query expansion using local and global document analysis. In *Proc. ACM-SIGIR Conference on Research and Development in Information Retrieval*, pages 4–11, Zurich, Switzerland, 1996.

[839] Yahoo!: Main page. http://www.yahoo.com, 1995.

[840] Byoung-Kee Yi, H. V. Jagadish, and Christos Faloutsos. Efficient retrieval of similar time sequences under time warping. In *ICDE'98*, pages 201–208, Orlando, Florida, Feb 1998.

[841] Degi Young and Ben Shneiderman. A graphical filter/flow model for Boolean queries: An implementation and experiment. *Journal of the American Society for Information Science*, 44(6):327–339, July 1993. With permission from University of Maryland, USA, Shneiderman & Young, 1993.

[842] C. T. Yu and G. Salton. Precision weighting — an effective automatic indexing method. *Journal of the ACM*, 23(1):76–88, January 1976.

[843] C. T. Yu, C. Buckley, K. Lam, and G. Salton. A generalized term dependence model in information retrieval. *Information Technology: Research and Development*, 2(4):129–154, October 1983.

[844] B. Yuwono and D. L. Lee. Search and ranking algorithms for locating resources on World Wide Web. In *Proc. of the Int. Conference on Data Engineering (ICDE)*, pages 164–171, New Orleans, USA, 1996.

[845] B. Yuwono and D. L. Lee. Server ranking for distributed text retrieval systems on the Internet. In *Proc. of the 5th Int. Conf. on Databases Systems for Advanced Applications (DASFAA)*, pages 41–50, Melbourne, Australia, 1997.

[846] L. A. Zadeh. Fuzzy sets. In D. Dubois, H. Prade, and R. R. Yager, editors, *Readings in Fuzzy Sets for Intelligent Systems*. Morgan Kaufmann, 1993.

[847] G. Zipf. *Human Behaviour and the Principle of Least Effort*. Addison-Wesley, 1949.

[848] J. Ziv and A. Lempel. A universal algorithm for sequential data compression. *IEEE Transactions on Information Theory*, 23(3):337–343, 1977.

[849] J. Ziv and A. Lempel. Compression of individual sequences via variable-rate coding. *IEEE Transactions on Information Theory*, 24(5):530–536, 1978.

[850] J. Zobel and A. Moffat. Adding compression to a full text retrieval system. *Software Practice and Experience*, 25(8):891–903, August 1995.

[851] Justin Zobel, Alistair Moffat, and Kotagiri Ramamohanarao. Inverted files versus signature files for text indexing. Technical Report CITRI/TR-95-5, Collaborative Information Technology Research Institute, Department of Computer Science, Royal Melbourne Institute of Technology, Australia, July 1995.

[852] Albert Y. Zomaya, editor. *Parallel and Distributed Computing Handbook*. McGraw-Hill, New York, 1996.

Note: some of the bibliography is only available on the Web, in particular conferences and electronic journals related to the Web itself or digital libraries. Most of these references are available on the Web page of the book (see Chapter 1).

Index